"Shepherd and Devine have done a signal service for anyone interested in the sociology of music, making the most important writing in the field available in one volume."
—*Howard S. Becker, author of* Art Worlds

"Ranging from seminal classics to the most up-to-date ideas and debates, this book gives the reader everything she needs to know about the sociological study of music. It is an indispensable guide to understanding the multiple ways in which music is socially structured and how music in turn impacts upon human societies."
—*David Inglis, University of Exeter*

"Is there life after the death of the social? Is there anything left to say about music and society after Max Weber or Theodor W. Adorno? This collection of classic texts and new work shows that the inquiry into the social life of music and the musical life of society is not only alive and well, it is also more diverse, more interdisciplinary, more theoretical—and perhaps also less 'sociological'—than ever. Musicologists, ethnomusicologists, media theorists, sociologists, anthropologists—read up!"
—*Veit Erlmann, University of Texas at Austin*

"The state of the art in the sociology of music. It combines insights from past and present, from musicology and sociology, all in one place. The Reader to own."
—*Ron Eyerman, Yale University*

"The sociology of music has come a long way since the days of the Frankfurt School and the Birmingham School, and this comprehensive Reader—the first of its kind—reveals the distance travelled. It includes some influential early texts as milestones, before proceeding to explore the role of music in social interaction, identity formation, politics, and industrial processes. The combination of senior scholars and those of a younger generation provides an overview of the field that could scarcely be bettered."
—*Derek B. Scott, University of Leeds and author of* Sounds of the Metropolis

"*The Routledge Reader on the Sociology of Music* is an important contribution to the area. Shepherd and Devine have created a volume that respects the multiple and varied interests that sociology brings to the study of music, music-making and the experience of music more generally. This volume provides the readers with classic theoretical statements in the area, more recent debates and essays that address current substantive issues. It is the sort of collection that readers will find to be of value for years to come."
—*Scott Grills, Brandon University*

THE ROUTLEDGE READER ON THE SOCIOLOGY OF MUSIC

The Routledge Reader on the Sociology of Music offers the first collection of source readings and new essays on the latest thinking in the sociology of music. Interest in music sociology has increased dramatically over the past decade, yet there is no anthology of essential and introductory readings. The volume includes a comprehensive survey of the field's history, current state and future research directions. It offers six source readings, thirteen popular contemporary essays, and sixteen fresh, new contributions, along with an extended Introduction by the editors. *The Routledge Reader on the Sociology of Music* represents a broad reference work that will be a resource for the current generation of sociologically inclined musicologists and musically inclined sociologists, whether researchers, teachers or students.

John Shepherd is Vice-Provost and Associate Vice-President (Academic) at Carleton University in Ottawa, where he is also Chancellor's Professor of Music and Sociology.

Kyle Devine is Lecturer in Music at City University London and a research associate with the Music and Digitization Research Group at the University of Oxford.

THE
ROUTLEDGE READER
ON THE SOCIOLOGY
OF MUSIC

edited by
John Shepherd and
Kyle Devine

Routledge
Taylor & Francis Group

NEW YORK AND LONDON

First published 2015
by Routledge
711 Third Avenue, New York, NY 10017

and by Routledge
2 Park Square, Milton Park, Abingdon, Oxon, OX14 4RN

Routledge is an imprint of the Taylor & Francis Group, an informa business

Library of Congress Cataloging in Publication Data
The Routledge reader on the sociology of music / John Shepherd and
 Kyle Devine.
 pages cm
 Includes bibliographical references and index.
 1. Music—Social aspects. 2. Sociology. 3. Arts and society.
 I. Shepherd, John, 1947– editor. II. Devine, Kyle, editor.
 ML3916.R676 2015
 306.4'842—dc23
 2015005915

ISBN: 978-0-415-85546-4 (hbk)
ISBN: 978-1-138-85636-3 (pbk)
ISBN: 978-0-203-73631-9 (ebk)

Typeset in Minion
by Florence Production Ltd, Stoodleigh, Devon, UK

Senior Editor: Constance Ditzel
Senior Editorial Assistant: Elysse Preposi
Production Editor: Sioned Jones
Marketing Manager: Amy Langlais
Project Manager: Anne Macdonald
Copy Editor: Carol Lee
Proofreader: Kilmeny MacBride
Cover Design: Jayne Varney

Contents

Preface

The Routledge Reader on the Sociology of Music provides an introduction to a rapidly developing and dynamic area of intellectual activity. It combines original contributions that summarize key topics and set agendas for future research with reprints of source readings and classic essays that have shaped the field.

For the better part of a century, scholars have questioned what exactly the sociology of music is, and what it could or even should be. The very fact that these questions remain open is part of what makes the field so vibrant and interesting—and it is an issue to which we will return in our Introduction. As a starting point for the book, though, we need to provide our understanding of what constitutes the field. We understand the sociology of music as a kind of conversation, an interdisciplinary meeting point where sociologists with interests in musical phenomena and musicologists with interests in social phenomena can work together to generate concrete and conceptual knowledge about music as a fact of life. The book is thus not about delimiting what music sociology can or cannot be. Rather, it is about feeding music studies and the social sciences into one another—an exercise that we believe enriches each discipline and affords deeper understandings of both music and society.[1]

Such an understanding means that the sociology of music is not merely the application to music of established sociological theories and empirics. It is instead an invitation to a cross-disciplinary conversation. We can say that the scholar at the intersection of these fields would be interested in the forms and roles of music in society, music's dynamic as a medium of human expression and communication, and its position within established social orders (including political, economic, institutional and technological systems). What is more, because what we call "music" is a phenomenon evident in all cultures, music sociology necessarily confronts some of the most fundamental questions about what it means to be human. Indeed, music sociology is open with respect to the kinds of music it studies. Although the field initially concerned itself largely with western art music, in recent years, scholars have championed the study of *all* music, from mashups to Machaut—including, and sometimes especially, those musics that may not seem "musicologically" significant.

The sociology of music is thus a broad and significant scholarly endeavor. Moreover, the field is growing. Such growth is a function of both the impact of "new" musicological thinking within music departments and the explosion of sociological interest in art and culture.[2] In addition to the steady flow of music-focused articles in journals such as *Cultural Sociology*, and in addition to the several conferences that have recently been devoted to the subject (see for example Brandl et al. 2012), journals such as *Poetics* (2002, 2004), *Social Studies of Science* (2004), *Leisure Studies* (2005), *American Behavioral Scientist* (2005), *Symbolic Interaction* (2006) and *Studies in Symbolic Interaction* (2010, 2014) have all released special issues focusing on music. Other recent works include a new survey of the field (McCormick 2012), an introductory textbook on popular music (Kotarba and Vannini 2009), an ethnographically-oriented guide to the subject (Towe Horsfall, Meij and Probstfield 2014) and an encyclopedia (Thompson 2014).

Despite all this activity, this Reader is the first of its kind. There are, of course, other general works of music sociology. However, most of the classic statements *on* the sociology of music are outdated and out of print (for example, Weber 1958, Silbermann 1963, Kunst 1968, Adorno 1976, Ballantine 1984, Dasilva, Blasi and Dees 1984, Supicic 1987, Honigsheim 1989, Blaukopf 1992). Additionally, while there are numerous exemplary studies *in* the sociology of music, these tend to be too specific to make for good reference works, in and of themselves (for example, Frith 1996, Peterson 1997, DeNora 2000). Our goal, then, is to present a broad and diverse book that introduces some of the field's main conceptual, methodological and empirical concerns, both past and present, and which serves as a resource for scholars, teachers and students working at the intersections of music and sociology.

About the Reader

Following a general Introduction, in which we examine the history, current state and possible future directions of music sociology, the Reader is organized into six sections: Source Readings; Approaches, Sites, and Debates; Politics, Social Issues, and Musical Cultures; Industries and Institutions; Technology and Mediation; and New Directions. Each section congregates around some of the field's main themes and is accompanied by a brief introductory essay that elaborates and contextualizes its content. As such, the purpose of this Preface is not to unpack the contents of the book, either chapter by chapter or section by section. Rather, the goal here is simply to attune readers to what they can expect in their exploration of *The Routledge Reader on the Sociology of Music*.

The Reader's thematic organization reflects what we think are some of the most formative and pressing issues in music sociology. The chapters have been newly commissioned and reprinted from world-leading authors. Of course, there are other ways of approaching the field. One book cannot provide a complete map; nor can it be all things to all people. For example, there are numerous theoretical issues that could stand more coverage than we are able to offer, while questions of methodology are addressed in ways that are mainly implicit.[3] There are also relatively distinct strands of the sociology of music itself, which have their own substantial bodies of literature, such as the sociology of music education (see Wright 2010) and the long-standing Institute for Music Sociology in Vienna (see Zembylas 2012).

For these reasons, this book is not an empirically, conceptually or culturally all-encompassing treatment of music sociology. Nevertheless, we have tried to present a representative range of issues from an illustrative range of perspectives. Our hope is to open up the world of music sociology. *The Routledge Reader on the Sociology of Music* is an introduction to a conversation—and an invitation to keep it going.

Thanks

As part of the background work for our introductory material, Kyle Devine undertook some archival research and interviewing. Our thanks go to Dina Kellams and Carrie Schwier of the Indiana University Archives for helping with our research into John H. Mueller, and to Howard Becker and Peter Martin for taking the time to answer Kyle's questions about the history of the discipline. Howard Becker went "above and beyond," making us aware of some of the French literature that we had not come across.

For expert and vital help in preparing the manuscript, we are enormously grateful to Gabrielle Kielich, a graduate student in Carleton University's master's program in Music and Culture. For administrative support, we are indebted to Meredith Warner, the Program Review Officer in the Office of the Vice-Provost and Associate Vice-President (Academic) at Carleton University. Georgina

Born, Dave O'Brien and Nick Prior were generous conversation partners at various stages of this project, while Stephen Cottrell and Tom Everett provided insightful feedback on the introductory material. Our editor at Routledge, Constance Ditzel, has from the beginning offered enthusiastic support and guidance to this project. Finally, we would like to thank the many reviewers who helped shape the volume with their excellent suggestions and input, including Veit Erlmann, Ron Eyerman, Scott Grills, David Inglis, Thomas Regelski, Mickey Vallee and others.

Notes

1   We use the terms "sociology of music" and "music sociology" interchangeably, notwithstanding some incisive critiques of the phrase "sociology *of* music" (see DeNora 2003, Hennion 2003; see also the first footnote in the Introduction).
2   Cultural sociology is, far and away, the most popular subfield in the American Sociological Association, and is strongly represented in the Australian, British, Canadian and European Sociological Associations. For additional background on so-called "new" musicology, see for example Williams (2001), Shepherd (2003), Stobart (2008) and the special issue of *Radical Musicology* (2010–2011). On the development and themes of cultural sociology and the sociology of the arts, see for example Inglis and Hughson (2003, 2005), Fuente (2007), Born (2010), Back et al. (2012), Alexander, Jacobs and Smith (2013), Alexander and Bowler (2014).
3   Indeed, producing a methodologically oriented introduction to music sociology would be a task of its own. While there are some excellent starting points (for example, Clarke and Cook 2004), it seems a comprehensive guide to research methods in the sociology of music would be a timely undertaking.

References

Adorno, T.W. 1976. *Introduction to the Sociology of Music*. New York: Continuum.
Alexander, A., R. Jacobs and P. Smith, eds. 2013. *The Oxford Handbook of Cultural Sociology*. Oxford: Oxford University Press.
Alexander, V. and A. Bowler. 2014. "Art at the Crossroads: The Arts in Society and the Sociology of Art." *Poetics* 43(1): 1–19.
Back, L., A. Bennett, L. Desfor Edles, M. Gibson, D. Inglis, R. Jacobs and I. Woodward. 2012. *Cultural Sociology: An Introduction*. Oxford: Wiley-Blackwell.
Ballantine, C. 1984. *Music and its Social Meanings*. New York: Gordon and Breach.
Blaukopf, K. 1992. *Musical Life in a Changing Society: Aspects of Music Sociology*. Portland: Amadeus Press.
Born, G. 2010. "The Social and the Aesthetic: For a Post-Bourdieuian Theory of Cultural Production." *Cultural Sociology* 4(2): 171–208.
Brandl, E., C. Prévost-Thomas and H. Ravet, eds. 2012. *Vingt-cinq ans de sociologie de la musique en France* (Tome 1). Paris: L'Harmattan.
Clarke, E. and N. Cook, eds. 2004. *Empirical Musicology: Aims, Methods, Prospects*. Oxford: Oxford University Press.
Dasilva, F., A.J. Blasi and D. Dees. 1984. *The Sociology of Music*. Notre Dame: University of Notre Dame Press.
DeNora, T. 2000. *Music in Everyday Life*. Cambridge: Cambridge University Press.
_____. 2003. *After Adorno: Rethinking Music Sociology*. Cambridge: Cambridge University Press.
Frith, S. 1996. *Performing Rites: On the Value of Popular Music*. Cambridge: Harvard University Press.
Fuente, E. de la. 2007. "The 'New Sociology of Art': Putting Art Back into Social Science Approaches to the Arts." *Cultural Sociology* 1(3): 409–425.
Hennion, A. 2003. "Music and Mediation: Toward a New Sociology of Music." In *The Cultural Study of Music: A Critical Introduction*, eds. M. Clayton, T. Herbert and R. Middleton, 80–91. New York: Routledge.
Honigsheim, P. 1989. *Sociologists and Music: An Introduction to the Study of Music and Society*. New Brunswick: Transaction.
Inglis, D. and J. Hughson. 2003. *Confronting Culture: Sociological Vistas*. Cambridge: Polity.
_____, eds. 2005. *The Sociology of Art: Ways of Seeing*. New York: Palgrave Macmillan.
Kotarba, J. and P. Vannini. 2009. *Understanding Society through Popular Music*. New York: Routledge.
Kunst, J. 1968. *Some Sociological Aspects of Music*. New York: De Capo.
McCormick, L. 2012. "Music Sociology in a New Key." In *The Oxford Handbook of Cultural Sociology*, eds. J.C. Alexander, R.N. Jacobs and P. Smith, 722–744. New York: Oxford University Press.

Peterson, R.A. 1997. *Creating Country Music: Fabricating Authenticity*. Chicago: University of Chicago Press.

Shepherd, J. 2003. "Music and Social Categories." In *The Cultural Study of Music: A Critical Introduction*, eds. M. Clayton, T. Herbert and R. Middleton, 69–79. New York: Routledge.

Silbermann, A. 1963. *The Sociology of Music*. London: Routledge.

Stobart, H., ed. 2008. *The New (Ethno)musicologies*. Lanham: Scarecrow.

Supicic, I. 1987. *Music in Society: A Guide to the Sociology of Music*. New York: Pendragon Press.

Thompson, W.F., ed. 2014. *Music in the Social and Behavioral Sciences: An Encyclopedia*. Thousand Oaks: Sage.

Towe Horsfall, S., J.-M. Meij and M.D. Probstfield, eds. 2014. *Music Sociology: Examining the Role of Music in Social Life*. Boulder: Paradigm.

Weber, M. 1958 [1921]. *The Rational and Social Foundations of Music*. Carbondale: Southern Illinois University Press.

Williams, A. 2001. *Constructing Musicology*. Aldershot: Ashgate.

Wright, R., ed. 2010. *Sociology and Music Education*. Farnham: Ashgate.

Zembylas, T., ed. 2012. *Kurt Blaukopf on Music Sociology: An Anthology*. New York: Peter Lang.

Acknowledgments

The following extracts were reproduced with kind permission. While every effort has been made to trace copyright holders and obtain permission, this has not always been possible in all cases. Any omissions brought to our attention will be remedied in future editions.

Adorno, T. 1976 [1962]. "Postscript—Sociology of Music." In *Introduction to the Sociology of Music*, 219–228. New York: Seabury.

Born, G. 2011. "Music and the Materialization of Identities." *Journal of Material Culture* 16(4): 376–388. © 2011. Reprinted by Permission of Sage.

Cohen, S. 2012. "Bubble, Tracks, Borders and Lines: Mapping Music and Urban Landscape." *Journal of the Royal Musical Association* 137(1): 135–170.

DeNora, T. 2003. "New Methods and Classic Concerns." In *After Adorno: Rethinking Music Sociology*, 35–58. Cambridge: Cambridge University Press. © Tia DeNora 2003. Reproduced by permission.

Frith, S. 2007. "Live Music Matters." *Scottish Music Review* 1(1): 1–17.

Gilbert, J. 2004. "Signifying Nothing: 'Culture,' 'Discourse,' and the Sociality of Affect." *Culture Machine* 6 (www.culturemachine.net/index.php/cm/article/view/8/7).

Grazian, D. 2004. "Opportunities for Ethnography in the Sociology of Music." *Poetics* 32(3/4): 197–210. © 2004 with permission from Elsevier.

Hennion, A. 2010. "Loving Music: From a Sociology of Mediation to a Pragmatics of Taste." *Comunicar* 27(34): 25–33.

Martin, P. 2006. "Music and the Sociological Gaze." In *Music and the Sociological Gaze: Art Worlds and Cultural Production*, 13–31. Manchester: University of Manchester Press.

McClary, S. 2000. "Turtles All the Way Down (on the 'Purely Musical')." In *Conventional Wisdom: The Content of Musical Form*, 1–31. Berkeley: University of California Press. © 2000 by the Regents of the University of California. Reprinted with permission.

Mueller, J.H. 1951. "Musical Taste and How it is Formed." In *The American Symphony Orchestra: A Social History of Musical Taste*, 380–405. Bloomington: Indiana University Press. © 1951. Reprinted with permission of Indiana University Press.

Peterson, R. 1992. "Understanding Audience Segmentation: From Elite and Mass to Omnivore and Univore." *Poetics* 21(4): 243–258. © 1991 with permission from Elsevier.

Pinch, T. and K. Bijsterveld. 2003. "Should One Applaud? Breaches and Boundaries in the Reception of New Technology in Music." *Technology and Culture* 44(3): 536–559. © 2003 The Society for the History of Technology. Reprinted with permission of Johns Hopkins University Press.

Prior, N. 2011. "Critique and Renewal in the Sociology of Music: Bourdieu and Beyond." *Cultural Sociology* 5(1): 121–138. © 2011. Reprinted by permission of Sage.

Santoro, M. 2011. "Production of Culture." In *The Encyclopedia of Consumer Culture*, ed. D. Southerton, 1154–1157. Thousand Oaks: Sage. © 2011. Reprinted by permission of Sage.

Schütz, A. 1951. "Making Music Together: A Study in Social Relationship." *Social Research* 18(1/4): 76–97. © 1951 New School for Social Research. Reprinted with permission of Johns Hopkins University Press.

Shepherd, J. 1991. "Music and the Last Intellectuals." *Journal of Aesthetic Education* 25(3): 95–114. © 1991 by the Board of Trustees of the University of Illinois.

Shepherd, J. and K. Devine. 2013. "Sociology of Music." In *The Grove Dictionary of American Music*, 2nd ed. New York: Oxford University Press.

Simmel, G. 1968 [1883]. "Psychological and Ethnological Studies on Music." In Georg Simmel: *The Conflict in Modern Culture and Other Essays*, ed. K.P. Etzkorn, 98–140. New York: Teachers College Press. © 1968 by Teachers College Press. All rights reserved.

Spencer, H. 1916 [1854]. "The Origin and Function of Music." In *Essays: Scientific, Political, and Speculative*, Vol. 2, 210–238. New York: Appleton.

Weber, M. 1958 [1921]. *The Rational and Social Foundations of Music*. Carbondale: Southern Illinois University Press.

Introduction

Music and the Sociological Imagination— Pasts and Prospects

JOHN SHEPHERD AND KYLE DEVINE

Our goal in this Introduction is to present some of the historical roots and promising future directions—the "pasts and prospects"—of what we might call the "sociological imagination" as it has been applied to musical culture. Of course, the phrase "sociological imagination" has a specific meaning: it was coined by the US sociologist C. Wright Mills (1959), who understood it as "a quality of mind" that "enables us to grasp history and biography and the relations between the two within society" (5, 6). In other words, the phrase designates a reflexive, critical orientation toward social conventions; it helps one see the constructed and mutable character of what might otherwise seem natural and unchanging.

Some of Mills's ideas about the sociological imagination were politically motivated and particular to his time and place (13–15). But Mills also believed that this "quality of mind" was a common denominator across many of the most insightful social analyses (6). As such, we want to relieve the sociological imagination of some of its Mills-specific historical and cultural connotations and, instead, to use the phrase to refer more generally to the various ways in which relationships between personal, social and musical experiences have been understood over time. In this way, the sociological imagination becomes a historical and analytical lens through which we can view over a century of shifting thought on music and the social[1]—that is, the various ways sociologists have engaged with music, on the one hand, and the various ways musicologists have engaged with the social, on the other. Using the sociological imagination as a kind of backdrop for an intellectual history, this Introduction initiates a sociology of music sociology.[2]

General Considerations, Early Histories

Although a broadly scholarly interest in music and the social extends back thousands of years (for example, Plato, Aristotle, Augustine, Boethius; see Bowman 1998), our investigation begins in the nineteenth century, when the modern academic world took shape. Without wishing to become mired in the complex intellectual genealogy of either musicology or sociology (see Duckles et al. 2001, Shepherd 2001), we can note a small irony in the development of their shared history: namely, that even as the academic world was driven toward the creation of specialized and distinct disciplinary domains, certain crosscurrents between music and sociology were nevertheless apparent from the outset. Several foundational social scientists, for example, drew on musical thought and scholarship.

1

Take, for instance, August Comte, who coined the very term "sociology" in the 1830s. Comte not only wrote on music; he believed that it "was the most social of all arts" (Etzkorn 1974: 44). Other founding figures of sociology such as Herbert Spencer, Georg Simmel and Max Weber also wrote on music (see also Elias 1993).

Such work suggests that the beginnings of music sociology were part of the intellectual formation of sociology writ large. Two characteristics have marked this work from the outset. First, scholars at the intersection of music and the social sciences often noted the lack of a community of scholars dedicated to examining the subject, and thus also a lack of continuity in the intellectual tradition. There is some validity to this claim, as the sociologists who did write about music tended to do so as an extension of their other activities. Consequently, their work was understandably characterized by their own theoretical and methodological predilections. For example, while Weber (1958) developed a detailed analysis of the system of functional tonality as an expression and incorporation of the rational instincts of modern western societies, Spencer and Simmel contributed to what has been described as "a somewhat futile debate about the origins of music" (Martin 1995: x). (While this debate may indeed have been "futile," not to mention problematic, we argue in the introduction to Section I that it is actually key to the development of the musical–sociological imagination during this period.) In early twentieth-century US sociology, too, studies of music also appeared as byproducts of broader, non-musical agendas. For example, several early ethnographic studies stemming from the so-called Chicago School explored dancehalls and musical careers as part of more general interests in labor and the effects of urbanization (for example, Becker 1951; see also Section II of this volume), while Paul Lazarsfeld of the Bureau of Applied Social Research (1946), as well as scholars such as David Reisman (1950) and Donald Horton (1957), examined the recording industry and audience patterns in order to understand phenomena such as mass culture, youth and deviance.

It has also been common in surveys of music sociology, both during this early period and since, to note that such work was carried out by scholars who were largely not cognizant of one another, and that the field has thus been diffuse and fragmented. For example, in an early doctoral dissertation on the subject, Kaplan (1951: 1) noted that the sociology of art in general "has almost completely been neglected," while later that decade Etzkorn (1959: 218) claimed that the sociology of music, too, had been "rather neglected." Becker (1964: 437) implicitly supported both positions in a review of Silbermann's *Sociology of Music* (1963): "Sociologists have not done much in the analysis of artistic behavior and I believe it is correct to say that very little of what has been done deals with music." Similar statements mark the sociology of music all the way down to the 1990s (for example, Rumbelow 1969, Bennett 1972). In 1995, for example, Martin (1995: vii) wrote that the state of the field was "rather inchoate." Again, there is some truth to this idea—and there appears to be agreement that, with the growth of the field around the year 2000, the field has at long last started to reach a more mature state (Martin 2006, Dowd 2007, Kwame Harrison 2010). We will return to this point. Here we simply want to suggest the possibility that the frequent assertions of music sociology's fragmented history and perpetually-emerging-but-never-arriving character have been exaggerated.

As simply one way of tempering such claims, we turn to the US sociologist John H. Mueller. Mueller was by no means exclusively concerned with music; indeed, he is perhaps most remembered for his work in general sociology and statistical reasoning. Yet he cultivated a sociological imagination in relation to music from at least the early 1930s. His major work on the subject appeared in 1951: *The American Symphony Orchestra: A Social History of Musical Taste*. It is a remarkably prescient book, as we explain in Section I. Here we want to focus initially on a correspondence that developed between Mueller and that most famous author of introductory music history, Donald J. Grout (see Burkholder, Grout and Palisca 2014).[3]

Although they had never met, Grout wrote to Mueller in the summer of 1948, because Cornell University was thinking about making a joint appointment in music and sociology. In part, Grout was seeking Mueller's opinion on a particular candidate. But the esteemed musicologist was also keen to "arrange to get together," as he thought Mueller might be able to clarify the relationship between musicology and sociology—a relationship that Grout found "annoyingly obscure." Unfortunately, perhaps, for the development of the field, Mueller did not know the candidate well enough to endorse him and Cornell, as far as we can tell, did not cross-appoint a scholar to music and sociology. In a follow-up note, though, Mueller obliged Grout's request to clarify the relationship between the fields, noting that the sociology of music was "certainly not yet a reality but rather the substance of things hoped for." Yet Mueller was nevertheless confident that the "blend of these disciplines . . . is not illusory." He proceeded to outline a variety of positions that are remarkably resonant with certain themes in music sociology today (see Section I).

In addition to Grout, Mueller served as a professional and personal point-of-contact for a number of other prominent sociologists working on musical problems during the early- to mid-twentieth century: for example, Etzkorn, Honigsheim, Kaplan, Schuessler, Silbermann and Sorokin. While none of these figures is today widely discussed in music sociology, the character of the associations formed around and through Mueller lend a coherence to this moment that is lost in the existing literature. There are additional clues that an early- to mid-twentieth-century music sociology may be less "illusory" than dusty. Such clues exist in the backpages of journals, in book reviews and obituaries, in acknowledgment sections, in letters and memos, in reminiscences, and even in what Becker (1964: 437) identified as "a movement to establish a Society of Sociological Musicians." All of this raises questions about how much the "disjointedness" of the field is a fact of history or an effect of the historiography—and it opens the door to a deeper sociology of music sociology than we are able to offer in this short Introduction.[4]

A second characteristic to mark early work in the sociology of music was a preoccupation with western art music (for example, Weber 1958). The reason for this concern with art music, rather than traditional or popular music, has lain in art music's privileged position, not only in society in general, but also in academia, where there has been an overwhelming tendency—abating during the second half of the twentieth century—to view it as the only form of music worthy of scholarly treatment. Thus, scholars such as Supicic (1987), not to mention the "civilizing" and "democratizing" agendas of larger cultural institutions such as the British Broadcasting Corporation (BBC) and US radio (Frith 1988, Goodman 2011; see also Section V), have understood a lack of interest in art music on the part of large sections of the population as a problem requiring resolution through the work of sociologists and the development of appropriate policies in the spheres of education and culture (see for example Frith 2012).

Nowhere, perhaps, does the privileged position of the art music tradition emerge more strongly than in the work of Theodor Adorno. A trained musician with a minor but not insignificant career as a composer, Adorno's principal contribution was as a philosopher and scholar of music. On the completion of his academic studies in 1931, he joined the Department of Philosophy at Frankfurt University and became associated with the Institute for Social Research directed by Max Horkheimer. When the Nazis came to power in 1933, Adorno left Germany, moving first to the United Kingdom and in 1938 to New York, where he rejoined the Institute of Social Research in exile. He moved to Los Angeles in 1941 and then, in 1949, returned to Frankfurt and became, with Horkheimer, co-director of the re-established Institute. The influence of the "Frankfurt School," the group of scholars associated with the Institute, began to grow in Germany and, subsequently, throughout circles of critical scholarship within English-speaking intellectual life.

The work and influence of the Frankfurt School can be understood in part as a reaction to the rise and fall of fascism in Germany, and also in part as a reaction to the alienation experienced by its members in the face of US popular culture. *Dialectic of Enlightenment*, by Horkheimer and Adorno (2002 [1947]), develops a theory of ideology in terms of which the culture industries are seen to instill in the majority of the population, through the mass production of cultural commodities, patterns of feeling and behavior commensurate with the needs of the dominant social form of industrial capitalism. Adorno was thus instrumental in developing an influential theory of mass culture that was pervasively Marxist and critical in its orientation, and that colored his understanding of popular music in particular. Adorno heard popular music—in his experience, apparently the dance-band music of the late 1930s and 1940s—as standardized and repetitive, hypnotically so in its alienating effects on the mass of people. However, to Adorno's credit, and unlike many who preceded and followed him, he paid attention to popular as well as to art music (Adorno 1976, 2002).

Adorno's work is clearly the product of a troubled and contentious period of history and of a severely dislocated biography. With the benefit of hindsight, many of his principal ideas on music are easy to criticize. However, his legacy can be argued to lie more importantly in the character and scope of the questions he asked than in the specifics of the answers he provided. Adorno understood the holistic character of the entire "musical–historical field." He saw that various musical traditions in modern western societies could be understood only through the character of their mutual relations, and that music needed to be understood not only in terms of its formal characteristics but also in terms of the relation of these to the circumstances of its production and reception. Adorno's work has been much discussed and much debated, and has been highly influential (see Middleton 1990, Paddison 1993, 1996; Martin 1995, Witkin 1998, Adorno 2002, 2009; DeNora 2003, Born 2005).

A reason for the influence of Adorno's work lies in the way in which, as a sociology of music, it can be positioned away from the more democratizing instincts of the discipline, and closer to the idealist and exclusionary tendencies of historical musicology and music theory. Adorno believed that it was the business of music sociology to make aesthetic judgments (for which he has been criticized: Martin 1995). This belief was part of a critical orientation that had little time for the kind of consensual and positivistic objectivity claimed by many sociologists (see for example Silbermann 1957). Indeed, Adorno saw such claims—which in the case of music pit the aesthetic and the emotional against social "facts"—as so much ideology, and reasoned that the aesthetic was necessarily social. But while this critical orientation, grounded in the wider Marxist project, generated the basis for later approaches to music that questioned the social and cultural *status quo* and the role in it of art music, it also allowed for the persistence of established beliefs concerning the relative value of art music and popular music. It was this retention of a recognizably traditional aesthetic that allowed many musicologists, faced with the cultural and aesthetic challenges of the 1960s and afterwards, to reconcile in an acceptable form two realms regarded previously as incommensurable: the sociological and the musicological.

Adorno is rightly regarded as an especially significant founder of music sociology, and his work has succeeded in giving shape—if in an idiosyncratic way—to an otherwise uneven field of study.

The 1970s and After

It can be argued that the cultural and intellectual shifts of the 1950s and 1960s, including various civil rights movements, anti-war protests and countercultural revolutions, marked the beginnings of a watershed in the academic study of music to which sociological and social–anthropological concerns contributed importantly. In the United States, this watershed first became apparent with the founding, in 1955, of the Society for Ethnomusicology. Ethnomusicology was a discipline developed in its initial formulation in the United States (it has a history that can be traced back to the years before the Second World War in Europe as well as the United States) from the disciplines of social anthropology and musicology. The advocacy of this society for the inclusion of traditional music in the curricula of university music departments was to have far-reaching implications in challenging the exclusivity of art music. Following on from this, the cultural and political challenges of the 1960s, intimately related as they were to various developments in rock, folk and popular music, gave rise to a generation of young people, some of whom, in obtaining academic positions in a range of disciplines in the 1970s, brought with them their cultural, political and musical affiliations. A similar phenomenon had occurred in the United States in the late 1930s and 1940s as a younger generation of scholars raised on jazz entered the academy: slowly but surely, jazz became accepted as a legitimate object of academic study.

The infusion of rock, folk and popular music into the academy had several consequences. First, the challenge to the exclusivity of art music posed by ethnomusicology was supplemented by an advocacy for the inclusion of popular music in education at both the secondary and post-secondary levels—an advocacy resting heavily on sociological arguments (see Vulliamy 1976, 1977, 1978; Vulliamy and Shepherd 1984). Second, the sociology of music itself became quickly and increasingly concerned with forms of popular music. As a field of study it began to manifest a recognizable community of scholars and, for a short while, a coherent intellectual trajectory. (The foundation of the US journal *Popular Music and Society* in 1971 and, in 1979, the International Association for the Study of Popular Music were in part expressions of these trends.) However, it also began to undergo two transformations: it began to be practiced as much by non-sociologists as sociologists (and, indeed, as much by non-musicologists as musicologists) and, in the formulation to emerge in the late 1970s, its democratizing and critical instincts spread readily and quickly outside the borders of its established concerns in conversations with ethnomusicology, as well as with interdisciplinary intellectual trajectories such as cultural studies and feminism. Sociology, through its relations with the study of music as in other areas of endeavor, was by the late 1980s evidencing the porous character of its disciplinary borders.

This changed character of the sociology of music became apparent first in the United Kingdom (see Chambers 1985, Shepherd 1994). The late 1970s saw the publication of *Whose Music? A Sociology of Musical Languages*, by Shepherd and others (1977), as well as Small's *Music–Society–Education* (1977). Both books cast a critical eye on the social constitution and character of art music and argue for the serious study of other music, including popular music, in terms and criteria drawn not from the study of art music but from within the cultural and social realities of the people creating and appreciating music of these other kinds.

In *The Sociology of Rock* (1978), Frith argued that the social relevance of popular music in the United Kingdom had to be understood as much in terms of generational as class differences. While "pop" music—seen as chart oriented and acquiescing in the conditions of its own commercial production—was relevant to youth culture and subcultures in the formation of their identities, it was rock music—judged as authentic and as carrying a critique of its own conditions of production— that more directly served the oppositional stances of many youth subcultures. *The Sociology of Rock* combined the instincts of symbolic interactionism with the insights of cultural Marxism (see also Frith 1983). This combination, characteristic of the conversation between British sociology and cultural studies at the time, received clearer theoretical formulation in the work of other scholars associated with the Centre for Contemporary Cultural Studies, University of Birmingham (see Willis 1978, Hebdige 1979). Although the work of Shepherd, Small and Frith emanated from the United Kingdom, much of what the work was concerned with was music of a US lineage—music that has made a major contribution to the development of popular music during the second half of the twentieth century.

If the work of the "Birmingham School" and its followers grew out of an engagement with subcultures and leisure, and emphasized the meanings music had for its audience, a sociological paradigm was developing concurrently in the United States that grew out of the study of institutions and work, and which examined how music was produced. The main architect of this highly influential approach, known as the "production-of-culture" perspective, has been Richard Peterson (see Peterson 1976, Dowd 2004a, Peterson and Anand 2004, Santoro 2008; see also Section II). For Peterson, cultural products like music were seen, not as the result of singular creative genius, but as outcomes of everyday institutional arrangements and processes of interaction that were broadly similar to other forms of work.

In addition to the production-of-culture perspective, other broadly conventional forms of music sociology continued to be practiced. One form approximates to social history in examining the history of the institutional, political and economic circumstances within which music has been practiced. Here the pioneering work of Raynor (1972, 1976) has been important in the context of European art music, as has the work of DeNora (1995, see also Johnson, Fulcher and Ertman 2009). Another form approximates to a more synchronic concern with such circumstances, as well as with the effects that music itself can have upon them. Important in the realm of art music have been the contributions of DiMaggio (1986), while in popular music studies the contributions of Garofalo (1992), Eyerman and Jamison (1998), as well as Bennett et al. (1993) should be noted. (See also Section III.)

At the same time, the boundaries between sociology, social anthropology, ethnomusicology, cultural studies, feminism and, indeed, some forms of musicology became less and less clear as the major task seemed that of constituting a critical, cultural musicology rather than of working within established disciplinary boundaries. In the late 1980s, Leppert and McClary published *Music and Society: The Politics of Composition, Performance and Reception* (1987), a book contributed to equally by sociologists, musicologists, cultural theorists and feminists. This period also witnessed the publication of four important volumes concentrating on ethnography, interviews and face-to-face interaction as the route to understanding the social constitution of musical realities. Two were by social anthropologists (Finnegan 1989, Cohen 1991), one by a sociologist (Weinstein 1991) and the other led by an ethnomusicologist (Crafts, Cavicchi and Keil 1993). Of equal importance was *Feminine Endings: Music, Gender and Sexuality* (1991) by feminist musicologist Susan McClary, which occasioned heated debate within musicology as to the gendered provenance of music.

The connections between ethnomusicology and the sociology of music that were discernible in the 1970s and 1980s became even closer in the 1990s. During this time there was a growing community of interest on the part of sociologists and social anthropologists in questions of ethnicity, difference, identity and globalization which found expression in the study of world popular music— popular music studies having been an area in which the study of western music had predominated and in which sociology had been more influential than ethnomusicology. This drew several important contributions to the study of popular and art music on a world basis and thus to the sociology of music broadly defined (Frith 1989, Waterman 1990, Stokes 1992, Guilbault et al. 1993, Slobin 1993, Erlmann 1996, Born and Hesmondhalgh 2000). This concern with how ethnicity and difference have figured in the social constitution of musical identities has also given rise in an era of globalization and late modernity to an interest in the concept of "place," "place" being understood more in terms of a community of intersecting musical interests and cross-fertilizations and less in terms of a notion of physically delimited space (Straw 1991). There have been important contributions from ethnic studies scholars (Lipsitz 1994), ethnomusicologists (Stokes 1994), cultural geographers (Leyshon, Matless and Revill 1998) and, indeed, interdisciplinary collaborations between music scholars and social scientists (for example, Whiteley, Bennett and Hawkins 2006; Toynbee and Dueck 2011; see also Section III). Recent scholarship in this area has increasingly drawn on anthropological and media theories in developing the notion of *circulation* as a framework for describing the migrations of music through culture and around the world (for a general overview see Straw 2010b; for an application see Novak 2013).

In these ways, the historical relationship between music and the sociological imagination evidences a tendency toward interdisciplinarity.

Music as Social Meaning

In contrast to the ideology of autonomy which saw western art music as the asocial fruit of absolute genius,[5] the sociological assumption that all human thought and action is socially constituted has given rise to the possibility that the structures and sounds of music are of social significance—that is, the meanings articulated through the structures and sounds of music may themselves be socially constituted. This line of thinking, implicit in the work of Weber and Adorno, became explicit around the 1970s (see Lomax 1968, Blacking 1973, Etzkorn 1974, Shepherd et al. 1977, Small 1977, Willis 1978, Keil 1979, Ballantine 1984).

All this work, with some variations, rested on the central idea that the character of social or cultural formations could find expression through musical structures and sounds, if not be in part constituted through them. Music could therefore reflect essential cultural forms, and thus serve as either a reinforcement of normative behavior (Lomax 1968) or a venue for social critique (Shepherd et al. 1977, Willis 1978, Ballantine 1984). For Shepherd and Ballantine, this critical potential is located in the presumed oppositional stances of various genres of popular music, a stance resting on a perceived homology between the technical characteristics of the musical genre in question and the character of the subcultural reality involved with the music. A detailed articulation of the homology thesis is found in Shepherd (1982), where he nuanced the work of Birmingham scholars Willis and Hebdige and identified in the technical musical characteristics of a wide range of popular music genres the potential for both social reproduction and resistance.

A significant weakness, shared by nearly all work on the social meaning of music, is a silence or lack of precision on the question of how "the social" gets into "the musical" (see Becker 1989, Hennion 1995, DeNora 2003, Martin 2006). A related question is that of how musical materials can have such meanings in the first place. There are two possibilities. One is that the meanings are endemic, "immanent" in some way to the specific character of the musical materials in question. Yet the presumed fixity of relation between meaning and music precludes the possibility for negotiation fundamental to the constitution of any social meaning. The alternative is that the characteristics of the sounds in question are assumed to play little role in the construction of the meanings articulated through them. From this perspective, musical meanings are not "immanent" but "arbitrary." This has been the position of Grossberg (1984, 1987), who has seen the sounds of music as little more than a ground of physiological and affective stimulation that can take on meaning only after being interpellated into the world of language.

A tension in the sociological analysis of musical meaning has thus lain in the need, on the one hand, to understand the characteristics of musical sounds as in some way being implicated in meaning construction and, on the other, to allow that processes of meaning construction through music are social in character. Martin (1995, 2006) has identified this tension as a basic difficulty in the so-called "new" musicology, and in particular the work of scholars such as Shepherd and McClary, which in turn has highlighted another problem: the tendency to reify both social structures and musical structures in the service of ensuring a smooth analytical fit between the two (for an attempt to resolve this tension see Shepherd and Wicke 1997).

Music as Social Interaction

An interest in music as social interaction at the level of micro-sociology appeared early on in the work of Schütz (1951). However, it has been argued for extensively and consistently by Becker, who has drawn a clear distinction between a more theoretical sociology of music, concerned with teasing out music's meanings, and an empirical sociology of music based on an examination of collective action. Sociologists working in this latter mode, he has observed, "aren't much interested in 'decoding' art works, in finding the work's secret meanings as reflections of society. They prefer to see those works as a result of what a lot of people do together" (Becker 1989: 282).

Becker's initial contributions to the sociology of music, based on studies carried out in the late 1940s, are represented in his book *Outsiders* (1963), a seminal contribution to the field of deviance studies in which two chapters deal with the distinctive way of life and careers of dance musicians. His foremost contribution to the sociology of art and music is *Art Worlds* (1982). Here Becker problematized received notions of art, understanding artistic works and other forms of cultural products as a consequence of the whole range of activities, hitherto taken for granted, involved in their production and consumption. For Becker, art worlds are constituted through the social interactions of a wide variety of players who act according to the opportunities, norms and constraints that typify the art world in question. The products of such worlds are thus shaped through the character of these actions which, in line with the general tenets of symbolic interactionism, may involve innovation as well as conformity.

Becker's work has exerted a strong influence, both directly and indirectly, on studies attempting to understand various aspects of the musical world using qualitative and ethnographic methods. Such studies examine the intricacies of music making and musical careers in areas as diverse as, for example, rock, Hollywood, the avant-garde, women's performance, karaoke, blues, jazz, opera and wind bands (Bennett 1980, Faulkner 1983, Born 1995, Bayton 1998, Drew 2001, Grazian 2003, Faulkner and Becker 2009, Benzecry 2011, Dubois, Méon and Pierru 2013). Indeed, Becker's influence has also been uniquely prevalent in France (see for example Bousson 2006, Buscatto 2007, Hammou 2014). At the same time, there is a developing body of scholarship that challenges and refines not only the work of Becker but the equally influential work of Peterson and Bourdieu (for example, McCormick 2006 on Becker; McCormick 2009 on Peterson; Hennion 2007, Prior 2008a and Born 2010a on Bourdieu; see also Sections II and VI).

Music as Social Identity

Toward the end of the 1980s, Frith observed that "the experience of pop music is an experience of placing: in responding to a song, we are drawn, haphazardly, into affective and emotional alliances with the performers and with the performers' other fans." He concluded that the "interplay between personal absorption into music and the sense that it is, nevertheless, something out there, something public, is what makes music so important in the cultural placing of the individual in the social." What Frith identified in this article was the way in which popular music in particular serves as a powerful force of identity for the individual within society, as well as a powerful force in forming the collective cultural and group identities from which individuals draw sustenance in constructing a sense of self. As he concludes, "the intensity of this relationship between taste and self-definition seems peculiar to popular music—it is 'possessable' in ways that other cultural forms are not . . . other cultural forms—painting, literature, design—can articulate and show off shared values and pride, but only music can make you *feel* them" (Frith 1987: 139–144; emphasis in original).

This interest in music as a basis for the formation of social identities, whether individual or collective, can be traced back to the late 1960s and early 1970s in work concerned to understand the relations between popular music and young people's perceived proclivity to challenge the social *status quo* (Denzin 1970, Hirsch 1971, Robinson and Hirsch 1972). Toward the end of the 1970s and going into the 1980s, this nascent interest took on a more explicit character in attempts to understand popular music as a force for the construction of gender and sexed identities (Frith and McRobbie 1978, Shepherd 1987; see also Section III). However, the major conceptual contribution to the understanding of popular music as a force for the construction of identities—beyond the largely ethnomusicological contributions to the study of world popular music and the related questions of ethnicity and place of the mid- to late-1990s—has lain in the work of Frith.

Like Grossberg, Frith has maintained a strong interest in what people say about music as a route to understanding the meanings that music holds for them. In this, he has demonstrated a strong affinity for the work of scholars such as Finnegan and Cohen in distancing himself from the more totalizing claims of studies in popular music emanating from British cultural studies of the 1970s, and for the work of Becker (1982) and Bourdieu (1984) in understanding how meaning and value are attributed to music (see Frith 1992, 1996). Frith does not understand various genres and styles of popular music as reflecting cultural and group realities so much as serving to constitute them in complex ways. A key to understanding his work is the way in which, as a sociologist, he has refused to take musical discourses at face value but to problematize them in the process of getting beneath their surface to grasp how they serve to constitute meaning and value for people in music. It was Frith who first importantly pointed out that notions of authenticity as attached to certain kinds of rock music in contrast to the perceived commercialism of pop music were in fact ideological in character: "the myth of authenticity is, indeed, one of rock's own ideological effects" (1987: 137).

The character of Frith's insights can be traced in part to the dual careers he has followed as a professional sociologist and a rock critic. The former career tended to be concerned with the development of dispassionate but committed social analyses, the latter with the world of value judgments: they came together in his book *Performing Rites: On the Value of Popular Music* (1996), a series of essays in which, as an academic critic, he seeks to understand the constitution of personal taste and emotional response in relation to music. Like Adorno, therefore, Frith has put aesthetic judgment at the center of his sociological agenda. But, unlike Adorno, he does not see the purpose of the sociology of music as the making of such judgments, but rather their understanding.

As a complement to scholars such as Frith (see also DeNora 2000), who have largely focused on the positive role of music in the construction of identity, Hesmondhalgh (2008: 342) has argued that "music's power to enable self-making is constrained, limited and damaged." As such, while acknowledging that the emphasis on music as a positive resource for identity has been valuable and illuminating (both inherently and as a reaction to the criticisms leveled by the Frankfurt School and its followers), Hesmondhalgh advocates a more balanced approach to the relationship between music and identity, one that takes better stock of music's negative potential. Some of this negative potential is readily apparent in forms such as musical manipulation and violence as well as the use of music in weaponry and torture (for example, Brown and Volgsten 2005, Johnson and Cloonan 2009, Goodman 2010, Cusick 2013). Perhaps the most influential account of such potentials, though, deals with more subtle ways that music can be put into the service of negative and exclusionary politics: Bourdieu's *Distinction* (1984).

Bourdieu has been significant in examinations of the relationship between social (and especially class-based) identity and musical taste. Part of his argument is that there are correlations between "high culture" and a taste for art music, and that individuals of high social status tend to use displays of their musical taste—through "cultural capital"—to distinguish themselves from those of lower social status. Because Bourdieu's analyses were conducted exclusively on French society, his theoretical generalizations have been called into question (but see Bennett et al. 2009). Other scholars, for example, using US survey data, found that high status individuals do not distinguish themselves from others through their "exclusive" taste for art music, but through their enjoyment of a wider variety of musics. This so-called "omnivore thesis" has generated considerable debate, a significant portion of which has played out in the pages of the journal *Poetics* (for summaries see Dowd 2007, Savage and Gayo 2011; see also Taylor 2009; Sections II, III and VI).

Other important contributions to understanding the role of music in constituting social identities have been made in relation to genres and subcultures (Grossberg 1992, Walser 1993, Thornton 1995), to communities and scenes at civic, national, global and virtual levels (Straw 1991, Shank 1994, Bennett and Peterson 2004, Biddle and Knights 2007) as well as technology (Bull 2007).

Music, Materiality, and Mediation

Looking back on these debates about the character of musical meaning, interaction and identity, it is possible to identify two sociologies of music. One has been practiced by sociologists with an interest in music, the other by music scholars with an interest in society. Each has been perceived as inadequate from the other's perspective. On the one hand, music scholars make connections between musical conventions and social structures/mores in ways that do not stand up to the empirical demands of sociology. Sociologists, on the other hand, describe the processes by which a musical work comes to be and the conditions in which it is used but fail to account for the specificity of the music itself. The challenge, in other words, has been to develop a *sociology* of music that is also a sociology of *music*.[6]

In addressing this challenge, scholars such as Hennion, DeNora and Born have developed theoretically sophisticated and empirically rigorous accounts of musical meanings and social identities as *co-constructed* in processes of cultural interaction (see also Marshall 2011, Sections II and VI). As a notion, "co-construction" (or "mutual mediation") takes seriously the materiality of musical sounds and aesthetics in a way that cuts a path between purely constructivist (arbitrary) and purely musicological (immanent) explanations of musical meaning and use (Shepherd 2002).

For example, in a series of publications stretching across four decades (1981, 1983, 1986, 1995, 1997, 2001, 2003, 2007, 2010, 2012, 2014), Hennion has argued against both an understanding of the art work as an independent object of beauty and a sociological approach that conceptually eradicates the specific and distinctive qualities of individual art works by reducing them to the conditions of reflective social symbols. In stressing the concept of mediation, Hennion understands the specific and distinctive character of cultural commodities as complex emanations of the social interactions that produce them, and the character of the material objects in and through which they are invested. He has thus striven to transcend a distinction customarily drawn in the sociology of culture between the circumstances of production and consumption (see also Peterson 2000, Peterson and Anand 2004, Santoro 2008, Straw 2010a).

Relatedly, DeNora (2000, 2003) focuses on the idea of musical "affordance." From this perspective, the specific material characteristics and properties of music can guide, shape and facilitate—but not determine—certain uses. However, it is necessary to observe how such musical materials are used by people before any conclusions about the meanings of musical objects or the identities of human subjects can be reached. This is to touch on another similarity of recent work bridging musical identity, meaning and interaction: a focus on process over product, and the (broadly) ethnographic study of music "in action" as opposed to a textual–analytic engagement with completed musical works. Calhoun and Sennett (2007: 5) succinctly describe this shift in the sociology of the arts more broadly: it is nowadays a study of painting more than paintings.

Born has developed a set of articles in which she outlines a theory of musical mediation (see for example Born 2005, 2010b, 2012a, 2012b). Building on the work of Hennion and DeNora, as well as Adorno and others, Born's argument is that music's social dimensions can be understood in terms of four intermediating "planes." While mediation is one of the most plastic concepts in contemporary music sociology, leading to many different uses and definitions (for an intelligent discussion see Valiquet 2015), Born's own understanding emerges intuitively in her elaboration of the planes. "In the first plane," she notes, "music produces its own diverse socialities in the guise of the intimate microsocialities of musical performance and practice.... In the second, music has powers to animate imagined communities ... In the third, music refracts wider social identity formations ... In the fourth, music is entangled in the institutional forms that enable its production, reproduction, and transformation." Although this fourfold framework emerges out of dissatisfaction with what she sees as the lopsidedly microsociological studies of scholars such as Hennion and DeNora (who arguably focus primarily on the first and second planes), Born wishes to avoid any simplistic call to macrosociological work. Indeed, she notes, invoking Deleuzian assemblage theory, "the four planes of music's social mediation are irreducible to one another and are articulated in contingent and non-linear ways through relations of affordance, conditioning, or causality" (2012a: 267). The promise of Born's catholic conceptual framework lies in its insistence that the aesthetic and affective dimensions of the first and second planes both inflect and are inflected by the social and institutional dimensions of the third and fourth. In other words, Born's theory of mediation advances the field's ability to produce analyses that are at once deeply social and deeply musical.

Questions of mediation and materiality serve as focal points not only for Hennion, DeNora and Born, but also an entire subfield: the sociology of musical media and sound technology (see Section V). This work pits itself against deterministic, inventor-based and "progress-oriented" understandings of the history of music technology, favoring instead studies that demonstrate how musical aesthetics and practices emerge in intimate and co-formative dialogues with scientific research and technological development. Taking influence from the field of science and technology studies, it could be said that the field has developed a "new" organology (Bijsterveld and Peters 2010; see also Born 1995, Théberge 1997, Waksman 1999, Taylor 2001, Pinch and Trocco 2002).

Such studies have been especially concerned with the introduction of new technologies—that is, with the cultural turbulence that often occurs when old technologies were new (see Marvin 1988). Recently, a body of radically material scholarship has emerged in relation to the opposite question: what happens when new technologies become old? Indeed, music formats, playback media and musical instruments (not to mention sheet music and concertgoing) are in this literature seen as more than facilitators of musical–aesthetic encounters and exchanges; they are "things" that must also be understood within global supply chains, stores of natural and raw materials such as plastics, as well as waste disposal and decomposition. Studies in media ecology and ecomusicology are thus beginning to focus attention on the environmental impact—or what we might call the political ecology—of modern music (Devine forthcoming; see also Straw 1999–2000, 2012; Acland 2007, Gabrys 2011, Maxwell and Miller 2012, Allen 2013).

Paralleling these emphases on the mediated and material character of musical sound has been a turn to other aspects of musical culture that are not easily studied in textual terms: experience (Shepherd and Wicke 2000), emotion and affect (DeNora 2001, Finnegan 2003, Stokes 2010), taste and attachment (Hennion 2003, 2007), feeling and embodiment (Johnson 2008), as well as listening, sound and vibratory phenomena more generally (Sterne 2003, Feld 2005, Born 2010b, Goodman 2010, Jasen 2012). Many of these scholars emphasize that an understanding of culture that privileges linguistic discourse and textuality—which has been the dominant conception in the humanities and social sciences since the alignment of psychoanalysis, semiotics and (post)structuralism that was achieved in the early-to-mid twentieth century—simply misses much of what makes music important to human relatedness. The implication, as with studies of music's social meaning, is that treating culture as a text to be read is not the favored mode of analysis. Indeed, such work suggests that we may have transitioned from a paradigm in which the sociological imagination assisted in the critique and reconsideration of orthodoxies in musical thought and scholarship, to one in which music, as a complex object of study, demands certain reconceptualizations of the sociological imagination and social theory writ large (see Shepherd and Wicke 1997; Born 2010c, 2012a: 266). Indeed, the growing emphasis on characteristics of music and musical experience that precede or in some sense evade cultural mediation (understood in its limited linguistic sense) has opened up the question of what music sociology might look like in the wake of "culturalism" as a dominant academic paradigm.

Music as Commercial and Industrial Process

The practice of music, and not just popular music, has since at least the middle of the nineteenth century become increasingly commercial and industrialized. Forces of mass production and mass consumption have, through different forms of mass dissemination (for example, radio, film, television and MP3 software) and commodification (for example, sheet music, cylinders, records, compact discs and ringtones), changed the practice of music from something necessarily embodied, local, face-to-face and located in the here-and-now, to something as often as not disembodied, global, impersonal and out of time and space. The influential theory of mass culture developed by Adorno and Horkheimer viewed these changes as having nothing but a deleterious effect on social and cultural life, although their contemporary Walter Benjamin (1961) argued a more positive case, seeing in the new technologies of mass production and mass dissemination creative possibilities for artists and cultural workers (see also Middleton 1990). The stage was set by Adorno's work in particular for the conventional view that music industries do little in their constant search for profits but create fantasy worlds of escapism for the vast majority of the population, thus serving the ideological needs of industrial capitalism as a social form and effectively marginalizing any possibility for opposition. This view, in essence, was replicated in the work of Chapple and Garofalo (1977) and, in a more measured way, Wallis and Malm (1984).

With the ongoing entrenchment of neo-liberal economic philosophies and the attendant changes to arts policy and funding practices, questions of politics and "value" are taking on new significance in the sociologies of music, arts and culture. Such discourses are less about "resistance" than the inherently political character of deciding how best to support vibrant music communities—questions that actually modulate long-standing tensions between ideas about music as commodity and music as culture. To an extent, these issues have come especially to the fore in relation to urban regeneration and cultural heritage (Cloonan 2007, Frith, Cloonan and Williamson 2009, Cohen 2010, Frith 2012, Taylor 2012, Hesmondhalgh 2013, Street 2013, O'Brien 2014, see also Sections III and VI).

Nevertheless, much work in the sociology of music since the 1970s has focused on the oppositional potential of many genres of popular music, while still acknowledging the undoubted influence and importance of the music industries in shaping public taste. Further, toward the close of the twentieth century, much work in popular music studies and on so-called world music concentrated more on the social interactions giving rise to particular music scenes and genres than on the development of all-inclusive theories. Such work began to reveal a more complex and nuanced understanding of the tensions between musicians and the music industries than could possibly be illuminated through an assumed stand-off between the forces of reproduction and resistance.

Here the work of Peterson has been influential. Peterson has sought to account for the pervasive influence of the music industries on the one hand and the fact that, on the other, the industries cannot actually determine tastes and buying habits: music sales are manifestly unpredictable which is why, in comparison to other commodities, cultural or otherwise, the music industries put out such a massive variety of product. In 1975 Peterson and Berger developed a cyclical theory according to which, during periods of oligarchy in the music industries (when a small number of major or transnational record companies command a high share of the marketplace) opportunities for artistic innovation and creativity are low and a high degree of control over public taste is maintained. By contrast, at the other end of the cycle, when the major companies command a relatively low share of the marketplace, independent record companies are seen to play a more significant role. The argument is that artists have more creative freedom and consumers a wider choice of product. In other words, Peterson and Berger argued that concentration and diversity are inversely correlated.

This work concentrates on the middle part of the twentieth century. During this period in the history of the music industries, when US companies dominated, it is arguable that the analyses presented in this work possessed considerable explanatory power. However, as the twentieth century progressed, the major record companies began on an increasingly international scale to use independent producers and companies as creative partners who assumed the initial risks in identifying and recording artists. As a result, it became more difficult to draw clear distinctions between major record companies and independents. This blurring, which was the result of decentralized production, became most noticeable during the 1980s (Lopes 1992). In examining the trend toward decentralization, Dowd has challenged Peterson and Berger's original research. Dowd suggests that high levels of concentration can be accompanied by high levels of diversity, provided that the major record labels operate according to a decentralized, "open" system of production, as opposed to the centralized, bureaucratic, and "closed" system described by Peterson and Berger (Dowd 2004b; see also Section IV).

In the late twentieth century, the pervasion of the internet and digital technologies significantly affected how music is recorded, heard and performed (Théberge 1997, Bull 2007, Prior 2008b), as well as the nature of musical enjoyment and fandom (Rojek 2004, Théberge 2005, Beer 2008). This pervasion also altered how music is bought and sold (see also Sections V and VI).

It is arguable that the rise of the MP3 digital audio format since the mid-1990s has effected the most significant shift in the character of the music commodity since recordings replaced sheet music in the early twentieth century (for measured accounts of this shift, see Hesmondhalgh 2009, Morris 2010, Sterne 2012, Gopinath 2013). Given the ease with which the MP3 format is uploaded and downloaded, shared and distributed, it has sparked academic, legal and public debates over the future of the music industry, as well as over the very nature of copyright and intellectual property (Frith and Marshall 2004; see also Section IV). Undeniably, parts of the music industry have struggled to adjust to these shifts and have suffered financially as a result.

However, given that there has been a problematic tendency in music industry scholarship "to privilege the *recording* industry as being *the* music industry" (Williamson and Cloonan 2007: 312; see also Sterne 2014), many scholars have been blinded to the fact that the sputtering record industry has been paralleled by a booming live music sector (Frith 2007a). In the United Kingdom during 2008, for example, the revenue of the live music business exceeded that of the recording industry (Frith et al. 2010; see also Frith et al. 2013).

Part of the reason for the buoyancy of live music as a business appears to be demographic: as the baby boomers age, they continue to use popular music as a resource for identity (Bennett 2006, Kotarba 2009) and continue to attend concerts put on by the idols of their adolescence. Indeed, the careers of the vast majority of pop and rock artists who toured the United States in 2002 began at least two decades prior (Connolly and Krueger 2006). While U2 is the best example here (their *U2 360°* tour was the most lucrative in history, grossing $772 million between 2009 and 2011), the trend holds for numerous other vintage and reunited acts.

Of course, the recent success of this sector is more complicated than pure demographics, and scholars are only beginning to understand the intricacies of the economic organization, state regulation and cultural value of live music (not to mention its increasingly complicated interrelationship with recording and webcasting). Conversely, the relationship between popular music and ageing is more complex than costly concerts and reunion tours. Since the Chicago School's early work on dance bands and jazz musicians, scholars have tended to focus on how popular music constitutes part of what it means to be young. Given contemporary demographic realities, studies of ageing and adulthood in music offer a necessary complement to such work (see for example Bennett and Hodkinson 2012, Bennett 2013; see also Keightley 1997). Indeed, while sociologists spent a large part of the twentieth century analyzing the connections between popular music and youth, studies are now emerging that take better stock of the relationship between popular music and a different but equally essential quality of late modern life: nostalgia (see for example Frith 2007b, Bijsterveld and van Dijck 2009).

Conclusion

In recent decades, interest in the sociology of music has undoubtedly increased. In addition to the growing amount of published work, Martin (2006: 1) goes so far as to suggest that, in contrast to the (ostensibly) scattered and fragmentary nature of the scholarship that has characterized the field since its earliest days, "since the mid-1990s the distinctiveness of a sociological approach to music has become increasingly apparent." Indeed, Martin's goal is to contribute to the establishment of that distinctive approach. Marshall (2011: 155) makes a similar point, albeit in a more specific context, noting that the sociology of popular music might be brought closer to the "sociological mainstream." Prior (2011) also presents a thoughtful case for the retention and solidification of specifically sociological approaches to music (see also Bennett 2008, Roy and Dowd 2010, Section VI).

But if recent scholarship in the sociology of music is marked by a degree of crystallization, or at least the desire for such a thing, we have shown in this Introduction that the musical–sociological imagination is at the same time marked by a proliferation of theories, methods and debates. This is the case not only with regard to the various topics outlined above. It is also necessary to mention recent developments in "big data" and digital information filtering systems, which use various algorithms to predict additional preferences in music (as well as movies, books and so on) based on existing listener behavior. Such developments not only offer new possibilities in mapping musical taste patterns and listening practices; they also offer new possibilities for musical encounter itself, potentially giving rise to new listening practices, aesthetic orders and forms of cultural capital (see Tepper and Hargittai 2009, Savage and Gayo 2011, Beer and Taylor 2013, Wilf 2013).

Similar approaches to pooling and analyzing data are also relevant in the so-called digital humanities, where they can be used to gain insight into historical shifts in performance practice, as in the so-called phonomusicology practiced currently by the Digital Music Lab (dml.city.ac.uk; see also Cottrell 2010). A significant forerunner of the Lab was the Arts and Humanities Research Council (AHRC) Research Centre for the History and Analysis of Recorded Music (CHARM), which developed software capable of digitizing, visualizing and comparing "large numbers of recordings in order to identify and characterise stylistic elements," both within particular periods and across time (Cook 2009: 221). One effect of such work has been to help establish a musicological paradigm that is focused less on scores than on the history of music as a performance art (see also Cook 2014). In a sense, the Digital Music Lab takes the work of CHARM to the next level by using larger-scale music collections: that is, bigger datasets. The possibilities of this approach in the digital humanities, which is sometimes called "distant reading," have been more thoroughly navigated thus far in the realm of literary studies, where similar methods were first established (see Moretti 2013). Distant reading is a methodological approach that looks at the history of cultural artifacts not as the detailed hermeneutic analysis of specific texts (the usual humanities approach) but, rather, by digitally amassing and analyzing tremendous swaths of data.

Other developments to do with the digital humanities and "new" social data include a possible turn, after decades of preference for qualitative research in music sociology, to the realm of quantitative (or at least mixed) methods. Such a possibility is evident in the continued importance of multiple-correspondence analysis (MCA, a method favored by Bourdieu; see also Bennett et al. 2009) as well as the rise of social network analysis (Crossley 2014; Crossley, McAndrew and Widdop 2014; McAndrew and Everett forthcoming; see also Sections V and VI). Each of these approaches has generated its own controversies. Indeed, the upshot of the relationship between the digital humanities, the musical–sociological imagination and what has been called the "social life of methods" (Savage 2013) remains to be seen.

Nevertheless, what these current research directions clearly show is a diversification of approaches to the interactions of the musical and the social. Such diversity is both valuable and welcome because it broadens the reach and scope of music sociology. But it also points to a rise in the porousness and interdisciplinarity that is characteristic of the academic study of culture more widely, which means that it is increasingly difficult to say exactly where the sociology of music ends and other humanities and social sciences approaches begin.

This leads to an ironic conclusion: if, after more than a century of scattered and fragmented scholarship, the twenty-first century is the moment in which the distinctiveness of a sociological approach to music has become apparent, it might also be the moment in which the *need* for a distinctively sociological approach to music is no longer clear.

Notes

1   A word is necessary on the phrase "music and the social." Language is a tricky thing in discussing the social character of music. Language is made up of words that appear discrete, particularly in their visual presentation. The temptation, then, becomes that of assuming that the phenomena to which the words refer are equally distinct, if not separate. This is an issue that has plagued attempts to understand the social character of music. We have therefore refrained from describing work in the sociology of music as addressing "the relation between music and society." "Music" and "society" in such formulations can easily be assumed to be distinct if not separate phenomena. The issue then becomes that of how they "relate." At its most extreme, this formulation can be taken to indicate that music exists outside the social, which then "influences" or even "constitutes" "it" in ways that need to be understood. For obvious reasons, we want to avoid these kinds of formulations. They reify both music and the social. We are therefore using the formulation "music and the social." However, the term "the social" has itself been criticized as a reification positing a static and structural "cause" of social action (see for example Latour 2005). By "the social," then, we simply mean "the condition of human interaction." Our assumption is that "the social" (which seems to be a slightly more action-oriented term than "society") *is* specific and concrete human interaction and that this human interaction *is* "the social." In this sense, we understand music to be a social phenomenon that is always the product of specific and concrete instances of human interaction. More precisely, we understand music not simply to be the sounds of music (which is how "music" as a social phenomenon itself comes to be reified) but to be *the* interaction between individual subjects as constituted through human interaction and the sounds that they recognize as musical (see Shepherd and Wicke 1997). In other words, music is an experience, not a thing.
2   Although an in-depth study on the scale of, say, Bourdieu's *Homo Academicus* (1988) seems possible, we present here only a tentative and skeletal foray into this territory.
3   All of the following references and quotations are taken from Mueller's correspondence files, which are held at the Indiana University Archives.
4   See Prior (2011: 124) for a brief but incisive comment that invites such a task.
5   For a summary and critique of this ideology, see Tagg and Clarida (2003).
6   We are paraphrasing here from Dahlhaus (1983: 129).

References

Acland, C., ed. 2007. *Residual Media*. Minneapolis: University of Minnesota Press.
Adorno, T.W. 1976. *Introduction to the Sociology of Music*. New York: Continuum.
_____. 2002. *Essays on Music*. Berkeley: University of California Press.
_____. 2009. *Currents of Music: Elements of a Radio Theory*. Cambridge: Polity Press.

Allen, A.S. 2013. "Ecomusicology." *The Grove Dictionary of American Music*, 2nd ed. New York: Oxford University Press.

Ballantine, C. 1984. *Music and its Social Meanings*. New York: Gordon and Breach.

Bayton, M. 1998. *Frock Rock: Women Performing Popular Music*. Oxford: Oxford University Press.

Becker, H.S. 1951. "The Professional Dance Musician and His Audience." *American Journal of Sociology* 57(2): 136–144.

_____. 1963. *Outsiders: Studies in the Sociology of Deviance*. London: MacMillan.

_____. 1964. Review of A. Silbermann, *The Sociology of Music*. *American Sociological Review* 29(3): 437.

_____. 1982. *Art Worlds*. Berkeley: University of California Press.

_____. 1989. "Ethnomusicology and Sociology: A Letter to Charles Seeger." *Ethnomusicology* 33(2): 275–285.

Beer, D. 2008. "Making Friends with Jarvis Cocker: Music Culture in the Context of Web 2.0." *Cultural Sociology* 2(2): 222–241.

Beer, D. and M. Taylor. 2013. "The Hidden Dimensions of the Musical Field and the Potential of the New Social Data." *Sociological Research Online* 18(2): online.

Benjamin, W. 1961. *Illuminationen*. Frankfurt. Eng. trans. and ed. H. Arendt, 1968.

Bennett, A. 2006. "Punk's Not Dead: The Continuing Significance of Punk Rock for an Older Generation of Fans." *Sociology* 40(2): 219–235.

_____. 2008 "Towards a Cultural Sociology of Popular Music." *Journal of Sociology* 44(4): 419–432.

_____. 2013. *Music, Style and Aging: Growing Old Disgracefully?* Philadelphia: Temple University Press.

Bennett, A. and P. Hodkinson, eds. 2012. *Ageing and Youth Culture: Music, Style and Identity*. New York: Berg.

Bennett, A. and R.A. Peterson, eds. 2004. *Music Scenes: Local, Translocal, and Virtual*. Nashville: Vanderbilt University Press.

Bennett, H.S. 1972. "Other People's Music." PhD diss., Northwestern University.

_____. 1980. *On Becoming a Rock Musician*. Amherst: University of Massachusetts Press.

Bennett, T., S. Frith, L. Grossberg, J. Shepherd, and G. Turner, eds. 1993. *Rock and Popular Music: Politics, Policies, Institutions*. London: Routledge.

Bennett, T., M. Savage, E. Silva, A. Warde, M. Gayo-Cal, and D. Wright. 2009. *Culture, Class, Distinction*. London: Routledge.

Benzecry, C. 2011. *The Opera Fanatic: Ethnography of an Obsession*. Chicago: University of Chicago Press.

Biddle, I. and V. Knights, eds. 2007. *Music, National Identity and the Politics of Location: Between the Local and the Global*. Aldershot: Ashgate.

Bijsterveld, K. and J. van Dijck, eds. 2009. *Sound Souvenirs: Audio Technologies, Memory and Cultural Practices*. Amsterdam: Amsterdam University Press.

Bijsterveld, K. and P.P. Peters. 2010. "Composing Claims on Musical Instrument Design: A Science and Technology Studies' Contribution." *Interdisciplinary Science Reviews* 35(2): 106–121.

Blacking, J. 1973. *How Musical is Man?* Seattle: University of Washington Press.

Born, G. 1995. *Rationalizing Culture: IRCAM, Boulez and the Institutionalization of the Musical Avant-Garde*. Berkeley: University of California Press.

_____. 2005. "On Musical Mediation: Ontology, Technology and Creativity." *Twentieth-Century Music* 2(1): 7–36.

_____. 2010a. "The Social and the Aesthetic: For a Post-Bourdieuian Theory of Cultural Production." *Cultural Sociology* 4(2): 171–208.

_____. 2010b. "Listening, Mediation, Event: Anthropological and Sociological Perspectives." *Journal of the Royal Musical Association* 125(1): 79–89.

_____. 2010c. "Music, Digitisation, Mediation: Towards Interdisciplinary Music Studies." European Research Council Advanced Grant proposal (249598).

_____. 2012a. "Music and the Social." In *The Cultural Study of Music: A Critical Introduction*, eds. M. Clayton, T. Herbert and R. Middleton, 261–274. New York: Routledge.

_____. 2012b. "Relational Ontologies and Social Forms in Digital Music." In *Bodily Expression in Electronic Music: Perspectives on Reclaiming Performativity*, eds. D. Peters, G. Eckel, A. Dorschel, 163–180. London: Routledge.

Born, G. and D. Hesmondhalgh, eds. 2000. *Western Music and Its Others*. Berkeley: University of California Press.

Bourdieu, P. 1984. *Distinction: A Social Critique of the Judgement of Taste*. Cambridge: Harvard University Press.

_____. 1988. *Homo Academicus*. Stanford: Stanford University Press.

Bousson, F. 2006. *Les mondes de la guitare*. Paris: L'Harmattan.

Bowman, W. 1998. *Philosophical Perspectives on Music*. Oxford: Oxford University Press.

Brown, S. and U. Volgsten. 2005. *Music and Manipulation: On the Social Uses and Social Control of Music*. New York: Berghahn.

Bull, M. 2007. *Sound Moves: iPod Culture and Urban Experience*. New York: Routledge.

Burkholder, P., D.J. Grout, and C.V. Palisca. 2014. *The History of Western Music*. New York: W.W. Norton.

Buscatto, M. 2007. *Les femmes du jazz: Séduction, fémininité(s), marginalisation.* Paris: CNRS Editions.

Calhoun, C. and R. Sennett. 2007. "Introduction." In *Practicing Culture*, ed. C. Calhoun and R. Sennett, 1–12. New York: Routledge.

Chambers, I. 1985. *Urban Rhythms: Pop Music and Popular Culture.* New York: Macmillan.

Chapple, S. and R. Garofalo. 1977. *Rock 'n' Roll is Here to Pay: The History and Politics of the Music Industry.* Chicago: Nelson-Hall.

Cloonan, M. 2007. *Popular Music and the State in the UK: Culture, Trade or Industry?* Aldershot: Ashgate.

Cohen, S. 1991. *Rock Culture in Liverpool: Popular Music in the Making.* Oxford: Clarendon Press.

_____. 2010. *Decline, Renewal and the City in Popular Music Culture: Beyond the Beatles.* Farnham: Ashgate.

Connolly, M. and A. Krueger. 2006. "Rockonomics: The Economics of Popular Music." In *Handbook of the Economics of Art and Culture*, eds. V. Ginsburgh and D. Throsby, 668–720. Amsterdam: Elsevier.

Cook, N. 2009. "Methods for Analysing Recordings." In *The Cambridge Companion to Recorded Music*, ed. N. Cook, E. Clarke, D. Leech-Wilkinson and J. Rink, 221–245. Cambridge: Cambridge University Press.

_____. 2014. *Beyond the Score: Music as Performance.* Oxford: Oxford University Press.

Cottrell, S. 2010. "The Rise and Rise of Phonomusicology." In *Recorded Music: Performance, Culture and Technology*, ed. A. Bayley, 15–36. Cambridge: Cambridge University Press.

Crafts, S.D., D. Cavicchi and C.M. Keil, eds. 1993. *My Music.* Hanover: Wesleyan University Press.

Crossley, N. 2014. *Networks of Sound, Style and Subversion: The Punk and Post-Punk Worlds of Manchester, London, Liverpool and Sheffield, 1975–80.* Manchester: Manchester University Press.

Crossley, N., S. McAndrew and P. Widdop, eds. 2014. *Social Networks and Musical Worlds.* New York: Routledge.

Cusick, S. 2013. "Towards an Acoustemology of Detention in the 'Global War on Terror'." In *Music, Sound and Space: Transformations of Public and Private Experience*, ed. G. Born, 275–291. Cambridge: Cambridge University Press.

Dahlhaus, C. 1983. *Foundations of Music History.* Cambridge: Cambridge University Press.

DeNora, T. 1995. *Beethoven and the Construction of Genius: Musical Politics in Vienna, 1792–1803.* Berkeley: University of California Press.

_____. 2000. *Music in Everyday Life.* Cambridge: Cambridge University Press.

_____. 2001. "Aesthetic Agency and Musical Practice: New Directions in the Sociology of Music and Emotion." In *Music and Emotion: Theory and Research*, eds. P. Juslin and J. Sloboda, 161–180. Oxford: Oxford University Press.

_____. 2003. *After Adorno: Rethinking Music Sociology.* Cambridge: Cambridge University Press.

Denzin, N.K. 1970. "Problems in Analyzing Elements of Mass Culture: Notes on the Popular Song and other Artistic Productions." *American Journal of Sociology* 75(6): 1035–1038.

Devine, K. Forthcoming. "Decomposed: A Political Ecology of Music." *Popular Music.*

DiMaggio, P. 1986. "Cultural Entrepreneurship in 19th Century Boston: The Creation of an Organizational Base for High Culture in America." In *Media, Culture, and Society: A Critical Reader*, eds. R. Collins, J. Curran, N. Garnham, P. Scannell, P. Schlesinger and C. Sparks, 194–211. London: Sage.

Dowd, T. 2004a. "Production Perspectives in the Sociology of Music." *Poetics* 32(3/4): 235–246.

_____. 2004b. "Concentration and Diversity Revisited" *Social Forces* 82(4): 1411–1455.

_____. 2007. "Sociology of Music." In *21st Century Sociology: A Reference Handbook*, Vol. 2, eds. C. Bryant and D. Peck, 249–260, 440, 505–512. Thousand Oaks: Sage.

Drew, R. 2001. *Karaoke Nights: An Ethnographic Rhapsody.* Walnut Creek: AltaMira Press.

Dubois, V., J.-M. Méon and E. Pierru. 2013. *The Sociology of Wind Bands: Amateur Music Between Cultural Domination and Authority.* Farnham: Ashgate.

Duckles, V. et al. 2001. "Musicology." In *The New Grove Dictionary of Music and Musicians.* New York: Grove's Dictionaries.

Elias, N. 1993. *Mozart: Portrait of a Genius.* Berkeley: University of California Press.

Erlmann, V. 1996. *Nightsong: Performance, Power, and Practice in South Africa.* Chicago: University of Chicago Press.

Etzkorn, K.P. 1959. "Musical and Social Patterns of Songwriters: An Exploratory Sociological Study." PhD diss., Princeton University.

_____. 1974. "On Music, Social Structure and Sociology." *International Review of the Aesthetics and Sociology of Music* 5(1): 43–49.

Eyerman, R. and A. Jamison. 1998. *Music and Social Movements: Mobilizing Traditions in the Twentieth Century.* Cambridge: Cambridge University Press.

Faulkner, R. 1983. *Music on Demand: Composers and Careers in the Hollywood Film Industry.* New Brunswick: Transaction Books.

Faulkner, R. and H.S. Becker. 2009. *Do You Know . . . ? The Jazz Repertoire in Action.* Chicago: University of Chicago Press.

Feld, S. 2005. "Places Sensed, Senses Placed: Toward a Sensuous Epistemology of Environments." In *Empires of the Senses: The Sensual Culture Reader*, ed. D. Howes, 179–191. Oxford: Berg.

Finnegan, R. 1989. *The Hidden Musicians: Music-Making in an English Town*. Cambridge: Cambridge University Press.

_____. 2003. "Music, Experience, and the Anthropology of Emotion." In *The Cultural Study of Music: A Critical Introduction*, eds. M. Clayton, T. Hebert, and R. Middleton, 181–192. New York: Routledge.

Frith, S. 1978. *The Sociology of Rock*. London: Constable. Rev. as *Sound Effects: Youth, Leisure and the Politics of Rock 'n' Roll*. New York: Pantheon, 1983.

_____. 1983. *Sound Effects: Youth, Leisure and the Politics of Rock*. London: Constable.

_____. 1987. "Towards an Aesthetic of Popular Music." In *Music and Society: The Politics of Composition, Performance, and Reception*, eds. R. Leppert and S. McClary, 133–150. Cambridge: Cambridge University Press.

_____. 1988. "The Pleasures of the Hearth: The Making of BBC Light Entertainment." In *Music for Pleasure: Essays in the Sociology of Pop*, 24–44. New York: Routledge.

_____, ed. 1989. *World Music, Politics, and Social Change*. Manchester: Manchester University Press.

_____. 1992. "The Cultural Study of Popular Music." In *Cultural Studies*, eds. L. Grossberg, C. Nelson, and P. Treichler, 174–182. London: Routledge.

_____. 1996. *Performing Rites: On the Value of Popular Music*. Cambridge: Harvard University Press.

_____. 2007a. "Live Music Matters." *Scottish Music Review* 1(1): 1–17.

_____. 2007b. "Reflections on the History of Popular Music." *Musicology* (Serbia) 7: 247–257.

_____. 2012. "The Sociology of Music in Britain." In *Vingt-cinq ans de sociologie de la musique en France* (Tome 1), eds. E. Brandl, C. Prévost-Thomas and H. Ravet, 63–69. Paris: L'Harmattan.

Frith, S. and L. Marshall, eds. 2004. *Music and Copyright*. Edinburgh: Edinburgh University Press.

Frith, S. and A. McRobbie. 1978. "Rock and Sexuality." *Screen Education* 29: 3–19. Reprinted in *On Record: Rock, Pop, and the Written Word* (1990), ed. S. Frith and A. Goodwin, 371–389. London: Routledge.

Frith, S., M. Brennan, M. Cloonan and E. Webster. 2010. "Analysing Live Music in the UK: Findings One Year into a Three-Year Research Project." *Journal of the International Association for the Study of Popular Music* 1(1): 1–30.

_____. 2013. *The History of Live Music in Britain, Volume 1: 1950–1967*. Farnham: Ashgate.

Frith, S., M. Cloonan and Williamson. 2009. "On Music as a Creative Industry." In *Creativity, Innovation and the Cultural Economy*, eds. A. Pratt and P. Jeffcutt, 74–89. New York: Routledge.

Gabrys, J. 2011. *Digital Rubbish: A Natural History of Electronics*. Ann Arbor: University of Michigan Press.

Garofalo, R., ed. 1992. *Rockin' the Boat: Mass Music and Mass Movements*. Boston: South End Press.

Goodman, D. 2011. *Radio's Civic Ambition: American Broadcasting and Democracy in the 1930s*. Oxford: Oxford University Press.

Goodman, S. 2010. *Sonic Warfare: Sound, Affect and the Ecology of Fear*. Cambridge: MIT Press.

Gopinath, S. 2013. *Ringtone Dialectic: Economy and Cultural Form*. Cambridge: MIT Press.

Grazian, D. 2003. *Blue Chicago: The Search for Authenticity in Urban Blues Clubs*. Chicago: University of Chicago Press.

Grossberg, L. 1984. "Another Boring Day in Paradise: Rock and Roll and the Empowerment of Everyday Life." *Popular Music* 4: 225–260.

_____. 1987. "Rock and Roll in Search of an Audience." In *Popular Music and Communication*, ed. J. Lull, 175–197. Newbury Park: Sage.

_____. 1992. *We Gotta Get Out of This Place: Popular Conservatism and Postmodern Culture*. London: Routledge.

Guilbault, J. with G. Averill, É. Benoit and G. Rabess. 1993. *Zouk: World Music in the West Indies*. Chicago: University of Chicago Press.

Hammou, K. 2014. *Une histoire du rap en France*. Paris: La Découverte.

Hebdige, D. 1979. *Subculture: The Meaning of Style*. London: Methuen.

Hennion, A. 1981. *Les professionnels du disque*. Paris: A.-M. Métailié.

_____. 1983. "The Production of Success: An Anti-Musicology of the Pop Song." *Popular Music* 3: 159–193.

_____. 1986. "La musique est une sociologie: points de méthode, à propos des théories musicales de Rameau." In *Sociologie de l'art*, ed. R. Moulin, 347–354. Paris: L'Harmattan.

_____. 1995. "The History of Art: Lessons in Mediation." *Réseaux* 3(2): 233–262.

_____. 1997. "Baroque and Rock Music: Music, Mediators and Musical Taste." *Poetics* 24(6): 415–435.

_____. 2001. "Music Lovers: Taste as Performance." *Theory, Culture and Society* 18(5): 1–22.

_____. 2003. "Music and Mediation: Towards a New Sociology of Music." In *The Cultural Study of Music: A Critical Introduction*, eds. M. Clayton, T. Hebert, and R. Middleton, 80–91. New York: Routledge.

_____. 2007. "Those Things That Hold Us Together: Taste and Sociology." *Cultural Sociology* 1(1): 97–114.

_____. 2010. "The Price of the People: Sociology, Performance and Reflexivity." In *Cultural Analysis and Bourdieu's Legacy*, eds. E. Silva and A. Warde, 117–127. London: Routledge.

_____. 2012. "'As Fast as One Possibly Can . . .': Virtuosity, a Truth of Musical Performance?" In *Critical Musicological Reflections: Essays in Honour of Derek B. Scott*, ed. S. Hawkins, 125–138. Farnham: Ashgate.

_____. 2014. "'Blowing in the Wind'? . . . A Response to the Author of 'Mastering the Jazz Standard: Sayings and Doings of Artistic Valuation." *American Journal of Cultural Sociology* 2(2): 253–259.

Hesmondhalgh, D. 2008. "Towards a Critical Understanding of Music, Emotion and Self-Identity." *Consumption Markets and Culture* 11(4): 329–343.

_____. 2009. "The Digitalization of Music." In *Creativity, Industry and the Cultural Economy*, eds. A. Pratt and P. Jeffcutt, 57–73. London: Routledge.

_____. 2013. *Why Music Matters*. Oxford: Wiley-Blackwell.

Hirsch, P.M. 1971. "Sociological Approaches to the Pop Music Phenomenon." *American Behavioral Scientist* 14(3): 371–388.

Horkheimer, M. and T.W. Adorno. 2002 [1947]. *Dialectic of Enlightenment*. Stanford: Stanford University Press.

Horton, D. 1957. "The Dialogue of Courtship in Popular Song." *American Journal of Sociology* 62(6): 569–578.

Jasen, P. 2012. "Bass: A Myth–Science of the Sonic Body." PhD diss., Carleton University.

Johnson, B. 2008. "'Quick and Dirty': Sonic Mediations and Affect." In *Sonic Mediations: Body, Sound, Technology*, eds. C. Birdsall and A. Enns, 43–60. Newcastle: Cambridge Scholars Publishing.

Johnson, B. and M. Cloonan. 2009. *Dark Side of the Tune: Popular Music and Violence*. Farnham: Ashgate.

Johnson, V., J. Fulcher and T. Ertman, eds. 2009. *Opera and Society in Italy and France from Monteverdi to Bourdieu*. Cambridge: Cambridge University Press.

Kaplan, M. 1951. "The Musician in America: A Study of His Social Roles—Introduction to a Sociology of Music." PhD diss., University of Illinois.

Keightley, K. 1997. "Frank Sinatra, Hi-Fi and the Formations of Adult Culture: Gender, Technology and Celebrity, 1948–1962." PhD diss., Concordia University.

Keil, C.M. 1979. *Tiv Song*. Chicago: University of Chicago Press. Reprinted as *Tiv Song: The Sociology of Art in a Classless Society*, 1983.

Kotarba, J. 2009. "Popular Music as a Meaning Resource for Aging." *Civitas* 9(1): 118–132.

Kwame Harrison, A. 2010. "Sociology and Cultural Studies." In *The Routledge Companion to Philosophy and Music*, eds. T. Gracyk and A. Kania, 557–568. New York: Routledge.

Latour, B. 2005. *Reassembling the Social: An Introduction to Actor-Network-Theory*. Oxford: Oxford University Press.

Lazarsfeld, P. 1946. *The People Look at Radio*. Chapel Hill: University of North Carolina Press.

Leppert, R. and S. McClary, eds. 1987. *Music and Society: The Politics of Composition, Performance and Reception*. Cambridge: Cambridge University Press.

Leyshon, A., D. Matless and G. Revill, eds. 1998. *The Place of Music*. New York: Guilford Press.

Lipsitz, G. 1994. *Dangerous Crossroads: Popular Music, Postmodernism, and the Poetics of Place*. London: Verso.

Lomax, A. 1968. *Folk Song Style and Culture*. Washington, DC: American Association for the Advancement of Science.

Lopes, P.D. 1992. "Innovation and Diversity in the Popular Music Industry, 1969–1990." *American Sociological Review* 57(1): 56–91.

Marshall, L. 2011. "The Sociology of Popular Music, Interdisciplinarity and Aesthetic Autonomy." *British Journal of Sociology* 62(1): 154–174.

Martin, P.J. 1995. *Sounds and Society: Themes in the Sociology of Music*. Manchester: Manchester University Press.

_____. 2006. *Music and the Sociological Gaze: Art Worlds and Cultural Production*. Manchester: Manchester University Press.

Marvin, C. 1988. *When Old Technologies Were New*. Oxford: Oxford University Press.

Maxwell, R. and T. Miller. 2012. *Greening the Media*. Oxford: Oxford University Press.

McAndrew, S. and M. Everett. Forthcoming. "Music as Collective Invention: A Social Network Analysis of Composers." *Cultural Sociology*: online pre-publication version.

McClary, S. 1991. *Feminine Endings: Music, Gender, and Sexuality*. Minneapolis: University of Minnesota Press.

McCormick, L. 2006. "Music as Social Performance." In *Myth, Meaning, and Performance: Toward a New Cultural Sociology of the Arts*, eds. R. Eyerman and L. McCormick, 121–144. Boulder: Paradigm Publishers.

_____. 2009. "Higher, Faster, Louder: Representations of the International Music Competition." *Cultural Sociology* 3(1): 5–30.

Middleton, R. 1990. *Studying Popular Music*. Milton Keynes: Open University Press.

Mills, C.W. 1959. *The Sociological Imagination*. New York: Oxford University Press.

Moretti, F. 2013. *Distant Reading: The Formation of an Unorthodox Literary Critic*. London: Verso.

Morris, J.W. 2010. "Understanding the Digital Music Commodity." PhD diss., McGill University.

Mueller, J.H. 1951. *The American Symphony Orchestra: A Social History of Musical Taste*. Bloomington: Indian University Press.

Novak, D. 2013. *Japanoise: Music at the Edge of Circulation*. Durham: Duke University Press.

O'Brien, D. 2014. *Cultural Policy: Management, Value and Modernity in the Creative Industries*. New York: Routledge.

Paddison, M. 1993. *Adorno's Aesthetics of Music*. Cambridge: Cambridge University Press.

_____. 1996. *Adorno, Modernism and Mass Culture: Essays on Critical Theory and Music*. London: Kahn and Averill.

Peterson, R.A. 1976. "The Production of Culture: A Prolegomenon." *American Behavioral Scientist* 19(6): 669–684.

_____. 2000. "Two Ways Culture is Produced." *Poetics* 28(2/3): 225–233.

Peterson, R.A. and N. Anand. 2004. "The Production of Culture Perspective." *Annual Review of Sociology 30*: 311–334.

Peterson, R.A. and D.G. Berger. 1975. "Cycles in Symbol Production: The Case of Popular Music." *American Sociological Review* 40(2): 158–173. Reprinted in *On Record: Rock, Pop, and the Written Word* (1990), eds. S. Frith and A. Goodwin, 140–159. London: Routledge.

Pinch, T. and F. Trocco. 2002. *Analog Days: The Invention and Impact of the Moog Synthesizer*. Cambridge: Harvard University Press.

Prior, N. 2008a. "Putting a Glitch in the Field: Bourdieu, Actor Network Theory and Contemporary Music." *Cultural Sociology* 2(3): 301–319.

_____. 2008b. "OK Computer: Mobility, Software and the Laptop Musician." *Information, Communication and Society* 11(7): 912–932.

_____. 2011. "Critique and Renewal in the Sociology of Music: Bourdieu and Beyond." *Cultural Sociology* 5(1): 121–138.

Raynor, H. 1972. *Social History of Music: From the Middle Ages to Beethoven*. New York: Barrie and Jenkins.

_____. 1976. *Music and Society Since 1815*. New York: Barrie and Jenkins.

Reisman, D. 1950. "Listening to Popular Music." *American Quarterly* 2(4): 359–371.

Robinson, J. and P.M. Hirsch. 1972. "Teenage Response to Rock 'n' Roll Protest Song." In *The Sound of Social Change: Studies in Popular Culture*, eds. R.S. Denisoff and R.A. Peterson, 222–231. Chicago: Rand McNally.

Rojek, C. 2004. "P2P Leisure Exchange: Net Banditry and the Policing of Intellectual Property." *Leisure Studies* 24(4): 357–369.

Roy, W. and T. Dowd. 2010. "What is Sociological about Music?" *Annual Review of Sociology* 36: 183–203.

Rumbelow, A.S. 1969. "Music and Social Groups: An Interactionist Approach to the Sociology of Music." PhD diss., University of Minnesota.

Santoro, M. 2008. "Culture As (And After) Production." *Cultural Sociology* 2(1): 7–31.

Savage, M. 2013. "The 'Social Life of Methods': A Critical Introduction." *Theory, Culture and Society* 30(4): 3–21.

Savage, M. and M. Gayo. 2011. "Unravelling the Omnivore: A Field Analysis of Contemporary Musical Taste in the United Kingdom." *Poetics* 39(5): 337–357.

Schütz, A. 1951. "Making Music Together: A Study in Social Relationship." *Social Research* 18(1): 159–178.

Shank, B. 1994. *Dissonant Identities: The Rock 'n' Roll Scene in Austin, Texas*. Hanover: Wesleyan University Press.

Shepherd, J. 1982. "A Theoretical Model for the Sociomusicological Analysis of Popular Musics." *Popular Music* 2: 145–177.

_____. 1987. "Music and Male Hegemony." In *Music and Society: The Politics of Composition, Performance, and Reception*, eds. R. Leppert and S. McClary, 151–172. Cambridge: Cambridge University Press.

_____. 1994. "Music, Culture and Interdisciplinarity: Reflections on Relationships." *Popular Music* 13(2): 127–142.

_____. 2001. "Sociology of Music." In *The New Grove Dictionary of Music and Musicians*. New York: Grove's Dictionaries.

_____. 2002. "How Music Works: Beyond the Immanent and the Arbitrary." *Action, Criticism, and Theory for Music Education* 2(2): 1–18.

Shepherd, J., P. Virden, G. Vulliamy and T. Wishart, eds. 1977. *Whose Music? A Sociology of Musical Languages*. London: Transaction.

Shepherd, J. and P. Wicke. 1997. *Music and Cultural Theory*. Cambridge: Polity.

_____. 2000. "Re-thinking Music: Disciplinary Implications." *Repercussions* 7–8: 105–146.

Silbermann, A. 1957. *Wovon lebt die Musik? Die Prinzipien der Musiksoziologie*. Regensburg: Gustav Bosse Verlag.

_____. 1963. *The Sociology of Music*. London: Routledge.

Slobin, M. 1993. *Subcultural Sounds: Micromusics of the West*. Hanover: Wesleyan University Press.

Small, C. 1977. *Music–Society–Education*. London: John Calder.

Sterne, J. 2003. *The Audible Past: Cultural Origins of Sound Reproduction*. Durham: Duke University Press.

_____. 2012. *MP3: The Meaning of a Format*. Durham: Duke University Press.

_____. 2014. "There Is No Music Industry." *Media Industries* 1(1): 50–55.

Stokes, M. 1992. *The Arabesk Debate: Music and Musicians in Modern Turkey*. Oxford: Oxford University Press.

_____, ed. 1994. *Ethnicity, Identity, and Music: The Musical Construction of Place*. Oxford: Berg.

_____. 2010. *The Republic of Love: Intimacy in Turkish Popular Music*. Chicago: University of Chicago Press.

Straw, W. 1991. "Systems of Articulation, Logics of Change: Communities and Scenes in Popular Music." *Cultural Studies* 5(3): 368–388.

_____. 1999–2000. "Music as Commodity and Material Culture." *Repercussions* 7–8: 147–172.

_____. 2010a. "Cultural Production and The Generative Matrix." *Cultural Sociology* 4(2): 209–216.

_____. 2010b. "The Circulatory Turn." In *The Wireless Spectrum: The Politics, Practices, and Poetics of Mobile Media*, eds. B. Crow, M. Longford and K. Sawchuck, 17–28. Toronto: University of Toronto Press.

_____. 2012. "Music and Material Culture." In *The Cultural Study of Music: A Critical Introduction*, eds. M. Clayton T. Herbert and R. Middleton, 227–236. New York: Routledge.

Street, J. 2013. "Music, Markets and Manifestos." *International Journal of Cultural Policy* 19(3): 281–297.

Supicic, I. 1987 [1964]. *Music in Society: A Guide to the Sociology of Music*. New York: Pendragon Press.

Tagg, P. and B. Clarida. 2003. *Ten Little Title Tunes: Toward a Musicology of the Mass Media*. New York: Mass Media Music Scholars' Press.

Taylor, T. 2001. *Strange Sounds: Music, Technology and Culture*. New York: Routledge.

_____. 2009. "Advertising and the Conquest of Culture." *Social Semiotics* 19(4): 405–425.

_____. 2012. "Music in the New Capitalism." In *The International Encyclopedia of Media Studies*. Oxford: Wiley-Blackwell.

Tepper, S. and E. Hargittai. 2009. "Pathways to Music Exploration in a Digital Age." *Poetics* 37(3): 227–239.

Théberge, P. 1997. *Any Sound You Can Imagine: Making Music / Consuming Technology*. Middletown: Wesleyan University Press.

_____. 2005. "Everyday Fandom: Fan Clubs, Blogging, and the Quotidian Rhythms of the Internet." *Canadian Journal of Communication*, 30(4): 485–502.

Thornton, S. 1995. *Club Cultures: Music, Media and Subcultural Capital*. Cambridge: Polity.

Toynbee, J. and B. Dueck, eds. 2011. *Migrating Music*. New York: Routledge.

Valiquet, P. 2015. "Mediation as Practice: Composing Technological Agents in Music and Social Theory." *Contemporary Music Review* 34 (forthcoming).

Vulliamy, G. 1976. "What Counts as School Music?" In *Explorations in the Politics of School Knowledge*, eds. G. Whitty and M. Young, 19–34. Driffield: Nafferton Books.

_____. 1977. "Music as a Case Study in the New Sociology of Education." In *Whose Music? A Sociology of Musical Languages*, eds. J. Shepherd, P. Virden, G. Vulliamy, and T. Wishart, 201–232. London: Transaction.

_____. 1978. "Culture Clash and School Music: A Sociological Analysis." In *Sociological Interpretations of Schooling and Classrooms: A Reappraisal*, eds. L. Barton and R. Meighan, 115–127. Driffield: Nafferton Books.

Vulliamy, G. and J. Shepherd. 1984. "Sociology and Music Education: A Response to Swanwick." *British Journal of Sociology of Education* 5(1): 57–76.

Waksman, S. 1999. *Instruments of Desire: The Electric Guitar and the Shaping of Musical Experience*. Cambridge: Harvard University Press.

Wallis, R. and K. Malm. 1984. *Big Sounds from Small Peoples: The Music Industry in Small Countries*. London: Constable.

Walser, R. 1993. *Running with the Devil: Power, Gender, and Madness in Heavy Metal Music*. Hanover: Wesleyan University Press.

Waterman, C. 1990. *Juju: A Social History and Ethnography of an African Popular Music*. Chicago: University of Chicago Press.

Weber, M. 1958 [1921]. *The Rational and Social Foundations of Music*. Carbondale: Southern Illinois University Press.

Weinstein, D. 1991. *Heavy Metal: A Cultural Sociology*. New York: Lexington Books.

Whiteley, S., A. Bennett and S. Hawkins, eds. 2006. *Music, Space and Place: Popular Music and Cultural Identity*. Farnham: Ashgate.

Wilf, E. 2013. "Toward an Anthropology of Computer-Mediated, Algorithmic Forms of Sociality." *Current Anthropology* 54(6): 716–739.

Williamson, J. and M. Cloonan. 2007. "Rethinking the Music Industry." *Popular Music* 26(2): 305–322.

Willis, P. 1978. *Profane Culture*. London: Routledge and Kegan Paul.

Witkin, R.W. 1998. *Adorno on Music*. London: Routledge.

I

SOURCE READINGS

Forerunners and Founding Figures

This section contains a chronologically ordered set of essays by some of the forerunners and founding figures of music sociology. The essays clearly show that sociologists were thinking about music and that musicologists were engaging with society long before the so-called "cultural turn" of the 1960s or the "new" musicology of the 1980s.

We have chosen to reproduce these particular essays, not because they should be taken as gospel or because we necessarily endorse their arguments, but because they tend to be dismissed, forgotten or only cursorily mentioned.[1] The main reasons for reprinting these essays, then, are for historical interest and for the benefit of teaching. We want to encourage readers to evaluate this work on its own terms and to understand it as part of the intellectual history of the musical–sociological imagination. Although part of our goal is to let these authors speak for themselves, we will also provide some brief introductory remarks.

On the surface, Spencer and Simmel seem to have been engaged in a "somewhat futile" (Martin 1995: x) and relatively harmless discussion of the origins of music. Essentially, they were debating whether speech evolved from music or music evolved from speech. Yet we must be careful to distance ourselves from their working paradigm because such ideas emerged during a time that was steeped in ethnocentric notions of evolution and poisonous nationalistic ideologies. Still, we do not wish to merely dismiss them. To do so would be to commit one of the cardinal sins of intellectual history: namely, to interpret the past using only the evaluative measures of the present. One thing that becomes clear if we abandon such anachronistic and "presentist" orientations is the gravity of this debate in the formation of music history: we see in these essays some of the tropes so commonly identified with "old" or "traditional" musicology—especially the idea of an inevitable evolutionary progression from primitive to modern, both in terms of comparative dimensions of western and non-western traditions, as well as in terms of the teleological development of tonal harmony toward complexity and sophistication within western culture (see also Grew 1928; Etzkorn 1964; Offer 1983, 2010; Trippett 2012). Such ideas are, of course, disagreeable. But it is no bad thing to understand more completely how sociological and musicological research agendas have developed, especially as scholars in fields such as biomusicology and evolutionary musicology begin refashioning questions about musical origins, evolutions and universals (see for example Wallin, Merker and Brown 2000, Tomlinson 2015).

Weber was also concerned with the long historical development and "foundations" of music, though his endeavor was not directly influenced by debates surrounding Darwin or evolution. As we mentioned in the general Introduction to this volume, Weber "developed a detailed analysis of the system of functional tonality as an expression and incorporation of the rational instincts of modern western societies." In doing so, he identified trends toward "rationalization" in both musical representation and instrument technology that arguably hold true, and which perhaps even intensified, in the digital age (see Born 1995, Théberge 1997, Section V). Moreover, Weber showed how music's foundational technologies and its aesthetic practices were historically and culturally dependent on one another, thereby foreshadowing one of the key arguments in the contemporary fields of sound studies and science and technology studies: co-formation. For an exceptional critical engagement with Weber and his place in the musical–sociological imagination, which includes a thorough bibliography, see Wierzbicki (2010; see also Braun 1999, Turley 2001, Botstein 2010, Pedler 2010, Darmon 2011).

Mueller's work begins to resemble a more contemporary sociology of music. Although the essay reproduced here comes from his magnum opus on music, *The American Symphony Orchestra: A Social History of Musical Taste* (1951), many of its basic ideas appeared in an article published in a 1935 issue of *Social Forces*: "Is Art the Product of Its Age?" This work is remarkable for its resonances with contemporary music sociology. For example, Mueller argues not only that taste can be accounted for, but that taste should be understood non-deterministically—that is, as he put it in his correspondence with Grout, taste is "the product of a long chain of conditioning factors, and is always changing as a result of continuous conditioning." He also advances a view of the relationship between musical sounds and social structures that is critical of the prevailing "zeitgeist" theories of his day, which saw art forms straightforwardly as the reflection of the "spirit of the age," thereby foreshadowing critiques of the "homology thesis" that have been leveled by Martin (1995) and others (see the general Introduction as well as Sections II and VI). Mueller also convincingly critiques the ideology of aesthetic autonomy—an exercise that was still taxing for the sociological imagination in the 1970s and 1980s (not to mention today). Generally, Mueller's history of the US symphonic repertoire foreshadows another key development in musicology and sociology: namely, the desire to see the history of music not in terms of static scores and finished "works" but as a range of shifting performances. In short, this is a fascinating and too little-known work, arguably well ahead of its time.

Of the six essays in this section, Schütz's is perhaps the best known. His argument about how musicians of all kinds must work to synchronize their "inner time" in performance situations—which he calls the "mutual tuning-in relationship"—remains influential for various phenomenological and interactionist scholars (see for example Weeks 1996, Faulkner and Becker 2009)—as well as scholarship on the problem of collective action writ large: namely, how do groups of individuals come to act together? (see for example Levi Martin 2011). Music has frequently served as a laboratory through which this larger question—which is fundamental to the social sciences—has been asked. In this context, one important development is that whereas Schütz's work on the subject can be considered that of an "armchair" theorist, other scholars have been inspired to put his thoughts to various empirical tests. Take for example Faulkner and Becker's study of jazz performance. They write:

> We began our study with the intuition that musicians could play together successfully without rehearsal or written scores because they all shared a repertoire of songs, "repertoire" serving as a specific instance of the idea of culture. We almost immediately realized that

"repertoire" wasn't strong enough to carry the weight that we were putting on it. . . . What we observed when we watched musicians playing, and when we ourselves played with others, was . . . a gradual fitting together of individual lines of action into a coherent collective act.

(2009: 190)

In finding that a reified notion of culture did not adequately describe the synchronous collectivization of action in jazz performance, Faulkner and Becker allow us to see similarities between Schütz's mutual tuning-in relationship, on the one hand, and more recent work that is critical of the idea that "the social" functions as a wellspring of collective action on the other (see for example Latour 2005). Such scholars think of established social orders less as pre-existing structures that somehow "cause" individuals to act than as "effects" of what people (and things) do together (see also the general Introduction and Sections V and VI).

As we outlined in the general Introduction, Adorno is one of the most foundational figures in music sociology. Yet his work is notoriously difficult to comprehend and full of controversial opinions. This has meant that students and scholars have been given to misrepresenting some of his basic positions. The essay included here, which was written as a postscript to his *Introduction to the Sociology of Music* (1976), covers several key themes in Adorno's musical oeuvre: ideology, the culture industry and mechanical reproduction, as well as the possibility for social critique and change through music. Yet it does so in a way that is uncharacteristically readable (if not perfectly reader-friendly) and thus serves as a good firsthand introduction to Adorno's sociology of music (see also Bowman 1998).

Taken together, these essays provide an intriguing and thought-provoking body of early scholarship that causes us to reflect on the way that research and scholarship are socially and historically contingent but, nonetheless, often prophetic in resonating with issues that later re-emerge—albeit usually in different guises.

Note

1 Certainly, we could have selected other essays by other key figures. Perhaps Bourdieu and Becker spring most readily to mind. However, such scholars are already widely read and widely cited, both within this volume and in music sociology more generally.

References

Born, G. 1995. *Rationalizing Culture: IRCAM, Boulez and the Institutionalization of the Musical Avant-Garde.* Berkeley: University of California Press.

Botstein, L. 2010. "Max Weber and Music History." *Musical Quarterly* 93: 183–191.

Bowman, W. 1998. *Philosophical Perspectives on Music.* Oxford: Oxford University Press.

Braun, C. 1999 "The 'Science of Reality' of Music History: On the Historical Background to Max Weber's 'Study of Music'." In *Max Weber and the Culture of Anarchy*, ed. S. Whimster. Basingstoke: Macmillan.

Darmon, I. 2011. "Weber on Music: Approaching Music as a Dynamic Domain of Action and Experience." *Cultural Sociology*: online prepublication.

Etzkorn, K.P. 1964. "Georg Simmel and the Sociology of Music." *Social Forces* 43(1): 101–107.

Faulkner, R. and H.S. Becker. 2009. *Do You Know. . .? The Jazz Repertoire in Action.* Chicago: University of Chicago Press.

Grew, E.M. 1928. "Herbert Spencer and Music." *Musical Quarterly* 14(1): 127–142.

Latour, B. 2005. *Reassembling the Social: An Introduction to Actor-Network-Theory.* Oxford: Oxford University Press.

Levi Martin, J. 2011. *The Explanation of Social Action.* Oxford: Oxford University Press.

Martin, P. 1995. *Sounds and Society: Themes in the Sociology of Music.* Manchester: Manchester University Press.

Mueller, J.H. 1935. "Is Art the Product of Its Age?" *Social Forces* 13(3): 367–375.

___. 1951. *The American Symphony Orchestra: A Social History of Musical Taste*. Bloomington: Indiana University Press.

Offer, J. 1983. "An Examination of Spencer's Sociology of Music and Its Impact on Music Historiography in Britain." *International Review of the Aesthetics and Sociology of Music* 14(1): 33–52.

___. 2010. *Herbert Spencer and Social Theory*. Basingstoke: Palgrave Macmillan.

Pedler, E. 2010. "Les sociologies de la musique de Max Weber et Georg Simmel: une théorie relationnelle des pratiques musiciennes." *L'Année sociologique* 60(2): 305–330.

Théberge, P. 1997. *Any Sound You Can Imagine: Making Music/Consuming Technology*. Middletown: Wesleyan University Press.

Tomlinson, G. 2015. *A Million Years of Music: The Emergence of Human Modernity*. New York: Zone Books.

Trippett, D. 2012. "Carl Stumpf: A Reluctant Revolutionary." In *The Origins of Music*, ed. D. Trippett. Oxford: Oxford University Press.

Turley, A. 2001. "Max Weber and the Sociology of Music." *Sociological Forum* 16(4): 633–653.

Wallin, N.L., B. Merker and S. Brown, eds. 2000. *The Origins of Music*. Cambridge: MIT Press.

Weeks, P. 1996. "Synchrony Lost, Synchrony Regained: The Achievement of Musical Co-ordination." *Human Studies* 19: 199–228.

Wierzbicki, J. 2010. "Max Weber and Musicology: Dancing on Shaky Foundations." *Musical Quarterly* 93: 262–292.

1

The Origin and Function of Music

HERBERT SPENCER

[. . .]

All music is originally vocal. All vocal sounds are produced by the agency of certain muscles. These muscles, in common with those of the body at large, are excited to contraction by pleasurable and painful feelings. And therefore it is that feelings demonstrate themselves in sounds as well as in movements. . . . Therefore it is that the angry lion roars while he lashes his sides, and the dog growls while he retracts his lip. Therefore it is that the maimed animal not only struggles, but howls. And it is from this cause that in human beings bodily suffering expresses itself not only in contortions, but in shrieks and groans—that in anger, and fear, and grief, the gesticulations are accompanied by shouts and screams—that delightful sensations are followed by exclamations—and that we hear screams of joy and shouts of exultation.

We have here, then, a principle underlying all vocal phenomena; including those of vocal music, and by consequence those of music in general. The muscles that move the chest, larynx, and vocal chords, contracting like other muscles in proportion to the intensity of the feelings; every different contraction of these muscles involving, as it does, a different adjustment of the vocal organs; every different adjustment of the vocal organs causing a change in the sound emitted;—it follows that variations of voice are the physiological results of variations of feeling; it follows that each inflection or modulation is the natural outcome of some passing emotion or sensation; and it follows that the explanation of all kinds of vocal expression, must be sought in this general relation between mental and muscular excitements. . . .

[. . .]

Thus we find all the leading vocal phenomena to have a physiological basis. They are so many manifestations of the general law that feeling is a stimulus to muscular action—a law conformed to throughout the whole economy, not of man only, but of every sensitive creature—a law, therefore, which lies deep in the nature of animal organization. The expressiveness of these various modifications of voice is therefore innate. Each of us, from babyhood upwards, has been spontaneously making them, when under the various sensations and emotions by which they are produced. Having been conscious of each feeling at the same time that we heard ourselves make the consequent sound, we have acquired an established association of ideas between such sound and the feeling which caused it. When the like sound is made by another, we ascribe the like feeling to him; and by a further consequence we not only ascribe to him that feeling, but have a certain degree of it aroused in ourselves: for to become conscious of the feeling which another is experiencing, is to have that feeling awakened in our own consciousness, which is the same thing as experiencing the feeling. Thus these various modifications of voice become not only a language through which we understand the emotions of others, but also the means of exciting our sympathy with such emotions.

Have we not here, then, adequate data for a theory of music? These vocal peculiarities which indicate excited feeling, *are those which especially distinguish song from ordinary speech*. Every one of the alterations of voice which we have found to be a physiological result of pain or pleasure, *is carried to its greatest extreme in vocal music*. For instance, we saw that, in virtue of the general relation between mental and muscular excitement, one characteristic of passionate utterance is *loudness*. Well, its comparative loudness is one of the distinctive marks of song as contrasted with the speech of daily life; and further, the *forte* passages of an air are those intended to represent the climax of its emotion. We next saw that the tones in which emotion expresses itself, are, in conformity with this same law, of a more sonorous *timbre* than those of calm conversation. Here, too, song displays a still highest degree of the peculiarity; for the singing tone is the most resonant we can make. Again, it was shown that, from a like cause, mental excitement vents itself in the higher and lower notes of the register; using the middle notes but seldom. And it scarcely needs saying that vocal music is still more distinguished by its comparative neglect of the notes in which we talk, and its habitual use of those above or below them and, moreover, that its most passionate effects are commonly produced at the two extremities of its scale, but especially the upper one.

A yet further trait of strong feeling, similarly accounted for, was the employment of larger intervals than are employed in common converse. This trait, also, every ballad and *aria* carries to an extent beyond that heard in the spontaneous utterances of emotion: add to which, that the direction of these intervals, which, as diverging from or converging towards the medium tones, we found to be physiologically expressive of increasing or decreasing emotion, may be observed to have in music like meanings. Once more, it was pointed out that not only extreme but also rapid variations of pitch, are characteristic of mental excitement; and once more we see in the quick changes of every melody, that song carries the characteristic as far, if not farther. Thus, in respect alike of *loudness, timbre, pitch, intervals*, and *rate of variation*, song employs and exaggerates the natural language of the emotions;—it arises from a systematic combination of those vocal peculiarities which are the physiological effects of acute pleasure and pain.

Besides these chief characteristics of song as distinguished from common speech, there are sundry minor ones similarly explicable as due to the relation between mental and muscular excitement; and before proceeding further these should be briefly noticed. Thus, certain passions, and perhaps all passions when pushed to an extreme, produce (probably through their influence over the action of the heart) an effect the reverse of that which has been described: they cause a physical prostration, one symptom of which is a general relaxation of the muscles, and a consequent trembling. We have the trembling of anger, of fear, of hope, of joy; and the vocal muscles being implicated with the rest, the voice too becomes tremulous. Now, in singing, this tremulousness of voice is very effectively used by some vocalists in highly pathetic passages; sometimes, indeed, because of its effectiveness, too much used by them—as by Tamberlik, for instance.

Again, there is a mode of musical execution known as the *staccato*, appropriate to energetic passages—to passages expressive of exhilaration, of resolution, of confidence. The action of the vocal muscles which produces this staccato style, is analogous to the muscular action which produces the sharp, decisive, energetic movements of body indicating these states of mind; and therefore it is that the staccato style has the meaning we ascribe to it. Conversely, slurred intervals are expressive of gentler and less active feelings; and are so because they imply the smaller muscular vivacity due to a lower mental energy. The difference of effect resulting from difference of *time* in music, is also attributable to the same law. Already it has been pointed out that the more frequent changes of pitch which ordinarily result from passion, are imitated and developed in song; and here we have to add, that the various rates of such changes, appropriate to the different styles of music, are further traits having the same derivation. The slowest movements, *largo* and *adagio*, are used where such depressing emotions as grief, or such unexciting emotions as reverence, are to be portrayed; while the more rapid movements, *andante, allegro, presto,* represent successively increasing degrees of mental vivacity; and do this because they imply that muscular activity which flows from this mental vivacity. Even the *rhythm*, which forms a remaining distinction between song and speech, may not improbably have a kindred cause. Why the actions excited by strong feeling should tend to become rhythmical, is not very obvious; but that they do so there are divers evidences. There is the swaying of the body to and fro under pain or grief, of the leg under impatience or agitation. Dancing, too, is a rhythmical action natural to elevated emotion. That under excitement speech acquires a certain rhythm, we may occasionally perceive in the highest efforts of an orator. In poetry, which is a form of speech used for the better expression of emotional ideas, we have this rhythmical tendency developed. And when we bear in mind that dancing, poetry, and music are connate—are originally constituent parts of the same thing, it becomes clear that the measured movement common to them all implies a rhythmical action of the whole system, the vocal apparatus included; and that so the rhythm of music is a more subtle and complex result of this relation between mental and muscular excitement.

But it is time to end this analysis, which, possibly we have already carried too far. It is not to be supposed that the more special peculiarities of musical expression are to be definitely explained. Though probably they may all in some way conform to the principle that has been worked out, it is obviously impracticable to trace that principle in its more ramified applications. Nor is it needful to our argument that it should be so traced. The foregoing facts sufficiently prove that what we regard as the distinctive traits of song, are simply the traits of emotional speech intensified and systematized. In respect of its general characteristics, we think it has been made clear that vocal music, and by consequence all music, is an idealization of the natural language of passion.

[. . .]

Not only may we so understand how more sonorous tones, greater extremes of pitch, and wider intervals, were gradually introduced; but also how there arose a greater variety and complexity of musical expression. For this same passionate, enthusiastic temperament, which naturally leads the musical composer to express the feelings possessed by others as well as himself, in extremer intervals and more marked cadences than they would use, also leads him to give musical utterance to feelings which they either do not experience, or experience in but slight degrees. In virtue of this general susceptibility which distinguishes him, he regards with emotion, events, scenes, conduct, character, which produce upon most men no appreciable effect. The emotions so generated, compounded as they are of the simpler emotions, are not expressible by intervals and cadences natural to these, but by combinations of such intervals and cadences: whence arise more involved musical phrases, conveying more complex, subtle, and unusual feelings. And thus we may in some measure understand how it happens that music not only so strongly excites our more familiar feelings, but also produces feelings we never had before—arouses dormant sentiments of which we had not conceived the possibility and do not know the meaning; or, as Richter says—tells us of things we have not seen and shall not see.

Indirect evidences of several kinds remain to be briefly pointed out. One of them is the difficulty, not to say impossibility, of otherwise accounting for the expressiveness of music. Whence comes it that special combinations of notes should have special effects upon our emotions?—that one should give us a feeling of exhilaration, another of melancholy, another of affection, another of reverence? Is it that these special combinations have intrinsic meanings apart from the human constitution?— that a certain number of aerial waves per second, followed by a certain other number, in the nature of things signify grief, while in the reverse order they signify joy; and similarly with all other intervals, phrases, and cadences? Few will be so irrational as to think this. Is it, then, that the meanings of these special combinations are conventional only?—that we learn their implications, as we do those of words, by observing how others understand them? This is an hypothesis not only devoid of evidence, but directly opposed to the experience of every one. How, then, are musical effects to be explained? If the theory above set forth be accepted, the difficulty disappears. If music, taking for its raw material the various modifications of voice which are the physiological results of excited feeling, intensifies, combines, and complicates them—if it exaggerates the loudness, the resonance, the pitch, the intervals, and the variability, which, in virtue of an organic law, are the characteristics of passionate speech—if, by carrying out these further, more consistently, more unitedly, and more sustainedly, it produces an idealized language of emotion; then its power over us becomes comprehensible. But in the absence of this theory, the expressiveness of music appears to be inexplicable.

Again, the preference we feel for certain qualities of sound presents a like difficulty, admitting only of a like solution. It is generally agreed that the tones of the human voice are more pleasing than any others. Grant that music takes its rise from the modulations of the human voice under emotion, and it becomes a natural consequence that the tones of that voice should appeal to our feelings more than any others; and so should be considered more beautiful than any others. But deny that music has this origin, and the only alternative is the untenable position that the vibrations proceeding from a vocalist's throat are, objectively considered, of a higher order than those from a horn or a violin. Similarly with harsh and soft sounds. If the conclusiveness of the foregoing reasonings be not admitted, it must be supposed that the vibrations causing the last are intrinsically better than those causing the first; and that, in virtue of some pre-established harmony, the higher feelings and natures produce the one, and the lower the other. But if the foregoing reasonings be valid, it follows, as a matter of course, that we shall like the sounds that habitually accompany agreeable feelings, and dislike those that habitually accompany disagreeable feelings.

Once more, the question—How is the expressiveness of music to be otherwise accounted for? may be supplemented by the question—How is the genesis of music to be otherwise accounted for? That music is a product of civilization is manifest; for though savages have their dance-chants, these are of a kind scarcely to be dignified by the title musical: at most, they supply but the vaguest rudiment of music, properly so called. And if music has been by slow steps developed in the course of civilization, it must have been developed out of something. If, then, its origin is not that above alleged, what is its origin?

Thus we find that the negative evidence confirms the positive, and that, taken together, they furnish strong proof. We have seen that there is a physiological relation, common to man and all animals, between feeling and muscular action; that as vocal sounds are produced by muscular action, there is a consequent physiological relation between feeling and vocal sounds; that all the modifications of voice expressive of feeling are the direct results of this physiological relation; that music, adopting all these modifications intensifies them more and more as it ascends to its higher and higher forms, and becomes music simply in virtue of thus intensifying them; that, from the ancient epic poet chanting his verses, down to the modern musical composer, men of unusually strong feelings prone to express them in extreme forms, have been naturally the agents of these successive intensifications; and that so there has little by little arisen a wide divergence between this idealized language of emotion and its natural language: to which direct evidence we have just added the indirect—that on no other tenable hypothesis can either the expressiveness or the genesis of music be explained.

And now, what is the *function* of music? Has music any effect beyond the immediate pleasure it produces? Analogy suggests that it has. The enjoyments of a good dinner do not end with themselves, but minister to bodily well-being. Though people do not marry with a view to maintain the race, yet the passions which impel them to marry secure its maintenance. Parental affection is a feeling which, while it conduces to parental happiness, ensures the nurture of offspring. Men love to accumulate property, often without thought of the benefits it produces; but in pursuing the pleasure of acquisition they indirectly open the way to other pleasures. The wish for public approval impels all of us to do many things which we should otherwise not do,—to undertake great labours, face great dangers, and habitually rule ourselves in a way that smooths social intercourse: that is, in gratifying our love of approbation we subserve divers ulterior purposes. And, generally, our nature is such that in fulfilling each desire, we in some way facilitate the fulfilment of the rest. But the love of music seems to exist for its own sake. The delights of melody and harmony do not obviously minister to the welfare either of the individual or of society. May we not suspect, however, that this exception is apparent only? Is it not a rational inquiry—What are the indirect benefits which accrue from music, in addition to the direct pleasure it gives?

But that it would take us too far out of our track, we should prelude this inquiry by illustrating at some length a certain general law of progress;—the law that alike in occupations, sciences, arts, the divisions that had a common root, but by continual divergence have become distinct, and are now being separately developed, are not truly independent, but severally act and react on each other to their mutual advancement. Merely hinting thus much, however, by way of showing that there are many analogies to justify us, we go on to express the opinion that there exists a relationship of this kind between music and speech.

All speech is compounded of two elements, the words and the tones in which they are uttered—the signs of ideas and the signs of feelings. While certain articulations express the thought, certain vocal sounds express the more or less of pain or pleasure which the thought gives. Using the word *cadence* in an unusually extended sense, as comprehending all modifications of voice, we may say that *cadence is the commentary of the emotions upon the propositions of the intellect*. This duality of spoken language, though not formally recognised, is recognised in practice by every one; and every one knows that very often more weight attaches to the tones than to the words. Daily experience supplies cases in which the same sentence of disapproval will be understood as meaning little or meaning much, according to the inflections of voice which accompany it; and daily experience supplies still more striking cases in which words and tones are in direct contradiction—the first expressing consent, while the last express reluctance; and the last being believed rather than the first.

These two distinct but interwoven elements of speech have been undergoing a simultaneous development. We know that in the course of civilization words have been multiplied, new parts of speech have been introduced, sentences have grown more varied and complex; and we may finally infer that during the same time new modifications of voice have come into use, fresh intervals have been adopted, and cadences have become more elaborate. For while, on the one hand, it is absurd to suppose that, along with the undeveloped verbal forms of barbarism, there existed a developed system of vocal inflections; it is, on the other hand, necessary to suppose that, along with the higher and more numerous verbal forms needed to convey the multiplied and complicated ideas of civilized life, there have grown up those more involved changes of voice which express the feelings proper to such ideas. If intellectual language is a growth, so also, without doubt, is emotional language a growth.

Now, the hypothesis which we have hinted above, is, that beyond the direct pleasure which it gives, music has the indirect effect of developing this language of the emotions. Having its root, as we have endeavoured to show, in those tones, intervals, and cadences of speech which express feeling—arising by the combination and intensifying of these, and coming finally to have an embodiment of its own; music has all along been reacting upon speech, and increasing its power of rendering emotion. The use in recitative and song of inflections more expressive than ordinary ones, must from the beginning have tended to develop the ordinary ones. Familiarity with the more varied combinations of tones that occur in vocal music, can scarcely have failed to give greater variety of combination to the tones in which we utter our impressions and desires. The complex musical phrases by which composers have conveyed complex emotions, may rationally be supposed to have influenced us in making those involved cadences of conversation by which we convey our subtler thoughts and feelings.

That the cultivation of music has no effect on the mind, few will be absurd enough to contend. And if it has an effect, what more natural effect is there than this of developing our perception of the meanings of inflections, qualities, and modulations of voice; and giving us a correspondingly increased power of using them? Just as mathematics, taking its start from the phenomena of physics and astronomy, and presently coming to be a separate science, has since reacted on physics and astronomy to their immense advancement—just as chemistry, first arising out of the processes of metallurgy and the industrial arts, and gradually growing into an independent study, has now become an aid to all kinds of production—just as physiology, originating out of medicine and once subordinate to it, but latterly pursued for its own sake, is in our day coming to be the science on which the progress of medicine depends;—so, music, having its root in emotional language, and gradually evolved from it, has ever been reacting upon and further advancing it. Whoever will examine the facts, will find this hypothesis to be in harmony with the method of civilization everywhere displayed.

It will scarcely be expected that much direct evidence in support of this conclusion can be given. The facts are of a kind which it is difficult to measure, and of which we have no records. Some suggestive traits, however, may be noted. May we not say, for instance, that the Italians, among whom modern music was earliest cultivated, and who have more especially practised and excelled in melody (the division of music with which our argument is chiefly concerned)—may we not say that these Italians speak in more varied and expressive inflections and cadences than any other nation? On the other hand, may we not say that, confined almost exclusively as they have hitherto been to their national airs, which have a marked family likeness, and therefore accustomed to but a limited range of musical expression, the Scotch are unusually monotonous in the intervals and modulations of their speech? And again, do we not find among different classes of the same nation, differences that have like implications? The gentleman and the clown stand in very decided contrast with respect to variety of intonation. Listen to the conversation of a servant-girl, and then to that of a refined, accomplished lady, and the more delicate and complex changes of voice used by the latter will be conspicuous. Now, without going so far as to say that out of all the differences of culture to which the upper and lower classes are subjected, difference of musical culture is that to which alone this difference of speech is ascribable; yet we may fairly say that there seems a much more obvious connexion of cause and effect between these than between any others. Thus, while the inductive evidence to which we can appeal is but scanty and vague, yet what there is favours our position.

Probably most will think that the function here assigned to music is one of very little moment. But further reflection may lead them to a contrary conviction. In its bearings upon human happiness, we believe that this emotional language which musical culture develops and refines, is only second in importance to the language of the intellect; perhaps not even second to it. For these modifications of voice produced by feelings, are the means of exciting like feelings in others. Joined with gestures and expressions of face, they give life to the otherwise dead words in which the intellect utters its ideas; and so enable the hearer not only to *understand* the state of mind they accompany, but to *partake* of that state. In short, they are the chief media of *sympathy*. And if we consider how much both our general welfare and our immediate pleasures depend upon sympathy, we shall recognise the importance of whatever makes this sympathy greater. If we bear in mind that by their fellow-feeling men are led to behave justly, kindly and considerately to each other—that the difference between the cruelty of the barbarous and the humanity of the civilized, results from the increase of fellow-feeling; if we bear in mind that this faculty which makes us sharers in the joys and sorrows of others, is the basis of all the higher affections—that in friendship, love, and all domestic pleasures, it is an essential element; if we bear in mind how much our direct gratifications are intensified by sympathy,—how, at the theatre, the concert, the picture gallery, we lose half our enjoyment if we have no one to enjoy with us; if, in short, we bear in mind that for all happiness beyond what the unfriended recluse can have, we are indebted to this same sympathy;—we shall see that the agencies which communicate it can scarcely be overrated in value.

The tendency of civilization is more and more to repress the antagonistic elements of our characters and to develop the social ones—to curb our purely selfish desires and exercise our unselfish ones—to replace private gratifications by gratifications resulting from, or involving, the happiness of others. And while, by this adaptation to the social state, the sympathetic side of our nature it being unfolded, there is simultaneously growing up a language of sympathetic intercourse— a language through which we communicate to others the happiness we feel, and are made sharers in their happiness.

This double process, of which the effects are already sufficiently appreciable, must go on to an extent of which we can as yet have no adequate conception. The habitual concealment of our feelings diminishing, as it must, in proportion as our feelings become such as do not demand concealment, we may conclude that the exhibition of them will become much more vivid than we now dare allow it to be; and this implies a more expressive emotional language. At the same time, feelings of a higher and more complex kind, as yet experienced only by the cultivated few, will become general; and there will be a corresponding development of the emotional language into more involved forms. Just as there has silently grown up a language of ideas, which, rude as it at first was, now enables us to convey with precision the most subtle and complicated thoughts; so, there is still silently growing up a language of feelings, which notwithstanding its present imperfection, we may expect will ultimately enable men vividly and completely to impress on each other all the emotions which they experience from moment to moment.

Thus if, as we have endeavoured to show, it is the function of music to facilitate the development of this emotional language, we may regard music as an aid to the achievement of that higher happiness which it indistinctly shadows forth. Those vague feelings of unexperienced felicity which music arouses—those indefinite impressions of an unknown ideal life which it calls up, may be considered as a prophecy, to the fulfilment of which music is itself partly instrumental. The strange capacity which we have for being so affected by melody and harmony, may be taken to imply both that it is within the possibilities of our nature to realize those intenser delights they dimly suggest, and that they are in some way concerned in the realization of them. On this supposition the power and the meaning of music become comprehensible; but otherwise they are a mystery.

We will only add, that if the probability of these corollaries be admitted, then music must take rank as the highest of the fine arts—as the one which, more than any other, ministers to human welfare. And thus, even leaving out of view the immediate gratifications it is hourly giving, we cannot too much applaud that progress of musical culture which is becoming one of the characteristics of our age.

2

Psychological and Ethnological Studies on Music[1]

Georg Simmel

Darwin writes in *The Descent of Man*: "We must suppose that the rhythms and cadences of oratory are derived from previously developed musical powers. We can thus understand how it is that music, dancing, song, and poetry are such very ancient arts. We may go even further than this and believe that musical sounds afforded one of the bases for the development of language (Darwin 1874: 595)."[2] In similar fashion he elaborates in his work, *On the Expression of the Emotions* (1872: 88), his view that the singing of birds serves especially the purpose of mating calls. It expresses sexual drives and charms the females. Man supposedly first used his voice for this purpose, and not in verbal language, which Darwin sees as one of the most recent products of human development. On the other hand, the use of musical tones for the attraction of females (or conversely of males) can be observed among animals of a very low order. Jaeger likewise observes that the singing of birds is not all that intimately related to articulated verbal language.[3] On the contrary, it corresponds precisely to the unarticulated wordless yodeling of man. It is "the expressive sound of sexual excitement, the tones of pleasure." But the meaning of birds singing should be more broadly interpreted, because it is also used to express pleasures derived from other sources, such as sunshine or the discovery of food. One should keep in mind, of course, that warmth and certain food items can also be stimulants. Human yodeling, however, is also connected with the sexual sphere, since it is said to be the sign of communication between boy and girl.

I should like to reply to these views that every expression of birds is vocal in nature. Just as birds express every other emotion through singing, so they must also express their sexual feelings. Even if these conditions were the most powerful, all others could rightfully serve for the same analogy. If this were so, it would be hard to understand why man should have progressed to verbal language, since he could express everything through the use of tones. Now I will even adopt Darwin's point of view: if man had found this non-verbal use of the singing voice, which he is said to have inherited from his ancestors, more natural than language, would he not have maintained it on the lowest cultural level as a survival, so that contemporary man, too, would express himself by wordless yodeling? With the exception of our mountain people, however, there is no evidence of it anywhere else in the world, as Professor Bastian assured me and as I convinced myself in my own studies. For birds, of course, singing is the natural expression of emotions, while man is more likely to shout. Why should man have searched for another form of expression for such a natural emotion as the sexual drive?

The priority of vocal singing over verbal language seems to me to be undemonstrable. Nor am I persuaded by the other argument that children are more likely in this fashion to imitate singing than speech. (A mother of five children, who later turned out to be musically talented, told me that none of her children sang in tones before their second or third years.) I believe that the reason for this is simply that children hardly understand the meaning of presented words. If they repeat anything, it is simply mechanical. The children must memorize the series of phonemes in order to reproduce them. Obviously this is difficult, and it is much easier for him to memorize and reproduce the speech melody, which makes a more precise sensual impression than the phonemes. If the speech melody now takes on a vocal melody, the child will naturally be able to imitate it more easily, since it will make an even more precise impression. It is only because it is mechanically easier to imitate the melody that it will be repeated by the child more readily than will the words. This would prove only that a child commences singing without words. But so far it has not been proven that the child will do so without imitating. Casual singing without words is only observed among adults, never among very small children, who always sing words.

[. . .]

II

It seems most likely to me that the source of vocal music is the spoken word, which is exaggerated by emotions in the direction of rhythm and modulation. My reasons are as follows. Language and mind develop through mutual support and strengthening. The progress of the one is built upon that of the other. "The essence of man is thought, and human thought is originally language," says Steinthal (see 1888). Therefore, wherever there are psychic processes among man, there is also language. Man's drive to express inner emotions through external action, which previously could only be satisfied by gestures and shouting, is given a richer and more appropriate form through language. This linguistic bridge from animal to human being cannot be retraced. Every emotion searches for expression in more and more characteristic linguistic form. Thinking and feeling among aborigines is expressed through speech. "Children and primitives speak almost continuously," observes Lazarus. More refined and emphatic psychic processes will search for a more exaggerated expression. Acute and intense processes will be very strong. For this reason the linguistic ability of primitive people will not provide an equivalent compensation for it, be it ever so intensified and expressive. For example, sudden terror will only cause us to scream as will intense pain.[4] On the other hand, there are emotions which "will not be strong enough to overcome the drive for linguistic expression. Nevertheless, they will not be able to find an adequate compensation in the usual modes and forms of language. Anger for example, finds expression in words, but with an intensified accentuation of voice level that is a far louder than usual one. Depression is expressed through words of softer and more monotonous character. There may also be additional emotions which amplify the rhythmic and modulatory elements of language. One example is the activities of war. The intensification of energies on this occasion seems to infuse all activities with rhythmic expression, as shown in the dancing and rhythmic steps used by many primitive peoples. When primitive man has progressed so far that he expresses his emotions through language (he must already have reached this stage when he engages in organized warfare)—so that, for example, specific expressions have been developed in a tribe for specific situations (for example, calls for bravery and for deprecating the enemy in warfare)—he then produces these sounds rhythmically and in keeping with the whole disposition and in step. Through the teaching of ethnology, we know that these rhythmically organized sounds are practiced throughout the world at the approach of the enemy. Rhythm, indeed, is the very beginning of music.

A second cause of the evolution of vocal song may have been a diffuse feeling of pleasure and enjoyment. We observe that people are more talkative when in happy spirits than when they are in quiet or depressed moods. Children especially, even when they are by themselves, will be observed speaking continuously when they are enjoying themselves. Primitive man, however, will employ the same words for all forms of emotional expression, only he will vary the tonal pitch and emphasis for expressions of joy. While his language has, as yet, not rigidified towards stabilized speech melody, he has at his disposal the fullness of modulation and differentiation.[5]

Even today we alter our mode of speech when we express joyful emotions. We then deflect our speech melody and produce a more melodious and harmonic speech pattern, as if we wished to give evidence of our inner harmony. Furthermore, one should observe that there seems to be a tendency towards rhythmic expression whenever we are happy. This is so, most likely, not only because there is an intrinsic link between rhythm and melody formation, but also for substantive reasons. The rhythmic motions of the dance are, among others, reproductions of the joyful mood (Lazarus 1882: 136).

In this category of emotions we may also include the sexual drive. I believe that I have already shown that it is impossible to prove in this manner the non-verbal origin of music. It may be possible, as Jaeger suggests, that the sexual excitement which accompanies verbal courting led, by its exaggeration, to vocal music (see Sections I and XVIII of this study). But then, one has to disregard the most primitive means known for satisfying the sexual drive, abduction, since it is not at all connected with courting. It is impossible to show that human singing is anywhere used merely as an animalistic expression. To this point, as to many others, Wilhelm Von Humboldt has added another seed of wisdom. He says,

> Words flow from the heart freely without necessity or intention. There may not have been in a desolate area any nomadic hunting horde which did not already own its own songs, for man, as an animal species, is a singing creature. He does, however, *connect thoughts with sound*.
>
> (Humboldt 1839: Paragraph 9)

A fourth emotion may be mentioned among the sources of vocal music: the mystical-religious. Almost all incantations, magic formulas, and prayers, as far as we can trace them in ethnographic materials, are produced with the greatest possible pathos, which approximates the tonal pattern of vocal music the most closely. Even today, speech is produced nowhere else in a more singing fashion than from the pulpit and during prayers. Indeed the ordinary begging tone noticeably approximates singing.[6] Also, the rhythmical element must be emphasized by the well-measured and elongated forms that are germane to mysticism. This is also demonstrated by the dance, which is employed in every primitive religion to express religious emotion.

The languages of [African] tribes supposedly consist almost exclusively of continuous recitations. The reason for this is certainly the easy excitability of these people, their emotional devotion and dedication to all fleeting ideas and impressions, so that the excitement at any given moment is probably too strong to be expressed in simple words, and therefore takes refuge in musical exaggeration. When in contrast to our harsh sounding idioms it has been said that the language of Greeks and Italians sound more like music, then his inclination to melody in speech is certainly not without connection to the more excited and simultaneously more emotional character of these people. What is commonly called musical talent of individuals and whole societies may, therefore, be derivable from such more general psychological qualities.

It seems to me that the first form of song stemmed from such origins. This first form, however, was quite different from what we today conceive of as vocal music. But one must not forget that music in this state was not yet art, just as the huts of the primitive people were not works of architectural art. In order for them to be developed into a form of art, a special impetus was needed which was not wholly conditioned by these first origins. No traveler has hesitated to recognize the songs of primitive peoples as music despite their unbelievable monotony or lack of harmony. Ammian describes the war songs of Bardal as songs, even though he compares their sound with the noise of the ocean when it beats against rocks. That the Chinese say, when they listen to European songs, that "the dogs are howling here," is characteristic of the difference in judgment concerning what is real and proper music. To European ears, Chinese music is equally incomprehensible. If, then, in our own time when music by no means approximates pure or natural sound any more, such differences in judgment occur—so that something can now be regarded as song and soon again be rejected—how much more must the boundaries between shouting, words and singing have vacillated during primeval days when the tonal material was in a more fluid condition. The reason that singing approximates unarticulated shouting more closely than spoken words seems to lie in the fact that whenever a larger number of untrained and uneducated individuals congregate for singing, the result, even today, is usually closer to noise than to musical tones.[7] Moreover, whenever excitement reaches a climax, vocal singing may not be an adequate compensation for these emotions, so that one has to resort to shouting. "Voluntary interjections are only employed when the suddenness or vehemence of some affection or passion returns men to their natural state" (Tooke 1806: 62).

[. . .]

VI

As language relates to concrete thought, so music does to diffuse emotional feelings. The first creates the second, because the second creates the first. Similarly, in poetry, the imagination of the poet kindles an analogous one in the listener. In the case of music, perceptual imaginations are replaced by far less defined emotions. In poetry these occur only intermediately. Among poets, the feelings precede the imaginations, while among listeners they follow them.

The assumption that music stimulates the emotions which precede the creative work of poets makes situations like the following easy to understand. Before writing poetry, Alfieri usually prepared himself mentally by listening to music. He once remarked, "almost all my tragedies were sketched in my mind while I listened to music or within a few hours thereafter." Milton was filled with solemn inspiration while he listened to the sound of an organ. For the sensitive poet Warburton, too, music was a necessity. A famous French preacher, Massillon, drafted the outline of his sermons which he had to deliver to the court, while he played his violin. Drawing on Streicher, Palleske refers to the stimulation which Schiller reputedly derived from music. The ancient custom of musical preludes before rhapsodies is likely related to this. Today the custom is preserved by composers who usually begin a song with a prelude of the accompanying instruments rather than with the immediate singing.

In order to understand properly the specific psychological characteristics of music, we cannot place enough stress on the transitional process from the affects and emotions of the performer through his music to the feelings and sensations of the listener. This process is cognitively understood much less for music than for any other art form. The superficial rationalistic conception of the eighteenth century's psychological research is characteristically represented by Euler (1840), who writes: "The enjoyment of music derives from ones ability to guess correctly the intentions and emotions of the composer, the execution of which will fill one's soul with a comfortable satisfaction if one considers the composition a fortunate one."

The enjoyment of music as art is contrasted with these relatively emotional patterns on the basis of only quantitative and not at all qualitative dimensions. Contemporary as compared with very primitive music produces such a myriad of feelings of great variety that an equilibrium ensues among them through their restraining relationships on one another. The result then is objectivity. Helmholtz writes:

> It would be important to discover whether the significant and highly varied expression of emotions which is produced by music cannot be derived from the very same form of emotional activity which is responsible for the movement of (bodily) limbs, just as the variations of the pitch level in song is caused by innervations of muscles. The recurrence of the sequence of physical-psychical phenomena of which we spoke here and earlier explains many effects of music. If, indeed, as I suppose, musical expressions are influenced by the rhythm of excited heartbeats, then it is natural that musical expression will be produced for the listener by the latter. This will be the result of physiological connections as well as of psychic associations and reproduction.
>
> (1879: Appendix F)

VII

During the course of its development, music rejects its natural characteristics more and more.[8] The further it advances, the closer it approximates the ideal of art. Through this process it approaches objectivity, which is the highest honor for the (performing) artist. This does not mean that all feelings, or only the very climatic and sanguine ones, disappear from music, nor that they should not become excited by it or should no longer excite themselves. It means only that music and its manner of presentation should not be the immediate result of these emotions, as it was originally; but instead, that it should become an image of them, which is reflected in the mirror of beauty. It is in this sense that the old explanation should be understood, according to which music, or any other art, is supposed to be imitation. Music imitates the tones which spring forth from the soul when elicited by a strong emotion. Above all this seems to me to be the decisive point in the explanation of music as an art form. Naturally it refers also to instrumental music, which in a very crude and initial approximation of art imitates those reflex-like rhythmic noises.

Even though the first production of musical sounds is originally accompanied by words, they can be omitted. Intense emotions produce the tones, and it is the latter, of course, which are important. I have observed singers who did not pay proper attention to the texts of their songs, and who thus sang all imaginable forms of contradictory meanings. Nevertheless, they performed the melodies with the truest and deepest emotional expression and comprehension. This is a perfect proof of the artistic character of music: music produces typical sensations which include completely the more individual sensations produced by words.

With deep insight, language refers to the making of music as "play" or "playing." Nowadays music is indeed play, and must be such if it is to be art. But in its inception music was serious to the same degree as speech and exclamation and all other natural sounds.

[. . .]

XV

The invention of musical themes for Greek melodies was restricted by the limited number of tones available on the stringed instruments. The charm and stimulation of this music could not, therefore, be based on the thematic constructions and novelty, but had rather to be found in the refinement and nuances of their performances. This is similar to Greek dramatic productions, which strove for perfect execution and variety within a frequently repeated dramatic plot and content. Schopenhauer remarks that the greater an artistic creation is, the less it owes its greatness to plot and content.

Polyphonic music marks the conclusion of the development of music towards art. Now it was in need of complicated rules. As was already noted, there were beginnings in this direction over extended periods of time. Nothing originated, however, which would resemble our own music. Hucbald (who died in 930 A.D.) made the first known attempt to connect several voices harmonically. He found it aesthetically pleasing to have parallel sixths and fourths proceed in musical sequences! Rousseau also desired to return to the simplicity of pure nature in music. Thus he devalued all polyphonic music. In an erroneous manner he frequently found the means for the fulfillment of his ideals in extrinsic or superficial aspects.[9] In consideration of the Greeks he composed an air of only four tones. Tartini entertained similar ideas.

In the more highly educated social circles, interest in music was created which had previously not been present. At the same time, the music of lower social strata lost more and more. Here I remind the reader of the phenomenon of the Meistersinger, who attempted to raise folk music to higher and more artistic perfection. But they succeeded only in creating confused artificial calculations similar to Gothic structures. The warmth of life was missing in their art which lacked the sunshine of personal genius.

Nevertheless, it is erroneous to believe that the nation is without influence upon musical developments. Probably nobody has any doubt concerning the developments in the other arts which have to be national if they are to reach and maintain the blossom of perfection. This does not at all mean that they have to be patriotic. Indeed, history even shows that the arts could produce the most beautiful examples in the most politically disorganized states—analogous to blooming flowers on the top of a rubbish heap. I wish simply to convey this: whatever great and well-developed talents an individual may bring into his life, only the life of his home country, which surrounds him from his very first day, will make him into what he is. It will form his character in him. It gives him his ends, and his means to them. The greater his talents are, the more he will accept from the material which is available to him in the national cultural heritage. This will take place without his specific action, without his becoming conscious of it during the years of his growth.

If an artist is to maintain a uniform style of work—without which it is impossible to become a great artist—he will not change the character of his drives as he receives them through the nature and culture of his society. He will have to guard his style, not because it is patriotic, not because it would be unpatriotic for a German to work in French mannerisms, but for the simple reason that his psycho-tendencies and the moral nature which he gained by his upbringing in his society form the best foundation for his form of art or style of creation. If he were to imitate models which are different from the national style, he would fracture his essence, and his art would decline. In this sense, then, he has to work on the basis of his national background and historical foundation. He does not necessarily have to be conscious of this, nor does he have to have nationalistic feelings.

It is not yet possible to state verbally the national differences in music, since the psychological dimension of music has not been adequately examined. If one considers the total development of the last 150 years of German music and compares it with the French and Italian, there can be no doubt that each is quite different, and not interchangeable with the others, either in character or in individual compositions. Obviously we cannot prove conclusively why a particular form of music necessarily had to be created by the particular characteristics of a people. The differentiation of music into national forms nevertheless demonstrates that such effects must take place. Further, just as even the most subjective and individualistic poetic product is, to a large extent, indebted to the linguistic usage of the national language in which it is written—there is a saying that it "imagines and thinks for everybody"—so there is an historically developed folk music present for everybody else. By folk music, of course, I do not mean only folk songs, that is, the type of music which the folk creates for its own consumption, but I include in the term all forms of the national musical literature.

The history of music shows in almost every case that a composer bases his creations on the precepts of his precursors. This implies that the sum of the historical musical development of a society forms the foundation of his musical culture. The composer, therefore, owes so much to the chain of his precursors that he would never have become what he is without them.[10] Of course, his musical taste is formed from his earliest day by continuous listening to the previously created national musical heritage. The frequent chance to listen to a given music would not be available—and in modern times one is almost continuously surrounded by it—if this music did not correspond completely with the culture of a people, and if it were not fully accepted by them. Thus the composer receives through tradition the music which directs his work.[11] This is similar to the poet who transforms through his own works the language of his people which is given to him.

In accordance with this line of argument, the foundations on which every composer has to build are of national character. We may further consider the influence which is exercised upon an artist who notices that a certain composition of an earlier composer is enthusiastically received by his people while another is neglected. Thus, if one considers the complete historical development of music, it is impossible to assume that musical history occurs independently of other national events as a sort of state within a state. We maintain this even though we have not yet discovered the formal relationship between the musical and other contents of the people's soul.

[. . .]

Notes

1 This essay had been submitted by Simmel as his doctoral dissertation to the Philosophical Faculty of the Humboldt University of Berlin. But his examining committee, composed of Professors Zupitza (chairman), Zeller, and Helmholtz, refused to accept it as submitted. Instead, they granted the degree for the previously written distinguished study on Kant's monadology. While Zupitza would have been willing to accept this study on music, if it were first "cleared of the numerous misspellings and stylistic errors," Helmholtz was more skeptical. "Regardless of my other reservations, Simmel is entirely too confident in his conclusions. And the manner in which he presented the faculty with this piece which is so full of misspellings and stylistic superficialities, which evidently was not proofread, in which sentences which are cited from foreign languages can hardly be deciphered, does not attest to a great deal of reliability. Insofar, however, as he has quite a few illustrious predecessors for what he evidently takes to be the method or lack of method of scientific study, he may let them serve as some kind of personal excuse. I, however, believe that we will be doing him a greater service if we do not encourage him further in this direction." [Michael Landmann (1958: 17)] As becomes evident from our text, Simmel must have published his study without paying heed to his professors, since footnotes and textual quotations reflect the shortcomings already criticized. Where it was possible to discern Simmel's likely source, fuller bibliographic information was supplied. We also compiled a bibliography of the works which Simmel might have used for his study. Hence, as chaotic as the documentation may still appear, it is already "improved" over Simmel's original.
2 The identical thought already occurred to Leibnitz (1847: III, 1). He observes, however: "One must also consider that man could speak, that is, make himself understood by the sounds of the mouth without forming articulate sounds, if one were to use musical tones for this effect. But it would need more art to invent a language of tones instead of that of words formed and perfected by degrees, by persons living in the natural simplicity."
3 Cited by Steinthal from *Ausland* 1867, No. 42.
4 The more the linguistic capacity increases, the more will automatic reflexes of this variety be drawn into the realm of language. This goes so far, if one is very strongly habituated to the use of language, that one will exclaim words even in situations which almost incapacitate us, and which in a natural state would produce only inarticulate shouts. When there is a sudden feeling of fear, we call out "Heaven!" or "Jesus!" and the like.
5 One might wish to compare here tonal modulations which are much more frequently employed for the significance of meaning in lower languages than in our own.

6 Cicero (1886): "Accentuation is employed in learning indistinct melodies." And during the Middle Ages it was said: "The accent is the mother of music."

7 Mere noise can be produced from musically pure tones by, for example, the simultaneous pressing of all the keys of a piano within several octaves. Compare Helmholtz (1863: 14).

8 How very early distortions of music's natural state occur is shown by a fragment of Democritus *(Philodemus de mus.* IV, in Vol. *Hercules* I, page 135, col. 36). This view has been maintained until Burney expressed his erroneous point of view in the 1789 Preface to his *History of Music*: "Music is an innocent luxury unnecessary indeed to our existence, but a great improvement and gratification of the sense of hearing."

9 "It is quite difficult not to surmise that our harmonies are nothing but Gothic and barbarian inventions of which we might never have become aware if it had not been for the truer and more artistic beauties of more truly natural music." Rousseau (1768), article on "Harmonie."

10 This can be most clearly illustrated by references to musical techniques and theory.

11 We can always see how important composers follow in the footsteps of their precursors before they develop their own styles. Goethe says that all true art will have to begin with "the tradition."

References

Burney, C. 1789. *A General History of Music.* 4 vols. London: Printed for the author.

Cicero, M.T. 1886. *De Oratore.* Leipzig: Verlag Von B.G. Teubner.

Darwin, C. 1872. *Über den Ausdruck der Gemütsbewegungen.* Leipzig: F.A. Brockhaus.

_____. 1874. *The Descent of Man.* Revised and Annotated Edition. New York: Hearst and Company.

Euler, L. 1840. *Letters Addressed to a German Princess on Natural Philosophy.* 2 vols. New York: Harper and Brothers.

Helmholtz, H.L.F. von. 1863. *Tonempfindungen.* Braunschweig: F. Viewey and Sohn.

_____. 1879. *Die Thatsachen in der Wahrnehmung.* Berlin: Verlag von August Hischwald.

Humboldt, W. von. 1839. *Einleitung zur Kawisprache.* Berlin: Druckerei der Königlichen Akademi der Wissenschaften.

Landmann, M. 1958. "Bausteine zur Biographie." In *Buch des Dankes an Georg Simmel,* eds. K. Gassen and M. Landmann, 11–33. Berlin: Duncker and Humblot.

Lazarus, M. 1882. *Leben der Secle.* 3 vols. Berlin: F. Dummler.

Leibnitz, G.W. von. 1847. *Nouveaux essais sur l'entendement humain.* Paris: Charpentier.

Rousseau, J.J. 1768. *Dictionnaire de Musique.* Paris: Chez la Veuve Duchesne.

Steinthal, C. 1888. *Der Ursprung der Sprache im Zusammenhange mit den letzen Fragen alles Wissens.* Berlin: F. Dummler.

Tooke, J.H. 1806. *The Diversions of Purley.* 2 vols. Philadelphia: A.M. Duane.

3

Rational and Social Foundations of Music

MAX WEBER

Peculiarities of Occidental Temperament

The peculiarity of modern temperament is found in the fact that the practical execution of the principle of distance is operative on our keyboard instruments as a temperament of tones gained harmonically. It is not like the so-called temperament in the tone systems of the Siamese and Javanese, merely a creation of a real distance scale rather than a harmonic scale. Beside the distance-wise measurement of the intervals is the choral and harmonic interpretation of intervals. Theoretically it dominates the orthography of notation.

Without this quality modern music would neither have been technically nor meaningfully possible. Its meaning rests on the fact that tone successions are not treated as an indifferent series of semitones. Despite all orthographic liberties taken even by the masters, it clings fast to the signation of the tones according to their harmonic meaning. Obviously the fact cannot be changed that even our notation, corresponding to its historical origins, is limited in the exactitude of its harmonic tone designation and reproduces, above all, the enharmonic but not the chromatic precision of the tones. For example, notation ignores the fact that the chord d–f–a according to the provenience of the tones is a genuine minor triad or a musically irrational combination of the Pythagorean and minor third. But, even so, the significance of our type of notation is great enough. Although explainable only from a historical viewpoint it is not merely an antiquarian reminiscence.

Our musical sensitivity also is dominated by the interpretation of the tones according to their harmonic provenience. We feel, even "hear," in a different fashion the tones which can be identified enharmonically on the instruments according to their chordal significance. Even the most modern developments of music, which are practically moving in many ways toward a destruction of tonality, show this influence. These modern movements which are at least in part the products of the characteristic, intellectualized romantic turn of our search for the effects of the "interesting," cannot get rid of some residual relations to these fundaments, even if in the form of developing contrasts to them.

There is no doubt that the distance principle which is akin to harmony and which is the basis of the subdivision of the intervals of our keyboard instruments, has an extensively dulling effect upon the delicacy of listening ability. The frequent use of enharmornic exchanges in modern music has a parallel effect on our harmonic feeling.

Though tonal ratio is hardly able to capture the living motion of musically expressive devices, it is, nevertheless, everywhere effective, be it ever so indirectly and behind the scenes, as a form-giving principle. It is particularly strong in music like ours where it has been made the conscious fundament of the tone system. Theoretically the modern tone system is not understandable without its effects. Nor has its influence fallen exclusively upon what already existed in musical practice. To be, sure, repeatedly it has tended to place our music in persistent dragging chains.

Certainly modern chordal harmony belonged to practical music long before Rameau and the encylopedists provided it with a theoretic basis (still somewhat imperfect) (Recy 1886, Oliver 1947, Helmholtz 1954: 356b). The fact that this occurred was productive of effects in musical practice quite in the same manner as the rationalization efforts of the medieval theorists for the development of polyvocality which existed before their assistance. The relations between tonal ratio and musical life belong to the historically most important and varying situations of tension in music.

[...]

The Great Instrument Makers and the Modern Orchestra

The numerous species of viols still found in the seventeenth and eighteenth centuries with very different, often very numerous stringing, recalling the rapid increase of strings on the Hellenic kithara, were a product of uninterrupted experimentation especially in the sixteenth century. It was also encouraged by the individually varied traditional practices and pretensions of the leading orchestras. These numerous types of viols vanished in the eighteenth century in favor of the three modern string instruments: the violin, viola, and cello. The superiority of these instruments was unambiguously demonstrated by violin virtuosity first appearing in full bloom since Corelli, and through development of the modern orchestra.

The violin, viola, and cello became the instruments for a special modern organization of chamber music, the string quartet as it was definitely established by Joseph Haydn. They constitute the kernel of the modern orchestra. They are a product of persistent experiments of the manufacturers of instruments from Brescia and Cremona.

The gap between the performance capacity of these instruments, which were in no way improved since the beginning of the eighteenth century, and their predecessors is very striking. Speaking with some exaggeration, the string instruments of the Middle Ages did not permit the legato playing which in our view is specific to them, although the ligatures of old mensural notation permit us to conclude they existed. The sustaining of tones, increasing or decreasing volume, melodious playing of fast passages, and all the specific qualities which we expect to be executed by the violin were still rendered only with difficulty until the sixteenth century. They were nearly impossible quite apart from the fact that the changes of hand position required today for the domination of the tone space of string instruments were almost excluded by the type of construction. Considering the quality of the family of instruments it is not surprising that the division of the neck through frets, thus mechanical tone production, prevailed. Virdung (1931 [1511]), therefore, still calls the hand fiddle together with the more primitive string instruments useless.

In connection with the demand of court orchestras the ascension of string instruments to their perfection began in the sixteenth century. The ever-present desire for expressive sonorous beauty, for a singing tone, and elegance of the instrument itself were the driving forces in Italy of the orchestras and the instrument makers. Even before the transfer of technical supremacy in violin construction to Brescia and Cremona, one notes in the sixteenth century, gradual approximations of various parts of the instrument (especially of the form of the bridge and the sound holes) toward its final form.

What such technical development offered in possibilities, once perfection was achieved, far surpassed what had been demanded. The performance capacity of the Amati instruments was not really exploited for many decades. In the same way as the single violin, following an ineradicable conviction, first had to be "played in" and had to wait a generation before it could reach the full height of its rendition potential, so the adaptation and introduction also as compared with other instruments occurred only very slowly. Ruhlmann's supposition that modern string instruments originate in a unique, unanticipated accident goes too far. However, it remains true that the tonal potential made available by the construction of the instrument was not immediately exploited. Its availability as a special solo instrument of virtuosi could not have been guessed beforehand by the builders.

It is to be assumed that the concerns of the Amati, Guarneri, and Stradivari were turned essentially toward achieving sensuous beauty and only then sturdiness in the interest of the greatest possible freedom of movement by the player. Their restriction to four strings, the omission of frets, therewith mechanical tone production, and the final fixing of all single parts of the resonant body and of the systems of conducting the vibration were aesthetic consequences. Other qualities devolved upon them in the form of "secondary products" as much unwilled as the atmospheric effects of Gothic inner rooms was initially. These were involuntary consequences of purely constructive innovations.

In any case the production of the great violin-builders lacked a rational foundation such as can be clearly recognized with organ, the piano and its predecessors, as well as the wind instruments. The crwth was improved on grounds belonging to the guild. The string instruments were developed on the basis of purely empirical knowledge gained gradually in time as to the most useful shape of the top, the sound holes, the bridge and its perforation, the core, the post, the raised borders, the best qualities of wood and probably also varnish. This resulted in those achievements which today, perhaps because of the disappearance of the balsam fir, can no longer be completely imitated.

Considering their technical construction, instruments created in such manner did not as such consist of a device to promote harmonic music. On the contrary, the lack of the bridge of the older instruments facilitated their use in bringing forth chords and the bourdon strings served as the harmonic support of the melody. This was omitted in the modern instruments which, on the contrary, seemed designed as vehicles of melodic effects. Precisely this was welcome to the music of the Renaissance, governed as it was by dramatic interests.[1]

[. . .]

Emancipation of the Piano and Its Emergence as the Instrument of the Middle Classes

French instrumental music showed the influence of the dance, determined by the sociological structure of France. Then, following the example of violin virtuoso performance, musical emancipation of piano music from the organ style of writing was carried out. Chambonnieres may be considered the first creator of specific piano works. Domenico Scarlatti, at the beginning of the eighteenth century, is the first to exploit in virtuoso fashion the peculiar sonorous effects of the instrument (Kirkpatrick 1953). Piano virtuosity developed hand in hand with a heavy harpsichord industry which was based on the demand of orchestras and amateurs. Continued development led on to the last great technical changes of the instrument and its typification. The first great builder of harpsichords (around 1600 the family Ruckers in Belgium [Closson 1935]) operated like a manufacturer creating individual instruments commissioned by specific consumers (orchestras and patricians) and thus in very manifold adaptation to all possible special needs quite in the manner of the organ.

The development of the hammer piano occurred by stages partly in Italy (Christoferi) partly in Germany. Inventions made in Italy remained unexploited there. Italian culture (until the threshold of the present) remained alien to the indoor culture of the Nordic Europe.

Italian ideals lacked the influence of the culture of the bourgeois-like home. They retained the ideal of *a cappella* singing and the opera. The arias of the opera supplied the popular demand for easily comprehensible and singable tunes.

The center of gravity of the production and technical improvement of the piano lies in the musically most broadly organized country, Saxony. The bourgeois-like musical culture derived from the *Kantorelen* virtuosi and builders of instruments proceeded hand in hand with an intense interest in the orchestra of the count. Beyond this it underwent continuous improvement and popularization. In the foreground of interest was the possibility of muffling and increasing the volume of the tone, the sustaining of the tone and the beautiful perfection of the chords played in the form of arpeggios at any tone distance. In contrast to these advantages was the disadvantage (especially according to Bach) of deficient freedom, in contrast to the harpsichord and clavichord, in playing fast passages. The removal of this disadvantage was of major concern.

In place of the tapping touch of the keyboard instruments of the sixteenth century, beginning with the organ a rational fingering technique was in progress, soon extended to the harpsichord. This presented the hands working into each other, the fingers crossing over one another. To our conception this was still tortured enough. Eventually the Bachs placed fingering technique, one would like to say, on a "physiological tonal" basis by a rational use of the thumb (David and Mendel 1945: 306ff). In antiquity the highest virtuoso achievements occurred on the aulos. Now the violin and, above all, the piano presented the most difficult tasks.

The great artists of modern piano music, Johann Sebastian and Philipp Emanuel Bach were still neutral toward the hammer piano. J.S. Bach in particular wrote an important part of his best work for the old types of instruments, the clavichord and harpsichord. These were weaker and more intimate than the piano and with respect to sonority calculated for more delicate ears. Only the internationally famous virtuosity of Mozart and the increasing need of music publishers and of concert managers to satisfy the large music consumption of the mass market brought the final victory of the hammer piano.

In the eighteenth century the piano-builders, above all, the German, were still artisans who collaborated and experimented physically (like Silbermann [Mooser 1857]). Machine-made mass production of the piano occurred first in England (Broadwood) then in America (Steinway) where first-rate iron could be pressed into construction of the frame. Moreover, iron helped overcome the numerous purely climatic difficulties that could affect adoption of the piano. Incidentally, climatic difficulties also stood in the way of adoption of the piano in the tropics. By the beginning of the nineteenth century the piano had become a standard commercial object produced for stock.

The wild competitive struggle of the factories played a role in the development of the instrument. So, too, did the virtuosi with the special modern devices of the press, exhibitions, and finally analogous to salesman techniques of breweries, of the building of concert halls, of the instrument factories of their own (with us, above all, those of the Berliner). These forces brought about that technical perfection of the instrument which alone could satisfy the ever increasing technical demands of the composers. The older instruments were already no match for Beethoven's later creations.

Meanwhile, orchestra works were made accessible for home use only in the form of piano transcriptions. In Chopin a first rank composer was found who restricted himself entirely to the piano. Finally in Liszt the intimate skill of the great virtuoso elicited from the instrument all that had finally been concealed of expressive possibilities.

The unshakable modern position of the piano rests upon the universality of its usefulness for domestic appropriation of almost all treasures of music literature, upon the immeasurable fullness of its own literature and finally on its quality as a universal accompanying and schooling instrument. In its function as a school instrument, it displaced the antique kithara, the monochord, the primitive organ, and the barrel-lyre of the monastic schools. As an accompanying instrument it displaced the aulos of antiquity, the organ, and the primitive string instruments of the Middle Ages and the lute of the Renaissance. As an amateur instrument of the upper classes it displaced the kithara of antiquity, the harp, of the North, and the lute of the sixteenth century. Our exclusive education toward modern harmonic music is represented quite essentially by it.

Even the negative aspects of the piano are important. Temperament takes from our ears some of the delicacy which gave the decisive flavor to the melodious refinement of ancient music culture. Until the sixteenth century the training of singers in the Occident took place on the monochord. According to Zarline, the singers trained in this manner attempted to reintroduce perfect temperament. Today their training occurs almost exclusively on the piano. And today, at least in our latitudes, tone formation and schooling of string instruments is practised from the beginning at the piano. It is clear that delicate hearing capacity possible with training by means of instruments in pure temperament cannot be reached. The notoriously greater imperfection in the intonation of Nordic as compared to Italian singers must be caused by it.

The idea of building pianos with twenty-four keys in the octave, as suggested by Helmholtz, is not promising for economic reasons. The building of the piano is conditioned by the mass market. It is the peculiar nature of the piano to be a middle-class home instrument. As the organ requires a giant indoor space the piano requires a moderately large indoor space to display its best enchantments. All the successes of the modern piano virtuosi cannot basically change the fact that the instrument in its independent appearances in the large concert hall is involuntarily compared with the orchestra and obviously found to be too light.

Therefore it is no accident that the representatives of pianistic culture are Nordic peoples, climatically house-bound and home-centered in contrast to the South. In southern Europe the cultivation of middle-class home comforts was restricted by climatic and historical factors. The piano was invented there but did not diffuse quickly as in the North. Nor did it rise to an equivalent position as a significant piece of middle-class furniture.

Note

1. By Renaissance Weber here means the early baroque period.

References

Closson, E. 1935. *La facture des instruments de musique en Belgique*. Brussels: Huy.
David, H. and Mendel, A. 1945. *The Bach Reader*. New York: Norton.
Helmholtz, H.L.F. 1954. *On the Sensations of Tone*. 2nd rev. Ed. A.F. Ellis, with a new Introduction by H. Margenau. New York: Dover Publications, Inc.
Kirkpatrick, R. 1953. *Domenico Scarlatti*. Princeton: Princeton University Press.
Mooser, A. 1857. *Gottfried Silbermann*. Langensalza: Schulbuchhandlung d. Th. L.B.
Oliver, A.R. 1947. *The Encyclopedists as Critics of Music*. New York: Columbia University Press,
Recy, R. 1886. "Rameau et les encyclopedistes." Revue des deux mondes 76: 138–164.
Virdung, S. 1931 [1511]. *Musica getutscht*. Ed. L. Schrade. Kassel: Bärenreiter.

4

Musical Taste and How it is Formed

JOHN H. MUELLER

[. . .]

It may seem embarrassing to raise, and impertinent to attempt to answer, questions on the nature of beauty which have occupied the thought of mankind at least since the time of the Greeks. Many may, in fact, feel that such questions are irrelevant to the enjoyment of great music. But they are implicit in history, and their tentative solutions in every epoch are a part of the very process of living. Man not only acts, but he also reflects on his actions in order to make them plausible to himself and to his fellow man.

During the nineteenth century, when most of the standard repertoire of today had its beginnings, the problems of art and beauty were considered the province of philosophy and metaphysics, in keeping with the revived Platonic theories which dominated the arts of that romantic era. Beauty was Truth, unencumbered by the vicissitudes of mundane life. It was a kind of Universal, compelling on every perceptive intelligence. This view still has many disciples in art pedagogy and in the critics' fraternity, and explains the passionate enthusiasm and missionary fervor with which certain tastes are promulgated, the esteem in which the artist is held, the conception which some artists have of their own role, and the awe of the layman before a creative work.

However, with the development of the social, anthropological, and psychological sciences (Mueller 1934, 1935, 1946; Farnsworth 1950), and their analysis of the diverse primitive and modern art forms, the tremendous variety of equally valid aesthetic standards could not but impress the conscientious and informed observer. The prestige that any given standard may command among its devotees takes on a rather provincial hue when examined in the light of the myriads of others that may be cherished with equal passion by their own adherents. In this great diversity of historically approved standards lies the reason for the supposed insolubility of the problem of beauty. Furthermore, new beauties are constantly being invented and old ones discarded. The solution is clearly not to be found exclusively in the nature of the beautiful objects themselves, nor exclusively in the human nature of the subject who enjoys them, but in the interaction or relation between both elements.

[. . .]

In explanation of . . . fluctuations in art tastes, it would be too simple and dogmatic merely to derogate as "decadent" those periods whose preferences differed significantly from the present, and to exalt those "golden" ages whose likings conformed to our own, only to have the next generation modulate, or even reverse, our judgments. A competent student of art history will easily demonstrate how such terms as Renaissance, Gothic, Baroque, Rococo, Romantic and other styles have some descriptive value, but are actually "loaded" abstractions which contain the retroactive judgments of another era, floated with conviction and great confidence, but signifying essentially a periodic re-evaluation of taste. It therefore has little meaning to state that, during his eclipse, critics were "mistaken" about Bach, and that his sons were "blind to his greatness"; that Brahms was long "undervalued" and Raff and Tschaikowsky "overrated"; or that "true" judgments cannot be ventured until after repeated hearings. The question is not intended to be facetious: Why should posterity always have the last word? Unless a given epoch exalts its own verdicts to a level of infallibility—as it often does—it must be acknowledged that every epoch, every age, is entitled to its own standards of judgment in matters aesthetic. The invidious distinctions so often drawn between epochs are psychologically and sociologically indefensible, and derive from a misconception of the nature of aesthetic "truth."

The standard of "truth" in matters aesthetic differs fundamentally from that of science. Aesthetic "truth" or appreciation is a psychologically *terminal* experience, a subjective and contemplative state of mind, in which every percipient differs from every other in slighter or greater degree according to his accumulated experience (Hevner 1937, Boas 1937, Schoen 1940). It is therefore essentially incommunicable except to the extent that the subjects' backgrounds are identical. Since aesthetic experiences are ends in themselves, and represent a state of personal fulfillment, they cannot be demonstrated as truthful or false by any external tests, for they reach their convincing termination in the subjective sense of gratification. Hence, aesthetic tastes cannot be "disputed," although their derivation may be traced and "accounted for."

[. . .]

Changes in aesthetic taste and judgment do not emanate solely from the dicta of aesthetes. They do not proceed from an exalted metaphysical realm, whence they are communicated to the chosen few who, like the apostles of old, feel called to share these privileged communications with the lay masses. The pattern of the repertoire, which constitutes musical taste, changing by small accretions, is formed by crosscurrents of many major and minor personal decisions and compromises made every time the program of a concert is selected or an annual series projected. The identity and strength of these forces differ from time to time and from place to place; but they are not capricious and whimsical—the patterns are too uniform for that. Nor are they automatic and preordained: the variations are too obvious for that. One can only conclude that musical opinions and tastes, like political and economic preferences, are forged in a matrix of social and psychological forces and, at any given time, represent a blend of both traditional factors and current experiences. One cannot come away from a study of a century of musical tastes without being struck by the perennial revision of human judgments, and the conviction that, under different circumstances, our tastes would have taken other channels with which we today would have been equally contented. And, unless human mentality reaches a saturation point, at which further development in forms, harmonies and rhythms cannot be absorbed or invented, society will continue to revise its most considered and hallowed judgments in the future, as it so obviously has in the past.

Of all the current theories designed to explain changes in aesthetic tastes, one of the most prevalent, and also the most suspiciously simple, is that art is a "reflection of the spirit of the age." According to this familiar principle, the stream of history is divided into broad periods, each of which is characterized by a "spirit" which pervades its totality and which binds it into a recognizable unit. There are many versions of this "spirit of the age," and not all exponents of this view would necessarily subscribe to the rather comprehensive formulation which avers that

> Some very general trend in the evolution of mankind controls all forms of human expression and all the ways in which they act, be they politics, economy, thought or art.
>
> (Sachs 1946: 326)

But no social scientist views society as a homogeneous entity in which an over-all "spirit" can be identified. Society is enormously more complex than the Hegelian *Zeitgeist* seems to assume. Instead of an integrated Society with a capital "S," society is rather a federation of various and diverse groups, each with its own interests and tastes, sometimes cooperating with one another, but quite frequently in mortal conflict. This unitarian view of Society, which has often been so congenial to totalitarian national aspirations as well, has lost much of its credibility in the more thoroughgoing, empirical methods of the twentieth century. This theory of an enveloping spirit has led to positing spurious relations between music, architecture, and other phases of life literally too numerous and too well-known to cite. The social approach to history is inconsistent with the synoptic notion of rolling into one the economic, technological, political, psychological, and other factors and labeling them with an intangible "spirit."

There is also the semantic objection, that an explanation of an event in terms of the "spirit" of that event is tautological. To explain rococo by the "spirit" of rococo, baroque by the "spirit" of baroque, is to explain something in terms of synonyms, which is no explanation at all. This is a grave methodological error that gives a satisfying sense of certainty for the simple reason that there is no possibility whatever of being contradicted. One reads the "spirit" from a few observed facts, and then reads it right back again into the unresistant period. "Spirituous" liquors analogously had their origin in similar verbalisms, but today modern chemistry and physiology have found more palpable explanations for the source of their potency.

[. . .]

We therefore cannot resist the conclusion that musical taste is a system of very specific tonal habits, conditioned by the incessant flow of experiences of the individual person as a participating member of a complex culture group. A great range of experiences might conceivably contribute to the end-result of finding pleasure in many given types of music, much as some trivial incident might influence the degree of affection for or aversion toward another person. In order to understand more fully how the aesthetic quality of a musical composition is acquired, it will be necessary to ascertain its psychological components, and to explore how the standards of beauty become established.

Because of the human propensity to read into the object what is actually in our heads—"the elliptical fallacy"—it is often thought that the merit of a composition resides within it; and once that has been established by some kind of authority, there is a certain aesthetic obligation imposed on the auditor to put himself *en rapport* with the established masterpieces, and to attempt to "discover" for himself the beauties resident in those works of art that have been vouchsafed by "qualified" listeners.

However, psychologically and sociologically speaking, this is an unfortunate assumption. Beauty is not a transcendental entity waiting, perhaps in some outer sphere, to be incorporated into a composition by a sensitive composer; nor is it a quality resident *in* the object, or in the relationship between its parts, waiting to he discovered and enjoyed by an observer—any more than pain is resident in a red-hot stove, or the essence of patriotism in a multicolored flag. Beauty in music is not a fact but rather a human *experience*, a judgment that results from the *contact* between the particular arrangement of sounds and the particular background of the auditor. Beauty "happens" to an object. If there were no observer, there would be no beauty; if there are two simultaneous observers, the same object could be—and usually is—both beautiful and ugly simultaneously. Two or more persons, with approximately the same training, background, and fund of experiences, observing the same object, would necessarily be in approximate agreement as to its degree of "beauty." Hence, the cultural agreement on many masterpieces. Any object can be beautiful if it is matched with the appropriate observer who has the corresponding accumulation of experiences and store of habits. Thus it is false dichotomy to segregate the thinking subject from the object of thought. The real issue does not lie in the segregation of the two, but in the manner of their collaboration (Lalo 1927: 3).[1]

[. . .]

There are those who may be offended at so prosaic a treatment of the arts, which suggests that good music is ephemeral and transient, and subject to the material vicissitudes of life. They would prefer to believe that Art secures its sanction from a higher realm, or that it at least possesses some distinctive objective trait to give it permanence and universality in its appeal to the discerning auditor. . . . It is the long dominance of such a figure as Beethoven, more recently joined by Sebastian Bach, which appears to give plausibility to the faith in a universal Beauty. It is such phenomena which create the illusion of timeless beauty that transcends the ages, the passing of which is uncomfortable to contemplate. A well-developed historical sense, however, will awaken the realization that a century—or a thousand years—is but a moment in civilization. Bach and Beethoven are not "universal"; they merely have lasted a long time.

Such an argument is not at all nihilistic. It does not proclaim the nonexistence of standards. For it is an error to suppose that, if norms cannot be absolute or eternal, there can be no norms at all. But so intense is the quest for certainty that the difference between absolute and period norms is often overlooked. However, it is the only point of view that makes the incessant fluctuations in taste plausible and is, above all, consistent with the current conceptions of the workings and nature of the human mind.

[. . .]

Changes in musical taste cannot be, and actually have not been, rushed . . . Even revolutionary changes are less rapid than is usually implied in the concept, for all these changes have their definite antecedents. The fact that musical tastes change slowly is consistent with the very requirements of social life. Without a certain degree of uniformity and continuity in norms, no publishing enterprise, no educational system, no critical standards, no concert organization—in fact, no common social existence would be possible. This fact confers on aesthetic taste its social nature. Although there is no psychological law which would prevent the development of a perfectly unique taste on the part of a hermit-like artist, it is a sociological impossibility that such a taste could survive in a social world. In a collective world, only collective tastes can qualify for survival, because the overhead in time, effort, and financial investment necessary for the implementation of a "taste system" is so great that only collective effort will sustain it.

Musical taste systems are further stabilized by having their material embodiment in huge financial investments in auditoriums, accoutrements for professional training, pedagogical institutions, printing of scores, manufacture of instruments; and have their nonmaterial formulation in a vast corpus of literature, theory and ideology which galvanize it into a major institution resistant to changes that threaten it with extinction. Under such circumstances, a composition may, indeed, possess an individuality, but its "uniqueness" is reduced to a mere variation of a general norm which constitutes the basis of critical judgment.

For norms to exist, it is not necessary for them to be eternal. Although anyone with even a modicum of historical sense must recognize the long-term inconstancy of norms, nevertheless they are relatively stable over a period of time, and evoke considerable sentimental, ethical, and special-interest attachments which get codified into legal, religious, or cultural and critical mandates. This holds for the economic and political systems as well as for aesthetic standards. In sociological language, these general social norms are called "folkways." After they have persisted for some time—as have the norms of family life, the folkways of government and religion, and the folkways of classic musical taste—they tend to sprout a halo of uncritical acceptance, creating the illusion of general and absolute validity which condemns all deviant forms of behavior as "immoral" or "in poor taste." This predisposition to universalize the standards of one's own culture is called, in technical jargon, "ethnocentricism."

Musical norms conform to these characteristics of social folkways. The norms are codified and transmitted from generation to generation with increments of change, but are also subject to considerable sectarian fervor. They are defended, not like scientific truths, but rather by an aesthetic "conscience" which may even proselytize for what is considered "true" beauty, and declare J.S. Bach "universal" when he is quite obviously attached to time, space, and circumstance, as is every other mortal, great and small.

[. . .]

The scientific and material world has also made its contribution to the formation of aesthetic taste, remote as science and art are popularly alleged to be. Certainly, much of the scientific activity is irrelevant to matters conventionally considered artistic; however, in the orchestral repertoire the science of physics and acoustics has revolutionized the repertoire simply by revolutionizing the instruments on which the repertoires are played. The old natural horns, with their removable crooks, had become increasingly awkward as the scores became more complex, demanding numerous key changes and chromatic passage work. The valves, of course, simplified the execution of these passages and made Wagner and Strauss, to say nothing of the later moderns, possible. The wood-winds, the violin (Tourte bow), the piano, and all other instruments were at various times the beneficiaries of corresponding technological improvements, with analogous evolution in the standards of musical structure and aesthetic tastes. It can therefore be unreservedly asserted that physical science is an integral element in the formation of aesthetic taste.

To these strictly musical applications of technology and science must be added the equally important technical advances in printing, architecture, communication and transportation, without which musical developments would have remained sterile. For, what benefit the chromatic creations of Wagner and Strauss without the facility to print the huge scores, to promulgate them rapidly and economically throughout the nation and beyond its borders, and the acoustical architectural setting to exploit them? It is said that the art of printing made democracy possible. A similarly daring generalization may be made about music; the art of printing probably exerted no less influence in the creation and dissemination of aesthetic tastes than in the formation and propagation of political beliefs.

The discussion of repertoires ultimately raises the problem of "good" taste and "good" music. There is no room here for the Olympian dictum that there are only "two kinds of music, good and bad." Such alternatives do not specify the concrete quality of the music to which these appellations are to be applied.

The question of "what is good music" is often shrugged off as being both impossible and unnecessary: impossible because the inner feelings of aesthetic conscience cannot be made rationally articulate; and unnecessary, because one need only to emulate those "qualified" persons who possess "good" taste. However, the whole foregoing text is a refutation of that dual evasion. If the repertoire is the result of individual choices, there should be no objection to an attempt to determine the possible criteria on which these choices are based.

The classification of our innumerable and diverse experiences into the desirable and undesirable, into the *good*, which we seek to perpetuate, and the *bad*, which we seek to avoid, is one of the most elementary human judgments. But it is complicated by the manifold use and meaning of the concept. The concept of "good," when applied to taste or action of man, can have only four basic meanings.

1. The instrumental or utilitarian meaning: an action or thing which is good *for something.*
   Spinach may be good as nutritious diet (but "I don't like it"). The study of mathematics may

be good for your efficiency, but you may not enjoy the discipline. A Strauss waltz may have therapeutic value in hastening convalescence, and coincidentally be quite thrilling and "good" to listen to.

2. Personal pleasure, as an aesthetic end in itself: an article of food may be consumed, a piece of music may be listened to, with utter delight, without any ulterior thought of health or prestige for having listened to it. It will earn from the consumer the pronouncement of "good" when he probably should proclaim more accurately, "I find it good," "I like it," "it gives *me* pleasure." He may experience such profound satisfaction that it will be difficult for him to realize that many another person may experience other and contrary reactions. However, this propensity to universalize and to dogmatize concerning beliefs and tastes that are intensely felt is a common phenomenon and results in attempts to impose on others our religious, political, and aesthetic beliefs whether or not they are appropriate. It emanates from a psychological myopia, which renders nothing more convincing than our own inner experiences and beliefs.

3. Conformity to an established social norm: moral behavior, styles of dress, and certain art forms are labeled "good" when they conform to certain pre-established standards or norms. These norms usually reside in certain authoritarian sources, such as historical and critical documents, in tradition, or in the behavior or tastes of a social class. Thus, monogamy is undoubtedly "good," though many enjoy violating it at times. A new hat may be in "good" style prescribed for the season—"that's what they are wearing"—though "it is not becoming to me." The concert patron who lacks confidence in his own judgment may say: "I suppose it is good music, but I don't like it." These well-established technical and aesthetic standards, representing as they do the composite judgments of large groups over long periods of time, carry the weighty sanction of tradition, and are therefore considered more valid than any individual judgment. The individual does not readily pit his momentary opinion against the judgment of time. These norms are received in the social heritage, give great intellectual security, and deserve the laudatory title of "good." They promote social solidarity, permit predictability, while social customs undergo their slow changes on the experimental growing edges.

4. Related to the definition of the social norm, but differing in its sanction, is the criterion of Truth or Goodness which is presumably independent of any human being's belief or judgment. This metaphysical notion, characteristic of the romantic doctrines of the nineteenth century, posits a Truth which resides in cosmic nature, inherent in the Universe, which finally gains acceptance through the agency of the clairvoyant leaders who possess the genius to translate it into mundane objects of art. This doctrine makes of the musician a kind of priest who interprets by inspirational and intuitive means, Truth and Beauty. This makes of Beauty an objective entity rather than a subjective human judgment. When fervently believed in, it confers on an artist and his interpreter a sense of self-confidence attained by no other means. It is a widespread dogma which, though not always articulately explained, lies at the root of many aesthetic pronouncements among pedagogues as well as laymen.

These familiar dilemmas testify to the necessity of coming to grips with the semantic implications of our terms. If "good" music is a social norm, and "taste," which approves it, is a more or less enduring and definable pattern of preferences under given conditions, then "good taste" will fluctuate and be subject to all the laws of social folkways. This definition conforms to all the observations which have been made throughout this work. But taste is never pure. It is a pluralistic phenomenon compounded of various ingredients which consist not only of spontaneous pleasure, but also of the overtones of fashion and prestige and technical erudition that emanate from the leaders. Conductors, musicians, and other members of the elite make the decisions for the public, very much as do the leaders in politics and public opinion. The norm may therefore be strengthened by the authority of a group which practices it, by a social ideology which sanctions it, and by the fervor with which it is promulgated. On the other hand, it may be weakened by competing groups, who are, for various reasons, opposed to the conventional norms, and seek to replace the "embalmed classics" with a modern style.

Ultimately, the established taste is a grand cooperative enterprise between the external physical object—which is neutral—and the audiences who endow it with "beauty," and who have been conditioned by their past experiences, their ethics and religion, the physical environment and the innumerable factors which impinge upon their lives and determine their choices. It would be more precise, therefore, to discard the "truism" that "good music survives," and to substitute the more realistic view that music which, through various social, material, and psychological circumstances survives, and which contains features that society values, is adjudged and labeled aesthetically "good." Sometimes this judgment is held in abeyance for years, while these forces are doing their work.

[. . .]

In spite of this, there is no end to the search for objective criteria of good music which would be compelling on all rational beings. In a strictly technical sense, there may be moderate consensus on this question. Probably most musicians would agree on certain standards of workmanship, clean handling of instrumentation, and many other processes. But fine workmanship is not inevitably translated into an aesthetic thrill. The sons of Sebastian Bach, the detractors of Stokowski's transcriptions, the critics of "atonalism," the auditors who hold themselves aloof from the flamboyant Wagner—all are the final refutation of a presumed identity between an objective description of an art object and the thrill of the listener. Technically, such music is "good"; aesthetically it is "bad" to many listeners.

[. . .]

Note

1   For a brief critical summary of Lalo's aesthetic see: Gilbert (1927), Mueller (1938).

References

Boas, G. 1937. *A Primer for Critics*. Baltimore: Johns Hopkins University Press.
Farnsworth, P.R. 1950. *Musical Taste, Its Measurement and Cultural Nature*. Stanford: Stanford University Press.
Gilbert, K. 1927. *Studies in Recent Aesthetic*. Chapel Hill: University of North Carolina Press.
Hevner, K. 1937. "The Aesthetic Experience; A Psychological Description." *Psychological Review* 44(3): 245–263.
Lalo, C. 1927. *Notions d'Esthétique*. Paris: F. Alcan.
Mueller, J.H. 1934. "Theories of Aesthetic Appreciation." In *Studies in Appreciation of Art*, Vol. IV, no. 6. Eugene: University of Oregon Publications.
_____. 1935. "Is Art the Product of its Age?" *Social Forces* 13(3): 367–375.
_____. 1938. "The Folkway of Art: An Analysis of the Social Theories of Art." *American Journal of Sociology* 44(2): 222–238.
_____. 1946. "Methods of Measurement of Aesthetic Folkways." *American Journal of Sociology* 51(4): 276–282.
Sachs, C. 1946. *The Commonwealth of Art*. New York: W.W. Norton.
Schoen, M. 1940. *Psychology of Music*. New York: Ronald Press.

5

Making Music Together
A Study in Social Relationship

ALFRED SCHÜTZ

Music is a meaningful context which is not bound to a conceptual scheme. Yet this meaningful context can be communicated. The process of communication between composer and listener normally requires an intermediary: an individual performer or a group of coperformers. Among all these participants there prevail social relations of a highly complicated structure.

To analyze certain elements of this structure is the purpose of this paper. The discussion is not aimed at problems commonly relegated to the realm of the so-called sociology of music, although it is believed that an investigation of the social relationships among the participants in the musical process is a prerequisite for any research in this field; nor is it concerned with a phenomenology of musical experience, although some elementary observations regarding the structure of music will have to be made. The chief interest of our analysis consists in the particular character of all social interactions connected with the musical process: they are doubtless meaningful to the actor as well as to the addressee, but this meaning structure is not capable of being expressed in conceptual terms; they are founded upon communication, but not *primarily* upon a semantic system used by the communicator as a scheme of expression and by his partner as a scheme of interpretation.[1] For this very reason it can be hoped that a study of the social relationships connected with the musical process may lead to some insights valid for many other forms of social intercourse, perhaps even to illumination of a certain aspect of the structure of social interaction as such that has not so far attracted from social scientists the attention it deserves.

[. . .]

As far as the question under scrutiny is concerned, the concrete researches of many sociologists and philosophers have aimed at certain forms of social intercourse which necessarily precede all communication. Wiese's "contact-situations," Scheler's perceptual theory of the alter ego, to a certain extent Cooley's concept of the face-to-face relationship, Malinowski's interpretation of speech as originating within the situation determined by social interaction, Sartre's basic concept of "looking at the other and being looked at by the other" (*le regard*), all these are just a few examples of the endeavor to investigate what might be called the "mutual tuning-in relationship" upon which alone all communication is founded. It is precisely this mutual tuning-in relationship by which the "I" and the "Thou" are experienced by both participants as a "We" in vivid presence.

Instead of entering here into the complicated philosophical analysis of this problem,[2] it may be permissible to refer to a series of well-known phenomena in the social world in which this precommunicative social relationship comes to the foreground. . . . It is typical for a set of similar interrelated activities such as the relationship between pitcher and catcher, tennis players, fencers, and so on; we find the same features in marching together, dancing together, making love together, or making music together, and this last-named activity will serve as an example for analysis in the following pages. It is hoped that this analysis will in some measure contribute to clarification of the structure of the mutual tuning-in relationship, which originates in the possibility of living together simultaneously in specific dimensions of time. It is also hoped that the study of the particular communicative situation within the musical process will shed some light on the nonconceptual aspect involved in any kind of communication.

II

[. . .]

   Musical notation is . . . just one among several vehicles of communicating musical thought. But musical notation is by no means identical with musical language. Its semantic system is of quite another kind than that of ideograms, letters, or mathematical or chemical symbols. The ideogram refers immediately to the represented concept and so does the mathematical or chemical symbol. The written word in our alphabetic languages refers to the sound of the spoken word and through it as an intermediary to the concept it conveys. As stated above, the meaning of a musical process cannot be related to a conceptual scheme, and the particular function of musical notation today as well as in its historical development reflects this situation. The musical sign is nothing but instruction to the performer to produce by means of his voice or his instrument a sound of a particular pitch and duration, giving in addition, at certain historical periods, suggestions as to tempo, dynamics, and expression, or directions as to the connection with other sounds (by such devices as ties, slurs, and the like). All these elements of the tonal material can only be approximately prescribed and the way to obtain the indicated effect is left to the performer. "The composer's specific indications are themselves not always a part of his original creation but rather one musician's message to another about it, a hint about how to secure in performance a convincing transmission of the work's feeling content without destroying its emotional and intellectual community," says a well-known composer and critic (Thompson 1948: 296). And the conductor, Furtwängler (1934: 609), is certainly right in stating that the composer's text "cannot give any indication as to the really intended volume of a *forte*, the really intended speed of a *tempo*, since every *forte* and every *tempo* has to be modified in practice in accordance with the place of the performance and the setting and the strength of the performing group" and that "the expression marks have intentionally a merely symbolic value with respect to the whole work and are not intended to be valid for the single instrument wherefore an "*ff*" for the bassoon has quite another meaning than for the trombone."

   Thus, all musical notation remains of necessity vague and open to manifold interpretations and it is up to the reader or performer to decipher the hints in the score and to define the approximations. These limits vary widely in the course of the historical development of musical culture. The more closely we approach the present in the study of the history of music, the lower the level of the general musical culture of performers and of listeners, and the stronger the tendency of the composer to make his system of notation as exact and precise as possible, that is, to limit more and more the performer's freedom of interpretation. To be sure, all signs of musical notation are conventional; but, as has been shown, the system of musical notation is more or less accidental to the process of musical communication. A social theory of music therefore does not have to be founded on the conventional character of the visual signs but rather on the sum total of what we have just called musical culture against the background of which the reader's or performer's interpretation of these signs takes place.

III

To make this web of social relationships called musical culture clearer, let us imagine a lonely performer of a piece of music sitting at his piano before the score of a sonata by a minor master of the nineteenth century which, we assume, is entirely unknown to him. Furthermore, we assume that our piano player is equally proficient as a technician and sight reader and that consequently no mechanical or other external obstacle will hinder the flux of his performance.

Yet, having hardly made these two assumptions, we hesitate. Are they indeed compatible with each other? Can we really maintain that the sonata in question is *entirely* unknown to our performer? He could not be an accomplished technician and sight reader without having attained a certain level of musical culture enabling him to read offhand a piece of music of the *type* of that before him. Consequently, although this particular sonata and perhaps all the other works of this particular composer might be unknown to him, he will nevertheless have a well-founded knowledge of the type of musical form called "sonata within the meaning of nineteenth century piano music," of the type of themes and harmonies used in such compositions of that period, of the expressional contents he may expect to find in them—in sum, of the typical "style" in which music of this kind is written and in which it has to be executed. Even before starting to play or to read the first chord our musician is referred to a more or less clearly organized, more or less coherent, more or less distinct set of his previous experiences, which constitute in their totality a kind of preknowledge of the piece of music at hand. To be sure, this preknowledge refers merely to the *type* to which this individual piece of music belongs and not to its particular and unique individuality. But the player's general preknowledge of its typicality becomes the scheme of reference for his interpretation of its particularity. This scheme of reference determines, in a general way, the player's anticipations of what he may or may not find in the composition before him. Such anticipations are more or less empty; they may be fulfilled and justified by the musical events he will experience when he starts to play the sonata or they may "explode" and be annihilated.

In more general terms, the player approaching a so-called unknown piece of music does so from a historically—in one's own case, autobiographically—determined situation, determined by his stock of musical experiences at hand in so far as they are typically relevant to the anticipated novel experience before him.[3] This stock of experiences refers indirectly to all his past and present fellow men whose acts or thoughts have contributed to the building up of his knowledge. This includes what he has learned from his teachers, and his teachers from their teachers; what he has taken in from other players' execution; and what he has appropriated from the manifestations of the musical thought of the composer. Thus, the bulk of musical knowledge—as of knowledge in general—is socially derived. And within this socially derived knowledge there stands out the knowledge transmitted from those upon whom the prestige of authenticity and authority has been bestowed, that is, from the great masters among the composers and the acknowledged interpreters of their work. Musical knowledge transmitted by them is not only socially derived; it is also socially approved,[4] being regarded as authentic and therefore more qualified to become a pattern for others than knowledge originating elsewhere.

IV

In the situation we have chosen to investigate—the actual performance of a piece of music—the genesis of the stock of knowledge at hand with all its hidden social references is, so to speak, prehistoric. The web of socially derived and socially approved knowledge constitutes merely the setting for the main social relationship into which our piano player (and also any listener or mere reader of music) will enter: that with the composer of the sonata before him. It is the grasping of the composer's musical thought and its interpretation by re-creation which stand in the center of the player's field of consciousness or, to use a phenomenological term, which become "thematic" for his ongoing activity. This thematic kernel stands out against the horizon of preacquired knowledge, which knowledge functions as a scheme of reference and interpretation for the grasping of the composer's thought. It is now necessary to describe the structure of this social relationship between composer and beholder,[5] but before entering into its analysis it might be well to forestall a possible misunderstanding. It is by no means our thesis that a work of music (or of art in general) cannot be understood except by reference to its individual author or to the circumstances—biographical or other—in which he created this particular work. It is certainly not a prerequisite for the understanding of the musical content of the so-called Moonlight Sonata to take cognizance of the silly anecdotes which popular belief attaches to the creation of this work; it is not even indispensable to know that the sonata was composed by a man called Beethoven who lived then and there and went through such and such personal experiences. Any work of art, once accomplished, exists as a meaningful entity independent of the personal life of its creator.[6] The social relationship between composer and beholder as it is understood here is established exclusively by the fact that a beholder of a piece of music participates in and to a certain extent re-creates the experiences of the—let us suppose, anonymous—fellow man who created this work not only as an expression of his musical thoughts but with communicative intent.

For our purposes a piece of music may be defined[7]—very roughly and tentatively, indeed—as a meaningful arrangement of tones in inner time. It is the occurrence in inner time, Bergson's *durée*, which is the very form of existence of music. The flux of tones unrolling in inner time is an arrangement meaningful to both the composer and the beholder, because and in so far as it evokes in the stream of consciousness participating in it an interplay of recollections, retentions, protentions, and anticipations which interrelate the successive elements. To be sure, the sequence of tones occurs in the irreversible direction of inner time, in the direction, as it were, from the first bar to the last. But this irreversible flux is not irretrievable. The composer, by the specific means of his art,[8] has arranged it in such a way that the consciousness of the beholder is led to refer what he actually hears to what he anticipates will follow and also to what he has just been hearing and what he has heard ever since this piece of music began. The hearer, therefore, listens to the ongoing flux of music, so to speak, not only in the direction from the first to the last bar but simultaneously in a reverse direction back to the first one.[9]

It is essential for our problem to gain a clearer understanding of the time dimension in which music occurs. It was stated above that the inner time, the *durée*, is the very form of existence of music. Of course, playing an instrument, listening to a record, reading a page of music—all these are events occurring in outer time, the time that can be measured by metronomes and clocks, that is, the time that the musician "counts" in order to assure the correct "tempo." But to make clear why we consider inner time the very medium within which the musical flow occurs, let us imagine that the slow and the fast movement of a symphony each fill a twelve-inch record. Our watches show that the playing of either record takes about three and a half minutes. This is a fact which might possibly interest the program maker of a broadcasting station. To the beholder it means nothing. To him it is not true that the time he lived through while listening to the slow movement was of "equal length" with that which he dedicated to the fast one. While listening he lives in a dimension of time incomparable with that which can be subdivided into homogeneous parts. The outer time is measurable; there are pieces of equal length; there are minutes and hours and the length of the groove to be traversed by the needle of the record player. There is no such yardstick for the dimension of inner time the listener lives in; there is no equality between its pieces, if pieces there were at all.[10] It may come as a complete surprise to him that the main theme of the second movement of Beethoven's Pianoforte Sonata in d-minor, Op. 31, No. 2, takes as much time in the mere clock sense—namely, one minute—as the last movement of the same sonata up to the end of the exposition (Tovey 1945: 57).

The preceding remarks serve to clarify the particular social relationship between composer and beholder. Although separated by hundreds of years, the latter participates with quasi simultaneity in the former's stream of consciousness by performing with him step by step the ongoing articulation of his musical thought. The beholder, thus, is united with the composer by a time dimension common to both, which is nothing other than a derived form of the vivid present shared by the partners in a genuine face-to-face relation[11] such as prevails between speaker and listener.

But is this reconstruction of a vivid present, this establishment of a quasi simultaneity, specific to the relationship between the stream of consciousness of the composer and that of the beholder? Can it not also be found in the relationship between the reader of a letter with its writer, the student of a scientific book with its author, the high school boy who learns the demonstration of the rule of the hypotenuse with Pythagoras? Certainly, in all these cases the single phases of the author's articulated thought are polythetically—that is, step by step—coperformed or reperformed by the recipient, and thus a quasi simultaneity of both streams of thought takes place. The reader of a scientific book, for instance, builds up word by word the meaning of a sentence, sentence by sentence that of a paragraph, paragraph by paragraph that of a chapter. But once having coperformed these polythetic steps of constituting the conceptual meaning of this sentence (paragraph, chapter), the reader may grasp the outcome of this constitutive process, the resulting conceptual meaning, in a single glance—monothetically, as Husserl (1931: 118, 119, 334ff) puts it—that is, independently of the polythetic steps in which and by which this meaning has been constituted. In the same way I may grasp monothetically the meaning of the Pythagorean theorem $a2 + b2 = c2$, without restarting to perform the single mental operations of deriving it step by step from certain assured premises, and I may do so even if I have forgotten how to demonstrate the theorem.

The meaning of a musical work,[12] however, is essentially of a polythetical structure. It cannot be grasped monothetically. It consists in the articulated step-by-step occurrence in inner time, in the very polythetic constitutional process itself. I may give a name to a specific piece of music, calling it "Moonlight Sonata" or "Ninth Symphony"; I may even say, "These were variations with a finale in the form of a passacaglia," or characterize, as certain program notes are prone to do, the particular mood or emotion this piece of music is supposed to have evoked in me. But the musical content itself, its very meaning, can be grasped merely by reimmersing oneself in the ongoing flux, by reproducing thus the articulated musical occurrence as it unfolds in polythetic steps in inner time, a process itself belonging to the dimension of inner time. And it will "take as much time" to reconstitute the work in recollection as to experience it for the first time. In both cases I have to re-establish the quasi simultaneity of my stream of consciousness with that of the composer described hereinbefore.[13]

We have therefore the following situation: two series of events in inner time, one belonging to the stream of consciousness of the composer, the other to the stream of consciousness of the beholder, are lived through in simultaneity, which simultaneity is created by the ongoing flux of the musical process. It is the thesis of the present paper that this sharing of the other's flux of experiences in inner time, this living through a vivid present in common, constitutes what we called in our introductory paragraphs the mutual tuning-in relationship, the experience of the "We," which is at the foundation of all possible communication. The peculiarity of the musical process of communication consists in the essentially polythetic character of the communicated content, that is to say, in the fact that both the flux of the musical events and the activities by which they are communicated, belong to the dimension of inner time. This statement seems to hold good for any kind of music. There is, however, one kind of music—the polyphonic music of the western world—which has the magic power of realizing by its specific musical means the possibility of living simultaneously in two or more fluxes of events. In polyphonic writing each voice has its particular meaning; each represents a series of, so to speak, autarchic musical events; but this flux is designed to roll on in simultaneity with other series of musical events, not less autarchic in themselves, but coexisting with the former and combining with them by this very simultaneity into a new meaningful arrangement.[14]

So far we have investigated the social relationship between composer and beholder. What we have found to be the outstanding feature of musical communication—that is, the sharing of the ongoing flux of the musical content—holds good whether this process occurs merely in the beholder's recollection,[15] or through his reading the score, or with the help of audible sounds. To believe that the visible signs of musical notation are essential to this process is no more erroneous than to assert, as even Husserl does, that a symphony exists merely in its performance by an orchestra. To be sure, the participation in the process of musical communication by means other than audible sounds requires either a certain natural gift or special training on the part of the beholder. It is the eminent social function of the performer—the singer or player of an instrument—to be the intermediary between composer and listener. By his re-creation of the musical process the performer partakes in the stream of consciousness of the composer as well as of the listener. He thereby enables the latter to become immersed in the particular articulation of the flux of inner time which is the specific meaning of the piece of music in question. It is of no great importance whether performer and listener share together a vivid present in face-to-face relation or whether through the interposition of mechanical devices, such as records, only a quasi simultaneity between the stream of consciousness of the mediator and the listener has been established. The latter case always refers to the former. The difference between the two shows merely that the relationship between performer and audience is subject to all variations of intensity, intimacy, and anonymity. This can be easily seen by imagining the audience as consisting of one single person, a small group of persons in a private room, a crowd filling a big concert hall, or the entirely unknown listeners of a radio performance or a commercially distributed record. In all these circumstances performer and listener are "tuned-in" to one another, are living together through the same flux, are growing older together while the musical process lasts. This statement applies not only to the fifteen or twenty minutes of measurable outer time required for the performance of this particular piece of music, but primarily to the coperformance in simultaneity of the polythetic steps by which the musical content articulates itself in inner time. Since, however, all performance as an act of communication is based upon a series of events in the outer world—in our case the flux of audible sounds—it can be said that the social relationship between performer and listener is founded upon the common experience of living simultaneously in several dimensions of time.

V

The same situation, the pluridimensionality of time simultaneously lived through by man and fellow man, occurs in the relationship between two or more individuals making music together, which we are now prepared to investigate. If we accept Max Weber's famous definition, according to which a social relationship is "the conduct of a plurality of persons which according to their subjective meaning are mutually concerned with each other and oriented by virtue of this fact," then both the relationship prevailing between intermediary and listener and that prevailing between coperformers fall under this definition. But there is an important difference between them. The listener's coperforming of the polythetic steps in which the musical content unfolds is merely an internal activity (although as an "action involving the action of others and being oriented by them in its course" undoubtedly a social action within Weber's definition). The coperformers (let us say a soloist accompanied by a keyboard instrument) have to execute activities gearing into the outer world and thus occurring in spatialized outer time. Consequently, each coperformer's action is oriented not only by the composer's thought and his relationship to the audience but also reciprocally by the experiences in inner and outer time of his fellow performer. Technically, each of them finds in the music sheet before him only that portion of the musical content which the composer has assigned to his instrument for translation into sound. Each of them has, therefore, to take into account what the other has to execute in simultaneity. He has not only to interpret his own part, which as such remains necessarily fragmentary, but he has also to anticipate the other player's interpretation of his—the other's—part and, even more, the other's anticipations of his own execution. Either's freedom of interpreting the composer's thought is restrained by the freedom granted to the other. Either has to foresee by listening to the other, by protentions and anticipations, any turn the other's interpretation may take and has to be prepared at any time to be leader or follower. Both share not only the inner *durée* in which the content of the music played actualizes itself; each, simultaneously, shares in vivid present the other's stream of consciousness in immediacy. This is possible because making music together occurs in a true face-to-face relationship—inasmuch as the participants are sharing not only a section of time but also a sector of space. The other's facial expressions, his gestures in handling his instrument, in short all the activities of performing, gear into the outer world and can be grasped by the partner in immediacy. Even if performed without communicative intent, these activities are interpreted by him as indications of what the other is going to do and therefore as suggestions or even commands for his own behavior. Any chamber musician knows how disturbing an arrangement that prevents the coperformers from seeing each other can be. Moreover, all the activities of performing occur in outer time, the time which can be measured by counting or the metronome or the beat of the conductor's baton. The coperformers may have recourse to these devices when for one reason or another the flux of inner time in which the musical content unfolds has been interrupted.

Such a close face-to-face relationship can be established in immediacy only among a small number of coperformers. Where a larger number of executants is required, one of them—a song leader, concert master, or continuo player—has to assume the leadership, that is, to establish with each of the performers the contact which they are unable to find with one another in immediacy. Or a nonexecutant, the conductor, has to assume this function. He does so by action in the outer world, and his evocative gestures into which he translates the musical events going on in inner time, replace for each performer the immediate grasping of the expressive activities of all his coperformers.

Our analysis of making music together has been restricted to what Halbwachs (for example, 1939, 1949) calls the musician's music. Yet there is in principle no difference between the performance of a modern orchestra or chorus and people sitting around a campfire and singing to the strumming of a guitar or a congregation singing hymns under the leadership of the organ. And there is no difference in principle between the performance of a string quartet and the improvisations at a jam session of accomplished jazz players. These examples simply give additional support to our thesis that the system of musical notation is merely a technical device and accidental to the social relationship prevailing among the performers. This social relationship is founded upon the partaking in common of different dimensions of time simultaneously lived through by the participants. On the one hand, there is the inner time in which the flux of the musical events unfolds, a dimension in which each performer re-creates in polythetic steps the musical thought of the (eventually anonymous) composer and by which he is also connected with the listener. On the other, making music together is an event in outer time, presupposing also a face-to-face relationship, that is, a community of space, and it is this dimension which unifies the fluxes of inner time and warrants their synchronization into a vivid present.

VI

At the beginning of this paper, the hope was expressed that the analysis of the social relationship involved in making music together might contribute to a clarification of the tuning-in relationship and the process of communication as such. It appears that all possible communication presupposes a mutual tuning-in relationship between the communicator and the addressee of the communication. This relationship is established by the reciprocal sharing of the other's flux of experiences in inner time, by living through a vivid present together, by experiencing this togetherness as a "We." Only within this experience does the other's conduct become meaningful to the partner tuned in on him—that is, the other's body and its movements can be and are interpreted as a field of expression of events within his inner life. Yet not everything that is interpreted by the partner as an expression of an event in the other's inner life is meant by the other to express—that is, to communicate to the partner—such an event. Facial expressions, gait, posture, ways of handling tools and instruments, without communicative intent, are examples of such a situation. The process of communication proper is bound to an occurrence in the outer world, which has the structure of a series of events polythetically built up in outer time. This series of events is intended by the communicator as a scheme of expression open to adequate interpretation by the addressee. Its very polythetic character warrants the simultaneity of the ongoing flux of the communicator's experiences in inner time with the occurrences in the outer world, as well as the simultaneity of these polythetic occurrences in the outer world with the addressee's interpreting experiences in inner time. Communicating with one another presupposes, therefore, the simultaneous partaking of the partners in various dimensions of outer and inner time—in short in growing older together. This seems to be valid for all kinds of communication, the *essentially* polythetic ones as well as those conveying meaning in conceptual terms—that is, those in which the result of the communicative process can be grasped monothetically.

It is hardly necessary to point out that the remarks in the preceding paragraph refer to communication within the face-to-face relationship. It can, however, be shown that all the other forms of possible communication can be explained as derived from this paramount situation. But this, as well as the elaboration of the theory of the tuning-in relationship, must be reserved for another occasion.

Notes

1 The system of musical notation, as will be shown, has quite another function and a merely secondary one.

2 Mead's (1932) is just one example of how investigations of this kind have to be carried out and where they lead.

3 All this is by no means limited to the situation under scrutiny. Indeed, our analysis has so far been merely an application of Husserl's masterful investigations into the structure of our experience. According to him the factual world is always experienced as a world of preconstituted types. To embark upon the importance of this discovery by Husserl, especially for the concept of type, so fundamental for all social sciences, is not within the scope of the present paper. This theory has been touched upon in Husserl's (1931: 149) *Ideas General Introduction to Pure Phenomenology*, translated by Gibson, and has been fully developed in his *Erfahrung und Urteil* (1939: 35ff., 139–143, 394–403).

4 With regard to the concepts of socially derived and socially approved knowledge, see my paper (1946: 463–478, especially 475ff), "The Well-Informed Citizen."

5 The term "beholder" shall include the player, listener, and reader of music.

6 This problem has been discussed for the realm of poetry by Tillyard and Lewis (1939) in their witty and profound book, *The Personal Heresy, a Controversy.*

7 An excellent survey of philosophical theories of music can be found in Langer (1942), Ch. 8, "On Significance in Music," and Ch. 9, "The Genesis of Artistic Import," although the author's own position seems unsatisfactory. It may be summed up in the following quotation: "Music has all the earmarks of a true symbolism, except one: the existence of an *assigned connotation* . . . It is a limited idiom like an artificial language, *only even less successful; for music at its highest, though clearly a symbolic form, is an unconsummated symbol.* Articulation is its life but not assertion; expressiveness, not expression."

8 Some of these specific means are essential to any kind of music, others belong merely to a particular musical culture. Rhythm, melody, tonal harmony, technique of diminution, and the so-called forms based on what Tovey calls the larger harmony, such as Sonata, Rondo, Variations, and so on, are certainly characteristic of the musical culture of the nineteenth century. It may be hoped that intensified research in the phenomenology of musical experience will shed some light upon the difficult problem which of these means of meaningful arrangement of tones is essential to music in general, regardless of what its particular historical setting may be.

9 This insight has been formulated in an unsurpassable way by St. Augustine in Book XI, Ch. 3R, of his *Confessions*.

10 We do not need the reference to the specific experience of listening to music in order to understand the incommensurability of inner and outer time. The hand of our watch may run equally over half the dial, whether we wait before the door of a surgeon operating on a person dear to us or whether we are having a good time in congenial company. All these are well-known facts.

11 This term, here and in the following paragraphs, is not used in the sense that Cooley (1937) used it in *Social Organization* Chs. 3–5; it signifies merely that the participants in such a relation share time and space while it lasts. An analysis of Cooley's concept can be found in my article, "The Home-Comer" (1945: 371).

12 Also of other time-objects such as dance or poetry (see endnote 13).

13 This thesis is simply a corollary to the other—that the meaning context of music is not related to a conceptual scheme. A poem, for instance, may *also* have a conceptual content, and this, of course, may be grasped monothetically. I can tell in one or two sentences the story of the ancient mariner, and in fact this is done in the author's gloss. But in so far as the poetical meaning of Coleridge's poem surpasses the conceptual meaning—that is, in so far as it *is* poetry—I can only bring it before my mind by reciting or reading it from beginning to end.

14 See, for instance, the Brahms song, "Wir wandelten wir zwei zusammen," in the introduction of which the walking together of the two lovers is expressed by the specific musical means of a canon, or the same device used in the Credo of Bach's B-minor Mass for expressing the mystery of the Trinity ("Et in unum").

15 In this connection, one recalls Brahms' dictum: "If I want to listen to a fine performance of 'Don Giovanni,' I light a good cigar and stretch out on my sofa."

References

Augustine. 1912. *St Augustine's Confessions*. New York: Macmillan.
Furtwängler, W. 1934. "Interpretation—eine musikalische Schicksalsfrage." In *Das Atlantisbuch der Musik*. Zurich.
Halbwachs, M. 1939. "La mémoire collective chez les musiciens." *Revue Philosophique* 121(3/4): 136–165.
_____. 1949. "Mémoire et société." *L'Année sociologique*. 3rd series, Vol. 1: 11–197.
Husserl, E. 1931. *Ideas General Introduction to Pure Phenomenology*. Translated by W.R. Boyce Gibson. London: George Allen and Unwin Ltd.
_____. 1939. *Erfahrung und Urteil*. Prague: Academia/Verlagsbuchhandlung.
Langer, S.K. 1942. *Philosophy in a New Key*. Cambridge: Harvard University Press.
Mead, G.H. 1932. *Philosophy of the Present*. LaSalle: Open Court.
_____. 1937. *Mind, Self, and Society*. Chicago: University of Chicago Press.
Schütz, A. 1945. "The Homecomer." *American Journal of Sociology*. 50(5): 369–376.
_____. 1946. "The Well-Informed Citizen." *Social Research* 13(4): 463–478.
Thompson, V. 1948. *The Art of Judging Music*. New York: A.A. Knopf.
Tillyard, E.M.W. and C.S. Lewis. 1939. *The Personal Heresy, a Controversy*. London: Oxford University Press.
Tovey, D.F. 1945. *Beethoven*. London: Oxford University Press.

6

Sociology of Music

THEODOR ADORNO

A question to be raised here is what a complete sociology of music, as distinct from a mere introduction, ought to look like. Its conception would have to differ from a systematics designed to develop or present, in strict continuity, something which in itself is discontinuous and not uniform. Nor could a method bent on a dubious completeness be expected to fit the phenomena as a schema of external order. Rather, a finished musical sociology should take its bearings from the social structures that leave their imprint on music, and on what we call musical life in the most general sense.

The social question about the relation of productive forces and circumstances of production can be applied to musical sociology without doing violence to it. What we mean there by "productive forces" is not just production in the narrow musical sense, i.e., the activity of composing, but also the work of living reproductive artists and the whole unhomogeneously compounded technology: the intramusical–compositorial one, the playing capacity of the reproducers, and the modes of mechanical reproduction which are today of paramount importance. Opposed to those as circumstances of production, are the economic and ideological conditions to which each tone, and the reaction to each tone, is tied. In this age of consciousness- and subconsciousness-industries the musical mentality and taste of audiences is also an aspect of the circumstances of production, in a measure the exploration of which would have to be a central task of musical sociology.

Musical productive forces and circumstances of production do not simply face each other as antagonists. Instead they interact in many reciprocal ways. Even in the socially particular sphere of music, circumstances of production can be changed, to some degree even created, by productive forces. The models are the transformations of public taste by great productions—abrupt ones as wrought by Wagner, for one, and imperceptibly slow ones in the entertainment music in which compositorial innovations, though diluted and neutralized, nevertheless leave their traces. For the present it was scarcely raised as a problem whether and to what extent the changes in public taste are actually determined by those in production, or whether both are equally dependent on a third factor whose cliché is the "changing spirit of the times." It seems plausible that the full bourgeois emancipation of the period around 1800 brought forth both Beethoven's genius and an audience to which he appealed. The question probably permits no clear-cut alternative; perhaps only the most discriminating analyses of contemporary reviews might do justice to the phenomenon. . . . Sometimes musical productive forces will explode the circumstances of production that have been sedimented in taste: jazz, for instance, which swept all nonsyncopated dance music out of fashion and demoted it to the realm of nostalgia.

Conversely, circumstances of production may shackle the productive forces, and in modern times this has become the rule. The music market has turned down progressive music and thus called a halt to musical progress; unquestionably the compulsion to adjust has made many composers suppress in themselves what they really would have liked to do—and by no means only since the mid-nineteenth century. What is called the alienation—a term that is gradually becoming hard to bear—of advanced production and audience would have to be reduced to its social proportions: as an unfoldment in which the productive forces cast off the leading-strings of circumstances of production and ultimately move into blunt opposition.

Let no one deny that this in turn has consequences for the production itself, that the specialization it is driven to can diminish its autonomous substance. A musical sociology focusing on the conflict between productive forces and circumstances of production would deal not only with what comes to be and is consumed but also with what does *not* come to be and is scuttled. Social pressures did and still do, perhaps, bar the unfoldment of important talents. Even the greatest were impaired. Some of Mozart's works in almost every category are written the way he really would have wished, and for all the unity of style they differ crassly from the ones he toiled over. Not only the productive force of individual artists is fettered, but the one potentially contained in the material. Stirring from the sixteenth century on was a desire for dissonances; an expression of the suffering, simultaneously autonomous and unfree subject, it was forced back time and again, down to the days of *Salome*, *Elektra*, and the atonal Schonberg, and mostly, as in Mozart's so-called "Musical Joke," was permitted satisfaction only in disguise, as humorous parody.

Now and then the circumstances of production have also enhanced the productive forces. Richard Strauss would not be conceivable without the rise of the German grande bourgeoisie and its influence on taste and institutions. Antitraditionalist qualities, subjective differentiation in particular, were as much elicited by the bourgeois music market as they later were socially limited in the course of the historical dialectic to which the bourgeoisie itself was subject, and finally revoked under totalitarian regimes. Even the autonomy of great music, the means of its most emphatic opposition to the dictates of the marketplace, would hardly have evolved otherwise than via the marketplace. Musical forms, even constitutive modes of musical reaction, are internalizations of social forms. Like all art, music is as much a social fact as an inner self-shaping, a self-liberation from immediate social desiderata. Even its socially unintegrated side is social in essence, confirming that emancipation of the subject whose idea was once envisioned by the bourgeois libertarians. The freedom of art, its independence of the demands made on it, is founded on the idea of a free society and in a sense anticipates its realization.

This is why the sphere of production[1] is not simply a basis for musical sociology as the sphere of production is a basis for the process of material living. As a matter of the mind, musical production is itself socially mediated, not something immediate. Strictly speaking, the only part of it that is a productive force is the spontaneity that is inseparable from the mediations. From the social point of view it would be the force that exceeds mere repetition of the circumstances of production as represented by types and species. Such spontaneity may harmonize with the social trend, as in the young Beethoven or in Schubert's songs; or it may offer resistance, as Bach and again the new music of today do, to submission to the market. The question to be raised is this: *How is musical spontaneity socially possible at all?* For it always contains social productive forces whose real forms society has not yet absorbed. Socially, of course, the objectification that generates musical texts has been largely preceded by what we now call musical reproduction: by the playing and singing of music.

Extremely crucial for any musical sociology is a task now being undertaken in several places: the exploration and analysis of the *economic base* of music, the element in which its relation to society is actualized. This concerns primarily questions of musical life: the extent and the effects of its determination, not only by economic motives but, more deeply and importantly, by economic legalities and structural changes. Fruitful, for instance, is the question whether forms of musical organization, composing, and taste were affected by the transition to monopoly capitalism. Whatever music may be summed up under the concept "fetishism of means" is likely to go back to the function of the "technological veil" in monopolism.

Musical interpretation and reproduction brings music close to society and thus has special relevance for the sociology of music. Economic analysis will have to deal chiefly with this sphere; it is there one can probably best put a finger on the components of a market that always remains in existence, and on the components of monopolistic manipulation. Technical requirements, the demands of a reproduction adequate to the composition, clash with the public's demand for glamour, perfection, and beautiful voices. The latter are cast for affects, to a degree exceeding all expectations. If you say from the musical point of view, for example, that even in opera beautiful voices are means of presenting the composition rather than ends in themselves, you will be answered in a tone of outrage out of all proportion to the rational gist of the controversy. The study of such outbursts and of their psychogenesis promises more insights into the function of musical activities in the psychological household of society than will result from inquiries about immediate likes or dislikes.

The reproduction of works, which delivers them to the marketplace, alters their function. In principle, except for the most obstreperous works of the avant-garde, the entire upper sphere of music can turn into entertainment music. The false consciousness of the reproducers, their objectively demonstrable inability to give the thing an adequate presentation—an inability shared by some very famous names—is socially wrong and simultaneously enforced by social circumstances. The right reproduction would amount to social estrangement. In principle, nothing but opposition, cancellation of its social contract, will still gain for music its content of social truth.

Something to be vigorously scrutinized is how the economic base, the social setup, and the production and reproduction of music are specifically linked. Musical sociology must not be content to state some structural congruence; it has to show how social circumstances are concretely expressed in types of music, how they determine the music. What this calls for is nothing less than a deciphering of music, that wordless and conceptless art. The realm in which the effort is most likely to succeed is technology. It is in the state of technology at a particular time that society extends into the works, and there are much closer affinities between the techniques of material and artistic production than are acknowledged by the scientific division of labor. The dissection of labor processes since the manufacturing period and the motive-thematical work since Bach, a simultaneously splitting and synthesizing procedure, are profoundly congruent; with Beethoven it is even more legitimate to talk of social labor. Society's dynamization by the bourgeois principle and the dynamization of music mean the same; yet how this unity is realized is quite obscure for the present. It may be quite correct to cite one and the same spirit as having jurisdiction in both places, but this is more a circumscription of the problem than a solution. Explanatory formulas are not infrequently mere masks to hide the thing that needs explaining.

Music is ideological where the circumstances of production in it gain primacy over the productive forces. What should be shown is what can make it ideological: engendering a false consciousness; transfiguring so as to divert from the banality of existence; duplicating and thus only reinforcing that existence; and above all, abstract affirmation. One may postulate that intramusical ideologies are recognizable by immanent discord in the works; the intention of my *Versuch über Wagner* was to combine, as far as possible, a critique of Wagnerian ideology with the intraesthetic critique. But diagnosis and analysis of ideologies do not exhaust the music-sociological interest in them. The same attention should be paid to the ways in which ideologies prevail in practical musical life, i.e., to the ideologies *about* music. Today ideology is apt to be entangled with violent naiveté. Music is unthinkingly accepted as a proffered consumer commodity, like the cultural sphere as a whole; it is affirmed because it is there, without much reference to its concrete nature. Checking such theses would be up to empirical research. It would be a partial aspect of its broader task: finding out to what extent the so-called mass taste is manipulated; to what extent it is that of the masses themselves; and to what extent, where it must be ascribed to the masses, it reflects what was drilled into them for centuries—and more yet, what they are social-psychologically constrained to feel by the total situation.

As far as musical sociology concerns itself with the ideological content and the ideological effect of music it becomes part of a theoretical critique of society. This imposes an obligation on it: to pursue the truth of music. Sociologically that amounts to the question of music as a socially right or wrong consciousness. Musical sociology would have to illuminate what it means to pursue the manifestations and criteria of such consciousness in music. We do not yet have enough analyses of what is rightly called "corn," the musical equivalent of mendacity; nor do we have analyses of the truth content of authentic works. Also to be researched are the historical, social, intramusical conditions of musical consciousness. One inescapable problem is whether in music there can be a clear-cut separation of a socially correct consciousness from ideology, or whether—which seems more plausible—the two permeate each other, and if so, why. The affirmative moment of all art, and that of music in particular, is inherited from the ancient magic; the very tone with which all music begins has a touch of it. It is Utopia as well as the lie that Utopia is here now. It would take an explication of the idea of truth to lend theoretical dignity to the sociology of music.

The question of the truth and untruth of music is closely linked with that of the relationship of its two spheres, the serious one and the lower, unjustly termed the "light Muse." The division probably originated in the social division of labor and in the oldest class relations, in which refined matters were reserved for the rulers and coarse ones for the populace. Ritual differences may have entered into the esthetic one. The division gradually congealed, was reified, finally came to be administered, and finds its echo among the listeners who seem to be insisting on either one or the other. Since the last rudiments of prebourgeois musical culture have withered, the spheres no longer touch. Administration and planning of the lower is the new quality into which the overwhelming quantity of entertainment music has recoiled. The antithesis of productive forces and circumstances of production becomes flagrant in the dichotomy: the productive forces are pushed into the upper, quasi-privileged sphere, are isolated, and are thus a piece of the wrong consciousness even where they represent the right one.

The lower sphere obeys the predominant circumstances of production. A critical sociology of music will have to find out in detail why today—unlike a hundred years ago—popular music is bad, bound to be bad, without exception. To be discussed in this context is the question raised by Erwin Ratz: how music can be mean. Meanness too is a *fait social*, incompatible with the immanent claim of any musically animated sound. Entertainment music no longer does anything but confirm, repeat, and reinforce the psychological debasement ultimately wrought in people by the way society is set up. The masses are swamped with that music, and in it they unwittingly enjoy the depth of their debasement. The proximity in which popular music besets them violates human dignity along with esthetic distance. It would be up to empirical research to develop methods subtle enough to track down such enjoyments and to describe their course.

Problems of this sort belong to the reception research of musical sociology. As a whole it has to go by categories and theorems objectively oriented on the matter, so as then, on its part, to correct and broaden the theorems. First to be clarified would probably be questions such as that of the difference between reception and consumption: in other words, wherein the assimilation of hearing music to the relation to material consumer goods consists; what esthetically adequate categories fall by the wayside; what new ones—one might think of sporting types—may possibly come into being. Passing mention might be made of the difficulty of distinguishing the new qualities from older ones since binding studies about the older qualities are not available. It is not even certain whether music ever was adequately received outside the fraternity of artists or whether such reception is a wishful image, conceived only as a negation of the present state of things.

Let me throw out some suggestions for a line of empirical inquiries designed on the basis of the theorems of my "Introduction" and from the outline sketched here. Historically one might compare technological changes in selected typical works with the changes in material technology, and also with those in forms of social organization. Questionable in this complex are the causal links; one would expect interdependence rather than strict dependence of one on the other.

Success with something like an analysis of musical content—in music, which has no immediately objective content, this would of course have to consist in materially deciphering facts of the "form"— could lead to efforts to determine just what parts of the resulting content are perceived, and how. Subjective research in reception would thus be meaningfully combined with object-directed analysis.

Radio Research has familiarized us with investigations concerning likes and dislikes, preferences and aversions, and these should now be related to the preferred or rejected qualities of music in itself. This might help to get an empirical grip on its ideological effects. It is hardly an accident that none of this was ever done even though the ways to pose the problems have been known for almost thirty years. Resistance comes from two facts: that the individual reactions and habitual behaviors to be researched are not conscious, and that most people—again due to cultural conditioning—are unable to put their musical experiences into appropriate words.

Added to this are idiosyncrasies on the researchers' own part. The alleged empirical inaccessibility of the dimension in question, the "deep stuff," is often merely a pretext to keep from jeopardizing the conservationist character of music and its alliance with very tangible interests. At first one will be able to approach the really meaningful questions of musical reception only indirectly, perhaps by establishing correlations between the musical likes and dislikes of the persons questioned, their extramusical ideologies, and their overall psychology.[2] A simpler way would be to have music described by test persons, to compare the description with the results of an object-directed analysis, and thus to recognize ideological elements in reception.

A study of the language people use in talking about music would unquestionably be worthwhile. It is a defensible hypothesis that this language consists in the main of socially prefabricated clichés that serve to screen a living relation to the matter. At the same time it is replete with ideological contents and psychological rationalizations which in their turn may affect the reception. A primitive experiment, yet instructive already, would be to take three groups—one made up to listeners of serious music, one of listeners to entertainment music, and a third of people who do not care—and to question them, not about music, but about their ideological views.

For some of these procedures there are models that would have to be repeated with representative samples and designed in line with a principle. I am thinking, for instance, of the attempts of Allport and Cantril to test immediate and manipulative-authoritarian factors in the effect of music, both serious and light. Also one should do what Malcolm McDougald did at the time, only in less personalized a manner: one should make descriptive analyses of the techniques of manufacturing hits with the aid of the mass media and locate the bounds of manipulation and the minimum requirements for its success. "Promotion research" would be especially interesting since the techniques that win prominence for a pop singer are presumably not very different from the ones that do it for a politician.

Empirical musical sociologists like Alphons Silbermann see the point of departure for all of musical sociology in the experience of music. Yet this concept must not be dogmatically accepted. It would have to be checked out on different types, most usefully, perhaps, in intensive individual case studies: in how far a musical experience actually occurs; in how far it is a ritual; by what means this supposedly first experience is socially mediated. The chances are that the primary thing will prove in fact to be a highly derivative one, and in that case the alleged musical experience should no longer be used as a basic category in a sociology of music. Instead, the guidelines are, on the one hand, presently prevailing cultural and anthropological qualities and, on the other, forms of organization and mechanisms with an effect on musical life, in which generally social mechanisms are disguised.

Suitable rudiments from the viewpoint of social psychology could probably be found in the theorems developed by this writer in a series of writings on jazz. Empirically one would have to trace the extent to which jazz, in the household of the masses, actually plays the role implied by its own structure—an adequacy which is no more a matter of course than the general one between a work and its reception. The exegeses of that music would have to be verified or falsified much further than was possible in their exposition. It could be done by including other branches of the culture industry, perhaps, branches independent of jazz but displaying analogous structures—as indicated, for example, in Herta Herzog's formula for the so-called soap operas: "Getting into trouble and back out again." Other ways would be comparison with Hollywood comedies or reference to the encompassing total schema of the "dirigist" mass culture.

Finally, the very widespread resistance to serious music and the social-psychological importance of hostility to music as a whole should probably, by means of clinical studies, be combined with characterological problematics and the general critique of ideologies. Just as diseases were able to tell us many things we did not know about the healthy organism, the social phenomena of hostility to music and estrangement from music would probably cast light upon the social function of music today, and also on its "dysfunction."

Suggestions of this sort sketch out a preliminary concept of the interrelation of the realms of musical sociology as well as that of the possibilities of dealing scientifically with much that has been developed here from thought and experience. It can, of course, not always be expressed according to the approved scientific rules of the game, no more than a critical theory of society can be couched in categories of the traditional one.

Notes

1   The writer's error in his essay "*Zur gesellschaftlichen Lage der Musik*," published in 1932 in *Zeitschrift für Sozialforschung*, was his flat identification of the concept of musical production with the precedence of the economic sphere of production, without considering how far that which we call production already presupposes social production and depends on it as much as it is sundered from it. This alone has kept the writer from reissuing that essay, the draft of a finished musical sociology.

2   Rudiments of such research now exist. At the University of Marburg, Christian Rittelmeyer of the Department of Psychology has shown empirically that the brusque rejection of progressive art, notably of music, accompanies complexes of a character structure tied to authority, such as rigid dogmatism and "intolerance for ambiguities"— which is to say that thinking in black-and-white stereotypes prevails among the sworn enemies of all things modern. Rittelmeyer went on to "investigate the effects regarding intolerance and an aversion to modern art which curricula in "*musische Bildung*" (works of art and the like) and in specific cultural education (specific visual aids) had on comparable groups," and he "came to the preliminary conclusion that the former method" (i.e., *musische Bildung*) "will either raise these values or leave them unchanged, while the latter will lower them." In the meantime we have received more concrete analyses of hit songs and the mechanisms of identification from Gunnar Sonstevold and Kurt Blaukopf (1968).

Reference

Sonstevold, G. and K. Blaukopf. 1968. "Musik der 'einsamen Masse'; Ein Beitrag zur Analyse von Schlagerschallplatten." In *Musik und Gesellschaft* no.4, ed. K. Blaukopf. Karlsruhe: Verlag.

II

APPROACHES, SITES, AND DEBATES

There is a discredited idea in media and communications theory which suggests that there is a direct, linear path between (1) "senders" or cultural producers, (2) "messages" or content and (3) "receivers" or audiences (see Hall 1980 for a well-known critique). This section might appear to impose a similar kind of linearity onto the social life of music: (1) musicians create some form of (2) musical sound that is then (3) heard and enjoyed (or not) by listeners. Indeed, to an extent these three sets of chapters do distinguish acts of "Creation" from both "The Music Itself" and acts of "Consumption." However, this is an analytical distinction that usually cannot be upheld when looking at actual musical practice. For example, the ideal–typical polarization of production and consumption can break down in contexts where making music means consuming technology (Théberge 1997) and where listening to music is itself a kind of performance (Frith 1996, Shepherd and Wicke 1997).

The first set of essays by McClary, Shepherd and Martin address a central issue in music sociology: namely, what is the relationship between musical sounds and non-musical phenomena? McClary discusses musical conventions as ideological formations that can be analyzed and interpreted according to their social meanings. Taking a retrospective tone, McClary reflects on the aims and stakes of her politically engaged, socially informed analyses of musical form, while also situating this so-called "new" musicology as a reaction against older positivist and absolutist strains of musical thought and scholarship.

Expanding on his earlier work on music as a kind of "social text," Shepherd argues that the primary semiotic tools of the new musicology were borrowed almost exclusively from the linguistic realm, and that such tools are in a sense inadequate because musical signification functions differently than linguistic signification. Paying special attention to the body, Shepherd calls for a conceptual framework that accounts for the specificity of musical sound as its own "signifying practice"—one that is not reducible to linguistic discourse. "Music," he notes, "goes behind the back of language and vision in speaking *directly to and through* the body" (emphasis in original).

Martin offers a thoughtful critique stemming partly from the work of McClary and Shepherd, identifying several "problems at the interface" of sociology and musicology. He clearly articulates one of the foundational tensions in music sociology: the idea that there have been, in a sense, two "social" approaches to the study of music, and that each has been perceived as inadequate from the other's perspective. From the side of musicology, sociologists are said to produce analyses that say very little about "the music itself," while sociologists complain that in simply "reading off" social meanings from a musical text, musicologists tend to fail an important test of sociological rigor—namely, explaining how those social meanings got into the music in the first place. These three chapters thus set the stage for several of the discussions in Section VI of this volume.

The chapters on "Creation" look at the issue of making music. Ethnography, which is a qualitative genre of research that involves the use of interviews and participant-observation to construct knowledge of groups of people, has been one of the main methods for gathering sociological insight into what musicians do and how musical culture works. Grazian offers a clear introduction to this key approach, including a historical sketch of the ethnographic perspective, a description of some contemporary ethnographic sites and suggestions for future research. Even with the current trend toward "big data" and quantitative methods in the social sciences (discussed in the Introduction), ethnography will surely continue to be one of music sociology's most essential tools for the foreseeable future.

McCormick addresses musical performance. In both sociology and musicology, "performance" is an important topic. But it tends to be treated in different ways. Sociologists think of music as a social performance in ways that invoke analyses of ritual and myth, while musicologists have recently constructed a history of performance from the traces left behind on recordings. McCormick outlines the consonances and dissonances between these approaches, suggesting that the question of "meaning" could serve as an especially significant point of interdisciplinary dialogue between music studies and the social sciences—and thus a crucial topic for future work on music as performance.

Part of McCormick's argument draws on work in the sociology of cultural production, a topic which is pursued centrally in Santoro's chapter. Santoro's exploration of "production" in the music sociology literature covers Peterson's "production of culture" perspective, Becker's "art worlds" approach, and Bourdieu's theory of the cultural field. The work of each scholar is unpacked carefully and critically, and is connected to influential conceptual and methodological developments both before and since. Santoro concludes by addressing a familiar theme in the sociology of music: the question, often raised by musicologists, of how researchers in cultural production might also get their hands dirty with musical sound.

The chapters on "Consumption" are concerned with how musical listening habits and purchasing patterns foster senses of community and self. Each of the chapters represents a different approach to this question. Bennett, for example, builds on classic research on subcultures and music scenes, as well as emerging studies in music and ageing, to illustrate how popular music can be used as a resource for the construction and maintenance of identities. This is significant as a rejoinder to early twentieth-century critics, such as Adorno, who believed that popular music was merely a distraction.

Peterson presents an early and foundational dialogue with the Bourdieuian idea that high social status is correlated with an exclusive taste for art music. Using US data, Peterson confirms that highbrows use musical taste to distinguish themselves from lowbrows; however, his novel—and controversial—suggestion is that the distinction is not made according to an exclusive taste for art music, but a more eclectic taste for many kinds of music.

Hennion, meanwhile, works against what he views as a dominant and Bourdieu-inspired research paradigm in music sociology. This "critical" paradigm, for Hennion, is prone to accounts of musical preferences that reduce both the activity of "taste" and the properties of the musical object to reflections of an individual's social background. Instead, Hennion develops a "pragmatic" orientation that understands musical taste and musical pleasure as "the result of an action performed by the taster, an action based on technique, bodily entertainment and repeated sampling, and which is accomplished over time, simultaneously because it follows a regulated development and because its success largely depends on moments" (see also Section VI).

As a group, these essays outline some of the research sites, conceptual paradigms and key debates that have shaped the contemporary musical–sociological imagination.

References

Frith, S. 1996. *Performing Rites: On the Value of Popular Music*. Cambridge: Harvard University Press.

Hall, S. 1980 [1973]. "Encoding/Decoding." In *Culture, Media, Language*, eds. S. Hall et al., 129–137. London: Hutchinson.

Shepherd, J. and P. Wicke. 1997. *Music and Cultural Theory*. Cambridge: Polity.

Théberge, P. 1997. *Any Sound You Can Imagine: Making Music/Consuming Technology*. Middletown: Wesleyan University Press.

A

THE MUSIC ITSELF

7

Music as Social Meaning

Susan McClary

An old legend tells of an earnest youth who went to a holy man seeking the meaning of life. In response to the disciple's questions about the world and its foundations, the guru explained that the earth sits on the back of a huge tiger, which stands on the flanks of an enormous elephant, and so on. When the cosmological series reached a giant turtle, the sage paused. His enraptured pupil—believing he had arrived finally at ultimate truth—exclaimed, "So the universe rests on that turtle!" "Oh, no," replied his mentor. "From there, it's turtles all the way down."[1]

I often find myself reflecting on this story as I experience the tensions between my work and the work of many others in my discipline. Over the course of the last fifteen years, I have engaged in what might appear to be a wide range of unrelated projects; yet in all of them, I have sought to explore the social premises of musical repertories. This fundamental concern motivates not only my accounts of how gender-related issues have intersected with music at different historical moments but also my studies of narrative strategies in Mozart or Schubert and my attempts at making sense of today's popular culture (e.g. McClary 1991, 1994a, 1994b, 1997).

Of course, I am not alone in my quest for cultural interpretations of western art music. Indeed, the numbers of those concerned with such matters have increased to the point where we are now widely known (for better or worse) as "the New Musicology." My colleagues in this endeavor include (most prominently) Rose Rosengard Subotnik, Lawrence Kramer, Richard Leppert, Philip Brett, Gary Tomlinson, Richard Taruskin, Robert Walser, and—the godfather of us all—Joseph Kerman, whose calls for music criticism and attacks on the "purely musical" date back several decades.

Yet despite the growing number of scholars committed to cultural interpretation and regardless of which project I happen to be pursuing, I continue to meet resistance from those who claim that most aspects of music—indeed, the ones that really matter—operate according to "purely musical" procedures. For while we all might agree that elements such as Baroque word-paintings or eighteenth-century *topoi* are referential, many musicologists and music theorists still like to assume that these elements simply perch on the surface of what underneath is autonomous bedrock. No gender, no narratives, no politics: just chords, forms, and pitch-class sets. And the discussion stops there.[2]

But those moments at which the investigation gets arrested have always intrigued me more than any others. Why does tonality emerge when and as it does in the seventeenth century? Because of "natural" evolutionary processes. Why does a sonata movement require that its second theme resolve into the key of the first? Because that's the way musical form works; end of conversation. But WHY? Like an unsatisfied child, I have pressed on beyond those limits to know more. And like a jaded culture critic, I have found it impossible to accept any kind of bedrock certainty, anything natural or purely formal in the realm of human constructs. Whichever position I take—that of child or culture critic—I always return to the conviction that "it's turtles all the way down."

Musicologists do grudgingly acknowledge one cluster of turtles: we refer to them as conventions. By "convention" we usually mean a procedure that has ossified into a formula that needs no further explanation. Why does a minuet repeat its opening section following the trio? Convention. Why do pop ballads end with fade-outs? Convention. Why did thousands of males undergo the knife in order to sing in the soprano range in Baroque opera? This last question—posed year after year by incredulous undergraduates in their music history surveys—is typically answered with the strangely threatening tone of voice parents reserve for inquiries about the Primal Scene: IT'S JUST A CONVENTION! Which translates—Don't ask (see McClary 2000).

Since the nineteenth century, western art has cultivated an aversion to conventions: we commonly exalt as "purely musical" the procedures that appear to have transcended signification, and we scorn conventions as devices that have hardened to the point where they no longer can mean anything at all. Thus, we have, on the one hand, patterns that operate beyond the petty concerns of cultural meaning and, on the other, clichés emptied of whatever communicative power they might once have possessed. We interpret reliance on convention as betraying a lack of imagination or a blind acceptance of social formula.[3] In either case, the individualistically inclined artist or critic shuns them with disdain and seeks value in those moves that escape the coercion of convention—that aspire, rather, to the condition of the "purely musical."[4]

Yet at the same time, we make concerted efforts to locate regularity within precisely those compositions that seem to have managed to escape the bounds of normative practice. The measuring sticks of Schenker graphs or the kabbalistic methods of set-based analysis strive to pull apparently unruly music back inside the horizons of the rational, the orderly, and (implicitly) the metaphysical.[5] Why, I have always wondered, do we not label the procedures such theories trace likewise as conventions? And why do we neglect to talk about why these procedures matter so very much to us?

In this book, I want to claim that this split between conventions and the "purely musical" is itself socially and historically contingent, that the procedures we regard at different moments as "purely musical" count rather as the most crucial set of conventional practices. I will scan through various stacks of turtles, sometimes teasing out the complex functions served by obvious conventions, sometimes addressing those clearly referential elements perched on the surface, sometimes prying into the shells of "purely musical" processes to examine their ideological premises. And while these turtles may occupy a range of positions within their respective stacks, I will not treat them as different in kind. No metaphysics—just cultural practice. Nothing but turtles. All the way down.

The periods in musical style that stand out for consistency in procedure—for example, the High Renaissance, the late eighteenth century—are those for which the hierarchy is at its most stable, though for a wide variety of historical and cultural reasons. If we remain exclusively within the domain of a particular style, we might well come to accept the premises characteristic of that repertory as Truth, just as our young disciple wanted to regard the giant tortoise as a *terminus ad quem*. We are less likely to do so, however, if we have witnessed the moments when the dominant turtles first slipped into those privileged positions and when they slipped back out again. During other times—for instance, the early 1600s or the late 1990s . . . —the scrambling is rather more apparent: an expressive device might become a standard procedure, a convention might be revived for use as a surface signifier, and so on. This is why I prefer in my work to take a rather wider view of history. For the jostling among expressive devices, conventions, and "purely musical" procedures becomes most apparent during those episodes of stylistic flux.

Enough of turtles for now, however. Even if we do not commonly approach music from this point of view, my project resembles several lines of inquiry long central to cultural studies and literary theory, including the work of Hayden White (1987, see also 1992), to whose *The Content of the Form* I pay homage in [the book from which this chapter has been excerpted]. I want to explore in music history the kinds of processes Raymond Williams (1977) calls "structures of feeling," Fredric Jameson (1981) the "political unconscious," Roland Barthes (1972) "mythologies," Thomas Kuhn (1962) "paradigms," Kaja Silverman (1992) "dominant fictions," or Ross Chambers (1984) simply the "social contracts" that establish the conditions for the production and reception of artworks. Whatever we label these structures, they are intensely ideological formations: whether noticed or not, they are the assumptions that allow cultural activities to "make sense." Indeed, they succeed best when least apparent, least deliberate, most automatic. Although musicologists and theorists often grant these kinds of formations the status of the "purely musical," I will treat them as conventions—albeit conventions that so permeate human transactions that we usually fail to notice their influence. And I want to examine the values they represent, the interests they reinforce, the activities they enable, the possibilities they exclude, and their histories within the contested field that music inevitably is.

I have chosen [the title of the book from which this chapter is excerpted], *Conventional Wisdom*, for two principal reasons. First, the phrase itself is a convention, a cliché that refers to commonly held but wrong-headed beliefs. We use it rhetorically to set up a surprising item of information: conventional wisdom has it that X; but in point of fact—Y! Just hearing the words "conventional wisdom" prepares us for that rude reversal, whereby something that seemed to have possessed truth-value gets relegated to the scrap heap of superseded misconceptions. Schoenberg's (1983: 128–129, *passim*) refiguring of tonality in his *Theory of Harmony* and Monteverdi's *seconda-prattica* manifesto both adopt something of this tactic, as they explain why the apparently universal laws of syntax they had inherited were "merely" conventions, why they felt free—even obligated—to push them aside.[6] My title draws on that same ironic stance, for I will seek to redefine what conventional wisdom has elevated as the "purely musical" to the status of social contract.

Yet my title also means to acknowledge the fact that genuine social knowledge is articulated and transmitted by means of shared procedures and assumptions concerning music. I want to insist that a great deal of wisdom resides in conventions: nothing less than the premises of an age, the cultural arrangements that enable communication, co-existence, and self-awareness. At the same time, none of them counts as anything more than artificial constructs human beings have invented and agreed to maintain—in particular contexts, for particular reasons, to satisfy particular needs and desires.

Consequently, conventions always operate as part of the signifying apparatus, even when they occupy the ground over which explicit references and encodings occur: in other words, it is not the deviations alone that signify but the norms as well. Indeed, the deviations of particular pieces could not signify if we did not invest a great deal in the conventions up against which they become meaningful.[7] Thus, while the traditional methods of hermeneutics often focus on explicating deliberate meanings, my project also factors in these seemingly automatic dimensions—which I take to be the most crucial because the most fundamental. In addition to paying attention to what individual compositions articulate on their surfaces, I will also examine the frames within which their strategies make sense as human endeavors.

The old question of form versus content has long been criticized as presenting a false dichotomy, especially perhaps in music. Theorists since the nineteenth-century critic Eduard Hanslick have generally solved the split by redefining everything as structure—thus the institutional prestige of our graphs, charts, and quasi-mathematical explanations of music. The more we have placed our trust in rigorous, self-contained analysis, the more we have had the impression that we might eventually explain it all on the basis of idealist abstractions.[8]

But too much is left out of such accounts, for the course of music history never did run smooth: the anxieties produced by collisions between incompatible practices or by the oedipal struggles between successive styles always involve far more than just notes. Plato warned that "the modes of music are never disturbed without unsettling of the most fundamental political and social conventions" (Shorey 1930: 333). The power of music—both for dominant cultures and for those who would promote alternatives—resides in its ability to shape the ways we experience our bodies, emotions, subjectivities, desires, and social relations. And to study such effects demands that we recognize the ideological basis of music's operations—its cultural constructedness. Even the urge to explain on the basis of idealist abstraction or to insist on an unbridgeable gap between music and the outside world stands in need of explanation, an explanation that would require a complex social history stretching back more than twenty-five centuries to Pythagoras (see McClary 1995, Eco 1995).

Thus, in contrast to Hanslick's resolution in the direction of form, I want to treat the entire complex as content—social, historically contingent content. As Adorno (1992: 6) puts it, "Form can only be the form of a content."[9] Moreover, I will claim that music (like other kinds of human artifacts) is assembled of heterogeneous elements that lead away from the autonomy of the work to intersect with endless chains of other pieces, multiple—even contradictory—cultural codes, various moments of reception, and so on. If music can be said to be meaningful, it cannot be reduced to a single, totalized, stable meaning. At the same time, its polysemousness does not justify our long-standing avoidance of interpretation. For if music frustrates our attempts at nailing down definitive meanings, it does so no more than poems, films, or paintings, all of which maintain a considerable degree of indeterminacy.

As even readers with little investment in what is called "postmodernism" have already no doubt discerned, my project shares many of the deconstructive assumptions animating much of the current work in literary criticism and film studies. Like similar investigations in those other disciplines, this book will strive to take apart into their constituent elements many of the procedures we have embraced as "natural." Yet my project differs tactically from that of most literary theorists.

Meaning has long seemed too immanent in verbal language. Accordingly, practices such as deconstruction strive to draw our attention to the opacity, constructedness, and undecidability of texts, literary and otherwise. But music studies have a different history—one that has long denied signification in favor of appeals to the "purely musical," that places music beyond the reach of "mere" social arrangements. And this history of denial, I would argue, has put us in what is no longer a tenable position for our understanding of musical cultures, either past or present. Thus before we can properly embark on programs that seek to destabilize musical signification, we have to recover some notion of how musical gestures, procedures, and forms do, in fact, produce their very powerful effects (see Subotnik 1996, Kramer 1990, 1995). Otherwise we simply hop from one brand of skepticism to another without ever having to consider how music actually operates as a cultural practice.

[. . .]

If I want to reject the possibility of the "purely musical" and to reassign those elements so often exalted as "purely musical" to the realm of convention, I also expect to reinfuse all these levels—whether expressive devices, explicitly conventional formulas, or deeply buried assumptions—with meaning. Not, to be sure, the giant turtle of transcendental meaning or even consistency; but human meanings, grounded in the historical contexts in which they performed—and, in many cases, *still* perform—crucial social functions. If in the final analysis we have nothing but turtles, our turtles ought to suffice.

[. . .]

The decentered approach to music history that will emerge over the course of this book differs considerably from the ones now generally circulating, which tend to take one repertory or another and create a narrative of origins and linear development. Without question, other historians would choose other elements—elements that would, of course, reflect their sense of the present as well as the kind of future they envision. But the existence of diverse historical narratives does not mean that such choices are either arbitrary or inconsequential. The recent canon wars revolve around which or whose turtles get to count in official records of cultural representation and reproduction. And a great deal is at stake in these debates, whether one claims on the one hand that a single tradition is to be maintained in the face of pluralism or, on the other, that such an account is no longer credible.

I should identify myself at this point as one who grew up listening to and playing virtually nothing but classical music. If I can be said to have a vernacular, western classical music would have to be it. Yet I can no longer tell the stories about music I was trained to tell, for those stories marginalize or even exclude many of the musics that have been most influential—in the west and elsewhere— for the past hundred years.

I sometimes think that we musicologists resemble those pedagogues at the end of the seventeenth century who continued to advocate the *prima-prattica* style of Palestrina, who failed to notice that their world had come to be dominated by opera and its musical languages. Like them, we too often take our "purely musical" procedures to be absolute and use them in evaluating musics that work on the basis of radically different premises. I prefer to take as my model the great medieval theorist Grocheo (1974), who impatiently pushed the "purely musical" speculations of Boethius to the side in order to produce a socially grounded inventory of the many distinct music cultures flourishing in Paris around 1300—an inventory that included explanations of the preferences of the aristocratic and ecclesiastical élites, the laboring classes, and even hot-blooded youths. What would our histories look like if we took note of the many kinds of music surrounding us—observing differences in social function and technique, to be sure, but acknowledging them all nonetheless as parts of a shared universe?

My history of western music contains Bach, Mozart, and Beethoven, but it also includes Stradella and the Swan Silvertones, Bessie Smith and Eric Clapton, k.d. lang, Philip Glass, and Public Enemy. And it treats all of them as artists who have negotiated with available conventions and in particular historical circumstances to produce musical artifacts of exceptional power and cultural resonance. If I can no longer privilege any one tradition, I find myself perpetually in awe of the countless ways societies have devised for articulating their most basic beliefs through the medium of sound; I share with philosopher Lydia Goehr (1992) the "sense of wonder at how human practices come to be, succeed in being, and continue to be regulated by one set of ideals rather than another." Just turtles, perhaps. But what magnificent turtles!

Notes

1 After I delivered the Bloch Lectures, I found that several other writers had drawn recently on the same story. Stephen Hawking (1988: 1) uses it to open *A Brief History of Time: From the Big Bang to Black Holes*. He tells a different version, albeit with the same punch line. Clifford Geertz (1973: 28–29) relates the story in *The Interpretation of Culture*, and Judith Becker and Lorna McDaniel (1991: 393–396) also employ it in "A Brief Note on Turtles, Claptrap, and Ethnomusicology." "Turtles all the way down" thus appears to have become a *locus classicus*—a particularly popular nugget of conventional wisdom—in this age of eroding certainties.

2 Equivalents of the "purely musical" exist also in the other arts. Zola, for instance, justified Manet's scandalous *Olympia* as "pure painting" thus erasing from consideration the disturbing content of that canvas. See the discussion in Bernheimer (1989: 16).

3 Conventions have been taken rather more seriously in a couple of areas of recent musicology. When scholars began to study nineteenth-century Italian opera in the 1980s, they had to learn to overcome the (largely German) prejudice against conventions and to focus on the ways Rossini or Verdi operated productively within shared procedures. Similarly, specialists in the eighteenth century have demonstrated the importance of topoi and conventions in the classic repertory. See, for instance, Allanbrook (1992). See also Allanbrook, Levy, and Mahrt, eds. (1992). Most of this work concentrates on structures of deliberate signification or particular formal devices rather than on the elements commonly understood as "purely musical."

4   Lydia Goehr's Bloch Lectures present a sympathetic account of the political and philosophical rationales behind the nineteenth-century notion of the "purely musical." See Goehr (1998). Despite what may at first glance appear as opposing positions, Goehr and I tend to agree about the history of this concept and also about the ways in which it has reified into a prohibition against cultural interpretation. For an exceptionally thoughtful treatment of the impact of such attitudes on nineteenth-century musical practice, see Meyer (1989).

5   For an investigation of similar longings to escape cultural contingency and to locate speech in the metaphysical, see Eco (1995).

6   Claudio Monteverdi's famous polemic opens his *Fifth Book of Madrigals* (1605); a gloss on this text by his brother, Giulio Cesare, followed in the 1607 publication of *Scherzi musicali*. For a translation of the glossed text, see Strunk, ed. (1950: 405–412).

7   Fred Maus has complained that an excessive amount of attention has been expended by the discipline on pieces that utilize moves to the minor sub-mediant. See Maus (1991: 20). As one of those guilty of writing extensively on this phenomenon and other "deviant" devices that seem to demand interpretation, I intend to do penance in this book by addressing the other side of the coin.

8   For the classic critique of this position, see Kerman (1994).

9   I wish here to acknowledge once again my debt to the work of Adorno and his foremost American explicator, Rose Rosengard Subotnik.

References

Adorno, T.W. 1992. "Music and Language: A Fragment." In *Quasi una Fantasia: Essays on Modern Music*. Translated by R. Livingstone, 1–8. London: Verso.

Allanbrook, W.J. 1992. *Rhythmic Gesture in Mozart*. Chicago: University of Chicago Press.

Allanbrook, W.J., J.M. Levy and W.P. Mahrt, eds. 1992. *Convention in Eighteenth- and Nineteenth-Century Music: Essays in Honor of Leonard G. Ratner*. Stuyvesant: Pendragon Press.

Barthes, R. 1972. *Mythologies*. Translated by A. Lavers. New York: Hill and Wang.

Becker, J. and L. McDaniel. 1991. "A Brief Note on Turtles, Claptrap, and Ethnomusicology." *Ethnomusicology* 35(3): 393–396.

Bernheimer, C. 1989. "The Uncanny Lure of Manet's Olympia." In *Seduction and Theory: Readings of Gender, Representation, and Rhetoric*, ed. Dianne Hunter, 1–27. Urbana: University of Illinois Press.

Chambers, R. 1984. *Story and Situation: Narrative Seduction and the Power of Fiction*. Minneapolis: University of Minnesota Press.

Eco, U. 1995. *The Search for the Perfect Language*. Translated by J. Fentress. Oxford: Blackwell.

Geertz, C. 1973. *The Interpretation of Culture*. New York: Basic Books.

Goehr, L. 1992. *The Imaginary Museum of Musical Works*. Oxford: Oxford University Press.

_____. 1998. *The Quest for Voice: Music, Politics, and the Limits of Philosophy*. Berkeley: University of California Press.

Grocheo, J. 1974. *De Musica*. Translated by A. Seay. Colorado Springs: Colorado College Music Press.

Hawking, S. 1988. *A Brief History of Time: From the Big Bang to Black Holes*. New York: Bantam Books.

Jameson, F. 1981. *The Political Unconscious: Narrative as a Socially Symbolic Act*. Ithaca: Cornell University Press.

Kerman, J. 1994. "How We Got into Analysis, and How to Get Out." In *Write All These Down: Essays on Music*. Berkeley: University of California Press, 12–32.

Kramer, L. 1990. *Music as Cultural Practice, 1800–1900*. Berkeley: University of California Press.

_____. 1995. *Classical Music and Postmodern Knowledge*. Berkeley: University of California Press.

Kuhn, T.S. 1962. *The Structure of Scientific Revolutions*. Chicago: University of Chicago Press.

Maus, F. 1991. "Music as Narrative." *Indiana Theory Review* 12: 1–34.

McClary, S. 1991. *Feminine Endings: Music, Gender, and Sexuality*. Minneapolis: University of Minnesota Press.

_____. 1994a. "Narratives of Bourgeois Subjectivity in Mozart's 'Prague' Symphony." In *Understanding Narrative*, eds. J. Phelan and P. Rabinowitz, 65–98. Columbus: Ohio State University Press.

_____. 1994b. "'Same as It Ever Was': Youth Culture and Music," in *Microphone Fiends: Youth Music and Youth Culture*, eds. A. Ross and T. Rose, 29–40. New York: Routledge.

_____. 1995. "Music, the Pythagoreans, and the Body." In *Choreographing History*, ed. S.L. Foster, 82–104. Bloomington: Indiana University Press.

_____. 1997. "The Impromptu That Trod on a Loaf: Or How Music Tells Stories." *Narrative* 5(1): 20–35.

_____. 2000. "Gender Ambiguities and Erotic Excess in Seventeenth-Century Venetian Opera." In *Acting on the Past: Historical Performance Across the Disciplines*, eds. M. Franko and A. Richards, 177–200. Hanover: Wesleyan University Press.

Meyer, L.B. 1989. *Style and Music: Theory, History, and Ideology*. Philadelphia: University of Pennsylvania Press.

Plato. 380 BCE [1930]. *The Republic*, ed. P. Shorey. London: Heinemann.

Schoenberg, A. 1983. *Theory of Harmony* (1911). Translated by R.E. Carter. Berkeley: University of California Press.

Silverman, K. 1992. "The Dominant Fiction." In *Male Subjectivity at the Margins*. New York: Routledge, 15–51.

Strunk, O., ed. 1950. *Source Readings in Music History*. New York: Norton.

Subotnik, R.R. 1996. "How Could Chopin's A-Major Prelude Be Deconstructed?" In *Deconstructive Variations: Music and Reason in Western Society*. 39–147. Minneapolis: University of Minnesota Press.

White, H. 1987. *The Content of the Form: Narrative Discourse and Historical Representation*. Baltimore: Johns Hopkins University Press.

_____. 1992. "Form, Reference, and Ideology in Musical Discourse." In *Music and Text: Critical Inquiries*, ed. S.P. Scher, 288–319. Cambridge: Cambridge University Press.

Williams, R. 1977. *Marxism and Literature*. Oxford: Oxford University Press.

8

Music, the Body, and Signifying Practice

John Shepherd

Recent years have witnessed an intensification of debate over the role and function of universities in North American society. A central feature of this debate has been an attack on scholarship which, in one way or another, could be described as "critical." The view that too much academic work was being politicized (that is, preoccupied with questions of race, gender, and class) or trivialized (that is, by a fascination with public culture) was made both by the conservative chair of the National Endowment for the Humanities, and later Ronald Reagan's Secretary of Education, William J. Bennett, and by Allan Bloom, author of *The Closing of the American Mind*.

Both Bennett (1984) and Bloom (1987) have argued against certain forms of criticism that became an important force in university life in the wake of the 1960s. These arguments can be read in the context of political cultures which, in the English-speaking nations of the northern hemisphere, have taken a marked turn to the right during the 1980s. The role of universities is being seen increasingly by governments and funding agencies in terms of the rhetoric of "human resources." Universities and the intellectual life they nurture are increasingly being inserted into the rhetoric of a narrow economic instrumentalism which can only conceive, or is only prepared to conceive, social usefulness and social responsibility in material as opposed to cultural terms. As Bill Graham (1989: 2), president of the Ontario Confederation of University Faculty Associations, has observed: "The university, according to the new mythology, is a key player in the on-rushing knowledge based, information economy. Post-secondary education becomes an engine of economic growth because universities supply much of the basic research needed for growth, and, along with colleges, they supply most of the 'human resources' as well."

It is not difficult to muster arguments in support of the view that, if universities are to function as an intellectual resource in society, their role should be inclusive of the full range of human activities, not restricted simply to the instrumental achievement of material reproduction. ... [W]ithin the humanities and social sciences, the study of music is just as important and just as crucial to the understanding of humanity as any other discipline. I now wish to illustrate how such a case could be made.

Music, the Body, and Signifying Practice

I would argue that "music"—as it is discursively constituted within specific conjunctures of social, cultural, and historical forces—displays unique and specific qualities that become partly constitutive of the signifying practices within which, as "nonlinguistic" sound, it is embedded. This uniqueness and specificity rest not on any one quality, but on a combination of three qualities. Firstly, music makes no direct appeal to the world of discrete objects and concepts. It is nondenotative. It completely elides Julia Kristeva's "symbolic order." Music evokes *directly* the textures, processes, and structures of the social world as that world is manifest in the external, public realm of social interaction *and* the internal, private realm of individual subjectivity. The prime focus of music's evocation distinguishes it quite radically from language as the other mode of human communication based in sound. Secondly, music's appeal is significantly iconic. That is, a strong *but not determining* element of necessity obtains between music as a sonic event and the particular meanings invested in the sonic event. This principle of iconicity again distinguishes music quite radically from language. Thirdly, music's appeal is primarily and initially somatic and corporeal rather than cerebral and cognitive. Music appeals directly and powerfully to the human body as an individual site of utterance (a word I am using purposively instead of "speech") and of political struggle. The corporeal foundation of music's communicative power again distinguishes it radically from language.

A problem in understanding the specificity of music as a social form is that, in the development of the discipline that could contribute fundamentally to understanding the interpenetration of context and text—the discipline, that is, of cultural theory—music has been almost totally absent and language omnipresent. Cultural theory has developed overwhelmingly from the study of language, either through the discipline of literature or the discipline of linguistics. The study of music, however, has hardly affected the development of cultural theory. Because of this, the presence of language in cultural theory or, more precisely, the implications of certain conceptualizations of language for the development of cultural theory, become hidden from view. The implications of certain conceptualizations of music for cultural theory are, on the contrary, rather more visible. To make the kinds of claims I have just made about music as a signifying practice and to make them before an audience of cultural theorists is, usually, to draw accusations of essentialism. To discuss language in terms of "signifiers" and "signifieds" does not, however, draw the same response. Cultural theory, developing in the main from the study of language, has folded within its diverse categories of analysis the "unique" and "specific" qualities of language as a signifying practice. The problem, then, is that to claim that language has specific qualities does not appear to essentialize it, since its study fits comfortably within the categories of analysis deemed appropriate to the study of culture as a wider phenomenon.

The distinctions being made here are important, because there is one possible route to understanding the signification of sound in music that rests on the traditional understanding of how sound in language signifies. According to this route, however, sounds in music work differently in the sense that they do not invoke or call forth signifieds coterminous with the world of objects, events, and linguistically encodable ideas as that world is understood to be structured and called forth by language. Sounds in music are understood to occasion a ground of physiological and affective stimulation which is subsequently interpellated into the symbolic order of language. It is at this point that the sounds of music enter the social world and take on significance. Sound in music is thus equally arbitrary in its relationship to processes of signification as is sound in language, except that, to the extent that sound in music depends upon the arbitrary signifying processes of language in order to take on meaning, it is more distanced from and not as immediately implicated in processes of meaning construction as is sound in language. Sound in music could thus be said to float even freer in its relationship to processes of signification than does sound in language because it is not as directly burdened by the conventions of traditional associations between signifiers and signifieds. There is more of a sense, according to this understanding of signifying processes in music, in which sound in music can take on *any* meanings assigned to it than can sound in language.

The objection can at this point be raised that although sound in music can be argued to be polysemic in theory, it never appears to be in practice. That is, people in specific social and historical circumstances appear to be affected only by certain orders of structures, processes, and textures in the sounds of music. Sound, in other words, does seem to be implicated in processes of meaning construction through music. This objection can, however, be effectively overcome by claiming that certain orders of structures, processes, and textures in the sounds of music are conventionally taken to be meaningful and certain other orders are not taken to be meaningful by people because there already exist embedded within the symbolic order of language, mutual agreements on what is and what is not meaningful among the range of such possible orders. This position on processes of signification in music is, in other words, logically defensible. It has the advantage of explaining how there can be a meaningful relationship between sounds, words, images, and gestures in music—something that is crucial to understanding meaning in popular music and something that has been almost completely ignored by the world of musicology.

Be that as it may, this position on significance in music is incompatible with the one I elaborated earlier on two grounds: (a) it drops the body, and affective states as corporeally constituted, out of the realm of the social construction of meaning as linguistically constituted; (b) relatedly, the symbolic order of language is taken to occupy a primary and exclusive position in processes of the structuring and constitution of meaning in the sense that processes of signification involving media other than language can take on meaning only by being interpellated into the world of language. This "linguistic" approach to understanding the significance of sound in music can thus be understood to drain music of its real signifying potential, to render it a colony of language. Although not without insight into the broader task of understanding significance within popular music, this view is not, however, grounded in the very materials fundamental to the ways in which music connects. Ungrounded consumerism in cultural theoretical accounts of music remains a constant possibility!

That views of music ungrounded in music's material substance can lead in directions that lack rigor can be illustrated by reference to attempts to construct alternative semiologies of extralinguistic discourses. A symptomatic reading of some of the dominant lines of thought within poststructuralism in particular reveals how views of language are not only ahistorical but exclusionary and unsympathetic to processes of social mediation that do not fall easily within their preferred categories. In fact, most views of language within cultural theory *as well as* the position on significance in music that I elaborated earlier are essential—essential, that is, if one wishes to extrapolate from the placements and practices of "language" and "music" within contemporary conjunctures of social and historical forces to those placements and practices of other times and other places. This tendency to reify and essentialize language affects even the work of those poststructuralists who have sought to ground discourse on extralinguistic forces and dispositions, as Richard Middleton observes in the context of Roland Barthes's writings on music. "Like other French poststructuralists who wanted to ground discourse on extralinguistic forces and dispositions," argues Middleton (1990: 266–267), "the later Barthes is open to the suspicion that 'anything goes': that along with meaning, the category of critique is abandoned, leaving the field open to political quietism, untheorized spontaneism, or apolitical hedonisms." Either we have language, meaning, discourse, and reality (the orderly, the rational, the cerebral), in other words, or we have the spontaneously unstructured world of ruptured, ecstatic *jouissance*, replete with luscious, Dionysian, hedonistic pleasures.

What is being suggested here is rather different: that music, in complex and multidimensional ways that go beyond language, is both structured and structuring. The pleasures of music are socially and historically situated and, as a consequence, display logics that can speak directly to complex conjunctures of social, cultural, and biographical forces. However, these pleasures are situated nondenotatively, iconically, and corporeally. Approached in this way, the understanding of the functioning of music as a moment of social and cultural negotiation could lead to the kind of understanding of affect that Lawrence Grossberg has recently called for as a future important development for cultural theory. The functioning of music is in a certain sense global, concrete, shaping, forming, and, crucially, internalized within the body. Social configurations are intensely yet dialectically related to bodily configurations, configurations that have both external and internal dimensions. The social body becomes the human body in much the same way as the human body becomes the social body. The internal states of the human body, somatically experienced, become the source of externally uttered movements, as John Blacking has argued:

> Crucial factors in the development of cultural forms are the possibility of shared somatic states, the structures of the bodies that share them, and the rhythms of interaction that transform commonly experienced internal sensations into externally visible and transmissible forms . . . The shared states of different bodies can generate different sets of rules for the construction of behaviour and action by means of repeated movements in space and time that can be transmitted from one generation to another.
>
> (1977: 9)

The internal dispositions and configurations of bodies that find expression in externally perceptible bodily movement affect fundamentally the dynamics of sound production from the most basic and inalienably human of all musical instruments, the human voice. The voice, says Middleton (1990: 262), "is the profoundest mark of the human. An unsounding human body is a rupture in the sensuousness of existence. Undoubtedly this is because vocalizing is the most intimate, flexible and complex mode of articulation of the body." It is also, presumably because the voice, as the most intimate, flexible, and complex mode of articulation of the body, is fundamental to the creation of human societies as quintessentially symbolic. Johann Sundberg discusses the relationships between body movements, human emotion, and the physiology of voice production:

> There is a close correlation between body movements observable with the naked eye and hidden body movements. Examples of normally invisible body movements can be found in laryngeal cartilages, most of which are involved in the regulation of pitch. If it is true that a particular pattern of expressive body movements is typical of a specific emotional mode, then we would expect a corresponding pattern of, for example, voice pitch in speech produced in the same emotional mode. In other words, it is likely that expressive body movements are translated into acoustic terms of voice production.
>
> (1987: 154–155)

The way in which internal states, somatically experienced, become the source of externally uttered movements and the way in which this dialectic affects the physiology of voice production is mirrored in the production of instruments as extensions of the human voice. Here there is an external, technological manifestation of sound production thoroughly implicated with the external movements of the body. John Baily has developed this theme in arguing that players' movements affect musical structures in fundamental ways. The motor patterns that are implicated in a particular kind of music results, in Baily's view, from interaction between the morphology of the instrument and the player's sensorimotor capacities. Equally, there has grown up an intimate relationship between instruments as imitators of the human voice and the human voice as an imitator of instruments. Middleton discusses *this* dialectic with specific reference to Afro-American music:

One of the importances of Afro-American music lies in the fact that often the voice seems to be treated more as an "instrument" (the body using its own resources to make sound) ... From work-song grunts through 1930s jazz styles (Louis Armstrong singing "like a trumpet"; Billie Holiday "like a sax") to the short mobile vocal phrases of funk and scratch textures (used like percussion, bass or synthesizer), we hear vocal "personality" receding as the voice is integrated into the processes of the articulating human body. Of course, at the same time, instruments in this tradition often sound like voices. But the often noted importance of "vocalized" tone is only part of a wider development in which "instrumental" and "vocal" modes meet on some intermediate ground: while it is true that the instrument-as-machine (technological extension of the body) becomes a gesturing body (the "voice" of the limb), at the same time the voice-as-a-person becomes a vocal body (the body vocalizing).

(1990: 264)

Whatever the complexities of the dialectics between body, voice, and instruments, we may nonetheless conclude, with Baily (1977: 330), that "music can be viewed as a product of body movement transduced into sound."

Music, through the body, does not therefore speak of a spontaneously unstructured world of ruptured, ecstatic *jouissance*, replete with luscious, Dionysian, hedonistic pleasures. I find it difficult to agree with Barthes (1975: 222) that in music the body "speaks, it declaims, it redoubles its voice: *it speaks but says nothing*: because as soon as it is musical, speech—or its instrumental substitute is no longer linguistic, but corporeal; it only says, and nothing else: *my body is put into a state of speech: quasi parlando.*" I would argue that, as somatically and corporeally manifest, music is both structured and structuring. As such, it resonates powerfully within the lived, somatic, and corporeal experience of the listener. To hear a voice, a musical sound, is frequently to know of the somatic and corporeal state which produced it. The reaction is both sympathetic and empathetic. "Listeners," says Middleton (1990: 243), "identify with the motor structure, participating in the gestural patterns, either vicariously, or even physically, through dance or through miming vocal and instrumental performance."

This principle of symbolism is important. For all Barthes's (1975: 225) talk of music as "madness," as only saying and nothing else, he does, in his claim that "the body passes into music through no other relay than the *significant*," point toward an alternative semiology. As Middleton concludes:

Barthes is writing of an extreme; but anyone who has participated actively or vicariously in intensely "executed" performance—who has felt the polyrhythmic interplay of hands in boogie-woogie piano, resonated with the intricacies of bluegrass texture, played along with a B.B. King guitar solo or the bass-line in Billy Ocean's "When the Going Gets Tough"— will recognize what he is pointing towards. At this extreme we would indeed find "a second semiology, that of the body in a state of music."

(1990: 265–266)

We are fulfilling Henri Lefebvre's (1971: 52–62) wish that clear correlations between signifiers and signifieds be abolished in attempting to understand music. However, it remains important to maintain a certain conceptual distance between music as a social medium in sound, somatically and corporeally immanent, and individual subjectivity as socially constituted and somatically and corporeally mediated. The body, the "real" body, concludes Middleton, "cannot actually be grasped in music, but only by the *hands*; in music, it is necessarily represented, positioned, analogized, (its movements) traced. There is an absence as well as a presence, and the body in a state of music is not the same as—and must coexist with—the music in a state of psychic-somatic cathexis" (Middleton 1990: 266).

This mode of signifying distinguishes music radically from language. Language, in its hegemonic visual forms and manifestations, makes an appeal that is essentially cerebral. Taking to its limits the capacity of thought to be independent of the world on which it operates, visual language, doubly arbitrary, eschews any tactile awareness, any direct awareness of the material world. Sound, the sense of touch "at a distance," as Murray Schafer (1973: 11) has called it, is effectively eradicated. In its hegemonic, visual forms and manifestations, language does not bring the body into play *directly*, either as a site for utterance or as a site for political struggle. Indeed, as we have seen, there is a strain of thought within poststructuralism that says that experience has meaning only when retrospectively located within the symbolic order—that is to say, retrospectively rationalized through language. The experience, knowledge, and meanings of the body cannot, according to this view of signification, speak *directly*, be spoken *directly*, or constitute *directly* the site of a politically efficacious awareness. There are resonances of this way of thinking in Middleton's comments on Baily's view that "music can be viewed as a product of body movement transduced into sound." This, says Middleton (1990: 243) "is moving us close to the limits of a semiotic approach. To some degree, the correlations or correspondences here seem so direct . . . that they have less to do with meaning than with processes in themselves, less with signs than *actions*."

Yet it does not follow from this that music simply evokes unmediated experience subsequently to be rendered meaningful within the fabric of language. As I have attempted to demonstrate elsewhere in analyzing voice types as gendered through the mediations of the body (Shepherd 1991: 152–173), the corporeal interface with music is quintessentially symbolic. Music is both structured and structuring. As Middleton (1990: 243) concludes, "Human movement and human action are never culture-free; rather . . . there are differences in kind and extent of mediation through which pre-semiotic human interaction acquires symbolic, logical and significatory superstructures." As Lefebvre (1971: 59–61) concludes, "Musicality communicates corporeality. It renders the body into social practice . . . deploying their resources, music binds bodies together (socialises them)."

Foucault perhaps seems to provide an exception to this trend within poststructuralism of separating experience from meaning when he claims that discourses constitute the body as well as the conscious and unconscious minds and the emotional lives of the subjects they seem to govern. The body, for example, is central to Foucault's analysis of sexuality in the modern world. He is concerned with how bodies have been perceived, given meaning and value, and with "the manner in which what is most material and most vital to them has been invested" (Foucault 1981: 152). In the modern world, Foucault argues, sex has become a focal point of the exercise of power through the discursive constitution of the body. Yet if the body is constituted discursively, then it is constituted through language and visual inscriptions and placements in a way that implicitly denies the body's very essence and corporeality as a material site for utterance and political struggle. It remains the case that the body *is* spoken for *indirectly* through the conscious and unconscious processes of the mind. Music, however, goes behind the back of language and vision in speaking *directly to and through* the body. In so doing, it reminds us that while language may be fundamental to the symbolic nature of human worlds, it may also, in its hegemonic, visual forms and manifestations, elide from knowledge the fluid materiality of human relations with the world that it nonetheless symbolically mediates. If language can effect a certain separation from the world on which it operates, then it may delude us into forgetting that it is through material relatedness that we are moved to think. As Blacking has so eloquently argued:

> If there are forms intrinsic to music and dance that are not modelled on language, we may
> look beyond the "language" of dancing, for instance, to the dance of language and thought.

As conscious movement is in our thinking, so thinking may come from movement, and especially shared, or conceptual, thought from communal movement. And just as the ultimate aim of dancing is to be able to move *without* thinking, to *be* danced, so the ultimate achievement in thinking is to be moved to think, to be thought . . . essentially it is a form of unconscious cerebration, a movement of the body. We are moved into thinking. Body and mind are one.

(1977: 22–23)

Conclusion

This is the point from which popular music studies can, through an interrogation and influencing of cultural theory, make an impact on wider academic discourses that attempt to understand people as social and signifying beings. But to do this, popular music studies needs to face in two directions at once. It needs, first of all, to exploit the way in which texture and process are heavily foregrounded in most of popular music's genres to establish corporeal textures and corporeal processes—socially and culturally mediated—as the seat for the analysis of all musics. It is in this sense that the subject matter of popular music studies makes the discipline an excellent apologist for the examination, within the academy, of the nonlinguistic use of sound. It needs to draw music analysis away from its traditional preoccupation with the socially decontextualized analysis of those parameters of music most susceptible to notational and therefore visual mediation: harmony, melody, and rhythm. This preoccupation still pervades much analysis within musicology and ethnomusicology. Analysis needs rather to concentrate on sound, and particularly the voice and the body in motion. Further, popular music studies needs to face ethnomusicology in drawing upon the work of figures such as John Blacking, Catherine Ellis, Charles Keil, and Steven Feld to force a cultural theoretical discourse to open up around their ideas and insights. Some of the most interesting work on the subject of music as a signifying practice within human communities has come from ethnomusicologists, yet their work has hardly begun to make an impact on understanding musical practices in the world in which we currently live.

Secondly, popular music studies needs to face cultural theory. It needs to subvert, forcefully, radically, and with vigor, the preeminence of the linguistic and the visual within poststructuralist and postmodern discourses. We are not, as scholars and academics, simply consumers, speculating cleverly over mute and silent sites about the kinds of meanings we like to think people construct around musical symbols. We must pay attention to the material ground of music, to the sounds that, in being structured, structure our being by facilitating some possibilities and constraining others. Ultimately, we must return to the empirical in grounding our analysis of meaning in music in (*inter alia*) the material substance of its articulation.

I would argue that we need a new kind of discipline to emerge out of the best of ethnomusicology and popular music studies. At the moment, the potential for that discipline lies within the new field of popular music studies, a field that, in studying a form of music that is undeniably social in its significance, is struggling to account for that sociality while at the same time not losing sight of music's specificity as a discursively constituted signifying practice. The realization of this struggle will have consequences not only for musicology. It will also have consequences for cultural studies. In the words of Middleton (1990: v): "Traditional musicology still banishes popular music from view because of its 'cheapness' while the relatively new field of cultural studies neglects it because of the forbiddingly special character of music. A breakthrough in popular music studies would reorient cultural studies in a fundamental way and would completely restructure the field of musicology."

Precisely because popular music lies outside the established canon of musicology and inevitably raises questions that cannot be dealt with in terms of the traditional ways in which the canon is conceptualized, it leads the study of music into those areas envisaged by McClary (1990) as legitimate territory for a feminist critique. There need be no conflict in this respect. McClary does not see all the issues raised by a feminist critique of musicology as being reducible to questions of gender, although, in many cases, she would rightfully claim that they fall back on the invidious masculine/feminine dichotomy that so pervades our society at the level of culture. What a thoroughgoing critique of music education at the university level reveals, and this regardless of the origins and motivations of the critique, is that it remains remarkably exclusionary. The point here is *not* that the traditional canon should not be taught—in one way or another. And it is *not* that the benefits (and there are some!) of dominant modes of western intellection should be jettisoned. The point is that if other musical traditions are not admitted to music education in ways that do not submit them to tokenism, peripheralization, and marginalization and if other ways of thinking about and engaging in the study of music are not seriously entertained, the public culture in which we all live will continue to live in ignorance of what it is music *can* be about other than unreflective leisure and pleasure or the uncritical maintenance of a particular form of musical capital. It is because music is placed in a "feminized" location in our world that it must be carefully controlled and monitored by the academy, subjected to the phallocentric and logocentric modes of intellection that McClary, in my view, so legitimately criticizes. But it is also because it is placed in a feminized location that it contains the residues of what it is that our culture, publicly, does not want to communicate with itself about. Blacking (1973), Catherine Ellis (1985), Charles Keil (1979) and Steven Feld (1982) have argued persuasively, in studying the musics and cultures of other times and places, that music is centrally important to processes of social and cultural reproduction. Our education systems—not to mention our public cultures as a whole—have become very skilled at persuading people, young and not so young, otherwise.

A central concern of the philosophy of music education should be why we teach music in the first place. There are obviously some very practical answers to this question. There is a need for performers, teachers, radio and television producers, music librarians, and others whose professional lives require knowledge of music. However, the training of professionals itself begs the more central question.

I would submit that disciplinary alignments within academic music, as well as the ways in which music is traditionally taught, have become so entrenched and routinized that sight has been lost of the central questions as to why all human societies have music and why and how it should as a consequence be taught. Music is an inalienable presence within human societies for reasons that dominant western cultures seldom admit to academic discourse: it is central to those processes within any society whereby individuals are collectively moved to think and organize themselves. I would submit that an important agenda for the philosophy of music education is to argue for readmission of these reasons as a basis for fundamental discussions about the role of music education. Music education has not traditionally been regarded as being in the intellectual forefront of academic music as a whole. Perhaps, for this very reason, it is the appropriate site from which to reinvigorate the academic study of music in such a way that it cannot only force meaningful dialogues with other disciplines, but constitute a platform from which the public in general can be made more aware of the central importance of music to the maintenance and recreation of human cultures.

References

Baily, J. 1977. "Movement Patterns in Playing the Herati Dutar." In *The Anthropology of the Body*, ed. J. Blacking, Association of Social Anthropologists Monograph 15, 275–330. London: Academic Press.

Barthes, R. 1975. "Rasch." In *Langue, discours, société*, eds. J. Kristeva, J.-C. Milner and N. Ruwet, 217–228. Paris: Editions du Seuil.

Bennett, W. 1984. *Reclaiming a Legacy*. Washington: National Endowment for the Humanities.

Blacking, J. 1973. *How Musical Is Man?* Seattle: University of Washington Press.

_____. 1977. "Towards an Anthropology of the Body." In *The Anthropology of the Body*, ed. J. Blacking, Association of Social Anthropologists Monograph 15, 1–28. London: Academic Press.

Bloom, A. 1987. *The Closing of the American Mind*. New York: Simon and Schuster.

Ellis, C. 1985. *Aboriginal Music: Education for Living*. St. Lucia: University of Queensland Press.

Feld, S. 1982. *Sound and Sentiment: Birds, Weeping, Poetics and Song in Kaluli Expression*. Philadelphia: University of Pennsylvania Press.

Foucault, M. 1981. *The History of Sexuality, Volume One, An Introduction*. Harmondsworth: Penguin.

Graham, B. 1989. "Premier's Council Has a Narrow View of Education." *Forum* 6(16): 2.

Keil, C. 1979. *Tiv Song*. Chicago: Chicago University Press.

Lefebvre, H. 1971."Musique et sémiologie." *Musique en jeu* 4: 52–62.

McClary, S. 1990. "Towards a Feminist Critique of Music." In *Alternative Musicologies*, ed. J. Shepherd, special issue of The Canadian University Music Review 10(2): 9–18.

Middleton, R. 1990. *Studying Popular Music*. Milton Keynes: Open University Press.

Schafer, R.M. 1973. *The Tuning of the World*. New York: Knopf.

Shepherd, J. 1991. *Music as Social Text*. Cambridge: Polity Press.

Sundberg, J. 1987. The *Science of the Singing Voice*. DeKalb: Northern Illinois University Press.

9

Music and the Sociological Gaze

PETER MARTIN

"The history of musicology and music theory in our generation," write Cook and Everist (1999: v), "is one of loss of confidence: we no longer know what we know." The reasons for this widely acknowledged crisis of confidence need not be rehearsed, but clearly arise from a series of challenges to the established discipline—from, for example, the critical and feminist theories of the "new" musicologists, from various claims about the proper relation of musicology to ethnomusicology, from the emergence of popular music studies, and so on. In this chapter I will be concerned with one aspect of these challenges and the response to them—an aspect which could be succinctly, if rather inadequately, characterised as a "turn to the social" in the study of music. Some authors have brought new life to a tradition of analysis which has come to be identified with Adorno, arguing that music inevitably bears the imprint of the societal conditions in which it was created. For John Shepherd,

> because people create music, they reproduce in the basic structure of their music the basic structure of their own thought processes. If it is accepted that people's thought processes are socially mediated, then it could be said that the basic structures of different styles of music are likewise socially mediated and socially significant.
>
> (1987: 57)

For Shepherd (1991: 122), therefore, it is not accidental that the conventions and procedures of functional tonality have achieved virtually hegemonic status in western societies, since in them is encoded a representation of the dominant ideology of industrial capitalism. Similarly, for Susan McClary (1991: 19), specific "gender/power relationships [are] already inscribed in many of the presumably value-free procedures of Western music." For these authors, musical analysis must go beyond the notes themselves to elicit the fundamentally social meanings which they convey.

Others have agreed with the proposal that musical works must be understood in terms of the social contexts from which they have emerged, but rather than seeking social meanings within the texts, so to speak, have sought to explore issues concerning the social circumstances of their production, performance and reception. An insistence on the fundamental importance of context, for example, permeated Olle Edström's (1997: 19, see also Tagg 1998: 228) discussion of the approach developed by the "Gothenberg School," specifically as a result of its members' reading of Adorno: "we gradually gained a deeper insight," he writes, "into the pointlessness of instituting theoretical discourses on music without a solid ethnomusicological knowledge of the everyday usage, function and meaning of music."

For present purposes, my initial concern is simply to suggest that, whether the focus is on music as a "social text" (Shepherd 1991), or on the societal contexts of its production and reception, the proposed analytical reorientation necessarily leads musicologists to engage with issues that are also of fundamental concern to sociologists, and have been so for many years. This much I take—perhaps optimistically—to be uncontentious. What I would argue, rather more polemically, is that in general this "turn to the social" in musicological studies has not led to a sustained engagement with the themes and traditions represented within the established discourse of sociology. In so saying, I do not intend either to reify or to ascribe a spurious unity to sociology—which, like musicology, has its warring factions, its doctrinal disputes, and a constant tendency toward fragmentation. Nevertheless, there are various ways in which sociological insights can illuminate all kinds of musical practices in their various contexts, so sociologists may therefore have a legitimate interest in such practices. Sociological concerns, however, arise from a rather different disciplinary discourse, and may well diverge from those of musicologists, whether old or new.

Put more simply, music, like any other phenomenon, may be approached from various different perspectives, of which the sociological is one. Yet whereas studies of music by historians, philosophers, psychologists and, to a lesser extent, economists, using their distinctive skills and insights, have apparently been quite acceptable to musicologists, the interface with sociology appears problematic, certainly when viewed from the sociological side of the fence. Part of the difficulty may well be that most sociologists lack the technical and theoretical knowledge required to undertake musicological analysis; but the same point could usually be made about historians, philosophers, and the rest. In fact, it could be argued that a similar lack of awareness—this time of the discourse of sociology—has hindered musicologists in their efforts to make the "turn to the social." It seems appropriate, therefore, to suggest some of the ways in which the agenda of the sociology of music may differ from that of musicology, but yet make a distinctive contribution to the understanding of musical practices in their cultural contexts.

Problems at the Interface

That the relations between musicologists and sociologists of music remain problematic is evident in their mutual responses. Indeed, for sociologists such responses usefully demonstrate the extent to which their efforts may be subject to misunderstanding and misapprehension. . . .

The Myth of Value-Freedom

This myth arises out of the quite fundamental contention that (despite all Adorno's arguments) it is not the business of the sociologist of music to make aesthetic judgments concerning music or its performers. To many musicologists and others with a background in the humanities, this position has on occasion been interpreted as a quite unworthy abdication of serious responsibilities, as a quite futile effort to achieve "value freedom," or even (as has been said of some work of mine) a presumption of "Olympian detachment" (Middleton 1996: 656). In fact, the position entails none of these criticisms. It is insufficiently appreciated that the approach, far from being value-free, derives from a different, but specific and identifiable, set of assumptions and values. The principle of "sociological indifference" is itself one of these values. It should also be emphasised that this principle is not a further example of superficial postmodern relativism, since those familiar with the sociological literature recognise it to be a methodological precept elaborated by Max Weber nearly a century ago. Weber (1978: 4) distinguished between sociology as a science concerned with "the interpretive understanding of social action," i.e. it formulates explanations of action based on "subjective meaning," whereas other "dogmatic disciplines . . . such as jurisprudence, logic, ethics, and aesthetics . . . seek to ascertain the 'true' and 'valid' meanings associated with the objects of their investigation." More concretely, the aim of the sociological exercise is not to decide on the justness of a law, or the rightness of a principle, or indeed the "real" meaning of a piece of music, but to understand the beliefs held and meanings taken by real people in actual situations, in order that their actions may be explained, and the course of events understood. To this end, it is essential that the sociologist attempts to remain indifferent to the claims and counterclaims made by the protagonists who are the subjects of the research: to take sides or to intervene would be to compromise the investigation itself—we would not, for example, expect a racist bigot to produce a credible study of inter-ethnic relations.

Sociologists' perspectives on these matters, then, are no more detached than those of musicological analysts—but the object of their studies, and their methodology, may be very different. In this context it is instructive to recall the remarks of Howard Becker on the relations between ethnomusicology and sociology, in which be points out that contemporary sociologists of art are no longer primarily concerned with the (often speculative) grand narratives relating art and society produced by European theorists of Adorno's generation, but focus on the collective activity through which things like music-making get done: "Sociologists working in this mode," says Becker, "aren't much interested in decoding art works, in finding the works' secret meanings as reflections of society. They prefer to see those works as the result of what a lot of people have done jointly." It is worth emphasising this point, for as Becker (1989: 281–282) himself suggests, the notion of investigating "what a lot of people have done jointly" is "deceptively simple." It's too simple in one sense, because as every sociologist knows, and a moment's reflection will confirm, the scientific analysis of the collaborative interactions which are the essence of human social life is an immensely difficult and complex undertaking. Earlier I referred to the "technical and theoretical knowledge" which is rightly regarded as essential if a person is to operate as a professional musicologist. At this point, it is worth noting that there is also an extensive domain of "technical and theoretical knowledge" which has been developed by sociologists concerned with the analysis, in various ways, of the routine accomplishment of orderly patterns of social organisation. Without some awareness of that domain, it may be hard to grasp what the sociologists' purposes are, and I strongly suspect that this is the source of some of the misapprehension of sociological work by some musicologists. . . .

[. . .]

Contrasting Approaches

Just as . . . there are now "old" and "new" musicologies, so have there been older and newer sociological approaches. In sociology, the older ones are generally concerned with "structural" phenomena and "macro" social processes which, as in the grand schemes of Marx, Durkheim and Parsons, are held to operate independently of real people, the newer ones starting from the fundamental reality of individuals in collaborative interaction, and examining the ways in which the social order is built up from that. And just as in musicology, the old and the new remain in uneasy coexistence. However, I think it is reasonable to detect in recent years a general drift away from "structural" approaches (on the grounds that they reify collective phenomena, and entail deterministic explanations of human behaviour). Certainly most theoretical sociologists have left behind them the conceptual baggage of structural and post-structural approaches, and seek to develop an understanding of social life in terms of practical action in interactional contexts. In such contexts, as Giddens (1987: 214–215) puts it, "meaning is produced and sustained through the use of methodological devices." Significantly, too, the work of Bourdieu (1990: 61), who explicitly saw his task as an "effort to escape from structuralist objectivism without relapsing into subjectivism" has attracted criticism precisely because he did *not* succeed in detaching his analyses from "structuralist" presuppositions, thereby failing to capture "the emergent processes inherent in the production and reproduction of the structure of daily life reasoning, language use, and practical action" (Cicourel 1993: 112). In general, then, and with varying emphases, much recent sociology has focused on the ways in which the "objective facticity" of the intersubjective world is produced, reproduced, and changed through organised practices which, however routine and regularly occurring, must nonetheless be enacted by real people in real situations.

What I wish to suggest, therefore, is that the application of this particular sociological "gaze" to the field of musical practices generates a rather different kind of discourse to that of musicology. As Becker suggested, the sociologist will not be concerned to decode or decipher the meaning of musical "texts," however defined, either from a syntactic or a semantic point of view. Nor, as argued above, is it any business of the sociologist to take sides in the inevitable and perpetual debates about their meaning or value. What will be of interest, however, are the many and varied ways in which such cultural objects are constituted and defined, the uses that are made of them, and the consequences of these activities, for it is through this sort of investigation that we may arrive at an understanding of the social organisation of the musical "worlds" (Becker 1982) in which all production, performance and reception take place.

One of the important contributions of Leonard B. Meyer was the recognition that aesthetic experience not only depends fundamentally on the kind of expectations the listener brings to the music, but that such expectations themselves are derived from particular kinds of cultural learning and experience. Individuals' responses and reactions, which are experienced as right and "natural," are nonetheless shaped by prior processes of social learning (Meyer 1970: 43). This is not quite as "paradoxical" as Meyer suggests, if we accept the point above that inculcation into the everyday intersubjective world *is* in fact the "natural" way in which human beings acquire the capacity to have any kind of experience, and so to engage in organised social life. But for present purposes the essential point is simply to emphasise the implications of the idea that the ways in which we hear music are profoundly influenced by our cultural experience, which varies both between and within societies: as Edström (1997: 16) has put it "the significance and meaning of music is created, like everything else, in its social environment." What this has been taken to mean, quite properly, is that the production, performance, and reception of music are "socially mediated," to use Shepherd's term, and in specific ways, so that—for example—styles of music are held to be capable of "implicitly coding an explicit world-sense" (Shepherd 1991: 85), which is then assumed to be characteristic of specific social groups. Now there are some general theoretical problems with this sort of analysis, and I have discussed these elsewhere (Martin, 1995: 160ff). At present what I wish to suggest as an extension of the points made above, and Becker's (1989) distinction between the old and the new sociologies of art, is that the things which are taken to constitute the "social environment"—such things as "societies," "social classes," musical "styles" and so on—are not entities "out there," so to speak, whose relationships can be unambiguously defined by the analyst. Rather, they are to be conceived as entities whose reality is constituted—and whose existence is normally taken for granted—through collaborative social interaction in specific situations. We need only reflect on the enormous range of actual sounds and musical styles which have been referred to as "jazz," for example, to realise the extent to which the meaning of the term—that is, what it signifies at any particular moment—is context-dependent.

It should be said straight away, in order to anticipate a frequent set of misunderstandings, that this sort of perspective does not commit us to philosophical idealism, to subjectivism or solipsism, or to a denial of the massive inequalities of wealth and power in societies. This theme cannot be pursued here, but is developed by Berger and Luckmann (1991: 78) in their discussion of objectification and the consequent "coercive power" of institutions; Blumer (1969: 75), too, asserts that any denial "of the existence of structure in human society . . . would be ridiculous." What I do wish to consider briefly, though, is the emerging importance of the social situation for the study of music as social practice. Again, Edström rightly includes the "situation" in considering the mutual interrelations of the factors involved in reception (the others being the "individual," the "music," and the "performance"). But the implication of the present argument is that we must go beyond a conception of the "situation" as, for example, "when and where music is performed" (Edström 1997: 64). Rather we must consider the social situation much more fundamentally as the focal point where all other factors—not least, the unique subjectivity of each individual—are brought together to constitute, what Schütz called a "vivid present" through the interactional "work" (DeNora 1986) of participants. As Goffman pointed out, perhaps because of its very ordinariness, the importance of the social situation is often neglected. All of us, as human beings operating in specific cultural contexts, constantly experience the world not as "social structures" or "institutions" but in terms of the exigencies and constraints of a succession of social situations. All of what we call "experience" is mediated in some way or other by social situations, from earliest infancy right through life; they, not "social facts," are ". . . a reality *sui generis*, as He used to say" (Goffman 1964: 136; the He in question is, presumably, Durkheim). Moreover, the dynamics of social life—from momentous political projects to tiny conversational details—do not consist in the operation of disembodied social processes; they must be *enacted* by culturally competent individuals. Again, Goffman made the point succinctly, by contrasting the vast amount of attention given to the study of "language" with the infinitely smaller number of studies of its actual use by speakers. However, asks Goffman, "where but in social situations does speaking go on?" (ibid.). In short, *from a sociological perspective* it is through the analysis of actual situations (rather than musical "works") that we will come to understand something of what Edström terms (1997:19) "the everyday usage, function, and meaning of music."

Consequently, studies of the reception, as opposed to the production or performance, of music assume a much greater significance, as Edström (1997: 58) has also argued, in relation to Cook's (1990) distinction between the "ways of hearing" characteristic of musicologists and non-specialists. Once it is accepted that the meaning of music is not to be found "within the text," so to speak, the analytical focus moves to concentrate on the meanings generated in the context of particular encounters, for they—and not the stipulations of some theoretician—will inform the subsequent conduct of the individuals concerned. (As Wittgenstein puts it: "You cannot prescribe to a symbol what it *may* be used to express. All that it CAN express, it MAY express" [quoted in Monk 1991: 165].) Furthermore, I suggest that the term "reception" is inadequate to convey what is involved here. The notion of reception is too passive, having the connotation of receiving a message which has been transmitted, as with radio and TV signals. What must be emphasised is the active and engaged process through which people "make sense" of their cultural environment. Something of this process may be found in the discussions of popular music which criticise mass-society theorists for their assumption of a homogenous aggregate of docile consumers, and examine instead the active "appropriation" of music, and the ways in which consumer goods may be ". . . taken over, transformed, reinterpreted, inserted into new contexts [and] combined to form a new style" (Middleton 1990: 157). But the implications of the view I am exploring go even further, in the sense that, as Blumer suggested, all cultural objects are themselves constituted in the constant process of collaborative interaction. Mundane as it may seem, it is through talk that we create, sustain—and change—the taken-for-granted world of commonsense reality, learning, using and arguing about concepts such as "the symphony," "bebop," "the orchestra," "delta blues," and so on. Of course, we do not have the freedom to define situations however we wish, precisely because of the "facticity" of institutions and cultural constraints. To paraphrase Marx, people make sense, but they do not make it as they please. Indeed, and I will return to this point, there is a "political" dimension to all this: such concepts and the meanings associated with them are constantly open to renegotiation, as when we argue against others' interpretations and advocate our own, or—often more significantly—as when organised interest groups attempt to impose authoritative "ways of hearing."

These and other considerations arise from the apparently straightforward, but still problematic, suggestion that the sociologist of music may be primarily concerned with the uses to which music is put, as much as the qualities or characteristics of music itself. Even phrasing the matter in this way can cause difficulties: many listeners, most musicologists, and—almost by definition—all "music-lovers" find it difficult or inappropriate to consider music in such prosaic, utilitarian, terms. Yet, quite apart from the process of demystification which is likely to result from any properly conducted sociological analysis, it is surely incontestable that music is "used" for various purposes in a whole range of social settings and occasions: to yield a profit or earn a wage, to sell commodities, to create a desired atmosphere, to project an image of one's self, to work, exercise, or make love to, to form part of a ritual, and so on. The list could be extended, but already what is evident is that, particularly in the electronic age, music's effectiveness in these sorts of circumstances does not necessarily depend on the "performance" of a "work," a dedicated setting, an "audience," or indeed attentive "listening." And while all such events can be of interest to the sociologist, the musicologist may, or may not, share this concern. That is to say, in each of these settings music plays a part, perhaps an important part, in the constitution of normatively organised social situations. Yet precisely because they *are* normatively organised and normally experienced as unproblematic, the organisational features through which this sense of order is created are simply taken for granted. As I have suggested, however, orderly collaborative interaction does not just happen; it involves, in Schütz's terms, the mutual orientation of the participants so as to secure a sense of intersubjective correspondence within an unproblematic "world" (Schütz 1972) and, further, the enactment of appropriate talk, gestures, actions, and so on in order to accomplish the event. These, I have argued, are matters of great technical interest to the sociologist who is concerned to understand the achievement of social order. But they may not be matters of much technical interest to the musicologist.

[. . .]

Conclusion

In considering these concerns of the sociologist, the musicologist may object that little or nothing has been said about the music, and that sociological interest appears to focus on contextual and circumstantial factors which, in principle, are distinct from the music itself. The objection is understandable, yet not sustainable, I submit, as a criticism of the sociology of music. What I have suggested is that there are various ways in which sociologists may wish to approach music as an organised social practice, but which do not necessarily depend on an analysis of the music itself. Indeed, the aim may well be to examine the process by which the "same" music is invested with quite different meaning and significance in different social contexts, in which case technical analysis, or decontextualised claims about how "it" has its "effects," will have little to contribute. If, as Edström (1997: 27) remarks, it is an "illusion" to imagine that there can be text without context: then it is important to recognise the ways in which social factors may be decisive in influencing the production of the "texts" themselves. It is easy for anyone with a background in the European tradition of "serious" music to overlook this important point, since in it the role of the "audience" at a performance is essentially passive. In other traditions, of course, interaction between performers and listeners is normal, as in the oral-aural traditions of African-American music (Jackson 2003: 67); in the informal settings in which these styles developed, "the audience . . . inevitably influences the performer's material" (Brown 2003: 121). Moreover, it is also important to recognise the extent to which those who create music in *any* style, take cognizance of the conventions of the "art world" (Becker 1982) in which they are operating (Martin 1995: 166).

So, as a final example, I will quote from Paul Berliner's *Thinking in Jazz* (1994), a magnificent ethnography of the process through which aspiring players learn to become recognisably capable jazz performers. Berliner is here describing an incident which occurred while the pianist Barry Harris was conducting one of his renowned workshops for young players:

> At a fifth student's performance . . . he shook his head and remarked "No, you wouldn't do that in this music." Stung by the rebuke, the student defended himself. "But you said to follow the rule you gave us, and this phrase follows the rule." "Yes," Harris admitted, "but you still wouldn't play a phrase like that." "But give me one good reason why you wouldn't," the student protested. "The only reason I can give you," Harris replied, "is that I have been listening to this music for over forty years now, and my ears tell me that the phrase would be wrong to play. You just wouldn't do it in this tradition. Art is not science, my son." The student left the workshop early that evening, not to return for months.
>
> (1994: 249)

The episode nicely captures some points which are relevant here. Firstly, there is the evident authority of Harris, the acknowledged master performer and the students' mentor. Secondly, the fact that his authority is brought to bear on the fine details of the students' playing, and thirdly that it is not concerned simply with technical correctness but with matters of stylistic appropriateness which can only be decided on the basis of prolonged experience of the musical community and its expectations. It is clear that what is being communicated to these neophyte improvisers are detailed ways of shaping performance practices which are dictated not only by formal musical requirements, or the creative energies of individuals, but by the norms and values of an established "interpretive community" (Fish 1980: 171). As in all interactions, the idiosyncrasies and interests of individuals must somehow be reconciled with what Wittgenstein called a "form of life" . . .

I have suggested that the perceived need to incorporate a "social" dimension into musicological studies may not be met successfully by developing the idea that music somehow expresses or conveys "social" messages of some kind, and that the sociological literature offers various alternative approaches, though these may not resonate particularly strongly with established musicological concerns. Musicological and sociological perspectives, then, are to be considered as emerging from, and grounded in, distinctly different academic discourses; as a consequence the way in which "music" is constituted in each will be different. With a recognition of these differences, though, may come an awareness of, and a mutual respect for the complementary strengths of the different disciplinary perspectives.

References

Becker, H.S. 1982. *Art Worlds*. Berkeley: University of California Press.
_____. 1989. "Ethnomusicology and Sociology: A Letter to Charles Seeger." *Ethnomusicology* 33(2): 275–85.
Berger, P. and T. Luckmann. 1991 [1966]. *The Social Construction of Reality*. London: Penguin.
Berliner, P. 1994. *Thinking in Jazz: The Infinite Art of Improvisation*. Chicago: University of Chicago Press.
Blumer, H. 1969. *Symbolic Interactionism: Perspective and Method*. Berkeley: University of California Press.
Bourdieu, P. 1990. *In Other Words: Essays Towards a Reflexive Sociology*. Cambridge: Polity Press.
Brown, C. 2003. *Stagolee Shot Billy*. Cambridge: Harvard University Press.
Cicourel, A.V. 1993. "Aspects of Structural and Processual Theories of Knowledge." In *Bourdieu*, eds. C. Calhoun, E. LiPuma and M. Postone, 89–115. Chicago: University of Chicago Press.
Cook, N. 1990. *Music, Imagination and Culture*. Oxford: Oxford University Press.
Cook, N. and M. Everist, eds. 1999. *Rethinking Music*. Oxford: Oxford University Press.
DeNora, T. 1986. "How is Extra-Musical Meaning Possible? Music as a Place and Space for 'Work.'" *Sociological Theory* 4(1): 84–94.

Edström, O. 1997. "Fr-a-g-me-n-ts: A Discussion on the Position of Critical Ethnomusicology in Contemporary Musicology." *Svensk Tidskrift for Musikforskning (Swedish Journal of Musicology)* 79(1): 9–68.

Fish, S. 1980. *Is There a Text in the Class? The Authority of Interpretive Communities.* Cambridge: Harvard University Press.

Giddens, A. 1987. "Structuralism, Poststructuralism, and the Production of Culture." In *Social Theory Today*, eds. A. Giddens and J.H. Turner, 195–223. Cambridge: Polity Press.

Goffman, E. 1964. "The Neglected Situation." *The Ethnography of Communication (American Anthropologist Special Edition)*, eds. J. Gumperz and D. Hymes, 66(6): 133–136.

Jackson, T.A. 2003. "Jazz Performance as Ritual: The Blues Aesthetic and the African Diaspora." In *The African Diaspora: A Musical Perspective*, ed. I. Monson, 23–82. New York: Routledge.

McClary, S. 1991. *Feminine Endings: Music, Gender and Sexuality.* Minneapolis: University of Minnesota Press.

Martin, P.J. 1995. *Sounds and Society: Themes in the Sociology of Music.* Manchester: Manchester University Press.

Meyer, L. 1970. *Emotion and Meaning in Music.* Chicago: Chicago University Press.

Middleton, R. 1990. *Studying Popular Music.* Buckingham: Open University Press.

_____. 1996. Review of P.J. Martin, Sounds and Society. *Music and Letters* 77(4): 656–657.

Monk, R. 1991. *Ludwig Wittgenstein: The Duty of Genius.* London: Vintage.

Schütz, A. 1972 [1932]. *The Phenomenology of the Social World.* London: Heinemann.

Shepherd, J. 1987. "Towards a Sociology of Musical Styles." In *Culture, Style, and the Musical Event*, ed. A.L. White, 56–76. London: Routledge.

_____. 1991. *Music as Social Text.* Cambridge: Polity Press.

Tagg, P. 1998. "The Goteborg Connection: Lessons in the History of Popular Music Education and Research." *Popular Music* 17(2): 219–242.

Weber, M. 1978. *Economy and Society.* Berkeley: University of California Press.

B

CREATION

10

Ethnography and Interaction

DAVID GRAZIAN

Ethnography literally refers to the art of writing about people. Within the social sciences it has come to refer to a broad set of practices through which scholars attempt to observe and interpret the cultural beliefs and practices of social groups by engaging them in some kind of interpersonal encounter. Traditionally, sociological ethnography has referred specifically to the task of the participant observer who "gathers data by participating in the daily life of the group or organization he studies" (Becker 1958: 652). However, in recent years the term has been appropriated by researchers who employ a broader range of qualitative methodologies, such as open-ended interviewing and biographical narrative collection. In this article I examine how these methodological tools have been employed in the sociological study of music, from the early ethnographic work of the Chicago school to more recent explorations of music-making in the contemporary city.

The Ethnography Tradition in Chicago

A founder of the Chicago school of urban sociology during the early decades of the 20th century, Robert E. Park introduced ethnographic fieldwork into the department's curriculum (Abbott 1999, Anderson 2001). Park himself was a former journalist, and under his guidance both graduate students and faculty alike researched and wrote ethnographic accounts of the otherwise hidden lives of Chicago's immigrant families, homeless men, working-class gangs, and juvenile delinquents.

Among these monographs, three in particular give an account of how popular music scenes operate within a larger cultural ecology of urban nightlife. In *Vice in Chicago*, Walter C. Reckless (1933) provides a detailed cartography of the city's Prohibition-era jazz venues, public dance halls, and vaudeville houses. In his analysis of the black-and-tan cabarets located in Chicago's segregated black neighborhoods, Reckless (1933: 102–103) uses ethnographic data to emphasize how consumers attach symbolic importance to the neighborhood context in which they experience live blues and jazz music: "To a slumming white patronage the Black Belt location of cabarets offered atmosphere and the colored man's music and patronage added thrill."

Like much of the Chicago school research on urban life, a moralistic social agenda informs *Vice in Chicago*. Similarly, Paul G. Cressey (1932) critically explores the underworld represented by the taxi-dance hall, a type of club popular during the 1920s where men could purchase three-minute dances with attractive female companions at ten cents per song. Cressey relies on close participant observation and in-depth interview data with dancers as well as their male patrons, the latter typically Asian immigrants who relied on these dance halls and their live music as entry points into the social world of American life. Another prominent Chicago researcher, Harvey Warren Zorbaugh, fills *The Gold Coast and the Slum* (1929) with anecdotes about the importance of music for the diverse residential communities of the city's Near North Side. In a chapter on the fashions of high-society, status-seekers measure their social worth in "invitations to certain box parties at the opera," exclusive balls and benefit concerts held for charity (Zorbaugh, 1929: 50–51). His account of the unmarried residents who inhabit the area's furnished rooming-house district includes a sad tale of an aspiring young pianist who flees Kansas for a chance to perform professionally in Chicago. (After a year, her music lessons grow more and more expensive until her teacher finally convinces her of the hopelessness of her ambition.) And in his research on Towertown, the city's bohemian entertainment zone, Zorbaugh (1929: 102) discovers the jazz musicians and "singing waiters" employed within its highly commercialized world of nightclubs and "Paris revues."

The legacy of these Chicago school investigations lies in (1) their use of the case study as a legitimate form of sociological inquiry; (2) an attention to participant observation and other types of ethnographic fieldwork; and (3) an emphasis on the interactional fields in which urban culture is produced, marketed and consumed. These examples would continue to influence ethnographic work in the sociology of music over the course of the twentieth century.

Producing Music

While the contributions of the Chicago school add to our knowledge of how music cultures operate in the urban milieu, it is clear that the study of music was always tangential to a more general examination of social organization and human ecology in the context of the American city. In contrast, the next wave of ethnography in music focused specifically on the world of musicians in the settings in which they lived and labored. The earliest of this research was conducted not by sociologists, but by folklorists and ethnomusicologists interested in capturing the indigenous musical cultures of the rural South. Through a variety of techniques, including extensive participant observation, interviewing, and recording songs and oral narratives, fieldworkers such as Alan Lomax (1993), Paul Oliver (1965), and David Evans (1982) created vivid and illustrative portrayals of the Mississippi Delta and its folk blues culture. This ethnographic work emphasized how blues musicians in that context drew on the reality of their surroundings, particularly chronic poverty and institutionalized racism, to infuse their songs with both ironic reflection and emotional intensity. In a similar vein, Charles Keil (1966) studied Chicago blues and soul singers, and Samuel Charters (1981) researched West African tribal performers (or *griots*) thought to be the originators of what would come to be the American blues tradition.

While productive, the ethnomusicological approach to blues research suffered from a number of related weaknesses: its presentation was generally impressionistic, rather than systematic; its intellectual goals were descriptive and explanatory, but not theoretical; and its orientation was romantic instead of critical. As a result, classic ethnomusicology evaded an analysis of how more contemporary professional, economic and institutional forces structure the production of popular music.

Sociology, on the other hand, was much better equipped to compensate for these gaps, and from the mid-1950s onward ethnographers explored the commercial contexts in which musicians produce their craft not only as inspired artists, but as employed professionals as well (Becker 1982). These ethnographic studies developed out of three related paradigms made popular within sociology at this time: the influence of Everett C. Hughes and his work on occupations; the rise of symbolic interactionism; and the strengths of labeling theory and the social construction of deviant behavior. In *Outsiders* (1963), Howard S. Becker (a student of Hughes) examines how jazz musicians negotiate between the demands of their audiences and their own artistic aspirations and establish career identities within an unstable job market. According to Becker (1963: 114–119), jazz musicians labored in a low-status profession regarded as "unconventional," "bohemian" and downwardly mobile by the reigning middle-class norms of the 1950s and 1960s, and this impacted how they conducted themselves in their domestic relationships as well as their professional lives. Becker demonstrates how close participant observation can yield both systematic empirical data and theoretical insight.

Becker's analysis of jazz players as an occupational group propelled future work on the professional lives of other types of musicians. Robert R. Faulkner (1971, 1973) explores the higher-brow world of classically trained orchestral musicians, particularly those who transition from live concert performance to studio recording for film and television. Like Becker, Faulkner's chief emphasis concerns how musicians organize and emotionally experience their careers as workers laboring in an inherently unpredictable field. The economics of musical work require that participants manage their ambitions and definitions of success accordingly, taking into account the challenges of finding employment as well as the benefits and costs of "going commercial."

In contrast to Faulkner, H. Stith Bennett (1980) researches the world of local rock musicians; however, like his predecessors, he addresses a wide range of their occupational strategies, including instrument acquisition, gig procurement, set programming, and techniques of performance. A student of Becker's, Bennett also performs as a musician and relies on his contact with fellow players as his primary source of data about not only professional practices, but the set of meanings that musicians attribute to those practices. Like Becker and Faulkner, Bennett draws on ethnographic methods in order to better understand how musicians develop subjectivities within a set of material constraints, commercial demands and professional expectations.

Subcultures and Style

Until the mid-1970s, ethnography in the sociology of music focused almost entirely on production. Why? In part, musicians made fitting case studies for research on occupations and on the social construction of deviance, two fields that exponentially grew in popularity among sociologists during the 1960s (Abbott 2001). But this focus was also due to an abandonment of ethnographic work on music *consumption*. The rise of the Frankfurt school's critique of mass culture, particularly Adorno's work on jazz and the "regression" of listening, contributed to growing attacks on the commodification of popular music by American public intellectuals during the 1940s and 1950s (Macdonald 1953, Hayakawa 1955, Adorno 1989, 1997; also see Rosenberg and White 1957). By portraying consumers of popular music as alienated, neurotic and childlike simpletons rather than discriminating human agents, this critique ultimately rendered such consumers unworthy of close ethnographic attention. Perhaps on the strength of this critique of popular culture, research on music consumption tended to employ varied approaches such as content analysis and survey methods but rarely ethnography (i.e. Clarke 1956, Horton 1957, Johnstone and Katz 1957). David Riesman (1950) provided an exception to this rule by conducting lengthy open-ended interviews with his students and a sample of younger teenagers. He found that American youth could be divided into two groups. The majority followed conventional adolescent tastes while a minority of active listeners exhibited their distaste for commercial music and celebrity performers. These latter consumers developed their musical preferences within the context of peer groups who expressed a disdain for conformity to the cultural mainstream.

Two decades later, observations like Riesman's would become the basis for an entire wave of ethnographic research on the consumption of music. Drawing on a amalgam of British social history, neo-Marxist theory and French post-structuralism, fieldworkers associated with the Centre for Contemporary Cultural Studies at the University of Birmingham produced accounts of how youth subcultures actively incorporate music into their overall lifestyles (Hall and Jefferson 1975, McRobbie and Garber 1975, Willis 1978, Hebdige 1979). In colorful studies of punks, skinheads, bikers, hippies, Rastafarians and other bohemian groups, researchers explored how young people rely on the creative potential of music to develop symbolic and aesthetic practices in concert with other elements of style, including fashion, body adornment, dance, drug use and slang. Reacting to the mass culture critique, these scholars argued that the consumption of music represented a class-conscious form of rebelliousness, or "resistance through rituals" (Hall and Jefferson 1975). By appropriating commodified forms of music for their own stylistic and expressive ends, music *consumers* could refashion themselves as *producers* as well.

While path-breaking in its own right, some of the research of the Birmingham school unfortunately emphasized the development of theory without empirical verification from ethnographic data, sometimes at the cost of substituting armchair sociology for the rigors of fieldwork. In contrast, more recent studies of subcultures and style employ intensive participant observation to reveal how young consumers use music to shape a set of collective identities and experiences in everyday life. In her late-1980s ethnography *Teenage Wasteland*, Donna Gaines (1991) hangs out in convenience store parking lots with working-class hard rock fans from suburban New Jersey, and details the enthusiasm with which they worship the songs and totemic symbols of their favorite bands—Led Zeppelin, Metallica, Bon Jovi, Suicidal Tendencies, the Grateful Dead. Through the consumption of heavy metal and glam rock, kids labeled as so-called "burnouts" invest their socially marginalized lives with meaning and affirmations of self.

Whereas previous accounts of youth subcultures explained how the consumption of music could also help foster in-group solidarity and integration, during the 1990s ethnographers began emphasizing how music tastes and rituals of consumption could lead to increased internal differentiation *within* subcultures. In her ethnographic study of British dance clubs, Sarah Thornton (1996) found that established acid house and techno music fans vie for subcultural status by mocking their less experienced counterparts within the scene. Clubbers criticize these novice thrill-seekers for exhibiting what they consider an amateurish lack of sophistication and style, and refer to the mainstream clubs that cater to them as "drunken cattle markets" where "tacky men drinking pints of best bitter pull girls in white high heels" (Thornton 1996: 99). Similarly, Ben Malbon (1999) explores how London dance clubs employees invoke the criteria of "coolness" to restrict entry into their establishments, thereby replicating the racist and sexist social norms of exclusion found in more mainstream cultural settings.

For Malbon's chatty informants, the achievement of "belonging" depends on their ability to negotiate among the various front and back stages of the club. Also with an ethnographic eye toward differentiation and spatial practices within music scenes, Wendy Fonarow (1997) draws on field observations and interviews to provide a mapping of the three spatial regions of British indie rock clubs inhabited by consumers during live shows. The youngest and most enthusiastic fans jump and shout at the front of the stage and in the mosh pit; older fans congregate on the floor behind the pit, where they can enjoy the performance without distraction; and industry personnel and other music professionals linger in the back regions near the bar, coolly consuming the whole scene with bemused detachment. Fonarow demonstrates how the participants of music performances differentiate themselves by engaging in varied strategies of consumption. At the same time, as these consumers get older they alter their affiliation with the band and their place within the club so that they eventually "move back through space until they are aged out of the venue all together" (Fonarow 1997: 369).

The Consumption of Music and the Self

While these accounts of music subcultures and scenes focus on collective processes and in-group interaction, other recent ethnographic research within the sociology of music emphasizes how consumers employ music to create more personal and individualized experiences for themselves. In *Common Culture* Paul Willis (1990) emphasizes the meanings and practices that young people attach to popular music. According to Willis's informants, music serves as a resource for generating meaning through the selective interpretation of memorable lyrics and styles of performance. He argues that through activities such as home recording and creating a "personal soundscape" inside one's head with the help of Walkman earphones, listening to music presents opportunities for developing a political consciousness, gaining spiritual nourishment, and making sense of pivotal milestones and life experiences (Willis 1990: 64).

The work of Tia DeNora (1999, 2000) offers a sophisticated framework for thinking about how individuals consume music. She argues that music operates as a "technology of the self," a resource for managing one's everyday life. Through open-ended interviews and ethnographic fieldwork conducted in sites such as aerobics classes and fashionable clothing shops, DeNora scrutinizes how consumers use music to orchestrate their daily routines from waking up to working out. In bedrooms and offices, music serves a variety of personal functions: it supplies mental preparation for the workday, encourages concentration during important tasks, alleviates stress, and acts as a device of organizing one's memory of key moments with romantic partners, family members or other intimates. In ethnographic forays into the world of music therapy and physical fitness, DeNora (2000) emphasizes the elemental relationship existing between music and the body. In aerobics, music operates not as background, but as *foreground*, as a tool employed to explicitly define the rhythm, pacing and progression of the workout, from warm-up to cool-down. Similarly, Rob Drew (2001) relies on fieldwork conducted in thirty karaoke bars to examine how individuals use their bodies to publicly express themselves musically. Through elaborate performances that attempt to imitate, embellish or parody the recordings of well-known entertainers, amateur crooners experience music in an earthly manner through their intensely drawn facial expressions, exaggerated dance styles and strained vocals.

Drew draws on his own experience as a participant observer to enrich his account, and in doing so he subjects himself to his own analysis. This may not be surprising, given that the last two decades have given rise to the postmodern critique of ethnography emanating from within the worlds of anthropology, gender studies and critical theory. This critique challenges traditional ethnography on several grounds, including (but not limited to): its unfair characterization of politically subjugated groups, including women and racial minorities; the false claim to objectivity made by fieldworkers; the inherent power discrepancies between researchers and subjects; and the resistance of ethnographers to reflect upon these issues and candidly introduce them into their written accounts from the field (Clifford and Marcus 1986, Clifford 1988, Rosaldo 1989, Abu-Lughod 1993, Behar and Gordon 1995, Marcus 1998).

This attention to reflexivity in ethnography has prompted a number of studies by researchers who examine their own experiences as music listeners and/or performers. In *Race Music*, Guthrie P. Ramsey, Jr. (2003) produces what he refers to as an "ethnographic memoir" by drawing on his own first-hand recollections as an African-American child growing up in Chicago, and his experiences as a professional jazz pianist and gospel performer. In addition, he draws on interviews with his immediate and extended family members who provide oral histories of their migration to Chicago from the Deep South and remembrances of life in the city's segregated black neighborhoods. Ramsey elegantly weaves together these materials to describe the relationship between music and memory as it thrives in the spaces of black urban culture, including its house parties, jazz clubs, churches, and roller-skating rinks.

Meanwhile, Stacy Holman Jones (2002) uses her field research as an opportunity for self-analysis. She combines her observations and a brief interview with a cabaret performer with her own musings on torch singing and fantasies about Sarah Vaughan to produce an ethnographic meditation on music and desire. Jones (2002: 739) herself refers to the piece as "a fiction and an autoethnography, an analysis and an argument, an irony and a literal rendition, a scrapbook and a fan letter." While these highly personal studies may lack the empirical reliability of more traditional field research, they emphasize the subjective and interpretive quality of ethnographic practice (see Geertz 1973).

[. . .]

Opportunities for Ethnography in the Sociology of Music

As demonstrated by past research, the promise of ethnographic methods presents a bounty of opportunities for the sociological study of music. Like music, ethnography is an interpretative practice; it requires participation and improvisation; its presentation invites a multiplicity of meanings as well as self-reflection. For these reasons, I conclude with three suggestions for new foci in ethnographic research in the sociology of music: the use of popular music in the marketing of urban areas; the production process within the culture industries; and the consumption of music in real time and space.

First, the contemporary literature on urban sociology proposes that elites often appropriate the local culture of their cities for political and entrepreneurial ends (Zukin 1995, Suttles 1984, Logan and Molotch 1987, Lloyd and Clark 2001, Lloyd 2002). In Chicago and Memphis, civic boosters promote blues clubs within their cities as a means of increasing tourism and generating revenue for their local economies, just as Nashville, New Orleans, and Liverpool rely on their own roots-oriented music heritages for their financial vitality (Grazian 2003). Ethnographic methods can help sociologists better understand these complex relationships existing between the political economy of urban areas and their music cultures. Specifically, by relying on three techniques—conducting participant observation at city-sponsored music festivals and other tourist attractions, engaging in open-ended interviews with civic leaders and the programmers of local cultural organizations, and collecting accounts of how musicians, residents, boosters and out-of-towners creatively employ images of "authenticity" to represent the city, ethnographers can add empirical weight to the more abstract paradigms indicative of much postmodern urban theory.

Second, ethnographic methods can enhance the historical and quantitative research currently conducted on the music industry itself. Over the past thirty years, the sociology of music has greatly benefited from the scholarly efforts made by those attempting to combine the fields of cultural production and organizational behavior. By treating the production of music as a commercial enterprise undertaken by large industrial conglomerates, sociologists have helped demystify the processes through which record labels and other media companies manufacture, market and distribute culture as a commodified form (Hirsch 1972, Peterson and Berger 1975, Peterson 1978, 1997; Frith 1978, 1981; Dowd and Blyler 2002).

In recent years, ethnographic work has contributed to this project as well by increasing our knowledge of how corporate cultures impact particular music genres; identifying the diverse artistic and economic interests that drive the production of music videos; uncovering how hip-hop impresarios rely on ideological considerations to successfully promote rap music; discovering how music critics organize themselves within the context of professional journalism; and exploring how the chaotic careers of session musicians are structured (Peterson and White 1979, Negus 1992, 1999; Regev 1997, McLeod 1999, Klein 2003). In future endeavors, ethnography may prove to be particularly useful for developing our understanding of how support personnel experience occupational marginality and gender segregation within the music industry; how the employees of independent record companies create alternative identities and professional presentations of self; and how ideologies that shape the industrial production of music eventually filter down to the level of the local music subculture or scene.

Finally, ethnographic methods provide an especially handy tool for sociologists interested in examining how people consume music in real time within spatial contexts of social interaction. To their credit, sociologists of culture have relied on sophisticated techniques to examine the tastes and participation rates among music consumers, and have identified the relationship between music genre appreciation and social class, race, educational background, and occupational status (Bourdieu 1984, DiMaggio and Ostrower 1990, Peterson 1992, Bryson 1996, 1997; Peterson and Kern 1996). But even the most rigorous quantitative studies of consumption can fail to account for how individuals actually experience music in their moments of consumption, whether during public concerts, small cabaret shows, or candlelit dinners. Of course, certain questions regarding the consumption of music can only be reliably answered by making inferences based on large population samples, and in these cases ethnography may only be appropriate as a complement to ongoing statistical data analysis. However, the pleasure (and occasional displeasure) produced by music rarely registers at the level of mere approval, but is often experienced in an emotional and visceral manner as expressed through bodily gestures, spontaneous applause, and welled tears of longing (see Malbon 1999, DeNora 2000, Drew 2001, Grazian 2003). Whether through participant observation, open-ended interviewing, or oral narrative collection, live performance and experiences provide among the most appropriate opportunities for ethnography in the sociology of music.

References

Abbott, A. 1999. *Department and Discipline: Chicago Sociology at One Hundred*. Chicago: University of Chicago Press.
_____. 2001. *Chaos of Disciplines*. Chicago: University of Chicago Press.
Abu-Lughod, L. 1993. *Writing Women's Worlds: Bedouin Stories*. Berkeley: University of California Press.
Adorno, T.W. 1989. "Perennial Fashion—Jazz." In *Critical Theory and Society*, eds. S.E. Bronner and D.M. Kellner, 199–212. New York: Routledge.
_____. 1997. "On the Fetish-Character in Music and the Regression of Listening." In *The Essential Frankfurt School Reader*, eds. A. Arato and E. Gebhardt, 270–299. New York: Continuum.
Anderson, E. 2001. "Urban Ethnography." In *International Encyclopedia of the Social & Behavioral Sciences*, eds. N.J. Smelser and P.B. Baltes, 16004–16008. New York: Elsevier Science.
Becker, H.S. 1958. "Problems of Inference and Proof in Participant Observation." *American Sociological Review* 23(6): 652–660.
_____. 1963. *Outsiders: Studies in the Sociology of Deviance*. Glencoe: Free Press.
_____. 1982. *Art Worlds*. Berkeley: University of California Press.
Behar, R. and D. Gordon, eds. 1995. *Women Writing Culture*. Berkeley: University of California Press.
Bennett, H.S. 1980. *On Becoming a Rock Musician*. Amherst: University of Massachusetts Press.
Bourdieu, P. 1984. *Distinction: A Social Critique of the Judgement of Taste*. Cambridge: Harvard University Press.
Bryson, B. 1996. "Anything But Heavy Metal: Symbolic Exclusion and Musical Dislikes." *American Sociological Review* 61(5): 884–899.
_____. 1997. "What About the Univores? Musical Dislikes and Group-Based Identity Construction Among Americans with Low Levels of Education." *Poetics* 25(2/3), 141–156.
Charters, S. 1981. *The Roots of the Blues: An African Search*. New York: Da Capo Press.
Clarke, A.C. 1956. "The Use of Leisure and its Relation to Levels of Occupational Prestige." *American Sociological Review* 21(3): 301–307.
Clifford, J. 1988. *The Predicament of Culture: Twentieth-Century Ethnography, Literature and Art*. Harvard University Press, Cambridge.
Clifford, J. and G.E. Marcus, eds. 1986. *Writing Culture: The Poetics and Politics of Ethnography*. Berkeley: University of California Press.
Cressey, P.G. 1932. *The Taxi-Dance Hall*. Chicago: University of Chicago Press.
DeNora, T. 1999. "Music as a Technology of the Self." *Poetics* 27(1): 31–56.
_____. 2000. *Music in Everyday Life*. Cambridge: Cambridge University Press.
DiMaggio, P. and F. Ostrower. 1990. "Participation in the Arts by Black and White Americans." *Social Forces* 63(3): 753–778.

Dowd, T.J. and M. Blyler. 2002. "Charting Race: The Success of Black Performers in the Mainstream Recording Market 1940–1990." *Poetics* 30(1/2): 87–110.

Drew, R. 2001. *Karaoke Nights: An Ethnographic Rhapsody*. Walnut Creek: Alta Mira.

Evans, D. 1982. *Big Road Blues: Tradition and Creativity in the Folk Blues*. Berkeley: University of California Press.

Faulkner, R.R. 1971. *Hollywood Studio Musicians*. Chicago: Aldine Publishing Company.

_____. 1973. "Career Concerns and Mobility Motivations of Orchestra Musicians." *Sociological Quarterly* 14(3): 147–157.

Fonarow, W. 1997. "The Spatial Organization of the Indie Music Gig." In *The Subcultures Reader*, eds. K. Gelder and S. Thornton, 360–369. London: Routledge.

Frith, S. 1978. *The Sociology of Rock*. London: Constable.

_____. 1981. *Sound Effects: Youth, Leisure, and the Politics of Rock 'n' Roll*. New York: Pantheon.

Gaines, D. 1991. *Teenage Wasteland: Suburbia's Dead End Kids*. New York: Pantheon.

Geertz, C. 1973. *The Interpretation of Cultures*. New York: Basic.

Grazian, D. 2003. *Blue Chicago: The Search for Authenticity in Urban Blues Clubs*. Chicago: University of Chicago Press.

Hall, S. and T. Jefferson, eds. 1975. *Resistance Through Rituals: Youth Subcultures in Post-War Britain*. London: Routledge.

Hayakawa, S.I. 1955. "Popular Songs Versus the Facts of Life". *Etc* 12(2): 83–95.

Hebdige, D. 1979. *Subculture: The Meaning of Style*. London: Routledge.

Hirsch, P.M. 1972. "Processing Fads and Fashions: An Organization Set Analysis of Culture Industry Systems."*American Journal of Sociology* 77(4): 639–659.

Horton, D. 1957. "The Dialogue of Courtship in Popular Songs." *American Journal of Sociology* 62(6): 569–578.

Johnstone, J. and E. Katz. 1957. "Youth and Popular Music: A Study in the Sociology of Taste." *American Journal of Sociology* 62(6): 563–568.

Jones, S.H. 2002. "Emotional Space: Performing the Resistive Possibilities of Torch Singing." *Qualitative Inquiry* 8(6): 738–759.

Keil, C. 1966. *Urban Blues*. Chicago: University of Chicago Press.

Klein, B. 2003. "Dancing about Architecture: Popular Music Criticism and the Negotiation of Authority." MA Thesis, Annenberg School for Communication, University of Pennsylvania.

Lloyd, R. 2002. "Neo-Bohemia: Art and Neighborhood Redevelopment in Chicago." *Journal of Urban Affairs* 24(5): 517–532.

Lloyd, R. and T.N. Clark. 2001. "The City as an Entertainment Machine." *Critical Perspectives on Urban Redevelopment* 6: 359–380.

Logan, J.R. and H.L. Molotch. 1987. *Urban Fortunes: The Political Economy of Place*. Berkeley: University of California Press.

Lomax, A. 1993. *The Land Where the Blues Began*. New York: Delta.

Macdonald, D. 1953. "A Theory of Mass Culture." *Diogenes* 1(3): 1–17.

Malbon, B. 1999. *Clubbing: Dancing, Ecstasy and Vitality*. New York: Routledge.

Marcus, G.E. 1998. *Ethnography Through Thick and Thin*. Princeton: Princeton University Press.

McLeod, K. 1999. "Authenticity Within Hip-Hop and Other Cultures Threatened with Assimilation." *Journal of Communication* 49(4): 134–150.

McRobbie, A. and J. Garber. 1975. "Girls and Subcultures." In *Resistance Through Rituals: Youth Subcultures in Post-War Britain*, eds. S. Hall and T. Jefferson, 209–222. London: Routledge.

Negus, K. 1992. *Producing Pop: Culture and Conflict in the Popular Music Industry*. London: Edward Arnold.

_____. 1999. *Music Genres and Corporate Cultures*. London: Routledge.

Oliver, P. 1965. *Conversation with the Blues*. Cambridge: Cambridge University Press.

Peterson, R.A. 1978. "The Production of Cultural Change: The Case of Contemporary Country Music." *Social Research* 45(2): 292–314.

_____. 1992. "Understanding Audience Segmentation: From Elite and Mass to Omnivore and Univore." *Poetics* 21(4): 243–258.

_____. 1997. *Creating Country Music: Fabricating Authenticity*. Chicago: University of Chicago Press.

Peterson, R.A. and D.G. Berger. 1975. "Cycles in Symbol Production: The Case of Popular Music." *American Sociological Review* 40(2): 158–173.

Peterson, R.A. and R.M. Kern. 1996. "Changing Highbrow Taste: From Snob to Omnivore." *American Sociological Review* 61(5): 900–907.

Peterson, R.A. and H.G. White. 1979. "The Simplex Located in Art Worlds." *Urban Life* 7(4): 411–439.

Ramsey, G.P., Jr. 2003. *Race Music: Black Cultures from Bebop to Hip-Hop*. Berkeley: University of California Press.

Reckless, W.C. 1933. *Vice in Chicago*. Chicago: University of Chicago Press.

Regev, M. 1997. "Who Does What with Music Videos in Israel." *Poetics* 25(4): 225–240.

Riesman, D. 1950. "Listening to Popular Music." *American Quarterly* 2(4): 359–371.

Rosaldo, R. 1989. *Culture and Truth: The Remaking of Social Analysis*. Boston: Beacon.

Rosenberg, B. and D.M. White. 1957. *Mass Culture: The Popular Arts in America*. New York: Free Press.

Suttles, G.D. 1984. "The Cumulative Texture of Local Urban Culture." *American Journal of Sociology* 90(2): 283–304.

Thornton, S. 1996. *Club Cultures: Music, Media and Subcultural Capital*. Hanover: Wesleyan University Press.

Willis, P.E. 1978. *Profane Culture*. London: Routledge.

_____. 1990. *Common Culture: Symbolic Work at Play in the Everyday Cultures of the Young*. Boulder: Westview.

Zorbaugh, H.W. 1929. *The Gold Coast and the Slum: A Sociological Study of Chicago's Near North Side*. Chicago: University of Chicago Press.

Zukin, S. 1995. *The Cultures of Cities*. Cambridge: Blackwell.

11

Performance Perspectives

Lisa McCormick

In both sociology and musicology, there has been a burst of research activity concerning "performance" in recent years. However, the two fields could not be more different in the way that they approach the topic, a contrast that has been sharpened by their independent development. Sociologists have tended to think about performance in terms of embodied social action, which has led them to investigate musical interaction rituals in a variety of social settings. Musicologists, on the other hand, have researched performance by "informing" it through an analysis of a work's formal structure or by gathering historical evidence about how it was played in the composer's time; they have also investigated the history of performance through recordings. In this chapter I will trace the development of performance research in these fields. To conclude, I will explore the possibility for a long overdue interdisciplinary synthesis.

Performance Perspectives in Sociology

The course of music sociology was decisively shaped in the 1970s and 1980s by the sequential emergence of the production perspective and the "art worlds" approach. While Bourdieu and the critical theory tradition had kept art and culture on the research agenda in Europe, these had to be established as suitable topics in US sociology (Santoro 2008). Peterson (1976; Peterson and Anand 2004) and Becker (1974, 1982) succeeded in making this case by crafting thoroughly sociological approaches to the study of music, but each did so in a way that sidelined performance in favor of other concerns. For those adopting Peterson's production perspective, the milieux in which music was created, manufactured, and evaluated was what mattered, so the aim was to understand the organizational and industry-wide structures that shaped the content and the form of cultural symbols. The pragmatic spirit of Becker's art worlds perspective encouraged a focus on the conventions co-ordinating artistic "work" and, by extension, the uses of music in everyday life. In declaring meaning and interpretation off limits, these perspectives helped to cement the "production/consumption paradigm" (McCormick 2012) that continues to dominate cultural analysis on both sides of the Atlantic, however "unhelpful" it becomes at times (Atkinson 2004: 158).

When performance did come up during this period, it tended to be in the more radical sub-disciplines. In the case of ethnomethodology, the exploration of embodied "doings" produced several classic essays on gender (Garfinkel 1967, West and Zimmerman 1987) as well as Sudnow's *Ways of the Hand* (1978).[1] What distinguishes Sudnow's (1978: xiii) study is that he deliberately avoided explaining the jazz piano style in order to describe the process of learning how to improvise, enhancing his account of "the knowing ways of the jazz body" with diagrams of fingerings and photographs of his hands placed in various chord positions at the keyboard. Sudnow (xiii) writes from the "standpoint of the performer," but the phenomenological motivation he embraces is less about "introspective consciousness" than about "examining" how the body sustains an "orderly activity" by managing "concrete problems." In locating the practical accomplishment of the jazz musician in the hands, the body is shown to be more than an executor of whatever the mind or the inner ear imagines; through the physical maneuvers that create sounds on the instrument, the body accumulates a thoroughly tactile knowledge that operates almost independently of the cognitive aspects of playing the piano.

The field of cultural studies is worlds apart from ethnomethodology in many respects, but here again what motivated an engagement with performance was a denial of the centrality of texts. In the Birmingham School's early ethnographic studies of subcultures, performance was implied rather than thematized in the investigation of rituals of resistance (see for example Hall and Jefferson 1976). In *Performing Rites*, Frith (1996) turned this around by proposing a resolution to the "value problem" in cultural studies with an aesthetics of popular music centered on performativity. In his view, structuralist approaches had proved inadequate because they could only relate popular music to social processes; it was only once the academic study of popular music moved away from "meaning and its interpretation—musical appreciation as a kind of decoding" and toward performance that music could be recognized as a social process in itself (1996: 272). This analytical move led Frith (210–211) to focus on the non-textual aspects of pop song performances beginning with the process of "double enactment" through which the singer contextualizes the "'act' of singing with the 'act' of performance"; his point is that the personality of the star remains distinct from the personality described in the lyrics, allowing the listener to attend to both the song and its performance. Like Sudnow, Frith addresses the physicality of performance but from the standpoint of the analyst rather than the performer; the pop star's voice and body are acknowledged to be expressive instruments, but their significance lies in the pleasure they produce for the listener and their function as a site of erotic desire.

Correspondingly, Frith (272) identifies the critical issue as "the coming together of the sensual, the emotional, and the social *as* performance," but unfortunately this aesthetic ideal is presented as the exclusive preserve of the popular. This radical position might have made sense when the cultural distinctions separating high and low were more firmly entrenched, but as these divisions have been eroded, the grounds have also been removed for overdrawing the distinction between popular and classical music. High art has always had its own occasions where the performance of music is intentionally foregrounded rather than the music itself, such as competitions (McCormick 2009). Neither can the case be made that technological mediation produces a uniquely popular aesthetic. What Frith (224) said of pop music videos applies equally to the high-definition broadcasts pioneered by the Metropolitan Opera, New York: they "dr[ew] on (and therefore br[ought] to our attention) established performing conventions and adapt[ed] them to new technological and selling circumstances."

Atkinson (2006) is one of the few sociologists to have ventured inside the rehearsal studio to observe how these established performing conventions inform the work of staging an opera production. For several years he conducted fieldwork with Welsh National Opera to investigate empirically the "practical work of theatricality" that makes an opera "work" (Atkinson 2010: 4). The key figure in these processes is the opera producer, who translates conceptual ideas about the opera text into embodied action through a form of cultural *bricolage*, drawing from sources as varied as literary antecedents and the mass media to supply motivations for singers' characters and thereby render staged interactions meaningful. Interpretive work is also how the producer embodies personal authority; in providing "dramaturgical direction," through demonstrative gestures, gazes and movement, an authoritative version of the production gradually becomes articulated (Atkinson 2004: 155). The opera production that results from these rehearsals serves as the foundation for a second-order performance to emerge; through occasions and material forms such as galas and programs, the opera company then performs itself to sponsors and patrons.

Atkinson's study is an exception; his "dramaturgy of dramaturgy" (2004: 151) compensates for the empirical grounding he found lacking in Goffman's (1959) elaboration of the dramaturgical metaphor. It is far more common for sociologists to import Goffmanian concepts wholesale into selected fieldsites to illuminate musical interactions. For example Dempsey (2008) takes Goffman's frame analysis as a starting point to identify the parameters that co-ordinate joint action and define appropriate utterances in the context of a jazz jam session. Lee (2009), on the other hand, builds on Goffman's theory of face-work by documenting the strategies used by emcees to avoid the embarrassment of interrupting the flow in freestyle rap ciphers. Similarly, Scarborough (2012) has examined how jazz and rock musicians attempt to save face—when their identity is threatened on stage, but with the added aim of explaining situational stratification; he expands Goffman's model by introducing Bourdieu's forms of capital, which allows him to identify how various face-work strategies depend on differentially distributed resources.

While auditions could have offered yet another site for an exploration of Goffmanian interaction rituals, Nylander (2014) deliberately rejected this sort of micro-analysis for his investigation of selection procedures into prestigious Swedish jazz schools. Instead, he follows Bourdieu; in taking a critical view of the practices of valuation and evaluation of jazz performance he sees through the romantic discourse that lace jurors' "sayings" to find the *doxic* principle that guides the selection of "heirs" and justifies the elimination of *epigones*, who disappoint by following the standard too closely, or *heretics*, who offend by straying too far from tradition. Predictably, a field theory framework collapses musical performance into the *habitus*; only musicians with the right upbringing can appear to be "naturally talented" and show "personality" by playing with the standard.

Reductive conclusions such as these are precisely what Hennion's (2003) sociology of musical mediations is meant to overcome. Rather than refute the lessons of critical sociology, the point here is to recognize its limitations, most notably the failure to account for the diverse ways in which actors experience aesthetic pleasure. For Hennion (2003: 85), the key to avoiding the dead-end of Bourdieuian deconstruction is to conceive of "mediations" both broadly and positively; they are not "mere carriers" of music or "substitutes that dissolve its reality" but all the "human and material intermediaries" that make music happen and allow for its appreciation. Accordingly, music can be seen as a contingent and possibly transformative event rather than a static object, while taste can be understood as performance rather than an indicator of the cultural capital associated with a socio-professional category (Hennion 2001: 3).

As this selective overview demonstrates, sociologists have investigated a wide range of musical genres guided by a diversity of perspectives, but they share a view of musical performance as embodied social action. However different the theoretical questions animating the research, they have all gravitated to ritual settings for their empirical observations, these running the gamut from everyday private practice sessions and impromptu jam sessions to formal concerts and regular gigs. An important advantage to this "ritualist" view is that it includes listening. Hennion (2001: 18) might resist the term "rites" to describe the ceremonies concocted by music-lovers in their efforts to achieve altered states, but this is only to protect their listening habits from the connotation of rigid codification. In contrast, Frith (1996: 275) embraces the term because identity is constructed through rites; it makes little difference whether ritual participation is in the form of "music making" or "music listening" because both are "bodily matters" or "social movements."

Performance Perspectives in Musicology

One might have expected performance perspectives to have a longer history in musicology than in sociology, but this is actually not the case. According to Leech-Wilkinson (2009: 791), the reason for this neglect is that musicology has had an "uncomfortable relationship" with performance for 100 years. Cook (2013a: 11) blames this discomfort on an unshakeable Platonic streak in music scholarship; by conceiving of music as an "abstract and enduring entity that is reflected in notation, with the notation itself being reflected" through performance, the role of the performer is reduced to that of a transmitter. At its most benign, this attitude encouraged musicologists to dismiss performance as mere matter of craft; in its more virulent form, performers were portrayed as a potential source of distortion, which stoked a moral discourse appealing to their sense of duty to the work and the composer's intentions. Either way, the (dead) composer was placed at the top of the musical hierarchy.

An important challenge to this uneasy status quo came from Small (1998), whose polemic was simple but effective: if "music" were a verb instead of a noun, new and better questions could be raised. He proposed an inclusive definition for his invented term, musicking: "To music is to take part, in any capacity in a musical performance, whether by performing, by listening, by rehearsing or practicing, by providing material for performance (what is called composing), or by dancing" (1998: 9). This was a profoundly sociological move; Small cast music as action in order to argue that the social relations modeled and enacted through music were just as important as the formal properties of the work being performed. This argument is developed through a "thick description" of a symphony concert, where he draws from Bateson's (1973) ritual theory to deconstruct the meaning of this event. Small's intervention paved the way for performance perspectives in sociology and musicology to converge, but this was not enough for the paths to cross.[2] Mainstream musicologists reluctantly conceded Small's (1998: 8) point that "musical works exist in order to give performers something to perform" and not the other way around, but they remain uncomfortable with the concept of music as an event, leaving it to ethnomusicologists and anthropologists to subject western classical music to the ethnographic gaze (see for example Kingsbury 1988, Born 1995, Nooshin 2014).

Rather than uproot the "textualist paradigm" (Cook 2013b) that has been deeply embedded in the field, musicological scholarship on performance has effectively reinforced it. This is not to diminish the revolutionary ambitions of the "early music movement" or its impact on the musical world; the notion of "historically-informed performance" (see Donington 1977, Kenyon 1988, Taruskin 1995, Butt 2002) that once bitterly divided performers, music scholars and audiences has now become institutionalized in conservatories, musicology departments and the recording industry. Initially, debates over the merits of period instruments and authentic performance practice were confined to the baroque repertoire, but they gradually expanded backward and forward in time to include everything from the medieval (Knighton and Fallows 1992) to the romantic period (Brown 1999). This agitation has resulted in the invention of a radically new performance style, but it would be inaccurate to call this development a "performative turn" in any meaningful sense; the arguments invariably center on the correct interpretation of notation and they are settled by mustering documentary evidence. Performers therefore remain subservient to musicologists, and the literary regime of scholarship remains intact.

The situation is no better when music theorists turn their attention to performance. In the subdiscipline known as "analysis and performance" (see especially Berry 1989), music theorists charge themselves with the task of exposing the structural relations that performers should realize in performance. The implied message is clear: it is possible but unlikely that performers left to their own devices could produce a correct performance, so in helping them to understand what they play, theorists ensure that compositional and listening "grammars" (Lerdahl 1988) will match. As both Lester (1995) and Cook (2001a) have complained, this approach amounts to an explanation of music without musicians because it deems performers irrelevant to the process of analysis. While Dunsby (1989) has challenged this Schenkerian and Schoenbergian legacy by arguing that performing music and explaining its structure are two distinct (if overlapping) activities, Rink (2002) has sought to find a middle ground with the concept of the "performer's analysis." The idea here is to draw a parallel; the analysis produced by theorists emphasizes structure but performers, being more attuned to the temporality of music, emphasize "shape." The performer's analysis is also more flexible; interpretations emerge gradually through the rehearsal process and are guided by an "informed intuition" rather than systematic rules (Rink 2002: 39).

Performers figure far more prominently in the analytic process when performance is studied by listening closely to recordings (for an overview see Bayley 2010). Unlike early music scholars, who must rely on fragmentary and often conflicting descriptions of techniques and performance practices, musicologists who study recordings can hear for themselves Toscanini's infamous fast tempi or Caruso's liberal use of *portamento*. The challenge that comes with this approach is taking into account the distortions introduced by technology. For recordings from the first part of the twentieth century, it is the limitations of recording devices that pose difficulties; with postwar recordings it is the sophistication of the equipment that is the problem because it allows the producer to manipulate what is heard. Complications such as these prevent analysts from treating recordings and live performances interchangeably, but if recordings are granted their own kind of authenticity, a large resource of evidence is gained for testing hypotheses about style.

For example, Bowen (1999) has conducted a statistical analysis of the eighty-year recorded history of the iconic first movement of Beethoven's Fifth Symphony. He found that while the tempo for the first theme has changed very little, the average initial tempo for the second theme has increased significantly, a trend he interprets as the decline of the nineteenth-century performance tradition of slowing down for the second theme. On the basis of this finding he criticizes traditional music theory analysis for gauging the proportional weight of themes and keys by the relative distribution of measures. If the movement's proportions are affected by the performance tradition, it follows that there is "no way to study *the* structure of a musical work; the structure of the music will vary depending on who is performing, when, where, and for whom" (Bowen 1999: 436). Through recordings, however, it is possible to trace how performance changes the structure of music. Leech-Wilkinson (2009, 2012) has also drawn on evidence from recorded performances to challenge conventional music theory but not to attack the methods of traditional analysis. Instead, he provocatively suggests that musicologists simply have not recognized how much performers have influenced them all along. Not only do contemporary performers supply the reference for the composer's or the theorist's idealized sound world; they also inspire new analytical techniques and theories by bringing out new aspects of the music through the style of performance.

The methods for studying recordings have varied in sophistication from the use of a stopwatch to extract timings to the use of spectrograms to measure vibrato and vocal inflections (Johnson 2002). However, the most elaborate scientific methods are found at the intersection of cognitive psychology and musicology (see Clarke 2004). For example, musical expression can be studied quantitatively by fitting a piano keyboard with the digital communications protocol "Musical Instrument Digital Interface" (MIDI) to capture features of the performance such as the identity of depressed keys, the time at which notes start and end, the velocity with which the hammer strikes the string and the timings of pedal depression and release. With such precise quantitative data available, the properties of a single performance can be charted in detail and larger samples can be compiled for statistical analysis. However, the limitations of MIDI-based studies are considerable; because data collection is restricted to the mechanism of the keyboard, the performer's use of other expressive tools, such as the instrument's acoustical properties and physical movements, cannot be captured.[3]

To study the visual component of musical performance, cognitive scientists have turned to video data. Davidson (1993), for example, employed the point-light technique to determine how much musical novices rely on visual information to gauge expressiveness. In this method, a reflective material is attached to the musician's major joints so that the camera captures the light bouncing off these points as they move during performance; in playback, brightness and contrast are adjusted to mask the performer's appearance, allowing viewers to concentrate only on physical movements. By preparing excerpts that could be shown to subjects in video-only, sound-only and video-and-sound versions, Davidson found that vision was a more effective indicator of performance manner than sound. In a similar vein, Tsay (2013) found that sight is a larger factor than sound in judgments about musical performance for both novices and professional musicians. In this study, participants were asked to identify the actual winners of a classical music competition using six-second clips of recordings which, depending on the conditions of the experiment, were played back with audio only, with video only or with sound and video together. The most striking finding was that subjects' selections were most reliable when they were based on the video recordings without sound; this was even the case with professional musicians who insisted most emphatically that sound was all that mattered.

While experiments such as these have produced intriguing results, the methods they employ share the same weakness as the more conventional performance perspectives in musicology: music is decontextualized. MIDI readings can only be collected, and video clips can only be played back, in a laboratory setting, but these bear little resemblance to the act of making music and listening *in situ*. As score-centered approaches, "analysis and performance" and historically-informed performance both reinforce a Platonic concept of music, which by definition denies the importance of context. As for the study of recordings, it only appears to be a radical departure from scores. Even proponents of phonomusicology have had to admit that it "gives a new lease on life to musicological textualism: recordings are taken out of context and analyzed as self-sufficient objects rather than as the traces of human actions in specific social and cultural situations" (Cook 2013b: 76).[4] For all the burgeoning interest in performance in the past fifteen years, musicology has yet to take a true "performative turn."

Toward an Interdisciplinary Synthesis: From Musical Ritual to Theater

The most promising development in this respect has been the intrusion of performance studies into musicology. The opening for this incursion appeared when Cook (2001b), a musicologist, dared to contemplate music *as* performance and pondered the possibilities of treating pieces of music as "scripts" rather than as texts or works. Auslander (2013), a performance studies scholar, subsequently set out to forge a new "discursive space" at the crossroads of the two fields, but he has met with some resistance. Performance studies could provide the antidote to the textualist orientation that would allow musicologists to "embrace the full implications of considering performance as constitutive of music" (Auslander 2013: 350), but even the most interdisciplinary among them will only go as far as advocating complementarity; musicologists continue to claim particular insight into sound and the "music itself" but readily acknowledge that performance studies can better attend to the social meanings that arise through performance (352). Auslander (355) rejects this distinction between "what music is and what it does" as a false dichotomy, arriving at the much more sociological position that "music *is* what musicians *do*."

It is therefore fitting that Auslander (2006) turns to Goffman to develop a performer-centered theory of musical performance. While he provocatively contends that "what musicians perform first and foremost is not music, but their own identities as musicians" (2006: 102), he still avoids a stand-off with musicology; unlike Small, he does not deny the normative status of musical works but treats them instead as part of the expressive equipment musicians use to create their personae. Auslander (102) also avoids making Frith's mistake of declaring performativity a genre-specific quality; instead, he insists that "all kinds of musicians (that is, singers, instrumentalists, conductors) in all genres (that is, classical, jazz, rock, etc.) enact personae in their performances." For example, self-effacing accompanists and anonymous members of a symphony orchestra are performing identities; they are simply more difficult to recognize because the defining characteristic of their personae is obscurity.

I have arrived at a similar position in my own work (McCormick 2006, 2009). By casting music as a mode of social performance, I am suggesting that sociologists have not gone far enough in suggesting that music is a resource in social action; music is in itself a social process through which social "actors, individually or in concert, display for others the meaning of their social situation" (Alexander 2004: 429). The cultural pragmatics model that I have modified for the analysis of musical performance distinguishes six elements of performance: the systems of collective representations, which comprise the cultural background for a performance and the components of the scripts; actors who enact the script and display meanings; the audience(s) for whom the performance is presented; the means of symbolic production including expressive equipment required to put on the performance; the *mise-en-scène*, which refers to the sequencing in time and space involved in bringing a script to life; and social power, which refers to the differential distribution of symbolic means and the freedom of social groups to create, perform, observe and evaluate performances. What this approach adds to the "presentation of musical self" explored by Auslander and the "ritualist" approaches described earlier is a macro-sociological dimension that can account for the dynamics of ritual-like processes in contemporary fragmented societies. What remains to be seen is whether a meaning-centered approach of this sort, given its potential for incorporating technical knowledge on sound, non-verbal communication and the "music itself," will ease musicologists' discomfort regarding performance, "extra-musical" context and the idea of music as an event.

Notes

1   A second version was published several years later. See Sudnow and Dreyfus (2001).

2   The "new" musicology was much more receptive to Small's critique, but this subfield also kept its distance from sociology despite its critical stance and the "social turn" that defined its early research agenda. Martin (2006: 33) has bluntly pointed out the consequences of this missed opportunity:

> while, in principle, interchange across disciplinary boundaries is to be welcomed, it has to be said that the sociologists' respect for the professional competencies and concerns of musicians and musicologists has not always been reciprocated. Indeed, as seen from the sociological side of the fence, a good deal of recent work on the social analysis of music, while usually interesting and often stimulating, is ultimately disappointing owing to the authors' evident lack of familiarity with the contours of contemporary sociological discourse and a consequent inability to engage with it.

3   MIDI controllers are available for other instruments, and pitch-to-MIDI conversion systems have improved, but the vast majority of studies using this technology have been conducted on the piano because it brings several advantages: its percussive character lends itself well to the analysis of timing; measurements can be taken unobtrusively; and the equipment has been commercially available (Clarke 2004).

4   Hennion (2003) has made a similar point about the role of recordings in jazz. Enthusiasts for the genre often argue that jazz, as an improvisational art form, is much freer than classical music because it is an oral tradition rather than a notated tradition. Hennion warns against accepting this contrast at face value:

> busy adorning the object of her love with these praises, the jazz lover forgets that this splendid transgression of centuries of written music did not come about by going back to the oral sources of a traditional music that

cannot be written down on paper, but on the contrary by going forward with the use of new means to overfix music, through a medium that no former genre could lean on: jazz has been written by recordings. (87)

References

Alexander, J.C. 2004. "Cultural Pragmatics: Social Performance Between Ritual and Strategy." *Sociological Theory* 22(4): 527–573.

Atkinson, P. 2004. "Performance, Culture and the Sociology of Education." *International Studies in Sociology of Education* 14(2):147–165.

———. 2006. *Everyday Arias: An Operatic Ethnography.* Lanham: AltaMira Press.

———. 2010. "Making Opera Work: Bricolage and the Management of Dramaturgy." *Music and Arts in Action* 3(1): 3–19.

Auslander, P. 2006. "Musical Personae." *TDR/The Drama Review* 50(1): 100–119.

———. 2013. "Afterword: Music as Performance: The Disciplinary Dilemma Revisited." In *Taking it to the Bridge: Music as Performance*, eds. N. Cook and R. Pettengill, 349–357. Ann Arbor: University of Michigan Press.

Bateson, G. 1973. *Steps to an Ecology of Mind.* St. Albans: Granada.

Bayley, A., ed. 2010. *Recorded Music: Performance, Culture and Technology.* Cambridge: Cambridge University Press.

Becker, H.S. 1974. "Art as Collective Action." *American Sociological Review* 39(6): 767–776.

———. 1982. *Art Worlds.* Berkeley: University of California Press.

Berry, W. 1989. *Musical Structure and Performance.* New Haven: Yale University Press.

Born, G. 1995. *Rationalizing Culture: IRCAM, Boulez, and the Institutionalization of the Musical Avant-Garde.* Berkeley: University of California Press.

Bowen, J.A. 1999. "Finding the Music in Musicology: Performance History and Musical Works." In *Rethinking Music*, eds. N. Cook and M. Everist, 424–451. Oxford: Oxford University Press.

Brown, C. 1999. *Classical and Romantic Performing Practice 1750–1900.* Oxford: Oxford University Press.

Butt, J. 2002. *Playing With History: The Historical Approach to Musical Performance.* Cambridge: Cambridge University Press.

Clarke, E. 2004. "Empirical Methods in the Study of Performance." In *Empirical Musicology: Aims, Methods, Prospects*, eds. E. Clarke and N. Cook, 77–102. Oxford: Oxford University Press.

Cook, N. 2001a. "Analysing Performance and Performing Analysis." In *Rethinking Music*, eds. N. Cook and M. Everist, 239–261. New York: Oxford University Press.

———. 2001b. "Between Process and Product: Music and/as Performance." *Music Theory Online* 7(2): n.p.

———. 2013a. *Beyond the Score: Music as Performance.* New York: Oxford University Press.

———. 2013b. "Bridging the Unbridgeable? Empirical Musicology and Interdisciplinary Performance Studies." In *Taking It to the Bridge: Music as Performance*, eds. N. Cook and R. Pettengill, 70–85. Ann Arbor: University of Michigan Press.

Davidson, J.W. 1993. "Visual Perception of Performance Manner in the Movements of Solo Musicians." *Psychology of Music* 21(2): 103–113.

Dempsey, N.P. 2008. "Hook-Ups and Train Wrecks: Contextual Parameters and the Coordination of Jazz Interactions." *Symbolic Interaction* 31(1): 57–75.

Donington, R. 1977. *The Interpretation of Early Music.* London: Faber and Faber.

Dunsby, J. 1989. "Guest Editorial: Performance and Analysis of Music." *Music Analysis* 8(1/2): 5–20.

Frith, S. 1996. *Performing Rites: On the Value of Popular Music.* Cambridge: Harvard University Press.

Garfinkel, H. 1967. "Passing and the Managed Achievement of Sex Status in an Inter-sexed Person, Part 1." In *Studies in Ethnomethodology*, 116–185. Englewood Cliffs: Prentice-Hall.

Goffman, E. 1959. *The Presentation of Self in Everyday Life.* Garden City: Doubleday.

Hall, S. and T. Jefferson, eds. 1976. *Resistance Through Rituals: Youth Subcultures in Post-War Britain.* London: Hutchinson.

Hennion, A. 2001. "Music Lovers: Taste as Performance." *Theory, Culture and Society* 18(5): 1–22.

———. 2003. "Music and Mediation: Toward a New Sociology of Music." In *The Cultural Study of Music: A Critical Introduction*, eds. M. Clayton, T. Herbert and R. Middleton, 80–91. New York: Routledge.

Johnson, P. 2002. "The Legacy of Recordings." In *Musical Performance: A Guide to Understanding*, ed. J. Rink, 197–212. Cambridge: Cambridge University Press.

Kenyon, N., ed. 1988. *Authenticity and Early Music: A Symposium.* Oxford: Oxford University Press.

Kingsbury, H. 1988. *Music, Talent, and Performance: A Conservatory Cultural System.* Philadelphia: Temple University Press.

Knighton, T. and D. Fallows, eds. 1992. *Companion to Medieval and Renaissance Music*. New York: Schirmer Books.

Lee, J. 2009. "Escaping Embarrassment: Face-Work in the Rap Cipher." *Social Psychology Quarterly* 72(4): 306–24.

Leech-Wilkinson, D. 2009. "Musicology and Performance." In *Music's Intellectual History: Founders, Followers, and Fads*, eds. Z. Blazekovic and B.D. Mackenzie, 791–804. New York: Répertoire International de Littérature Musicale.

_____. 2012. "Compositions, Scores, Performances, Meanings." *Music Theory Online* 18(1): 1–17.

Lerdahl, F. 1988. "Cognitive Constraints on Compositional Systems." In *Generative Processes in Music: The Psychology of Performance, Improvisation, and Composition*, ed. J.A. Sloboda, 231–259. Oxford: Oxford University Press.

Lester, J. 1995. "Performance and Analysis: Interaction and Interpretation." In *The Practice of Performance: Studies in Musical Interpretation*, ed. J. Rink, 197–216. Cambridge: Cambridge University Press.

Martin, P.J. 2006. *Music and the Sociological Gaze: Art Worlds and Cultural Production*. Manchester: Manchester University Press.

McCormick, L. 2006. "Music as Social Performance." In *Myth, Meaning, and Performance: Toward a New Cultural Sociology of the Arts*, eds. R. Eyerman and L. McCormick, 121–144. Boulder: Paradigm Publishers.

_____. 2009. "Higher, Faster, Louder: Representations of the International Music Competition." *Cultural Sociology* 3(1): 5–30.

_____. 2012. "Music Sociology in a New Key." In *The Oxford Handbook of Cultural Sociology*, eds. J.C. Alexander, R.N. Jacobs and P. Smith, 722–744. New York: Oxford University Press.

Nooshin, L., ed. 2014. *The Ethnomusicology of Western Art Music*. London: Routledge.

Nylander, E. 2014. "Mastering the Jazz Standard: Sayings and Doings of Artistic Valuation." *American Journal of Cultural Sociology* 2(1): 66–96.

Peterson, R., ed. 1976. *The Production of Culture*. Beverly Hills: Sage Publications.

Peterson, R. and N. Anand. 2004. "The Production of Culture Perspective." *Annual Review of Sociology* 30: 311–334.

Rink, J. 2002. "Analysis and (or?) Performance." In *Musical Performance: A Guide to Understanding*, 35–58. Cambridge: Cambridge University Press..

Santoro, M. 2008. "Culture As (And After) Production." *Cultural Sociology* 2(1): 7–31.

Scarborough, R.C. 2012. "Managing Challenges on the Front Stage: The Face-Work Strategies of Musicians." *Poetics* 40(6): 542–64.

Small, C. 1998. *Musicking: The Meanings of Performing and Listening*. Hanover: Wesleyan University Press.

Sudnow, D. 1978. *Ways of the Hand: The Organization of Improvised Conduct*. Cambridge: Harvard University Press.

Sudnow, D. and H.L. Dreyfus. 2001. *Ways of the Hand: A Rewritten Account*. Cambridge: MIT Press.

Taruskin, R. 1995. *Text and Act: Essays on Music and Performance*. New York: Oxford University Press.

Tsay, C.-J. 2013. "Sight Over Sound in the Judgment of Music Performance." *Proceedings of the National Academy of Sciences* 110(36): 14580–14585.

West, C. and D.H. Zimmerman. 1987. "Doing Gender." *Gender and Society* 1(2): 125–151.

12

Production Perspectives

Marco Santoro

Stressing the eminently *social* nature of musical experience, sociology as a discipline has contributed concepts and models useful for capturing the related phenomena of music production, consumption and appreciation: in short, the *social organization* of musical life. Three approaches or perspectives have hegemonized the sociological study of the arts in the last few decades, exerting influence on the field of popular music studies as well: the production-of-culture perspective, the art world approach and the cultural field theory. Others concepts or ideas, such as "subculture" and "scene," have informed in recent times research on the social organization of popular music (Straw 1991, Gelder and Thornton 1997, Bennett 1999, Bennett and Peterson 2004). However, it is around these three principal concepts—production of culture, art world, and field—that the sociological debate on arts and music has been mainly articulated, and the most fruitful and influential insights have been developed (see Alexander 2003; van Maanen 2009).

The expression "production of culture" identifies a perspective originally developed from the field of industrial sociology in the 1970s and 1980s, mainly through the work of the late US sociologist Richard A. Peterson (see DiMaggio 2000, Santoro 2008a, 2008b). The worlds of jazz, rock and especially of country music originally provided the empirical ground for the development of this perspective, which Peterson has been successful in generalizing on many occasions beyond the boundaries of his own case studies (Peterson 1976, 1979, 1994, 1997; Peterson and Anand 2004). In the years during which the production-of-culture perspective developed as an intellectual movement, it strongly influenced the formation of a specialized sub-discipline of sociology devoted to the study of culture: the sociology of culture (sometimes called "cultural sociology"). This production perspective has numerous affinities and even some historical links with the two other influential approaches developed in sociology to account for the arts. These are the "art world" approach proposed by Becker in a series of studies culminating in the now classic book *Art Worlds* (1982), and the sociological analysis of cultural production developed by the French scholar Pierre Bourdieu beginning in the 1960s (Bourdieu 1966, but see especially Bourdieu 1992) and grounded in both structuralism and theories of practice.

While the "art world" approach focuses on interpersonal ties and networks explored mainly at the micro-social level, the production perspective shared by Peterson and Bourdieu focuses on meso-social and macro-social levels of institutional life with a strong emphasis that is particularly explicit in Bourdieu on *objective* relations, that is, relations existing behind and beyond the agents' consciousness and their concrete, effectual interactions. At the same time, while Peterson's perspective shares with Bourdieu's a focus on social structure, it is less critically oriented, less theoretically argued and more open to historical and ethnographical contingencies. In short, these three approaches to the sociological analysis of the collective dimensions of cultural, artistic and musical life have both commonalities—which contribute to the sense of consistency and soundness they convey—and differences—which explains why they persist as distinct and somewhat competing ways of undertaking cultural research and making sense of its outcomes.

While emphasizing the production dimensions of cultural practices, these three approaches do not neglect other dimensions such as consumption, education and evaluation. We could say "production" is a strategic point of access into a sphere—the cultural sphere—which has long been subject to "unsociological" if not "antisociological" criticism. These criticisms tend to come from those for whom the notions of individual creative talent and the inherent value of artworks are unquestionable and reflective of phenomena that in their opinion are beyond the realm of social constitution. Shifting the focus to production has been a main strategy by which sociologists have attempted to enter this realm and overcome the legacy of traditional and conservative approaches to understanding culture espoused by the humanities (see Abbott 2004). It is against this backdrop that these concepts and perspectives need to be assessed.

The Production-of-Culture Perspective

As envisioned and practiced by Peterson and his close followers, the production-of-culture perspective focuses on the ways in which the meanings of symbolic phenomena (or cultural objects) are significantly shaped by the environments within which they are created, distributed, evaluated, taught, preserved and even consumed. Indeed, albeit originally conceived of as a tool for studying the production of cultural items, the perspective has subsequently been extended to situations, environments and places where cultural production is not consciously sought—for example, the production of identities and lifestyles by ordinary (and usually young) people through the recombination of cultural industries products in highly original and sometimes subversive ways. This application of the production-of-culture perspective creates a link with British cultural studies' emphasis on forms of symbolic and ritual resistance to the dominant culture. The idea of "production" referred to in this approach is therefore a very broad one, and includes all those processes and actions that contribute to molding the cultural object, including the production of meanings through appropriation by consumers, a practice Peterson (2000) calls "auto-production."

The cultural objects investigated under the aegis of this perspective are many and different, and drawn from different historical epochs. The initial focus was on expressive symbols such as art works, scientific reports, instances of popular cultures such as songs and soap operas, religious practices and doctrines, legal judgments, news, novels and so on. However, along the way the perspective came to be increasingly applied to symbolic structures and forms generated not by purposeful action on the part of some professional cultural producer, but to symbolic phenomena existing as a by-product or unintended effect of the collective activities of ordinary people in their everyday lives, be they organized in subcultures or networks (Crane 1992, White 1993, Peterson and Anand 2004).

The historical, intellectual relevance of the production-of-culture approach lies in its challenge to the long dominant idea in the social and human sciences that cultures (mainly conceived as values and norms) and social structures mirror or reflect each other, a view subscribed to by most traditional Marxists and functionalist sociologists (including the prominent social theorist Talcott Parsons) but apparent also in the humanities. Breaking with this well-established reflective or mirror model, the production perspective conceives of "culture" and "social structure" as interdependent but relatively autonomous spheres in an ever-changing "patchwork" (see Peterson 1979, see also Griswold 1994).

In fact, one of the main features of the perspective, which has strongly contributed to its success, is its catholic gaze and its openness toward theories and methods used in other branches of sociology and the social sciences. Historical, quantitative and ethnographic techniques have all been used by practitioners of this approach. So have conceptual tools drawn from a wide range of intellectual traditions, including industrial economics, structural anthropology, neo-Weberian theory, ritual theory and Marxism. Concepts borrowed from symbolic interactionism, neoinstitutional theory of organizations, and European sociological and cultural theory (such as British subcultural theory and Bourdieu's generative structuralism) have also contributed to the development of the perspective. Over the years, this has made the perspective theoretically more sophisticated and attentive to both micro-interactions and large historical forces. It can be thought of as a central insight, and not some preferred method or self-sufficient theory that sets its boundaries vis-à-vis other schools or ways of studying culture. The approach's distinctiveness is to be found in its focus on the *organizational features* of social activities conceived of as factors influencing the structure and form of cultural items. Every method and tool that can help in exploring and studying these features is welcomed by its practitioners.

In a more narrow sense, however, the production perspective could be described as the creative application principally of organizational theory, institutional economics (for example, Caves 2000) and, more recently, network analysis (for example, White 1993) to the study of cultural objects. These objects can be thought of as the more or less intended products of the concerted activities of individuals acting in organizations, industrial settings and social circles. All such practices can be conceived of as "systems of cultural production," susceptible to analysis through the application of this perspective. The central tenet of the approach is that the variations of these systems are key for explaining variations in cultural objects.

As variation in cultural production is a major focus of analysis, it is not surprising that historical change is at the heart of the perspective, both as a topic and as a testing device. Cultural production systems normally change slowly, but rapid changes that drastically alter the aesthetic principles of some cultural forms are also possible, as illustrated by the pioneering study of French impressionism by Harrison and Cynthia White, *Canvases and Careers* (1965). Peterson contributed to the study of cultural change in the main through his research on the Nashville music industry. The major outcomes of this research are contained in his book, *Creating Country Music: Fabricating Authenticity* (1997).

The production of culture, then, is a perspective and not a formalized theory. The closest to the latter is the so-called "six facets model" delineated by Peterson in a series of publications. According to this model, six factors can be identified as being of relevance to the process of cultural production. These include law and regulation, technology, industrial structure or field, organizational structure, occupational careers, and the consumer market. These six facets are not strictly theorized in their differential relations and priorities, but are considered together as parts of an interdependent production network whose structure has to be described and assessed locally (Peterson and Anand 2004; see also Ryan 2007). The emphasis on contingency is in this sense one of the main features of the approach, and this distinguishes it from established functionalist approaches, Marxist-oriented cultural theory, and even Bourdieu's sociology of cultural production (see below).

Law and regulation impact on the ways in which cultural practices and styles develop. For example, copyright laws have often influenced the kinds of fiction and songs that are published, while notions of intellectual property influence the range of cultural expressions, both inhibiting (when restrictive) and promoting (when enlarging). One of the major institutions here is censorship. This can have a direct impact on cultural content. In addition, regulation of ownership (for example, of media) as well as policies of deregulation can influence the degree of diversity and variety of cultural products. *Technology* identifies the tools and means through which people and institutions communicate and through which cultural content circulates. Changes in technology profoundly affect the culture that can be produced, providing new creative opportunities or making previous ways of producing obsolete. Technology includes innovations in media such as radio, phonograph records, movies, television, electric musical instruments and digitalized communication, as well as pre-modern and modern devices such as writing and printing. To the extent that cultural production occurs in organizations, both *organizational structures* and the larger *organizational fields* (or industries) in which production processes are embedded can influence the cultural product's form and content. For example, there is a difference between the many small firms that compete in producing a diversity of products and the few vertically integrated oligarchical firms that mass-produce a few standardized items. Another contrast can be drawn between for-profit organizations, which are typical of cultural industries specializing in large-scale production, and not-for-profit organizations, which are commonly established in high culture arts to reduce commercial pressures and create a haven from conventional market forces (DiMaggio 1982).

As Becker (1982) also emphasizes, work is a crucial factor in the production of art and the ways in which work is organized also have an impact on cultural objects. *Occupational careers* can be quite diversified (for example, creative careers, craft-like careers, bureaucratic careers and entrepreneurial careers). Careers tend to be more or less standardized. Less conventional careers tend to generate innovation in so far as they attract creative people likely to challenge conventions and rules. Finally, there are *consumer markets*, typically conceived of by Peterson as being constructed by producers in order to organize, understand and predict consumer taste. It is characteristic of this approach that it accounts for the subjectivities of consumers from the point of view of production as "product images" (see Ryan and Peterson 1982).

The production-of-culture perspective has been developed by Peterson and his associates (including sociologist Paul DiMaggio) through a series of studies on jazz, rock, country music and, especially, the recording industry. While sensitive to macro- and meso-levels of social organization, the production-of-culture perspective has also inspired research at the micro level (see Fine 1992, Hughes 2000, Bennett and Peterson 2004). If Peterson's ideas on culture as a phenomenon of production have been influential well beyond the study of music (see Santoro 2008a for an evaluation of their contribution to the development and institutionalization of cultural sociology at large), their impact has been pivotal for the legitimation of popular music and the music industry as mainstream research topics in sociology in the United States and elsewhere (see Dowd 2007 for a broad and enlightening international review of work in this area).

Becker's Art World Approach

A common wisdom among sociologists is that Becker has developed a theory with respect to what Peterson has propounded through empirical research. In fact, things are more complex. Even if Peterson has never claimed to be developing a theory but only a "perspective," it is clear his work goes beyond a mere collection of empirical case studies and generalizations derived therefrom. His work cannot be reduced to a simple listing of variables or concepts. The production-of-culture perspective is grounded on a set of assumptions about the nature of cultural phenomena and the agency of cultural creators and consumers. It has generated a series of concepts useful in analyzing the social processes of the production and consumption of cultural items. Finally, it has developed hypotheses about the workings and the transformation of those same cultural items as embedded in larger and changing environments.[1]

Becker's approach to the sociology of art (and music) has a different background and genesis. It is firmly rooted in the well-known Chicago sociological tradition and, more specifically, that brand of Chicago sociology commonly referred to as *symbolic interactionism*. As a student of Blumer (who was in turn a student and assistant of George Herbert Mead, a leading proponent of the US philosophical tradition of pragmatism), Becker inherited some basic principles of this theoretical tradition, that is, the centrality of meaning and of human interaction in the social fabric (for a good introduction to symbolic interactionism, see Charon 2007). In addition, as a fellow student of another influential teacher at the University of Chicago in the 1940s and 1950s—Everett C. Hughes—Becker absorbed a second crucial ingredient of the Chicago tradition: the ethnographic approach to the study of social life, together with a special concern for the marginal and/or "deviant" social institutions that Hughes considered to be strategic research sites for the cultivation of a sociological imagination. In particular, Hughesian social research focused on occupations, including low status ones, as essential social institutions through which people make their living and participate in society. Work is conceived, not only as a source of income, but also as a crucial ingredient for any social activity (on the assumption that even that which is entertainment or free time for one person is usually work for someone else). This focus on work is also a crucial ingredient of the art world approach. The idea is that making art is in its core a work activity, an occupation, and that an artwork is something made by people cooperating together through work.

An art world may thus be defined as "the network of people whose cooperative activity, organized via their joined knowledge of conventional means of doing things, produces the kind of works that art world is noted for" (Becker 1982: x). The circularity of the definition is a symptom of what the art world approach is, which is to say that it is, not a logically organized sociological theory but simply "an exploration of the potentialities" of an idea. To be sure, the term and possibly the idea of "art world" is not Becker's invention, but is drawn from philosophy and aesthetic theory, notably Danto's and Dickie's so-called institutional theory of art (Danto 1964, Dickie 1974). As a sociologist, however, Becker is concerned less with abstract concepts than with actual people doing concrete things in real-world settings. He sees concepts as useful devices for making sense of empirical material in the form of historical documents or actual observations *in situ*. In a word, what Becker claims to add to the institutional aesthetic theory is "meat," that is, human actors engaged in human activities.

It is a crucial point of the art world approach as developed by Becker that human activities are "cooperative activities" and that the social worlds where art is made (created, produced, distributed, received, consumed) are made up of networks of persons interacting with each other, and among whom exists a consensus sufficient to enable collective work. As is clear, full autonomy is deemed impossible for artists in the art world approach. Artists always have to rely on the work of other people—especially those Becker calls *support personnel* (Becker 1982: 77): craftsmen, technicians, organizers, copy editors and even service personnel inasmuch, for example, as they bring a cup of coffee every morning to the writer, thus creating the conditions necessary for the production of the work of art. The artist is, indeed, just one of the many agents who contribute in Becker's eyes to the production of the artwork—and they may not necessarily be the most important agent. More precisely, we should say the artist is just someone to whom a label (that of "artist") has been successfully applied—not in any way different from the application of the label of "deviant" or "criminal" to certain other individuals, classes of individuals who formed the subject of a previous seminal book by Becker, the now classic *Outsiders* (1963). It is only through communicative interaction, the negotiation of meanings among interacting persons, that something called "art" could be produced and someone called "the artist" might be acknowledged. But what kind of work and how much work must someone do in order to be recognized as an artist or for their work to be recognized as artwork? Becker makes a fine distinction between the work of all the cooperating people involved in making an artwork and what he names the "core activity," that is, that bundle of tasks "without which the work would not be art" (Becker 1982: 25). This is not an easy distinction to manage empirically. The problem is that it is not clear what exactly is or should be that core bundle of tasks. These tasks change over time and there is evidence that the core activity may be minimal, for example, the addition of a signature on a urinal (Duchamp's famous and scandalous artwork, *Fountain*) or staying still and silent in front of a piano for four minutes and thirty-three seconds (*4' 33"*, the famous John Cage composition for piano). Indeed, Becker knows that people can sometimes stop cooperating and claim more credit or authority than is appropriate. This can produce disagreement and conflict. In contrast to Bourdieu—who considers disagreement, conflict and competing claims to occupy an important social status (the common stuff of social life), and consensus to be the more or less stable effect of symbolic as well as material domination—Becker has a more optimistic view. This view is not so much a view of human nature as of the potentially infinite chances to make things and "find one's way" in social life (see Becker and Pessin 2006). More than constraints and conflicts, Becker (1982: x) focuses his "exploration of the potential of the idea of an art world" on opportunities and cooperative interactions, looking for their conditions of existence and their variations one from another.

This introduces us to another central concept of the art world approach: the notion of *convention*. This is drawn also from a tradition of analytical philosophical thinking (Lewis 1969) but reshaped by Becker in more sociological terms. Conventions are what make cooperative interactions and links socially possible, establishing the norms and standards for artists and their support personnel, audiences and the people who manage the relationships between them, often known as distributors. Conventions determine which materials are to be used, which forms are appropriate, and which rights and obligations pertain to the various agents of the art world. It is because of a previous knowledge of conventions as standardized and agreed upon ways of doing things that, for example, people in a jam session who have never have met before can produce music, or that people watching a film in a cinema or a drama in a theater may understand and enjoy their sometimes subtle contents and stylized forms. Conventions, or shared ways of doing things together are, indeed, the stuff of culture. What is produced is contingent upon conventions. This makes it easier to produce conventional artworks than experimental ones. However, there is always room for challenge, transgression and innovation in Becker's view, even if all situations or arrangements are not equally suitable to encourage such activity. Artists can be classified according to their different dispositions toward innovation on a sort of scale, from the more conventional artists (such as the "integrated professional" or the "folk artist," both accepting established ways of doing things even if in two very different contexts, the first modern and industrialized, the second traditional and rural) to the less conventional ones (such as the "naïve artist," who innovates because they have no real knowledge of conventions, and the "maverick," who consciously and intentionally goes beyond established conventions).

The art world approach has been applied to the study of popular music by Becker himself, as well as some of his students. In a sense, it is from the study of popular music, and in particular of jazz (especially more commercial and dance-oriented jazz) that Becker in the early 1950s began his sociological exploration of the social world of the arts. This exploration eventually produced his 1982 book on "art worlds." Building on his early ethnographic studies of jazz musicians, and adding new empirical evidence, Becker has recently focused on jazz improvisation as a collective action made possible by the development of conventions. These conventions include standard works that everybody participating or aspiring to participate in the jazz art world has to know and master (Becker and Faulkner 2009). Becker's ideas have inspired studies of rock music, especially at a grass roots level (Bennett 1980), as well as of the recording industry (for example, Kealy 1990 [1979]). The idea of the art world has also been appropriated by British scholar Simon Frith in his book *Performing Rites* (1996) as a conceptual device for distinguishing among different spheres of music appreciation as well as between the spheres of production and distribution. This has given rise in Frith's work to the notions of the art music world, the commercial music world and the folk music world. Another British sociologist, Peter Martin (1995, 2006), has built around the art world approach a general framework for the sociological study of music. US sociologist Paul Lopes (2002) has used the approach to make sense of the social and cultural transformations of jazz music since its inception, especially the rise of jazz to the status of "art." In recent times, Becker's ideas have been especially influential in France, where there has been a marked contribution to the development of the sociology of music more as a truly sociological enterprise than as a derivative of aesthetic theory (for example, Buscatto 2007a, 2007b; Perrenoud 2007). Indeed, as Becker himself has recognized, the art world approach has been informed also by his reading of early French research in the sociology of art, especially painting (Moulin 1967). It in addition has affinities with Latour's (2005) actor-network theory. All this makes Becker's work prone to a favorable reception by French scholars. But probably the most extensive application of the idea of the art world to the study of popular music is to be found in British anthropologist Ruth Finnegan's (1989) ethnographic research on the music life of Milton Keynes (UK). Finnegan used Becker's conceptual framework in order to map the articulation of music life in its various spheres (from classic to folk to rock to jazz) as well as to reconstruct the different links and paths through which those segments are interconnected.

Cultural Production as a Field (in Practice): The Contribution of Bourdieu

In sociological writing, the idea of art world is often compared to another idea: that of the "field" as elaborated by French sociologist Pierre Bourdieu. Indeed, it is also because of its apparent suitability as an alternative to Bourdieu's sociological theory that some French scholars have felt themselves encouraged to accept Becker's approach. Whereas the art world approach presents itself as sensitive to contingency, change and (inter)subjectivity, Bourdieu's sociology is heir to a structuralist vision of the social world where actors appear as both self-interested (strategically pursuing status and distinction) and constrained by social circumstances out of their control. However, things are indeed a bit more complex, as we shall see. In its most simple formulation (see Bourdieu and Wacquant 1992, Bourdieu 1992), a field consists of a set of objective, historically given relations between positions anchored in certain forms of power (or capitals, as Bourdieu says). What people do is contingent upon their position in a field, that is, the volume and composition of capital(s) that they command. Fields exist everywhere human activities (or practices) are sufficiently differentiated and a certain degree of autonomy has been gained, for example, through the establishment of specialized institutions. Bourdieu suggests looking at a field as if it were a game with its own rules and stakes. For a field to develop, a set of rules and a special stake, as well as a set of boundaries that separate the field (and its practitioners) from other fields, have to develop and to be accepted by at least a few agents. To give just one example, a field of rock music has developed—in the United States, in the United Kingdom, then in other countries, and finally at the transnational level. At the same time, within the more general field of music, a certain set of rules and stakes specifically associated with rock as a special kind of music, and with rock musicians as specialized performers, became differentiated from the more general rules and stakes at work in the musical field as a whole. This is no more than to delineate a geometric locus wherein a series of specialized music (sub)fields, for example, classical music, opera, rock, jazz, rap, techno, and so on, intersect and variously interact (see Savage 2006). What the concept of "field" suggests, then, is that it is not enough for a musical innovation to be conceived and articulated to be established and recognized as a new style or even a genre. It also needs the emergence and institutionalization of a new system of social relations, practices and identities (which Bourdieu tries to capture with his twin concepts of *habitus* and field). What the concept of field underlines, then, is the temporal embeddedness of any cultural practice, as well as the historical nature of any cultural field (see Steinmetz 2011). This is what makes

Bourdieu's structuralism different from other structuralist theories, that is, the fact that it is a *genetic* form of structuralism (Bourdieu 1986).

An important point is that a few invariant features are common to all fields (these are their structural properties). One is the antagonism between those who are already well established in the field, and those who are newcomers. The former have an interest in conservation and orthodoxy, the latter in transformation and transgression. Antagonisms of this sort are common in (popular) music history, and become especially prominent when new genres or styles emerge. Such antagonisms can also be found inside genres that have gained a certain degree of cultural legitimation ("old school" versus "posers" and so on). A second structural property is that anyone in the field has an interest in playing the game of the field, which involves acting in ways that build cultural capital and legitimation, and that effectively serve to preserve the existence of the field.

Indeed, as this outline already suggests, the concepts of "world" and "field" share a few features that allow them to overlap while not becoming interchangeable (see Alexander 2003; Crossley and Bottero 2011). Both are spatial metaphors, both are focused on relations, both are sensitive to the institutional dimensions of social life, both are strategic devices in a sociological understanding of culture and art that is focused on production more than consumption, and both are eager to debunk traditional visions of art as a "special," "superior," "spiritual" sphere. Like Becker, Bourdieu also considers art as a very mundane activity driven by often prosaic and profane interests and motivations. But whereas Becker emphasizes cooperative links, usually at the personal, micro level, Bourdieu gives primacy to agonistic and typically impersonal, or *super*personal, "objective," relationships—that is, relations that exist independently of agents' consciousness and their concrete interactions (this is something Bourdieu inherits from both Marxism and Levi-Straussian structuralism). Indeed, the concept of field strives to precisely capture the deep structure of that which the concept of the art world describes at its surface: from the field perspective, the art world as a network of cooperative links is just the visible and emergent side of a much more complex and structured system of relations among not so much individuals as positions. It is the structure of the field—a structure to be discovered and reconstructed by the scholar and not immediately observable in real life—that governs and drives production as well as consumption and appreciation of what the field recognizes as art.

What for Becker is an indefinite world of opportunities and chances is for Bourdieu a "space of possibles" which is finite and at risk of not being exploited: not everyone can do the same thing in the same space, as not everyone is equally endowed with resources (capitals) and, above all, not everyone possesses the "right" *habitus*, that set of acquired dispositions through which agents classify the world and perceive it. When *habitus* and field are complicit, agents act as if they were following a rule, the right rule, even if there is no rule or they are unaware of the rule. But *habitus* and field are not always so in line. This creates space for failure as well as for innovation.

It is the structure of the field, and what happens in this structure through conflict and struggle, which *makes* the field as a structured space of the possible, which defines *what* can be and what is "art" and who can be legitimately identified as an artist. Conflict and struggle occur among people differently placed within the various positions of the field's structure and variously endowed with both capital(s) and *habitus*. Every field has its own specific rules and principles, its own specific forms of capital in the form of valuable sets of resources. In the rock music field, for example, this capital takes the form of the knowledge and mastery of rock music traditions and rock music techniques, thereby giving rise to status. In the jazz field this same knowledge and skill would not work as resources to the same degree, if at all. However, both fields have the same basic structure and, indeed, all fields function according to the same general logics. These may be summarized as the struggle for differentiation and for achieving the greatest share of legitimacy or authority inside the field. Bourdieu insists that to exist in a field means to distinguish oneself from others who compete for the same or even greater attention or status. What makes the field so important for Bourdieu is, however, less its form than its effects. As a space of positions a field has a structure or even *is* a structured space. What people make or like or appreciate or accept with respect to adopting their position is contingent upon the location of their position in this space. Every field has a center as well as margins and boundaries, and exactly where these boundaries are to be traced (that is, where the limits of the field are) is one of the main stakes of the games that are played in the field. (Indeed, Bourdieu often makes use of the metaphor of the game to make sense of the field.) Being at the margins is different than being at the center, and even if someone would prefer to stay at the margins (and this is hardly usual), this choice would have consequences for what they like, what they produce, what they evaluate as worthwhile, what they can expect from critics and audiences.

Peterson was well aware of what was happening in France around Bourdieu when he set forth his production-of-culture perspective in the 1970s. Indeed, we can consider Bourdieu's work on cultural production and consumption as a crucial source for the US renovation in the 1970s and 1980s of a sociological analysis of culture around Peterson and his followers (see Santoro 2008a, 2008b), as well as for the natural linkage of Peterson's production-of-culture approach to sociological institutional theory. (This not to be confounded with aesthetic institutional theory as exemplified by Danto and especially Dickie.) Like Bourdieu, Peterson has a strong sense of structure, surely stronger than Becker, who relies upon a sociological tradition (that of interactionism together with Chicago ethnography) more sensitive to process and action than structure, to change than persistence or reproduction. This does not mean that Bourdieu or Peterson are insensitive to change: both are strongly interested and, indeed, have long worked on the moments of "creation," "genesis," "revolution" and "transformation" that have literally generated, created and produced a certain field or genre, and have governed its transformation and even decline (see for example Bourdieu 1992, 2013; Peterson 1972, 1997). But what for Becker is part and parcel of social life, that is, change, is for Bourdieu—and to a lesser measure Peterson—exactly what needs to be explained and carefully reconstructed for being relatively exceptional. That which for Becker is fluid and always changing appears to Bourdieu as organized and constraining, as a source of inertia and resistance more than openness and opportunities. Changes occur, but only in special moments and within specific conditions (we could say that change for Bourdieu is always an event, something that has deep and heavy consequences and rarely happens without struggle and crisis, while for Becker it is just an occurrence, the accumulation of small modifications that can be accommodated in everyday life).

Bourdieu never produced a field analysis wholly devoted to music—neither serious nor popular music—focusing his research on other forms of culture, such as photography, literature, and painting. However, popular music—in the form of French *chanson*—is of course present in his magnum opus *Distinction* (1984) as one of the cultural genres invoked in measuring social differences in tastes. For many reasons (including a certain suspicion of popular music and popular culture that is apparent in Bourdieu's writings), French studies on popular music have been typically driven by a critical stance toward Bourdieuian sociology, and heavily influenced by symbolic interactionism and pragmatism (for example, Hennion 1993). This goes some way to explain the success of the art world approach in French studies of popular music (for notable exceptions see Fabiani 1986, Dubois and Méon 2013). The concept of field (alone or together with other concepts developed by Bourdieu such as those of cultural capital, *habitus* and practice) has nonetheless been employed as a strategic conceptual device in many empirical studies on popular music (and popular music criticism) in various countries such as the United Kingdom (Thornton 1995, Toynbee 2000, Gudmunsson et al. 2002, Savage 2006), Israel (Regev 1989), Italy (Santoro 2002, 2006), Sweden (Trondman 1990, Roe 1993), as well as in comparative studies of value in popular music (van Venrooij and Schmutz 2010).

Conclusion

One of the central criticisms advanced against the production-of-culture perspective is its relative neglect of the cultural basis of cultural production, that is, the symbolic dimension of the organizational environments in which cultural items are fabricated (Negus 1997). These environments included the aesthetic and cognitive dimensions of the production process itself (Fine 1992, Born 2010, Prior 2011). This line of research is currently pursued, *inter alia*, by so-called *production studies*, which recently emerged in media studies at the same time as capitalizing on the sociology of cultural production (see Mayer, Banks and Caldwell 2009). Another criticism is related to the neglect of the cultural object itself. Since the production of culture focuses on the social conditions of the existence of cultural objects, analysis of the latter is usually left to other disciplines whose research field is the art work itself. Musicology and art history number among these disciplines. The neglect of the work of art has been acknowledged as a real limit by practitioners of the production approach, who have recently shifted their focus to this dimension (for example, Becker, Faulkner and Kirshenblatt-Gimblett 2006; see also Griswold 1987). To be sure, the cultural object has not been totally neglected in the past—as Bourdieu's (1992) analysis of Flaubert's *The Sentimental Education* demonstrates. Peterson too has studied the lyrics contents of country songs (McLaurin and Peterson 1992) as well as the classificatory practices at work in processes of genre construction (Lena and Peterson 2008). It is true, however, that the focus of the production approach has been predominantly on contexts rather than texts, on working conditions rather than the works themselves. The latter is customarily conceived as the proper sphere of humanities. Another major criticism has been advanced by Alexander and Smith (2001), who read the perspective as an epitome of what they label "weak programs" in the sociological analysis of culture. These "weak programs" are conceived of as those research paradigms that study culture as a "soft" or non-independent variable that can only be explained with reference to "harder" social structures. In other words, Alexander and Smith argue that "weak programs" reductively view social structure as the "base" and culture as the "superstructure." This criticism is only partially fair, as people working in this tradition (Peterson included) have not been insensitive to cultural codes and texts even while focusing on contexts and environments. The strength of this research program—or family of research programs—is, indeed, precisely their focus on social structure and organizational issues in a field of study too often left to the humanities, journalism and fans with their emphasis on individual creativity, exceptional talent and (supposedly) autonomous artworks (Santoro 2011). The challenge of future studies, therefore, is to persuasively integrate a (sociologically timely) focus on social structure and social organization with the recognition as well as the understanding of other dimensions of the entire musical process, or "musicking" as Small refers to it (1998; see also Crossley and Botero 2014, Santoro and Solaroli 2015).

Note

1   Probably the better way to capture a theoretical glimpse of Peterson's work is to read it as a form of (neo)institutionalism—something his major work, *Creating Country: Fabricating Authenticity* (1997), claims openly. It is not by chance that DiMaggio, one of the major figures in contemporary sociological institutional theory (see for example DiMaggio and Powell 1983, 1991), started his academic career working with Peterson (see for example, DiMaggio and Peterson 1975, DiMaggio 2000 and Santoro 2008a).

References

Abbott, A. 2004. *Methods of Discovery: Heuristics for the Social Sciences*. New York: Norton.
Alexander, J.C. and P. Smith. 2001. "The Strong Program in Cultural Theory: Elements of a Structural Hermeneutics." In *The Handbook of Sociological Theory*, ed. J. Turner, 135–150. New York: Kluwer.

Alexander, V. 2003. *The Sociology of the Arts*. London: Wiley-Blackwell.

Becker, H.S. 1963. *Outsiders: Studies in the Sociology of Deviance*. London: Free Press.

———. 1982. *Art Worlds*. Berkeley: University of California Press.

Becker, H.S. and R.R. Faulkner. 2009. *"Do You Know. . .?" The Jazz Repertoire in Action*. Chicago: University of Chicago Press.

Becker, H.S., R.R. Faulkner and B. Kirshenblatt-Gimblett. 2006. "Editors' Introduction." In *Art from Start to Finish: Jazz, Painting, and other Improvisations*, eds. H.S. Becker, R.R. Faulkner and B. Kirshenblatt-Gimblett, 1–20. Chicago: University of Chicago Press.

Becker, H.S. and A. Pessin 2006. "A Dialogue on the Ideas of 'World' and 'Field'." *Sociological Forum* 21(2): 275–286.

Bennett, A. 1999. "Subcultures or Neo-Tribes? Rethinking the Relationship Between Youth, Style and Musical Taste." *Sociology* 33(3): 599–617.

Bennett, A. and R.A. Peterson, eds. 2004. *Music Scenes: Local, Trans-Local and Virtual*. Nashville: Vanderbilt University Press.

Bennett, H.S. 1980. *On Becoming a Rock Musician*. Amherst: University of Massachusetts Press.

Born, Georgina. 2010. "The Social and the Aesthetic: For a Post-Bourdieuian Theory of Cultural Production." *Cultural Sociology* 4(2): 171–208.

Bourdieu, P. 1966. "Champ intellectuel et projet créateur." *Les Temps Modernes* 246 (November): 865–906.

———. 1984. *Distinction: A Social Critique of the Judgement of Taste*. London: Routledge and Kegan Paul.

———. 1986. "Fieldwork in Philosophy." In *Choses Dites*. Paris: Minuit.

———. 1992. *The Field of Cultural Production: Essays on Art and Literature*. Cambridge: Polity.

———. 2013. *Manet, une révolution symbolique*. Paris: Seuil.

Bourdieu, P. and L.J.D. Wacquant. 1992. *An Invitation to Reflexive Sociology*. Chicago: University of Chicago Press.

Buscatto, M. 2007a. *Femmes du jazz: Musicalités, féminités, marginalités*. Paris: CNRS.

———. 2007b. "Contributions of Ethnography to Gendered Sociology: The French Jazz World." *Qualitative Sociology Review* 3(3): 46–58.

Caves, R.E. 2000. *Creative Industries*. Cambridge: Harvard University Press.

Charon J.M. 2007. *Symbolic Interactionism: An Introduction, An Interpretation, An Integration*, 9th ed. Upper Saddle River: Pearson Prentice Hall.

Crane, D. 1992. *The Production of Culture: Media Industries and Urban Arts*. Newbury Park: Sage.

Crossley, N. and W. Bottero. 2011. "Worlds, Fields and Networks: Becker, Bourdieu and the Structures of Social Relations." *Cultural Sociology* 5(1): 99–119.

———. 2014. "Music Worlds and Internal Goods: The Role of Convention." *Cultural Sociology*, forthcoming.

Danto, A. 1964. "The Art World." *Journal of Philosophy* 56(19): 571–584.

Dickie, G. 1974. *Arts and the Aesthetic*. Ithaca: Cornell University Press.

DiMaggio, P.J. 1982. "Cultural Entrepreneurship in Nineteenth Century Boston, I: The Creation of an Organizational Basis for High Culture in America." *Media, Culture and Society* 4(1): 33–50.

———. 2000. "The Production of Scientific Change: Richard Peterson and the Institutional Turn in Cultural Sociology." *Poetics* 28(2/3): 107–136.

DiMaggio, P.J. and R.A. Peterson. 1975. "From Region to Class, the Changing Locus of Country Music: A Test of the Massification Hypothesis." *Social Forces* 53(3): 497–506.

DiMaggio, P.J. and W.W. Powell. 1983. "The Iron Cage Revisited: Institutional Isomorphism and Collective Rationality in Organizational Fields." *American Sociological Review* 48(2): 147–160.

———. 1991. "Introduction." In *The New Institutionalism in Organizational Analysis*, eds. W.W. Powell and P.J. DiMaggio, 1–38. Chicago: University of Chicago Press.

Dowd, T. 2007. "Innovation and Diversity in Cultural Sociology: Notes on Peterson and Berger's Classic Article." *Sociologica: Italian Journal of Sociology Online* 1(1): www.sociologica.mulino.it/doi/10.2383/24213.

Dubois, V. and J-M. Méon. 2013. "The Social Conditions of Cultural Domination: Field, Sub-field and Local Spaces of Wind Music in France." *Cultural Sociology* 7(2): 127–144.

Fabiani, J-L. 1986. "Carrières improvisées: théories et pratiques de la musique de jazz en France." In *Sociologie de l'art*, ed. R. Moulin, 231–245. Paris: La Documentation française.

Fine, G.A. 1992. "The Culture of Production: Aesthetic Choices and Constraints in Culinary Work." *American Journal of Sociology* 97(5): 1268–1294.

Finnegan, R. 1989. *The Hidden Musicians: Music-Making in an English Town*. Cambridge: Cambridge University Press.

Frith, S. 1996. *Performing Rites: On the Value of Popular Music*. Cambridge: Harvard University Press.

Gelder, K. and S. Thornton, eds. 1997. *The Subcultures Reader*. London: Routledge.

Griswold, W. 1987. "The Fabrication of Meaning: Literary Interpretation in the United States, Great Britain, and the West Indies." *American Journal of Sociology* 92(5): 1077–1117.

_____. 1994. *Cultures and Societies in a Changing World*. Thousand Oaks: Pine Forge Press.

Gudmundsson, G., U. Lindberg, M. Michelsen and H. Weisethaunet. 2002. "Brit Crit: Turning Points in British Rock Criticism, 1960–1990." In *Pop Music and the Press*, ed. S. Jones, 41–64. Philadelphia: Temple University Press.

Hennion, A. 1993. *La Médiation Musicale*. Paris: Métailié.

Hughes, M. 2000. "Country Music as Impression Management: A Meditation on Fabricating Authenticity." *Poetics* 28(2/3): 185–205.

Kealy, E.R. 1990 [1979]. "From Craft to Art: The Case of Sound Mixers and Popular Music." In *On Record: Rock, Pop, and the Written Word*, eds. S. Frith and A. Goodwin, 207–220. New York: Pantheon Books.

Latour, B. 2005. *Reassembling the Social: An Introduction to Actor-Network-Theory*. Oxford: Oxford University Press.

Lena, J.C. and R.A. Peterson. 2008. "Classification as Culture: Types and Trajectories of Music Genres." *American Sociological Review* 73(5): 697–718.

Lewis, D. 1969. *Convention*. Cambridge: Harvard University Press.

Lopes, P.D. 2002. *The Rise of a Jazz Art World*. Cambridge: Cambridge University Press.

Martin, P.J. 1995. *Sounds and Society: Themes in the Sociology of Music*. Manchester: Manchester University Press.

_____. 2006. *Music and the Sociological Gaze: Art Worlds and Cultural Production*. Manchester: Manchester University Press.

Mayer, V., M.J. Banks and J.T Caldwell. 2009. *Production Studies: Cultural Studies of Media Industries*. New York: Routledge.

McLaurin, M.A. and R.A. Peterson. 1992. *You Wrote My Life: Lyrical Themes in Country Music*. Philadelphia: Gordon and Breach.

Moulin, R. 1967. *Le Marché de la peinture en France*. Paris: Éditions de Minuit.

Negus, K. 1997. "The Production of Culture." In *Production of Culture/Cultures of Production*, ed. P. DuGay, 67–118. London: Sage.

Perrenoud, M. 2007. *Les musicos. Enquête sur des musiciens ordinaires*. Paris: La Découverte.

Peterson, R.A. 1972. "A Process Model of the Folk, Pop, and Fine Art Phase of Jazz." In *American Music: From Storyville to Woodstock*, ed. C. Nanry, 135–151. New Brunswick: Transaction.

_____., ed. 1976. *The Production of Culture*. Beverly Hills: Sage Publications.

_____. 1979. "Revitalizing the Culture Concept." *Annual Review of Sociology* 5: 137–166.

_____. 1994. "Cultural Studies Through the Production Perspective." In *The Sociology of Culture*, ed. D. Crane, 163–189. Oxford: Blackwell.

_____. 1997. *Creating Country Music: Fabricating Authenticity*. Chicago: University of Chicago Press.

_____. 2000. "Two Ways Culture is Produced." *Poetics* 28(2/3): 225–233

Peterson, R. and N. Anand. 2004. "The Production of Culture Perspective." *Annual Review of Sociology* 30: 311–334.

Prior, N. 2011. "Critique and Renewal in the Sociology of Music: Bourdieu and Beyond." *Cultural Sociology* 5(1): 121–138.

Regev, M. 1989. "The Field of Popular Music in Israel." In *World Music, Politics and Social Change*, ed. S. Frith, 143–155. Manchester: Manchester University Press.

Roe, K. 1993. "Academic Capital and Music Tastes Among Swedish Adolescents." *Young* 1(3): 40–55.

Ryan, J. 2007. "The Production of Culture Perspective." In *21st Century Sociology*, eds. C. Bryant and D. Peck, 222–230. Thousand Oaks: Sage.

Ryan, J. and R.A. Peterson. 1982. "The Product Image: The Fate of Collaboration in Country Music Songwriting," *Sage Annual Reviews of Communication Research* 10: 11–32.

Santoro, M. 2002. "What is a 'Cantautore'? Distinction and Authorship in Italian (Popular) Music." *Poetics* 30(1/2): 111–132.

_____. 2006. "The Tenco Effect. Suicide, San Remo, and the Social Construction of the Canzone d'Autore." *Journal of Modern Italian Studies* 11(3): 342–366.

_____. 2008a. "Culture As (And After) Production." *Cultural Sociology* 2(1): 7–31.

_____. 2008b. "Producing Cultural Sociology: An Interview with Richard A. Peterson." *Cultural Sociology* 2(1): 33–55.

_____. 2011. "From Bourdieu to Cultural Sociology." *Cultural Sociology* 5(1): 3–23.

Santoro, M. and M. Solaroli. 2015. "Contesting Culture: Bourdieu and the 'Strong Program' in Cultural Sociology." In *The International Handbook of the Sociology of Art and Culture*, eds. L Hanquinet and M. Savage. London: Routledge.

Savage, M. 2006. "The Musical Field." *Cultural Trends* 15 (2/3): 159–175.

Small, C. 1998. *Musicking: The Meanings of Performing and Listening*. Hanover: Wesleyan University Press.

Steinmetz, G. 2011. "Bourdieu, Historicity, and Historical Sociology." *Cultural Sociology* 5 (1): 45–66.

Straw, W. 1991. "Systems of Articulation, Logics of Change: Communities and Scenes in Popular Music." *Cultural Studies* 5(3): 368–388.

Thornton, S. 1995. *Club Cultures: Music, Media and Subcultural Capital.* Cambridge: Polity Press.

Toynbee, J. 2000. *Making Popular Music.* London: Arnold.

Trondman, M. 1990. "Rock Taste—On Rock as Symbolic Capital. A Study of Young People's Music, Taste and Music Making." In *Popular Music Research,* eds. K. Roe and U. Carlsson, 71–85. Gothenburg: Nordicom.

van Maanen, H. 2009. *How to Study Art Worlds: On the Societal Functioning of Aesthetic Values.* Amsterdam: Amsterdam University Press.

Van Venrooij, A. and V. Schmutz. 2010. "The Evaluation of Popular Music in the United States, Germany and the Netherlands: A Comparison of the Use of High Art and Popular Aesthetic Criteria." *Cultural Sociology* 4(3): 395–421.

White, H.C. 1993. *Careers and Creativity: Social Forces in the Arts.* Boulder: Westview Press.

White, H.C. and C. White. 1965. *Canvases and Careers: Institutional Change in the French Painting World.* Chicago: University of Chicago Press.

C

CONSUMPTION

13

Identity

Music, Community, and Self

ANDY BENNETT

> ... it seems of greater importance to people what they like musically than whether or not they enjoyed a film or television program ... [individuals own] their favorite music in ways that [are] intense and important to them ... mak[ing] it part of [their] identity and build[ing] it into [their] sense of [them]selves.
>
> (Frith 1987: 140, 143)

There is little doubt that music, in each of its myriad forms, plays a key part in the formation and articulation of identity. There are various aspects to, and thus ways of understanding, this quality of music. Thus, music can become a strong marker of national identity, for example, in the form of national anthems and similar pieces of music or songs with a strong patriotic flavor (see Stokes 1994). It can also work as a symbol of taste and a way for particular social groups to mark themselves off as "cultured" in a highbrow sense of this term, as is often seen in the case of audiences for classical music, opera and jazz (see Hennion 1993, Martin 1995). Or music can be used to denote an alternative lifestyle and/or radical stance in opposition to what are perceived as mainstream societal and political values. Examples of this latter manifestation of music and identity are contemporary popular musical styles such as punk (Hannerz 2013), hardcore (Haenfler 2006) and rap, the last of these also embodying strong aspects of ethnic and racial identity particularly as these relate to oppressed minorities in urban contexts around the world (see for example Rose 1994, Lipsitz 1994, Mitchell 1996). In more recent times the relationship between music and identity has also been examined in the context of locality (Cohen 1991, Bennett 2000), memory (DeNora 2000, Strong 2011), the body (Dodds 2011, Driver 2011) and technology (Bull 2000, Beer 2010, Nowak and Bennett 2014).

The purpose of this chapter is to examine and critically evaluate these and other ways in which music and identity have been studied and theorized in sociology. The chapter will also draw on some work from cognate disciplines, notably media and cultural studies, social anthropology and ethnomusicology. As the chapter will endeavor to illustrate, a key contribution of sociological studies of music, particularly in the wake of the cultural turn (see Chaney 1994), has been an in-depth understanding of the importance of music as a resource drawn on by individuals on the co-production of culture in an everyday context. In other words, more contemporary sociological work on music and identity has been concerned to look beyond the significance of socio-cultural responses to music as a reflection of the structural conditions underpinning social relationships in a given societal context, and to recast music as a resource through which individuals negotiate such structural forces and engage in the co-production of their social-cultural identities.

Music and National Identity

As noted above, a key way in which music assumes a socio-cultural relevance is through its use as maker of national identity. From the performance of national anthems at sporting events (another forum in which national identity is often keenly felt) to the singing of patriotic songs at concerts, national celebrations and other events, music and national identity become interwoven in highly complex ways. In considering the way music functions in this context, Stokes (1994: 3) suggests that it plays a critical function in informing "our sense of place." Music, in this sense, embeds a series of aural signifiers through which listeners articulate a sense of identity as inherently linked to nation. A highly pertinent example of this is seen in Warren's analysis of the part played by music in the generation of nationalistic fervor in Nazi Germany. As Warren comments:

> National Socialist songs . . . occup[ied] a place of permanence in the national life . . . Their primary focus [wa]s to arouse the emotions of the singers to a point where they [we]re more sensitive to the impact of the words . . . of the speaker. But they also fulfil[led] the derivative function of exercising a lasting influence over the attitude of the individual . . .
>
> (1972 [1943]: 73)

Through this function, suggests Warren, music became a medium through which national-socialist values were adopted and widely endorsed in Germany during the 1930s, culminating in the Nazis' rise to power in Germany. This admittedly extreme example from twentieth-century history illustrates the mobilizing power of music in this respect. Indeed, as Frith (1987: 141) argues: "Only music seems capable of creating this sort of spontaneous . . . identity, this kind of personally felt patriotism."

However, it is not just in such extreme examples that music's resonance with notions of national identity can be seen to manifest itself. Thus, another, more mundane, instance of this is seen in the context of folk music. As Frith (1987) points out, "in London's Irish pubs . . . 'traditional' Irish folk songs are still the most powerful way in which to make people feel Irish and consider what their 'Irishness' means." Similarly, MacKinnon (1994) in his study of the British folk music scene has observed how the singing of traditional folk songs in folk clubs provides people with what they perceive to be a link to the past—a link that, as McKinnon argues, is actually quite problematic given the highly romanticized notions of the past that are often embedded in folk music discourse.

Indeed, in an era where articulations of a *pure* national identity are highly contradictory—and yet increasingly held on to as a means of creating a shared sense of what could be termed socio-cultural security—popular music has also often become a platform for articulations of national distinctiveness. Thus, for example, during the early 1980s, *Neue Deutsche Welle* (New German Wave) comprised a group of guitar-based groups, among them Bapp and Flatsch, from German cities such as Berlin, Düsseldorf, Hamburg, Hanover and Hagen, performing songs in local dialect. Similarly, the emergence of "Britpop" a decade later saw the British music press attempting to create a sense of "Englishness" through the ascription of home-grown characteristics to a musically varied collection of groups such as Blur, Oasis and Pulp. Typically, accent was focused on as a key driver for Britpop's national distinctiveness with the "mockney" twang of singers such as Blur's Damon Albarn being interwoven by music journalists into a discourse of Cool Britannia promoted by successive governments during the 1990s (see Bennett and Stratton 2010). Again, the Britpop phenomenon was emblematic of a radically imagined notion of Englishness, which conflated "England" and

"Britain" while simultaneously fixating in a highly insensitive fashion on the concept of England as a "white" nation, airbrushing out of existence the other ethnic groups that have progressively settled in England and other parts of the British Isles since the 1940s (Bennett 1997).

Music, Space, and Place

Moving beyond the sphere of the national, music has also been considered as an important signifier of "community" at local, trans-local and affective levels. An early attempt to conceptualize the significance of music in this respect from a social perspective is seen in the British subcultural theory studies of the early 1970s. Taking inspiration from the Chicago School sociologists of the early twentieth century, British cultural studies theorists argued that the stylized identities of post-war British youth cultures were not examples of youth deviance, as had been widely reported in the British press (see Cohen 1987) but were contemporary examples of a class-struggle that had been ongoing in Britain for a century or more. The spectacular style of successive youth cultures, from Teddy boys and skinheads, through mods and rockers, to punk in the mid-1970s all reflected, it was suggested, an antagonism toward the hegemonic authority (Gramsci 1971) of dominant institutions such as school, work and law-enforcement agencies. Hebdige (1979), whose seminal study of punk is often regarded as a high point in this era of subcultural theory, suggested that the punk style appropriated what he referred to as a rhetoric of crisis that dominated the British media in the late 1970s as the United Kingdom slipped into a post-industrial economic depression. As Laing (1985) among others has argued, however, although purporting to examine the importance of youth style and music as a means through which young people could negotiate a new cultural space for themselves or—as Cohen (1972) put it—magically recover a sense of cohesive working-class community, for the most part subcultural theory was heavily focused around style with music taking something of a back-seat. Only Willis (1978) made any sustained attempt to examine the significance of music in relation to the collective identities of youth cultural groups. Using the examples of working-class bikers and middle-class hippies, Willis suggested that the former's preference for rock 'n' roll singles and the latter's preference for album-orientated progressive rock represented and reaffirmed characteristic values associated with their contrasting class positions. Thus, according to Willis, for the bikers, the short, musically straightforward rock 'n' roll songs that formed the audio backdrop for their socializing and dancing resonated with their internalized working-class values of male camaraderie and bravado. For the hippies, on the other hand, argues Willis, their more educated and artistically orientated middle-class values made them more amenable to the abstract soundscapes of progressive rock. Willis has subsequently been criticized due to the inherently class-biased focus of his analysis. Thus, according to Bennett:

> For Willis, what appear on the surface as spontaneous responses to music, are, in fact pre-determined by the structural experience of class. Far from being reflexive and creative agents, choosing music because of the way in which its rhythm, tempo, melody, sound, lyrical content, production, packaging, and so on, appeals to them as individuals, the bikers and hippies are depicted by Willis's study as acting unconsciously and in accordance with structurally embedded antecedents which basically "tell" them "how" to react to particular aural and visual stimuli.
>
> (2008a: 422–423)

While subcultural and, more recently, post-subcultural studies have continued to maintain a presence in academic work (see for example, Muggleton 2000, Bennett and Kahn-Harris 2004), the study of music and its relationship to aspects of space and place has also evolved in different directions while also expanding the range of cultural practices that connect with music in an everyday context. In their highly instructive work on local music-making, Finnegan (1989) and Cohen (1991) consider the micro-social importance of music as a medium through which individuals are able to both connect with and narrativize their relationship to specific places in locally nuanced ways. In Finnegan's case, this involves a survey of a broad range of local music-making practices in the English town of Milton Keynes. For Cohen, the focus is on amateur and semi-professional rock and pop groups in Liverpool. Despite the contrasting geographical locations of the two places focused on in Finnegan's and Cohen's respective studies, and the contrasting ways in which music is historically located in each site, what crucially emerges from each study is the sense in which music serves as a highly tangible way through which individuals are able to feel a sense of collective identity and belonging in which participation in common musical activities and a feeling of connection to place are simultaneously realized and articulated through each other.

This perspective on music, space and place and its impact on notions of local identity is further developed in subsequent work by Shank (1994) and Bennett (2000). Thus, Shank considers how conflicting notions of local identity are articulated through the various music scenes clustered within the city of Austin, Texas, particularly in the contrasting examples of cowboy song and punk, the former articulating relatively conservative notions of Texan identity while the latter radically contests such representations of identity through its satirical take on male Texan values and the broader political values of the region. Bennett's work similarly focuses on what he terms multiple narratives of the local as these are articulated through various contemporary popular music styles, including dance, rap and rock. For Bennett, however, the significance of music in the context of locality and the articulation of local identity is not necessarily tied to obvious creative innovation, such as locally produced music with locally themed lyrics, but can also evolve through the collective appropriation and aesthetic re-articulation of non-locally produced music as well. To illustrate this point, Bennett observes how, in the northern English city of Newcastle upon Tyne, particular notions of local identity are expressed through the appropriation of dance and progressive rock music. In the case of the former, dance music fans incorporate their musical taste into an aesthetic discourse that rejects what they consider to be the cultural conservatism of the traditional "Geordie" (the term used to describe a person from Newcastle) identity. In the case of progressive rock, and with specific reference to a local Pink Floyd tribute band, Bennett notes how through their creative working of local symbolism, in-jokes and banter into their performances, the band effectively celebrates traditional Geordie values and the stereotypical notion of the Geordie identity.

While examples of local music-making and consumption have often been referred to using the term community, the concept of scene is also often used in this context. According to Straw (1991: 379), who is commonly cited as one of the first academic theorists to position scene as a conceptual framework for use in the critical analysis of music, scenes often transcend particular localities "reflect[ing] and actualiz[ing] a particular state of relations between various populations and social groups, as these coalesce around specific coalitions of musical style." Straw's work is significant in that, through casting scene as both a local and trans-local concept, he expands our understanding of how, in acquiring shared musical tastes, individuals are able to connect and forge a common sense of identity and belonging that transcends the boundaries of physical communities.

A further important contribution of the music scenes literature has been to illustrate the highly diverse ways in which individuals, through their involvement in a specific scene, are able to acquire a sense of cultural participation and belonging. Thus, as Stahl (2004) observes, rather than merely encompassing music performance and consumption, scenes embrace a wide range of creative and entrepreneurial activities, including music-making, production, promotion and distribution. Scenes also rely on individuals who manage and provide infrastructural resources, such as venues, clubs, rehearsal space, recording studios, record/music shops, needed to sustain such activities (see also Spring 2004). In more recent research on the independent music scene in Milan, Tarassi (2012) notes how in many cases the roles performed by individuals in the creation and sustaining of a scene over time are not necessarily distinct but often combine. As such, many individuals' associations with music scenes often involve them performing a multi-tasking role—their sense of belonging being articulated through a range of knowledges, experiences and competencies as musicians, promoters, sound engineers, journalists and audience members.

Music, Taste, Memory, and Identity

The work on music scenes has done much to broaden an understanding of how music acts as a form of social glue that bonds individuals together into particular forms of micro-social clusters, with both local and trans-local dimensions. However, it has been suggested by some researchers that music offers other opportunities for examining the nature of collective identity and belonging in contemporary social settings. Indeed, over thirty years ago Frith (1981) suggested that the key to understanding the then fashionable concept of the "rock community" was to appreciate that this stood not for a physical community but rather for an *aesthetic* community of geographically dispersed fans whose consumption of rock and its expressed political and cultural values gave rise to a sense of shared experience—and a series of lifestyle preferences—through which individual fans were able to create a sense of commonality and unity embedded in the rock aesthetic. While later work on scenes has produced a more complex and multi-layered understanding of the relationship of rock and other popular music genres to questions of community and belonging, the central point of Frith's argument regarding the aesthetic power of music to create affective bonds retains credence. For example, in more recent work on music and ageing, Bennett argues that, through their engagement with the affective qualities of music, individuals often find a means of culturally "connecting" that may involve little or no actual social interaction as such. In exploring this point, Bennett refers to ageing fans of musics such as rock and punk who have withdrawn from the physical local or trans-local scenes that they were once part of but still continue to associate with these musics and the cultural scenes they have engendered through a process of affectivity. This may involve, for example, reading particular retro music magazines, watching music-related films and documentaries on TV, surfing the internet and downloading material, or playing their old albums and singles at home. As Bennett explains:

> Ageing music audiences may use such mediums to affectively situate themselves within a community of like-minded others. As with Anderson's (1983) "imagined communities" of newspaper readers in particular national settings, affective scenes are underpinned by a knowingness on the part of isolated individuals that many others are listening to the same music, reading the same music literature, watching the same music-related films and documentaries and—above all—making a similar sort of sense out of what they are hearing, reading and watching, based upon their shared generational memories and cultural experience of that music.
>
> (2013: 60)

Strong (2011) similarly suggests in her work on grunge and memory that ageing fans of grunge, while no longer necessarily involved in a physical grunge scene or wearing the types of clothing associated with the grunge style, retain a connection to the scene through listening to grunge music and reliving the memories associated with this experience. Across a range of other styles, including dance, hardcore and rap, it is clear that a similar processes of ongoing attachment to these musics for ageing fans is being achieved through memory and a deeply inscribed set of aesthetic understandings of how a particular music and style have shaped the individual over time (see Bennett and Hodkinson 2012). Further insight into the importance of music in constructing and articulating a sense of affective belonging, specifically from a female perspective, is offered by Vroomen (2004). Focusing on the example of Kate Bush, a singer-songwriter from Britain who first rose to stardom in the late 1970s with her hit single "Wuthering Heights," Vroomen considers how Bush's ageing female fans continue to display a deep sense of connection with the artist. A core motive here, argues Vroomen, is that through listening to Kate Bush these older fans are able to keep in touch with themselves, their values and aspirations—with many of the highly personalized themes explored in Bush's music closely resonating with the lives of her female fans. In this sense, suggests Vroomen, these fans maintain a sense of affective connection with each other—even though they are often barely aware of this. Thus, as Vroomen (2004: 240) observes: "The fact that these women were keen to take part in [my] research and to share their experiences with me—encouraged by our mutual recognition as fans—suggests the possible existence of a scene, albeit a more loosely defined one based on shared feelings and knowledge."

A further significant aspect of Vroomen's redefinition of scene in this way is its bypassing of discourses of style and musical value as common demarcators of music fandom. In the case of Vroomen's research, the centrally binding factor is the artist, the emotional and memory investment in the artist and the way that discourses of authenticity woven around an artist resonate with the individual fan and thus become a means of forging an affective bond. Lewis (1992), in work focusing on the concept of what he terms taste cultures, suggests that these can cut across aspects of demography through their creation of affective bonds between individuals based on their common preference for particular artists and or genres of music. This is a pertinent step forward in helping us disentangle some of the conventional theoretical baggage that connects music, style and spectacular cultural practice into a form of given understanding as to how music "works" in a social context at the expense of looking instead at how more mundane practices can also give rise to forms of musical association, identity and community. Caviccihi's (1998) study of Bruce Springsteen fans is an interesting case in point here. As Cavicchi observes, the common articulation of "Bruce stories" by Springsteen fans bespeaks highly personalized narratives of association with Springsteen while at the same time articulating a common point of reference for a highly diverse fan base.

Lewis's concept of taste culture and the increasing dimension of cultural memory embedded within it arguably also has critical resonances with the shifting age composition of popular music fan bases and audiences. Thus, whereas popular music was once considered primarily a youth music, this definition no longer holds true; popular music scenes and audiences for concerts and festivals are no longer uni-generational, but rather omni-generational. To speak of popular music exclusively, or even primarily, in relation to "youth" culture then is becoming increasingly problematic and new terminologies need to be developed to explain what is going on here. Indeed, it is becoming increasingly clear that a number of artists from genres spanning the full range of musical developments during the last sixty years now draw broad and diverse audiences whose key point of commonality is a particular expression of taste and aesthetic preference, for which a primary point of reference is music. Moreover, given that many artists whose work is celebrated in this way have careers spanning several decades, cultural memory also plays a significant part in the way that these artists are received and understood by old and young fans alike (see Bennett 2008b).

Music, Belonging, and the Internet

Since the late 1990s, discussions of the socio-cultural significance of music have become increasingly inseparable from discussions of the internet. The proliferation of internet sites for the downloading (legally and illegally) of music and the amount of information—including videos, films and documentaries posted on sites such as YouTube—featuring and/or about music mean that the internet has become perhaps the primary medium for music in the twenty-first century. The use of the internet for peer-to-peer (P2P) file-sharing has been a critical area of concern for a number of years given the issues of copyright and intellectual property it raises (see Rojek 2005). At the same time, however, it is clear that, from an academic point of view, the internet offers a broader range of opportunities to consider how the individual's interactions with music give rise to new means of understanding the connection between music, self and community.

In their analysis of popular music scenes, Peterson and Bennett suggest that increasing access to the internet for music fans has given rise to a new form of scene that they refer to as a "virtual scene":

> Whereas a conventional local scene is kept in motion by a series of gigs, club nights, fairs, and similar events, where fans converge, communicate, and reinforce their sense of belonging to a particular scene, the virtual scene involves direct net-mediated person-to-person communication between fans ... This may, involve, for example, the creation of chat-rooms or list-serves dedicated to the scene and may involve the trading of music and images on-line.
>
> (Peterson and Bennett 2004: 11)

The concept of the "virtual" scene is important in that it offers a way of framing participation in musical life in which face-to-face interaction is replaced by engagement using internet technology. Several studies have focused on this phenomenon. Thus, Kibby (2000) examines how fans of cult music artist John Prine have used the internet as a means of engaging in a form of cultural enshrinement of this artist and his work. Bennett (2002, 2004) considers how fans of the Canterbury Sound, a sub-scene of the English progressive rock movement of the late 1960s and early 1970s, have used the internet as a means of both reviving and critically engaging with the scene. Through engagement between fans online, new discourses of the Canterbury Sound are constructed and provide, among other things, historical depth to a musical moment that is now over forty years old. Indeed, as well as providing a basis for fans, including younger generations of fans, to celebrate and reassess the contribution of particular genres and artists to contemporary popular music history and development, the internet has also provided a basis for the emergence of scenes that would not otherwise have come into existence at a global level. A pertinent example here is post-rock, a genre which, as Hodgkinson (2004) notes, could hardly have been described as a scene at all were it not for the opportunity for small groups of globally dispersed fans to connect and converse on the internet and also through other more traditional print media forms such as fanzines.

The capacity of the internet to allow new forms of fan engagement with, and indeed feel a sense of ownership over, music and artists has also become a topic of focus for academic researchers in recent years. As work in this area has illustrated, through actively promoting emerging genres of music through posting on blogs, swapping files and creating websites, music fans can also create a sense of community and collective belonging. A pertinent case in point here is K-pop. As Jung (2014) observes, the rapid emergence of K-pop (an abbreviation used to describe a brand of boy- and girl-band pop produced in Korea), initially across Asia and subsequently more globally, is closely bound up with the online practices of fans. Indeed, according to Jung (2014: 115), K-pop is indicative of "newly arising youth-led media cultural transmissions in the global creative industries." Developing this argument, Jung goes on to illustrate how in different parts of Asia, including Korea, Japan, Taiwan and Hong Kong, the efforts of fans to draw attention to K-pop were instrumentally important in creating an initial fan base for the genre. That particular clusters of fans based in specific geographical regions were able to communicate with other young people in different countries via the internet was critically important in this respect. As Jung concludes, such an evolution of K-pop in the Asian and subsequently global popular music landscape marks a radical departure in the way that popular music genres are "discovered" and become established. Similarly, it offers a new way of seeing the role of fans in relation to music and adds an additional dimension to the type of interaction between fans and the music industry in which the fan moves from being a consumer to a prosumer, that is to say a co-producer of the musical artifact.

Conclusion

This chapter has examined the relationship between music, identity and community as this has been addressed in academic research. As the account presented here has endeavored to illustrate, a number of themes and concepts have been applied in attempting to explain how music serves as a cultural resource in the formulation and articulation of individual and collective identities in contemporary social settings. The work discussed in this chapter focuses variously on music in a national context as well as looking at more micro-social local and trans-local contexts through which music is appropriated and inscribed with discourses of identity, community and belonging. Similarly, it has been shown how more recent work builds on these ideas while incorporating new frames of conceptual reference including memory and affect or considering the impact of new forms of digital connectivity as enabled by the internet and the opportunities for online communication that this affords.

References

Anderson, B. 1983. *Imagined Communities: Reflections on the Origins and Spread of Nationalism.* London: Verso.

Beer, D. 2010. "Mobile Music, Coded Objects and Everyday Spaces." *Mobilities* 5(4): 469–484.

Bennett, A. 1997 "'Village Greens and Terraced Streets': Representations of 'Britishness' in Britpop." *Young: Nordic Journal of Youth Research* 5(4): 20–33.

_____. 2000. *Popular Music and Youth Culture: Music, Identity and Place.* Basingstoke: Macmillan.

_____. 2002. "Music, Media and Urban Mythscapes: A Study of the Canterbury Sound." *Media, Culture and Society* 24(1): 107–120.

_____. 2004. "New Tales from Canterbury: The Making of a Virtual Music Scene." In *Music Scenes: Local, Trans-Local and Virtual*, eds. A. Bennett and R.A. Peterson, 205–220. Nashville: Vanderbilt University Press.

_____. 2008a. "Towards a Cultural Sociology of Popular Music." *Journal of Sociology* 4(4): 419–432.

_____. 2008b. "'Things They Do Look Awful Cool': Ageing Rock Icons and Contemporary Youth Audiences." *Leisure/Loisir* 32(1): 259–278.

_____. 2013. *Music, Style, and Aging: Growing Old Disgracefully?* Philadelphia: Temple University Press.

Bennett, A. and P. Hodkinson, eds. 2012. *Ageing and Youth Cultures: Music, Style and Identity.* Oxford: Berg.

Bennett, A. and K. Kahn-Harris, eds. 2004. *After Subculture: Critical Studies in Contemporary Youth Culture.* Basingstoke: Palgrave Macmillan.

Bennett, A. and J. Stratton, eds. 2010. *Britpop and the English Music Tradition.* Aldershot: Ashgate.

Bull, M. 2000. *Sounding Out the City: Personal Stereos and the Management of Everyday Life.* Oxford: Berg.

Cavicchi, D. 1998. *Tramps Like Us: Music and Meaning Among Springsteen Fans.* New York: Oxford University Press.

Chaney, D. 1994. *The Cultural Turn: Scene Setting Essays on Contemporary Cultural History.* London: Routledge.

Cohen, P. 1972. "Subcultural Conflict and Working Class Community." In *Working Papers in Cultural Studies* 2, 5–51. Birmingham: Center for Contemporary Cultural Studies.

Cohen, S. 1987. *Folk Devils and Moral Panics: The Creation of the Mods and Rockers.* Oxford: Basil Blackwell.

_____. 1991. *Rock Culture in Liverpool: Popular Music in the Making.* Oxford: Clarendon Press.

DeNora, T. 2000. *Music in Everyday Life.* Cambridge. Cambridge University Press.

Dodds, S. 2011. *Dancing on the Canon: Embodiments of Value in Popular Dance.* Basingstoke: Palgrave.

Driver, C. 2011. "Embodying Hardcore: Rethinking 'Subcultural' Authenticities." *Journal of Youth Studies* 14(8): 975–990.

Finnegan, R. 1989. *The Hidden Musicians: Music-Making in an English Town*. Cambridge: Cambridge University Press.

Frith, S. 1981. "'The Magic That Can Set You Free': The Ideology of Folk and the Myth of Rock." *Popular Music* 1: 159–168.

_____. 1987. "Towards an Aesthetic of Popular Music." In *Music and Society: The Politics of Composition, Performance and Reception*, eds. R. Leppert and S. McClary, 133–149. Cambridge: Cambridge University Press.

Gramsci, A. 1971. *Selections from the Prison Notebooks*. London: Lawrence and Wishart.

Haenfler, R. 2006. *Straight Edge: Clean-Living Youth, Hardcore Punk, and Social Change*. Piscataway: Rutgers University Press.

Hannerz, E. 2013. *Performing Punk: Subcultural Authentications and the Positioning of the Mainstream*. Uppsala: Uppsala University Press.

Hebdige, D. 1979. *Subculture: The Meaning of Style*. London: Routledge.

Hennion, A. 1993. *La Passion musicale*. Paris: Métailié.

Hodgkinson, J.A. 2004. "The Fanzine Discourse Over 'Post Rock.'" In *Music Scenes: Local, Trans-Local and Virtual*, eds. A. Bennett and R.A. Peterson, 221–237. Nashville: Vanderbilt University Press.

Jung, S. 2014. "Youth, Social Media and Transnational Cultural Distribution: The Case of Online K-Pop Circulation." In *Mediated Youth Culture: The Internet, Belonging and New Cultural Configurations*, eds. A. Bennett and B. Robards, 114–129. Basingstoke: Palgrave Macmillan.

Kibby, M.D. 2000. "Home on the Page: A Virtual Place of Music Community." *Popular Music* 19(1): 91–100.

Laing, D. 1985. *One Chord Wonders: Power and Meaning in Punk Rock*. Milton Keynes: Open University Press.

Lewis, G.H. 1992. "Who Do You Love? The Dimensions of Musical Taste." In *Popular Music and Communication*, 2nd ed., ed. J. Lull, 134–151. London: Sage.

Lipsitz, G. 1994. *Dangerous Crossroads: Popular Music, Postmodernism and the Poetics of Place*. London: Verso.

MacKinnon, N. 1994. *The British Folk Scene: Musical Performance and Social Identity*. Buckingham: Open University Press.

Martin, P.J. 1995. *Sounds and Society: Themes in the Sociology of Music*. Manchester: Manchester University Press.

Mitchell, T. 1996. *Popular Music and Local Identity: Rock, Pop and Rap in Europe and Oceania*. London: Leicester University Press.

Muggleton, D. 2000. *Inside Subculture: The Postmodern Meaning of Style*. Oxford: Berg.

Nowak, R. and A. Bennett. 2014. "Analyzing Everyday Sound Environments: The Space, Time and Corporality of Musical Listening." *Cultural Sociology* (14 May, online pre-print version): 1–17.

Peterson, R.A. and A. Bennett. 2004. "Introducing Music Scenes." In *Music Scenes: Local, Trans-Local and Virtual*, eds. A. Bennett and R.A. Peterson, 1–15. Nashville: Vanderbilt University Press.

Rojek. C. 2005. "P2P Leisure Exchange: Net Banditry and the Policing of Intellectual Property." *Leisure Studies* 24(4): 357–369.

Rose, T. 1994. *Black Noise: Rap Music and Black Culture in Contemporary America*. London: Wesleyan University Press.

Shank, B. 1994. *Dissonant Identities: The Rock 'n' Roll Scene in Austin, Texas*. London: Wesleyan University Press.

Spring, K. 2004. "Behind the Rave: Structure and Agency in a Rave Scene." In *Music Scenes: Local, Trans-Local and Virtual*, eds. A. Bennett and R.A. Peterson, 48–63. Nashville: University of Vanderbilt Press.

Stahl, G. 2004. "'It's Like Canada Reduced': Setting the Scene in Montreal." In *After Subculture: Critical Studies in Contemporary Youth Culture*, eds. A. Bennett and K. Kahn-Harris, 51–64. London: Palgrave.

Stokes, M. 1994. "Introduction: Ethnicity, Identity and Music." In *Ethnicity, Identity and Music: The Musical Construction of Place*, ed. M. Stokes, 1–27. Oxford: Berg.

Straw, W. 1991. "Systems of Articulation, Logics of Change: Communities and Scenes in Popular Music." *Cultural Studies*, 5(3): 368–388.

Strong, C. 2011. *Grunge: Music and Memory*. Farnham: Ashgate.

Tarassi, S. 2012. "Independent to What? An Analyis of the Live Music Scene in Milan." PhD diss., The Catholic University of Milan.

Vroomen, L. 2004. "Kate Bush: Teen Pop and Older Female Fans." In *Music Scenes: Local, Trans-Local and Virtual*, eds. A. Bennett and R.A. Peterson, 238–253. Nashville: Vanderbilt University Press.

Warren, R.L. 1972 [1943]. "The Nazi Use of Music as an Instrument of Social Control." In *The Sounds of Social Change*, eds. R S. Denisoff and R.A. Peterson, 72–78. Chicago: Rand McNally and Company.

Willis, P. 1978. *Profane Culture*. London: Routledge and Kegan Paul.

14

Taste as Distinction

Richard A. Peterson

Between World Wars I and II it was widely accepted in intellectual circles that the emerging *mass media* were spawning an equivalent *mass audience*, an audience that was unthinking, herd-like, and inherently passive yet easily swayed by skilled political and commercial demagogues (Gans 1974). The interpretation proffered by Hadley Cantril and his associates of what happened following Orson Welles' 1938 radio dramatization of an invasion from Mars typifies this view. They quite wrongly interpreted the reaction to the broadcast as widespread panic (Cantril et al. 1940). As Rosengren and his associates were clearly able to show in a similar case in Sweden, reports about mass panics tend to be strongly exaggerated or downright false, based as they often are on hearsay and newspaper sensationalism (Rosengren et al. 1978). But things today are different. Researchers, as Jensen and Rosengren (1990) have recently found in their careful review of the five major traditions in communications research on audiences, no longer see the audience as an undifferentiated mass.

Some of the correlates of this discredited "massification" perspective are, nevertheless, still part of many researchers' taken-for-granted view of the world. In particular the standard view of stratification in the United States holds that at the top there is an educated and discerning elite with well-refined tastes and at the bottom an ignorant and stimulus-seeking mass (Goffman 1951, Glenn 1969, Sobel 1983). The "high brow" is set off against the "low brow" (Brooks 1958); the "superior" is contrasted with the "brutal" (Shils 1961); and, in common parlance, the "snob" is counterpoised to the "slob."

It is the purpose of this paper to suggest that the elite-to-mass hierarchy, which may once have been an accurate depiction of how the class hierarchy was seen, at least from the top (Goffman 1951, Baltzell 1964), does not now fit patterns of leisure time activities and media consumption in the United States. After outlining the implications of the snob-to-slob conception, data from a recent study will be presented, showing that this earlier view does not fit with this data. In conclusion, an alternative conception, one that pairs what I have reason to designate the *omnivore* with its counterpart, the *univore*, will be proposed as being more in line with the contemporary status hierarchy of the United States.

The Received View of the Status Hierarchy

Inspired by the early work of Weber (1946) and Veblen (1899), sociologists developed a view of status groups ranked in terms of their appreciation of the arts and letters, their styles of clothes and language, and their use of leisure time. They also noted the close association between such status rankings and ranking by stratification variables including income, occupation and years of schooling (Goffman 1951, Warner 1953, Form and Stone 1957, Gans 1974, 1985).

Evidence of the importance of symbolic indicators for stratification has come from a wide range of different studies. The bifurcation between fine art and popular culture in the nineteenth century and the increasing use of the former as a marker of class position has been traced by DiMaggio (1982) and Levine (1988). Ethnographic studies of the workings of cultural status indicators have been shown among elements of the American elite by Baltzell (1964) and Domhoff (1974). Sennett and Cobb (1973), LeMasters (1975), Halle (1984), and Fantasia (1988) have also shown that symbolic status markers work as powerfully in differentiating various segments of the working classes. The importance of cultural indicators in the identities of occupational groups has been documented by Hughes (1958) and by Bensman and Lilienfeld (1991). Finally, the concept of cultural capital developed by Pierre Bourdieu has given further theoretical importance to the place of symbolic forms in class socialization by showing how arts appreciation and other cultural indicators get used in crystallizing and in maintaining the status hierarchy (Bourdieu 1984, 1985; Bourdieu and Passeron 1977, DiMaggio and Mohr 1985, Lamont and Lareau 1988).

The hallmark of those at the top of the hierarchy according to the received elite-to-mass theory is patronizing the fine arts, displaying good manners, wearing the correct cut of clothes, using proper speech, maintaining membership in the "better" churches, philanthropic organizations and social clubs, and especially for the women of the class, cultivating all of the attendant social graces. The term "snob" applied to such people is of course pejorative. It is, nonetheless, a fair characterization of the attitude of those at the upper end of the status hierarchy because of their moralistic contempt for and distancing from all cultural manifestations that do not exactly fit with what is taken to be proper. Thus, within the purview of the elite-to-mass perspective, it is incumbent on members of the cultural elite not only to *do the right thing*, but as importantly, to *absolutely shun* all other sorts of cultural practices. This distancing from other than proscribed speech, music, dance, and behavior is so wrapped in moral fervor that Veblen (1899) and Warner (1953) quite correctly speak of caste-like barriers of ritual cleanliness and uncleanliness, because to partake of any of the elements of "common" or "popular" or "mass culture" is to jeopardize one's class standing. Even the "serious study" of popular culture by academics is a threat to "standards" because, within the received perspective, it is seen as lending legitimacy to that which is vulgar, and it thus threatens the sanctity of the status boundaries distinguishing between what is fine and what is common (Browne 1991).

According to the received theory, those in the middle of the status hierarchy, the "middle-brows," tend to imitate—or rather emulate—those above them but without the requisite knowledge of taste standards or the resources of time and money needed to fully participate. The resulting middle-brow taste culture is characterized by light classical music, romantic painting and literature, the ready-made versions of the high fashion clothes of the previous season, and a simplified, if prudish, etiquette (Gans 1974).

Within the elite-to-mass theory several characterizations are given of the lower end of the status hierarchy. The earliest authors characterize it in terms of folk, peasant, or ethnic culture (Veblen 1899), while more recent authors tend to characterize the bottom as an undiscriminating mass which seeks out easily understood elements that stimulate the emotions (Brooks 1958, Wilensky 1964). Thus the bottom has been characterized in two quite different ways: as a set of distinct tradition-bound taste cultures based in ethnic, racial and religious customs, on the one hand, and on the other as an undifferentiated mass. Different as these two characterizations sound at first, they are not so different as applied in contemporary America because recent studies of working-class culture in the massification tradition suggest that the once distinct working-class sub-cultures are being broken down into a mass by the combined forces of urbanization, industrialization, and exposure to advertising and the mass media (Ewen 1976).

The received elite-to-mass theory thus makes clear predictions about the arts and leisure choices of groups at different levels of the status hierarchy. Those at the top will choose the fine arts and related leisure activities while shunning all others. Those near the middle will choose derivative works and activities, while those groups at the bottom will shun the fine arts and indiscriminately choose sensational and mass-mediated entertainments.

A Fortuitous Test of the Theory

The study by Albert Simkus and myself that triggered these speculations was originally developed to test ideas about the empirical structuring of occupational status groups, about their hierarchal ranking, and about the patterns of cultural choices made by these occupational status groups. Our study was based on the Survey of Public Participation in the Arts (SPPA), a national area-probability sample of adults gathered in 1992 by the U.S. Bureau of the Census for the National Endowment for the Arts.[1] The theory, data, methods, and results of the study are more completely reported in Peterson and Simkus (1993). Fortuitously, the study brings into question the received theory of the status hierarchy and points the way toward a quite different conception of the hierarchy.

Based on recent research ranging from that of Pierre Bourdieu (1984, 1985) to that of Eric Olin Wright (1985) on the nature and structure of social classes, Simkus and I defined nineteen distinct groups of occupations. . . . For reasons fully explained in Peterson and Simkus (1993) we chose to rank the occupational groups in terms of the form of music most often chosen as their favorite by the members of the group. . . .

The type of music liked best was chosen as the indicator of aesthetic taste because, unlike questions about activities attended, time or money spent, all respondents are equally able to respond no matter where they live and whatever other demands there are on their resources. At the same time, respondents are free to make choices quite at variance with their behavior. So how well does the aesthetic ranking of musical taste correlate with the data on elite arts activities?

. . . [R]anking by type of music does correspond well with the available behavioral measures. The two groups at the top of the hierarchy, Higher and Lower Cultural Professionals do, in fact, rank high on all the cultural activities including attending classical music concerts, grand opera, Broadway musical shows, jazz concerts, theatrical plays, ballet and modern dance performances, art museums, and reading novels and poetry. In addition, the occupations in the top group have all of the high rates and, with one minor exception all of the occupations with low rates are in the bottom group of occupations. Many of the slight anomalies in the specific rankings make sense. For example, Farmers, who are at the top of the lower group of occupations show lower rates of participation in those elite arts activities, including opera, jazz, theatrical plays, and ballet, that are generally available only in the larger cities far from where Farmers live. These findings show the type of music liked best to be a good proxy for taste more generally.

The data reported so far are in line with the elite-to-mass theory, but other data in the same study bring the received theory into question. To begin with, just 30% of those in the highest status group say they like classical music best and only another 6% say they like opera best. Thus, 64% of the top group do not fit the model of the aesthetically exclusive snob. Indeed 9% of this top status group say they like country and western music best—the music with the lowest prestige of all! Is this finding some sort of aberration? According to the received theory, the high status groups should be exclusive in their taste and not even like the non-elite music forms. Accordingly they should rank low on all of these non-elite musical forms.

. . . Before proceeding, note that in each case the "high" and "low" are defined relative to that one type of music. Thus for example, if 20% of an occupational group like barber shop quartet music this is high relative to the other groups because only 13.4% of the entire sample like the music, while 20% liking hymns and gospel music is low because the average for the entire sample is 33%, and over half of those in several occupational groups like these kinds of religious music. If the received theory is correct, the occupational groups near the top will show the lowest rates of liking these forms of music, and those liking them most will be at or near the bottom of the hierarchy.

[Our] data . . . do not show this clear pattern of aesthetic exclusivity. Indeed, the occupational groups at the top are much more likely to be high on liking these non-elite forms while the occupational groups at the bottom are likely to be low on their rate of liking them. Only one category of music, country and western, fits the predicted pattern, while three groups, mood music, big band, and barber shop music, show just the opposite of the predicted ranking, and the other types of music show patterns that are quite mixed.

These findings so radically at variance with the received theory of elite-to-mass led us to check the available data on the non-elite leisure activities of the occupational groups. . . . If anything, these findings are more at variance with the received theory than are those shown for musical tastes. Most of the high scores are held by the higher status occupational groups, and with only two exceptions the low occupational groups tend to be low on these activities. One exception is repair of the home or automobile, which has a pattern of high and low rates among the high and low occupational groups. The proportion watching television three or more hours comes closest to fitting the predicted pattern. Nevertheless, according to these data, the couch potatoes—the stereotypic way of characterizing heavy TV viewers—are more likely to be found among the middle level white or pink collar occupations than among blue collar workers. This curvilinear relationship between class and TV viewing has been reported by others. See for example Frank and Greenberg (1980), Roe (1985) and Rosengren and Windahl (1989).

How to explain the findings that the higher status occupational groups tend to show high rates of participation in non-elite activities? They do not tend to have more leisure time to indulge their interests, for those in high status occupations tend to work longer hours than those below. They do tend to have more money, and much leisure in the U.S. today is costly or capital intensive. Money is not a prohibitive factor, however, in most of these items except for persons who are destitute. Attending a high school sports game, for example, counts as well as attending a high-priced professional event, and Plants-Garden asks about having plants in the apartment as well as having an outdoor garden.[2] There may be, however, other types of activities, such as professional wrestling and betting on the numbers—not measured in this survey—that are distinctive of the lower class. Nonetheless, it is quite clear from the systematic nature of the contra-theoretical findings . . . that many of those at the top do not exhibit the snob-like disdain for all non-elite forms of music and leisure activities. This suggests the need for an alternative explanation to the received elite-to-mass theory of the status hierarchy.

The Top: Elitist to Omnivore

Does this mean that the U.S. is becoming a more egalitarian society, or does it mean that leisure activities and taste in music are losing their efficacy as status markers for the elite? Perhaps, but I think not. It may just mean that the image of the taste-*exclusive* highbrow, along with the ranking from "snob" to "slob," is obsolete.

There is mounting, if fragmentary, evidence from other studies that high status groups do not only participate more than do others in high status activities, they tend to participate more often in most other kinds of leisure activities as well (DiMaggio 1987, DiMaggio and Useem 1978, Peterson and Hughes 1984). In effect, elite taste is no longer defined simply as the expressed appreciation of the high art forms and a corresponding moral disdain of, or patronizing tolerance for, all other aesthetic expressions. In so far as this view is correct, the aesthetics of elite status are being redefined as the appreciation of all distinctive leisure activities and creative forms along with the appreciation of the classic fine arts.[3] Because status is gained by knowing about, and participating in (that is to say, by consuming) many if not all forms, the term "omnivore" seems appropriate for those at the top of the emerging status hierarchy.[4]

There is one other bit of information in the data set at hand that can be used to add further corroboration to the idea of omnivore. When asked to choose their one favorite genre of music, some respondents were unable to pick just one. These respondents who were coded as "liking no one category best" were not evenly distributed among the occupational status groups. In line with the omnivore image of liking many kinds of music, all of the groups with 10% or more who could not choose just one favorite are clustered at or near the top of the status hierarchy, while all those with less than 3% who could not choose just one are at or near the bottom.

The Bottom: Mass to Univore

If the top of the taste pyramid is conjectured to be the omnivore, how best to characterize those at its base? The standard appellation "mass taste" seems out of place because . . . the occupational groups near the bottom are not more likely to spend more hours watching television. What is more, the information just cited on "liking no one category of music best" is contrary to the characterization of the tastes of those at the bottom of the status hierarchy as "mass tastes" because virtually all of their members were able to choose one kind of music as their favorite. As Herbert Gans observed in 1974, the appellation "mass culture" is more a reflection of the prejudices of the "massification theorists" than a description of the realities of working-class life in the United States. . . .

The information on the favorite type of music provides the best clue for how to characterize those near the bottom of the occupational status hierarchy. In the preparation of our article, Simkus and I ran log-multiplicative analyses for sub-samples based on gender, race and age. We found that the taste scale developed here discriminates better at the upper end of the occupational prestige hierarchy than further down. In each of the sub-samples tested, classical music emerged as clearly the most prestigious. There is, thus, general agreement among Americans, our results suggest, that classical music anchors the upper end of the taste hierarchy and thus constitutes cultural capital as shown by Bourdieu (1984).

At the same time, the ranking of music genres further down the line varied greatly from one gender- race- and age-specific sub-sample to another. This may be because of the nature of the survey instrument,[5] but it may also reflect the realities of the use of music to mark boundaries in the United States today. If this is so, the data suggest that there is less and less consensus on the ranking as one moves down the hierarchy of taste. Instead there is an increasingly large number of alternative forms having more or less equal taste value. As indicated by the results of this analysis, below classical music we find Folk, then Jazz, followed by Middle-of-the-Road and Big Band music near the middle, with Rock, Religious music, Soul, and Country music all near the bottom.

Insofar as this is a fair description of the underlying structure of tastes, the taste hierarchy does not so much represent a slim column of taste genres one on top of the other as it does a pyramid with one elite taste at the top and more and more alternative forms at about the same level as one moves down the pyramid toward its base. Thus as one approaches the bottom, musical taste can serve not only to horizontally mark the status *level* but also to vertically mark the status *boundaries between taste groups* defined by age, gender, race, region, religion, lifestyle, etc. that are at roughly the same stratum level.[6] This model fits with the finding mentioned earlier that the lower status occupational groups much more often are able to choose one genre of music that they like the best.

The most descriptive appellation for those near the base of the pyramid would seem to be "univore," suggesting that, unlike the high status "omnivore," members of this group tend to be actively involved in just one, or at best just a few, alternative aesthetic traditions.

Conclusions

Putting together these conjectures, one can hypothesize two pyramids. One right side up and the other upside down. In the first representing taste cultures there is at the top one elite taste culture constituting the cultural capital of the society and below it ever more numerous distinct taste cultures as one moves down the status pyramid. In the inverted pyramid representing concrete individuals or groups, there is at the top the omnivore who commands status by displaying any one of a range of tastes as the situation may require, and at the bottom is the univore who can display just one particular taste. This taste is nonetheless greatly valued by the univore because it is a way to assert an identity and to mark differences from other status groups at approximately the same level.

With the data available we have been able to glimpse most clearly the workings of these two pyramidal structures in the case of music taste. Here the elaborated musical taste code of the omnivore member of the elite can acclaim classical music and yet, in the proper context, show passing knowledge of a wide range of musical forms. At the same time persons near the bottom of the pyramid are more likely to stoutly defend their restricted taste preference, be it religious music, country music, the blues, rap, or some other vernacular music, against persons espousing other lower status musical forms.[7]

This study clearly highlights the inadequacies of both the "elite" and the "mass" elements of the received theory of status hierarchy. Has it always so poorly fit the data? It may be that the elite-mass theory was once correct, and has only become inaccurate as U.S. society has changed. The available evidence suggests the answer—"Yes and no." The answer is "Yes" because the studies of high status persons cited above suggest that a self-conscious elite that believed in the exclusive high status fine culture had consolidated in the U.S. before World War I. The answer is "No" because the characterizations of the lower end of the status hierarchy as a "mass" were based on crude social surveys that, like most contemporary surveys, were not designed to discriminate among the many elements of the U.S. lower class. What is more, all early 20th-century ethnographic studies of the lower orders of the society report a variegated mix of distinct communities based on religion, race, occupation, and national origin. Thus, in effect, the univore has a venerable heritage while the omnivore has emerged recently.

This is not the place to explore for the reasons for the emergence of the omnivore, but a number of possibilities deserve further attention. These include: (1) the fundamental humanist belief in the moral superiority of fine culture was sharply contradicted by the realities of the two World Wars. (2) Technical education, to an important degree, has displaced birth and cultural breeding as requisite for elite status. (3) Many mobile persons of diverse traditions value the customs of their past. At the same time, many forces have operated to tame and make respectable ethic and working-class cultural expressions. These agents include liberal education, the democratic effort to find something good in the traditions of all groups, the exposure via the mass media of diverse cultural expressions, and the commercialization of a wide range of folk and ethnic-based customs, foods, and music.

If the omnivore has indeed emerged and gradually displaced the elitist in recent decades, it should be possible to show this using survey data on leisure activities. The proportion of omnivores to elitists should grow with each succeeding birth cohort. If the causes for the change mentioned in the paragraph just above are operative, omnivores should predominate in all cohorts raised since World War II, that is to say those born since 1940.

The pyramidal hierarchy proposed here ranging from omnivore down to univore is just that, *a proposal*. The conception must undergo rigorous testing before it can claim to be an adequate successor to the elite-to-mass conception which was proposed a century ago and was fully elaborated in the 1930s.

Notes

1 For a complete report of the 1982 Survey of Public Participation in the Arts see Robinson et al. (1985).
2 Other possible sources of explanation for the differences between occupational groups including race, gender, and age differences are pursued by Peterson and Simkus (1993). While not unimportant, they do not explain away all of the counter-theoretical findings.
3 Some of the dynamics of this process of aesthetic transformation as applied to the field of "art music" have been sketched by Peterson (1990).
4 The word "dilettante" has been suggested, but this connotes a person who dabbles in a number of aesthetic forms and performs for a more or less disinterested elite audience. The omnivore is more like the "other-directed" character type described by David Riesman in his 1950 book, *The Lonely Crowd*. In common they change to fit the circumstances of their immediate surroundings. The two are different in that Riesman's character characteristically found safety in adapting the blandest of tastes and values while the omnivore may display a range of quite different tastes as the circumstances demand.
5 The SPPA survey used in this study was created to better understand the dynamics of participation in the fine arts and may not, therefore, have adequately canvassed the range of popular and quasi-folk music choices available as alternatives to art music.
6 This substantive conjecture is in line with the research findings of Judith Blau (1986a, b), DiMaggio and Ostrower (1990) Peterson and Hughes (1984), and Peterson (1972).
7 Musical tastes may well operate in a way roughly parallel to Bernstein's findings for linguistic codes. See Basil Bernstein (1977), who distinguishes between the elaborated linguistic code of the well educated English elite and the restricted linguistic code of the poorly educated working class.

References

Baltzell, E.D. 1964. *The Protestant Establishment*. Glencoe: Free Press.
Bensman, J. and R. Lilienfeld. 1991. *Craft and Consciousness: Occupational Technique and the Development of World Images*. New York: Aldine de Gruyter.
Bernstein, B. 1977. *Class, Codes and Control*. Vol. 3. London: Routledge and Kegan Paul.
Blau, J. 1986a. "High Culture as Mass Culture." *Society* 23(4): 65–69.
_____. 1986b. "The Elite Arts, More or Less de rigueur: A Comparative Analysis of Metropolitan Culture." *Social Forces* 64(4): 875–905.
Bourdieu, P. 1984 [1979]. *Distinction: A Social Critique of the Judgement of Taste*. Cambridge: Harvard University Press.
_____. 1985. "The Social Space and the Genesis of Groups." *Theory and Society* 14(6): 723–744.
Bourdieu, P. and J-C.Passeron. 1977 [1970]. *Reproduction in Education, Society and Culture*. Beverly Hills: Sage.
Brooks, V.W. 1958. *America's Coming of Age*. Garden City: Doubleday.
Browne, R. 1991. *Against Academia: A History of the Popular Culture Movement*. Bowling Green: Popular Press.
Cantril, H., H.G. Wells, H. Koch, H. Gaudet and H. Herzog. 1940. *The Invasion from Mars*. Princeton: Princeton University Press.
DiMaggio, P. 1982. "Cultural Entrepreneurship in Nineteenth-Century Boston: The Creation of an Organizational Base for High Culture in America." *Media, Culture and Society* 4(1): 33–50.
_____. 1987. "Classification in Art." *American Sociological Review* 52(4): 440–445.
DiMaggio, P. and J. Mohr. 1985. "Cultural Capital, Educational Attainment, and Marital Selection." *American Journal of Sociology* 90(6): 1231–1261.
DiMaggio, P. and F. Ostrower. 1990. "Participation in the Arts by Black and White Americans." *Social Forces* 68(3): 753–778.
DiMaggio, P. and M. Useem. 1978. "Social Class and Arts Consumption: The Origins and Consequences of Class Differences in Exposure to the Arts in America." *Theory and Society* 5(2): 141–161.
Domhoff, G.W. 1974. *The Bohemian Grove and Other Retreats*. New York: Harper and Row.
Ewen, S. 1976. *Captains of Consciousness*. New York: McGraw-Hill.
Fantasia, R. 1988. *Cultures of Solidarity*. Berkeley: University of California Press.
Form, W.H. and G.P. Stone. 1957. "Urbanism, Anonymity, and Status Symbolism." *American Journal of Sociology* 62(5): 504–514.
Frank, R.E. and M.G. Greenberg. 1980. *The Public's Use of Televison*. Beverly Hills: Sage.
Gans, H.J. 1974. *Popular Culture and High Culture*. New York: Basic Books.

_____. 1985. "American Popular Culture and High Culture in a Changing Class Structure." *Prospects: An Annual of American Cultural Studies* 10: 17–37.

Glenn, N.D. 1969. *Social Stratification*. New York: Wiley.

Goffman, E. 1951. "Symbols of Class Status." *British Journal of Sociology* 2(4): 294–304.

Halle, D. 1984. *America's Working Man*. Chicago: University of Chicago Press.

Hughes, E.C. 1958. *Men and Their Work*. Glencoe: Free Press.

Jensen, K.B. and K.E. Rosengren. 1990. "Five Traditions in Search of the Audience." *European Journal of Communication* 5(2): 207–238.

Lamont, M. and A. Lareau. 1988. "Cultural Capital: Allusions, Gaps and Glissandos in Recent Theoretical Developments." *Sociological Theory* 6(2): 153–168.

LeMasters, E.E. 1975. *Blue-Collar Aristocrats*. Madison: University of Wisconsin Press.

Levine, L.W. 1988. *Highbrow/Lowbrow: The Emergence of Cultural Hierarchy in America*. Cambridge: Harvard University Press.

Peterson, R.A. 1972. "A Process Model of the Folk, Pop, and Fine Art Phases of Jazz." In *American Music: From Storyville to Woodstock*, ed. C. Nanry, 135–151. New Brunswick: Trans-Action Books and E.P. Dutton.

_____. 1990. "Audience and Industry Origins of the Crisis in Classical Music Programming: Toward World Music." In *The Future of the Arts: Public Policy and Arts Research*, eds. D.B. Pankratz and V.B. Morris, 207–227. New York: Praeger.

Peterson, R.A. and M.J. Hughes. 1984. "Social Correlates of Five Patterns of Arts Participation." In *Contributions to the Sociology of the Arts*, ed. E. Nikolov, 128–136. Sofia: Bulgarian Research Institute for Culture.

Peterson, R.A. and A. Simkus. 1993. "How Musical Taste Groups Mark Occupational Status Groups." In *Cultivating Differences: Symbolic Boundaries and the Making of Inequality*, eds. M. Lamont and M. Fournier, 152–168. Chicago: University of Chicago Press.

Riesman, D. 1950. *The Lonely Crowd*. New Haven: Yale University Press.

Robinson, J.P., C.A. Keegan, T. Hanford and T.A. Triplett. 1985. *Public Participation in the Arts: Final Report on the 1982 Survey*. College Park: University of Maryland.

Roe, K., 1985. "The Swedish Moral Panic Over Video 1980–1984." *Nordicom Review of Nordic Mass Communications Research* (June): 20–25.

Rosengren, K.E., P. Arvidson and D. Sturesson. 1978. "The Barsebeck 'Panic': A Case of Media Deviance." In *Deviance and Mass Media*, ed. C. Winick, 131–149. Beverly Hills: Sage.

Rosengren, K.E. and S. Windahl. 1989. *Media Matter: TV Use in Childhood and Adolescence*. Norwood: Ablex.

Sennett, R. and J. Cobb. 1973. *The Hidden Injuries of Class*. New York: Random House.

Sobel, M.E. 1983. "Life Style Differentiation and Stratification in Contemporary U.S. Society." *Research in Social Stratification and Mobility* 2: 115–144.

Shils, E. 1961. "The Mass Society and Its Culture." In *Culture for the Millions*, ed. Norman Jacobs, 1–27. Princeton: Van Nostrand.

Veblen, T. 1899. *The Theory of the Leisure Class*. New York: MacMillan.

Warner, W.L. 1953. *American Life: Dream and Reality*. Chicago: University of Chicago Press.

Weber, M. 1946. "Class, Status, Party." In *From Max Weber: Essays in Sociology*, eds. H. Gerth and C.W. Mills, 180–195. New York: Oxford University Press.

Wilensky, H.L. 1964. "Mass Media and Mass Culture: Interdependence or Independence?" *American Sociological Review* 29(2): 173–197.

Wright, E.O. 1985. *Classes*. London: New Left.

15

Taste as Performance

ANTOINE HENNION

This text presents the challenges and first results of an ethnographic investigation in progress into the music fans of today. This study is particularly focused on the theoretical and methodological problems that accompany an investigation of this type if it is not conceived as the only explanation of external determinisms that direct the analysis towards the social origins of the fan or the aesthetic properties of the songs. On the contrary, the objective is to focus on the gestures, objects, media, devices and relationships included in a listening or a playing that are not limited to the forming of a taste already there, but which are redefined in the process of the action, and produce a more uncertain result. What has been constituted thanks to the media and the invention of the listener throughout the slow "discomorphosis" (Hennion et al. 2000) of music in the 20th century, joined today by "internetization," is that the sheet music of places and centuries past has been transformed into a repertoire that is available here and now for those who want it. The analysis of the music fan and taste need to be placed within this double transformation: that of the music which becomes a repertoire and that of the participant who becomes purchaser-listener-releaser.

This is why the fan's attachments and modes of action can be articulated and form subjectivities (not only responding to social labels), and have a history that is irreducible to that of the works. Therefore, it is necessary to conceive a more pragmatic sociology that is closer to what the actors think and do, as opposed to the critical conception that the culture of sociology has got us used to. The question of cultural inequalities and uneven access to the works has hidden the very production of the works as an accessible repertoire. In terms of music fans, this has led us to adopt a broader definition that includes all the practices of music. There is no reason to endorse the idea that some are but a passive consumption (attending a concert or listening to a record) and would not be worthy of appearing in a study of music fans. A highly active form of listening to music exists, in the sense of an enthusiastic development of competence (a no less traditional acceptance of the word fan, but more usual if we speak of cigars, wine or coffee). Undoubtedly, it is also wise to abandon the use of a single word, like taste for example, with so many connotations and mainly referring to the consumption of a precious object. Love, passion, taste, practices, habits, obsessions: there is an abundance of vocabulary that better defines the variety of configurations that link to music. It is not so important to determine it a priori; above all it is not necessary to measure it only by the standard of taste for an object whose appreciation requires an erudite learning. It is not just about the choice of an over-selective social format but about not making premature hypotheses on the meaning of these practices, in which the place and status of the music itself are very far from being determined. Music is made, we like it, we listen to it, we like this genre or that music. The verbs are more adequate as they force less a collective practice with the objects to enter a substantive category directed towards an object.

In terms of the method, the sociologist cannot just observe taste from the outside, which is how he/she believes an amateur observes a work of art: as an object that can be contemplated and not as an effect that can or cannot emerge. Taste, pleasure or the effect of things are neither exogenous variables nor automatic attributes of the objects.[1] They are the result of an action performed by the taster, an action based on technique, bodily entertainment and repeated sampling, and which is accomplished over time, simultaneously because it follows a regulated development and because its success largely depends on moments. Taste is a bodily practice that is collective and instrumented, regulated by methods that are incessantly argued over, and that centres around the appropriated perception of uncertain effects. Thus, we prefer to talk about "attachments."[2] This beautiful word destroys the opposition that accentuates the dualism of the word "taste," between a series of causes that come from outside and the "hic et nunc" of the situation and the interaction. In terms of music fans, there is less emphasis on labels and more on states, less on self-proclamations and more on people's activity; regarding the objects that motivate taste, their right to reply and their ability to coproduce what is happening, what arises from the contact, remains open.

Taste as Reflexive Activity

So, another way of presenting this text would be to say it aims at articulating the musical taste in the act, the situation, with its tricks and traps, far removed from the space of public justification, focusing only on its own success. The practices of the music fan studied produce a marked variance in the base elements of taste that our study has elucidated (Hennion 2004): the relationship to the object, the support on a collective, the entertainment of oneself, and finally the constitution of a technical device (understood in the broad sense of a more or less organized set of favourable conditions for the development of the activity or of the appreciation). Taste is neither the consequence (automatic or induced) of the objects that provoke taste by themselves, nor a mere social arrangement projected onto the objects or the simple pretext of a ritual or collective game. It is a reflexive, instrumented arrangement to test our sensations. It is not a mechanical process, it is always "deliberate"; it is an "accomplishment," as expressed by English-speakers, who use Latin better than we, Latin languages-speakers, do . . .

The crucial point is the way in which taste depends on the returns of the object tasted, on what it does and what it makes people do. This is no paradox, except for sociologists, who consider everything within the relationship of taste, except the presence and effects of the product that causes taste. Speaking of "returns" is not to say either that the object contains its effects but that it is discovered precisely at the point of non-determination, variance and the deepening of the effects that the product produces; effects that are not due only to the product but to its momentums, unfoldings, and to circumstances. Also it is the idea of mediation (Hennion 2007). The very media we give ourselves to capture the object (the record, song, dance or collective practice) form part of the effects that this can produce. Our research consequently centres on the analysis of taste as a collective, instrumented and reflexive activity, with the underlying idea that sociology has a lot of work to do if it wants to give an account of attachments, firstly on itself, in terms of its supposed theories and perhaps, fundamentally, on its means of investigation and the type of relationship it has with what it observes. If one has to get involved, in time and with its body, in commerce with the object in question, it is that relationship that imposes itself, also for the analyst. Listening is a challenge that the sociologist is confronted with. What can we say about music without involving our own love for it and, in the first instance, without listening? Therefore, the word listening is perfect because it avoids the duality of the relationship with the object (whether it is known or unknown, loved or unloved, "let yourself be deceived," believing in it or showing up taste as being just belief. . .), to bring together a wide range of varied aspects of musical activity: the attention of an I, the presence of others or the reference to them, the headphones, the instruments of sound production, the bodily reaction and the reflexive development of sensitivity.

You Keep Loving but What You Have Been . . .

But it would be selfish to reduce the problem to questions about the sociologist's situation towards what he/she observes. Sociology itself has long affected tastes, influenced the amateur. When we ask somebody about what he/she likes, today the answer comes with an excuse: his/her family was upper class, a brother played the violin, of course not everyone has the money to buy the best Bordeaux wines . . . We have reached the ultimate extreme, paradoxical, of criticism, where criticism becomes the doxa and not the paradox and makes the very reality of what it criticises disappear inside the actors it wishes to analyse. This vulgarization of its thesis determines the reception the sociologist receives henceforth: the amateur feels guilty or an object of suspicion, feels ashamed of what he/she likes, decodes and anticipates the meaning of what he/she says, stands accused of a practice that is too elitist, accepts the ritualistic nature of his/her rocking nights, wine tastings among friends or his/her love of opera. And what is worse, the amateur does not dare any longer speak of neither the objects, the gestures, the feelings he/she experiences, nor his/her uncertainties. Instead of that, the amateur places him/herself within those cases presumably assigned to him/her and only has one concern: that he/she does not seem to be ignorant of the fact that his/her taste falls into the domain of sociology. Far from revealing the hidden social character of tastes that the amateur would consider personal, irreducible and absolute, from now sociology is for some amateurs the first repertoire available to talk about them, and they put up no resistance, on the contrary, on presenting (among other registers, it is true, according to the circumstances and the speakers) their objects of attachment as arbitrary signs determined by social origin that they consider to be relative, historic and pretexts for various rituals.

A curious paradox: it is the turn of the sociologist to de-sociologize the amateurs so that they can talk not about their determinisms but about ways of doing things, less about what they love. How can we make them stop warning the sociologist they know that their choices are determined, and speak again about ways of listening, drinking and playing, and about pleasure, of what overwhelms them, of the forms their practices take, of the surprising techniques they develop as amateurs to gather the conditions of their happiness, without any guarantee that it will be achieved? Far from being an agent manipulated by unknown forces, the amateur is a virtuoso of aesthetic, social, technical, mind and body experimentation. He/she is not the last one to argue the effects of belief and of distanciation: the amateur also wonders if excessive proximity to the object can blind him/her. Taking up a curious challenge, the truth about his/her tastes, the amateur is sparing, according to the moments, of participation and withdrawal, of enthusiastic immersion and resorting to mechanisms of objectivising, analysis, guides and references. Put into another way, there is no debate that is so inherent in sociology that it escapes to the reflexive activity of the amateurs.

The sociologization of the actors themselves also functions in another way, as a pragmatic resource to work on the tastes. A chance example came to my mind that is independent of our investigations. In an argument between some rockers (that I, the sociologist, had not provoked), one evening I heard one say to the other: "You keep loving but what you have been." I didn't give it much thought but I think that comment made an impression on me. I recalled it some time later when discussing this subject. What could be more reflexive than this . . . reflection? On the one hand, this reflection mobilizes a sociology of social determinisms: your tastes are your past in sediment (family, school, social . . .), it forms your identity. Once liberated from the temptation to declare that the social is a hidden dimension that determines everything, we can recognize that the fact that some people's micro-statement on taste carries immediate social identifications forms part of everyone's broad common knowledge. But this mobilization by people themselves completely changes the state of such a knowledge: first, it is not that unconscious; and, most importantly, this initial determination is not the end of the matter: it can be put to work (or not), it can be considered a support to go further or simply as a sign, it can be reinforced or surpassed. In sum, it is part of taste itself, as is its availability for debate with those that are closest. If the rocker in question offers this reflection to his friend, it is because he also thinks that tastes are negotiated in the exchange with others. This leads us quite far from a vision of taste as a game played by actors just considered as "believing" in the object of their taste and being blind to its social determinisms.

They select one from all the possible determinisms. Here, on our rocker's case, it was the history of taste as a definition of oneself, considered by the rest of his friend's as a type of highly stereotyped repetition; but by reproaching him his perpetual return to the rock of the 70s, they are not determinist: on the contrary, they make their assertion active, performing. They would not point it out without having in mind the uncertain hope that this might help him move a little forward . . .

In short, we are obliged to make a curious redress. It consists of giving back to the amateur the competences of a sociologist, and to the sociologist his/her right and duty to be an amateur as well. But the effort is worth it. The speaker who was distrustful is now in a position to talk about his/her tastes and becomes somebody who is incredibly ingenious in describing what he/she does, referring less to what he/she likes and more to how he/she likes it, with whom, how he/she does it, what carries him/her away, more or less according to the moments or given circumstances.

Philippe: The Music Library as Imagined Harem

One of the first amateurs I questioned at the start of the investigation provided me with a caricature of a good interview for a postgraduate student. He talked of his family background, his sister played the violin, his uncle took him to concerts as a young lad, the first time he went to the opera (an unforgettable experience), his current job (doctor), his tastes (opera and chamber music).

By chance, as he is a friend of mutual friends of ours, I had the chance to converse with him again, not in a second interview, but in a different kind of meeting, two years later, at a dinner for friends at his house. After dinner, he took me to the music room he had built himself, to which his wife, children and even his dog were forbidden access. There, with all the objects and places of his passion, in front of another amateur, it was another man who revealed himself to me. He didn't try to show the sociologist that an interviewee is no less intelligent than the interviewer, nor that he could politely display the series of determinisms of his own taste. Neither did he begin to recite a boring list of his favourite classics, anticipating my answers according to amateurs' ritual when first meeting. What he did was show me what he does, his gestures, his obsessions, his things, his installation. He also showed me how he experienced his moments of pleasure, the choice of his uncountable records, the ways in which he acquired them, even his critical notes (taken from magazines but never followed up when he is in a store) or the way in which he characterizes his states of mind and translating his fatigue into the terms of a possible repertoire.

He had two walls filled to the ceiling with shelves of records, CDs and cassettes. Then, laughing, he showed me how he sorted his objects; like everybody else, he had ordered them chronologically and alphabetically, which makes home record shelves look like a mini-Fnac. He is an overworked doctor and buys a lot. He had left some shelves empty on the lower right side where his latest purchases were piled up awaiting "classification." But they were also there as priority listening because they were new. And that is how he got the idea of transforming into a criteria of order this "lack of classification." So, he places the recordings he has just listened to on the lower right side of his record shelves, and so lets them pile up inside his library according to how much he likes each one over a period of time. He began with boxed sets of opera, his favourite genre, and he liked this system so much that he generalized it. His record collection gradually became a photograph in which his gestures pile up by strata. The physical space of the record library has become a trail of the amateur's personal history.

He uses it as such, knowing that he has to turn to the right to listen to new music or music he wishes to hear again, and on the left he will find rarer objects or music he has forgotten he had. He himself made me aware that had invented an absolutely idiosyncratic form of classifying music: Who, apart from him (and sometimes it was hard work . . .) would know where a specific record was kept? But most importantly, the amateur asserts himself over the musicologist. His taste is what determines classification, not the history of music. Between the pleasure of so keeping up a memory of what he has listened to, the satisfaction of being wrong, of evaluating his false impressions about the last time he listened to a record, the pleasure of forcing himself to step out of his own routine thanks to his ingenuity, or when he must bend down to pick up a record he has put to one side, it is easy to see an expression of happiness that says he has not wasted his time with his invention.

Listening is not only an instant, it is also a history. Its reflexivity is also its ability to build itself as the framework of its own activity. This time we no longer consider it in the present of a contact with the sounds that happen, but in the improbable duration of a slow invention, that of an art and a technique of listening for the sake of listening. The production of its own spaces and duration, of dedicated scenarios and mechanisms, the progressive evolving constitution of a repertoire, the entertainment of the body and spirit, the formation of a media of professionals, of a trade of criticism and a circle of amateurs, this is the other side of its reflexivity: music as a delegation of the power to move our emotions to a set of works converted into the objective of a privileged listening. This historic aspect of music listening is extremely awkward due to its false evidence. The very fact of listening to music is a strange position of which it is difficult to perceive the paradoxical nature once we occupy it and it becomes something natural.[3] To stand before an identified object, which must be listened to (consequently, for this object we have equipped the perception with techniques, words and all necessary prostheses) and which is able to rise to this expectation, is at the same time the most fundamental, the gesture that makes the music just as we perceive it, and the least visible part of our musical operations. At least, when we are with so-called serious or learned musicians: it is enough to move away from their tight circles and drift towards other musics, be them ethnic or popular, to get back to finding the heterogeneous multiplicity of mixed relations, "events" (in the sense of producers of shows), from which it is hard to pull away between the pleasure of the collective, bodily sensations, the formats of an organized moment and the musical elements of a performance.[4]

[. . .]

Conclusion: The Object of the Music

To leave behind an objectivist conception of taste, as if it were no more than the consequence of the physical properties of the objects that cause taste, does not mean substituting it for a social, ritual or interactive analysis in which belief in the object replaces the role of first cause that the object itself had before. The previous analyses aimed to show the opposite: the awkward presence of the object in taste. It is definitively the agreed place, or not, for the returns of the music, for the answer of the objects, which makes the difference. By being socially constructed, the object does not cease to exist: on the contrary, thus it is more present. We cannot keep on alternating indefinitely between natural-linear interpretations (taste arises from things in themselves) and circular-cultural interpretations (the objects are what we make of them). It is necessary to get rid of this "zero-sum game" between the object and the social in order to show how taste comes to things thanks to its amateurs. Here we stick closely to the suppositions of pragmatism.

This is what takes us out of a dual world (on the one hand, autonomous but inert things and on the other, pure social signs) to let us into a world of mediations and effects in which they are produced together, one by the other, the body that experiences the taste and the taste for the object, the collective which loves and the repertoire of loved objects.[5] The attachments mean all this, the body and the collectives, the things and the mechanisms, all these are mediators. They are determinants and the determined at the same time: they determine the impositions and renew the course of the things.

This co-production, the co-formation of an object and of those things that make it possible demand a more balanced sociology of taste in which the amateurs have as much to learn from sociology as vice-versa.[6] The very objective of our research (the amateur's and more precisely the big amateur's) was somewhat controversial in terms of the sociology of culture. Research strategies have led to an absolute rejection of taste as an individual and collective experience, a deliberate activity that requires considerable commitment and which multiplies the invention of mechanisms and social and bodily techniques.

The highly productive development of an attachment through an object that is produced and shared is interpreted, paradoxically, as its exact opposite, a free game determined by social labels in which the qualities and classifications of the object of appreciation only appeared as secondary or illusory. Meanwhile no interest was shown in the frameworks within which this taste or passion operated, nor in the mechanisms or the times and places that the amateur's invented to develop the collective and instrumented appreciation of their common object.

In conclusion, tastes, not as independent variables that gather together in order to guarantee a result but as uncertain mediations that support each other to make states arise, to bring about responses to objects, to transform beings, to make the moments that matter coherent. We can dream: and what if sociology was to cease fighting once and for all against the imaginary power that the objects supposedly hold over us? And what if, by listening to the amateurs, sociology was to recognize this power, or in other words, the art of a more intense and reflexive relationship which, through taste, humans slowly by surely establish with the objects, with others, with their bodies and with themselves?

Notes

1 The main interest of the DEP research into amateurs (Donnat 1996) is to break with this model in order to focus on effective practices, like historians did, for example, with regard to collecting (Pomian 1987) or reading (Chartier 1987, 1992).

2 Concerning the notion of attachment, see Callon (1999), Gomart and Hennion (1999) and Latour (1996, 2000).

3 The social historian W. Weber posed the question, with regard to the concert, asking himself whether people did listen to music in the 18th century (Weber 1997). There is an anachronism in the use of the same words (listening, music, work) to describe situations that are so historically opposed, such as court music, the modern concert and the record. As P. Szendy (2001) points out, the ear has a history.

4 At this point we can ask ourselves, perhaps stretching the reasoning to the limit, whether today's technology and all-powerful music systems are not media that impede listening, or at least purposeful listening, to make music pass over to the side of the social techniques of emotion and collective fusion, tearing it away from the selective attention invented by classic mechanisms.

5 The sociology of taste owes a lot here to the works on sciences and techniques of CSI and the Actor-Network Theory, for example, Callon (1986), Latour (1991) and Law and Hassard (1999).

6 Thus, I conclude a critical journey through the sociology of art and culture (Hennion 2007) with an invitation to abandon its submission to what I call the theory of generalized belief. P. Bourdieu (1979) has radicalized a critical formulation in the sociology of culture but via the notion of convention, it is the same model of belief that dominates the sociology of art as H.S. Becker's (1988), even if in a much more liberal and closer to the actors mode.

References

Becker, H.S. 1988. *Les mondes de l'art.* Paris: Flammarion.

Bourdieu, P. 1979. *La distinction. Critique sociale du jugement.* Paris: Minuit.

Callon, M. 1986. "Some Elements for a Sociology of Translation: Domestication of the Scallops and the Fishermen of St-Brieuc Bay." In *Power, Action and Belief: a New Sociology of Knowledge?* ed. J. Law, 196–229. London: Routledge and Kegan Paul.

_____. 1999. "Ni intellectuel engagé, ni intellectuel dégagé: la double stratégie de l'attachement et du détachement." *Sociologie du travail* 99(1): 1–13.

Chartier, R. 1987. *Lecture et lecteurs dans la France d'Ancien Régime.* Paris: Seuil.

_____. 1992. *L'Ordre des livres: lecteurs, auteurs, bibliothèques en Europe entre le XIVe et le XVIIe siècle.* Aix-en-Provence: Alinea.

Donnat, O. 1996. *Les amateurs. Enquête sur les activités artistiques des Français.* Paris: DEP/Ministère de la Culture-DAG.

Gomart, É. and A. Hennion. 1999. "A Sociology of Attachment: Music Lovers, Drug Addicts." In *Actor Network Theory and After,* eds. J. Law and J. Hassard, 220–247. Oxford: Blackwell.

Hennion, A. 2004. "Pragmatics of Taste." In *The Blackwell Companion to the Sociology of Culture,* eds. M. Jacobs and N. Hanrahan, 131–144. Oxford: Blackwell.

_____. 2007. *La passion musicale. Une sociologie de la médiation.* Paris: Métailié.

Hennion, A., S. Maisonneuve and É. Gomart. 2000. *Figures de l'amateur. Formes, objets, pratiques de l'amour de la musique aujourd'hui.* Paris: La Documentation Française.

Latour, B. 1991. *Nous n'avons jamais été modernes. Essai d'anthropologie symétrique.* Paris: La Découverte.

_____. 1996. *Petite réflexion sur le culte moderne des dieux faitiches.* Paris: Les empêcheurs de tourner en rond.

_____. 2000. "Factures/fractures. De la notion de réseau à celle d'attachement." In *Ce qui nous relie,* eds. A. Micoud and M. Peroni, 189–208. La Tour d'Aigues: Éds de l'Aube.

Law J. and J. Hassard, eds. 1999. *Actor Network Theory and After.* Oxford: Blackwell.

Pomian, K. 1987. *Collectionneurs, amateurs et curieux: Paris-Venise, XVIe-XVIIIe siècles.* Paris: Gallimard.

Szendy, P. 2001. *Écoute. Une histoire de nos oreilles.* Paris: Minuit.

Weber, W. 1997. "Did People Listen in the 18th Century?" *Early Music* XXV(4): 678–691.

III

POLITICS, SOCIAL ISSUES, AND MUSICAL CULTURES

Each of these chapters does something similar but in a different musical context. The goal is to sketch a variety of musical "worlds" (Becker 1982) and some of their attendant political and social issues. Drott addresses the question of politics most directly and most broadly, providing a sophisticated discussion of music's role in protest, resistance and social movements. Drawing on examples from a variety of genres, one of Drott's crucial points is that the political potential of music should be understood within a wider spectrum of sonic practice, including noise-making, through which groups assert their presence and make their voices heard.

Other chapters address musical politics and social inequalities in more particular contexts. Leonard, for example, looks at gender in the popular music industries. She begins by underlining the foundational role that social constructionist and feminist theories of gender played in disrupting the ideology of aesthetic autonomy that has long informed musical discourse. From there, Leonard outlines various gender dynamics and stereotypes in three main areas of the music industries: employment and work settings, genre worlds and audiovisual representation. Kwame Harrison offers a similar examination in relation to hip hop, which, he argues, is "one of the foremost arenas in which discussions of race, racial injustices and the transformation of racial meanings occur." This is a nuanced, almost historographic analysis of four main themes that have tended to recycle in both public and academic discussions of hip hop and race in the US (especially blackness and whiteness). Kwame Harrison thus ends with a call for additional ethnographic research into hip hop, which seems to hold promise for moving beyond entrenched views of the genre.

Regev's chapter examines the hybrid musical aesthetics and identity formations that have emerged in an era of globalization and cosmopolitanism. In particular, he identifies the proliferation of a "cluster of styles and genres" called "pop-rock music." Without falling into overly simplistic debates about cultural imperialism or postmodernism, which defined an earlier generation of work on "world music" (for a critical summary see Born and Hesmondhalgh 2000), Regev outlines the processes by which pop-rock became a kind of globalized aesthetic, affective and even embodied framework for making music.

As Regev's chapter suggests, questions of music and place, of the relation between the global and the local, have become especially important in recent decades. Cohen's chapter explores the musical construction of place in the urban context, focusing on Liverpool. Using a unique method in which musicians were asked to draw maps of the city and its music, Cohen shows how material metropolitan environments affect musical memories and practices of music-making, while also drawing attention to the key roles of creative industries and cultural policy in urban regeneration. Cohen is a key part of a growing literature on music and the city (for example Scott 2008, Baker and Knighton 2011, Holt and Wergin 2012, musicinlondon.org) as well as growing bodies of research at the intersection of music, urban geography, policy and cultural heritage (for example Krims 2006, Cohen et al. 2015).

Michelsen and Weber outline issues of taste and cultural capital in relation to two rather different musical worlds. Michelsen discusses the central but under-researched role of music journalism and music criticism in the formation and maintenance of popular music "taste cultures." His chapter includes clear historical overviews of ideas about taste and culture, as well as music journalism and criticism writ large. Weber, meanwhile, outlines the complexities of social class and cultural capital in the world of nineteenth-century art music (though he also touches on popular music). Weber's analysis is based on a deep reading and careful reconsideration of Bourdieu. This leads Weber to questions of "omnivorous" musical taste in the nineteenth-century upper class, as well as how the relationship between social class and music in the nineteenth century can help in deciphering listening practices in the twentieth century.

Fogarty's chapter begins by noting a curiosity: although music and dance are inextricable in most cultures, relatively little work in the sociology of music has taken stock of this relationship. After unpacking what amounts to a dual marginalization of dancing and bodies in both certain areas of scholarship and certain areas of society, Fogarty builds toward a theory of the kinesthetic in music. Her focus is less on "the" body than on various *bodies* (such as the difference between youthful and ageing bodies) and her discussion is based in a reflexive account of the role of ethnography in constructing knowledge about dance cultures. In the end, Fogarty's chapter provocatively suggests that the most promising future research directions may exist, not in the sociology of music and dance, but in the sociology of sound and movement.

Collectively, the authors in this section address a wide range of musical genres (from popular music to art music) and time periods (from the early 1800s to today). The intended benefits of this section are thus twofold: not only do these chapters present sociological insights into the organization and functioning of various musical worlds (which is valuable and interesting in and of itself); they also show readers what it means to apply a sociological imagination to musical culture—and therefore also how they might do so themselves.

References

Baker, G. and T. Knighton, eds. 2011. *Music and Urban Society in Colonial Latin America.* Cambridge: Cambridge University Press.

Becker, H.S. 1982. *Art Worlds.* Berkeley: University of California Press.

Born, G. and D. Hesmondhalgh, eds. 2000. *Western Music and Its Others: Difference, Representation and Appropriation in Music.* Berkeley: University of California Press.

Cohen, S., R. Knifton, M. Leonard and L. Roberts. 2015. *Sites of Popular Music Heritage: Memories, Histories, Places.* New York: Routledge.

Holt, F. and C. Wergin, eds. 2012. *Musical Performance and the Changing City: Post-Industrial Contexts in Europe and the United States.* New York: Routledge.

Krims, A. 2007. *Music and Urban Geography.* New York: Routledge.

Scott, D. 2008. *Sounds of the Metropolis: The Nineteenth-Century Popular Music Revolution in London, New York, Paris and Vienna.* Oxford: Oxford University Press.

16

Resistance and Social Movements

Eric Drott

If ever there were any doubts regarding music's significance for political protest, the wave of unrest that has swept the globe since the financial crisis of 2008 should have laid them to rest. Consider the following: the role of Tunisian rapper El Général in catalyzing the Jasmine Revolution; Manu Chao's impromptu performance before Barcelona's Indignados encampment in May 2011; the drum circle whose rhythms resounded through Zuccotti Park during Occupy Wall Street; the transformation of Ramy Essam's refrain "*Irhal, irhal*" ("Leave, leave") into the rallying cry of those demanding Hosni Mubarak's ouster in Tahrir Square; Brazilian demonstrators' playful appropriation of "*Vem pra rua*" ("Come into the street"), a song originally commissioned for a Fiat commercial. These and other examples too numerous to cite attest to music's enduring capacity to mobilize individuals and encourage their participation in contentious action. At a minimum, recent events refute popular media narratives regarding the declining status of protest music since its putative glory years in the 1960s (Hajdu 2004, McKinley 2011). Yet the prominence accorded to music in journalistic accounts of the post-2008 protest wave, while salutary in some respects, has given rise to its own distortions. Only a narrow range of musical practices, performing an equally narrow range of functions, has attracted journalistic attention. This is particularly true of protest anthems, songs deemed to speak on behalf of the anonymous multitudes. Judging from contemporary press accounts, what captures the mediatic imagination above all else are those rare yet memorable occasions when musicians are able to crystallize the spirit of a movement, giving voice to its grievances and aspirations (Bohlman 2012).

A principal concern of this chapter is to expand upon this widespread but overly restrictive conception of music's place in political action. Much as demonstrations, occupations and strikes are but the visible surface of activism, behind which hides the mundane work of recruitment, organization and education, so too does the canonization of certain songs or the consecration of certain artists deflect attention away from the variety of ways music serves social movements and the cause of political resistance. In addition, placing too great an emphasis on protest song encourages a neglect of the broader range of sound- and noise-making practices used in acts of public contention. To this end the conclusion of this chapter seeks to resituate music within a broader continuum of sonic practices encountered in protest actions.

Resistance

The diversity of ways music can be implicated in contentious politics is already suggested by the title of this chapter, which, in juxtaposing the terms "resistance" and "social movements," gestures toward two distinct conceptions of political action. While these conceptions interpenetrate to a large degree—clearly many social movements see themselves as resisting some hegemonic order—the two are not coextensive. Resistance implies the existence of a totalizing system against which struggle is waged, if only to secure a space of relative autonomy within its bounds (McKay 1996, Duncombe 2002). The struggles of social movements, by contrast, need not be defined in anti-systemic terms. Rather, their targets run the gamut from specific local grievances to entire ideological regimes (patriarchy, ethnocentrism, the contemporary "culture of death," and so on). Concomitant with this difference in scale is a more fundamental divergence in how the space of politics is conceived. Both the theory and practice of cultural resistance assumes society to be structured by radical disparities in wealth, power and prestige, which dominant groups perpetuate by means of persuasion, coercion and violence when necessary. This conflict-model of society—by and large a legacy of Marxist thought—also animates many social movements, though not all. Particularly among single-issue groups operating within liberal–democratic polities, a more pluralistic, less antagonistic vision of the social world commonly prevails. Finally, and most importantly, cultural resistance has the potential to embrace a much wider swath of activities than are usually associated with social movements. This is in large part due to the fact that resistance is such a fluid, unstable concept, especially compared to social movements. Although a hard-and-fast definition of the latter is difficult to formulate, a few basic features may be identified: they are collective enterprises that in order to contest existing social arrangements engage in a sustained campaign against power holders, with an eye toward effecting a change in policy, customs, practices and so on (Tarrow 1998, Mathieu 2012). Of these characteristics, only one—a conflictual or contestatory stance—is an invariant trait of cultural resistance. Coordinated, collective action is not obligatory: one can undertake acts of resistance at an individual level, even if this risks limiting their effectiveness. Likewise, resistance need not endure through time. As often as not it is episodic, flaring up whenever opportunities to register discontent present themselves. Neither can one assume that resistance aims at effecting substantive change. Even if certain forms of cultural resistance are marked by actors' ambition to radically overturn existing social relations, others fail to move past symbolic gestures of defiance, or function as coping mechanisms to palliate the daily humiliations of social, economic and/or political subordination.

Many of the distinctions outlined above are implicit in Scott's influential model of "everyday resistance" (Scott 1985, 1989, 1990). Focusing principally on settings characterized by rigid stratifications of power, wealth and prestige (traditional peasant societies, slave economies, caste systems), Scott emphasizes the strategic necessity for dominated groups to adopt forms of resistance that are covert, deniable and thus unlikely to result in the sanctions that open defiance would garner. Common actions include poaching, work slowdowns, sabotage, desertion, or pilfering. As Scott (1989) observes, such small-scale interventions are seldom recognized as genuinely political, since they are neither "openly declared" nor a product of "group action in the usually understood sense of collective action." The same is true of the discourses, traditions and symbolic forms—including music—that provide the ideological corollary of transgressive conduct. Unable to express discontent openly for fear of retribution, subordinate groups develop what Scott (1990) dubs a "hidden transcript," counter-traditions of critique that can only be performed out of earshot of dominant groups. Outside of rare exceptions, the only traces of this "offstage" talk discernible in the public sphere are those that assume veiled or ambiguous forms. As is the case with low-level acts of material resistance like pilfering or sabotage, deniability is crucial: hence the frequent recourse to metaphor, euphemism, allegory, insinuation and other techniques that allow individuals to say one thing while implying another.

Music has long served subordinate groups as a vehicle for expressing discontent with the prevailing social order. Such musical resistance may manifest itself episodically, in individual songs or performances, though it commonly assumes a more enduring form, in the styles, practices and aesthetic ideologies cultivated by certain subcultures and music scenes (Hall and Jefferson 1976). For instance, in her pioneering study of rap music Tricia Rose (1994: 101) characterizes the genre as it had developed up to the early 1990s as "a hidden transcript" in Scott's sense, in which rappers "act out inversions of status hierarchies" and "tell alternative stories of contact with police and the education process." The marriage of text, music and performance in song offers numerous avenues for the expression of such resistance. Lyrics can give voice to counterhegemonic ideals, at times explicitly, at other times only implicitly. The latter is typical of cultural production under repressive regimes, where censorship, the specter of professional sanctions, and the menace of physical violence make musicians' dissimulation of critical content imperative. In apartheid-era South Africa, for example, music producers developed ingenious forms of word-play to evade censors; a compilation released by the label Shifty Records in 1985 bearing the seemingly innocent if nonsensical Afrikaans title *A Naartjie in Our Sosatie* ("A Tangerine in Our Kebab") revealed its subversive intent when rendered phonetically into English ("Anarchy in Our Society") (Drewett 2003: 158). Certain musics may likewise convey a sense of "resistance" at a sonic or stylistic level, though music's semiotic indeterminacy renders such significations elusive, liable to divergent interpretations. Far from being a shortcoming, however, the non-representational and intensely connotative nature of musical meaning makes it a powerful medium for political contention. The opposition it expresses appears to derive from a profoundly corporeal or affective level of experience, beyond verbalization. But to the extent that a particular performance, practice, subculture, or genre can be heard as resistant, it is through the mutual mediation of sociopolitical oppositions and distinctions specific to the musical field. A song or a genre only embodies an oppositional stance in relation to other songs or other genres, which, by virtue of their cultural prestige, institutional backing, economic dominance, or association with social elites, are identified as mainstream or hegemonic (Thornton 1996, Drott 2011).

It follows from this that music is not invariably an instrument of resistance, but can serve equally well as an instrument of social control. In such cases music becomes precisely that which dominated groups resist. Willis's ethnography of the "counter-school culture" developed by working-class adolescents in the industrial city of Hammertown captures this dynamic vividly. In one interview his informants relate how the rejection of school authority—and the dominant ideology it embodies— is enacted through a refusal to participate in the singing of hymns during school assemblies: "I was just standing there, moving my mouth," one lad relates. Another adds that "when we do sing we make a joke of it," singing the wrong verses at the wrong times (Willis 1977: 30). Collective music-making, and the group cohesion it is supposed to instill, become the terrain on which the conflict between superordinate and subordinate groups is carried out.

Apart from serving as a *medium* for resistance, or—negatively—as an *incitement* to acts of cultural defiance, music may become the *grounds* for dissensus, the object whose alleged misuse or exploitation prompts transgressive action. Its co-optation by political authorities, commercial enterprises and other institutional forces often elicits counter-movements within the musical field that struggle against the perceived offenses committed both through and against this charged site of aesthetic and political investment. At its limit, the hostility engendered toward music's co-optation by a corrupted social order can circle back on music itself, as is the case with the critique of the institution of art undertaken by Dada and neo-vanguard movements like Fluxus or Situationism (Bürger 1984). Less extreme but more commonplace are forms of resistance that target specific policies deemed detrimental to musical life. For instance, certain commentators have interpreted the practice of illegal file-sharing as a form of "everyday resistance." Abetting the free circulation of MP3 files over the internet represents in this reading a response to the progressive enclosure of the musical commons by large media conglomerates. Opposition to increasingly restrictive intellectual property laws leads people to engage in a kind of digital poaching, waged against a modern-day rentier class (Howard-Spink 2004, Burkart 2010).

As the last example indicates, a key question in the study of cultural resistance concerns the interpretation of activities that, when viewed from a different angle, appear apolitical. Consider file-sharing. While cyberlibertarians and hacktivists may defend it as a form of civil disobedience, record industry personnel prefer to empty the practice of political import, describing it as theft or piracy. Even if one rejects the industry's framing as transparently self-interested, it is difficult to say how many of those who download MP3 files illicitly are animated by principled objections to intellectual property law, and how many are driven by more selfish motives. Similar hermeneutic problems arise in connection to other forms of musical resistance. Are the transgressive qualities associated with a genre like noise music properly understood as an expression of resistance? Its anti-commercialism and breaches against norms of musicality might suggest so. But unless musicians, fans and other members of this scene corroborate such a reading, one risks mistaking strategies of subcultural distinction for acts of symbolic dissent (Thornton 1996). More problematically, treating cultural practices as coded political utterances lends itself to reductivist accounts, as a desire to recognize the political agency of subaltern groups paradoxically robs them of aesthetic agency (Kelley 1997). Scott's theory of cultural resistance exemplifies this risk. In stressing the need to expand our definition of what counts as political conduct lest the tactics of disempowered groups elude our grasp, Scott's interpretive method compels scholars to look past appearances, to uncover the subtext hidden beneath the text—in short, to cultivate an inverted hermeneutics of suspicion that presumes subordinate groups cannot be trusted to mean what they say. Lacking criteria for assessing their validity, such readings cannot help but be implicated in the acts of contention they purport to describe.

Social Movements

Unlike resistance, which encompasses the sporadic interventions of individuals, social movements are sustained, collective initiatives. To this we might add another distinction: "resistance" refers to an activity, whereas the term "movement" conventionally refers to a social form or entity. Conceiving social movements along substantialist lines like this is problematic, however, in that it reifies what is in reality a more fluid phenomenon. A movement is not something that is given but something that is achieved. It exists only insofar as it is enacted and re-enacted through a variety of inter-connected practices. Social movement theorist Sidney Tarrow (1998: 4) has identified three sets of activities that may be regarded as constitutive of movements: "first, mounting collective challenges; second, drawing on social networks, common purposes and cultural frameworks; and, third, building solidarity through connective structures and collective identities to sustain collective action." Paraphrasing Tarrow, one might say that outside of periodic acts of public contention activists are obliged to engage in continuous cultural and organizational work: framing issues, forging shared identities, drawing symbolic boundaries, recruiting participants, procuring resources and mobilizing support, to name a few.

Disaggregating social movements into the diverse practices by which they are performed points to the variety of ways music may contribute to their enactment. Of these, one of the most conspicuous concerns the framing of injustices. As Snow (2008: 384) observes, framing is a vital part of the "signifying work" and "meaning construction" that activists pursue in their efforts to focus attention on and mold perceptions of an issue. Typically this involves reinterpreting a situation heretofore tolerated, casting it as unjust and in need of rectification. But such "diagnostic framing" does not suffice by itself. In addition, there must be "prognostic framing": the problem identified must not be perceived as inevitable or unchangeable, but as the outcome of contingent political choices—and hence liable to change via concerted political action. Finally, to incite action participants must also engage in "motivational framing," mobilizing support by emphasizing a problem's severity or urgency (Snow and Benford 2000: 615).

While much work in frame alignment theory has stressed the cognitive and evaluative dimensions of activists' signifying practices, it is clear that their efficacy depends in large part upon the emotions they arouse (indignation, anger and so on) (Goodwin, Jasper and Polletta 2001, Traïni 2008: 19). It is here that music proves a powerful resource, given its unparalleled capacity to generate and transmit affective states. A case in point is El Général's "*Rais Lebled*," whose lyrics voiced frustration with the police and governmental corruption rampant in Tunisia prior to the Jasmine Revolution. By directing its criticisms at president Ben Ali, the song suggested that it was not only in his power to put such abuses to an end, but that his failure to do so made him culpable for the wrongs committed against the Tunisian people. Both El Général's flow and the timbre of his voice make his disgust palpable, while the use of double-tracking in the song's chorus lends weight to his denunciation of the regime, as if the song was not just an individual but a collective expression of outrage. Throughout, the looped minor-mode riff that accompanies El Général's rap imbues the song with a grim, inexorable quality. In short, it is not simply that the song identifies an injustice and intimates how it might be addressed (that is, through a change of government); it also invests this framing with expressive force, materializing in sound the affect that the song aims to engender in listeners.

That El Général's music had been banned from state-run media, compelling him to use Facebook to distribute "*Rais Lebled*," underlines the degree to which music's ability to frame an issue depends on how it is mediated, not just stylistically or generically, but also institutionally, discursively and technologically. On the one hand, such mediating factors shape the perception and interpretation of music—that is, what *effects* it has as well as what *affects* it imparts. It is worth noting in this connection that a song or performance, in framing a subject of political contention, itself comes to be framed, colored by its association with the cause in question. The fate of the *Internationale* is instructive, its value for activists fluctuating in tandem with the vicissitudes of both the international socialist movement and the communist regimes that embraced the anthem. On the other hand, music's mediation not only shapes its character and content; it also shapes the size and composition of the public(s) it is able to address. In contexts where media and culture industries are either directly controlled by the state or structured along oligopolistic lines, activists have often been compelled to develop alternative communication channels (newspapers, independent press agencies, community radio stations) to circumvent limits on political expression (Rucht 2004). To a certain extent such endeavors resemble the role played by independent record labels and alternative distribution systems in certain "alternative" music scenes. While it would be a mistake to assume the latter are universally political in their intent or effect, sites of underground musical production and distribution may on occasion be harnessed to contestatory movements. An example is the North Indian "cassette culture" described by Manuel (1993). He observes that tapes proved "ideal vehicles for sociopolitical mobilizations" insofar as they were "resistant to censorship and inexpensive enough to be produced as well as consumed by lower-class as well as affluent activists" (Manuel 1993: 238). The advent of the internet, mobile telephones and social media offer musical and political actors still other avenues for bypassing media gatekeepers, as the case of "*Rais Lebled*" illustrates.

Another way music participates in the constitution of movements is through the construction of collective identities. The association of certain genres and scenes with certain social formations makes music a privileged vehicle for imagining, enacting and/or reaffirming one's attachment to a broader collectivity. But music does more than reproduce extant identities; as scholarship since the mid-1990s has insisted, it is also generative of social groups, creating new communities and reshaping the contours of existing ones (Born 2011). Music's power to both produce and reproduce collectivities parallels processes of identity-formation in social movements, which often build upon affective bonds already in place within a community, even as they cultivate their own distinctive group identities (Eyerman and Jamison 1998, Polletta and Jasper 2001). In explicitly identitarian movements, music along with other cultural traditions often figures prominently as subordinated groups endeavor to invert the stigma attached to them by a dominant national culture. The fusion in Bahian *blocos afro* of elements drawn from the *afoxé* and other afro-diasporic musics (such as reggae), part of a strategy of contesting the material and cultural subordination of Afro-Bahians with the self-proclaimed "racial democracy" of Brazil, offers but one example (Dunn 1992). Yet even when the revalorization of ascribed identities is not a principal objective, music's capacity to engender a sense of membership within a broader community can prove crucial to a mobilization's success. As Roscigno and Danaher (2004) have persuasively argued, the broadcast of millworker songs on independent radio stations in and around North Carolina during the 1920s and 1930s was instrumental in creating a sense of shared identity within this geographically dispersed labor force. Lacking the solidarity mill songs instilled, it is unlikely that the strike movement that swept the region in 1934 would have been as significant as it was (Roscigno and Danaher 2004: 102–109).

Among activists participatory forms of music-making have long been privileged as a way of fostering solidarity and shared identity. The development of an identifiable repertoire of songs is one way a distinctive "movement culture" may come into existence, as the prominence of the Wobblies' *Little Red Songbook* or the freedom songs of the African-American civil rights movement attest. Equally notable are practices of group singing or musical performance that punctuate the collective life of many movement organizations. It is not difficult to see why this kind of activity is so widespread. Group singing is something virtually anybody can take part in, while the synchronization of physical gesture required of collective performance enables individuals to experience solidarity at a corporeal level. Further heightening the potency of this joint action is the way in which musical vibrations penetrate the body, permeating it, even as the individual body contributes to the collective sound that envelops it. The collapse of clear-cut boundaries between self and other in auditory space—boundaries that persist within physical space—affords participants a way of transcending themselves and becoming part of a larger, social body (Traïni 2008: 24–26, Roy 2010: 16).

The foregoing suggests that the analytical distinction drawn above between the cultural and organizational work constitutive of movements blurs in practice. For one thing, the elaboration of collective identities is crucial for ensuring that contentious action persists over time. This is because the resulting sense of solidarity and mutual obligation counteracts the "free rider" problem that afflicts collective action, the temptation to forego participation on the assumption that one might still enjoy the fruits of others' labors (Olson 1965). In addition, both collective identity and movement culture vary according to the social relations and institutional models that govern participants' interaction (Roy 2010: 5). A clear illustration of how cultural and organizational work converge is apparent in efforts to recruit potential "converts" by exploiting the social networks embedded in music scenes. As Tarrow (1998: 23) notes, a movement is less an aggregation of discrete individuals than an "interlocking network of small groups"; and as Della Porta and Diani (2006: 117) remark, this network structure reflects the fact that most individuals are mobilized via "personal contacts developed either in private settings (family, personal friendship circles, colleagues) or in the context of other associational activities." Music scenes offer one such "associational activity." For instance, white power activists have frequently targeted fans of Oi! and black metal, genres whose aesthetic extremism and violent rhetoric seems to offer potentially ripe targets (Corte and Edwards 2008: 6–7). Other examples include the anarcho-punk and straight-edge scenes, which for some have provided a route into anarchist and radical environmentalist movements (McKay 1996: 73 ff., Haenfler 2006: 58–59). In some cases, however, music scenes may not feed into activism so much as provide competing sites of affective investment. As I have observed elsewhere, the fact that both musical and political communities "mobilize individuals around a common cause, the one artistic, the other ideological" means that the "points of contact between these two domains can easily turn into points of rivalry" (Drott 2011: 8).

Conclusion: The Sound of Contention

To conclude, let us turn to the point where music, resistance and movements intersect: in acts of public contention. Music is a perennial adjunct to demonstrations, occupations, sit-ins and strikes, most often in the form of collective singing, but also as performed by street bands, samba groups, drum circles, sound systems and other musical formations. This is not surprising, given that acts of public contention are themselves performances of a sort, staged for a number of audiences: power holders, against whom claims are lodged; the general public, whose opinion is decisive for the outcome of a mobilization; and the media, which has the power to amplify an action's impact or diminish it, depending on the coverage it provides (Tilly 2008). Yet the performativity of protest is only effective when it successfully wins the attention of its target audiences. For this reason a common denominator of contentious action is its disruptive character. By preventing the normal conduct of business or flow of traffic protesters can thereby demonstrate their determination, signal their solidarity to observers, and potentially "broaden the circle of conflict," depending on how authorities react (Tarrow 1998: 96). Scholl (2012: 44) sums up the appeal of disruptive action by saying that it enables groups to "become visible." But it does more than that. It also makes groups *audible*.

This last point indicates the importance of sonic practices for public protest—practices that include but are not limited to music-making. From the *charivaris* and "rough music" of pre-modern Europe to the pots and pans that accompanied the 2012 "casserole" protests in Montreal, the tactical deployment of sound has long provided protesters a means of asserting their presence to adversaries and bystanders alike (Sterne 2012, Born 2013). Such practices allow activists to occupy auditory space at the same time as their bodies occupy physical space, imposing on the rhythms of everyday life another, different rhythm:

> Our first act of mischief was to invade a Starbucks where people were having their routine coffee break before work. Marching in, we formed a circle and played for a few minutes to general consternation and astonishment before clattering back out onto the streets again . . . It was like we were announcing, "Hey, normal life ends here folks, there is a marching band in your Starbucks, you're not going to work today!"
>
> (Whitney 2003: 224)

This is not to say that the strategic use of sound is the sole province of activists. The increasing recourse of security forces to "sound cannons" to disperse crowds makes this clear, painfully so for the protesters affected. Nor is it to suggest that disruption is the only way sonic practices may prove useful for contentious acts. They may also serve to express a movement's ideals via chants and singing; lift the spirits of participants; engender a sense of shared purpose; create a virtual "safe space"; rhythmically entrain activists and induce a state of heightened awareness in them; disorient police forces; offer a much-needed source of diversion; and reclaim public space. Yet regardless of what is heard, by whom and to what end, the precondition for whatever positive effects that might accrue to the deployment of sound and noise in protest is the bare fact that it allows people to be heard. To this end future research into music's relation to resistance and social movements must situate it within the broader soundscape of political protest, that is, within the continuum of sounds, noises and silences that animate the work of contentious action.

References

Bohlman, A. 2012. "Activism and Music in Poland, 1978–1989." PhD diss., Harvard University.
Born, G. 2011. "Music and the Materialization of Identities." *Journal of Material Culture* 16(4): 376–388.
___. 2013. "Introduction—Music, Sound, and Space." In *Music, Sound and Space: Transformations of Public and Private Experience*, ed. G. Born, 1–69. Cambridge: Cambridge University Press.
Bürger, P. 1984. *Theory of the Avant-Garde*. Minneapolis: University of Minnesota Press.
Burkart, P. 2010. *Music and Cyberliberties*. Middletown: Wesleyan University Press.
Corte, U. and B. Edwards. 2008. "White Power Music and the Mobilization of Racist Social Movements." *Music and the Arts in Action* 1(1): 4–20.
Della Porta, D. and M. Diani. 2006. *Social Movements: An Introduction*, 2nd ed. Oxford: Blackwell.
Drewett, M. 2003. "Music in the Struggle to End Apartheid: South Africa." In *Policing Pop*, eds. M. Cloonan and R. Garofalo. Philadelphia: Temple University Press.
Drott, E. 2011. *Music and the Elusive Revolution: Cultural Politics and Political Culture in France, 1968–1981*. Berkeley: University of California Press.
Duncombe, S. 2002. *The Cultural Resistance Reader*. London: Verso.
Dunn, C. 1992. "Afro-Bahian Carnival: A Stage for Protest." *Afro-Hispanic Review* 11(1/3): 11–20.
Eyerman, R. and A. Jamison. 1998. *Music and Social Movements: Mobilizing Traditions in the Twentieth Century*. Cambridge: Cambridge University Press.
Goodwin, J., J. Jasper and F. Polletta. 2001. *Passionate Politics: Emotions and Social Movements*. Chicago: University of Chicago Press.
Haenfler, R. 2006. *Straight-Edge: Clean-Living Youth, Hardcore Punk, and Social Change*. New Brunswick: Routledge.
Hajdu, D. 2004. "Where Has 'Where Have All the Flowers Gone' Gone?" *The New Republic* 230(24): 33–36.
Hall, S. and T. Jefferson, eds. 1976. *Resistance through Rituals: Youth Subcultures in Postwar Britain*. London: Hutchinson.
Howard-Spink, S. 2004. "Grey Tuesday, Online Activism, and the Mash-Up of Music and Politics." *First Monday* 9(10): online.
Kelley, R.D.G. 1997. *Yo' Mama's Disfunktional! Fighting the Culture Wars in Urban America*. Boston: Beacon Press.
Manuel, P. 1993. *Cassette Culture: Popular Music and Technology in North India*. Chicago: University of Chicago Press.
Mathieu, L. 2012. *L'Espace des mouvements sociaux*. Broissieux: Editions du Croquant.
McKay, G. 1996. *Senseless Acts of Beauty*. London: Verso.
McKinley, J. 2011. "At the Protests, the Message Lacks a Melody." *New York Times* (19 October): C1.
Olson, M. 1965. *The Logic of Collective Action: Public Goods and the Theory of Groups*. New York: Schocken.
Polletta, F. and J. Jasper. 2001. "Collective Identity and Social Movements." *Annual Review of Sociology* 27: 283–305.
Roscigno, V. and W. Danaher. 2004. *The Voice of Southern Labor: Radio, Music, and Textile Strikes, 1929–1934*. Minneapolis: University of Minnesota Press.
Rose, T. 1994. *Black Noise: Rap Music and Black Culture in Contemporary America*. Middletown: Wesleyan University Press.
Roy, W. 2010. *Reds, Whites, and Blues: Social Movements, Folk Music, and Race in the United States*. Princeton: Princeton University Press.
Rucht, D. 2004. "The Quadruple 'A': Media and Strategies of Protest Movements Since the 1960s." In *Cyberprotest: New Media, Citizens and Social Movements*, eds. W. Van De Donk, B. Loader, P. Nixon and D. Rucht, 25–48. London: Routledge.
Scholl, C. 2012. *Two Sides of a Barricade: (Dis)order and Summit Protest in Europe*. Albany: State University of New York Press.
Scott, J. 1985. *Weapons of the Weak: Everyday Forms of Peasant Resistance*. New Haven: Yale University Press.
___. 1989. "Everyday Forms of Resistance." *Copenhagen Papers in East and Southeast Asian Studies* 4: 33–62.
___. 1990. *Domination and the Arts of Resistance: Hidden Transcripts*. New Haven: Yale University Press.
Snow, D. 2008. "Framing Processes, Ideology, and Discursive Fields." In *The Blackwell Companion to Social Movements*, eds. D. Snow, S. Soule and H. Kriesi, 380–412. Oxford: Blackwell.
Snow, D. and R. Benford. 2000. "Framing Processes and Social Movements: An Overview and Assessment." *Annual Review of Sociology* 26: 611–639.

Sterne, J. 2012. "Quebec's #Casseroles: on Participation, Percussion and Protest." *Sounding Out!* http://sound studiesblog.com/2012/06/04/casseroles.

Tarrow, S. 1998. *Power in Movement: Social Movements and Contentious Politics.* Cambridge: Cambridge University Press.

Thornton, S. 1996. *Club Cultures: Music, Media, and Subcultural Capital.* Middletown: Wesleyan University Press.

Tilly, C. 2008. *Contentious Performances.* Cambridge: Cambridge University Press.

Traïni, C. 2008. *La Musique en colère.* Paris: Sciences Po.

Whitney, J. 2003. "Infernal Noise: The Soundtrack to Insurrection." In *We Are Everywhere: The Irresistible Rise of Global Anticapitalism*, ed. Notes From Nowhere Collective, 216–227. London: Verso.

Willis, P. 1977. *Learning to Labor: How Working-Class Kids Get Working-Class Jobs.* New York: Columbia University Press/Morningside.

17

Gender and Sexuality

MARION LEONARD

There is a very considerable literature that explores the way in which gender and sexuality are manifested, performed, inscribed and played out within music texts, genres, instrumentation, cultures, locations, environments, practices and institutions. Scholars have attended to a host of dimensions ranging, for example, from how music is shaped by and also informs notions of gender and sexuality (McClary 1991, Shepherd 1991) to the gendering of musical education (Comber, Hargreaves and Colley 1993, Glover 1993, Green 1997), and from examinations of masculinity in popular music (Jarman-Ivens 2007, Hawkins 2009) to studies presenting queer readings of music texts and examining queer identities in music-related scenes (Brett, Wood and Thomas 1994, Whiteley and Rycenga 2006, Taylor 2010). Some of this work has been approached using the empirical investigation methods that are core to sociology, while other studies have developed out of musicology and other disciplines such as cultural studies and anthropology. This work has been motivated by the need to examine the relationship between music and wider social worlds and to consider how music and its cultures represent, construct and engage with presentations of gender and sexuality. A review of the depth and scope of this work is far beyond the capacity of one chapter. To narrow the discussion this chapter will concentrate on some issues related to the careers and representation of women within the contemporary (popular) music industries. This is not to suggest that an analysis of gender necessarily or chiefly involves attention to the experience of women. Instead, the concentration on women will be used as a way to draw out some broader points about how gender is related to the practice, texts, distribution and experience of music. To focus the chapter still further, three dimensions will be considered, concentrating on the music industries of the United Kingdom and United States: employment and the work environment, genre worlds, and modes of representation within music video.

Gender, while treated in everyday encounters as a seemingly knowable label for dimensions of personal identity, is produced, structured and shaped within social communities. As Butler has argued:

> gender is a kind of a doing ... [but] one does not "do" one's gender alone. One is always "doing" with or for another, even if the other is only imaginary ... the terms that make up one's own gender are, from the start, out-side oneself, beyond oneself in a sociality that has no single author (and that radically contests the notion of authorship itself).
>
> (Butler 2004: 1)

Similarly, sexuality is defined and regulated by social processes and can be understood as "a cultural and historical phenomenon; the discourses, institutions, and practices that create it are those of particular times and places" (Maus 2014). Analysis of music in relation to gender and sexuality must necessarily consider the social contexts, structures and discourses that have shaped, influenced or otherwise informed music practices, texts and contexts. Yet the study of gender and sexuality should not be considered as a discrete topic, distinct from and additional to the broader field of music criticism. Feminist studies and gender theory have worked as effective critical tools, producing new understandings and enabling fresh analyses of music, its cultures and systems of representation. The discipline of musicology, as critics have pointed out (McClary 1991, Brett, Wood and Thomas 1994, Shepherd 1995), has not traditionally been attentive to and reflexive about the implications of difference related to concepts such as age, class, ethnicity and gender. Gender analysis has been one method through which scholars have challenged the idea that music should be understood on its own terms as an artistic practice with its own systems of organization. By attending to the issues of gender and sexuality scholars have highlighted that music production, analysis, institutions, histories, aesthetics and practices cannot be divorced from the social worlds in which they have been produced.

Gender and Music at Work

Gender has been seen as a side issue to the business of music. Scholarly accounts of the music industries have generally either failed to touch on gender issues or have made only passing reference to them. However, gendered discourses pervade the music sector and inform how business is done within it. Attending to this provides another way of understanding the logics, unspoken assumptions and cultures within music businesses and how they shape careers, promotion and critical reception. Developing a deeper understanding of these factors provides a way to identify and potentially address areas of inequality and concerns about workforce diversity. This is a complex subject, not least because the music industries involve a wide range of different businesses, roles and practices. Indeed the "core music industry" has been defined as including not only the traditional players such as musicians, record labels and music trade bodies, but also music festival organizers, music promoters, music agents, ticketing agents, concert venues and arenas, and online music distributors (UK Music 2013: 17). Discussion of gender in the music industries needs to keep pace with the changing dynamics of the sector to consider how the shifts in working practices and the new landscape of media industries are impacting those working in the field. Moreover, it is important to take into account the experience of people working across a range of different areas and specialisms, from musicians and producers to publishers and promoters.

A significant number of challenges to women working in the music sector have been identified, including the male dominance of the profession, barriers to entry, a limited number of role models in particular male-dominated spheres of practice, and a lack of women within senior industry positions. For example, research into leadership in the creative and cultural industries in the United Kingdom has found that women held only 15 percent of executive roles within a sample of 1,201 music firms (Cultural Leadership Programme 2008: 33). Further research in the United Kingdom has found that only 39 percent of music employees are women (Creative & Cultural Skills 2010) and almost half of women working in music earn less than £10,000 per year, compared with 35 percent of men (Creative & Cultural Skills 2009). This is not to downplay the achievements of women in leadership roles such as those celebrated by *Billboard*'s 2013 Women in Music Awards. Yet, despite these positive role models, women continue to be under-represented within the music sector. The music sector is far from unique in having a workforce with these issues. However, in unpacking these factors research can reveal how gendered attitudes inform employment, career advancement and decision making.

Different roles within the music industries and related media professions have been identified as highly gender segregated. For instance, Negus's (1992: 126) research, conducted between 1988 and 1992, found women had developed a strong presence in the areas of marketing and publicity. However, "higher management and key decision-making jobs were dominated by an 'old boys network'." Women were socially excluded from roles in A&R and recording studios, which had highly gendered casual work cultures and "a bantering male camaraderie" (58). These findings align with Nixon and Crewe's (2004: 134) more recent research into working environments within the creative industries, where "the informality of office life allowed strident forms of masculinity and homosociability to flourish." Other research, such as Sandstrom's (2000) study of women sound-mixing engineers and Hutton's (2006) discussion of women DJs and club promoters, has expanded knowledge of how work environments are produced as gendered. Issues identified include the perception of certain jobs as more suitable for men or women, pressure to perform gender in restrictive ways, lack of role models and sexist behavior. Gender discrimination can also influence recruitment practices and hiring decisions even to entry-level positions. Frenette's ethnographic research with interns in the music industries of New York provides an example. This largely unpaid form of work, while offering no guarantee of securing a position in the future, is considered by many to be a necessary step on the path to paid employment. While not focused on gender issues, Frenette's study found that interns "are mostly female (though gender distribution varies between departments), whereas the employees with the longest tenure tend to be male" (Frenette 2013: 392). The reasons for this require examination. However, it might be supposed that, as has been found in other areas of the creative industries, perceptions of "ideal employees" are not gender neutral (Milestone and Meyer 2012: 78–79).

Attending to issues of gender has produced a greater depth of understanding concerning the challenges of work structures and the processes of securing work. Many people working in the music sector are doing so on a freelance basis rather than as paid employees (Armstrong 2013, Watson 2013). This echoes the nature of employment within the broader creative industries (Hesmondhalgh and Baker 2010). This employment is characterized by "a preponderance of temporary, intermittent and precarious jobs; long hours and bulimic patterns of working; the collapse or erasure of the boundaries between work and play" (Gill and Pratt 2008: 14). Armstrong's (2013: 300) empirical study of female musicians found that sustaining a freelance career in music can be viewed as "simultaneously fulfilling and rewarding, and insecure and potentially exploitative." While both men and women are affected by the pressure of job uncertainty and the requirement to continually look for new opportunities, some dimensions of this work environment intersect with gender issues. A small-scale study with women working in areas such as tour management, A&R and concert promotion found that the requirement to keep pace and stay engaged with work networks influenced one respondent to take only a short period of maternity leave and caused others to consider alternative employment. These individuals felt that the expected long hours of work and punishing travel schedules were not compatible with family life (Leonard 2014).

Freelance workers need to build networks, gain professional recommendations and secure regular project work. However, this can be challenging for women trying to break into male-dominated fields of practice. Farrugia and Swiss's (2008: 85) study of women DJs and producers in San Francisco's electronic/dance music scene provides an illustration. They found the majority of local artist booking agents, record label owners and club managers were men "perpetuating a 'boy's club' mentality" and that women often found it difficult to access the "vital social networks that consist of male DJs, label owners, and producers" (88). Hesmondhalgh and Baker's (2010: 14) research into working conditions in the creative industries identified music industry professionals who considered socializing to be a "compulsory element" of their job, with one artist manager explaining that he felt marginalized because he was not a "pub person." Pubs are key sites for social interaction, informal meetings and, of course, live music performance. They have historically also been gendered spaces. Some women may be less inclined to work in sectors that involve late-night networking and socializing in a predominantly male sphere. Women's organizations such as Women in Music in New York and Women's Music Business Association in Nashville have attempted to overcome such obstacles: facilitating social interaction and networking with other women professionals by organizing mixers, brunches and speed networking events. The continuing need for such support is demonstrated by the launch in 2012 of the Women's International Music Network and the establishment of the Network of Women in Events in 2013 as a forum for professional women working in live and outdoor events.

Gender and Genre

Particular modalities of gender are often produced within music cultures that structure the experiences of those who participate. Research has focused on a range of music practices and I shall take rock music as one such example. Frith and McRobbie's (1990) article, first published in 1978, is an important early discussion of how rock music signifies in terms of gender and sexuality. The authors commented on how control and production within rock are male dominated and, focusing in on the sub-genre of "cock rock," considered how the performance style is "aggressive, dominating and boastful" (1990: 374). Subsequent studies have explored this subject in more depth, examining the music styles, performance conventions, gendered discourses and modes of representation within rock and its various sub-genres. Walser's (1993) work provides one such example, exploring the construction of gendered identities through the music, lyrics, behavior and visual images of heavy metal.

Studies drawing on in-depth interviews with women musicians have helped to develop an understanding of how rock is produced as a gendered field of practice (Bayton 1998, Leonard 2007, Reddington 2007). This research has revealed how women have experienced and navigated rock culture as a masculine practice. For example, Cohen's (1991: 206) ethnographic study of rock culture in Liverpool revealed that women were understood by male musicians to be intruders or a threat. Outside of performances, female musicians "were often mistaken for girlfriends of male band members." This culture of masculinity has persisted over time and women musicians continue to report similar instances (Leonard 2007: 57–58). More generally, the backstage arena of live music— the workspace for road crew, sound engineers and security—has frequently been articulated and reinscribed as a male space (Smaill 2005: 16). It should be noted that the music worlds of many genres are similarly gendered. Interviews with women working in other spheres have revealed comparable experiences (for example, Tucker 1999).

The gendering of music also extends to musical instruments. A clear example of this in rock is the association of the guitar with masculinity. Sociologist Mavis Bayton (1997) has discussed how the electric guitar has been culturally produced as masculine in a range of ways, which include performance conventions, instrument design, promotional advertising and the retail environment in guitar shops. Focusing on the world of guitar retailing, Sargent's (2009) ethnographic research has further explored how both specialist independent guitar shops and large chain "big-box" stores in the United States continue to reproduce hegemonic masculinity despite women's increased visibility in rock. Her findings were that different types of shops generated different modes of masculinity: "competitive fraternization in big-box stores and geeky paternalism in mom-and-pop shops," both of which fitted into "the overall gendered culture of rock music and the stores as work environments" (2009: 671). The electric guitar is so privileged as a symbol of masculinity that Clawson (1999) found that women in alternative rock bands have instead tended to play the bass. Men tended to monopolize guitar playing. The bass was a less socially prized instrument, enabling women an entry point into bands. This suggests that there are structural reasons for the predominance of women bass players. However, Clawson, who interviewed male and female band members, found that it was chiefly women who proffered gendered explanations for why they might be more "naturally" suited to the instrument. This reveals how powerful gendered conceptions can be, both in channeling opportunities for participation and in naturalizing the status quo.

Gender and sexuality also inform the critical reception of artists, the processes of history and how performers are validated and remembered. The ways in which artists are reviewed, critiqued and appraised through music criticism has often been influenced by gendered attitudes (Davies 2001, Railton 2001, Johnson-Grau 2002, Feigenbaum 2005). Kruse (2002: 138) has argued that rock and pop criticism has traditionally "presented its subject matter in a way that assumes writer and reader coexist in a phallocentric world in which women are peripheral." The explanations for this gender bias are complicated and may include the historical male dominance of music journalism as well as the targeting of music magazines toward an imagined male audience (Théberge 1991). Moreover, rock criticism has tended to reproduce ideologies that valorize links between rock, masculinity and notions of authenticity (McLeod 2001). Such gendered music criticism is influential in reinforcing the discourse of rock music culture and shaping views on artists. These appraisals in turn become part of the documentary evidence that informs how musicians and artists are evaluated over time. Reddington's (2007) study of British women musicians of the punk era has explored how women became lost from punk histories. The original interview material generated through the research helps to address this absence. Similarly, Strong's (2011: 398) research on women in grunge makes a convincing argument about "the processes of remembering and forgetting" to explain how "women are generally written out of historical accounts of music in order to reinscribe the creative dominance of men in this field." This has the effect of "the status quo [remaining] ultimately unchallenged."

Music Video, Representation, and Distribution

Music video is a key site through which codes of gender and sexuality are represented and enacted. This media form intersects with many issues that are important within the sociology of music because these audiovisual texts are shaped by genre conventions; produce, critique and/or reflect wider social norms about gender and sexuality; and are products of commercial and industrial processes. Since the 1980s, with the launch of MTV and other music television channels, music video became a central method of promotion for popular music and a major factor in the establishment of the success and iconicity of many global stars such as Madonna and Michael Jackson. Music video established new modes of display, performance and ways of "knowing" an artist. Responding to the importance of video as a promotional medium a considerable body of scholarship developed in the 1980s and 1990s. This scholarship examined how gender was constructed within this medium (Kaplan 1987, Lewis 1990, Walser 1993). Some of this work, as well as subsequent work, has focused on the problematic way in which women have been presented, objectified and marketed through this media (Vincent, Davis and Boruszkowski 1987). Critical attention has also been given to how some artists have used video to offer alternative ways of navigating gender identities (Shelton 1997). Madonna's video work has been especially singled out (for example, Brown and Schulze 1990, McClary 1991, Vernallis 2004) because of the ways in which it has often consciously played with, parodied and inhabited different productions of gender and modes of sexual display. Many of these videos stirred controversy and provoked debate on the issue of artist agency and control over self representation. These debates continue in relation to artists such as Lady Gaga and Beyoncé (Durham 2012).

As this media form has matured, its aesthetics and modes of representation of gender have developed and conventions have become established. As Railton and Watson (2011: 11) have argued, music video can be understood as "a site where normative constructions of race, gender and ethnicity are put on display, confirmed, reinforced and, sometimes, challenged." The representation of artists in video is tied into genre, imagined audiences and industrial logics. For example,

Fitts' (2008) qualitative research on rap music video production highlights how formulaic representations such as the "booty video" become replicated in the hope that the videos will receive airtime. However, in discussing the gender politics of contemporary music video, it is important not only to examine aesthetic and stylistic conventions but also to attend to the social and industrial changes that have taken place within the music and media industries. The way in which music video now operates has been rearticulated in response to the global decline in music sales since the 1990s and the shift by television channels away from music video programming. Music video budgets have been cut in response to these changes but, as Edmond (2014) has discussed, far from signaling an end to the importance of music video its distribution has shifted to a variety of video sharing sites such as YouTube and Vevo. Videos are also regularly embedded within blogs and social networking pages. The demand for this content is such that music video-related content is in YouTube's "charts for 'most-viewed,' 'most-popular,' and 'most-discussed' videos." As well, "at the end of 2011, the Vevo channel on YouTube was the most watched channel globally, generating a huge 56 billion views" (Edmond 2014: 307).

The debate over sexual exploitation in music video came to global media prominence again in 2013 with the releases of "Wrecking Ball" by Miley Cyrus and "Blurred Lines" by Robin Thicke, featuring Pharrell Williams and the rapper TI. The Cyrus video featured the star, in a literal translation of the lyrics, swinging naked on a wrecking ball and suggestively licking a sledgehammer. It was "the most popular music video ever on Vevo. Attracting 19.3 million views in the first 24 hours" (Gillette 2013: 22). The video has, at the time of writing, received over 720 million views and was the second most watched music video on YouTube in 2013 (Allocca 2013). A parody of the video also became the fourth top-trending video on the site for 2013. Also featuring in the top ten chart of most viewed music videos was the catchy and deeply problematic "Blurred Lines." The song, whose lyrics were labeled by one critic as "rapey," was promoted by a video featuring scantily clad women (who were topless in the unrated video version) provocatively dancing and being ogled by the three male musicians. It was the sixth most watched music video on YouTube in 2013 and has, to date, attracted nearly 350 million views. Both videos provoked controversy, highlighting the sexist and sexualized way in which women are regularly portrayed to invite a presumed heterosexual male gaze. As Goodwin (1992: 186) observed, a very problematic issue with the way that the form developed was "the routine denial of subjectivity to women in music videos and their repeated display as helpers, assistants, objects of lust, groupies, backup singers, and so on." By contrast, "Men appear as objects, but also as actors." The Thicke video can be compared to numerous earlier examples, such as Robert Palmer's "Simply Irresistible," in which women were featured as sexualized objects. The popularity of the Cyrus video relied upon the fact that the star appeared naked. Critical opinion was divided between whether the musician had been exploited or was in control of her own image. Regardless, the video is a high-profile example of how women are regularly portrayed on screen. Beyond this, these two videos also illustrate how music is promoted within the contemporary media landscape.

Music videos were originally considered purely as promotional vehicles to drive music sales. However, they recently have come to be re-evaluated because they can also generate revenue streams through means such as product placement and advertising on the distributor's site (Edmond 2014). Financial agreements with companies such as YouTube mean that rights holders profit from the popularity of streaming music videos. This income stream is not insignificant as YouTube has "over the last several years" paid the music industry "over $1 billion" (Pham 2014). Moreover, music companies UMG and Sony Music Entertainment have taken more control over the distribution of music video and its potential advertising revenue by partnering in the syndication hub Vevo, thereby offering access to videos on their own sites and distributing content to platforms such as YouTube. Controversial or sexually provocative videos such as the two under discussion have proved effective in this media landscape. They become "viral" by being shared through social networks. They also benefit from discussion within traditional media. This in turn increases online viewers. Moreover, since February 2013, the *Billboard* charts have reflected not only sales, audio streaming and airplay data but also the streaming of official videos and user-generated clips that use authorized audio. Thus the business motivation to harness very high volumes of viewers (to raise the profile of an act, generate revenue streams and achieve higher chart placings) can encourage the persistence of particularly restrictive productions of gender and sexuality in music video.

The issue of how artists are represented is tied up with how audiences are conceived and targeted by video directors, record companies, broadcasters and distributors. This point is well argued by Lewis (1990) in her critical account of MTV, which details how the programming of the station at its outset produced a "preferred male address," tailored to reach a white male adolescent audience. Lewis balances this observation with an account of "female-address video." This account examines the way in which some female musicians in the early to mid-1980s developed videos designed to engage female audiences and resonate with some of their cultural experiences. Other scholars have undertaken audience research to tease out the complex way in which gender and sexuality is interpreted by viewers (Kalof 1993). For example, Hurley's (1994) qualitative research with young people in Australia explored the ways in which pleasure and meaning in music video were produced by adolescents who were actively constructing their gender subjectivity. More recently, Reid-Brinkley (2008) has focused on online responses to portrayals of black femininity in rap music and video. The research examines how viewers reproduce and resist intersecting identity positions of race, gender, class and sexuality. Developments in technology with inexpensive editing software and the free distribution of content on sites such as YouTube has enabled users to upload their own videos as tributes or parodies of official releases. These texts visualize and materialize the active way in which "audiences" are also creative agents producing a further bank of texts, some of which critique, exaggerate, re-imagine and provide resistance to the way in which gender and sexuality have been mediatized. User-generated material broadens the way in which music video is defined. Its content is worthy of study, along with how it is trended and received and the different enactments of gender produced through this "unauthorized" media.

Conclusion

This chapter has only touched on a small fraction of the scholarship that has contributed to our understanding of music and its relation to gender and sexuality. Work within the sociology of music has unpacked how discourses about sexuality and gender: inform the value given to music; are played out within music cultures; influence how audiences respond to and engage with music; structure the promotion and reception of artists; and have a bearing on industrial logics. By focusing on women within the (popular) music industries this chapter has discussed how gender is implicated within employment structures, working environments, genre cultures, the production of histories and conventions of representation. Conceptions of gender and sexuality are deeply embedded in our social worlds, intersecting with other discourses of ethnicity and class, and it is important that we continue to investigate how these shape our experience and understanding of music.

References

Allocca, K. 2013. "You Tube Rewind: What You Watched in 2013." *You Tube Official Blog*, 11 December. http://youtube-global.blogspot.co.uk/2013/12/youtube-rewind-2013.html.

Armstrong, V. 2013. "Women's Musical Lives: Self-Managing a Freelance Career." *Women: A Cultural Review* 24(4): 298–314.

Bayton, M. 1997. "Women and the Electric Guitar." In *Sexing the Groove: Popular Music and Gender*, ed. S. Whiteley, 37–49. London: Routledge.

_____. 1998. *Frock Rock: Women Performing Popular Music*. Oxford: Oxford University Press.

Brett, P., E. Wood and G.C. Thomas, eds. 1994. *Queering the Pitch: The New Gay and Lesbian Musicology*. New York: Routledge.

Brown, J.D. and L. Schulze. 1990. "The Effects of Race, Gender, and Fandom on Audience Interpretations of Madonna's Music Videos." *Journal of Communication* 40(2): 88–102.

Butler, J. 2004. *Undoing Gender*. New York: Routledge.

Clawson, M.A. 1999. "When Women Play the Bass: Instrument Specialization and Gender Interpretation in Alternative Rock Music." *Gender and Society* 13(2): 193–210.

Cohen, S. 1991. *Rock Culture in Liverpool: Popular Music in the Making*. Oxford: Oxford University Press.

Comber, C., D.J. Hargreaves and A. Colley. 1993. "Girls, Boys and Technology in Music Education." *British Journal of Music Education* 10(2): 123–134.

Creative & Cultural Skills. 2009. *Music Impact and Footprint 08–09*: www.data-generator.co.uk.

_____. 2010. *Creative & Cultural Skills: Sector Skills Assessment for the Creative and Cultural Industries. An Analysis of the Skills Needs of the Creative and Cultural Industries in the UK*: www.data-generator.co.uk.

Cultural Leadership Programme. 2008. *Women in Leadership in the Creative and Cultural Sector*. TBR: Newcastle upon Tyne.

Davies, H. 2001. "All Rock and Roll is Homosocial: The Representation of Women in the British Rock Music Press." *Popular Music* 20(3): 301–319

Durham, A. 2012. "'Check On It': Beyoncé, Southern Booty, and Black Femininities in Music Video." *Feminist Media Studies* 12(1): 35–49.

Edmond, M. 2014. "Here We Go Again: Music Videos after YouTube." *Television and New Media* 15(4): 305–320.

Farrugia, R. and T. Swiss. 2008. "Producing Producers: Women and Electronic/Dance Music." *Current Musicology* 86: 79–99.

Feigenbaum, A. 2005. "'Some Guy Designed This Room I'm Standing In': Marking Gender in Press Coverage of Ani DiFranco." *Popular Music* 24(1): 37–36.

Fitts, M. 2008. "'Drop It Like It's Hot': Culture Industry Laborers and Their Perspectives on Rap Music Video Production." *Meridians: Feminism, Race, Transnationalism* 8(1): 211–235.

Frenette, A. 2013. "Making the Intern Economy: Role and Career Challenges of the Music Industry Intern." *Work and Occupations* 40(4): 364–397.

Frith, S. and A. McRobbie. 1990. "Rock and Sexuality." In *On Record: Rock, Pop and the Written Word*, eds. S. Frith and A. Goodwin, 371–389. New York: Pantheon Books. Reprinted from *Screen Education* 29 (1978): 3–19.

Gill, R. and A. Pratt. 2008. "Precarity and Cultural Work in the Social Factory? Immaterial Labour, Precariousness and Cultural Work." *Theory, Culture and Society* 25(7/8): 1–30.

Gillette, F. 2013. "Vevo Takes a Wrecking Ball to MTV." *Bloomberg Businessweek* 4347 (September 23): 22–23.

Glover, J., ed. 1993. "Music, Gender and Education Special Issue." *British Journal of Music Education* 10(3).

Goodwin, A. 1992. *Dancing in the Distraction Factory: Music Television and Popular Culture*. Minneapolis: University of Minnesota Press.

Green, L. 1997. *Music, Gender, Education*. Cambridge: Cambridge University Press.

Hawkins, S. 2009. *The British Pop Dandy: Masculinity, Popular Music and Culture*. Aldershot: Ashgate.

Hesmondhalgh, D. and S. Baker. 2010. "'A Very Complicated Version of Freedom': Conditions and Experiences of Creative Labour in Three Cultural Industries." *Poetics* 38(1): 4–20.

Hurley, J.M. 1994. "Music Video and the Construction of Gendered Subjectivity (Or How Being a Music Video Junkie Turned Me Into a Feminist)." *Popular Music* 13(3): 327–338.

Hutton, F. 2006. *Risky Pleasures? Club Cultures and Feminine Identities*. Aldershot: Ashgate.

Jarman-Ivens, F. 2007. *Oh Boy! Masculinities and Popular Music*. New York: Routledge.

Johnson-Grau, B. 2002. "Sweet Nothings: Presentation of Women Musicians in Pop Journalism." In *Pop Music and the Press*, ed. S. Jones, 202–218. Philadelphia: Temple University Press.

Kalof, L. 1993. "Dilemmas of Femininity: Gender and the Social Construction of Sexual Imagery." *The Sociological Quarterly* 34(4): 639–651.

Kaplan, E.A. 1987. *Rocking Around the Clock: Music Television, Postmodernism, and Consumer Culture*. New York: Methuen.

Kruse, H. 2002. "Abandoning the Absolute: Transcendance and Gender in Popular Music Discourse." In *Pop Music and the Press*, ed. S. Jones, 134–155. Philadelphia: Temple University Press.

Leonard, M. 2007. *Gender in the Music Industry: Rock, Discourse and Girl Power*. Aldershot: Ashgate.

_____. 2014. "Putting Gender in the Mix: Employment, Participation and Role Expectations in the Music Industries." In *The Routledge Companion to Media and Gender*, eds. C. Carter, L. Steiner and L. McLaughlin, 127–136. New York: Routledge.

Lewis, L. 1990. *Gender Politics and MTV: Voicing the Difference*. Philadelphia: Temple University Press.

Maus, F.E. 2014. "Sex, Sexuality." *Grove Music Online*. *Oxford Music Online*. Oxford University Press, www.oxfordmusiconline.com/subscriber/article/grove/music/A2257260.

McClary, S. 1991. *Feminine Endings: Music, Gender, Sexuality*. Minnesota: University of Minnesota Press.

McLeod, K. 2001. "'*1/2': A Critique of Rock Criticism in North America." *Popular Music* 20(1): 47–60.

Milestone, K. and A. Meyer. 2012. *Gender and Popular Culture*. Cambridge: Polity.

Negus, K. 1992. *Producing Pop: Culture and Conflict in the Popular Music Industry*. London: Edward Arnold.

Nixon, S. and B. Crewe. 2004. "Pleasure at Work? Gender, Consumption and Work-Based Identities in the Creative Industries." *Consumption Markets & Culture* 7(2): 129–147.

Pham, A. 2014 "YouTube Has Paid Out $1 Billion to Music Industry In Last Few Years." *Billboard.biz* (February 03): www.billboard.com/biz/articles/news/digital-and-mobile/5893900/youtube-has-paid-out-1-billion-to-music-industry-in.

Railton, D. 2001. "The Gendered Carnival of Pop." *Popular Music* 20(3): 321–331.

Railton, D. and P. Watson. 2011. *Music and the Moving Image: Music Video and the Politics of Representation*. Edinburgh: Edinburgh University Press.

Reddington, H. 2007. *The Lost Women of Rock: Female Musicians of the Punk Era*. Aldershot: Ashgate.

Reid-Brinkley, S.R. 2008. "The Essence of Res(ex)pectability: Black Women's Negotiation of Black Femininity in Rap Music and Music Video." *Meridians: Feminism, Race, Transnationalism* 8(1): 236–260.

Sandstrom, B. 2000. "Women Mix Engineers and the Power of Sound." In *Music and Gender*, eds. P. Moisala and B. Diamond, 289–305. Urbana and Chicago: University of Illinois Press.

Sargent, C. 2009. "Playing, Shopping, and Working as Rock Musicians: Masculinities in 'De-Skilled' and 'Re-Skilled' Organizations." *Gender and Society* 23(5): 665–687.

Shelton, M.L. 1997. "Can't Touch This! Representations of the African American Female Body in Urban Rap Videos." *Popular Music and Society* 21(3): 107–116.

Shepherd, J. 1991. *Music as Social Text*. Cambridge: Polity.

_____. 1995. "Difference and Power in Music." In *Musicology and Difference: Gender and Sexuality in Music Scholarship*, ed. R.A. Solie, 46–65. Berkeley: University of California Press.

Smaill, A. 2005. *Challenging Gender Segregation in Music Technology: Findings and Recommendations for Music Education and Training Providers in the North-West*. A Report for the Regional Equality in Music Project. University of Salford.

Strong, C. 2011. "Grunge, Riot Grrrl and the Forgetting of Women in Popular Culture." *The Journal of Popular Culture* 44(2): 398–416.

Taylor, J. 2010. "Queer Temporalities and the Significance of 'Music Scene' Participation in the Social Identities of Middle-aged Queers." *Sociology* 44(5): 893–907.

Théberge, P. 1991. "Musicians' Magazines in the 1980s: The Creation of a Community and a Consumer Market." *Cultural Studies* 5(3): 270–293.

Tucker, S. 1999. "Telling Performances: Jazz History Remembered and Remade by the Women in the Band." *Oral History Review* 26(1): 67–84.

UK Music. 2013. *The Economic Contribution of the Core UK Music Industry*. London: UK Music.

Vernallis, C. 2004. *Experiencing Music Video: Aesthetics and Cultural Context*. New York: Columbia University Press.

Vincent, R.C., D.K. Davis and L.A. Boruszkowski. 1987. "Sexism on MTV: The Portrayal of Women in Rock Videos." *Journalism Quarterly* 64(4): 750–941.

Walser, R. 1993. *Running with the Devil: Power, Gender, and Madness in Heavy Metal Music*. Middletown: Wesleyan University Press.

Watson, A. 2013. "'Running a Studio's a Silly Business': Work and Employment in the Contemporary Recording Studio Sector." *Area* 45(3): 330–336.

Whiteley, S. and J. Rycenga, eds. 2006. *Queering the Popular Pitch*. New York: Routledge.

18

Hip Hop and Race

Anthony Kwame Harrison

Hip hop, as a form of music and popular culture, has become one of the foremost arenas in which discussions of race, racial injustices and the transformation of racial meanings occur. Through song and celebrity, hip-hop voices offer immediate commentaries on newsworthy racial events as well as critical observations on historical and ongoing patterns of race-based inequality. Some scholars of hip-hop music have hailed it as a postmodern multicultural form that reflects the fluidity and malleability through which young people today fashion their identities; still others view it as perpetuating some of the most damaging ideologies of race and models of racialized behavior in contemporary society.

In this chapter, I survey how sociological researchers and commentators have examined and understood hip hop in relation to race.[1] My discussion is primarily set within the United States. I do this with the awareness that hip hop is a global phenomenon and that racial issues are not unique to the United States. Nevertheless, most conventional treatments situate hip hop's crystallization within a US context. Furthermore, the racial dynamics that saturate US society—historically and contemporarily—are among the most dynamic and globally consequential. Indeed, some have suggested that hip hop's worldwide spread has contributed to exporting US notions of race to a generation of global youth.

Conceptually, this chapter is organized around two central dyads as well as four related core questions. Where the first dyad is concerned, I separate the music's production from its consumption in considering hip hop as a cultural product. Second, in considering race—and given the canonical scholarly treatment of rap as black music—I distinguish between hip hop's relationship to black people (individuals and communities) and non-black people.[2] In terms of the latter, most attention and scrutiny have customarily been given to white hip-hop fans (see Allinson 1994, Roediger 1998, Tate 2003, Hess 2005). Finally, where I have previously used a chronological framework to outline hip-hop scholarship's treatment of race (Harrison 2008), here I de-emphasize the timeline approach largely to show the consistency and resiliency of key debates.

In the late 1980s, Chuck D of the group Public Enemy famously referred to rap music as black America's CNN—suggesting that it functioned as "an alternative, youth-controlled media network" (Chang 2005: 251) that narrated the experiences of being young and black in the urban United States. In the ensuing "culture wars" that accompanied hip hop's rise to mainstream prominence, numerous advocates would adopt this perspective in response to conservative critics, who were quick to blame the music for inspiring a host of social ills (Lipsitz 1998). The sociological studies on rap that first appeared within this context by and large sought to defend hip hop and the artists/communities that created it. Rose (1994: 184), for example, located hip hop's emergence within the shifting capitalist structures and rising inequality of post-industrial New York, adding that "although rappers are some of the most prominent social critics in contemporary culture, they remain some of the most institutionally policed and stigmatized."

These pivotal years were marked by a shift in music industry structure that saw many small independent hip-hop record companies being bought up or bought out by large corporate labels (Henderson 1996, Basu 2005). Concurrently, rap's foremost authenticating tropes were transformed from *Afrocentric* bases to *ghettocentric* ones (Smith 1997)—that is, the politically conscious rap of the late 1980s gave way to images of violence, drugs and sexuality associated with "gansta" lifestyles. To some this change continued the well-worn US practice of fetishizing racial differences in order to appeal to white audiences (Quinn 2005, Heaggans 2009). Out of this conflation one of the most salient debates surrounding hip-hop music as it relates to blackness and black performance emerged.

Question 1: Do hip-hop songs and by extension video representations—which are mediated through historically white-controlled, profit-driven entertainment industries—offer genuine windows into black-US experiences and perspectives or are they carefully engineered racial representations designed to appeal to mainstream consumer tastes?

Sociologists of popular music are typically suspicious of the distance between a music style's community-based origins and the music industry corridors that produce it as a commodified product. Yet many sociological studies of rap music understand it as a form of *hidden transcript* (Scott 1990), which follows from a tradition of subversive black aesthetics (McDonnell 1992, Lusane 1993, Stapleton 1998, Neff 2009, Gosa 2011).[3] One of the principle proponents of this view, Rose (1994: 99), elaborates: "Under social conditions in which sustained frontal attacks on powerful groups are strategically unwise or unsuccessfully contained, oppressed people use language, dance, and music to mock those in power, express rage, and produce fantasies of subversion."

Whereas much of this scholarship appears to be inspired by some allegiance to hip hop, sociologists who are seemingly less allied question the authenticity of rap's dominant images and consider the various interests such images serve. This is particularly relevant since, according to Jeffries (2011), most hip-hop listeners make little to no connection between the operations of the cultural industries that stand behind the proliferation of certain rap songs and their commercial success.

Two astute and influential sociological commentaries on the importance of white culture-brokers in rap music's formative years came from non-academic writers Samuels (1991) and George (1998). Neal historicized these developments by illustrating how the post-civil-rights entertainment industries sought to supplant black culture as a legitimate community resource and recast it as a commodity that could be bought and sold. He concluded that "Hip-Hop emerge[d] as the first black popular music form to develop largely unmediated by communal critique from the formal and informal structures of the traditional Black Public Sphere" (Neal 1997: 133–134). Negus (1999) similarly drew attention to the disjuncture between music industry organizational structures and the cultural practices through which rap music is made, emphasizing the constraints imposed by an industry culture that is itself part of a wider society that harbors racial anxieties about rap music and the people who make it.

The correspondence between rap's popular ascendance and prevailing imagery that conformed to stereotypes about dangerous black bodies (Sharpley-Whitney 2007, White 2011)—later augmented by visions of extravagant consumerism (Quinn 1996, Pattillo-McCoy 1999)—strongly suggested that the one-time youth-controlled information network had fallen under the jurisdiction of the corporate United States. Reflecting on this, De Genova (1995: 130) asked, "how is it that the commodification of hip-hop in the mass media so obviously prioritized its blackness, at the expense of its distinctive Latino attributes?" De Genova's query introduces a second crucial issue that surrounds hip-hop "originalism" (Perry 2004) and race.

Question 2: Should rap music's community of origin be understood as solely black and in doing so are hip-hop historians ignoring the cultural contributions of Latinos, particularly Puerto Ricans?

Several early treatments of hip hop uncritically described its community of origin as exclusively black (Toop 1984, Henderson 1996). Yet almost as soon as definitive sociological scholarship on rap began appearing, a handful of works sought to address the omission of Latinos as founders. As Flores explained, "Puerto Ricans from the South Bronx and El Barrio have been involved in . . . rap music since the beginnings of hip hop" (Flores 1996: 85, see also del Barco 1996). At times, this issue has been settled through a hip-hop division of labor that emphasizes African Americans' prominence in musical endeavors while highlighting Puerto Ricans' contributions to dancing and graffiti (Harrison 2008). Yet, more commonly, scholars call attention to the intercultural hybridity reflected in the percussive rhythms and musical aesthetics that were popular in New York City at the time of hip hop's formation (Perkins 1996, Chang 2005). Rivera (2003) pointedly argues that, as fellow African-diasporic racial subjects, Puerto Ricans' racial location—which has a bearing on their connection to hip hop—stands between blackness and *Latinidad* (see also Ogbar 2007).

Despite the importance of highlighting these cultural dynamics, most efforts to champion the creative and resilient power of rap locate it within definitively black oral traditions. Keyes (1996), for example, presents rapping as part of an African-diasporic expressive practice of achieving meaning through tones, rhythms and the creative fluidities of oral texts. In her ethnography of emceeing in the Mississippi Delta, Neff (2009) understands distinct rap styles as emerging through combinations and ongoing conversations between various black expressive traditions rather than singular precise pathways. Neff furthermore draws attention to the generative and transformative power of speech and musical aesthetics. Similarly, in describing hip hop as "trickster music," Perry (2004: 31, see also Stapleton 1998) focuses on the oral textures through which hip-hop songs offer a "subtextual critique of society, and particularly white supremacy." Gosa (2011: 191) builds on this idea by exploring hip hop's potential as counterknowledge—defined as "an alternative knowledge system intended to entertain while challenging white dominated knowledge industries such as academia or the mainstream press." Where colorblind ideology and notions of a post-racial society have served to obscure racial inequities, Gosa (2011: 200) argues that counterknowledge seeks to "expose the architecture of stratification." Other works in this tradition pivot to examine how hip hop's formation within contexts of social subjugation enables its intercultural mobility. Morgan (2009: 14, 189), for instance, locates the lyrical performances of Los Angeles underground emcees within a tradition of "African American cultural, political, social, and artistic expression," which she argues makes itself available to other marginalized groups as a global symbol of resistance to "bigotry, stereotypes, and injustices of many kinds."

Rap's diffusion across race, social class and geographic spaces raises questions about the legitimacy of its various non-black manifestations. Concerns regarding cultural appropriation, that is, "the taking—from a culture that is not one's own—of intellectual property, cultural expressions or artifacts, history and ways of knowledge" (Ziff and Rao 1997: 1), saturate the history of scholarship on black music in the United States (Hall 1997). In a context in which the boundaries between cultural, if not racial, groups appear to be increasingly blurred, many hip-hop scholars seek to investigate the nature of this appropriation.

Question 3: Should non-black hip-hop artists—and especially white artists—be interpreted through traditional cultural appropriation frameworks or is something notably different going on?

In examining hip hop as black oppositional expression, Martinez (1997) allowed for the possibility that it could speak to other groups facing similar systematic injustices within the dominant social order. Delgado (1998) took this a step further by presenting early-1990s Chicano rappers as examples of Gramscian *organic intellectuals* who (re)articulated Chicano ideology and galvanized Mexican-American communities. Likewise, Irving (1993: 112) saw rap music as attempting to "overcome . . . exclusionary tactics and construct a multi-subjectivized position" across race and gender. Regarding race, she writes: "it is thus no contradiction that thriving Mexican and Asian hip hop cultures have sprung up, as the discourse of rap constructs an equivalence between the subject position of Blacks and other ethnic groups on the basis of their mutual oppression and desire for self determination" (113). A more comprehensive treatment is offered by Ogbar (2007), who interrogates the salience of race among emcees identifying as black, Latino, Asian-American and white. Through discussing instances of figurative passing, cultural appropriation and cultural melding among non-black rappers, Ogbar argues for the ability to simultaneously affirm non-black identity and appropriate black cultural styles.

Recently, sociologists have focused on hip-hop production within specific Asian-American communities. Sharma (2010), for example, looks at hip-hop Desi (South-Asian US) artists who use music as a way to identify *with* rather than as black people. Sharma (2010: 279) sees these artists as atypical South-Asian Americans whose critical consciousness enables them to "exert agency by pushing back on imposed identities and narrow expectations." Similarly, Harrison (2012) describes how west coast Filipino-American youths' recognition of their historically racialized social location inspires them to embrace hip hop as a mode of politically conscious knowledge building. By examining Asian-American rappers' use of "strategic 'preemptive strike[s]'" to anticipate critiques of their racial identity, Wang (2007: 38) complicates such readings. Wang (2006: 159) is hesitant to characterize cross-racial participation in hip hop as inherently liberating, arguing that "despite its long-standing cross-cultural appeal, [hip hop] is not an ideal space in which AfroAsian relations should be forged and developed." Such concerns become even more contentious when applied to white hip-hop artists.

Authenticity has emerged as the primary conceptual framework through which debates over white artists' appropriation of rap are discussed. The seminal piece of scholarship addressing hip-hop authenticity was authored by McLeod (1999: 139) who, through an analysis of how artists, fans and the press talk about rap, offered a binary model of "realness" and "fakeness." Not surprisingly, with regard to race, McLeod found that "real" hip hop was associated with blackness while "fake" hip hop was associated with whiteness.[4]

Some of the most notable applications of racial authenticity within hip-hop studies have specifically focused on the white rapper Eminem. Hess (2005), for example, examined Eminem's authentic rap performance against the backdrop of earlier white artists including the Beastie Boys and Vanilla Ice. He specifically cites the latter's crucial role in setting the terms through which all white rappers who came after him negotiated their authenticity claims.[5] Post-Vanilla-Ice white rappers were compelled to foreground their whiteness as a way of critically reflecting on their place within a black music tradition (see also Armstrong 2004). This reading parallels Wang's observations about Asian-American artists' preemptive efforts, thus raising questions about the extent to which these authenticating practices should be historically contextualized rather than attributed to Vanilla Ice's signature influence. Kajikawa (2009) considers Eminem's racialized performance within the context of evolving meanings of whiteness in US society. Kajikawa offers several potential readings of Eminem; yet rather than deciding on one, he advocates continuing to look to popular culture as an important space in which changing racial meanings play out.

Shifting the focus from popular stardom to localized music scenes, Harkness's (2011) exploration of the processes through which white rappers in Chicago pursue authenticity rests on a conceptual division between gangsta-oriented (street) and backpacker-oriented (suburban) rappers. Presenting the gangsta and backpacker as ideal types, Harkness illustrates how both groups situationally prioritize being perceived as genuine and aspire to transgress black–white racial boundaries. In his ethnographic study of Bay Area underground hip hop, Harrison (2009) similarly discusses the way hip hoppers of various races and ethnicities deploy situational processes of racialization to assert their claims to and/or affiliations with hip-hop culture.

Several of the aforementioned works spotlight non-black rappers' efforts to foreground their racial identities; studies that specifically focus on the lyrical strategies used in emcee battling shed light on this practice. Cutler (2009), for example, describes how white rappers' double-consciousness— of how they are being perceived by black people—impacts their performative stances during battles. Alim, Lee and Carris (2010) extend Cutler's analysis by exploring how, in the context of battling, emcees perform and are performed—through parody and stylization—into racial and ethnic otherness. Although acknowledging black rappers' abilities to temporarily invert racial hierarchies in these performative spaces, the authors are reluctant to view this as a legitimate challenge to society's existing racial order.

Taken collectively these studies showcase the increased racial visibility of non-black rappers either as an effort to anticipate and stave off potential criticism and/or to secure a particular market. At the same time, more critical attention is paid to the representations of blackness, especially when they conform to stereotypical themes. There is also ambivalence regarding the political possibilities of a racially integrated hip-hop performance sphere, with the most hope lying where the music is pointedly political and attempts to speak foremost to a particular ethno-racial experience as opposed to across experiences.

Philosopher Paul C. Taylor and anthropologist John L. Jackson, respectively, have authored two of the most important pieces that seek to critically explore theories of culture and authenticity as they relate to hip hop, appropriation and race. In an essay entitled "Does Hip Hop Belong to Me?" Taylor questions which communities and, by extension, which individuals have a right to claim hip hop as theirs. By challenging the nature of authenticity as applied to culture, arguing that the concept obscures more than it reveals, Taylor presents hip hop as an ongoing process rather than a static thing. He concludes that "once we start to attend to the complexities of history, to the details of cultural borrowings and cross-fertilizations, it becomes hard to say when a culture really belongs to any single group" (Taylor 2005: 91). Jackson (2005: 182), in turn, outlines hip hop's cultural project as "constructing and deconstructing the social, cultural, and political boundaries placed around black bodies . . . in situation-specific ways." In critiquing how the meanings associated with blackness have been fabricated and propagated, Jackson (175) develops a notion of hip-hop sincerity that can potentially subvert the power connected to authenticity.

Question 4: What impact does rap music have on those who listen to it and in what ways does it work to support or undermine existing structures of racial inequality?

Justifiably or not, for many in the United States, hip hop is viewed as a window into the lives and lifestyles of urban black youth. This is certainly true for many white hip-hop consumers who are far removed from sizable communities of black people (Chideya 1999); yet it also holds true for black youth whose lives hip hop is purported to represent (Pattillo-McCoy 1999), as well as many hip-hop listeners situated between these two racial poles. Forman (2002: 9) discusses how the spatial discourses surrounding hip hop have provided young people of all races with "a distinctive understanding of the social terrains and conditions under which 'real' black cultural identities are formed and experienced." Although Forman (344) is critical of the problematic implications of "realness," he concludes that hip hop serves as a site "for social debate on the contemporary convergences of youth, race, space, and place."

In the early 1990s, statistics began to show that upwards of 70 percent of rap consumers were white teenagers.[6] Such figures undoubtedly contributed to the public outcry regarding hip hop's damaging influence. Examining media representations during the late 1980s, Binder (1993) argued that rap's dangerous image was directly connected to the music's association with blackness. In surveying Toronto high school students, Tanner, Ashbridge and Wortley (2009) found that rap listeners who were black appreciated the music's resistant representations and were comparatively skeptical of its claims to gangsta authenticity; white and Asian youth who listened to rap, on the other hand, were more likely to be involved in criminal or delinquent activities.[7] Likewise, Jeffries (2011) noted that black hip-hop listeners used the music as a form of identity development and consciousness-raising, and were therefore critically engaged and invested in evaluating its images of blackness, whereas white listeners were not.

A number of sociological studies explore rap music's impacts on black gender relations and gender identities. Hutchinson's (1999) ethnographic study of African-American male-female relations in a Houston gangsta rap nightclub, and Sharpley-Whitney's (2007) examination of sexualized and misogynistic imagery in commercial hip hop both emphasize the more damaging effects that rap music can have on young black women. White (2011) looks comparatively at portrayals of black masculinity in the US racial imaginary, and how hip hop continues a legacy from earlier malevolent representational forms (see also Delaney 1997, Heaggans 2009). Kubrin (2005), in turn, argues that gangsta rap offers an interpretive resource through which young black men make sense of their lives that renders masculinity, violence, danger and unpredictability as normative.

Scholars have varied interpretations of white rap consumption. Whereas several view it as signaling shifting implications of race, with white youth seemingly rejecting the privileges of their status (Chideya 1999, see also Stephens 1991, Potter 1995), others see it as "a more complex expression of racism" that involves vicariously experiencing the perceived adventures of black urbanity (Watkins 2005: 97, see also Allinson 1994).[8] Roediger (1998) grapples with these different understandings, ultimately concluding that white hip-hop fans are a "work in progress." He notably sees them as different from previous generations of "white negroes" in the extent to which they essentialize views of black culture as "male, hard, sexual, and violent" (1998: 362). This issue is even more pointedly tackled by Yousman (2003) who, emphasizing the fine line between fascination and fear, discusses the similarities between gangsta rap and imagery used by the far right to promote anxieties around racial difference.

Fernandes (2011: 105), in her exploration of hip hop's global appeal, encountered a predominantly Asian-American hip-hop scene in Chicago, which she viewed as a rather pedestrian effort by middle-class Asian youth to rebel against the conformities of suburban life. Maira similarly described how second-generation South Asians in New York have drawn on hip hop as a cultural idiom to address tensions surrounding the politics of their ambiguous position in the existing racial order. Maira (2000: 360) sees such cultural borrowing as an assertive act of positioning South-Asian identities within the US racial order; yet, like Fernandes and Wang, she concludes that this orientation toward black urban styles "fails to materialize a politics of alliance-building." Two ethnographic studies both centered in seemingly progressive college-town venues take differing perspectives on this issue. Dowdy (2007) suggests that local hip-hop shows serve as interactive political spaces that, through coordinated actions between performers and audiences, engender collective agency and identity across racial lines. In contrast, Rodriquez (2006) argues that the white show-goers he interviewed adopted a colorblind ideology that allowed them to position themselves as hip-hop insiders. Rodriquez ultimately reads this as an illustration of how white privilege works to neutralize racially coded forms of expression.

In conclusion, there is no question that hip-hop music offers an important platform for examining and discussing racial issues in contemporary US society. Yet, throughout the history of sociological scholarship on hip hop and race, several key debates have been recycled. These center around questions over what hip hop represents, who controls its representation, the social impacts of such representations, and how to interpret hip hop's appeal across cultural and racial lines. Over the years, more races have joined the discussion, yet the central issues, by and large, continue to be framed through orientations away from whiteness and toward blackness. Although this chapter has not focused on methodology, I believe the recent appearance of ethnographic studies on hip hop and race (see Harrison 2009, Morgan 2009, Neff 2009, Sharma 2010, Harkness 2011) offers great promise in terms of extending well-worn cycles, developing more nuanced understandings of existing readings, and pointing toward new directions of inquiry.

Notes

1　Recognizing that there are disagreements surrounding the use of the terms "hip hop" and "rap," for the purposes of this chapter I use them interchangeably. Although hip hop is generally thought to include the expressive practices of graffiti-writing, b-boying/b-girling and deejaying, I focus on hip hop as a music commodity.

2　I present these organizing structures as either/or options largely in the practical interest of framing my discussion. They are in fact much more blurred than this model suggests.

3　Perkins (1996) locates rap as the most recent in a line of black US oral traditions.

4　Harrison (2008) builds on McLeod's study by examining applications and understandings of racial authenticity over fifteen-plus years of hip-hop scholarship.

5　Specifically, Ice's feigned claim to cultural immersion within a predominantly black hip-hop world.

6　Remarkably little sociological attention has been given to actual statistics on rap sales by race.

7　Recognizing that this study is outside my stated US focus, I nevertheless believe its relevance warrants inclusion.

8　Delaney (1997) suggests that when white hip-hop consumers enter adulthood many of them abandon their hip-hop fandom in favor of more mainstream interests.

References

Alim, H.S., J. Lee and L.M. Carris. 2010. "'Short Fried-Rice Eating Chinese MCs' and 'Good-Hair-Havin Uncle Tom Niggas': Performing Race and Ethnicity in Freestyle Rap Battles." *Journal of Linguistic Anthropology* 20(1): 116–133.

Allinson, E. 1994. "It's a Black Thing: Hearing How Whites Can't." *Cultural Studies* 8(3): 438–456.

Armstrong, E.G. 2004. "Eminem's Construction of Authenticity." *Popular Music and Society* 27(3): 335–355.

Basu, D. 2005. "A Critical Examination of the Political Economy of the Hip-Hop Industry." In *African Americans in the U.S. Economy*, eds. C.A. Conrad, J. Whitehead, P. Mason and J. Stewart, 258–270. Lanham: Rowman and Littlefield.

Binder, A. 1993. "Constructions of Racial Rhetoric: Media Depictions of Harm in Heavy Metal and Rap Music." *American Sociological Review* 58(6): 753–67.

Chang, J. 2005. *Can't Stop Won't Stop: A History of the Hip-Hop Generation*. New York: St. Martin's Press.

Chideya, F. 1999. *The Color of Our Future*. New York: William and Morrow Company.

Cutler, C. 2009. "'You Shouldn't be Rappin', You Should be Skateboardin' the X-Games': The Coconstruction of Whiteness in an MC Battle." *In Global Linguistic Flows: Hip Hop Cultures, Youth Identities, and the Politics of Language*, eds. H.S. Alim, A. Ibrahim and A. Pennycook, 79–94. New York: Routledge.

De Genova, N. 1995. "Check Your Head: The Cultural Politics of Rap Music." *Transition* 67: 123–137.

Delaney, P. 1997. "Pop Culture, 'Gangsta Rap' and the 'New Vaudeville'." In *The Media in Black and White*, eds. E.E. Dennis and E.C. Pease, 83–88. New Brunswick, NJ: Transaction Publishers.

del Barco, M. 1996. "Rap's Latino Sabor." In *Droppin' Science: Critical Essays on Rap Music and Hip Hop Culture*, ed. W.E. Perkins, 63–84. Philadelphia: Temple University Press.

Delgado, F.P. 1998. "Chicano Ideology Revisited: Rap Music and the (Re)articulation of Chicanismo." *Western Journal of Communication* 62(2): 95–113.

Dowdy, M. 2007. "Live Hip Hop, Collective Agency, and 'Acting in Concert.'" *Popular Music and Society* 30(1): 75–91.

Fernandes, S. 2011. *Close to the Edge: In Search of the Global Hip Hop Generation.* New York: Verso.

Flores, J. 1996. "Puerto Rocks: New York Ricans Stake Their Claim." In *Droppin' Science: Critical Essays on Rap Music and Hip Hop Culture*, ed. W.E. Perkins, 85–115. Philadelphia: Temple University Press.

Forman, M. 2002. *The 'Hood Comes First: Race, Space, and Place in Rap and Hip Hop.* Middletown: Wesleyan University Press.

George, N. 1998. *Hip Hop America.* New York: Viking Penguin.

Gosa, T.L. 2011. "Counterknowledge, Racial Paranoia, and the Cultic Milieu: Decoding Hip Hop Conspiracy Theory." *Poetics* 39(3): 187–204.

Hall, P.A. 1997. "African-American Music: Dynamics of Appropriation and Innovation." In *Borrowed Power: Essays on Cultural Appropriation*, eds. B. Ziff and P.V. Rao, 31–51. New Brunswick: Rutgers University Press.

Harkness, G. 2011. "Backpackers and Gangstas: Chicago's White Rappers Strive for Authenticity." *American Behavioral Scientist* 55(1): 57–85.

Harrison, A.K. 2008. "Racial Authenticity in Rap Music and Hip Hop." *Sociology Compass* 2(6): 1783–1800.

_____. 2009. *Hip Hop Underground: The Integrity and Ethics of Racial Identification.* Philadelphia: Temple University Press.

_____. 2012. "Post-Colonial Consciousness, Knowledge Production, and Identity Inscription within Filipino American Hip Hop Music." *Perfect Beat* 13(1): 29–48.

Heaggans, R. 2009. *The 21st Century Hip-Hop Minstrel Show: Are We Continuing the Blackface Tradition.* San Diego: University Readers.

Henderson, E.A. 1996. "Black Nationalism and Rap Music." *Journal of Black Studies* 26(3): 308–339.

Hess, M. 2005. "Hip-Hop Realness and the White Performer." *Critical Studies in Media Communication* 22(5): 372–389.

Hutchinson, J.F. 1999. "The Hip Hop Generation: African American Male-Female Relationships in a Nightclub Setting." *Journal of Black Studies* 30(1): 62–84.

Irving, K. 1993. "'I Want Your Hands On Me': Building Equivalences through Rap Music." *Popular Music* 12(2): 105–121.

Jackson Jr., J.L. 2005. *Real Black: Adventures of Racial Sincerity.* Chicago: University of Chicago Press.

Jeffries, M.P. 2011. *Thug Life: Race, Gender, and the Meaning of Hip Hop.* Chicago: University of Chicago Press.

Kajikawa, L. 2009. "Eminem's 'My Name Is': Signifying Whiteness, Rearticulating Race." *Journal of the Society for American Music* 3(3): 241–363.

Keyes, C. 1996. "At the Crossroads: Rap Music and Its African Nexus." *Ethnomusicology* 40(2): 223–248.

Kubrin, C.E. 2005. "Gangstas, Thugs, and Hustlas: Identity and the Code of the Street in Rap Music." *Social Problems* 52(3): 360–378.

Lipsitz, G. 1998. "The Hip Hop Hearings: Censorship, Social Memory, and Intergenerational Tensions among African Americans." In *Generations of Youth: Youth Cultures and History in Twentieth-Century America*, eds. J. Austin and M.N. Willard, 395–411. New York. New York University Press.

Lusane, C. 1993. "Rap, Race, and Politics." *Race and Class* 35(1): 41–56.

Maira, S. 2000. "Henna and Hip Hop: the Politics of Cultural Production and the Work of Cultural Studies." *Journal of Asian American Studies* 3(3): 329–369.

Martinez, T.A. 1997. "Popular Culture as Oppositional Culture: Rap as Resistance." *Sociological Perspectives* 40(2): 265–286.

McDonnell, J. 1992. "Rap Music: Its Role as an Agent of Change." *Popular Music and Society* 16(3): 89–107.

McLeod, K. 1999. "Authenticity within Hip Hop and Other Cultures Threatened with Assimilation." *Journal of Communication* 49(4): 134–150.

Morgan, M. 2009. *The Real Hiphop: Battling for Knowledge, Power, and Respect in the LA Underground.* Durham: Duke University Press.

Neal, M.A. 1997. "Sold Out on Soul: The Corporate Annexation of Black Popular Music." *Popular Music and Society* 21(3): 117–135.

Neff, A.C. 2009. *Let the World Listen Right: The Mississippi Delta Hip-hop Story.* Jackson: University Press of Mississippi.

Negus, K. 1999. "The Music Business and Rap: Between the Street and the Executive Suite." *Cultural Studies* 13(3): 488–508.

Ogbar, J.O.G. 2007. *Hip-Hop Revolution: The Culture and Politics of Rap.* Lawrence: University Press of Kansas.

Pattillo-McCoy, M. 1999. *Black Picket Fences: Privilege and Peril among the Black Middle Class.* Chicago: University of Chicago Press.

Perkins, W.E. 1996. "The Rap Attack: An Introduction." In *Droppin' Science: Critical Essays on Rap Music and Hip Hop Culture*, ed. W.E. Perkins, 1–45. Philadelphia: Temple University Press.

Perry, I. 2004. *Prophets of the Hood: Politics and Poetics in Hip Hop*. Durham: Duke University Press.

Potter, R.A. 1995. *Spectacular Vernaculars: Hip-Hop and the Politics of Postmodernism*. Albany: State University of New York Press.

Quinn, E. 2005. *Nuthin' but a 'G' Thang: The Culture and Commerce of Gangsta Rap*. New York: Columbia University Press.

Quinn, M. 1996. "Never Shoulda Been Let Out The Penitentiary: Gangsta Rap and the Struggle over Racial Identity." *Cultural Critique* 34: 65–89.

Rivera, R.Z. 2003. *New York Ricans from the Hip-Hop Zone*. New York: Palgrave McMillan.

Rodriquez, J. 2006. "Color-Blind Ideology and Cultural Appropriation in Hip-Hop." *Journal of Contemporary Ethnography* 35(6): 645–668.

Roediger, D. 1998. "What to Make of Wiggers: A Work in Progress." In *Generations of Youth: Youth Cultures and History in Twentieth-Century America*, eds. J. Austin and M.N. Willard, 358–366. New York: New York University Press.

Rose, T. 1994. *Black Noise: Rap Music and Black Culture in Contemporary America*. Middletown: Wesleyan University Press.

Samuels, D. 1991. "The Rap on Rap: The Black Music That Isn't Either." *New Republic* 205(20): 24–29.

Scott, J.C. 1990. *Domination and the Arts of Resistance: Hidden Transcripts*. New Haven: Yale University Press.

Sharma, N.T. 2010. *Hip Hop Desis: South Asian Americans, Blackness, and Global Race Consciousness*. Durham: Duke University Press.

Sharpley-Whitney, T.D. 2007. *Pimps Up, Hoes Down: Hip Hop's Hold on Young Black Women*. New York: New York University Press.

Smith, C.H. 1997. "Method in the Madness: Exploring the Boundaries of Identity in Hip Hop Performativity." *Social Identities* 3(3): 345–374.

Stapleton, K.R. 1998. "From the Margins to Mainstream: the Political Power of Hip Hop." *Media, Culture and Society* 20(2): 219–234.

Stephens, G. 1991. "Rap Music's Double-Voiced Discourse: A Crossroads for Interracial Communication." *Journal of Communication Inquiry* 15(2): 70–91.

Tanner, J., M. Asbridge and S. Wortley. 2009. "Listening to Rap: Cultures of Crime, Cultures of Resistance." *Social Forces* 88(2): 693–722.

Tate, G. 2003. *Everything but the Burden: What White People Are Taking from Black Culture*. New York: Broadway Books.

Taylor, P.C. 2005. "Does Hip Hop Belong to Me? The Philosophy of Race and Culture." In *Hip Hop and Philosophy: Rhyme 2 Reason*, eds. D. Darby and T. Shelby, 79–91. Chicago: Open Court.

Toop, D. 1984. *Rap Attack: African Jive to New York Hip Hop*. London: Pluto Press.

Wang, O. 2006. "These Are The Breaks: Hip-Hop and AfroAsian Cultural (Dis)Connections." In *AfroAsian Encounters: Culture, History, Politics*, eds. H. Raphael-Hernandez and S. Steen, 146–166. New York: New York University Press.

_____. 2007. "Rapping and Repping Asian: Race, Authenticity, and the Asian American MC." In *Alien Encounters: Popular Culture and Asian America*, eds. M.T. Nguyen and T.L. Nguyen Tu, 35–68. Durham: Duke University Press.

Watkins, S.C. 2005. *Hip Hop Matters: Politics, Pop Culture, and the Struggle for the Soul of a Movement*. Boston: Beacon Press.

White, M. 2011. *From Jim Crow to Jay-Z: Race, Rap and the Performance of Black Masculinity*. Urbana: University of Illinois Press.

Yousman, B. 2003. "Blackophilia and Blackophobia: White Youth, the Consumption of Rap Music, and White Supremacy." *Communication Theory* 13(4): 366–391.

Ziff, B. and P.V. Rao. 1997. "Introduction to Cultural Appropriation: A Framework for Analysis." In *Borrowed Power: Essays on Cultural Appropriation*, eds. B. Ziff and P.V. Rao, 1–27. New Brunswick: Rutgers University Press.

19

Cultural Globalization
Pop-Rock and Musical Cosmopolitanism

Motti Regev

Cross-fertilization, mutual inspiration, multi-directional influences, transference of stylistic elements and simple copying or imitation have characterized the relations between musical cultures around the world for centuries, and certainly so since early modernity. Still, the notion of musical nationalism or musical ethnicity has been an essential, practically unquestionable premise that dictated the nature of much musical activity in almost every country during most of the twentieth century. That is, nations at large or certain sectors within them, as well as ethnic groups of various formations, have all worked to preserve and reproduce, or invigorate and invent, musical idioms, genres and styles that they could claim as their own. Musical styles and genres, in other words, have functioned throughout modernity as signifiers of ethno-national cultural uniqueness. Regardless of their genuine musicological "purity" in terms of nativeness or indigenousness, musical styles and genres have been proclaimed by nations and ethnic entities to be expressions of their cultural singularity and authenticity.

The process of intensified cultural globalization that took accelerated shape during the last decades of the twentieth century has disrupted this state of affairs. Cultural globalization facilitated greater contact between musical cultures, affording stylistic mixtures and hybrids that blurred the supposed clarity of musical mapping according to nation and ethnicity. Traditional musical idioms, stylistic elements and creative practices have been deterritorialized from their native habitats, and then localized and indigenized in various ways into the fabric of totally different cultural contexts. Against this tide, numerous musical cultures have taken defensive measures, opting for stylistic orthodoxies and strict preservation tactics. Ethnomusicology has been the major scholarly discipline to try and analyze these processes through empirical research and theorization. Extensive research has uncovered the complexity and intricacies of musical transformations, followed by theorizations of the nature and causes of the revamped global order of musical cultures (Slobin 1993, Taylor 1997, Erlmann 1999, 2003; Turino 2000). Stokes (2004, 2007) has provided two excellent comprehensive reviews of this state of affairs in the musics of the world and corresponding scholarly literature.

Except for some notable cases, however, research and theory in ethnomusicology have seldom focused on one of the major processes in world musical culture brought about by cultural globalization. It is a process through which a cluster of interconnected musical styles and genres—a musical idiom—has been globally institutionalized as a signifier of universal modernity. I call this cluster of styles and genres *pop-rock music*, and refer to its worldwide proliferation as the *pop-rockization* of world popular music. Omnipresent and ubiquitous throughout the world in both public and private spheres, the sonic vocabularies of pop-rock music embody the emergence and consolidation of cultural cosmopolitanism or, in this regard, musical cosmopolitanism. This chapter thus focuses on pop-rock as a global phenomenon. It offers a brief summary of the socio-cultural context that brought pop-rock music to worldwide legitimacy. This is followed by a discussion of certain consequences of pop-rockization. The chapter extracts and distills points and ideas elaborated broadly in Regev (2013).

Pop-Rock

The elements that interconnect all styles and genres of pop-rock music and that render them prominent expressions of contemporaneous modernity are primarily their creative technologies. Electric and electronic instruments, sound manipulation equipment of all types (in recording studios or as accessories to instruments), amplification and the targeting of creativity toward the sonic materiality of a recorded product are the essential components that jointly characterize pop-rock music as an aesthetic realm, a musical art. For pop-rock musicians, these technologies of sonic expression are not just aids for enhancing or capturing sound produced by traditional acoustic instruments and the human voice, but rather creative tools for generating sonic textures that cannot be produced otherwise (Wicke 1990, Gracyk 1996). In addition, pop-rock is culturally organized around a stylistic genealogy and a historical narrative for which the emergence of the rock 'n' roll style in the mid-1950s in the United States serves as a mythical moment of "birth" (Peterson 1990). The history of pop-rock tends to be narrated—even when focusing on local, national cases in countries other than the United States or the United Kingdom—as an unfolding lineage of styles, organized around a symbolic divide between earlier periods and the "rock era." All styles of pop-rock are characterized in such narrations as developments, mutations and expansions derived from the original style of rock 'n' roll and from the successive styles that developed from it. Moreover, pop-rock styles and genres have been portrayed over the years as suppliers of aesthetic languages and packages of meaning around which consecutive generations of teenagers and young adults all over the world have defined their late modern sense of particularity, of distinction. By the early twenty-first century, the stylistic genealogy of pop-rock includes forms, periods, fashions, trends and fads of music known by names such as hard rock, alternative rock, punk, progressive rock, power pop, soul, funk, disco, dance, house, techno, hip hop, heavy metal, extreme metal, reggae, country rock, folk rock, psychedelic rock, singer-songwriters and, notably, pop—as well as many more. These are augmented in countries around the world by various labels that refer to local, indigenous and national variants of such phenomena (*rock nacional* in Argentina and Brazil, *Anadolu rock* in Turkey, *yéyé* in 1960s France, Afropop of various forms, Algerian *pop-rai*, J-pop, K-pop, and many other uses of nation names as adjectives, such as *Ruski rock*, *hip-hop Italiano*, and so on). The set of creative practices around which pop-rock is organized, the cluster of sonic textures associated with these practices, together with the perceptual scheme that organizes the historical narrative, the cultural meanings and the stylistic lineage of pop-rock, may well be called the "pop-rock aesthetic."

Pop-Rockization

When examined globally, one cannot but assert that by the early twenty-first century world culture is calibrated to a large extent to the sounds of pop-rock music. Rock ballads, electro-dance pop tunes and hip-hop hits fill up the background music in fashion stores, supermarkets and malls, car radios, TV commercials, internet websites and many other channels all over the world. Electric and electronic sounds, pulsating beats and guttural vocals have become trivial, ubiquitous components in popular music styles in almost every country. Pop-rock songs serve as soundtracks for films and television dramas in all languages, functioning as sonic signifiers of moods, periods, generations and locations. Pop-rock styles and genres provide aesthetic idioms and bundles of meaning around which generational and lifestyle groupings, as well as ethnic factions and other prominent sectors within and across national societies, define their sense of late modern identity.

Sociologically, pop-rockization of global musical culture can be envisaged as one major component in the re-arrangement of cultural hierarchies in late modernity. This process is closely connected to the correspondence between the intensified fragmentation of modern societies and the accelerated pace of stylistic innovation in all forms of art and expressive culture. Reading the global proliferation of pop-rock genres and styles along this theoretical framework constitutes an elaboration of Bourdieuian sociology, and especially an adaptation of Bourdieu's (1993) notion of homology between the supply and demand sides of culture to popular music.

In Bourdieu's work, homology refers to an unintended correspondence between struggles within artistic fields, which result in a constant invention and reinvention of genres and styles, and the emergence of class fractions and sub-fractions demanding recognition and legitimacy. The constant supply of new cultural products by the former caters to the expanding social market for such products, created by the demands of the latter. Connected to this, DiMaggio (1987) points to a strong correlation that exists in modern social formations between the intensity and amount of status differentiation or fragmentation, and the system of classification and hierarchization of art forms and genres. Intensified status differentiation will typically go hand in hand with growing ritualized classification in the arts—that is, classifications that dramatize the differences between forms and genres through various ritualistic practices. Taken together, the complex ritualized diversification, as well as constant innovation of styles and genres in popular music, can be sociologically theorized in light of the decomposition of late modern social formations into small and ever-changing social units of life style groupings, and the quest of each one of them for cultural materials around which they can do "boundary work" (Lamont and Fournier 1992, Lamont and Molnár 2002) and thus shape their sense of difference, distinction and uniqueness.

Perceived from an early stage as the musical expression of a neutral and universal modernity, pop-rock music became from the 1960s onwards a supplier of musical materials that functioned as a prominent focus for these socio-cultural processes. Consecutive styles and genres of pop-rock became objects of worship, encapsulated in various practices around the world. These practices have given rise to a musical art that is embraced and followed by musicians and fans alike. Motivated by a creative interest in keeping up with stylistic innovations, musicians adapted and indigenized pop-rock genres or stylistic elements in a cultural strategy that continuously expanded, re-formulated and re-mapped the musical repertoire within national fields of popular music. Their musical output served the cultural interests of fans who demanded local pop-rock styles "of their own" in order to update their sense of contemporaneous national identity along models of global modernity. Consequently, pop-rock music became a dominant force in many national fields of music.

The process of pop-rockization—that is, the diachronic process through which pop-rock music gained recognition, legitimacy, esteem and dominance in national fields of popular music across the globe—can be portrayed—in the manner of an ideal type—as a *longue durée* event consisting of four phases. In an early phase, local musicians introduce pop-rock into a local national culture for the first time. However, although their initial contribution to the emergence of a national pop-rock is acknowledged by critics and historical narratives, these musicians and their work are typically regarded, in most cases, as essentially mimicking Anglo-American pop-rock, and as lacking in artistic quality and authenticity. The second phase is one of initiating consecration, a mythologized period regarded as constituting the "birth" of national pop-rock, the moment when its proper local "history" begins. This occurs in terms of ritual practices of periodization. This process of consecration consists of the early work of musicians that, according to conventional wisdom, are the first to make local rock music "worthy of its name," and in two senses: music that matches—according to local critics— artistic standards set by leading Anglo-American artists of the period; and music that could properly be called locally "authentic"—because of the language it uses, the content of its lyrics, a typical sonic texture, the social sources from which it emanates and, most notably, the self-authorship of the musicians.

In the third phase, pop-rock music arises to dominance in many countries in a national field of popular music, gaining along the way legitimacy as a viable form of local musical art. Writing about pop-rock in Argentina, Alabarces (1993) talks about an "explosion" in the amount and public impact of rock produced in Argentina in the early 1980s, while Regev and Seroussi (2004), referring to Israel, write about "the coming of rock" during this phase. The firm consolidation of pop-rock as a leading force in national fields of music and culture takes shape along two complementary channels. Genres and styles, and the pop-rock aesthetic in general, become increasingly indigenized by merging and hybridizing them with local forms of popular music, while some local and traditional genres go through a process of pop-rockization by way of electrification, amplification and other pop-rock creative practices. In addition, during this phase, traditional melodic pop, or popular song, are transformed into styles known as *soft rock* or *adult oriented rock*, rendering the rock aesthetic more commercial and accessible to wider publics.

The final phase of the musical historical event of pop-rock typically consists of a stylistic diversification in accordance with current trends in global pop-rock—most notably electronica, hip hop, metal and alternative rock. Many countries have witnessed the flourishing of local variants of these styles. Also characteristic of this phase has been the development of indigenous styles of pop-rock, decoupled from trends in the global field. In addition, local musicians have made forays into the global field with occasional success, thus giving rise to a pride in their artistic quality and ability to match Anglo-American dominance. Most importantly, perhaps—and in what amounts to ritualistic self-appraisals—this phase also witnesses the appearance of written or televised histories of national pop-rock and the introduction of prizes and awards by the industry, the media and the state to honor and glorify the work of pop-rock musicians. In sum, it is the phase in which pop-rock becomes not only fully accepted, but rather gains a national self-confidence to the point of celebrating its own achievements and writing its own history in a self-glorifying manner.

Beginning in the 1960s, these four phases have roughly coincided—in the cases of Western Europe, Latin America and Japan—with the last four decades of the twentieth century. By the 1990s, and certainly into the current century, pop-rockization had become, globally speaking, a *fait acompli*. World musical culture has become calibrated to the electric and electronic sounds of pop-rock, as well as to the pace of successive pop-rock styles and genres.

Pop-Rock Impact: Spaces and Bodies

One major impact of pop-rockization, and one that has been less explored by research thus far, pertains to everyday cultural experience as affected by the ubiquitous presence of pop-rock sonic vocabularies of electric, electronic and amplified sounds. It is a cultural change that exemplifies McClary's (1991: 25) dictum that "music is a powerful social and political practice precisely because in drawing on metaphors of physicality, it can cause listeners to experience their bodies in new ways," as well as DeNora's (2003: 47) assertion that music has the potential to "structure things as styles of consciousness, ideas, or mode of embodiment." Once encountered and absorbed into musical cultures and personal tastes, new sonic textures have the potential to usher new modes of individual and collective experiences, alter the physical reality of public spaces, and in general affect cultural performance at the individual and collective levels. This is indeed one of the major cultural consequences of pop-rockization. Pop-rock genres and styles have acted as agents of cultural change at the material, physical levels of human bodies and urban spaces by introducing new sonorities, sound patterns and textures generated by electric and electronic instruments as well as by amplification and the wide dissemination of the resulting music. Pop-rock has ushered in the emergence and consolidation of *global electro-amplified soundscapes* and *aesthetic cosmopolitan bodies*. The constitution of such soundscapes and bodies has been a direct outcome of a growing and habitual familiarity, a familiarity shared by individuals around the world by virtue of the typical sonorities of pop-rock and its characteristic sonic and musical units of signification. These, as repertoires consisting of auditory communicative elements, as vocabularies of sounds and stylistic elements, have become building blocks for modes of bodily experience and patterns of spatial consciousness. These were new in the 1960s, becoming ubiquitous and omnipresent through subsequent decades.

In the remaining part of this chapter I will look at the physicality of pop-rock music as sound, at its materialization in bodies and spaces. The discussion is based on two premises. One is that, as an art form organized around recording, pop-rock's stylistic history has been an exploration of sonic vocabularies and the continuous introduction of new sonorities; the second is that one of pop-rock music's essential contributions to modern global cultural reality is to be found in the permeation of its typical sonorities into everyday lifeworlds.

Spaces

Music is territorial; its sounds fill up both closed and open spaces. There are "many ways in which popular music is spatial—linked to particular geographical sites, bound up in our everyday perceptions of place, and a part of movements of people, products and cultures across space" (Connell and Gibson 2003: 1; see also Leyshon, Matless and Revill 1998, Johansson and Bell 2009). One particular and prominent way is to be found in the construction of ethno-national space, of cultural locality and domesticity. Territories are domesticated to become environments culturally possessed, owned by national or ethnic communities. Such domestication shapes a given territory as the "homeland" of a given ethnic group or national community. Music is one major element that greatly contributes to the specificity of cultural spaces, to the aesthetic uniqueness that sets apart one ethno-national space from another, and therefore to the perceived familiarity, the sense of "being at home" shared by members of ethno-national communities in the territories they inhabit and possess (Stokes 1994). Originally referring to all sounds and to the confined space of the house, Barthes (1991: 246) asserted that "for the human being . . . the appropriation of space is also a matter of sound: domestic space . . . is the space of familiar, recognized noises whose ensemble forms a kind of household symphony." Narrowing down this assertion to the sounds of music, and extending it to public, collective space, it holds also for the appropriation and domestication of space by national, ethnic and other communities. This is achieved by filling the space they inhabit with sounds of familiar music, music they consider their "own." This practice has been associated conventionally with indigenous folk and popular musical idioms.

The growing presence of Anglo-American pop-rock in the musical space of many countries in the world since the 1960s has disrupted the soundscapes that previously existed in them. By breaching existing musical soundscapes with the new tones and timbres of electric, electronic and amplified sound, Anglo-American pop-rock music initially created a clear-cut division between the local, folk or traditional musics that have conventionally comprised the uniqueness of ethno-national musical space, and the new foreign music, which has been perceived as cultural invasion. However, once local, national and ethnic styles of pop-rock started to emerge and gain legitimacy if not dominance in local fields of popular music, the nature of the uniqueness of ethno-national musical spaces became significantly transformed. The experience of being culturally "at home" in a person's own country, originally associated in the case of musical space with sonic vocabularies of traditional, indigenous music, has been gradually converted to noticeably include sounds of electric and electronic instruments, of music conceived for amplification and emitted from loudspeaker systems. With repertoires of songs and sonic structures already known to local audiences as their "own", national pop-rock has naturalized electric sounds into public spaces. With the legitimacy gained by local pop-rock, electric sounds were no longer perceived as intrusions, but rather as conventional elements of domestic cultural space.

In many urban settings around the world, pop-rock in indigenous repertoires of national pop-rock has become smoothly woven together with Anglo-American pop-rock to create one public musical soundscape composed primarily of electric and electronic sonic vocabularies. The local elements in the sonic environment render it domestic, creating the feeling of Italian-ness, Israeli-ness or Thai-ness, to mention some examples. They afford the sense of being at home to members of the national community, to individuals for whom such countries are a cultural home. Yet the presence of Anglo-American pop-rock hits, as well as the electric and electronic nature of local music, turns such space into one that shares much aesthetic common ground with the spaces of other urban settings around the world. Local urban musical environments thus become global electro soundscapes, places where one feels local and global at the very same time. Culturally, they become aesthetic cosmopolitan landscapes.

Bodies

The permeation of pop-rock's sonic vocabularies and song repertoires within the public cultural sphere, together with its dominance of cultural landscapes in urban settings worldwide, means that it has become a major musical "device of social ordering" (DeNora 2000). This is especially the case in consumerist contexts. By the 1990s and into the current century, the sonic vocabularies of practically all kinds of pop-rock have come to be used intensively in the media, marketing and advertisement industries in order to project moods and images into film and television dramas and onto consumer goods. Such projection takes the form either of licensed excerpts from well-known songs, or of commissioned original music (Taylor 2007). In addition, historical repertoires of Anglo-American or other national pop-rock that enjoy the status of "classics" come to be featured prominently in various urban settings as background music—most prominently in shopping centers (Sterne 1997).

This development has been made possible because of an acquired familiarity and acquaintance with the tones and timbres of pop-rock, as well as a habitual and intuitive capacity to decipher its rhetorical patterns. All over the world, successive generations of adolescents and young adults since the 1960s have either participated actively in the aesthetic cultures of pop-rock or developed taste preferences for one or more genres of pop-rock. By and large, by the turn of the century, numerous adults the world around were already equipped with the corporeal knowledge relevant to deciphering pop-rock music and enjoying it. The bodies of all these individuals have become intuitively receptive to the sonorities of pop-rock.

One significant effect of this long-term impact of pop-rock sonorities on the bodies of individuals the world over has to do with the cultural performance of musical nationalism. As it has been typically constituted by national movements and nation states in their formative phases, musical nationalism has been organized around traditional forms of music that are played on acoustic and often indigenous instruments. Such forms of music have served the interests of nationalism in establishing itself as a direct continuation of ancient traditions and as a reflection of existing folklore. National culture and its embodiment in individuals' sense of identity thus became associated with the sounds and sonic textures of these instruments, and therefore with concomitant modes of corporeality. Many of the musical idioms associated with specific national and ethnic cultures have been based on the typical sonorities of certain musical instruments, on ensembles in which they are prominently featured, and on typical sonic patterns produced by such ensembles. The tones and timbres as well as typical sonic patterns associated with instruments such as the sitar and *tabla, ûd, bouzouki, balalaika, bandoneon* and *charanga*, accordion and *zourna* (or associated with ensembles in which these instruments are featured prominently) might immediately evoke notions of Indian, Arab, Greek, Russian, Argentinean, French and Armenian cultural uniqueness respectively. This evocation may connote identifiable and possibly exotic otherness to listeners who are not themselves members of these national cultures. For individuals who are native members of these cultures, however, the corporeality evoked by the typical sonic textures of these instruments amounts to a bodily performance of membership in their national cultures. Upon listening to such music and recognizing in it, spontaneously and intuitively, their collective identity, they are engaged in the cultural performance of musical nationalism. The daily encounters with music, especially with music one knows and likes, amount to "performing rites," as Frith (1996) calls them. In such rites, he contends, music "both articulates and offers the immediate experience of collective identity" (1996: 273). Intuitive, spontaneous bodily recognition of a given musical piece as one we know or like, one that "belongs" to our collective cultural identity, amounts to a performance of membership in this collective entity. In the case of national identity, such recognition amounts to a cultural performance, a re-assertion, of membership in the nation.

The cultural transformation encapsulated in the sonic vocabulary of pop-rock therefore means, at the individual level, an alteration of the corporeality through which memberships in nations or ethnicities are performed. With the growth of sectors within national societies who adopt national pop-rock styles as the music that expresses and symbolizes their collective identity, the bodily experience and performance of national identity have been transformed. The bodily experience associated with folk and traditional acoustic instruments has been augmented and at times replaced by the bodily experience associated with pop-rock. It became a bodily disposition that affords experiences of cultural hominess and domesticity through sonic vocabularies that are simultaneously native and foreign, indigenous and alien. Put differently, when bodies come to identify and experience the sense of a cultural home—as this is mediated through musical sound—through the sonic vocabularies of pop-rock, they become aesthetic cosmopolitan bodies.

An aesthetic cosmopolitan body is a body that articulates its own local identity by incorporating elements from alien cultures. Aesthetic cosmopolitan bodies are bodies whose very corporeality is inscribed with cultural dispositions and sensibilities, schemes of aesthetic perception and evaluative criteria shared by many other bodies across the world. Once the bodies of modern individuals adapt their senses, and knowingly incorporate elements from other cultures into the experiential repertoires through which they articulate cultural locality and hominess, their bodies become aesthetic cosmopolitan bodies.

With the auditory perceptual schemes of individuals all over the world becoming accustomed to the distorted sounds of electric guitars and to the indefinable timbres of electronic music; with the tones and timbres of pop-rock being absorbed into the canonical auditory knowledge of listeners across the world; with pop-rock's units of meaning becoming familiar and recognizable as musical elements by listeners in almost any culture, ethnic group and nation; when all the above become elements in the cultural performance of contemporary musical nationalism, it becomes plausible to assert that pop-rock music has constituted its listeners as aesthetic cosmopolitan bodies, that is, as bodies inscribed with musico-aural knowledge that affords a sense of being local and trans-local at the same time. As the stylistic idioms and sonorities of pop-rock became a steady influx, a constant and regular feature of contemporary national music cultures, the bodies of members in such national societies became accustomed to the mixture of traditional and new, native and alien tastes as practices of contemporary locality.

The sonic vocabulary of pop-rock has modified the state of affairs in the global musical and cultural fields. In Latour's (2005) terminology, and in that of actor-network theory in general, the sounds of pop-rock qualify as actants, as "things" in the world whose presence has a certain transformative effect on reality. Pop-rock music has generated and provided a repertoire of actants that mediated new ways of experiencing the body, new styles of consciousness and modes of embodiment, new designs of the musical public sphere, new patterns of performing national and ethnic identity.

Conclusion

Given the constant emergence of styles and genres of pop-rock, where each one expands the palette of the sonic vocabulary, pop-rock history can be envisaged as the serial appearance of clusters of actants. One significant modification brought about in world culture by these serial clusters of actants, by the long and expanding stylistic lineage of pop-rock genres, is the growing cultural propinquity between national formations. The corporeality evoked by the sounds of these genres and the qualities they radiate on cultural spaces have grown to become a conventional and legitimate ingredient in the experience of national cultural specificity in many different countries. Pop-rock sounds have thus brought formerly distant and separate cultural spaces into greater proximity. If, as Frith (1996: 272) asserts, music "gives us a way of being in the world, a way of making sense of it," then the particularity of that mode of being in the world, which is the experience of membership in a given national formation as it is mediated by music, has been transformed by pop-rock. It is no longer a way of being in the world that is, or at least strives to be, totally different from that of national formations other than one's own. Rather, it is a way of being in the world whose particularity shares much common expressive ground with that of other national formations. That is, as the same expressive materials—electric and electronic sonic vocabularies, pop-rock genres, styles and musical works—are used to produce the experience of musico-cultural uniqueness of different national formations, the cultural overlap between these formations is enhanced and intensified. The mutual sense of otherness between different national or ethnic formations is reduced, shrunk to a minimum, while the proportion of shared aesthetic perceptions grows and expands. Pop-rock music stands at the core of what aesthetic cosmopolitanism is all about—the shriveling and withering of cultural otherness—not its disappearance, but its mutation into something always familiar, never fully alien or strange. Listening to girl groups from Japan, to hip hop from Turkey, to flamenco-tinged rock from Spain and to a female or male rock auteur from any country, pop-rock fans anywhere in the world will always encounter in each of the above some electric and electronic sounds, vocal techniques and musical phrases familiar from their very own national music.

References

Alabarces, P. 1993. *Entre Gatos y Violdores: el Rock Nacional en la Cultura Argentina*. Buenos Aires: Ediciones Colihue.
Barthes, R. 1991. *The Responsibility of Forms*. Berkeley: University of California Press.
Bourdieu, P. 1993. *The Field of Cultural Production*. Cambridge: Polity.
Connell, J. and C. Gibson. 2003. *Sound Tracks: Popular Music, Identity and Place*. London: Routledge.
DeNora, T. 2000. *Music in Everyday Life*. Cambridge: Cambridge University Press.
_____. 2003. *After Adorno: Rethinking Music Sociology*. Cambridge: Cambridge University Press.
DiMaggio, P. 1987. "Classification in Art." *American Sociological Review* 52(4): 440–455.
Erlmann V. 1999. *Music, Modernity and the Global Imagination*. Oxford: Oxford University Press.
_____. 2003. "Hybridity and Globalization." In *The Continuum Encyclopedia of Popular Music of the World*, vol. 1, eds. J. Shepherd, D. Horn, P. Oliver and P. Wicke, 279–290. New York: Continuum.

Frith, S. 1996. *Performing Rites: On the Value of Popular Music.* Cambridge: Harvard University Press.

Gracyk, T. 1996. *Rhythm and Noise: An Aesthetic of Rock.* Durham: Duke University Press.

Johansson, O. and T.L. Bell. 2009. *Sound, Society and the Geography of Popular Music.* Aldershot: Ashgate.

Lamont, M. and M. Fournier, eds. 1992. *Cultivating Differences: Symbolic Boundaries and the Making of Inequality.* Chicago: University of Chicago Press.

Lamont, M. and V. Molnár. 2002. "The Study of Boundaries in the Social Sciences." *Annual Review of Sociology* 28: 167–195.

Latour, B. 2005. *Reassembling the Social: An Introduction to Actor-Network-Theory.* Oxford: Oxford University Press.

Leyshon, A., D. Matless and G. Revill, eds. 1998. *The Place of Music.* New York: Guilford Press.

McClary, S. 1991. *Feminine Endings: Music, Gender, and Sexuality.* Minneapolis: University of Minnesota Press.

Peterson, R.A. 1990. "Why 1995? Explaining the Advent of Rock Music." *Popular Music* 9(1): 97–116.

Regev, M. 2013. *Pop-Rock Music: Aesthetic Cosmopolitanism in Late Modernity.* Cambridge: Polity.

Regev, M and E. Seroussi. 2004. *Popular Music and National Culture in Israel.* Berkeley: University of California Press.

Slobin, M. 1993. *Subcultural Sounds: Micromusics of the West.* Hanover: Wesleyan University Press.

Sterne, J. 1997. "Sounds Like the Mall of America: Programmed Music and the Architectonics of Commercial Space." *Ethnomusicology* 41(1): 22–50.

Stokes, M., ed. 1994. *Ethnicity, Identity and Music: The Musical Construction of Place.* Oxford: Berg.

_____. 2004. "Music and the Global Order." *Annual Review of Anthropology* 33, 47–72.

_____. 2007. "On Musical Cosmopolitanism." *The Macalester International Roundtable 2007.* Paper 3: http://digitalcommons.macalester.edu/intlrdtable/3.

Taylor, T.D. 1997. *Global Pop: World Music, World Market.* London: Routledge.

_____. 2007. "The Changing Shape of the Culture Industry; Or, How Did Electronica Music Get into Television Commercials?" *Television and New Media* 8(3): 235–258.

Turino, T. 2000. *Nationalists, Cosmopolitans, and Popular Music in Zimbabwe.* Chicago: University of Chicago Press.

Wicke, P. 1990. *Rock Music: Culture, Aesthetics and Sociology.* Cambridge: Cambridge University Press.

20

Music Criticism and Taste Cultures

Morten Michelsen

Music criticism has profoundly influenced musical practice as well as how various publics have understood and related to various kinds of music. This chapter explores that relationship, situating the practice of music criticism both historically and within the contexts of music journalism and the music press more broadly.

As the chapter argues, the formation and dynamics of taste cultures are central to understanding how people, both individually and collectively, relate to music. The chapter therefore begins with a discussion of the development of the concept of "taste cultures," the relationship of this concept to others such as "subcultures," "scenes" and "tribes" that have been used to understand the cultural practices of various groups, and the relationship of this concept to others of a similar provenance ("taste publics," "taste groups," "taste structures," "interpretive communities" and so on).

The chapter then proceeds to delineate the principal characteristics of music journalism and music criticism and to explore the relations between music criticism and taste cultures as a way of grasping the considerable influence music criticism has had on the formation of taste cultures and thus on how people relate to music. These explorations are situated historically. The chapter concludes by reflecting on the somewhat peripheral status of research on music criticism and music journalism within popular music studies, and of the role played by the concept of taste cultures within the sociology of music. A case is made for broadening the scope of research in both cases.

Taste Cultures

Questions about music and taste are extremely relevant as starting points for research concerning what music means to listeners and musicians, what they use it for (if anything) and how it contributes to establish and transcend borders in and between individuals and collectives. General questions regarding taste have been discussed in other chapters. Here we will focus on one specific function of taste, namely how it may be used to produce, maintain and change communities or cultures organized around music. The discussion will focus on popular as opposed to art music cultures because the different notions of taste cultures that have been developed have in fact been mainly relevant to understanding popular culture in more detail. Art music cultures are obviously taste cultures as well, but there has been much less interest in understanding how they worked as they appeared "natural" to many traditional musicological and sociological gazes.

During the twentieth century, sociologists developed different kinds of categories in order to point to larger or smaller groupings within complex societies, very often within a class perspective. Also, within the sphere of culture, different subcultures have been explained as class-based, and distinctions between high culture and low culture, or "lowbrow," "middlebrow" and "highbrow," have also been seen as class-related. In the early 1950s, US sociologists David Riesman and Howard Becker changed this perspective and claimed that the cultural fault line did not necessarily run only between the classical and the popular. It could be observed just as well *within* popular music culture. Riesman distinguished between two main categories in US youth cultures: a consumption-oriented majority culture and a hot jazz-oriented minority culture. The latter he described in the following way:

> The rebelliousness of this minority group might be indicated in some of the following attitudes toward popular music: an insistence on rigorous standards of judgment and taste in a relativist culture; a preference for the uncommercialized, unadvertised small bands rather than name bands; the development of a private language and then a flight from it when the private language (the same is true of other aspects of private style) is taken over by the majority group; a profound resentment of the commercialization of radio and musicians.
>
> (Riesman 1950: 365–366)

Riesman draws a picture much more detailed than this. Nevertheless, we see clearly the contours of a youth culture using a specific musical genre—including its discourse—as a mark of superior taste. This marker then serves as one of the main tools of identification for the culture in question. While Riesman looked at audiences, Becker (1951) investigated musicians and discovered the same distinction between a mainstream and a more artful, bebop-related jazz.

The early cultural studies tradition in the United Kingdom focused on another type of category, subcultures, which conceptualized a series of British male youth cultures within a neo-Marxist framework. These subcultures were related to music, often superficially: teds (teddy boys) to rock 'n' roll, mods to beat, punks to punk, and so on (see for example Willis 1978). These analytical syntheses of musical tastes and musical and social practices became a watershed. They provided an important source for a sociological dominance of popular music studies that developed during the early 1970s. Since then, notions of subculture have been criticized, not least for the homological logic that was used to bind together taste and the social. Although subcultures in some senses could constitute taste cultures, the difference would be that "subculture" is a more encompassing term than "taste culture." The latter stresses matters of taste and sociality and leaves it to other types of categorization to grasp a bigger picture.

Hesmondhalgh (2005) discusses why different ways of conceiving musically-based groupings within popular music are not entirely satisfactory. He critiques the theories of scenes, tribes and subcultures, which have been used quite extensively to grasp specific musical–social formations. He argues that the first two concepts are too vague and general as analytical tools with regard to what actually belongs to specific scenes or tribes and how their borders are constituted. Discussing subcultures, Hesmondhalgh (2005: 32) points out the automatism of the homological argument and concludes that subcultural theory has not contributed much to socio-musical analysis. Instead of these concepts, Hesmondhalgh suggests turning to the concepts of genre and articulation. He argues that these can be used in less totalizing ways than has been the norm for the other concepts. Such concepts, he concludes, point to debates about borders and to a relationalism and dynamism lacking in the other concepts.

Moving from general social categorizations related to music toward taste-related ones, it needs pointing out that all the categories and fields of study mentioned so far are in some way or another related to taste, to sets of complex relations concerning liking and disliking between individuals, groups and musical sounds. In 1966, sociologist Herbert Gans suggested the concepts of "taste cultures" and "taste publics" (see Gans 1999 [1974]) to discuss this topic. In 1980, literary scholar Stanley Fish introduced the notion of "interpretive communities." These concepts are the ones most theorized, but other related concepts have occurred in the academic literature: "taste communities" (McLeod 2001), "taste groups" (Frith 1996: 36), "protocommunities" (Willis 1990: 114) and "affective alliances" (Grossberg 1992: 80) are some of them.

Here we will focus on Gans's concepts. Entering the high culture / low culture debates that developed after the Second World War, Gans introduced the concept of taste cultures in order to demonstrate that an abstract and general dichotomy of high and low (fine art and mass) culture was too simplistic. His point was that low culture, or popular culture as he preferred to call it, included so many divergent phenomena that it did not make sense to group them together under one umbrella term. Instead, from looking at US culture in the 1960s, Gans sketched out five major taste cultures, based mainly on class indicators (education, income and occupation). Departing from the, by then, accepted trichotomy of highbrow, middlebrow and lowbrow, he referred to these taste cultures as "high," "upper-middle," "lower-middle," "low" and "quasi-folk low" (Gans 1999 [1974]: 100–120). These cultures could then be modified in various ways by reference to the parameters of religion, region, race, sex and age. Deciding on the actual number of taste cultures that could thus be identified becomes "an empirical and a conceptual problem." Gans also attempted to avoid the concomitant dichotomy of the aesthetic and the non-aesthetic by arguing that different sets of aesthetic standards and values give rise to different taste cultures (92–93).

Gans (92) distinguished between taste cultures (values and standards) and taste publics (people who make the same choices for the same reasons). As he explains:

> Taste cultures are not cohesive value systems, and taste publics are not organized groups; the former are aggregates of similar values and usually but not always similar content, and the latter are aggregates of people with usually but not always similar values making similar choices from the available offerings of culture. Moreover, they are analytic aggregates which are constructed by the social researcher, rather than real aggregates, which perceive themselves as such . . .
>
> (94)

Gans (135 ff.) also refers to "taste structures" as providing an overall context for taste cultures and taste publics. Taste structures make it possible for individuals to "shop around" in different taste cultures, but also provide the mechanism that keeps taste cultures in place in the socioeconomic hierarchy. Gans's terminology is quite general. One of his points is that empirical studies are needed to further develop the analysis he suggests.

Sociologist Giselinde Kuipers comments on Gans's approach in one of the relatively few empirical studies that followed his work. Kuipers' point of departure is that taste is not only "a pattern of preferences and aversions, but [also] . . . a form of cultural knowledge" (Kuipers 2006: 360). It is taste as knowledge that sustains the cultural hierarchy, and it is taste in this sense that is the basis for taste cultures. Taste may be related to objects and it might be seen as part of a Bourdieuian *habitus*. Also, taste cultures must be seen in relation to other taste cultures as they normally are aware of each other and react to each other in different ways. Kuipers (361–362) suggests four types of relation: opposition (conflict), side by side (accept or ignorance), mainstream versus margin (matters of size) and fragmentation (many small).

This indicates that taste culture is a concept that may grasp cultures in many sizes and in many forms. It is possible to "zoom out" and study cultures the size of Gans's upper-middle culture, or it is possible to "zoom in" and study very small groupings. Size does not matter, and spatial relations among members are not important either. Neither is the sometimes very loose organization of taste communities (for example, classical music or jazz lovers around the world) held together in imagined communities by the same views on specific musics.

To get an even more detailed understanding of how taste cultures work, we will turn to the work of British popular music scholar Simon Frith. Apart from having served as a rock critic for about twenty years, he has written quite extensively on matters of taste and music, not least in *Performing Rites: On the Value of Popular Music*. Here, Frith (1996: 19) begins from the Gansian assumption that judgments of value take place in all kinds of cultures and that differences between high and low cultures can be considered only as a social fact, not an ontological difference. He subscribes to the Riesmanian notion that the most important—and interesting—divide is that between the margins and the mainstream (35). He argues that:

> For most rock critics . . . the issue in the end isn't so much representing the music to the public (the public to the musician) as creating a knowing community, orchestrating a collusion between selected musicians and an equally select part of the public—select in its superiority to the ordinary, undiscriminating pop consumer. The critic is, in this respect, a fan . . . with a mission to preserve a perceived quality of sound, to save the musicians from themselves, to define the ideal musical experience for listeners to measure themselves against. . . . the language of music criticism . . . depends on the confusion of the subjective and the objective, on the championing not so much of music as a way of listening to music.
>
> (67)

Here, Frith describes the workings of intellectually-inclined types of musical taste cultures and the interdependence of audiences, musicians and critics, with critics placed as intermediaries between audiences and musicians. His example involves rock critics. However, I would argue that these mechanisms work for all kinds of intellectually inclined musical taste cultures, be they oriented toward jazz, art music, rock or world music genres. The discourses erect borders, define canons within genres, create relations between musical sounds and words, argue for a specific (high) placement in the cultural hierarchy, and advise on how to use and talk about the music.

The concept of taste culture has been used mainly in relation to popular music cultures. The above quotation could make one think that discussing popular music taste cultures is the same as discussing non-mainstream taste cultures, that is, reproducing the high–low split by ascribing a word-based taste to minority groups and non-taste to mainstream cultures. Frith's take on this is to point to mainstream cultures' articulation of taste as "common sense" and, more importantly, as a feeling that cannot only take "one out of oneself," but also "take one deep inside" (73). This means that mainstream cultures articulate themselves differently compared to non-mainstream ones. I would argue that, instead of a principal reliance on language to justify their positions, they tend to treat music as part of a broader set of cultural practices, for example, those of dance and fashion. Music is often judged according to how well it fits in with such practices, something that does not need much verbal explanation. Such mainstream cultures have hardly been analyzed as taste cultures, an omission that demonstrates that the hierarchical organization of taste cultures remains effective, and that Gans's analysis of different taste cultures as cultural practices remains relevant.

In her influential study of musical life in Milton Keynes, Finnegan (2007 [1989]: 329) has challenged the view that class background strongly influences the formation of taste cultures by arguing that citizens' musical tastes and practices are not bound to any significant degree by class background: "its relevance for musical differentiation is elusive and at best only partial." Hesmondhalgh (2013: 122) argues against this assertion by pointing out that the issue of class is not important to Finnegan, and that she never substantiates her claims with data, but uses only "quasi-quantitative statements."

While there are debates around the parameters that should be used to underwrite the concept of taste cultures as well as about the ways that the concept can be applied to an understanding of issues of cultural value, the concept remains highly appropriate to grasping the profound influence that music criticism has had on the ways in which various publics have understood and related to various kinds of music. In the following, therefore, we will take a closer look at a certain type of popular music taste culture, namely those taste cultures that are articulated in journalistic and critical practices in newspapers and magazines.

Music Journalism and Music Criticism: What Are They?

Following Lindberg et al. (2005: 7), music criticism can be seen as a subset of a broader tradition of music journalism. Music journalism includes all journalistic genres concerned with music, be they "non-critical" genres such as celebrity gossip sheets and news reports, or "critical" genres such as reviews, in-depth interviews or serious articles and essays (that is, genres that have argumentative or interpretative intentions but are not strictly speaking academic). Music journalism in a modern sense dates back to the early eighteenth century, and has developed as part of bourgeois culture in tandem with changes in musical practices and the production of music that have occurred since then. Highbrow and middlebrow musical genres such as art music, jazz and rock have existed in close relation with the practice of criticism. The genres' critical practices have much in common, challenging as they do the age-old problem of how to talk and write about sound and music. The field of music criticism has in addition exchanged ideas with other fields of cultural practice. For example, rock critics such as Robert Christgau were involved in the "New Journalism," a form of literary, non-fiction writing as exemplified in the work of Tom Wolfe and Hunter S. Thompson.

Historically, journalism and criticism have appeared in general newspapers (quality dailies, tabloids, weeklies) and in specialized magazines (for example, fanzines, teen glossies, inkies, style bibles, industry and musicians' magazines). From the 1980s onwards, pop and rock journalism spread to a wide variety of publications such as men's and women's general interest magazines. The 1990s saw the beginning of music journalism on the internet. As of the writing of this chapter, several internet "magazines" have become established along with the web pages of well-established publications such as *Gramophone*, *Rolling Stone* and *NME*. The latest phenomenon at the time of writing is the blogger: individuals or small groups presenting their take on a chosen genre on the internet. Some of these bloggers have been very successful, much more so than the fanzine producers of the previous century. Books, of course, have been and remain an important medium as well. They range from fast-written, brief and glossy productions about the latest musical phenomenon to in-depth and well-researched volumes dealing with biography, music history and culture. Radio and television have carried some music journalism, but their role has primarily been to mediate new or well-loved music. The balance between these different media changes through time and varies significantly from country to country.

Music journalists and critics come from diverse backgrounds. Historically, art music critics often had and still have a conservatory or university education in music. By contrast, jazz critics tend to be amateur experts and fans, but often have some kind of background in academic education. Rock critics also tend to be fans and amateurs. Because they have been or are relatively young they often lack a formal post-secondary educational background. Only a few music critics have graduated from post-secondary institutions in journalism. Critics have overwhelmingly been white men. A few women and people of color entered the field before the 1990s; however, they have become more visible in the last two or three decades. Music journalism, on the other hand, was often undertaken by women, especially fan-oriented writing. Apart from writing criticism, critics often have journalistic responsibilities as well: doing interviews, brushing up press releases for inclusion in their publications and writing news stories, for example. It is in these ways that music professionals and music lovers enter the business of journalism and some eventually become critics (cf. Frith 2002).

Together with other mass media newspapers and magazines, journalists and editors act as gatekeepers, to an extent controlling what becomes popular and what does not. While radio and television programs simply play music (or choose not to), music magazines and music journalists need to justify in words what they let through the gates. Such justification or support can take the form of a simple picture caption endorsing an artist, or be an extended piece of writing based on research and interviews. In this way, journalism has probably become the most important vehicle for establishing in the public mind why certain songs and artists are good (or bad). Journalism also influences the ways in which different genres are structured with regard to values and standards, with regard to who "belongs" and who does not, and with regard to which expressions and writing styles are important to writing about the music. In short, journalism has been influential in the formation and articulation of musical taste cultures.

Music Criticism and Taste Cultures

The development of taste cultures goes back to the early eighteenth century when the bourgeoisie began to appear as a distinct social class. Music (for example Italian operas by, among others, Handel) formed part of the discussions that appeared in the London journals *The Tatler* and *The Spectator*. These discussions often took the form of reviews. In the course of the eighteenth century two separate taste cultures formed: *Die Kennern* (the learned) and *Die Liebhabern* (the amateurs). In Germany in particular magazines began to appear that catered to one culture or the other. Each culture was thus valorized—one by using technical language and academic reasoning to analyze and evaluate the music for a select public, the other by using metaphorical language to describe and evaluate the music for a much broader public. As Tadday (1997) observes, both approaches had aesthetic as well as social functions, the first contributing to the articulation of the aesthetics of autonomy, the second teaching a broader public the basics of music's functions. This latter was achieved, for example, by writing entertaining reviews of concerts by famous traveling virtuosi. In this way, members of the bourgeoisie were able to demonstrate that they belonged to these cultures by being able to communicate about their music.

Even though new scores were reviewed in specialist magazines, most nineteenth-century criticism focused on reviews of performances. With the advent of records, a new kind of criticism emerged that provided advice on whether or not a particular record was worth purchasing. From the 1920s on, publications devoted to record reviews came into being. A good example is provided by the British magazine *Gramophone* (established in 1923). Record criticism published in specialist magazines became central to the articulation of the most important new taste culture of the 1920s, jazz. Early on, jazz criticism discovered what art music had known for several centuries: that disagreements between different positions on a particular issue boosted interest in the genre in question, as well as sales of magazines and concert tickets. In the world of jazz, there was first of all "hot" versus "sweet," then "mouldy figs" versus "sour grapes" (in effect, Dixieland versus swing), and then swing versus bebop (Gendron 1995, Gennari 2006). Defining oneself as a jazz fan often meant taking a stand against one taste culture while being for another. Such debates served to articulate the aesthetics of jazz and entrench different taste publics within the taste culture of jazz as a whole.

While jazz criticism took quite some time to coalesce into an identifiable discourse, rock criticism was surprisingly quick in reaching the equivalent stage. Scholars seem to agree that rock criticism came into being in the second part of the 1960s (Lindberg et al. 2005, Powers 2013). The first traces of rock criticism began to appear in 1965 as small groups of young intellectuals with a working-class background and little university training entered the tabloids and the morning newspapers. After an initial rush of daily rock criticism between 1967 and 1971, rock and its critics lost their news value and cultural section editors downgraded the topic. Since the late 1970s, when punk rock made headlines, the amount of newspaper rock criticism grew again and has since then been relatively stable, taking in new genres such as hip hop, electronic dance music and even pop.

In the United Kingdom, some pop music papers adapted quickly to the advent of rock in the later part of the 1960s (for example, *Melody Maker*), while others were quite slow (for example, *New Musical Express*). In the United States, new magazines inspired by underground papers emerged (for example, *Rolling Stone* and *Creem*). They all came to thrive on rock and served to define the aesthetics and the ideology of this new taste culture, not least through an articulation of the well-established split between highbrow and lowbrow—in this case, between rock and pop. What rock was not became as important as what it was. From one perspective, rock could be analyzed as an international taste culture. From another, rock and pop became a tangle of more or less related taste cultures depending upon geography and genre.

In the 1970s, three weeklies in the United Kingdom, *Melody Maker*, *NME* and *Sounds*, came to represent three slightly different taste cultures, with *NME* being the most spectacular. In order to re-launch the publication as a rock paper in 1972, the *NME* editor recruited new staff from the London underground press. Two of these individuals, Charles Shaar Murray and Nick Kent, became journalistic stars in their own right. This was because of their writing style, their "carnival of words" (Lindberg et al. 2005: 204), and their general lack of respect. The magazine made fun of itself while at the same time developing a rock aesthetic in a quite serious manner. For example, under a tangle of headlines and subheadings including

"It's real, it's natural, it's rock 'n' roll, it's . . ."

Hot poop for Hoople people

. . . part the first (in which Charles Sortof Monay stands awestruck in a wonder Winterland, pointing idiotically at a gang of colourful rascals from Hereford doin' their thang) . . .

Murray (Charles Sortof Monay) tells the story of Mott the Hoople in San Francisco. He makes good-humored fun of all the people involved, linking them together with all sorts of bizarre, on-the-spot associations. But despite the general laid-back narrative, Murray suddenly turns serious in his last few sentences:

> Mott the Hoople matter. They matter a lot, because they are one of the few, the very few bands currently operating whose work is intellectually consistent, who seem to have a solid idea of exactly what they're here for. . . . They may not be the best rock-and-roll band in the world, and they may not be the most important, but right now, they're certainly the most valuable.
>
> (Murray 1974: 29)

Murray jumps right into one of the most central claims in the aesthetics of rock: rock matters. One can hardly be more bombastic than that while staying within the limits of rock's discourse. The bombastic can "balance on the edge" because of the rest of the article.

Murray and his *NME* colleagues appeared as extremely self-assured taste leaders, as articulators of a specific brand of rock taste that 150,000–200,000 readers consulted each week during the 1970s and 1980s. Their subjects, photos and writing styles became nodal points in a discourse on rock that celebrated both rock transcendence and pop fun. They formed a "hip" taste culture that could support several taste publics from the latest in hip pop (Bolan "yes," Elton John "no") to the latest in avant-garde (Throbbing Gristle "yes," Gentle Giant "no") and US roots music (blues "yes," country "no").

All through the 1980s, *NME* and the other inkies were challenged by a range of glossy publications. First, as pop became still more accepted, the runaway success *Smash Hits* became a magazine for the knowing pop fan. In 1982, its circulation passed the 500,000 mark (Long 2012: 143). Then the so-called style bibles (for example, *The Face*, *i-D*) created links between music, fashion and popular culture in a somewhat avant-garde, intellectually stimulating and "hip" way. *The Wire* began as primarily a jazz magazine but slowly turned toward all things experimental, placing rock-related experiments at the center but also commenting on jazz and modern art experiments. *Kerrang!* went for the developing heavy metal genre, and *Q Magazine*—with Paul McCartney on its first cover—went for the then new, older, male rock demographic. Both *Smash Hits* and *Q* turned toward rock journalism as consumer guidance rather than criticism in the sense in which the term is being used here.

All this indicated a multilevel diversification of rock criticism. The inkies became less influential and narrowed their focus to rock-related music as the magazine industry flourished and big publishing houses like IPC and Emap used modern marketing techniques to target different age groups and genre preferences. These developments also indicated a general shift toward music journalism as consumer guidance rather than criticism. Most of the magazine-led taste cultures changed from being reflexive in a traditional, wordy sense to being among the leaders of life styles in a broad sense.

While the inkies in many ways straddled the divide between mainstream and margins, it seems that, at the time of writing, the glossies are reserved for a broad range of mainstream consumerist taste cultures. Specialist magazines still cater to marginal taste cultures and use traditional aesthetic discourse to cast light on all kinds of non-mainstream music. These divisions have been reproduced on the internet. Currently, every magazine has a webpage, *Rolling Stone*'s and *NME*'s probably being the largest. Yet there is a plethora of internet sites serving either mainstream or minority taste cultures, the US website pitchfork.com being one of the most successful examples.

Conclusions

Frith did argue in the early 1980s for establishing music journalism and criticism as central research topics in popular music studies. But despite a few articles in the 1990s, the area has only received more sustained attention after the onset of the millennium. US- and British-related primary materials have become more readily available because of digitization (for example, rocksbackpages. com). Fans of criticism have also collected different kinds of British and US materials (for example, rockcritics.com). A few academic books have been published (Jones 2002, Lindberg et al. 2005, Powers 2013) and a handful of articles can be found, with Brennan (for example, 2006) and Powers (for example, 2009) being the most frequent contributors in English. Articles in German or one or other of the Scandinavian languages are not that rare either. Nearly all research has been qualitative in character, as researchers have analyzed individual texts within an aesthetic-cultural framework. Only recently have some sociologists brought in quantitative statistics (for example, Schmutz 2009) in order to compare changes in the balance between highbrow and lowbrow in different countries.

Notions of "taste cultures" and other, related and similar concepts are pervasive in the scholarship on the sociology of music. This is so because such research includes in its discussions the dimension of taste important to various musical–social groupings. These discussions have been restricted mainly to taste cultures for which written discourses have been central. It will be important to develop analyses of taste cultures in which the written or spoken word is of less value: for example, in different kinds of pop and dance taste cultures. While researchers using the concept may study larger or smaller groups, taste cultures' borders need further analysis: what belongs and what does not and when is there not enough cohesion in a grouping to render the label "taste culture" appropriate. The relation between taste cultures and taste publics should in addition be made clearer, as should their relations to other concepts such as genre (Hesmondhalgh 2005) that are used to grasp the character of complex musical–social groupings.

References

Becker, H.S. 1951. "The Professional Dance Musician and His Audience." *American Journal of Sociology* 57(2): 136–144.

Brennan, M. 2006. "The Rough Guide to Critics: Musicians Discuss the Role of the Music Press." *Popular Music* 25(2), 221–234.

Finnegan, R. 2007 [1989]. *The Hidden Musicians: Music-Making in an English Town*. Middletown: Wesleyan University Press.

Fish, S. 1980. *Is There a Text in This Class? The Authority of Interpretive Communities*. Cambridge: Harvard University Press.

Frith, S. 1996. *Performing Rites: On the Value of Popular Music*. Cambridge: Harvard University Press.

_____. 2002. "Fragments of a Sociology of Rock Criticism." In *Pop Music and the Press*, ed. S. Jones, 235–246. Philadelphia: Temple University Press.

Gans, H. 1966. "Popular Culture in America: Social Problems in a Mass Society or Social Asset in a Pluralist Society?" In *Social Problems: A Modern Approach*, ed. H.S. Becker, 549–620. New York: John Wiley & Sons.

_____. 1999 [1974]. *Popular Culture and High Culture: An Analysis and Evaluation of Taste* (revised and updated edition). New York: Basic Books.

Gendron, B. 1995. "Mouldy Figs and Modernists: Jazz at War (1942-1946)." In *Jazz among the Discourses*, ed. K. Gabbard, 31–56. Durham: Duke University Press.

Gennari, J. 2006. *Blowin' Hot and Cool: Jazz and its Critics*. Chicago: Chicago University Press.

Grossberg, L. 1992. *We Gotta Get Out of This Place: Popular Conservatism and Postmodern Culture*. New York: Routledge.

Hesmondhalgh, D. 2005. "Subcultures, Scenes or Tribes? None of the Above." *Journal of Youth Studies* 8(1): 21–40.

_____. 2013. *Why Music Matters*. Malden: Wiley-Blackwell.

Jones, S., ed. 2002. *Pop Music and the Press*. Philadelphia: Temple University Press.

Kuipers, G. 2006. "Television and Taste Hierarchy: The Case of Dutch Television Comedy." *Media, Culture and Society* 28(3): 359–378.

Lindberg, U., G. Gudmundsson, M. Michelsen and H. Weisethaunet. 2005. *Rock Criticism from the Beginning: Amusers, Bruisers and Cool-Headed Cruisers*. New York: Peter Lang.

Long, P. 2012. *The History of the NME: High Times and Low Lives of the World's Most Famous Music Magazine*. London: Portico Books.

McLeod, K. 2001. "A Critique of Rock Criticism in North America." *Popular Music* 20(1): 47–60.

Murray, C.S. 1974. "Hot Poop for Hoople People." *New Musical Express* (11 May): 28–29.

Powers, D. 2009. "'Bye Bye Rock': Toward an Ethics of Rock Criticism." *Journalism Studies* 10(3): 322–336.

_____. 2013. *Writing the Record: The Village Voice and the Birth of Rock Criticism*. Amherst: University of Massachusetts Press.

Riesman, D. 1950. "Listening to Popular Music." *American Quarterly* 2(4): 359–371.

Schmutz, V. 2009. "Social and Symbolic Boundaries in Newspaper Coverage of Music, 1955–2005: Gender and Genre in the US, France, Germany, and the Netherlands." *Poetics* 37(4): 298–314.

Tadday, U. 1997. "Musikkritik." In *Musik in Geschichte und Gegenwart, Sachteil*, vol. 6, ed. L. Finscher, 1362–1378. Kassel and Stuttgart: Bärenreiter and Metzler.

Willis, P. 1978. *Profane Culture*. London: Routledge and Kegan Paul.

_____. 1990. *Common Culture: Symbolic Work at Play in the Everyday Cultures of the Young*. Milton Keynes: Open University Press.

21

Art Music and Social Class

WILLIAM WEBER

The fields of music history, sociology and history proper ("plain" history, as a musicologist once said) have been relating with one another more closely and effectively in the last twenty years. Just as interest in music history has spread among historians, so larger social and cultural problems have captured the interest of musicologists. I will never forget when a Los Angeles graduate student challenged me for not mentioning the Industrial Revolution after I gave a talk on nineteenth-century concert programming. Rethinking the ideas of Bourdieu has recently provided a fluent language by which fields communicate with one another, thanks mostly to publications by DiMaggio, Bennett, Fulcher, Steinmetz and Charle (discussed during the course of this chapter). The concepts of *"habitus,"* "eclecticism" and "legitimation" have helped bring new perspectives on matters of the past as well as the present, most importantly regarding the hoary problem of social class (Weber 1979). How did the middle and the upper classes relate to one another in their musical interests? Can we speak of eclectic musical tastes in the nineteenth century? Discussing such patterns in Europe and the United States can help understand listening habits in recent decades.

The Complexities of Social Class

Treatment of social classes in musical life has been problematic for a long time, thanks to the persistence of clichés in the historical and sociological literature. Discussion of the July Revolution of 1830 in France that led to a constitutional monarchy is an important case in point, since scholars from various fields have assured their readers that the middle class, even though in existence from the eleventh century, rose like a phoenix after July of that year, bringing modern politics, operatic life and serious musical listening with it (Johnson 1995, Petrey 2001). Undue credit for the rise of "grand opera" is often given to Louis Véron, director of the Paris Opéra from 1831, even though those productions began in 1828 under the modernizing leadership of the Vicomte de La Rochefoucauld, a civil servant from an ancient noble family. Whereas the old viewpoint of a self-conscious new bourgeoisie still survives (Maza 2003), other historians think that the leaders of the July Monarchy sold the regime to the public as bourgeois because they were scared of the revolutionary workers and did not want to expand the voting population very much (Pilbeam 1991). For that matter, close interaction between bourgeois and aristocratic publics was a long tradition at the Opéra; in 1780 there were a lot more businessmen with boxes there than in London's King's Theatre, and the number of bourgeois among subscribers remained relatively stable in Paris during the first half of the nineteenth century (Fulcher 1987, Huebner 1989, Weber 1993).

Historians and sociologists have moved in parallel directions in reshaping conceptions of social class. Both fields now favor studying social classes as being made up of disparate occupational groups with fractionalized cultural orientations. Historian William M. Reddy (1992: 24) summed up this viewpoint by saying that "it is no longer acceptable to examine the socio-economic position and experiences of a given group and from there to leap to consciousness and ideology." He argued for identifying "intermediary steps" to explain "how, why, and by whom the necessary communication is established to make political action possible" (ibid.). Any use of the time-honored terms for social classes must be examined critically. Writing in a key volume on European social classes, Kocka and Mitchell (1993) and Mosse (1993) warned of the "precarious unity" to be seen either in *Bürgertum* or *bourgeoisie*, terms that evolved from designating civic status and taxation into vague and conflicted notions about superordinate social groups (see also Kocka 1995). Mosse provided the most succinct definition of what European historians now see happening within the nobility and bourgeoisie in the course of the nineteenth century: each group was made up of a complicated set of professions, regional origins and cultural tendencies from which a *composite elite* emerged around 1880. Mosse (70–102) outlined how "This new elite, increasingly based on wealth, developed a distinctive culture made up of both aristocratic and bourgeois elements," their influence then being "transmitted by educational institutions and processes of socialization." A political ruling cadre emerged parallel to the composite elite but was by no means identical with it. There were obvious differences in how these dynamics played in various countries with the United Kingdom being an outlier where such differences were concerned. There were also significant differences in France and Russia.

This analysis helps identify the new upper class among the subscribers to the premier opera houses and the leading classical music concert series. Despite the impressive growth of middle-class musical life, the separation of the upper-middle class to join the new composite elite blurred any distinct identity of the middle class as such. Moreover, we shall see that major tension over social and musical values grew up between the worlds of opera and classical music, originating in what Bourdieu calls *class fractions*. The dynamics of that tension are of great interest to sociologists; indeed, a recent survey of leisure habits in the United Kingdom found music to be "the most divided, contentious cultural field of any" (Bennett et al. 2009: 75).

One of the traditional misconceptions is that bourgeois culture overwhelmed the aristocratic. It is clear that much of eighteenth-century aristocratic culture lasted through the nineteenth century (Mayer 1991). The suave, graciously articulated sound of orchestras dominated by string instruments originated in court music rooms and was transposed to municipal concert and opera houses involving bourgeois publics. The Concert of Ancient Music, the first public institution devoted to canonic repertoire, was founded in London in 1776 by a group of noblemen, and most concert societies that grew up subsequently involved aristocratic families to some extent. Early notions of Beethoven's greatness likewise grew out of Austrian aristocrats who were particularly active in musical life (DeNora 1997). The prestigious boxes at the premier opera houses continued to endow an aristocratic identity to the new composite elite. That tradition was absorbed by the increasingly commercial management of such halls, confirming Mosse's analysis of the integration of bourgeois and noble elites. Moreover, the frequent performance of music in salons knit together upper-class groups in intimate quarters. Interestingly, in France, the main country in which the nobility was disempowered politically, noblewomen led salons focused on new music at a time when old operas and symphonies had come to dominate repertoires. Winnarreta, the Princesse de Polignac, devoted a great deal of her life to supporting composers of the time (Kahan 2003).

Aristocratic cultural traditions became transmuted into genteel society in the early nineteenth-century United States. Bushman (1992: 306) showed how "the lingering allure of aristocracy" spread from the gentry to better-off urban families in choices of furniture, clothing and manners. That meant that Italian opera companies were welcomed warmly in New York and then the provinces; a specialized musical taste was reconceived by some commentators as *democratic* to justify its lofty prestige (Ahlquist 1997). Orchestras established in New York City and Boston followed British practices in offering a refined taste of repertoire, even though they occasionally included songs that the directing board of the Philharmonic Society of London would not tolerate. Levine (1990) demonstrated how theaters generally became focused on a smaller upper-class public and were increasingly defined as *high culture* institutions toward the end of the century.

DiMaggio has developed a fertile framework by which to compare European with US cities, with respect to the class structure inherent in cultural life. He showed that the relative unity or fragmentation of elites determined much concerning the relations between institutions of high culture generally. Whereas in Boston tightly-bound elites knit the Boston Symphony Orchestra together with the Elizabeth Gardner Museum, in New York a dispersed structure allowed separate orchestras and museums to flourish (DiMaggio 1982, 2009, 2010). I find it useful to apply these models to European cities in the eighteenth and nineteenth centuries to explain the extent of eclecticism in repertoires. In Vienna, where musical and cultural institutions were tightly intertwined, the Vienna Philharmonic Orchestra performed a much narrower repertoire than the other major European orchestras and prevented any other professional ensemble from appearing until 1900. By comparison, in Paris, the fragmentation of the elites in the sequential revolutions and the liberalization of rules over concerts and opera stimulated the rise of four separate orchestras in the second half of the century. A similar comparison can be made for the eighteenth century. Whereas rigid monopolies were imposed over musical institutions in Paris, in London concerts proliferated thanks to the fragmentation of municipalities and political groups (Weber 2008).

Rethinking Bourdieu on Music

A rethinking of the sociological principles of social class has developed in a close relationship with a rethinking of what Bourdieu proposed for the study of social and cultural distinction. As Wacquant (1991: 57) put it, the middle class, like any social group, "does not exist ready-made in reality" but rather "must be constituted through material and symbolic struggles waged simultaneously over class and between classes." He cited Bourdieu's argument that "it is these intermediate zones of social space that the indeterminacy and the fuzziness of the relationship between practices and positions are the greatest" (ibid.). Through the concept of social space, Bourdieu brought into being a multidimensional process through which to view the creative strategies he perceived going on in processes of social distinction (Bourdieu 1987, Wacquant 1991: 52, Weininger 2005).

The key concept needed to evade misconceptions about social class is Bourdieu's notion of class fractions. Understanding the fractionalization of class provides valuable insights into the ways social formations of musical taste interact and change. Bourdieu (1984: 14) argued in *Distinction* that "the dominant class constitutes a relatively autonomous space whose structure is defined by the distribution of economic and cultural capital among its members, each class fraction being characterized by a certain configuration of this distribution to which there corresponds a certain life-style." Bourdieu often spoke about how his thinking evolved out of an awareness of these differences in taste as the *habitus clivé*. Steinmetz (2011: 52) pointed out that Bourdieu spoke of a *destabilized habitus* and saw some cases as "the result of socially heterogeneous situations [that] are therefore internally *riven* or 'cleft'" (emphasis in original). Bennett (2007: 203) likewise pointed out that "Bourdieu usually allows for a tension, in the case of artists and intellectuals, between their class *habitus* and the *habitus* associated with their distinctive position in a specific artistic or intellectual field."

Historians and sociologists have followed parallel paths in identifying contrasting social and cultural paths taken by occupational groups. Revisionistic thinking about the French Revolution of 1789 made clear that men elected to the Third Estate were rarely businessmen but rather members of the "liberal" professions (law, medicine or the civil service). Work on the nineteenth century has likewise shown that businessmen and members of the liberal professions—who usually were less wealthy—tended to play quite different roles politically (Weber 1979, 2003 [1975]; Kocka 1995). In my study of middle-class publics in the 1830s and 1840s, I found such differentiation to be substantial: subscribers to the early concerts of classical music were most often from the liberal professions, and patrons of opera singers most often were from high levels of business. That pattern fits an argument made by Bennett and Silva (2011: 440–441), namely, that Bourdieu saw cultural capital as "the chief means of occupational preferment for the *dominated fraction* of the dominant class, and not for its *dominant (that is, its owning) fraction*" (emphasis added). Thus did lawyers and journalists propound a high aesthetic for classical repertoire (*musical idealism*, in my terminology) in attacking the opera world for becoming crudely commercialized through the sale of easy-to-sing editions of opera tunes. The first generation of self-empowering professional music critics arose in this period; they attracted much public attention by propounding idealistic musical values against "superficial" playing done by virtuoso pianists. That dialogue fits what recent studies have shown regarding the manipulation of cultural capital, which is "always linked to a field . . . in which agents battle relationally for strategic advantage and position" (Prieur and Savage 2011: 570). "For Bourdieu," note Prieur and Savage, "capital is a relational concept that designates a social force that works within a field in which it is subject to contestation" (569).

Still, we can be sure that by the 1860s people in both occupational groups had at least some experience with both grand opera and classical music. Does that mean that an *omnivorous* taste existed among the upper classes in the nineteenth century? What evolved was not so much an uncritical liberalism toward contending tastes since this would involve the negotiation of different musical tastes according to a sense of contrasting social needs, seen to some extent in hierarchical terms. Eclecticism of taste took its most explicit form in events called *promenade concerts* that brought together waltzes, virtuoso solos, medleys of opera tunes and movements from classical symphonies. In some cases, one could walk around during the performances of these promenade concerts. Begun most prominently at the Vauxhall Gardens in eighteenth-century London, such concerts were given a more extravagant form in the 1830s—a form that was condemned by idealistic critics for barbarizing musical taste. A recent study has demonstrated the nervous relationship between promenade concerts and the main classical music orchestra in Chicago in the late nineteenth century (Vaillant 2003).

The concept of *legitimation* has proven a key tool for understanding how musical tastes interacted in particular social spaces in the nineteenth century. I would argue that legitimation occurred not within musical culture as a whole, but specifically within each of the forms of *habitus* found in the contrasting fields of nineteenth-century musical culture—opera and related virtuosity, classical music concerts and early forms of popular song. The three fields related with one another by carefully negotiated exchanges of music on a short- or a long-term basis. That process was governed as much by the conditions of social class in each *habitus* as by assumptions of taste. When an orchestra performed pieces from Gluck's *Orphée* or Mozart's *Don Giovanni*—thus decontextualizing them in each case from the complete opera—it reshaped assumptions about the character of the music significantly.

For all the eclecticism of tastes and the fractionalization of social classes, musical culture did not hold back the reproduction of class hierarchies. DiMaggio and Useem (1982) have led thinking in this area, arguing that forms of high culture contributed to the ongoing concentration of wealth and dominance of the upper classes in the United States during the late nineteenth and twentieth centuries (cf. DiMaggio 1982). Much the same process can be seen in the stabilizing effect that musical institutions brought to society in nineteenth-century Europe. The legitimizing process within and between the separate forms of *habitus* encouraged a functioning cultural unity within the new composite elite and the more prosperous middle classes. The exchange between musical fields in the negotiation of their relationships aided control of cultural life as a whole by upper social strata. The worlds of opera and classical music coexisted despite their differences as the new unitary bourgeoisie emerged. Thus did promenade concerts gain publics on many levels, from upper-class bath towns to parks in poor cities. Offering a mix of music from the two disparate forms of musical *habitus* yielded a stabilizing sense of social unity.

Opera versus Classics: Two Forms of *Habitus*

The aesthetic status of the opera world is the most problematic aspect of the nineteenth century when viewed in contrast to the classical music world. It is valid to apply the term *high culture* in a neutral sense to elite-influenced culture in both the opera world and concert life. However, doing so conflicts with the notion of *high taste* claimed by proponents of the classical music world. The idealism of such thinking broke with the traditional belief in the primacy of the general public by endowing a new authority exerted variously by the philosopher, the critic or the musician. That led to musical training through the study of great works sanctioned as canonic by such intellectuals. String quartets established the purest model of taste by banishing vocal music from their events and in some cases the piano, since that instrument was such a force for commercializing musical culture (Weber 2008). One can apply the term *univore* to such an ideology for classical music as a "high" taste of an uncompromising nature that ought not be identified as *snobbish*. Yet most listeners at classical music concerts must also have valued opera and virtuoso music to some extent within an eclectic set of tastes.

By contrast, the world of opera and virtuosity grew out of the traditional assumption that the public governed musical taste. In the eighteenth century journalists had reported what the public and the connoisseurs said about a piece or a performance, indicating that the former had premier authority. Opera criticism of the kind that emerged at the turn of the nineteenth century did not achieve the kind of intellectual standing that reviews of classical music concerts did; indeed, the reviews were usually by the same writers. The musical theater was much more commercially active than classical music concerts since the burgeoning of sheet music for popular opera tunes made it difficult to see an aesthetically purified culture in that context. Thus critics often reported how much money came in at a theater on a good night as evidence of public commitment, something that was quite unusual for the concerts.

All of which suggests why I am reluctant to apply the term *sacralization* to the world of opera, at least for the nineteenth century. Levine (1990) was justified in arguing that opera achieved the status of *high culture* in the United States in the late nineteenth century. But the opera world involved such a varied set of genres that no broad aesthetic emerged among old operas that was comparable to the notion of *classics*. Commentators did not see *a single version of cultural truth*, because opera with spoken text, such as *opéra-comique*, *Singspiel*, "English" opera, the operetta and the US musical, stood at a great distance from grand opera and Wagnerian music drama. No unifying aesthetic developed around works by such composers as Mozart, Bellini, Auber, Meyerbeer, Wagner and Offenbach.

A broad new public emerged with international significance with the productions of grand opera, which began in 1828. It was quickly assumed that virtually everyone could and, indeed, would enjoy these spectacular productions, which filled the Opéra much more consistently than had ever been done. The Théâtre-Italien, which had been the preserve of the connoisseurs and the nobility, became overshadowed by the Opéra, the bastion of the emerging composite elite. The sense that everybody "had to go" that arose with operas from *Guillaume Tell* (1828) through to *Le Prophète* (1849) resembles the popularity later achieved by Andrew Lloyd Webber's *Evita* (1978) and *Cats* (1981). Attracting the large new public drove up production costs, and grand new halls were built to provide spectacle for the expanding public. All of which led directors to put on more revivals than new works, stimulating a canonic repertoire to form around particularly popular pieces.

The premier opera houses in the main cities found themselves in the ironic situation of being increasingly dependent on drawing the middle-class public to seats in the galleries. Those listeners in effect represented the mass public that was buying sheet music of popular opera pieces. They influenced what was happening in opera life as much as the elite subscribers. Charle (2008, 2012, 2015) has shown that French works dominated the international market for opera for the rest of the nineteenth century. This was especially true for pieces from the Opéra-Comique. The sophisticated charm of these shows drew audiences even more widely than grand opera, for pieces by Daniel Auber, Fromenthal Halévy and Adolphe Adam were the principal fare at provincial theaters all over Europe. Indeed, only a few theaters in capital cities produced pieces by Christoph-Willibald Gluck or Italian composers of his time.

Taste for foreign and indigenous opera became divided, to a certain extent, between the upper and the middle classes in the United Kingdom. British musical culture was influenced in the long term by the intensely cosmopolitan culture that grew up among the families of the nobility and gentry in the late seventeenth century. Italian opera became the musical equivalent of the Grand Tour in the world of art, deterring the upper classes from investing their theatrical lives in English opera. From the founding of the Queen's (or King's) Theatre in 1705, a wide gulf opened up between all-sung Italian opera and "ballad" or "English" opera of songs and spoken dialogue—indeed, almost no pieces by British-born composers were presented there until the late 1830s. Theaters offering English opera had longer seasons for a much larger public than the cosmopolitan premier theater. While families of the gentry might sing songs from English opera at home, they did not identify with it to nearly the same extent as did equivalent French families, which would go regularly to the Opéra-Comique.

Popular Classes and Popular Music

Writings on the social history of music during the twentieth century tended to portray bourgeois initiatives aimed at stimulating musical activities among the lower-middle class and well-to-do workers. Music historians wrote on how efforts arose to bring "music to the millions" in western and central Europe through music lessons, choruses and orchestral ensembles. The French choruses, which were referred to as "the Orphéon clubs," and British schools for musical training stimulated national competitions among ensembles. But in the last twenty years the tendency has been to see initiatives growing out of long-standing traditions of music-making on the local level. Conventions of singing in taverns, churches and community organizations usually provided the basis from which local musical entrepreneurs expanded the scale and public profile of musical activities.

British historians and musicologists have further developed this topic. As Marsh (2010) has shown, British musical life became rooted on the local level in the sixteenth and seventeenth centuries in villages, stately homes and cathedrals. The British genres of the glee and the catch were enjoyed among a wide range of social classes from the late eighteenth century, either in elite dinner parties or lower-middle class taverns. Guiguet (2010) has shown that such songs were performed at dinners supporting the Conservative party in the 1830s, among workers as well as landowners. While owners of local industries helped out bands and choruses, the main stimulus came from community groups—local clubs, trade associations or political parties—from which national meetings or competitions then developed (Waters 1990, Joyce 1991). By the same token, in France, the Orphéon clubs had local roots among people at extremes of the social spectrum (Ellis 2007). In Germany, choruses for men and a few for women likewise were found in almost every city—over 200 were found in Münster alone (Friedrich 1961, Heemann 1992).

Music clubs like these often cropped up on a wide variety of social levels and usually did not manifest strong class consciousness. In a formative study of British activities, Russell (1987: 151) argued that "music rivaled politics . . . [and] could form an uneasy link between potentially antagonistic social classes." He reported that a small but significant rise in income occurred by the 1880s that was crucial to the spread of brass bands and choruses. In a key study of popular song, Scott (2008: 9) likewise suggested that "Popular culture was a site for the contested meanings of social experience, and functioned frequently as an area of compromise over values, allowing the working class to adopt evasive or resistant strategies." Scott illustrates how translating "authentic" Cockney talk might pass on attributes of middle-class values.

City governments and private entrepreneurs usually collaborated in developing musical entertainment on a local level. In Lille around 1910, for example, a city bureau supervised theaters, concert halls and performing groups, bringing businessmen together with performers and trying to keep entertainment districts orderly. The most important events were festival performances on holidays where bands, choruses and soloists would offer middlebrow-like programs similar to those of promenade concerts—opera selections, instrumental solos, marches and short symphonic movements. Composers identified with classical music were involved in these occasions in Lille. On Bastille Day 1912, pieces by Jules Massenet, Camille Saint-Saëns and local composers were performed by an Orphéon chorus, as well as the brass band of the typographers union and an ensemble called the Berlioz Circle (Anon. 1912: 1). Pasler (2009) has argued that broad notions of Republican politics underlay such musical activity.

But by far the most important phenomenon was the rise of modern-day popular song in venues referred to as music halls in the United Kingdom, *cafés-concerts* in France, *Variété* in central Europe, and vaudeville in the United States. In the early nineteenth century, the song tradition rooted in taverns grew with the commercialization of theater songs and, from the 1840s, expanded into shows involving dance groups, acrobats and opera selections. The centerpiece of such theater shows was made up of character songs for one or two locally well-known singers, but an evening often ended with a string of opera duos whose diversity in genre and period indicates a knowledgeable public. The theaters expanded to an extraordinary extent: in London by 1866 there were thirty music halls that could hold more than 1,500 people, and the upper classes sometimes went to those in the West End that offered twenty-five singers, an orchestra of sixty and a ballet of 150. By contrast, local music halls had no more than ten musicians, drawing prosperous artisans as well as clerks and their families (Weber 2008).

Intellectual legitimation became more conflicted for popular musical culture toward the end of the nineteenth century. Whereas idealists ceased uttering harsh words about promenade concerts that were put on for the more wealthy sections of the middle class, commentary turned increasingly against the word *popular*, changing it from a neutral sign of public interest to a derogatory indication of low taste. Still, French critics began legitimating the leading singers at the *cafés-concerts* by the late 1860s; one declared that the famous Mlle Thérèsa (Emma Valadon) had given "a Corneille-like tirade, artfully done" (Anon. 1875). By contrast, the British music halls developed a public rooted more deeply in the working class. This public was not thought of as being "artful." Arguably, the music halls laid down a cultural basis for British rock 'n' roll in the 1950s (Weber 2008: 299).

Continuity or Change in the Twentieth Century?

The very fact that recently developed sociological concepts prove useful for studying musical culture of the nineteenth century suggests continuity in the roles played by social class since that time. For better or for worse, the social authority exerted by opera houses and concert societies from the early nineteenth century continued to help reproduction of the upper classes from generation to generation and to provide cultural stability during the ravages of the period demarcated by the First and Second World Wars (1914–1945). Indeed, that very experience may well have contributed significantly to the ossification of a canonic repertoire that made new works seem like oddities to most audiences. Yet it is clear that the economic boom and political liberalization of the following three decades unleashed profound changes in both class structure and musical culture. For one thing, a taste for rock 'n' roll became ubiquitous and pervasive within musical life through processes that were not controlled by elite institutions such as the church or state. Rock groups in middle-class garages are the present-day equivalent of the old British bands, but they are based on a new and significant kind of commercialism. Additionally, a compositional avant-garde emerged that was subsidized by government and elite charities in ways radically different from the patronage enjoyed by composers a hundred years before. Enlightened government leaders now make efforts—which can be frustrating—to further musical modernism for the small public eager to hear the music.

References

Ahlquist, K. 1997. *Democracy at the Opera: Music, Theater and Culture in New York City, 1815–60*. Champaign: University of Illinois Press.

Anon. 1875. *L'Eldorado et la question des cafés-concerts*. Paris: Hugonis, 1882, 25–26, citing 1867 text.

Anon. 1912. *Lille Echo* (July 14): 1 (untitled).

Bennett, T. 2007. "*Habitus* Clivé: Aesthetics and Politics in the Writing of Pierre Bourdieu." *New Literary History* 38(1): 201–228.

Bennett, T. and M. Savage, E. Silva, A. Warde, M. Gayo-Cal and D. Wright. 2009. *Culture, Class, Distinction*. London: Routledge.

Bennett, T. and E. Silva. 2011. "Introduction: Cultural Capital—Histories, Limits, Prospects." *Poetics* 39(6): 427–443.

Bourdieu, Pierre. 1984. *Distinction: A Social Critique of the Judgement of Taste*. Cambridge: Harvard University Press.

———. 1987. "What Makes a Class? On the Theoretical and Practical Existence of Groups." *Berkeley Journal of Sociology* 32: 1–17.

Bushman, R.L., 1992. *The Refinement of America: Persons, Houses, Cities*. New York: Knopf.

Charle, C. 2008. *Théâtres en Capitales: Naissance de la Société du Spectacle à Paris, Berlin, Londres et Vienne, 1860–1914*. Paris: Albin Michel.

———. 2012. "Circulations Théâtrales entre Paris, Vienne, Munich et Stuttgart (1815–60): Essai de Mésure et d'Interprétation d'un échange Inégal." In *Der literarische Transfer zwischen Großbritannien, Frankreich und dem deutschsprachigen Raum im Zeitalter der Weltliteratur (1770–1850)*, ed. N. Bachleitner, 229–260.Wiesbaden: Harrassowitz Verlag.

———. 2015. "La Constitution d'un Panthéon de la Musique et de l'Opéra au XIXe Siècle." In *The Oxford Handbook of Opera Canon*, eds. W. Weber and C. Newark. New York: Oxford University Press.

DeNora, T. 1997. *Beethoven and the Construction of Genius: Musical Politics in Vienna, 1792–1803*. Berkeley: University of California Press.

DiMaggio, P. 1982. "Cultural Entrepreneurship in Nineteenth-Century Boston." *Media, Culture and Society* 4(1/4): 33–50, 303–322.

———. 2009. "Introduction." *Organizzare la Cultura: Imprenditoria, Istituzioni e Beni Culturali*. Bologna: Mulino.

———. 2010. "The Problem of Chicago." In *The American Bourgeoisie: Distinction and Identity in the 19th Century*, eds. S. Beckert and J. Rosenbaum, 209–233. London: Palgrave Macmillan.

DiMaggio, P. and M. Useem. 1982. "The Arts in Class Reproduction." In *Cultural and Economic Reproduction in Education: Essays on Class, Ideology and the State*, ed. M.W. Apple, 181–201. London: Routledge and Kegan Paul.

Ellis, K. 2007. "A Tale of Two Societies: Class, Democratisation and the Regeneration of Early Choral Musics in France, 1861–74." In *Les Sociétés de Musique en Europe 1700–1920: Structures, Pratiques Musicales, Sociabilités*, eds. H. Bödeker and P. Veit, 269–288. Berlin: Berliner Wissenschafts-Verlag.

Friedrich, A. 1961. *Beiträge zur Geschichte des Weltlichen Frauenchores im 19. Jahrhundert in Deutschland*. Regensburg: Gustav Bosse Verlag.

Fulcher, J.F. 1987. *The Nation's Image: French Grand Opera as Politics and as Politicized Art*. Cambridge: Cambridge University Press.

Guiguet, K. 2010. "Music and Power: A Conservative Musical Soundscape in Britain, 1830–1850." PhD diss., Carleton University.

Heemann, A. 1992. *Männergesangvereine im 19. und frühen 20. Jahrhundert: Ein Beitrag zur städtischen Musikgeschichte Münsters*. Frankfurt am Main: Peter Lang.

Huebner, S. 1989. "Opera Audiences in Paris, 1830–1870." *Music and Letters* 70(2): 206–225.

Johnson, J.H. 1995. *Listening in Paris: A Social History*. Berkeley: University of California Press.

Joyce, P. 1991. *Visions of the People: Industrial England and the Question of Class*. Cambridge: Cambridge University Press.

Kahan, S. 2003. *Music's Modern Music: A Life of Winnaretta Singer, Princesse de Polignac*. Rochester: University of Rochester Press.

Kocka, J. 1995. "The Middle Classes in Europe." *Journal of Modern History* 67(4): 783–806.

Kocka, J. and A. Mitchell, eds. 1993. *Bourgeois Society in Nineteenth Century Europe*. Oxford: Berg.

Levine, L. 1990. *Highbrow/Lowbrow: The Emergence of Cultural Hierarchy in America*. Cambridge: Harvard University Press.

Marsh, C. 2010. *Music and Society in Early Modern England*. Cambridge: Cambridge University Press.

Mayer, A. 1991. *The Persistence of the Old Regime: Europe to the Great War*. New York: Pantheon.

Maza, S. 2003. *The Myth of the French Bourgeoisie: An Essay of the Social Imaginary, 1750–1850*. Cambridge: Harvard University Press.

Mosse, W. 1993. "Nobility and Middle Classes in Nineteenth-Century Europe: A Comparative Study." In *Bourgeois Society in Nineteenth-Century Europe*, eds. J. Kocka and A. Mitchell, 70–102. Oxford: Berg.

Pasler, J. 2009. *Composing the Citizen: Music as Public Utility in Third Republic France*. Berkeley: University of California Press.

Petrey, S. 2001. "Robert le Diable and Louis-Philippe the King." In *Reading Critics Reading: Opera and Ballet Criticism in France from the Revolution to 1848*, eds. R. Parker and M.A. Smart, 137–154. New York: Oxford University Press.

Pilbeam, P. 1991. *The Revolution of 1830 in France*. London: Macmillan.

Prieur, A. and M. Savage. 2011. "Updating Cultural Capital Theory: A Discussion based on Studies in Denmark and in Britain." *Poetics* 39(6): 566–580.

Reddy, W.M. 1992. "The Concept of Class." In *Social Orders and Social Classes in Europe Since 1500: Studies in Social Stratification*, ed. M.L. Bush, 13–25. London: Longman.

Russell, D. 1987. *Popular Music in England: A Social History*. Montreal: McGill-Queen's University Press.

Scott, D. 2008. *Sounds of the Metropolis: The Nineteenth-Century Popular Music Revolution in London, Paris, and Vienna*. New York: Oxford University Press.

Steinmetz, G. 2011. "Bourdieu, Historicity, and Historical Sociology." *Cultural Sociology* 5(1): 45–66.

Vaillant, D. 2003. *Sounds of Reform: Progressivism and Music in Chicago, 1873–1935*. Chapel Hill: University of North Carolina Press.

Wacquant, L.J.D. 1991. "Making Class: The Middle Class(es) in Social Theory and Social Structure." In *Bringing Class Back In: Contemporary and Historical Perspectives*, eds. S. McNall, R. Levine and R. Fantasia, 39–64. Boulder: Westview Press.

Waters, C. 1990. *British Socialists and the Politics of Popular Culture, 1884–1914*. Manchester: Manchester University Press.

Weber, W. 1979. "The Muddle of the Middle Classes." *19th-Century Music* 3(2): 175–185.

———. 1993. "L'Institution et son Public: l'Opéra à Paris et à Londres au XVIIIe siècle." *Annales Economie/Société/Civilisation* 48(6): 1519–1539.

———. 2003 [1975]. *Music and the Middle Class: Social Structure of Concert Life in London, Paris and Vienna, 1830–1848*. London: Croom Helm/Ashgate.

———. 2008. *The Great Transformation of Musical Taste: Concert Programming from Haydn to Brahms*. Cambridge: Cambridge University Press.

———. Forthcoming. "The Problem of Eclectic Listening in French and German Concerts, 1860–1910." In *The Art of Listening and Its Histories*, eds. C. Thorau and H. Ziemer. Oxford: Oxford University Press.

Weininger, E.B. 2005. "Foundations of Bourdieu's Class Analysis." In *Approaches to Class Analysis*, ed. E.O. Wright, 82–119. Cambridge: Cambridge University Press.

22

Cityscapes

SARA COHEN

[. . .]

Between 2007 and 2009 I conducted a two-year project on music and urban environments with a research associate, Brett Lashua.[1] One of our main aims was to examine musical creativity and local distinctiveness in a context of urban regeneration and through ethnographic research, and the project focused on amateur rock, pop and hip-hop musicians, and involved a case study on music-making in Liverpool. We were interested in how musicians interacted with material urban environments for the purposes of music-making: the places they played in, for example, and their journeys to and from those places. We were also interested in places represented through music and the ways in which musicians experienced and thought about the city and about urban change. . . .

Whilst participant observation and interviews provided the foundation of our methodological approach, the project also involved archival research and the use of maps and mapping. In civic and music archives we consulted historical maps, as well as photographs, architectural drawings, newspaper articles, leaflets and other documents that helped us to situate the research within a historical context. We also created our own maps through which we could share our research findings with musicians and others (Cohen 2012). They included maps of the walking tours we had undertaken with musicians; digital, multimedia and interactive maps of local music sites and sounds; and maps created through Geographic Information Systems (GIS) mapping technology, a digital means of storing spatial information that allows for the display of multiple layers of information searchable via various themes, and also for the interrogation of research data. Most importantly, once we had got to know musicians, we invited them at appropriate points during our conversations to draw us their own maps illustrating their music-making routes and routines.

These kinds of hand-drawn map (also commonly referred to as cognitive, conceptual or sketch maps) have long been used to study the ways in which people describe places and remember what is where; people's subjective sense of space and place; and differences between people in terms of their spatial knowledge and understanding. . . .

[W]hilst drawing their maps, musicians talked to us about their music-making activities and experiences and some of the sites involved. In doing so, they showed how at particular moments, and within particular circumstances, the act of mapping can prompt memories and stories of music and place; hence, in the words of Marc Augé (2002: 4), a map can act as a "memory machine." Drawing the maps helped musicians to express musical experience and knowledge in spatial terms, and provided them with a means of connecting music to memories of material urban environments and associated identities, emotions and relationships.

At the same time, the maps helped us to learn about the city from the perspective of musicians, prompting us to consider what mattered to musicians and why, what made places distinctive and gave them value, and how those places might have changed. The stories of the musicians fleshed out the maps, helping to bring their patterns to life and make them fluid. . . .

[. . .]

Map

[One such map] was drawn by a 22-year-old black hip-hop MC named Pyro, a contemplative and sharply observant musician who had been rapping in public for around five years, and whose reflections on life were delivered hesitantly but with a tone of gravity and wisdom that belied his young age.[2] The map is of his south Liverpool neighbourhood of Wavertree, which he had renamed, as a pun, "Shake-a-bush" (as opposed to Wave-a-tree). It is populated with the domestic homes (referred to as "cribs") of Pyro and his fellow musicians, in which they created and recorded their music, as well as local gathering spots such as the football pitch and corner shop. Other sites, such as the city centre, record shop and college seem worlds apart.

On his map, Pyro has clearly drawn a place marked as "Bingo" along the border of his neighbourhood, a place he also referred to as "the Pivvy." "The Pivvy" is a colloquial term for the Pavilion, which opened in 1908 as the last of several new music halls built outside the city centre in Liverpool's fast-expanding suburbs. It later became a variety theatre, and the Beatles performed there once in 1962. Following a fire, part of the building was reconstructed, and the Pavilion is now a bingo hall. . . .

Just beyond the Pavilion lies Toxteth, or Liverpool 8, which has a different postcode from Pyro's turf in Wavertree (Liverpool 15). In many UK hip-hop and grime-music scenes, postcodes and home territories matter, and gang wars have been fought over these boundaries, boundaries that musicians involved with other local, genre-based musical cultures might not notice or might attend to or care about in alternative ways.[3] Pyro told us of a dramatic increase in local gang rivalries over the previous five years, a phenomenon that he attributed to urban deprivation, and of the palpable web of "invisible borders" that criss-cross the city so that "you just know" when you have crossed a line. Thus, to some the Pivvy represents one small part of the Beatles' story in Liverpool; to others it represents an older, bygone era of music hall; to a young musician like Pyro it marked a dangerous edge.

Whilst drawing his map, Pyro explained: "I don't venture too far from my crib. I don't even go out much. It's not my map, it's my bubble [. . .] That's me isn't it? Me extended family, me football, and the roads." . . . According to Pyro's map, Wavertree was thus a bubble (and he labelled it as such) that encompassed his everyday social world, and in a faltering voice he described that place and world thus:

> Down here, there is not, there is not a lot of light. So when people are down, like, if you fall off track from when you are young, you're pretty much, ain't no help, that you're pretty much done. Do you know what I'm saying? That's probably universal to a lot of slums and to a lot of places, but it's just, for me, growing up in Liverpool, it's just, it's just fucked.

[. . .]

Music Genre and Urban Environments

[M]aps and accompanying conversations prompt reflection on the relationship between music and cities, and on the micro-topographies of local music-making. They show how musicians interact with material urban environments through memory, mapping and storytelling, and highlight ways in which musicians not only think about and reflect on those environments and make them meaningful, but also inhabit and experience them. Material urban places and venues are thus sites of musical memory, mythology and imagination, as well as of music-making and social interaction. At the same time . . . [there are] differences as well as similarities in the micro-topographies of music-making and in how musicians categorize and conceptualize music and urban space. This second section of the article explores and explains these differences by relating them first to music genre, and secondly to urban environments shaped and distinguished by particular social, economic and historical circumstances.

Music Genre

Musicians performing hip-hop, rap, rhythm & blues, and grime (styles now encompassed by the broader marketing category known as Urban Music) tended to produce maps of Liverpool that differ from those of rock musicians. Pyro's map of the south Liverpool neighbourhood of Wavertree, for example, draws on the social and ideological conventions of rap and hip-hop culture, where spatial categories and identities have been a central component. The various subgenres of hip hop represent urban environments in different ways, but a spatial concept that has been fundamental to the genre is the 'hood, a shortened version of "neighbourhood" and a more localized version of "the ghetto," a concept promoted through 1970s soul and funk music. Scholars such as Murray Forman (2002) and Tricia Rose (1994) have examined how rap and hip hop have taken cities and depressed inner-city neighbourhoods as their creative foundation. Along with "the street," the notion of the 'hood has become a key site for the construction and commercial marketing of hip-hop authenticity, and through hip hop both street and 'hood have been commonly associated with images of urban discontent, of crews and posses, and of social, economic and racial divisions. Dan Sicko (2004: 111), for example, describes certain styles of Detroit hip hop as an "extreme, almost parodied" version of inner-city life, which he links to the extremities of urban decline in that city. Hip-hop crews such as Insane Clown Posse and Esham and (to a lesser extent) the multi-platinum-selling Eminem draw on horror-themed lyrical content and imagery, or on shocking (and blatantly over-the-top) narratives to give an exaggerated, almost cartoon-like, version of urban deprivation in Detroit.

These genre conventions help to explain the way in which Pyro described his life in Liverpool in terms of marginality and clear boundaries marking divisions of class, age and territory, as well as the references to "lines" and "tracks" in the verbal narrative that accompanied his mapping, and also in his musical compositions. The lyrics to Pyro's songs refer to a "hard life" in a particular urban neighbourhood (the 'hood), as illustrated by the first verse of a song entitled "On and On":

> Yo, this is that real-life stuff that we all go through, all of us.
> I lost a friend to a car crash, another to a stab wound.
> Both young men didn't have to go that soon.
> I grew up fast, before I left the classroom,
> A bit of fist and a lot more attitude,
> No gratitude, I couldn't see my future.
> [. . .]

Pyro . . . associated himself with a local "hip-hop community" and spoke of the need for people like him to contribute to that community and help to build it up. Liverpool is not generally known for hip hop, and since the early 1990s hip-hop musicians in that city have complained about the difficulty of performing in the city centre owing to policing and access or door policies operated by club, bar and venue managers and local authorities, who automatically assume that hip-hop events will attract drug-taking and violence (Cohen 2007: 27). In fact this situation is by no means peculiar to Liverpool, but is replicated in other parts of the UK, as is illustrated by Phil Kirby's (2009) account of hip hop in Manchester. Gun crime has been a growing problem in major UK cities, and scenes based around hip hop, grime and other forms of Urban Music have suffered from being associated with such crime. In London, for example, hip hop and grime have been affected by the risk-assessment strategy of the "Clubs Focus" initiative, which demands that club owners and promoters pass the names of musicians and MCs to the police several weeks in advance of their appearance at a club. The police often advise against the appearance of certain performers and against certain types of club nights. As a result of this initiative, even commercially successful performers such as Dizzee Rascal and Roll Deep have enjoyed fewer opportunities to perform live.

[. . .]

Urban Environments

The hand-drawn maps and accompanying conversations suggest the relevance for understanding the relationship between music and material urban environments, not only of music genre but also of specific socio-economic circumstances that shape and distinguish cities and urban neighbour-hoods. This includes a combination of circumstances that has been peculiar to Liverpool, as well as global and historical trends influencing the restructuring of Liverpool and other cities within a wider political economy.

Whilst creating their maps, for example, the musicians drew on local narratives of music and place, including familiar stories of river-crossings and the tunnel bus, and of the distinctiveness of Liverpool, its neighbourhoods and other places within the city. During the nineteenth century, the port brought Liverpool great wealth, but it depended upon a large and unskilled workforce, and brought into the city destitute immigrants fleeing from hardship elsewhere. The fortunes of the port fluctuated throughout the twentieth century, but those circumstances shaped the geography of the city, producing distinctive patterns of local settlement, strong neighbourhood identities and territorial boundaries of class, ethnicity and religion (see Belchem 2000). This may help to explain how Pyro described Wavertree and related the neighbourhood's troubled borders to urban deprivation and its negative impact on the lives of the young people around him, and to geographical centres and margins. He spoke to us, for example, about the official marketing and regeneration of Liverpool as European Capital of Culture 2008 and how they had misrepresented the city. He described Liverpool as a city that had been "left behind" in terms of urban regeneration, offering to take us on a walk around the streets of Wavertree to show us "the real Liverpool." He had devoted one of his recent songs to that topic and to exposing what lay behind the official celebrations of Liverpool as European Capital of Culture. The song's lyrics and accompanying video invite the listener to accompany the singer on a tour of the city's streets, describing Liverpool as a capital of drugs and crime, and juxtaposing images of the struggles and hardship of everyday life in the marginalized 'hood with images of the privileged city-centre enclaves of the urban elite.

Pyro's concerns are supported by a 2010 UK government report showing that, nationally, the gap between rich and poor had increased substantially since the 1970s, and whilst a succession of regeneration programmes had transformed parts of Liverpool, some of the city's neighbourhoods continued to be classified as among the most deprived in Europe (Hills et al. 2010). Nevertheless, the award to Liverpool of the title European Capital of Culture 2008 marked the city authorities' embrace of culture as a resource for urban regeneration.[4] In Liverpool, across Europe and beyond, efforts have been made to use culture to remodel cities as part of a wider process of social and economic restructuring governed by the politics and economics of neo-liberalism (Harvey 2001,

Hall and Miles 2003, Yudice 2003, Zukin 2005). The global economic recession of the 1970s, resulting from a crisis in the capitalist economy based upon so-called "Fordist" methods of mass production, provoked dramatic changes in Liverpool and in many other port and industrial cities. Among other things, traditional manufacturing industries collapsed, encouraging a process of de-industrialization and depopulation that gave rise to intense debates about the future of such cities and their role and significance within the global economy.

As a means of compensating for and overcoming such problems, many cities launched programmes of economic restructuring and turned to more specialized, "post-Fordist" systems of production involving new information technologies and knowledge-based industries, and more flexible and decentralized labour processes targeted at markets that were more specialized or niche. There was a parallel emphasis on the rebranding of such cities and on their physical regeneration involving strategic economic development targeted at specific urban areas. Increasingly, attention was also paid to the contribution that culture and the so-called "cultural" or "creative industries" could make to that process. This has involved initiatives aimed at branding cities as centres of consumption; attracting investment into them from corporate capital and property developers in addition to the spending of city visitors and young, middle-class professionals; encouraging the development of residential properties in newly gentrified city-centre locations and in tandem with the development of the night-time economy; and using the arts and cultural activity as a stimulus for regeneration initiatives based on the development of retail sales and tourism.

In Liverpool, these developments have led, among other things, to an increasing privatization, regulation and surveillance of city-centre areas, and concerns about the exclusion of youths and other groups from those areas.[5] At the same time, black musicians have pointed us to racist policing and licensing policies that regulated and constrained black music-making throughout the twentieth century, restricting it to particular areas of the city (Cohen 2007: 26–29). Until the 1980s a so-called "colour bar" had also operated informally in some city-centre clubs and performance venues in order to prohibit entry to black audiences. Given such circumstances, it is perhaps not surprising that a young black hip-hop musician such as Pyro from the run-down district of Wavertree would represent his life and music in terms of a "bubble" and social and cultural marginalization. However, racism was not something Pyro mentioned to us explicitly, and differences between the rock and hip-hop maps cannot be attributed to race or ethnicity, given the mix of black and white musicians involved in the mapping of hip hop in Liverpool, but might rather be inflections from a combination of previously more race-based sets of policies and contemporary representations of hip hop.

[. . .]

Clearly . . . music-making in Liverpool can be related to the city's position within the global political economy, and to events and trends that have influenced the restructuring not only of Liverpool but also of cities in other parts of the world. As Sharon Zukin and others have shown, the association of many urban areas with culture and creativity has made them a focus for physical regeneration. Property developers and city planners, for example, have sought to capitalize on the bohemian image and artistic reputation of certain areas by developing them into residential districts and cultural quarters targeted at young professionals wanting to be based in a city-centre location and to benefit from its proximity to bars, restaurants, clubs and entertainment venues. Yet those developments have commonly resulted in the gentrification and privatization of such areas, and subsequent increases in rental rates and surveillance practices have commonly resulted in the exclusion from those areas of the artists, small cultural businesses and young people who had made them so attractive for development in the first place (Zukin 1989, Cohen 2007). Thus city planners execute plans about how cities should be which create contradictions, anomalies and gaps: people and places that do not fit the plan (De Certeau 1988: 94).

Music Genres, Mediation, and Urban Environments

. . . This . . . part of the article . . . consider[s] what the maps suggest about the relationship between music and material urban environments. So far, the discussion suggests that this relationship must be understood in terms of complexity. First, it has shown how the maps relate to particular material sites (including streets, neighbourhoods, homes, venues) and to urban landscapes that are continually being shaped and transformed by the organization and reorganization of urban space within a wider political economy. Secondly, it has shown how those material sites are related to music events and practices (including music performance, sound recording and songwriting), which are in turn related to particular music genres . . .

In order to examine this complexity, and the kinds of relations involved, the following discussion draws on insights from anthropological, sociological and musicological research. It begins by considering notions of homology, articulation and mediation, and their usefulness for understanding relations between music and material urban environments. It then explores some of these ideas further by returning to the detailed lines and patterns of the hand-drawn maps and the stories they tell, and considering their broader implications.

Music Genres, Social Groups, and Urban Environments

Both genre and urban environments have been fundamental for understanding popular music and how it is practised, categorized and conceptualized. Keith Negus (1999), for example, provides an in-depth account of how genre has operated as an organizing factor for music corporations involved with the production and dissemination of music recordings, as well as a way of organizing audience expectations of music as sound. Other scholars have focused on those audiences and how particular music genres have been embraced by, and been seen to represent, various audience groups (Bennett 1999, Bennett and Peterson 2004). Genre has thus provided a basis for the development of musical cultures and identities, as illustrated by studies of youth subcultures, scenes and tribes, and the work of Fabian Holt (2007). In addition to this, Ruth Finnegan (2007) illustrates how important genre is for understanding the work that musicians do, whilst numerous scholars have examined the influence of genre codes and conventions on musical composition (Frith 1998, Brackett 2000, Toynbee 2000). At the same time, music scholars and critics have commonly explained popular-music genres by relating them to cities and urban settings, as illustrated by the titles of classic books about popular music such as *The Sound of the City* and *Urban Rhythms* (Gillett 1983, Chambers 1985).

Within such music scholarship, relations between music genres, social groups and urban environments have been conceptualized in various ways, and this section considers the work of scholars who have argued that music either reflects or produces social structures, or does both. In doing so, it illustrates differences between scholars in terms of how far they see music as shaped and constrained by social structures and processes, or as the outcome of collaborative interaction, human agency and the ability of people to create and transform the world.

Music and Structural and Environmental Determinism

Music scholars, journalists and audiences have commonly discussed ways in which musical sounds and practices are influenced by social groups and genre-based cultures, and by particular urban environments. Hip hop and punk music, for example, have been closely related to "post-industrial" cities, and the film *Once Upon a Time in New York* provides just one illustration of this.[6] Using a cartographic map of New York as a central motif and narrative device, the film traces the chronological and spatial development of hip hop, punk and disco in and across that city. In particular, it focuses on how the three genres emerged from specific New York neighbourhoods during the mid- to late 1970s, a period of post-industrial urban decline. It describes how those neighbour-hoods provided the social, cultural, economic and material conditions necessary for the emergence of particular kinds of youth cultures related to the three genres, and how they also provided musicians with a source of creative inspiration. This is illustrated through interviews, archival film footage and accounts of legendary punk bands such as the Velvet Underground, New York Dolls and Ramones, and disc jockeys such as Kool Herc, Grandmaster Flash and Afrika Bambaataa, who have often been credited by journalists and fellow musicians as the founding fathers of hip hop.

By suggesting that music tells us something about cities at particular historical moments, this film supports the work of Adam Krims (2007) on music and urban geography. Krims argues that whilst different kinds of musical representations of the city exist at any one time, and whilst those representations and images change over time, there are nevertheless limits to this. In order to explain those limits he introduces the notion of "the urban ethos," a "regime of representation" that interacts significantly with the structures of real cities; thus the spatial restructuring of cities imposes limits of musical possibility, and changes in the structure of cities are accompanied by changes in how cities are represented musically (Krims 2007: 8). Krims illustrates this argument by contrasting two particular songs. The first is the classic pop song "Downtown," released by Petula Clark in 1964 and inspired by New York, which he describes as a cheerful, enthusiastic and upbeat song that celebrates "downtown" as a place of affluence, fun and adventure (2). Krims argues that in the early twenty-first century this kind of musical representation of the city is no longer possible, and instead alternative representations of the city have emerged, such as the rap song "In My Hood" by 50 Cent. Krims describes that song as a "relentlessly bleak and nightmarish" image of city life that would be "unimaginable to contemporary audiences of Petula Clark's 'Downtown'," and as an example of how "the vision of a worry-free, hospitable city life had disappeared" (4). According to Krims, therefore, 1990s hip hop, with its dense combinations of musical layers self-consciously out of tune with one another, provides an example of how changes in cities wrought by the reorganization of urban production have implanted themselves in patterns of musical sounds.

Krims supports his argument about the relationship between music and urban environments by adopting an approach that nicely combines detailed micro-analysis of lyrics and musical sounds with a macro-perspective that situates music within a context of urban change and restructuring, and thus in relation to the historical development of cities within the global political economy. He also provides a subtle account of how music genres offer metaphorical mappings of the city through sounds, lyrics and music video, mappings that are "often tied to notions of origin and authenticity" (Krims 2007: 16–18). At the same time, however, he deliberately ignores the practices and perspectives of music-makers and audiences, and questions of individual agency (an absence highlighted both by Krims himself and by Philip Bohlman [2009: 323]), and this contributes to an overemphasis on how music is determined by urban environments. For Krims (2007: 13), the urban ethos "poses a set of basic stances concerning the relationship of subjects to their urban setting: who can go where and do what? Who is constrained by the city, and who is freed by it?" Yet to appreciate the complexities of that relationship, and the musical possibilities and constraints involved, requires a focus on people and their music practices. The maps, songs and verbal narratives of Pyro and other musicians certainly point to ways in which music-making in Liverpool is influenced by genre-based musical cultures as well as by local circumstances and local/global relations. However, to suggest that music is determined by those environments would be to undermine the agency of the music-makers involved, as well as the ways in which relations are routed through people and created through interactions between people themselves, and between people, sounds and material things (including physical, geographical and built locations and venues for music practice and performance).

[. . .]

Multiple Articulations Between Music and Urban Environments

Toynbee (2000: 128) highlights the ambiguous position of musicians: on the one hand they are creative agents, and "on the other they are constrained by generic codes and the expectations of communities." To explain the relationship between music-making, genre and community, Toynbee uses the metaphor of "articulation." He is particularly drawn to the ways in which John Clarke and others (1993), on the one hand, and Stuart Hall (1999), on the other, developed the notion of articulation to account for complexities in the relationship between culture and social class. Toynbee notes how music genres can be connected to a sense of community and communal experiences of urban life, but emphasizes that at the same time other kinds of connections are also possible, so music can have multiple articulations to the social. Using the example of hip hop and rap, he points out that whilst rap musicians make conscious use of communal experience in the post-industrial city, "Hip hop homologies constitute just one level of articulation in the symbolic practice of rap." To illustrate this, he refers to the work of Tricia Rose (1994), which shows how hip hop incorporates and parodies white mainstream media, such as horror films, as well as referencing previous African American musics and other aspects of African American culture (Toynbee 2000: 114–115).

Toynbee thus critiques Franco Fabbri's (1982) description of music genre as a static system of classification. Building on the work of Stephen Neale (1980), and on Pierre Bourdieu's concepts of "field" and "*habitus,*" he describes genre instead as constituting a "radius of musical creativity" (Toynbee 2000: xxi). This radius is governed by recognizable and relatively stable genre conventions and musical traditions and parameters, but it also offers music-makers possibilities for exploring the limits of repetition and thus for destabilization, transformation and innovation (106). It therefore involves the regulation of tensions between repetition and difference. For Hesmondhalgh (2005), Toynbee's work shows that although music scholars have put the metaphor of articulation to use in such different ways that its usefulness has become limited, when combined with the key concept of genre it nevertheless provides a promising way of thinking about the relationship between music and the social. In this way Toynbee also provides a promising means of accounting for the complexities of the relationship between music and material urban environments in Liverpool and the multiple articulations that this involves. Yet his use of articulation to conceptualize relations between musical creativity, genres and social groups could be further developed with the help of Born's work on music's mediations.

Music, Environment, and Mediation

Hesmondhalgh (2005) suggests that Toynbee's approach has much in common with that of Born (2000: 32), who seeks to account for the fact that music can variably both reflect existing social identities and produce new ones. More recently, however, Born has sought to develop such an account through Hennion's (2003) sociologically informed notion of "mediation." Music, she argues, can be understood only in terms of its mediations, and in an article on music listening, mediation and event she supports this argument by reviewing various sociological and anthropological studies of music (Born 2005, 2010). She uses these studies to show how focusing on music experience, rather than on narrower categories such as music "listening," allows "questions of the encultured, affective, corporeal and located nature of musical experience to arise in a stronger way than hitherto" (2010: 89). The studies also illustrate the benefits of an approach that focuses on music events, and that takes into account human subjectivity and agency as well as the social and historical conditions of musical experience, its material circumstances and transformations, and the multiple relations and influences that it brings into play.

[. . .]

Born's approach . . . has much in common with that promoted by Finnegan (2003) in an earlier publication. There, Finnegan argues for abandoning the notion of music "text" because it directs attention away from experience and multiplicity, and "from people's diverse experiences back into that limiting approach of locating emotion in the work" (189). Like Born, therefore, Finnegan argues for a focus on experience and social difference. Furthermore, she . . . argue[s] for a situated, relational, empirical approach to research on how people engage with music, and how those engagements are variously practised and conceptualized in different contexts.

The Journeys and Boundaries of Music and Music-Making

The notions of articulation and mediation explored above help to conceptualize the relationship between music and material urban environments in ways that move beyond divisions of reflection and production, structure and agency. They also help to address the complexities of that relationship, avoiding simplistic notions of music on the one hand and material environments on the other, in order to attend instead to the multiple relations between material sites, music practices, sounds, genres and social groups. The following discussion explores these relations further by returning to the maps of music-making in Liverpool and their various lines and patterns, and by focusing on the mapping process, a process that prompted, and was accompanied by, stories of music and place. . . .

Journeys

[. . .]

The maps of music-making in Liverpool feature lines that represent not only the journeys of musicians across a page and through memory and verbal narratives and stories, but also their spatial and biographical journeys. The hip-hop maps, for example, draw attention to mundane, everyday, circular routes and routines within and across urban space, such as the regular river-crossings of one hip-hop crew, and Pyro's journeys around the houses of his fellow musicians and the neighbourhood street corner. . . . In these ways the maps highlight pathways forged by musicians across space and through time. In her seminal book on amateur musicians in the English town of Milton Keynes, Finnegan (2007) adopts this metaphor of "pathways" in order to reconceptualize the notion of bounded musical "worlds."[7] She begins by describing genres such as "classical music," "rock and pop" and "country and western" as musical worlds distinguishable not only by musical style, but also by collective and conventional ways of structuring and organizing music-making, as well as shared understandings of music. However, by comparing and contrasting music-making across these genre-based worlds she shows that the boundaries between them are of course not fixed. Musicians participate in different worlds at the same time and with varying degrees of involvement, and these worlds overlap and intersect, and are also bound into complex relationships with music institutions and events elsewhere, thus extending beyond local boundaries.

Consequently, Finnegan abandons the term "world," with its implied sense of immersion and enclosure, and explores alternative ways of describing local music-making:

> One way of looking at people's musical activities is therefore to see them as taking place along a series of pathways which provide familiar directions for both personal choices and collective actions. Such pathways form one important—if often unstated—framework for people's participation in urban life, something overlapping with, but more permanent and structured than, the personal networks in which individuals also participate. They form broad routes set out, as it were, across and through the city. They tend to be invisible to others,

but for those who follow them they constitute a clearly laid thoroughfare both for their activities and relationships and for the meaningful structuring of their actions in space and time.

(2007: 323)

Musical pathways thus comprise "a series of known and regular routes" that people take through life and across urban space; routes that extend through time and criss-cross the city (317). They are pathways that people choose to form and re-form through their music-making activities and all the hard work and commitment that this involves, and they also provide "settings in which relationships could be forged, interests shared, and a continuity of meaning achieved in the context of urban living" (306). Some pathways are narrow, highly individual and particularistic, whilst others are wider, well-trodden and more familiar (324). Moreover, people can forge new and innovative paths whilst also maintaining paths that are older, established and traditional (306–307). These musical pathways are just some of the many pathways in people's lives, and they can be left and rejoined.

By describing music-making and music genres in terms of "pathways" rather than "worlds," Finnegan thus adopts a metaphor that is more open and dynamic, and more suited to the flux and flow of local music-making. In this sense, although she has been criticized by Holly Kruse (1993: 37–38) and others for concentrating on music-making in just one particular town, her approach nevertheless complements a more general shift in social theory over the past three decades, a shift away from fixed and bounded notions of place and culture and encouraged by globalization. The work of many anthropologists has contributed to that trend by showing how place and culture are created and recreated through movement and everyday practice, and are thus always in process of becoming, and by emphasizing the openness and fluidity of culture and inter-cultural exchange. This is evident in the language of mobility and in-betweenness that such scholars have used to describe contemporary global culture, a language of travel, mixing and hybridity, border-crossings and borderlands (Clifford 1992, Hannertz 1997). Arjun Appadurai (1996), for example, provides a seminal account of how modernity involves deterritorialized global and cultural flows or "scapes" of people, images, products and so on.

As a highly mobile cultural form, music provides an excellent example of this process. Musicianship is commonly spoken and written about using metaphors of mobility: musicians go out on the road and on tour, and around club or performance circuits. Musicians' tours have also played a significant part in mythological accounts of popular music that have been circulated and recycled through films and the music press, whilst the value of musicians within a particular locality is often connected to their ability to "make it" and thus leave and escape from that locality, moving up the "ladder of success" and beyond, and the ability of their music to transcend local boundaries, occupy trans-local worlds and appeal to heterogeneous audiences (Cohen 1991, 2007). Meanwhile, music also involves the movement of sounds through time; musical sounds and products are disseminated across space through music and media technologies, including new mobile technologies; and descriptions of those sounds tend to be suffused with metaphors of movement (Lashua and Cohen 2010: 71).

[. . .]

Boundaries

The lines of the hand-drawn maps thus help draw attention to the journeys taken by musicians as they mapped their music-making activities and experiences in Liverpool, as they talked about what they were mapping, and as they traced their musical pathways. In addition, they point to relations between music genres, social groups and material urban environments that were forged through this process and as the musicians went along. Yet the maps feature lines suggesting that music and music-making should be understood not just in terms of journeys and movement but also in terms of boundaries, and that descriptions of culture as "flow" can thus make things seem rather smooth and easy (Hannertz 1997). . . .

Such boundaries differ from one musician and musical group to another, and they are generated and shaped by particular moments and circumstances. Pyro, for example, described his music as a hybrid "mesh," yet he also placed it in a spatial bubble, the boundaries of which were rather ambiguous. At certain points in our conversation about his life and music the bubble seemed to suggest an enclosed, isolated and protective space, but at others it suggested limited opportunities, restricted movements and curtailed freedoms. Thus whilst Massey (2000: 228) described how cartographic maps flatten culture and leave people stuck and silent, stuck and silenced is how people sometimes feel and/or are. Clearly, therefore, the boundaries of music-making are socially constructed, multiple and complex, and they may be created by individuals, groups or institutions and have social, cultural, moral or economic significance. They include, for example, boundaries that are generic, legal, aesthetic, geo-political and so on. Some of these boundaries are created by musicians to facilitate their music-making practices and discourses, but musicians also confront and push against boundaries that lie outside their control, such as those that prevent access to musical places and resources and are enforced and maintained by strategies of policing and surveillance. This suggests that some boundaries are less permeable and easily crossed or dissolved than others . . .

[. . .]

In western modernity, music has been commonly thought of (much like the notion of place) as a bounded object, product, text or thing with a fixed and definable essence, as suggested by the notion of "the music itself." Yet the mapping of music-making in Liverpool suggests that music should be thought of instead as a dynamic process involving the negotiation of boundaries. Boundaries are part of the everyday lives of musicians, and to understand music-making is to understand how musicians live and engage with them; how they remember and imagine them and make them meaningful.

Conclusion: Music and Urban Landscape

To conclude, I want to bring together the main points that have been made in this article, including those relating to the previous section on the journeys and boundaries of music-making and music's mediations. The article has explored the relationship between music and material urban environments through ethnographic research on amateur rock and hip-hop musicians in Liverpool and the use of conceptual mapping. This involved focusing in micro-sociological detail on particular music maps and their various lines and patterns, on the process of mapping music and the stories involved, and on music practices and perspectives in specific localities. At the same time, however, that focus was integrated with discussion on global trends and urban change, and on theoretical approaches to people, cultures and environments drawn from anthropological, sociological and musicological research. . . . On the basis of this, three general points can be made . . .

The first point is that musicians interact with material environments to create and recreate musical landscapes. This approach to landscape is influenced and supported by the work of numerous anthropologists who have studied how landscapes are lived in and through, and experienced and embodied, rather than just observed, attended to and represented (Jackson 1989, Hirsch and O'Hanlon 1995, Feld and Basso 1996). The article illustrated this by focusing on landscapes created through conceptual mappings of music-making and the material sites and experiences involved, and through music-making practices such as songwriting, sound recording and live performance.

These musical landscapes matter to musicians and are shared by them. They emerge through music practices that are regular, routine and collaborative, as well as through the individual and collective memories, stories and imaginations of musicians.

The second point is that these musical landscapes are diverse and contested, multi-layered and intersecting. This was illustrated through comparison between the hand-drawn maps, which helped to highlight landscapes shaped not only by individuals and personal situations and circumstances, but also by music genre and by urban conditions connected to the global political economy. More specifically, it showed how the maps featured material sites that were related to music events and practices, and to urban landscapes that were being continually transformed, and how those events and practices were in turn related to musical sounds and genres and to various social groups. This highlighted the complexities of the relationship between music and material urban environments. To try to account for this complexity and the kinds of relations involved, the article turned to studies of music informed by social anthropology, sociology and musicology before returning to the hand-drawn maps and their detailed lines and patterns. This led to the third and final point, which is that the concept of musical landscape helps to show how music and music-making are mediated by material urban environments, a process involving the navigation of journeys and boundaries and the forging of multiple relations along the way (relations between people, practices, sounds, genres, material sites and so on).

[. . .]

Further research could deepen understanding of amateur music-making and urban landscape, and this article has argued for research that focuses on what people do when they engage in music-related practices and on the processes involved, and for an approach to music that is situated, relational and comparative. Most importantly, the article has made a case for the contribution of maps and mapping to music research. Whilst acknowledging the problematic nature of maps, it has nevertheless shown that, when combined with ethnographic research, maps can provide a useful methodological and analytical research tool. In particular, the act of mapping can prompt memories and stories of music-making, and the maps' detailed lines and patterns can tell us something about the spatial aspects of that music-making, and about how and why music matters.

Notes

1 I would like to thank Brett for his contribution to the project; the Arts and Humanities Research Council UK (Landscape and Environment) for supporting it; our project partners, English Heritage, National Museums Liverpool and Urbeatz; and all the musicians who participated in the project and gave their permission for us to use their maps and lyrics. In addition, I would like to thank the organizers and participants of seminars and conferences at which Brett and I presented papers on aspects of the research, but above all the Royal Musical Association, which gave me the opportunity to present a keynote conference address ("Boundaries," RMA Annual Conference, University College London, 17 July 2010) that provided the basis for this article. My thanks are also due to David Horn for his comments on drafts of that address, and to Michael Spitzer and the two anonymous reviewers who commented on the version that was submitted to JRMA.

2 MC is an acronym for Master of Ceremonies that originates from the dance halls of Jamaica, where the Master of Ceremonies would introduce the different acts, make announcements and deliver a toast in the style of a rhyme. It is commonly used to refer to a "rapper," that is someone engaged in the performance and rhythmic delivery of rhyming lyrics. Rapping is closely associated with hip-hop music and also commonly referred to as "emceeing" or "MCing."

3 Grime is a style of music influenced by hip-hop and various other musical styles, such as UK garage, breakbeat and punk.

4 The European City of Culture competition was launched in 1985, and in 1999 it was relabelled the Capital of Culture competition. Since 2007 the award has been made to two cities each year.

Nominations are submitted to the European Parliament and must include a cultural project of European dimension. These nominations are judged by a selection committee established by the European Commission, and each winning city must "organise a programme of cultural events highlighting its own culture and cultural heritage as well as its place in the common cultural heritage, and involving people concerned with cultural activities from other European countries with a view to establishing lasting cooperation" (http://europa.eu/legislation_ summaries/other/l29005_ en.htm >).

5 Henry A. Giroux (2004: 85) describes how in US cities neo-liberal policies have intensified the political, social and economic problems faced by young people, and encouraged a view of youth as "a threat to be feared and a problem to be contained."

6 Once Upon a Time in New York: The Birth of Hip-Hop, Disco and Punk, dir. Ben Whalley, exec. producer Mark Cooper (BBC, 2007).

7 The metaphor is inspired by Howard Becker's (1984) notion of "art worlds."

References

Appadurai, A. 1996. *Modernity at Large: Cultural Dimensions of Globalization*. Minneapolis: University of Minnesota Press.

Augé, M. 2002. *In the Metro*. Minneapolis: University of Minnesota Press.

Belchem, J. 2000. *Merseypride: Essays in Liverpool Exceptionalism*. Liverpool: Liverpool University Press.

Bennett, A. 1999. "Subcultures or Neo-Tribes? Rethinking the Relationship between Youth, Style and Musical Taste." *Sociology* 33(3): 599–617.

Bennett, A. and R.A. Peterson, eds. 2004. *Music Scenes: Local, Trans-Local and Virtual*. Nashville: Vanderbilt University Press.

Bohlman, P. 2009. Review of Krims, Music and Urban Geography. *Music and Letters* 90(2): 322–324.

Born, G. 2000. "Music and the Representation/Articulation of Sociocultural Identities." In *Western Music and its Others: Difference, Representation, and Appropriation in Music*, eds. G. Born and D. Hesmondhalgh, 31–36. Berkeley: University of California Press.

_____. 2005. "On Musical Mediation: Ontology, Technology and Creativity." *Twentieth-Century Music* 2(1): 7–36.

_____. 2010. "Listening, Mediation, Event: Anthropological and Sociological Perspectives." *Journal of the Royal Musical Association* 135(Supplement 1): 79–89.

Brackett, D. 2000. *Interpreting Popular Music*. Berkeley: University of California Press.

Chambers, I. 1985. *Urban Rhythms: Pop Music and Popular Culture*. Basingstoke: Macmillan.

Clarke, J., S. Hall, T. Jefferson and B. Roberts. 1993. "Subcultures, Cultures and Class: A Theoretical Overview." In *Resistance through Rituals*, eds. S. Hall and T. Jefferson, 3–59. London: Routledge.

Clifford, J. 1992. "Traveling Cultures." In *Cultural Studies*, eds. L. Grossberg, C. Nelson and P. Treichler, 96–116. New York: Routledge.

Cohen, S. 1991. *Rock Culture in Liverpool: Popular Music in the Making*. Oxford: Clarendon Press.

_____. 2007. *Decline, Renewal and the City in Popular Music Culture: Beyond the Beatles*. Aldershot: Ashgate.

_____. 2012. "Urban Musicscapes: Mapping Music-Making in Liverpool." In *Mapping Cultures: Place, Practice, Performance*, ed. L. Roberts, 123–143. London: Palgrave Macmillan.

De Certeau, M. 1988. *The Practice of Everyday Life*. Berkeley: University of California Press.

Fabbri, F. 1982. "A Theory of Musical Genre: Two Applications." In *Popular Music Perspectives* 1, eds. D. Horn and P. Tagg, 52–81. Gothenburg and Exeter: International Association for the Study of Popular Music.

Feld, S. and K.H. Basso, eds. 1996. *Senses of Place*. Santa Fe: School of American Research Press.

Finnegan, R. 2003. "Music, Experience and the Anthropology of Emotion." In *The Cultural Study of Music: A Critical Introduction*, eds. M. Clayton, T. Herbert and R. Middleton, 181–192. London: Routledge.

_____. 2007. *The Hidden Musicians: Music-Making in an English Town*. 2nd ed. Middletown: Wesleyan University Press.

Forman, M. 2002. *The 'Hood Comes First: Race, Space, and Place in Rap and Hip-Hop*. Middletown: Wesleyan University Press.

Frith, S. 1998. *Performing Rites: On the Value of Popular Music*. Cambridge: Harvard University Press.

Gillett, C. 1983. *The Sound of the City: The Rise of Rock and Roll*. London: Souvenir Press.

Giroux, H.A. 2004. *The Terror of Neoliberalism: Authoritarianism and the Eclipse of Democracy*. Boulder: Paradigm Publishers.

Hall, S. 1999. "Cultural Studies and its Theoretical Legacies." In *Stuart Hall: Critical Dialogues in Cultural Studies*, eds. K.-H. Chen and D. Morley, 262–275. London: Routledge.

Hall, T. and M. Miles, eds. 2003. *Urban Futures: Critical Commentaries on Shaping the City*. London: Routledge.

Hannertz, U. 1997. "Flows, Boundaries and Hybrids: Keywords in Transnational Anthropology." Working Paper WPTC-2K-02, Department of Social Anthropology, Stockholm University.

Harvey, D. 2001. *Spaces of Capital: Towards a Critical Geography*. New York: Routledge.

Hennion, A. 2003. "Music and Mediation: Toward a New Sociology of Music." *The Cultural Study of Music: A Critical Introduction*, eds. M. Clayton, T. Herbert and R. Middleton, 80–91. London: Routledge.

Hesmondhalgh, D. 2005. "Subcultures, Scenes or Tribes? None of the Above." *Journal of Youth Studies* 8(1): 21–40.

Hills, J., M. Brewer, S.P. Jenkins, R. Lister, R. Lupton, S. Machin, C. Mills, T. Modood, T. Rees and S. Riddell. 2010. "An Anatomy of Economic Inequality in the UK: Report of the National Equality Panel."

Hirsch, E. and M. O'Hanlon, eds. 1995. *The Anthropology of Landscape: Perspectives on Place and Space*. Oxford: Clarendon Press.

Holt, F. 2007. *Genre in Popular Music*. Chicago: University of Chicago Press.

Jackson, M. 1989. *Paths Toward a Clearing: Radical Empiricism and Ethnographic Inquiry*. Indiana: Indiana University Press.

Kirby, P. 2009. "The Regulation of Urban Music in Manchester." MA diss., University of Liverpool.

Krims, A. 2007. *Music and Urban Geography*. London: Routledge.

Kruse, H. 1993. "Subcultural Identity in Alternative Music Culture." *Popular Music* 12(1): 33–41.

Lashua, B.D. and S. Cohen. 2010. "Liverpool Musicscapes: Music Performance, Movement and the Built Urban Environment." In *Mobile Methodologies*, eds. B. Fincham, M. McGuinness and L. Murray, 71–84. London: Palgrave Macmillan.

Massey, D. 2000. "Travelling Thoughts." In *Without Guarantees: In Honour of Stuart Hall*, eds. P. Gilroy, L. Grossberg and A. McRobbie, 225–232. New York: Verso.

Neale, S. 1980. *Genre*. London: British Film Institute.

Negus, K. 1999. *Music Genres and Corporate Cultures*. London: Routledge.

Rose, T. 1994. *Black Noise: Rap Music and Black Culture in Contemporary America*. Middletown: Wesleyan University Press.

Sicko, D. 2004. "Bubble Metropolis: Expanding Detroit's Identity Through Music." In *Shrinking Cities: Detroit*, ed. P. Oswalt, 108–114: www.shrinkingcities.com/fileadmin/shrink/downloads/pdfs/WP-Band_III_Detroit.pdf

Toynbee, J. 2000. *Making Popular Music: Musicians, Aesthetics and the Manufacture of Popular Music*. London: Arnold.

Yudice, G. 2003. *The Expediency of Culture*. Durham: Duke University Press.

Zukin, S. 1989. *Loft Living: Culture and Capital in Urban Change*. New Brunswick: Rutgers University Press.

_____. 2005. *Cultures of Cities*. Oxford: Blackwell.

23

The Body and Dance

Mary Fogarty

Although dance is inseparable from music in most cultures, their relationship has been most thoroughly navigated from ethnomusicological, ethnochoreological and anthropological perspectives. Comparatively little has been written at the interstices of sociology and music studies. This chapter considers the ways in which dance and the body more broadly have been conceptualized, and how the productions of meanings thus generated can be accessed for sociological studies of music. Particular attention will be paid to ethnography as a sociological method. In doing so, traces of the body and embodied experience within sociological studies of music are also held up as signs of a nascent but as yet underdeveloped area of great significance: the sociology of movement. As a foundation for all this, the following section surveys various disciplinary approaches to dance, and the issues to which such approaches have given rise.

Disciplines and Issues

Early dance scholarship stemmed largely from anthropology and its parent field, ethnology. While such accounts clearly demonstrated the significant role of dance in society, they inherited problematic conceptual paradigms from ethnology and anthropology—most notably "primitivism" and "functionalism." These paradigms encouraged understandings of dance (not to mention the body more generally) as principally those activities that, in "primitive" societies, were performed ritualistically in relation to hunting, sexual selection, worship, sickness and so on. In effect, scholars positioned such dances as early steps on the evolutionary path toward "civilized" western dance practices. Critiques of the overly simplistic and ethnocentric character of such conceptions have been directed at several foundational studies of dance—including, perhaps most notably, Sachs (1937) and Rust (1969) (see also Williams 1974, Youngerman 1974).

Other areas of dance studies focused on "modern" societies, often suggesting that certain "high" forms of dance (such as ballet) were inherently more sophisticated and valuable than those of both "primitive" (or traditional) cultures and "low" (or popular) cultures. In the case of "high" cultural forms of dance, such forms could work to enact differences between the upper class and peasants (for a critique see Kealiinohomoku 1980 [1970]). Dance scholarship has thus historically evidenced the same elitist proclivities as certain branches of musicology and sociology of the arts, for which the notion of "art" was a value judgment and only the cultural forms that achieved this condition were deemed worthy of serious attention. Although non-ethnocentric and non-hierarchical modes of inquiry have emerged, the problems of elitism and "lingering evolutionism" are still relevant concerns in certain areas of dance scholarship (Buckland 1999).

According to Thomas (1995), a more critically informed, sociological type of dance scholarship began to take hold in the 1970s and 1980s, partly as an epiphenomenon of the rise of cultural studies and the academy's increasing attention to popular and youth culture. At the same time, Thomas, voicing a concern that could be leveled at vast swaths of music scholarship before and since, criticizes the contemporaneously emerging fields of music sociology and popular music studies for privileging music over dance, noting that scholars such as Frith "shie[d] away from carefully situating the popular dance styles ... in preference for a more critical examination of music" (Thomas 1995: 3).

Thomas thus provides one of the first detailed accounts of modern dance from a critical sociological perspective, and her oeuvre represents perhaps the most sustained sociological research program in relation to dance. Recent edited collections such as Malnig's *Ballroom, Boogie, Shimmy, Sham, Shake* (2009) and Dodds's and Cooks's *Bodies of Sound* (2013) have built on and extended the pioneering work of Thomas, casting light on social and popular dance practices from interdisciplinary cultural studies perspectives, informed by both historical and ethnographic accounts of dance and music. This way of thinking about dance—*all* dance—as a form of social production has taken root in contemporary dance studies. As we will see in more detail below, this is in contrast to previous paradigms in which dance was understood variously as the mark of either "primitive" or "civilized" cultures, or "high" or "low" (that is, "deviant") cultures.

A review of some key themes in the sociology of the body and dance is thus important to this chapter (see also Thomas 1995), as is a review of some aspects of the body and dance that are nascent in the literature on the sociology of music. The chapter will discuss ethnographic approaches and their limitations, review sociological accounts of how dance is mediated, and analyze the historical roots of various contemporary dance practices. The chapter also proposes an account of listening practices, as performed by our bodies within social groups, as a viable starting point to understanding the intersection of music and dance. Listening has many implications for a sociological approach to *music* that accounts for the body, as well as for one of the physical activities most commonly associated with music consumption, experience, participation and expression: dance.

Ethnographic Sites of Resistance and Rebellion

Early studies of subcultures in the United Kingdom focused initially on the spectacular expressions of young men (Willis 1978, Hebdige 1979), the everyday dance practices of girls and young women (McRobbie 1984) and later focused on the 1990s experiences of club cultures (Malbon 1999). Some of these experiences included the articulation of elitist views by "serious" participants in these popular worlds. Thornton (1995) drew attention to the distinctions that are made by participants in popular culture, and designates dance performance as a form of "subcultural capital." Those with minimal "subcultural capital" danced around their handbags and were inferred to be incompetent (read "feminine") or uncool by snobbish club goers. However, most of the sociological accounts addressing youth culture and music avoided ethnographic descriptions of movement "itself," as recently pointed out by dance scholar Sherril Dodds (2011). What is clear from Thornton's account, like other studies since, is that dance is a performance of (musical) tastes (see also Fogarty 2012b).

In another context, French sociologist Pierre Bourdieu (2007) looked at ageing bachelors in his home region of Béarn, France. He saw peasant men unable to find partners, both in life and in dance, as women flooded to the urban centers to learn the latest dance steps and dress in the most current fashions. By contrast, uncoordinated peasant bachelor men hung out in the corner of the neighborhood ball as the shift to urban lifestyles passed them by. Bourdieu thus shows how social change is something that is felt at the very center of the body, as anguish and humiliation imposed on the values of participants whose world is forever transformed as their potential partners dash away.

Similarly, in New Zealand, Kopytko (1986) points out that aboriginal young people brought to the city are drawn to breakdancing. Crews provide a sort of family relationship that is missing in the shift to the urban lifestyle as young people are separated from their language and their elders. They use the practice of dance to form strong ties, to protect themselves against the weight of the city and threats from others. Bailey's recent study (2013) of inner-city ballroom culture likewise demonstrates how the ball-going LGBT community forms competing groups, each known as a "house." This "house" serves as a tight-knit family unit and an alternative to biological and familial bonds that often become strained and estranged by homophobia. At balls, vogue dancers interact not only with the music but with their competitors. They also interact with the sounds of the commentator on the microphone and the crowd, synching movement not only to the sonic environment but also to social impulses and rhythms. They do this in order to impress the crowd with spectacular and unpredictable spins and dips.

Sociological studies of dance have focused on how dancers' use of space customarily distinguishes participants: amateurs from professionals, insiders from outsiders. Writers such as Urquia (2004) have built on Bourdieu's theory of *habitus* to discuss the ways in which salsa practitioners and teachers compete for resources and space through their embodied practices and claims to authenticity and authority. Bourdieu's (1993) broader claims about the production of tensions between participants in the field of cultural production provide a useful model for understanding dance worlds in which tensions and competition between participants often take on a tone of exasperation and make their way quickly into ethnographic writing.

The mediation of youth has been a neglected area of popular dance studies. If the media contributed to the "labeling" of social deviance (as accounted for in sociological theories of deviance— see for example Becker 1963) then the later work of British scholars, notably Cohen (1971), made a more pronounced case for a sociology of "moral panics" that involved authorities and the media (McRobbie and Thornton 1995). Notably, "breakdancing" was represented in early to mid-1980s newspaper accounts as being linked either to gang violence in the ghettos or to the pursuit of leisurely, amateur fun by "suburban housewives" (Rivera 2003). In a later section I discuss how French newspapers did an about-face on this issue, and began to treat onstage *hip hop danse* as a theatrical art form worthy of criticism and interpretation (Shapiro 2004). Meanwhile, "b-boys" and "b-girls" used the media resources they could obtain to produce underground video magazines that were circulated internationally. This resulted in "imagined affinities" between participants who had little in common besides their shared dance practice (Fogarty 2012a). The internet accelerated the abilities of street dancers to share videos that at first were ordered online and mailed internationally but later uploaded to the World Wide Web (Fogarty 2011). At the time of writing, websites such as YouTube were making the acquisition of many skillsets readily available, including those of dance moves. In doing so, these new forms of interaction have served to challenge the earlier claims of Thornton (1995), who argued that popular dances are ephemeral because they are embodied and do not circulate widely in the same way as music.

Most of the aforementioned studies rely on ethnography as their primary methodology. While several early writers on club cultures do reflect on the limitations and impacts of their chosen method, Wacquant advocates an especially reflexive form of ethnography, arguing that to engage in ethnographic research on issues of embodiment is to engage in social action and social justice. This act of engagement, which Wacquant (2005) terms "carnal sociology," is rooted in participation in embodied practices where mastery of one's body is an organizing social force. Accounts of body-focused practices often engage the ways in which people are not only organized according to the actions and appearances of their bodies, but also punished, silenced and contained. Prioritizing the transformations of the ethnographer at the visceral level foregrounds an embodied knowledge of practice.

Valuable though such ethnographic work is, it has two main limitations. The first is that the role of music is virtually ignored. It is rare to find a dance scholar who does not pepper their ethnographic accounts with discussions of their attempts to master the dance in question, and with detailed and descriptive accounts of the movement itself from their own experiences. However, acts of listening are not typically dealt with.

The second limitation is of a more general character, and has to do with issues of access. This is especially the case when considering the practices of elites and the underprivileged. How many studies of the sociology of dance, for example, consider populations in jail? And yet prison represents one of the key societal restraints that have spawned a considered analysis of bodies in society. This is highlighted in the work of Turner (1984), which is informed by Foucault's arguments about the containment and control of bodies in society.

Similarly, dancing continues to be treated not only as one of the most trivial physical activities afforded by music, but also as an ongoing and serious threat to public order. For example, in July 2014 a *New York Times* article reported that arrests of New York City subway street dancers had quadrupled over the past year, with 203 arrests at the time of writing (Flegenheimer and Goodman 2014). In May 2014, *The Guardian* reported the arrest of a group of Iranians who made a dance video dedicated to Pharrell Williams' hit song "Happy" (Dehghan 2014). It would appear that dance—that leisurely activity often seen to promote fun, pleasure and togetherness—has been foregrounded by virtue of moral panics as a site for political activity. Of course, these stories are placed within a larger history of dance and the body in which both have been targeted as sites of resistance and rebellion (see Fanon 1965). Dancers are not only regulated but also punished and contained, and these issues are central to sociological considerations of the structuring of society. This also demonstrates the limitations of a methodological approach that claims special insight through embodied movements: the ethnographer may not encounter the same limits to their freedom through the physical constraint or violence imposed on those they study.

Writing about Dance

Ethnography constitutes one major contribution to writing about dance. However, other forms of writing have concerned themselves with establishing dance as a legitimate topic for serious discussion. An important background to this writing is the major distinction that has, indeed, been drawn on so many fronts between "serious" art and "fun," and the manner in which this invokes the mind/body dualism articulated by Descartes and implicated in popular discourse. Although the validity of the mind/body dualism has been seriously challenged, the distinctions between fun and seriousness persist not only in the high/low divide of music, but also within most other aspects of popular music culture. Ostensibly, serious music is listened to carefully and fun music is sensual, hedonistic and best expressed through social dancing (Frith 1996). Goehr (1992) demonstrates how, since the industrial age, serious music has moved into the concert hall where it can be contemplated quietly from a seated position. (The expectations around concentration in relation to musical practices in western societies will emerge later in the section on phenomenology.) The intriguing question for the current discussion is this: how did dance attempt to distinguish itself as a serious practice (as opposed to a "fun" or "hedonistic" activity) when so much thinking around the mind/body distinction located all things about the body on the side of sensual and "mindless" pleasure?

In 1939, dance critic John Martin argued for the importance of dance. For him, human movement was *the* crucial medium and the human body its instrument (Morris 2006). He suggested that all humans have "movement sense," with its physiological base and emotional content (2006: 67). As dance sociologist Gay Morris suggests, Martin's other intention besides prioritizing and valuing dance was to suggest the superiority of modern dance as a platform to express the universal message of dance. In fact, newspaper critics, often music critics writing for newspapers without a designated dance critic, were critical of the rise of US modern dance at the same time as they educated the general public on the intentions of the practice and elevated its meanings (Conner 1997).

For French sociologist Roberta Shapiro (2004), French newspaper accounts of hip-hop dance and "breakdancing" as a theatrical art form worthy of criticism inspired theorizations about the "artification" of popular practices. Shapiro looked at the emergence of *hip hop danse* in France as a theatrical form, and pointed to some causes for this transformation of status for the dance in French society. These causes included the support of social workers, choreographers and producers interested in the form and its practitioners. "Artification" is the term Shapiro and Heinich (2012) use to suggest the existence of a set of processes that enable the legitimation of a practice as "art" in public perceptions.

The written word, through dance criticism, has therefore played a crucial role in the legitimation of specific dance art genres. I have argued that mediated oral accounts documented in "underground" videos elevated the practices of b-boys and b-girls in the estimations of viewers to an art form worthy of appreciation through its own aesthetic frameworks as created by dancers (Fogarty 2012a). In academic debates, lovers of dance music have fought to have their electronic music of choice treated as a "serious" cultural form, worthy of its own journals and conferences, at the expense of "bad" pop music. The next section will further interrogate how, often, one type of dance or music is held up at the expense of another, and how problematic this can be for the rigorous study of music and dance in societies.

Dance Distinctions

Discourses about dance have illuminated conflicts among dance styles and their various aesthetics which have played out in the literature and in public discourses. Their starting point is the dispute over the value of various art forms that took place in the eighteenth century. Some philosophers argued that dance was the ultimate art form, whereas others denigrated the status of dance. Part of the strategy of dance practitioners and their advocates was to reject music as a bedfellow in order that dance be considered an art "in its own right." The fallout of this divorce has been that dance scholarship and movement analysis have only slowly developed ways to talk about the relationship between music and dance (see Jordan 2000, Mroz 2011).

First, and as mentioned previously, one style of dance has often been valorized at the expense of others despite a common predilection to see dance as a "universal language" that transcends all cultures (this myth of the universal language is also often attributed to music). In the case of so-called modern dance, the form was often opposed to the trivial and sensuous US jazz dancing that was seen as a reflection and sign of the defects of modernity. US modern dance, on the other hand, was celebrated as expressing "the" human condition. And yet, as Banes (1998) notes, many of the modern dancers had their first performances on entertainment stages and even incorporated aspects of popular entertainment into their later and more "serious" work. As I mentioned in the last section, critics of US modern dance contributed to the establishment of the centrality of this form in the high art categories of theatrical dance.

Second, within theatrical performances, evaluations of many dance forms come to be organized around the aesthetic preferences and conventions of the dominant "serious" dances as these preferences and conventions become institutionalized. This process remains racialized, classed and gendered. Contemporary debates play out in the aesthetic choices and evaluations gathered up for theatrical dance. One common trope within theatrical dance communities is that dance *artists* do not always face the front of the stage, but instead use the kinesthetic space behind them. This is understood to be in opposition to hip-hop or commercial dance, which is frontal and thus "two-dimensional." Playing with recorded music or interpreting popular music is often viewed as a gimmick, as opposed to the mastery of "pure movement." So, it seems, dance advances its seriousness at the expense of apparently less serious dances, which are argued to be less contained, organized or theoretically informed.

Third, choreographers respond to these discourses of "seriousness" through their artistic creations. For example, hip-hop dance that aspires to be treated seriously on a theatrical stage will typically start by altering the musical genres and styles selected for dancing (Shapiro 2004). Again, choreographers such as Alain Platel and William Forsythe will use pop song references to "make fun" of their "high art." In both cases, the choices of music for dance are predictably unpredictable, a play on the blurring of lines between high/low. However, in practice, the divides of dance worlds are reinforced daily, from the types of dancers' bodies that are encouraged in educational contexts to the ethnicities, genders and sexualities accepted in both the performance and representation of societal interests.

Phenomenological Accounts of Dance and Thinking about Music

> We have bodies, but we are also, in a specific sense, bodies; our embodiment is a necessary requirement of our social identification so that it would be ludicrous to say "I have arrived and I have brought my body with me."
>
> (Turner 1984: 7)

In 1984, Turner argued that a sociology that aspires to be comprehensive must account for the embodiment of social actors. When sociologists move away from social constructionism in pursuing questions of the body and dance, they often enter the realm of phenomenology to understand embodied experiences. Questions are here organized around what it *feels* like to dance.

For Wainwright and Turner (2006), the answer to the question of what it feels like to dance is explored by interviewing ballet dancers on their experiences of ageing. This line of inquiry is undertaken not to assert that the dancers have complete authority over their experiences and actions, but rather to demonstrate the interplay of action and institutions, social roles and social organization, and individual expressions of experience. Similarly, Tarr and Thomas (2011) focus on contemporary dancers' experiences of pain and injury. Their methodology involved a visual component through which participants created maps of their bodily pain with body-scanning technology. Their approach is informed theoretically by the work of phenomenologist Maurice Merleau-Ponty (1962). The term "cultural phenomenology" is invoked to express not only the experiences of dancers but also the "ways in which these are culturally shaped and mediated" (Tarr and Thomas 2011: 145).

The philosopher Ludwig Wittgenstein (1953) observed that we can never know what someone else is going through when they are in pain. We can ask them about the pain, where it is and what it feels like (here analogy would be crucial). Wittgenstein pointed this out to demonstrate some of the limitations of language and, later, to further a critique of the emerging discipline of psychology. However, his observations provide an interesting basis for a phenomenological approach to the sociology of music and dance. First, in applying his insight to music, we can never know what someone else is listening to in a song. I have elsewhere argued that this is part of the intrigue and part of the pleasure that audiences observing popular dance performances experience through their shared aesthetic attention to the music (Fogarty 2014). When we look at someone performing dance with certain competences we feel as though we are seeing what they are listening to in the music. When dancers are incompetent, audiences often comment that they are "not listening to the music." Dance competence, then, gives us a sense that we are getting an insight into a certain experience and the articulation of qualities within the music through the quality of the performers' "serious" listening practices while dancing. Frith (1996) argues that all musical listening is a type of performance. He suggests that there are social conventions of how best to listen, which are constrained by historical precedents, contemporary practices and distinctions of taste.

One of the most significant evaluations of popular dance involves a consideration of the relation between dancers' movements and the music. Buckland (1983) has argued that popular dance practices have been distinguished from art dance through their tight relationship to popular music recordings. Let us compare this argument to recent studies by experimental psychologists (Mitchell and MacDonald 2006) in which the relationship between musical tastes and pain were tested. Participants were asked to put a hand in a cold water press while, for example, looking at an aesthetically pleasing painting or listening to a recording of a song they liked. Researchers found that participants were likely to keep their hand in the water longer while listening to the music they liked. This has implications for sociologists interested in questions about the intersection of music and dance.

First, we realize that, when listening to music we like, it is possible that we will pay less attention to our bodies. This may go a long way toward appreciating the experiences of injured dancers who love the music to which they are dancing (and especially the experiences of those who listen to amplified music that sonically envelopes them in sound!). Second, the music we like does something to pain. This "something" has possibly to do with the phenomenon of concentration. Sociologist Antoine Hennion (2007) has argued that concentration should not be treated as a mere psychological issue and that sociology might be adept at exploring this phenomenon. What are we doing when we are listening to music while dancing? This depends, as I have suggested, on a number of things. There are social and aesthetic conventions of listening to consider (that is, when is it appropriate to dance to music?). There are issues of concentration and how concentration is socially rewarded (that is, the concentration of the competent social dancer and the engaged audience). And, of course, there are those moments when the way we listen to music is challenged by the dance that goes with it (for example, when a folk band uses trendy onstage movement sensibilities and gestures that give them crossover appeal; see Dodds 2013).

Second, Frith (2014) has recently suggested that listening to music has never been solely about concentration. However, discourses about "serious" listening continue to privilege situations where the convention and assumption have been that audiences are concentrating intently. Yet as Frith points out, even in the concert hall where the conditions are set up for serious concentration, most listening experiences involve daydreaming and wandering thoughts. These do not necessarily constitute a bad or unwelcome experience.

Third, the skin is the body's largest sensory organ. When sound is amplified this amplification draws out the connection through active engagement of the body as felt presence and the musical source. These physiological responses are informed by social situations and conditioning. For example, much of the tension that occurs between audience members and between audiences and performers arises when conflicting conventions of how to treat music either seriously or pleasurably are played out live. One instance of this is when half the audience wants to dance and the other half wants to sit comfortably in their seats and watch the performance without visual impediments.

These considerations raise new questions at the intersections of music and dance studies. How does theorizing amplification change when dance is considered (Devine 2013)? How has the "modernization" of sound affected how listening is organized in relation to the body and social space (Sterne 2003)? And, as I have argued here, what might thinking about sound and listening contribute to the study of dance?

Conclusion

What we require, then, is the emergence of a discipline that accounts for dance and movement more broadly defined in relation to sounds and music within and across societies. This work, which would need to engage the sociology of music in productive ways, lies at the intersection of a nascent sociology of movement and music studies. A sociology of movement would ideally not ignore the listening practices of dancers and audiences, but would instead focus the discussion of movement around a broad range of issues. I have tried to provide an example where a sociology of movement (including gestures) might fit with a sociology of music to account for a range of multisensory experiences (such as amplification).

Dancers have been treated socially either as outcasts (as in the cases both of ballet and modern dancers in years gone by and of contemporary street dancers in New York City) or as body specialists whose value lies in their capacity to move through space and time in detailed ways. We are most often struck by dancers as presenters of the physical capacities of the body. This is not unlike our views of kung fu masters or Olympic stars. Our awe lies in their capacity to do with their bodies what most of us could only dream of. The specialized knowledge of dancers is thus linked to the spectacular for most audiences, even as the "spectacular" is rejected not only by dance forms and choreographers aspiring to the condition of high art, but also by sociologists interested in accounting for the lives of young girls and women who are often represented as marginalized in studies of deviance, youth cultures and symbolism (see McRobbie 1984, Gaunt 2006).

Dancers are also seen to have specialized knowledge of the body in a different way. They are kinesthetic movers. They have somatic knowledge. They are the experts of proprioception. But rarely do we think of dancers in relation to music, rarely are they encountered as sound or music experts in academic literature. And yet many dancers have been championing their love of music as a sign of their seriousness in a popular culture that feminizes dance but treats lovers of records as "serious" (read "masculine") musical connoisseurs. Accounts of salsa (Urquia 2004), breaking (Fogarty 2011) and ballroom (Bosse 2013) have demonstrated as much.

This chapter has considered the body and dance, not only as a set of physical capabilities and capacities, but also as bodies of knowledge that activate specialized listening practices in both performers and audience members. It has touched on some of the key issues of interest for a sociology of movement that incorporates considerations of music and sound. We know that mastery of movement is learned, that skills develop over time, that bodies age and change, and that the experiences of our bodies are not necessarily shared across individuals in a society—and certainly not across lines of gender, ethnicity and age. What we do not know is what the future of researching the social interactions of music and dance will look like. As acclaimed music video choreographer Ryan Heffington suggests, "the body has the ability to transform the world" (Cills 2014). However, we want to know what that will *feel* like as people live longer, continue to modify their appearances in novel ways, experience changing relationships to biological powers, medications and health, and choose to dance professionally or not. An added dimension to all these human factors results from the ways in which the entertainment industries continue to shift and change economic focus. We also want to know how institutions constrain or enhance our abilities to experience dance and music together or as separated entities, and how the circulation of mediated encounters with dance can shape our understanding not only of music but also of ourselves—bodies included.

References

Bailey, M.M. 2013. *Butch Queens Up in Pumps: Gender, Performance, and Ballroom Culture in Detroit*. Ann Arbor: University of Michigan Press.
Banes, S. 1998. *Dancing Women: Female Bodies on Stage*. London: Routledge.

Becker, H.S. 1963. *Outsiders: Studies in the Sociology of Deviance*. London: Free Press of Glencoe.

Bosse, J. 2013. "Sound Understandings: Embodied Music Knowledge and 'Connection' in a Ballroom Dance Community." In *Bodies of Sound: Studies Across Popular Music and Dance*, eds. S. Dodds and S. Cook, 39–54. Farnham: Ashgate.

Bourdieu, P. 1993. *The Field of Cultural Production: Essays on Art and Literature* Cambridge: Polity Press.

_____. 2007. *The Bachelors' Ball: The Crisis of Peasant Society in Béarn*. Chicago: University of Chicago Press.

Buckland, T. 1983. "Definitions of Folk Dance: Some Explorations." *Folk Music Journal* 4(4): 315–352.

_____. 1999. "All Dances Are Ethnic, but Some Are More Ethnic Than Others: Some Observations on Dance Studies and Anthropology." *Dance Research: The Journal of the Society for Dance Research* 17(1): 3–21.

Cills, H. 2014. "The Choreographer Behind 'Chandelier' Knows Just How to Move You." *BuzzFeed* (06 June): www.buzzfeed.com/hazelcills/the-choreographer-behind-chandelier-knows-just-how-to-move-y#1egkr3.

Cohen, S., ed. 1971. *Images of Deviance*. Harmondsworth: Penguin.

Conner, L. 1997. *Spreading the Gospel of the Modern Dance: Newspaper Dance Criticism in the United States, 1850–1934*. Pittsburgh: University of Pittsburgh Press.

Dehghan, S.K. 2014. "Iranian Pharrell Williams Fans Detained Over 'Obnoxious' Video." *The Guardian* (20 May): online.

Devine, K. 2013. "Imperfect Sound Forever: Loudness Wars, Listening Formations and the History of Sound Reproduction." *Popular Music* 32(2): 159–176.

Dodds, S. 2011. *Dancing on the Canon: Embodiments of Value in Popular Dance*. New York: Palgrave MacMillan.

_____. 2013. "Bellow Head: Re-Entering Folk through a Pop Movement Aesthetic." In *Bodies of Sound: Studies Across Popular Music and Dance*, eds. S. Dodds and S. Cook, 25–38. Farnham: Ashgate.

Dodds, S. and S. Cook, eds. 2013. *Bodies of Sound: Studies across Popular Music and Dance*. Farnham: Ashgate.

Fanon, F. 1965. *The Wretched of the Earth*. New York: Grove Press.

Flegenheimer, M. and D. Goodman. 2014. "On Subway, Flying Feet Can Lead to Handcuffs." *New York Times* (28 July): online.

Fogarty, M. 2011. *Dance to the Drummer's Beat: Competing Tastes in International B-Boy/B-Girl Culture*. PhD diss., University of Edinburgh.

_____. 2012a. "Breaking Expectations: Imagined Affinities in Mediated Dance Cultures." *Continuum: Journal of Media and Cultural Studies*, Special Issue on "Mediated Youth Cultures," eds. A. Bennett and B. Robards, 26(3): 449–462.

_____. 2012b. "Each One Teach One: B-Boying and Ageing." In *Ageing and Youth Cultures: Music, Style and Identity*, eds. P. Hodkinson and A. Bennett. Oxford: Berg.

_____. 2014. "Gene Kelly: The Original, Updated." In *The Oxford Handbook of Dance and the Popular Screen*, ed. M. Blanco Borelli, 83–97. Oxford: Oxford University Press.

Frith, S. 1996. *Performing Rites: On the Value of Popular Music*. Oxford: Oxford University Press.

_____. 2014. "What Are We Doing When We Are Listening to Music?" Public Presentation with Chris Frith and Fred Frith, *Studying Music—An International Conference in Honour of Simon Frith*. University of Edinburgh, 10–12 April.

Gaunt, K.D. 2006. *The Games Black Girls Play: Learning the Ropes from Double-Dutch to Hip-Hop*. New York: New York University Press.

Goehr, L. 1992. *The Imaginary Museum of Musical Works: An Essay in the Philosophy of Music*. Oxford: Oxford University Press.

Hebdige, D. 1979. *Subculture: the Meaning of Style*. London: Routledge.

Hennion, A. 2007. "Those Things that Hold Us Together: Taste and Sociology." *Cultural Sociology* 1(1): 97–114.

Jordan, S. 2000. *Moving Music: Dialogues with Music in Twentieth Century Ballet*. London: Dance Books.

Kealiinohomoku, J.W. 1980 [1970]. "An Anthropologist Looks at Ballet as a Form of Ethnic Dance." *Journal for the Anthropological Study of Human Movement* 1(2): 83–97.

Kopytko, T. 1986. "Breakdance as an Identity Marker in New Zealand." *Yearbook for Traditional Music* 18: 21–28.

Malbon, B. 1999. *Clubbing: Dancing, Ecstasy and Vitality*. London: Routledge.

Malnig, J., ed. 2009. *Ballroom, Boogie, Shimmy Sham, Shake: A Social and Popular Dance Reader*. Urbana: University of Illinois Press.

McRobbie, A. 1984. "Dance and Social Fantasy." In *Gender and Generation*, eds. A. McRobbie and M. Nava, 130–161. London: Macmillan.

McRobbie, A. and S.L. Thornton. 1995. "Rethinking 'Moral Panic' for Multi-Mediated Social Worlds." *British Journal of Sociology* 46(4): 559–574.

Merleau-Ponty, M. 1962. *Phenomenology of Perception*. Translated by C. Smith. London: Routledge.

Mitchell, L.A. and R. MacDonald. 2006. "An Experimental Investigation of the Effects of Preferred and Relaxing Music on Pain Perception." *Journal of Music Therapy* 63(4): 295–316.

Morris, G. 2006. *A Game for Dancers: Performing Modernism in the Postwar Years, 1945–1960*. Hanover: Wesleyan University Press.

Mroz, D. 2011. *The Dancing Word: An Embodied Approach to the Preparation of Performers and the Composition of Performances*. Amsterdam: Rodopi.

Rivera, R.Z. 2003. *New York Ricans from the Hip Hop Zone, New Directions in Latino American Cultures*. New York: Palgrave Macmillan.

Rust, F. 1969. *Dance in Society: An Analysis of The Relationship Between the Social Dance and Society in England from the Middle Ages to the Present Day*. London: Routledge and Kegan Paul.

Sachs, C. 1937. *World History of the Dance*. New York: W.W. Norton.

Shapiro, R. 2004. "The Aesthetics of Institutionalization: Breakdancing in France." *The Journal of Arts Management, Law, and Society* 33(4): 316–335.

Shapiro, R. and N. Heinich. 2012. "When is Artification?" *Contemporary Aesthetics* 4: online.

Sterne, J. 2003. *The Audible Past: Cultural Origins of Sound Reproduction*. Durham: Duke University Press.

Tarr, J. and H. Thomas. 2011. "Mapping Embodiment: Methodologies for Representing Pain and Injury." *Qualitative Research* 11(2): 141–157.

Thomas, H. 1995. *Dance, Modernity and Culture: Explorations in the Sociology of Dance*. London: Routledge.

Thornton, S. 1995. *Club Cultures: Music, Media and Subcultural Capital*. Cambridge: Polity.

Turner, B.S. 1984. *The Body and Society*. Oxford: Oxford University Press.

Urquia, N. 2004. "'Doin'it Right': Contested Authenticity in London's Salsa Scene." In *Music Scenes: Local, Translocal, and Virtual*, eds. A. Bennett and R.A. Peterson, 96–100. Nashville: Vanderbilt University Press.

Wacquant, L. 2005. "Carnal Connections: On Embodiment, Apprenticeship, and Membership." *Qualitative Sociology* 28(4): 445–474.

Wainwright, S. and B.S. Turner. 2006. "'Just Crumbling to Bits': An Exploration of the Body, Ageing, Injury and Career in Classical Ballet Dancers." *Sociology* 40(2): 237–255.

Williams, D. 1974. "Dance in Society: An Analysis of the Relationship between the Social Dance and Society in England from the Middle Ages to the Present Day by Frances Rust." *CORD News* 6(2): 29–31.

Willis, P.E. 1978. *Profane Culture*. London: Routledge and Kegan Paul.

Wittgenstein, L. 1953. *Philosophical Investigations*. Oxford: Basil Blackwell.

Youngerman, S. 1974. "Curt Sachs and His Heritage: A Critical Review of World History of the Dance with a Survey of Recent Studies That Perpetuate His Ideas." *CORD News* 6(2): 6–19.

IV

INDUSTRIES AND INSTITUTIONS

It is possible to suggest that some of the most innovative recent developments in music sociology, such as those of Hennion and DeNora, have occurred at the level of "microsociology" (Born 2005). Without subscribing to any fundamental division between "macro" and "micro" levels of social life—because it is always possible to see the micro in the macro and the macro in the micro—this section nevertheless focuses primarily on larger musical–institutional and musical–industrial frameworks, as well as longer musical–historical processes.

Around 1900, the phrase "music industry" referred primarily to music publishing and the instrument trade (Majeski 1990). However, as record sales grew during the twentieth century it became increasingly common to view the recording industry as "the" music industry writ large (for critiques of this tendency see Williamson and Cloonan 2007, Sterne 2014). Recognizing that the music industries are in fact plural, Laing's chapter outlines some of the history of the recorded music industry, as well as key sociological perspectives on recording. Marshall notes that the institution of copyright shares an intimate historical connection, not only with recording, but also with music publishing. Indeed, Marshall shows how with the rise of digital music sales and distribution (see also Section V), issues of copyright, licensing rights and royalty payments have become increasingly central to any understanding of the relationship between music and commerce.

The rise of digitalization and online music affected the music industries in other significant ways. While it is necessary to mention the shifts and controversies that surround user-generated content and free labor in the context of the so-called Web 2.0 (see Terranova 2000, Hesmondhalgh 2010, Morris 2014), the most frequently discussed issue in this context is the economic turmoil created by illegal downloading and P2P file-sharing (see David 2010). Interestingly, in recent years this ostensible downturn in the recorded music industry has been met by an increase in the buoyancy of the live music sector. As Frith argues below, such an economic development is tied up with the enduring centrality of musical performance as a form of social interaction.

Other questions emerge in relation to the ebbs and flows of capitalism in the late modern world, especially with regard to globalization, the so-called "network society" and neo-liberalism (see for example Burckhardt Qureshi 2002; Taylor 2007, 2012a, 2012b; see also Boltanski and Chiapello 2006,

Harvey 2011, Piketty 2014). Such developments have reconfigured the relationship between music, the arts and culture on the one hand, and the state and public policy on the other. As Behr shows, such shifts reanimate a long-standing ideological tension between art and commerce, or "the relationship between music as culture and music as industry" (Frith, Cloonan and Williamson 2009: 74). They also raise urgent political questions about how to define and measure cultural "value" and how to support artistic and musical work in conditions of uncertainty and precariousness (see also Menger 2014).

There are of course numerous other industrial and institutional contexts that could be explored here, such as the role of music and sound in issues of health, well-being and the medical professions (see for example DeNora 2013, Rice 2013). Other significant institutions include those of musical training and education. Such institutions cannot be seen as "neutral" grounds of teaching and rehearsal. Rather, they perform important functions in terms of the production and reproduction of aesthetic regimes, value systems and class-bound forms of cultural capital, as well as gendered and ethnic social inequalities (see Vulliamy and Shepherd 1984, Green 1997, Armstrong 2011, Born, Devine and Taylor 2013). Of course, the sociology of music education shares a history with music sociology more generally (as well as ethnomusicology and popular music studies, as outlined in the Introduction). However, the field has also developed a distinct identity and community of scholars, served by its own journals, conferences, degree programs—and, of course, its own literature. It is possible and desirable that the fields might be brought into closer and more regular dialog. But building such a bridge would require a book unto itself. In the meantime, we direct interested readers to some of the current work in the sociology of music education (see for example Wright 2010, Swanwick 2012).

References

Armstrong, V. 2011. *Technology and the Gendering of Music Education*. Farnham: Ashgate.
Boltanski, L. and E. Chiapello. 2006. *The New Spirit of Capitalism*. London: Verso.
Born, G. 2005. "On Musical Mediation: Ontology, Technology and Creativity." *Twentieth-Century Music* 2(1): 7–36.
Born, G., K. Devine and M. Taylor. 2013. "Music, Digitization and Mediation in British Higher Education." Presented at Music and Digitisation Research Group workshop, University of Oxford (May).
Burckhardt Qureshi, R., ed. 2002. *Music and Marx: Ideas, Practice, Politics*. New York: Routledge.
David, M. 2010. *Peer to Peer and the Music Industry: The Criminalization of Sharing*. London: Sage.
DeNora, T. 2013. *Music Asylums: Wellbeing Through Music in Everyday Life*. Farnham: Ashgate.
Frith, S., M. Cloonan and J. Williamson. 2009. "On Music as a Creative Industry." In *Creativity, Innovation and the Cultural Economy*, eds. A. Pratt and P. Jeffcut, 74–89. London: Routledge.
Green, L. 1997. *Music, Gender, Education*. Cambridge: Cambridge University Press.
Harvey, D. 2011. *The Enigma of Capital: And the Crises of Capitalism*. London: Profile.
Hesmondhalgh, D. 2010. "User-Generated Content, Free Labour and the Cultural Industries." *Ephemera* 19(3–4): 267–284.
Majeski, B., ed. 1990. *The Music Trades 100th Anniversary Issue: A History of the US Music Industry*. Englewood: Music Trades.
Menger, P.-M. 2014. *The Economics of Creativity: Art and Achievement under Uncertainty*. Cambridge: Harvard University Press.
Morris, J. 2014. "Artists as Entrepreneurs, Fans as Workers." *Popular Music and Society* 37(3): 273–290.
Piketty, T. 2014. *Capitalism in the Twenty-First Century*. Cambridge: Harvard University Press.
Rice, T. 2013. *Hearing the Hospital: Sound, Listening, Knowledge and Experience*. Canon Pyon: Sean Kingston Press.
Sterne, J. 2014. "There Is No Music Industry." *Media Industries* 1(1): 50–55.
Swanwick, K., ed. 2012. *Music Education* (4 vols). New York: Routledge.
Taylor, T. 2007. "The Commodification of Music at the Dawn of the Era of 'Mechanical Music'." *Ethnomusicology* 51(2): 281–305.
_____. 2012a. "Music in the New Capitalism." In *The International Encyclopedia of Media Studies*. Oxford: Wiley-Blackwell.

_____. 2012b. *The Sounds of Capitalism: Advertising, Music and the Conquest of Culture*. Chicago: University of Chicago Press.

Terranova, T. 2000. "Free Labor: Producing Culture for the Digital Economy." *Social Text* 18(2): 33–58.

Vulliamy, G. and J. Shepherd. 1984. "Sociology and Music Education: A Response to Swanwick." *British Journal of Sociology of Education* 5(1): 57–76.

Williamson, J. and M. Cloonan. 2007. "Rethinking the Music Industry." *Popular Music* 26(2): 305–322.

Wright, R., ed. 2010. *Sociology and Music Education*. Farnham: Ashgate.

24

Recorded Music

DAVE LAING

While the technologies essential to the recording of sound were established in the late nineteenth century, it was not until the 1950s that recordings became the primary sector of the music industry, particularly in the various genres of popular music. Coincidentally, the second half of the twentieth century saw a swift increase in the range and volume of sociological interest in music, much of which centered on the analysis of the effects of recorded music on various audiences, and on the processes and impacts of the recorded music industry.

In this chapter, the sociological study of recorded music will be examined through the following categories: first, the sequence and history of technologies of sound recording; second, the practices of listening produced by recorded music; third, the effects of music recordings on the evolution of popular music and its genres; fourth, the character and development of the industry of recorded music, notably through the institution of the record company; fifth, the concept of the independent label and the "concentration and diversity debate"; finally, the ontological and epistemological implications of the ability to copy and preserve sound through recording.

Technologies of Sound Recording

As succinctly related most recently by Osborne (2012: 8–16), the history of sound recording begins in a flurry of activity in Europe and the United States in the final decades of the nineteenth century. Several inventors made progress toward the capture of sound. However, most histories of recorded music cite the innovations of Thomas Edison as crucial to the crystallization of recorded sound as a technology and a consumer product. Edison has been the subject of numerous biographies, the most recent of which are by Israel (2000) and Millard (1993). Such studies tend to cast their subject in the role of the genius inventor, and there is some justice in Sterne's (2003: 28) stricture on "the cult of Edison in phonographic historiography." Nevertheless, it was Edison who was the first to articulate the potential uses of his "invention." In 1878, he made a list in his notebook of eight such uses:

- To make Dolls speak, sing, cry and make various sounds
- & also to apply it to all kinds of Toys such as Dogs animals, fowl, reptiles, human figures; to cause them to make various sounds
- to Steam Toy Engines exhausts and whistles
- to reproduce from sheets music both orchestral instrumental and vocal, the idea being to use a plate machine with perfect registration & stamp the music out in a press from a die or punch

259

previously prepared by cutting it in steel or from an Electrotype or cast from an original or tin foil

- a family may have one machine and 1000 sheets of the music thus giving endless amusement
- I also propose to make toy music boxes and toy talking boxes playing several tunes
- Also to clocks and watches for calling out the time of day or waking a person
- For advertisements continually rotated by clockwork.

(Quoted in Conot 1979: 107)

It is noteworthy that almost all these possible applications of the invention are in the field of entertainment (especially for children) or "amusement." Only two refer more or less directly to the recording of musical performances. The processes by which music became the principal focus of recording technologies by the first decade of the twentieth century have been under-researched. However, the factors involved included the earlier history of mechanical music devices such as musical boxes, barrel pianos, organs and pianolas (player pianos), and the associated growth in domestic musical entertainment typified in the nineteenth century by the expansion in the ownership of pianos and printed sheet music.

The evolution of the means to consume recordings was crucial in the process of the formation of recorded music. To begin with, Edison favored the transfer of recorded music onto cylinders, while his rivals preferred discs, which eventually became the industry standard format. For domestic consumption, the playback equipment was housed in often elaborate pieces of furniture, similar in design to cabinets and cupboards.

The first generation of recording technologies, which were mechanical and derived from the work of Edison and such contemporaries as Emile Berliner, were to be supplanted in the 1920s by electrical recording, a method developed to add a soundtrack to formerly silent cinema films (for an account of the introduction of electrical recording see Gelatt 1977: 219–228). One important response to this apparently progressive development was the negative reaction of many experts (including Edison) as well as consumers who were attached to the auditory experience supplied by the earlier mechanical format.

In this context, it is worth considering the concept of a recorded music "format," a term widely used throughout the scholarly literature as well as in magazines and advertising. For most writers it merely signifies a distinct and scientifically definable technology for producing and consuming recordings. However, Sterne has convincingly proposed that a format is a more complex assemblage:

> *Format* denotes a whole range of decisions that affect the look, feel, experience, and workings of a medium. It also names a set of rules according to which a technology can operate. In an analog device, the format is usually a particular utilization of a mechanism . . . In a digital device, a format tells the operating system whether a given file is for a word processor, web browser, a music playback program, or something else . . . Most crucial dimensions of a format are codified in some way—sometimes through policy, sometimes through the technology's construction and sometimes through sedimented habit.

(2012: 7–8)

Sterne's definition is a useful corrective to the ever-present tendency in this field to submit to technological determinism, an ideology defined by Williams (1974: 7) in the following terms: "New technologies are discovered, by an essentially internal process of research and development, which then sets the conditions for social change and progress. Progress, in particular, is the history of these inventions, which 'created the modern world'."

Sterne's inclusion of "sedimented habit" echoes the argument of Edgerton's (2006) *The Shock of the Old*, which shows that "innovation-centric" approaches to new technologies should be countered with the fact that "the time of maximum use is typically decades away from invention, or indeed innovation" (2006: 4). The concept of "sedimented habit" also assists in understanding certain residual features of newer formats, such as the strong tendency to limit the length of compact disc albums to the ten or twelve songs common on LPs, even though compact disc (CD) technology enables over eighty minutes of music to be inscribed onto the disc.

Electrical recording was the most important innovation in the analog age in terms of recording and reproducing initial performances with higher degrees of sonic definition and clarity (fidelity), not least because its microphone technology enabled the sound of larger ensembles from jazz groups to orchestras and choirs to be satisfactorily reproduced (an achievement difficult if not impossible with mechanical recording, which was better suited to recording small, loud ensembles). However, it has been less celebrated by commentators and historians than the advent in the 1940s of vinyl discs of varying sizes and speeds. This is mainly because electrical recording affected only the production side of the industry. Existing means of consumption, in the form of 78-rpm shellac discs and playback devices, remained the same.

A so-called "battle of the speeds" ensued, with two major US companies introducing competing formats. While Columbia proposed a long-playing record of twelve inches in diameter and revolving at 33⅓ rpm, its rival the Radio Corporation of America (RCA) came forward with the 45-rpm, single-play disc of seven inches, containing only one or two short tracks on each side. Equally important was the material from which the new discs were constructed. Unlike shellac, which was known to be heavy and brittle, the new records were made from polyvinyl chloride (a petroleum-based plastic) and were claimed to be lightweight and unbreakable.

In many countries, the 45- and 33-rpm records coexisted with the older 78-rpm disc for much of the 1950s. To play the newer formats it was necessary to purchase special record players and, in the United States, jukeboxes had to be replaced with machines designed to play at the new speeds. It should in this context be noted that the important role of the jukebox in the dissemination and consumption (not to mention the economics) of popular music between the 1930s and 1980s has been under-researched.

During this vinyl era, the new discs became known as "singles" and "albums." While the term "single" was new, the term "album" had previously described sets of 78-rpm discs that together made up, for example, a recording of an orchestral symphony, and were interleaved in a book-like package. There was also an extended play (EP) format, a seven-inch disc containing four songs instead of the single's two.

In 1963, the Dutch electronics company Philips demonstrated a tape cassette at the Berlin Audio Fair. A small minority of audiophiles had previously adopted reel-to-reel tape technology, but this was a cumbersome way to play recorded sound. The compact cassette was the smallest and most portable recorded music artifact to date. It soon became a formidable rival to disc formats. Its use spread globally, and it was especially popular in "less developed" regions of the world, such as South India, whose cassette industry was the subject of a classic study by Manuel (1993). The appeal of the cassette was immensely enhanced by the fact that this was a format that could be used by consumers to make their own recordings, the first such dual-purpose format since Edison's by then long-extinct cylinder.

In later years, the versatility of the cassette was reinforced when Sony introduced its Walkman system. This consisted of portable headphone stereo sets that allowed listeners to form their own intimate, personal, aural space while on the move. This was the fulfilment of a process that Williams (1974, 1983) had termed "mobile privatization." Studies of Walkman culture have been published by du Gay et al. (1997) and Bull (2000).

By the early 1950s, a distinct tribe of audio enthusiasts had emerged, first in the United States, and then in Japan and Europe. In the late 1970s, for example, the monthly circulation of high-fidelity (hi-fi) magazines grew from 50,000 to 200,000 (Breh 1982). The discourse of such journalism and its relation to consumer culture and ideologies of listening are expertly analyzed by Keightley (1996). Innovations in music reproduction embraced by these early enthusiasts included stereo, which separated the sound into two streams, quadraphonics (which separated sound into four streams) and, later, digital technology.

Recording studios had introduced various forms of computer-based equipment in the 1970s. However, the first extension of digital technology to playback systems took the form of the CD format. This technology was developed jointly by two of the leading transnational electronics conglomerates, Sony of Japan and Philips of the Netherlands (Nathan 1999). The introduction of the CD reignited a controversy over the purposes and goals of music recording. In a strikingly similar manner to the debates that have haunted the history of photography, those who held to the somewhat naïve view that recordings should aim to mirror the sound and ambience of live performances often regarded the application of digital technology to be inferior to the "natural" process of acoustic recording. The CD sound was held to be cold and clinical in contrast to the warmth supplied by music encoded onto vinyl.

The CD was nevertheless a remarkable success. Within a few years it had overtaken both the vinyl LP and the cassette in terms of unit sales. Between 1983 and 1989, annual global sales of the format grew from 5 million to 400 million. In this early phase, individual consumers purchased large numbers of CDs as replacements for their favorite vinyl or cassette albums.

Because CD discs were premium priced, often 50 percent more than the equivalent LP or cassette, they provided record companies with very high profits, thus engendering a hubris that did not serve the industry well when the next technological advance occurred in the late 1990s. This advance was the transmission of information between computers through the medium of the internet, a digital communication system using the genuinely revolutionary technology of the World Wide Web. The early history of the provision of music files on the internet is recounted by Alderman (2001). The subsequent misadventures of the industry as a consequence of this innovation have been discussed by several authors (Knopper 2009, Hardy 2012, Marshall 2013). The eventual emergence of an industry standard format, the MP3 (layer 3 of the Motion Pictures Experts Group-1 audio standard) is documented and impressively contextualized by Sterne (2012), while Collins and Young (2014) have mapped the range of prototypes of online music sites.

In industrial terms, the control of the recorded music market has now moved decisively from the record companies and their distribution and marketing systems to the giant companies of the computer and internet sectors, notably Apple and Amazon. Apple's leading position is based on its three-fold dominance of online retail (through its iTunes websites), personal music players (through the iPod: a Walkman for the internet age) and the mobile or cell phone market (through the iPhone). The iPhone and its rivals are the present focus of the search by new technology firms for a format that can undertake a multitude of functions, including the acquisition and immediate playback of music recordings. The iTunes model is based on an "analog" model of the sale of discrete commodities (discs or tapes). However, it may be outflanked by the "streaming" of music offered by such European companies as Spotify and Deezer. These companies use a broadcast and subscription model whereby the listener can request a recording for immediate consumption without the necessity of purchasing it.

There are several narrative accounts of this sequence of recording formats, each of which tends to focus on interweaving its subject with another dimension of the history of recorded music. Milner (2009) prioritizes studio technologies applied only to popular music, while Gelatt (1977) is equally devoted to the relationship between recording technologies and western art music. The most comprehensive account remains that of the Finnish scholars Pekka Gronow and Ilpo Saunio (1998), although it was written before the age of the internet and MP3s. Gronow and Saunio are, however, even-handed in their consideration of the impact of recording technology on the various genres of music.

Although he has not published a similar narrative history, the sociologist who has done most to explore and explicate the workings of the industry of recorded music is Simon Frith. From his first book, which contained a chapter called "Making Records" (Frith 1978) to his magnum opus, *Performing Rites* (1996), Frith has continually interrogated the implications of recording for music listeners, critics and creators.

Listening to Recorded Music

Turning to the consumers of recorded music, there have been a number of sociological studies of the character of the listening experience provided for audiences by recorded music. An early theme of such work was the relationship between such experience and that of hearing "live" performances of music. Keightley's (1996) work emphasizes how hi-fi enthusiasts were encouraged to design the layout of their stereo systems to recreate the concert context, with the armchair listener situated in the equivalent of the front row of the concert hall. However, there has been an increasingly consensual view that recordings as such provide distinct and separate musical events. This was recognized at an early stage for popular music of the 1950s and after because of the application of studio techniques: double-tracking of voices, fade-out endings and so on. Even scholars whose primary concern was with western art music argued for the difference, sometimes proclaiming the superiority of recordings for the purpose of bringing "every musical work into being in its optimum and thus adequate form," rather than undertaking to "picture a concert hall with its positive and negative characteristics" (Breh 1982: 173). The case of "live albums" in the popular music sphere—where the recording was made at a concert before an audience—complicates this issue further, as these have frequently been improved by record producers to eradicate errors in singing or playing.

Some work on listener response has focused on individual listeners and their use of recorded music to instigate or enhance an affective response (for example, Crafts, Cavicchi and Keil 1993, DeNora 2000). In addition to Bull's (2007) widely-cited study of iPod users, as well as numerous statistical surveys of online file-sharing, studies are now emerging that address the various new possibilities and cultural nuances of online music consumption (for example, Beer 2008, Tepper and Hargittai 2009, Wilf 2013).

There are important sites of communal response to recorded music, notably the discotheque or dance club and the karaoke room. Each of these sites has generated considerable amounts of research, often of the participant observer type. In the case of the discotheque, the rise to popularity of "disco" as a dance music genre in the 1970s, together with its consequent sequence of recorded genres (house music, garage and so on) inspired studies of consumer behavior (Thornton 1995, Malbon 1999), histories of "disc-jockeyism" and efforts to specify the practice of DJing as a cultural form (Brewster and Broughton 2006). Karaoke is a practice whereby consumers add vocals to recorded backing tracks of well-known popular recordings. It originated in Japan, the source also of much research on karaoke (Mitsui and Hosokawa 1998).

Music Recording and Genres

In addition to the study of recorded music formats, scholars have considered the impact of recording on the topography of music genres, in particular its role in "discovering" and disseminating subaltern sounds throughout academic communities and the wider community of music and media consumers.

A very early use of recording was as a tool for ethnomusicologists to accurately capture the musical expression of ethnic, tribal or social groups whose cultures were transmitted orally. US scholars such as Frances Densmore recorded songs and dances of native Americans while the Library of Congress established an Archive of American folk song (Oliver 2003). In various parts of Europe, composers responding to the sentiment for a national culture sought inspiration by "collecting" the music of rural popular classes. Examples include Percy Grainger and Ralph Vaughan Williams in the United Kingdom, as well as Béla Bartók and Zoltán Kodály in Hungary and Romania. The geographical locus of such work moved in later generations to Africa and Asia. The issues and dilemmas facing both ethnomusicology and indigenous music makers were summed up strikingly by Feld (2000) in his meditation on the world music phenomenon.

The generic name for such practice—"field recordings"—indicates that these recordings were made *in situ* with the performers rather than in specially designed studios. Field recordings have also been commercially motivated. In the United States, the 1920s saw recording engineers head for the west and south to find singers and instrumentalists whose recordings could be marketed to their own communities. The musician Fred Gaisberg had operated in much the same way two decades earlier when he visited countries in Asia, the Middle East and Southern Europe and recorded popular singers for the Gramophone Company (see Moore 1999). Two classic examples of journeys to the south and west of the United States involved Ralph Peer's trip to Bristol, Tennessee in 1927, where he made the first recordings by the Carter Family and Jimmie Rodgers, and the 1936 and 1937 sessions in a Texas hotel room where the influential blues singer and guitarist Robert Johnson was recorded.

These early examples can be utilized to make a vital general statement about sound recordings: that they have the potential to transcend the limitations of the time and space in which they originated. This has at least two important and connected consequences. First, recordings can serve to define and codify a music genre through their direct influence on other musicians in the ethnic or geographical group, as happened with both Rodgers and the Carter Family. Second, such an influence can reach forward through time and outwards both geographically and culturally. For example, in his autobiography, Keith Richards (2010) of the Rolling Stones describes the impact of Johnson's 1930s tracks on him as a white British teenager in the early 1960s. Third, on a more theoretical level, because of its ability to transcend its time and place of origination, recorded music is an essential component of the type of music "scene" specified by Straw (1991: 373) as "that cultural space in which a range of musical practices coexist, interacting with each other within a variety of processes of differentiation."

The Industry of Recorded Music and the Record Company

As well as the subject of a technological history and a creator of cultural and aesthetic effects, recorded music is the product of a cultural industry whose own history stretches for a century and a half from Edison's successful experiments of the 1870s to the present day. The institutional heart of this industry is the record company. The record company has shared some features with consumer goods manufacturers in general, as well as with manufacturers within the cultural industries more specifically. However, the record company also has unique characteristics which are determined by the specific vectors of recorded music as a commodity.

The earliest recorded music industry companies were founded by patent owners to market their gramophones and phonographs. In some cases, the company also traded in other consumer products, notably the British-owned Gramophone and Typewriter Company. In order to attract purchasers these companies built up a catalogue of recordings. These were generally drawn from songs or tunes familiar to owners of pianos or vaudeville and music hall audience members. The same strategy was adopted when the Gramophone Company (having dropped the reference to typewriters) expanded internationally. In 1901, it made a cartel agreement with the Victor Company of the United States. The companies agreed to divide the globe and not to compete in each other's sphere of influence.

During the 1920s, the recording industry was negatively affected by the Great Depression, the global economic crisis and by competition from the new media of radio and films with soundtracks. This led to a series of mergers. In Europe, the Gramophone Company combined forces with its main competitor, the regional branch of Columbia. In the United States, both Columbia and Victor were acquired by radio hardware manufacturers and network broadcasters, and became the Columbia Broadcasting System (CBS) and RCA respectively. Edison's record company closed in 1929, shortly after the Wall Street crash.

By the late 1940s and early 1950s the remaining large record companies had evolved bureaucratic structures which would remain broadly in place until the present day. The structures were made up of divisions to deal with manufacturing, distribution, finance, marketing, business affairs and A&R (artists and repertoire). Negus (1992, 1999) has produced studies of the structures of British record companies and the strategic systems of transnational firms.

The difficulties suffered by the record industry in the internet era have attracted a substantial, though often superficial, degree of analysis. Some authors were not able to resist *Schadenfreude* ("pleasure derived from the misfortune of others"—witness, for example, the title of Knopper's (2009) book: *Appetite for Self Destruction: The Spectacular Crash of the Record Industry in the Digital Age*). Others placed these changes in the context of corporate political economy (see for example Hardy 2012). The corporate context of this industry crisis was a further reduction in the number of major companies, which by 2012 was reduced to three—Universal, Sony and Warner.

While some activities of the record industry are structurally similar to those of other businesses, marketing, business affairs and A&R have characteristics peculiar to this industry. From the 1940s onwards, a principal objective of record industry marketing has been to secure radio airplay for newly released popular recordings. The methods used were sometimes tantamount to bribery of radio station personnel and were widespread enough to be given a neologism for a name: "payola." Segrave (1994) has written a somewhat pedestrian history of this practice. Dannen's (1990) investigative journalism analyzed payola practices in the 1980s.

Business affairs departments in record companies are staffed by lawyers whose principal activity is to draw up recording contracts. Historically, these contracts—sometimes called industry standard contracts—have been lengthy and complex, introducing esoteric concepts such as breakage allowances, packaging deductions and contract periods. They were often criticized for unfairly favoring the record company and were sometimes challenged in the courts (Laing 2000). In this context Stahl (2012) and Jones (2012) have opened up discussion on the nature of musicians' labor power.

According to Frith (1978: 78), "an A&R man [sic] is responsible for what music goes out on a company's label—for getting artists signed to the label, for keeping them there (or dismissing them) and for the records that are issued in their name." As this indicates, the artist and repertoire function is pivotal for the record industry. Here, risk-taking is a vital part of the search for commercial success. However, the elimination of risk is equally important for profitability.

There have been a number of accounts of national recorded music markets outside the anglophone sphere that complement the study of record companies. Of particular interest are those of Wallis and Malm (1984), dealing with Africa, Asia and the Caribbean in the 1970s, and of Marshall (2013), with its case studies of the contemporary industries of Brazil, France, Japan and elsewhere.

Independent Labels and the Concentration and Diversity Debate

The availability of apparently robust statistical information on total unit sales of recorded music and (through the charts) the comparative popularity of individual recordings has provided opportunities for analyses of the influence of record companies on the evolution of popular music. One instance of this is provided through the "concentration and diversity debate."

This debate is about whether there was an inverse correlation between the proportion of best-selling records produced by the major companies ("concentration") and the variety of top-selling recordings ("diversity") (see for example Burnett 1992). The historical background to the debate was the rise of a new breed of small record companies in the United States following the Second World War. These companies were seen as the carriers of new forms of African-American music (generally termed "rhythm & blues") and of rock 'n' roll itself. The role of independent record companies in the rise of rock 'n' roll was detailed most thoroughly in Gillett's influential *The Sound of the City*, first published in 1970, a book based on a master's thesis supervised by the eminent US sociologist Herbert Gans. The new small companies were known as "independents" to contrast them with the "majors," the descendants of the turn-of-the-century companies, Columbia, Victor and Gramophone.

Among these are studies by Bowman (1997, on the soul music of Stax), Cohadas (2001, on the rhythm & blues and rock 'n' roll of Chess), Cook (2001, on the jazz label Blue Note), Escott and Hawkins (1991, on the rock 'n' roll of the Sun label), Gillett (1974, on the rhythm & blues and pop of Atlantic), Goldsmith (1998, on the Folkways label and folk music), Houghton (2010, on the folk and rock of Elektra), Ro (1998, on the hip-hop label Death Row) and Young (2006, on the "indie" music of Rough Trade).

Soon after the publication of Gillett's book, the production-of-culture theorist Richard Peterson, together with David Berger (Peterson and Berger 1975), put forward a "four-firm thesis" that showed how the rise of rock 'n' roll was linked to a significant rise in the number of record companies responsible for Top 10 hits in the United States in the late 1950s. This thesis was intermittently tested and critiqued over the next forty years by Christianen (1995), who applied it to the Netherlands, as well as by Lopes (1992) and Dowd (2004). Using a modified methodology, Christianen argued that the structure of the Netherlands' national market differed significantly from that of the United States. Lopes was able to show that, despite retaining their grip on overall record sales, the major companies had adopted an "open" structure of multiple A&R centers in competition with each other, thus contributing to diversity. For his part, Dowd introduced a new model, measuring the diversity both of recording artists and record companies.

Ontology and Epistemology

One type of response to the emergence of sound recording has been to regard it as representing a fundamental break or dislocation in a scientific, experiential or cultural field or sector, even a Kuhnian paradigm shift or a Foucauldian change of episteme. This approach to the study of recorded music has sometimes been called "phonography," as in the title of *Phonographies: Grooves in Sonic Afro-Modernity* (Weheliye 2005). This book also argued for a privileged role for music recording in the transition from oral communication to a modernist sensibility in African-American culture. Sterne's approach is to place recording in a more general history of "audile technique" and of acoustic space. Kittler (1999) is more concerned to focus on the historical moment of invention and technological advances, as the title of his book—*Gramophone, Film, Typewriter*—indicates. A different emphasis on the field of listening and sound is placed by authors who emphasize the "acousmatic" character of listening, that is, the definitive absence of a visual dimension in sound recording, its presentation of "a voice without a face" (Laing 1991, Richardson 2012). The addition of a visual dimension to audio tracks to create music videos can be seen as the most ambitious attempt to surmount the limitations of acousmatic listening. The early popularity of this audiovisual format following the launch in the United States of the MTV cable channel in 1981 inspired a rush of academic work on music video, of which the best known are the books by Kaplan (1987) and Goodwin (1992). In the early twenty-first century, such visualizations of recorded music have become even more prominent in both the aesthetic and the political economy of recorded music through such online outlets as YouTube and Vevo. A definitive sociological study of this phenomenon is overdue.

References

Alderman, J. 2001. *Sonic Boom: Napster, P2P and the Future of Music*. London: Fourth Estate.

Beer, D. 2008. "The Iconic Interface and the Veneer of Simplicity: MP3 Players and the Reconfiguration of Music Collecting and Reproduction Practices in the Digital Age." *Information, Communication and Society* 11(1): 71–88.

Bowman, R. 1997. *Soulsville USA: the Story of Stax Records*. New York: Schirmer Books.

Breh, K. 1982. "High Fidelity, Stereophony, and the Mutation of Musical Communication." In *The Phonogram in Cultural Communication*, ed. K. Blaukopf, 165–177. Vienna: Springer.

Brewster, B. and F. Broughton. 2006. *Last Night a DJ Saved My Life: The History of the Disc Jockey*. London: Headline.

Bull, M. 2000. *Sounding Out the City: Personal Stereos and Everyday Life*. New York: Berg.

_____. 2007. *Sound Moves: iPod Culture and Urban Experience*. New York: Routledge.

Burnett, R. 1992. "The Implications of Ownership Changes on Concentration and Diversity in the Phonogram Industry." *Communication Research* 19(6): 749–769.

Christianen, M. 1995. "Cycles in Symbol Production? A New Model to Explain Concentration, Diversity and Innovation in the Music Industry." *Popular Music* 14(1): 55–93.

Cohadas, N. 2001. *Spinning Blues into Gold. Chess Records: the Label that Launched the Blues*. London: Aurum Press.

Collins, S. and S. Young. 2014. *Beyond 2.0. The Future of Music*. Sheffield: Equinox.

Conot, R. 1979. *A Streak of Luck*. New York: Da Capo.

Cook, R. 2001. *Blue Note Records. The Biography*. London: Secker and Warburg.

Crafts, S., D. Cavicchi and C. Keil. 1993. *My Music. Explorations of Music in Daily Life*. Middletown: Wesleyan University Press.

Dannen, F. 1990. *Hit Men: Power Brokers and Fast Money inside the Music Business*. New York: Times Books.

DeNora, T. 2000. *Music and Everyday Life*. Cambridge: Cambridge University Press.

Dowd, T. 2004. "Concentration and Diversity Revisited: Production Logics and the US Mainstream Records Market 1940–1990." *Social Forces* 82(4): 1411–1455.

Du Gay, P., S. Hall, L. Janes, H. Mackay and K. Negus. 1997. *Doing Cultural Studies: The Story of the Sony Walkman*. London: Sage.

Edgerton, D. 2006. *The Shock of the Old: Technology and Global History Since 1900*. London: Profile.

Escott, C. and M. Hawkins. 1991. *Good Rockin' Tonight: Sun Records and the Birth of Rock 'n' Roll*. New York: St Martin's Press.

Feld, S. 2000. "A Sweet Lullaby for World Music." *Public Culture* 12(1). 145–71.

Frith, S. 1978. *The Sociology of Rock*. London: Constable.

_____. 1996. *Performing Rites: On the Value of Popular Music*. New York: Harvard University Press.

Gelatt. R. 1977. *The Fabulous Phonograph*, 2nd revised ed. New York: Collier Books.

Gillett, C. 1974. *Making Tracks: Atlantic Records and the Growth of a Multi-Billion Dollar Industry*. New York: Dutton.

_____. 1996 [1970]. *The Sound of the City. The Rise of Rock 'n' Roll*, 3rd revised ed. London: Souvenir Press.

Goldsmith, P.D. 1998. *Making People's Music: Moe Asch and Folkways Records*. Washington, DC: Smithsonian Institution Press.

Goodwin, A. 1992. *Dancing in the Distraction Factory: Music Television and Popular Culture*. Minneapolis: University of Minnesota Press.

Gronow, P. and I. Saunio. 1998. *An International History of the Recording Industry*. London: Cassell.

Hardy, P. 2012. *Download! How the Internet Transformed the Record Business*. London: Omnibus.

Houghton, M. 2010. *Becoming Elektra: the True Story of Jac Holzman's Visionary Record Label*. London: Jawbone.

Israel, P. 2000. *Edison: A Life of Invention*. New York: Wiley.

Jones, M.L. 2012. *The Music Industries: From Conception to Consumption*. Basingstoke: Palgrave Macmillan.

Kaplan, E.A. 1987. *Rockin' Around the Clock: Music Television, Postmodernism and Consumer Culture*. London: Methuen.

Keightley, K. 1996. "'Turn it Down!' She Shrieked: Gender, Domestic Space and High Fidelity, 1948–59." *Popular Music* 15(2):149–177.

Kittler, F. 1999. *Gramophone, Film, Typewriter*. Stanford: Stanford University Press.

Knopper, S. 2009. *Appetite for Self-Destruction: The Spectacular Crash of the Record Industry in the Digital Age*. New York: Simon & Schuster.

Laing, D. 1991. "A Voice without a Face: Popular Music and the Phonograph in the 1890s." *Popular Music* 10(1): 1–9.

_____. 2000. "George Michael's Contract or Copyright and Power in the Contemporary Record Industry." In *Changing Sounds. New Directions and Configurations in Popular Music. Papers from the 10th International Conference of the International Association for the Study of Popular Music*, eds. T. Mitchell and P. Doyle, 256–259. Sydney: University of Technology.

Lopes, P.D. 1992. "Innovation and Diversity in the Popular Music Industry." *American Sociological Review* 57(1): 56–71.

Malbon, B. 1999. *Clubbing: Dancing, Ecstasy, Vitality*. London: Routledge.

Manuel, P. 1993. *Cassette Culture: Popular Music and Technology in North India*. Chicago: University of Chicago Press.

Marshall, L., ed. 2013. *The International Recording Industries*. London: Routledge.

Millard, A. 1993. *Edison and the Business of Innovation*. Baltimore: Johns Hopkins University Press.

Milner, G. 2009. *Perfecting Sound Forever: The Story of Recorded Music*. London: Granta.

Mitsui, T. and S. Hosokawa, eds. 1998. *Karaoke Around the World*. London: Routledge.

Moore, J.N. 1999. *Sound Revolutions: A Biography of Fred Gaisberg, Founding Father of Commercial Sound Recording*. London: Sanctuary.

Nathan, J. 1999. *Sony: The Private Life*. London: Houghton Mifflin.

Negus, K. 1992. *Producing Pop: Culture and Conflict in the Popular Music Industry*. London: Hodder Arnold.

_____. 1999. *Music Genres and Corporate Cultures*. London: Routledge.

Oliver, P. 2003. "Field Recording." In *Continuum Encyclopedia of Popular Music of the World Volume 1: Media, Industry and Society*, eds. J. Shepherd, D. Horn, D. Laing, P. Oliver and P. Wicke, 25–26. London: Continuum.

Osborne, R. 2012. *Vinyl: A History of the Analogue Record*. Farnham: Ashgate.

Peterson, R. and D. Berger. 1975. "Cycles in Symbol Production: The Case of Popular Music." *American Sociological Review* 40(2): 158–173.

Richards, K. 2010. *Life: Keith Richards*. London: Phoenix.

Richardson, J. 2012. *An Eye for Music: Popular Music and the Audiovisual Surreal*. New York: Oxford University Press.

Ro, R. 1998. *Have Gun Will Travel. The Spectacular Rise and Violent Fall of Death Row Records*. New York: Doubleday.

Segrave, K. 1994. *Payola in the Music Industry: A History, 1880–1991*. Jefferson: McFarland.

Stahl, M. 2012. *Unfree Masters: Recording Artists and the Politics for Work*. Durham: Duke University Press.

Sterne, J. 2003. *The Audible Past: Cultural Origins of Sound Reproduction*. Durham: Duke University Press.

_____. 2012. *MP3: The Meaning of a Format*. Durham: Duke University Press.

Straw, W. 1991. "Systems of Articulation, Logics of Change: Communities and Scenes in Popular Music." *Cultural Studies* 5(3): 368–388.

Tepper, S. and E. Hargittai. 2009. "Pathways to Music Exploration in a Digital Age." *Poetics* 37(3): 227–239.

Thornton, S. 1995. *Club Cultures: Music, Media and Subcultural Capital*. Cambridge: Polity.

Wallis, R. and K. Malm. 1984. *Big Sounds from Small People: The Music Industry in Small Countries*. London: Constable.

Weheliye, A.E. 2005. *Phonographies: Grooves in Sonic Afro-Modernity*. Durham: Duke University Press.

Wilf, E. 2013. "Toward an Anthropology of Computer-Mediated, Algorithmic Forms of Sociality." *Current Anthropology* 54(6): 716–739.

Williams, R. 1974. *Television: Technology and Cultural Form*. London: Fontana.

_____. 1983. *Towards 2000*. London: Chatto and Windus.

Young, R. 2006. *Rough Trade*. London: Black Dog.

25

Live Music

SIMON FRITH

The Economics of Performance

It has long been an academic commonplace that the rise of mediated music (on record, radio and the film soundtrack) meant the decline of live music (in concert hall, music hall and the domestic parlour). For much of the last 50 years the UK's live music sector, for example, has been analysed as a sector in decline. Two kinds of reason are adduced for this.

On the one hand, economists, following the lead of Baumol and Bowen (1966), have assumed that live music can achieve neither the economies of scale nor the reduction of labour costs to compete with mass entertainment media. To cite a familiar example, "in 1780 four quartet players required forty minutes to play a Mozart composition; today forty minutes of labour are still required" (Cowen 1996: 208). And, at the same time, the size of paying audience a live quartet can reach is still restricted by acoustics: its sound can only fill a limited space. It is inevitable, then, that as a matter of economic survival concert promoters have to raise ticket prices faster than overall inflation. Meanwhile, the mass media, taking full advantage of both economies of scale (a single master recording can supply a global market with the same Mozart CD) and technological means of reducing production costs (live performers replaced by recorded performances) can keep the rising prices of its goods well below inflation. In these circumstances, performance of classical and contemporary art music has become entirely reliant on state subsidy. To price tickets according to concerts' true costs would be to restrict entry to a small super-rich elite (like the market for original art works). Hence the recurring predictions of orchestral demise and the fact that the level of state support of the UK's orchestras and opera houses remains an ongoing and well publicised political issue for both the Arts Council England and the Scottish Arts Council.

On the other hand, popular music sociologists and historians have documented the impact of recording technology on public and private uses of music, and shown how job opportunities for live musicians have declined while musical activity has been increasingly domesticated (see, for example, Frith 1987, Sanjek and Sanjek 1991). Cinema organists were made redundant by talking pictures; pit orchestras were replaced by pre-recorded tapes, pub singers by juke boxes, dance halls with dance bands by discos with DJs. As people spent more time listening to music at home (on record, radio and television) so they spent less time going to hear live performers in bar rooms and public halls. At the same time, the domestic use of music has been personalised: family entertainment moved from the piano to the phonogram, from the living room radiogram to the bedroom transistor, from the hi-fi system as household furniture to the walkman and the iPod as personal music accessories. For socio-cultural as well as economic reasons, then, the live music sector seemed doomed to extinction, surviving only as the result of state-subsidised conservation.

Of course the story has never been this simple and in the last decade, in particular, there has been increasing evidence that the "decline of live music" describes a more complicated situation. Recent surveys of the UK music industry suggest that live music is one of its more buoyant sectors. Williamson et al. (2003) found that live music was the only Scottish music activity attracting inward investment. The latest UK-wide music industry survey (by Creative and Cultural Skills, a government agency set up to support training in music and other creative industries) found that the live business was the biggest employer in the music sector (*Music Week*, August 19 2006, pp. 4–5). In March 2006 *Music Week* had anticipated the annual meeting of the International Live Music Convention by reporting that "the live industry is in rude health" and predicting continued growth on the back of two years of record-breaking ticket sales.

[. . .]

Faced with such evidence, it is difficult to avoid the conclusion that the decline of live music, inevitable according to economists and sociologists, has been reversed. The UK live sector is, in Feargal Sharkey's words, experiencing a "boom" (Ashton 2006). How can we explain this? In addressing this question this paper is divided into two parts. In Part 1, I describe why and how live music remains an essential part of the music industry's money making strategies. In Part 2, I speculate about the social functions of performance by examining three examples of performance-as-entertainment: karaoke, tribute bands and the Pop Idol phenomenon.

Performance and Economic Value

To begin with the economics. It is important to stress that the basic premises of Baumol and Bowen's original argument remain valid. There are still limits on the size of the audience one can physically reach in a live show and the costs of live music do continue to rise faster than general inflation. In the USA, for example, the average ticket price for rock concerts rose 82% between 1996 and 2003 while the Consumer Price Index rose by only 17% (Krueger 2005). While comparative data for the UK isn't available, it is safe to assume that similar price rises lie behind the economic health of the sector reported by *Music Week*. Such data suggest that the live sector does indeed suffer from Baumol and Bowen's disease. But the disease hasn't been fatal.

The immediate reason for this is that live music doesn't, in fact, compete with mediated music for leisure spending but, rather, has been absorbed together with recorded music into a single, more complicated music market. And the underlying point here is not that economists got things wrong but that sociologists did. The value of music (the reasons why people are prepared to pay money for it) remains centred in its live experience, and record companies and broadcasters have had to take this into account.

Because live music matters to its audiences, its promoters have been able to follow two strategies, in particular, for dealing with their cost problem. They have, first, expanded audience size—by increasing the capacity of venues, by broadening the scope of "the tour," and, above all, by growing a new sort of musical event, the festival. (All these strategies have been dependent, in turn, on the technological and aesthetic valorisation of *volume*, enabling musicians to be heard by far more people in much bigger spaces.) These developments can be traced most clearly in the history of the live rock music industry. The live rock circuit began in the late 1960s with ballrooms (such as Bill Graham's Fillmore West and East, with capacities of c.2000) but in the early 1970s moved into arenas and stadiums with capacities of 20,000 and upwards (see Chapple and Garofalo 1977, 137–154, and, for a stimulating study of Grand Funk Railroad as the pioneer of arena rock, Waksman 2007). In Britain the Exhibition Centres built in Birmingham, Glasgow and Manchester in the 1970s and 1980s (with 10,000+ seats) became essential for the live rock business, not least because without venues of such size the UK risked losing out on what were now the biggest bands' global touring schedules.

But for British promoters the most significant means of expanding the size of the live audience has undoubtedly been the festival. Festivals are the key asset in the portfolios of the international corporations now dominating British concert promotion and the economic reasons for this are obvious. Not only can the crowd size be expanded (to 50,000 plus over a weekend—the Glastonbury Festival was relaunched in 2007, following its 2006 suspension while its facilities were being improved, with ticket sales of 175,000) but economies of scale can kick in (a great variety of bands are covered by the same staging, ticketing and marketing costs). The British rock industry is now organised around the summer festival season—Glastonbury, T in the Park, Reading and Leeds—and, of course, festivals are equally essential in other music worlds—folk (Cambridge), jazz (Brecon), classical (Edinburgh), world (WOMAD), etc. 2006 saw the launch of a new generation of "niche" or "boutique" festivals, following the growing success of the long-established All Tomorrow's Parties. Mean Fiddler mounted the Latitude Festival in Suffolk, for example. It combines music with politics, comedy and literature for an audience of 12–15,000 (Larkin 2006b).

Music Week's survey of the live sector's UK earnings in 2005 gives some measure of the success of these rock strategies: REM's Hyde Park concert grossed almost £2.5 million; Duran Duran's gig at Birmingham City's football stadium, almost £1 million; Live Nation's (relatively small) Download Festival, £1.1 million. . . .

But such survival isn't just a matter of larger audiences and higher ticket prices. Promoters' (and artists') second solution to the cost disease has been to expand the earnings potential of a live event. Historically, of course, live venues have not only made money from ticket prices, but also from the sale of drink and food, from programmes and from cloakroom and parking costs. But what is now key to rock performers' earnings is merchandise—the ever expanding range of tee-shirts, sweatshirts and other clothing, posters, bags and other souvenirs. Now in one sense what is being exploited here is simply an occasion—the gathering of fans in one place is a good opportunity to sell them products that they could, in fact, buy elsewhere. Thus jazz, folk and classical concerts have long been important opportunities for performers to sell their CDs. But something more is at stake in rock merchandise: what is being sold is a memento of *being there*, a product unique to the event (and digital technology has made available a new sort of CD for sale—an instant recording of the concert itself, available only to the concert goers).[1]

The point I want to stress here, then, is not simply the economic importance of concert merchandise (acts get a much higher percentage of the returns on merchandise sales than on ticket sales; for some acts merchandise income certainly matches and may even surpass their performance fee) but its indicative importance. A live concert is not simply a transitory experience but also symbolises what it means to be a music fan. This is not just a sociological argument; it has economic consequences too. The conventional argument in rock analysis has been that live concerts exist courtesy of the record industry: their function is to promote records, to which they are subordinate (and for which purpose they are subsidised). But this argument no longer seems valid.

On the one hand, there are certainly now major acts (the Rolling Stones being the best example) who gross more from live performance than from record sales and for whom a new record release acts to promote a new tour rather than vice versa. Indeed, this seems to be part of the trajectory of the rock career: acts who can command the highest ticket prices and hence the biggest live earnings, are those whose peak popularity in terms of record sales was years ago. Connolly and Kreuger have calculated that only 4 of the top 35 rock/pop artists who toured the US in 2002 earned more from their recordings/publishing than from live concerts (the four being Eminem, Jay-Z, Linkin Park and Brian "Baby" Williams). 28 of the remaining 31 acts (led by Paul McCartney) had had careers stretching back at least 20 years, and for all of these performers live earnings were far, far greater than recording/publishing earnings. (Interestingly, the Red Hot Chili Peppers, who could be said to be in mid-career, earned the same, £6.1 million, from performance and recordings/publishing—see Connolly and Kreuger 2005: Table 1.1)

On the other hand, in the context of downloading, Myspace and declining record sales, the straightforward relationship between live performance and record promotion has anyway broken down. Kreuger hypothesises that the large increase in rock concert prices in the US in the 1990s reflects the fact that acts (and/or their record companies) no longer had any incentive to keep prices down in the expectation that bigger audiences would translate into higher record sales. Rather, they seek now to maximise profits from concerts as unique events:

> new technology that allows many potential customers to obtain recorded music without purchasing a record has severed the link between the two products. As a result concerts are being priced more like single-market monopoly products.
>
> (Kreuger 2005: 26)

Kreuger calls his hypothesis "the Bowie theory" in reference to David Bowie's prediction that "music itself is going to become like running water or electricity," and his advice to fellow performers that, "You'd better be prepared for doing a lot of touring because that's really the only unique situation that's going to be left" (quoted in Kreuger 2005: 26).

It is this suggestion that the live show is the only "unique situation left" that both accounts for the value that audiences are willing to put on their attendance (hence the above inflationary price rises) but which also, paradoxically, puts live music promoters in a potentially beneficial relationship with music mass media. For record companies, their acts' live concerts offer something new to market. . . .

Performance and Cultural Value

Paradoxically, then, the digital revolution in the storage and distribution of music has only served to underline the continued cultural—and therefore economic—importance of live music, which remains vital for almost all music genres. Baumol and Bowen's predictions have not been borne out. Mediated forms of music have not displaced live performance. Rather, it has adapted itself to new economic and social circumstances. Indeed, one could argue the converse: the record industry itself was shaped by consumer understanding of recorded music as live music. This is perhaps most obvious in the classical music world, in which the "concert hall experience" is still the ideal of classical music recording. . . .

The same argument can be applied to most forms of popular music. According to the much discussed notion of "authenticity," for example—the central value term in rock, folk and jazz music (see Moore 2002)—the live show is the truest form of musical expression, the setting in which musicians and their listeners alike can judge whether what they do is "real."[2] These arguments are familiar and, as with classical music, one can point to the ways in which record, radio, television and video producers have developed ways of representing music that make reference to the ideal live show. But three further aspects of the popular belief in live music are worth noting here.

First, the emergence of the festival as the high point of many people's musical year suggests that what is valuable for the festival audience is not the live performance of a particular group for its particular fans, but "live performance" as a kind of abstract ideal. 2006's T in the Park, for example, was sold out within minutes of the tickets going on sale (on the Web), at which time *no acts had been announced.*

Second, live gigs and venues are essential to the mythology of rock, folk, jazz and country music fans. Read the history of any local scene in the UK and you will come across a paean of nostalgic praise to a now defunct venue, a place which for all its filth and seediness (the reason it is now defunct) is nonetheless seen as *essential* to a city's musical soul (in Glasgow, for example, such a legendary venue is the Apollo).[3]

Third, it is noticeable that even those genres which are not "authentic" in these terms nevertheless use live shows to cement their fan base. The boy band, McFly, grossed more than £500,000 from its three nights at the Scottish Exhibition Centre in 2005 while the Backstreet Boys grossed £1.1 million from its four dates in London, Manchester and Birmingham. (Larkin 2006a). And even the dance music scene, which was at one time taken to mark the end of the valorisation and romanticisation of live music (see Thornton 1995) developed its own "live" values with the rise of the superstar DJ and the drawing power of their "in person" performance.

So far in this paper I have been concerned to show, first, that despite well founded predictions from both economists and sociologists, the live music sector continues to flourish and, second, that across genres the concert (its format remarkably unchanged by music's mediation by record, radio and television) continues to be the experience which for most music lovers defines their musical values. (We would, on the whole, be baffled by someone who said they loved particular performers but had no desire to see them live.)[4] What I want to do now is turn to a different question: *why* does live music matter so much in popular culture, given the overwhelming presence and availability of "piped" and "canned" music or, to use less negative terms, the ever increasing size of people's private musical archives (whether as record collections or iPod files)? To put this question another way: what is live music *for*?

The Sociology of Performance

In addressing this question I want to focus on the emergence over the last 20 years of three new forms of performance-as-entertainment (or entertainment-as-performance): karaoke, tribute bands, and reality TV shows like *Pop Idol*. Each of these phenomena has become a familiar part of the leisure economy and each combines live and mediated music.

[. . .]

Karaoke, tribute bands and reality TV shows occupy quite different positions in the music economy but as forms of entertainment they have significant common features. They all involve a "pretend" performance that has something to do with a "real" one (though they are in themselves all real performances with real audiences). Their various performances have different kinds of relationship with their originals—appropriation, imitation, approximation—but all might be called *secondary* performances: a primary performance, the "proper" way of doing, it is always being evoked.[5] This aspect of these performances—the comparison with the real thing—is explicit. These performances involve *evaluation*, by both formally appointed judges and by the public/audience. This is even true of tribute bands: their continuing success depends on their audiences' assessment of their authenticity as copies!

There are a number of issues that can be pursued here but I want to focus on one: what is the relationship of these kinds of performance to primary performance? Are the pleasures the same?

Not exactly. To begin with these performers aren't stars and their non-stardom is part of the performing point, though one might know or get to know them as personalities.[6] Such shows therefore have a high potential for embarrassment, obvious, for example, in the early audition rounds of *X Factor*. Here the mismatch between performing ambition and ability can be quite startling (as, indeed, it often is at a pub's karaoke night). For the audience, secondary performances involve a great deal of laughter and astonishment.

This is related to my second point above: the element of judgement means that the audience is in a way detached from the performance, observing it *as a performance* rather than being drawn into it or imaginatively and emotionally becoming part of it. Such detachment is obviously most marked when appointed judges publicly comment on these would-be performers and decide which of the *Pop Idol* contestants or karaoke singers is the best, but it is in the nature of secondary performance that everyone in the audience is judging what they see and hear. And the question then is this: what does such evaluation reveal about the social meaning of the primary performances to which these performers implicitly (and often explicitly—as with tribute bands) refer?

The answer lies, I think, in the tension in popular cultural ideology between performance as something *learnt* (a matter of technique, the appropriate gestures) and performance as something *meant* (self-expressive, heartfelt, revealing something of the performer's "real" personality). The good secondary performance is therefore something both obviously fake (because it involves acquiring abilities performers don't just have, inherently; abilities determined and shaped from the outside by teachers, mentors, other performers, audiences) and real (because a matter of truth-to self and honesty to one's audience—what's at stake in the way judgements work here is always the performer's perceived *sincerity*).

The issues raised here are not peculiar to popular culture. They reflect a general understanding of musical talent and what that talent means and are equally apparent in conservatories which similarly distinguish between technical efficiency, the learnt ability to play properly, and musicality, the expressive, individual ability that comes from within. (For an illuminating ethnographic study of a US conservatory see Kingsbury 1988) As I've already noted, in the classical music world live performance is taken to be the moment when the music itself speaks most directly to its listeners. Critics are suspicious of performers who too obviously revel in their artifice or virtuosity. Here is *Guardian* critic Tim Ashley on singer Cecilia Bartoli. Bartoli, he writes, "could be accused of unearthing second-rate music for the express purpose of showing off, for what she now presents us with is a vocal Olympiad, at which we are primarily invited to marvel at her technique . . . Bartoli is always impressive but rarely moving. It is artifice rather than art" (quoted in Frith 2004: 16).

The conservatory ideal, then, is the performance that doesn't draw attention to itself, either with missed notes and technical infelicity or with too self-conscious a display of performance as process, but which is, nevertheless, clearly expressive of both composer's and musician's personality. Quite what this means in performing practice is not necessarily easy to assess, and it is entertaining to compare the expert comments on the performers in the BBC's *Young Musician* (a biennial competition for classical instrumentalists) with the expert comments on the performers in such shows as *X Factor*. The criteria of excellence are obviously different, but they are not articulated any more clearly, and this is a source of considerable stress for trainee performers, for music students for whom part of the educational process is, in fact, the separation of potential professionals from those who will never be more than amateurs (Dibben 2006).

Historically these pressures haven't faced popular performers, or at least not in these terms. Their training is less formalised and the amateur/professional distinction less clear cut. One striking feature of the reality TV pop shows, though, is the way in which the account of performance offered (by both competitors and judges) reflects the emerging influence on British pop of stage schools. The 1980s success of the US television show (and live touring act), *Fame*, inspired the opening of a host of private stage schools around the country and the UK now has two national performing academies (supported by a mix of industry and state funds): the Brit School for the Performing Arts and Technology, opened in London in 1992, and the Liverpool Institute for Performing Arts, opened in 1996. These academies are based on the premise that pop stardom can be just as much a matter of proper instruction and assessed achievement as a classical performing career.[7] But whereas in the classical conservatory the learning process happens behind closed doors, as it were, as part of the "mystery" of the musical craft, in pop music it has become part of the public process of star-making itself.

For rock ideologues reality TV pop shows are despicable for this very reason. Here we can *see* that pop is just as a matter of commercial artifice, has nothing to do with the authentic musical expression of emotions and ideas. In the rock, jazz and folk worlds, the amateur/ professional divide may be blurred, but other distinctions do matter—between the talented and the talentless, between those who have paid their dues and those who haven't. "These days you don't really need it," complains Brad Paisley in his country song about the decline of musical talent, "Thanks to reality TV."

I am describing a tension here between two attitudes to performance. In the classical tradition, for rock, jazz and folk fans, musical performance is valuable because it offers us access to something remarkable and unique, to genius or talent which only select individuals have (even if as a result of long years of technical training and/or dues paying). This is what I call primary performance. In the cases I've been describing of secondary performance the pleasure on offer is quite different. Here what matters is not the performance as such but the process of becoming a performer, and failure is as interesting—as entertaining—as success. The ordinariness of the performers, their lack of credentials or charisma, is here essential. Rob Drew (2001: 121–122) describes the hostility of karaoke audiences in US bars to performers who are thought to be moonlighting professionals. The 2006 run of *X Factor* had to dump competitors who, scandalously, turned out already to be on agents' books.

Conclusion: What is Performance For?

I will end by posing a new question. Why do people want to be performers? How can we explain the popularity of karaoke, the vast number of applicants for *Pop Idol* and *X Factor*, the continued pull of conservatories and stage schools (even though the vast majority of their graduates will not make a living from performing)? In asking this question I am reversing the familiar academic use of "performance" as a metaphorical description of social identity and instead wondering what "being a performer" means as a social role. What is its function for society?

My answer is this. Over the last hundred years or so, for both cultural and technological reasons, the western experience of music has been individualised (this is the sociological argument underlying the predicted decline of the performance sector). Music is now tied up with people's sense of self. Listening to music has become a way of laying claim to one's own physical and emotional space. We therefore make both a new demand on music (to meet our personal needs) and a new commitment to it, as a symbol of our individuality.[8]

This egocentric and essentially lonely aesthetic is shaped, though, by an equally passionate drive to *share* our musical tastes. Music has become more important too for our social intercourse, in gift relations and the understanding of collective identities, to intimacy and our reading of our own and other people's feelings. Live musical performance matters, then, for two reasons. On the one hand, it is a public celebration of musical commitment, a deeply pleasurable event at which our understanding of ourselves through music is socially recognised. On the other hand, it is a site in which to explore—for ourselves—how performance works. And, of course, where there are social desires, there will be entrepreneurs—promoters, ready, at a price, to meet them.

Notes

1   While most fan clubs organize special events, hotel deals, etc. as part of the show "packages" they sell, some acts are more enterprising than others. Wet Wet Wet fans can buy tickets for the group's soundcheck; Iron Maiden fans can—at a price—be flown to the gig by Bruce Dickinson! Thanks to Martin Cloonan for this information.

2 For illuminating ethnographic studies of the importance of the live event for people's understanding of what rock and jazz "mean," see Cavicchi 1998 and Berger 1999.
3 For a recent example of such a history (of Southampton), see Gray (2006).
4 Though as John Butt reminds me, there are dedicated fans of dead performers.
5 There are obviously echoes here of the pursuit of authenticity in the early music movement in the classical world—performers refer to the primary (historical) performance by adopting authentic (period) instruments, performing styles, settings and acoustics. But the primary/secondary model isn't applicable to the usual way in which classical music listeners and critics judge a realized, material performance against the abstract, ideal performance imagined in the score—for discussion of the concept of the ideal performance, see Goehr (1995–1996).
6 This argument is perhaps complicated by such shows as *Celebrity Stars in Their Eyes* or *Celebrity Fame Academy* in which participants are minor stars, but such shows have never had the impact of the programmes they copy and they work, on the whole, as conventional TV entertainment.
7 The Brit School's most successful graduates so far are Katie Melua and Amy Winehouse.
8 For an important critical view of these developments see Hesmondhalgh (2007).

References

Ashton, R. 2006. "Industry Partners Seek Live School." *Music Week* (30 September): 3.

Baumol, W.J. and W.G. Bowen. *1966. Performing Arts: The Economic Dilemma*. New York: Twentieth Century Fund.

Berger, H.M. 1999. *Metal, Rock and Jazz: Perception and the Phenomenology of Musical Experience*. Hanover: University Press of New England.

Cavicchi, D. 1998. *Tramps Like Us: Music and Meaning among Springsteen Fans*. New York: Oxford University Press.

Chapple, S and R. Garafalo. 1977. *Rock 'n' Roll is Here to Pay*. Chicago: Nelson-Hall

Connolly, M. and A. Kreuger. 2005. "Rockonomics: The Economics of Popular Music." *Working Paper No. 11282*, National Bureau of Economic Research.

Cowen, T. 1996. "Why I Do Not Believe in the Cost Disease." *Journal of Cultural Economics* 20(3): 207–214.

Dibben, N. 2006. "The Socio-Cultural and Learning Experiences of Music Students in a British University." *British Journal of Music Education* 23(1): 91–116.

Drew, R. 2001. *Karaoke Nights: An Ethnographic Rhapsody*. Walnut Creek: AltaMira Press.

Frith, S. 1987. "Towards an Aesthetic of Popular Music." In *Music and Society: The Politics of Composition, Performance and Reception*, eds. R. Leppert and S. McClary, 133–149. Cambridge: Cambridge University Press.

_____. 2004. "What is Bad Music?" In *Bad Music*, eds. C.J. Washburne and M. Derno, 15–36. New York: Routledge.

Goehr, L. 1995–1996. "The Perfect Performance of Music and the Perfect Musical Performance." *New Formations* 27: 1–22.

Gray, O. 2006. *Access One Step: the Official History of the Joiners Arms*. Winchester: Sarsen Press.

Hesmondhalgh, D. 2007. "Musique, émotion et individualisation." *Réseaux* 25(141/142): 203–230.

Kingsbury, H. 1988. *Music, Talent and Performance: A Conservatory Cultural System*. Philadelphia: Temple University Press.

Kreuger, A. 2005. "The Economics of Real Superstars: the Market for Rock Concerts in the Material World." *Journal of Labor Economics* 23(1): 1–30.

Larkin, J. 2006a. "Live Boom Raises Data Questions." *Music Week* (11 March): 10–11.

_____. 2006b. "New Niche Festivals Bubble Up." *Music Week* (29 September): 3.

Moore, A. 2002. "Authenticity as Authentication." *Popular Music* 21(2): 209–233.

Sanjek, R. and D. Sanjek. 1991. *American Popular Music Business in the Twentieth Century*. New York: Oxford University Press.

Thornton, S. 1995. *Club Cultures: Music, Media and Subcultural Capitals*. Cambridge: Polity.

Waksman, S. 2007. "Grand Funk Live! Staging Rock in the Age of the Arena." *In Listen Again: A Momentary History of Pop Music*, ed. E. Weisbard, 157–171. Durham: Duke University Press.

Williamson, J., M. Cloonan and S. Frith, 2003. *Mapping the Music Industry in Scotland: A Report*. Glasgow: Scottish Enterprise.

26

Cultural Policy and the Creative Industries

Adam Behr

A post occasionally prevalent on social media websites, usually coinciding with cuts to arts funding, harks back to the Second World War: when Winston Churchill was asked to cut arts funding in favor of the war effort, he simply replied "Then what are we fighting for?"

No such exchange took place. However, its continuing appeal speaks to both the intensity of feeling around the arts and the question of what government's role in managing or supporting them is supposed to be. In placing "arts funding" within a national value system, it also infers specific types of activity, governmental and artistic—subsidy in the former case and subsid*ized*, rather than market driven, in the latter. But "the arts" exist in a wider context, notably so in the mass market of the twentieth and twenty-first centuries, and government interventions in the arts take place amidst a welter of other concerns. Neither "cultural policy" nor the "creative industries" are straightforwardly discrete areas of activity or investigation. Indeed the term "creative industries" itself is partly a factor of how cultural policy has been enacted, particularly in the anglophone world, over the last three decades and how these industries have, in turn, had an effect on policy formation.

This complexity is compounded by the fact that "culture" is a multivalent term. It can be taken loosely to mean sets of customs and behaviors in social groupings (with boundaries that are, themselves, blurry) or, more specifically, to refer to the practices and products of artistic pursuits. Regarding policy decisions, however, it leans toward the latter—toward those spheres of activity that have, as Hesmondhalgh (2013: 166) writes, "an impact on the primary symbolic domain." But here too, the distinctions between "cultural" and other types of activity and effect—notably economic—are not altogether clear, as the trend toward a policy emphasis on the creative *industries* suggests.

The study of both the creative industries and their policy context is also multifaceted, drawing on "a wide repertoire of research methodologies from a raft of academic discourses" (Scullion and Garcia 2005: 113); sociology, economics, political science and cultural studies are all represented and interwoven. But while it is beyond the scope of this chapter to give a comprehensive account of the history and full reach of the area, it is possible to indicate some key threads.

I begin with a brief overview of the scope of cultural policy, its general remit and some of the primary tensions within its enactment. I then move on to a discussion of a key thrust in recent times, the rise to prominence of the "creative industries" in the policy framework, notably in the west although with echoes elsewhere, particularly in rising economic powers such as China. Some implications of this are teased out through examples illustrating the intersection—and complications—of policy at local, regional and national levels, as well as internationally. Finally, I point toward some current debates and the challenges facing academics in addressing them.

Culture and the State

First, while it seems obvious, it is worth stating that "cultural policy" is inherently political. It is an intentional strategy applied within a power structure and, as such, is informed by ideological and practical concerns. Politics is, of course, intimately connected to both regulatory and economic concerns—often the former in service of the latter. As Street notes (2013: 281), "cultural policy—like all policy—is about allocating scarce resources and resolving coming demands . . . [it] is also about attributing value to the objects of cultural policy—the artistic and cultural forms that are supported and regulated."

But there are choices implicit in this, and opportunity costs. Allocating resources in one direction means not doing so elsewhere and ideology has a role in guiding these choices. Beyond this, there is the matter of *where* these choices apply. Most obviously, but not exclusively, policy is implemented by governments of nation states. In this context, there are different emphases toward culture, historically and geographically. Cloonan (1999: 203–204) outlines three broad strategies: the "authoritarian," which seeks strict controls of culture, found in its most extreme version in the harsh censorship of totalitarian regimes; the "benign state," which adopts a broadly *laissez-faire* approach but will intervene in a reactive way (for example, to restore order, or respond to perceived obscenity); and the "promotional" tendency, which views culture as an asset to be fostered by policies such as those, in France and Canada, of radio-play quotas to protect "national" content.

Cloonan is referring to popular music, but similar attitudes are evident in the case of other arts as well. A nation that heavily censors its musicians, for instance, or adopts an economically protectionist attitude to broadcast content, may well operate similar policies in other fields: the absolutist regimes of Nazi Germany and Stalinist Russia were as unforgiving of theater and cinema as they were of music, for instance, and modern day France imposes levies on cinema and television to support national output which, like broadcast quotas for music, are part of a strategy of *l'exception culturelle*. It should be noted, as Cloonan (1999) acknowledges, that these tendencies are often overlapping and not mutually exclusive.

To this end, it warrants mention that cultural policy touches on other aspects of policy, some of which relate to the management of infrastructure and business, notably broadcasting and media ownership. More specifically, it is also the case that many policies that have a marked effect on cultural provision do not directly refer *to* it. Frith (2013) gives the examples of alcohol licensing and health and safety regulation with regard to live music, and much the same could be said about the impact of education, transport and broader economic policies. But those policies that do relate specifically to cultural products and activities must negotiate between discourses within the arts that fall across long-standing fault-lines, highlighted by theorists from the Frankfurt School onwards, between "high" and "mass" culture—between "art" and "commerce." This tension is most obvious in the relationship between "the arts" and the "marketplace," the key question being: is it the role of the state to support those activities that the market either cannot, or will not?

One potential dichotomy is between "excellence" and "diversity" (Street 2011), between competing claims for resources to promote quality work, or to promote wider access to a range of arts. The former criterion was historically given precedence in British arts funding during the post-War emergence of the Arts Council of Great Britain (ACGB) from the Council for the Encouragement of the Arts. The ACGB was formed during the Second World War to boost morale (Cloonan 2007: 26). It and its successors adopted a broadly paternalistic *modus operandi* until the 1980s, favoring the "high arts" in the allocation of funding as a means of preserving and nurturing work that was seen as uplifting. Under the initial auspices of John Maynard Keynes—whose work as an economist was central to much of post-War settlement—fostering "excellence," free from state intervention, was set as the template for cultural policy.

Baked into this preservation of artistic integrity, however, was a relatively restricted conception of quality art that excluded mass culture in both its folk and commercial forms. This extended to suspicion of forms imported from the United States. "Preservation" in other words extended to a sense of national culture, with implications for the marketplace. Not only could "pop" (like Hollywood movies) be seen to look after itself in the market; it also—echoing Adorno's arguments—failed to meet the criteria for "excellence" and spiritual uplift.

This consensus was increasingly shaken as the 1960s wore into the 1970s and popular culture made a pitch for respectability and authenticity on high-cultural terms. However, the broader mechanisms in place for *funding* the arts and government policy were ultimately disrupted more by the increasingly wide-ranging international shift from Keynesian to Chicago School economics, which in both the United Kingdom and the United States saw the role of the state diminished. Where Keynes had advocated strong government intervention to manage markets and keep the economy on an even keel, economists and politicians influenced by the thinking of Milton Friedman and others at the University of Chicago (as well as Austrian economists like Friedrich Hayek) believed that the role of government should be restricted, and focused on the generation of wealth rather than on spending and regulating markets.[1] Broadly speaking, the emphasis on a free-market economy was inimical to state funding of the arts on both ideological and practical grounds.

A consequence of this was the drive among arts organizations to alter the way in which they framed their contribution to the nation to one that appealed to the prevailing neo-liberal economic philosophy, which favors minimal state spending and holds that society is best served by an unfettered market.[2] With high-culture values no longer central to governmental thinking, the emphasis shifted toward making the case for *investment* rather than support. Money spent on the arts came to be spoken of in relation to the returns it generated: profits, tax revenues and jobs. The key value of culture, in other words, was "instrumental" rather than "intrinsic."

I will return to these different conceptions of cultural value, since they continue to inform both policy and theoretical discussions, but it is worth discussing first some of the terrain—cultural and geographical—within which they are implemented. Cloonan's framework of different strategies refers to nation states but these, of course, are made up of numerous smaller jurisdictions. Local and national policies are not congruent; neither are they always happy bedfellows. The application of policy at the level of the city reveals much about the roots of the broader shift from "cultural policy" to a "creative industries" policy.

Culture and the City

The arts in their broadest sense have been perceived as a mechanism for "uplift," not just in the moral and spiritual realms—as with a Keynesian view—but also in practical and material ways. They have been lauded and deployed for their regenerative effect. Certainly, insofar as the United Kingdom has had a popular music policy, it began at a local level. Frith (1993: 15–24) describes the growth of a "culture industry policy," originating with the Greater London Council (GLC), but spreading to other city authorities throughout the 1980s. As he observes, "the policy meant thinking about local culture in terms of employment and industry—how many jobs were there in the local arts?—and trying to develop new opportunities for artistic production—how many jobs could there be?" (1993: 15).

It is worth noting that several of these authorities were starkly at odds with the prevailing Thatcherite ethos of the time. The GLC fell prey to the Local Government Act of 1986, which the national government used to shut down such centers of opposition (Cloonan 2007: 19). Again, it is difficult to divorce cultural policy from politics more generally. However, the turn toward a view of culture as a material means rather than a symbolic end in itself was to be wide-ranging and enduring.

City authorities have had frequent recourse to both highly specific and diffuse cultural initiatives to drive economic growth or mitigate the effects of funding cuts and unemployment to foster community cohesion. Glasgow, for instance, has used international events and festivals—from the European Commission's City of Culture award in 1990 to the Commonwealth Games in 2014—to bring in funding and regenerate the post-industrial environment (Behr, Brennan and Cloonan 2014: 14). This phenomenon is not uniquely British. For instance, Toronto has benefitted from $1.13 billion of film and television industry activity (Sutherland 2013: 371), while Calgary sought to develop its local music industry (373). Austin, Texas provides another notable example: The presence there of South by Southwest (SXSW), an internationally significant music and technology showcase, is now a key driver of the local economy, a situation that other cities worldwide have sought to emulate.

But tensions remain regarding *who* specifically benefits and *what* counts as either culture or a "creative industry." Cohen's (2007, 2013) work on Liverpool, which also leveraged Capital of Culture[3] status in the name of urban renewal, provides a salutary picture of such activities and their complications. A range of events drew on Liverpool's musical history to present it as a symbol of transformation from post-industrial decline to vibrant urban cultural hub (Cohen 2013: 577). A centerpiece, "People's Opening," decorated the city center, as musicians from Ringo Starr to the Liverpool Philharmonic played, and acrobats performed across landmark buildings. A "musical map" with an accompanying written history made much of high-profile aspects of the city's musical past such as the Cavern Club—home to the early Beatles—and the dance music nightclub "Cream."

These and other events—the re-release of a celebratory book about the city's past emblazoned with the Capital of Culture logo—validated a particular type of cultural memory, bringing such memories within the fold of "heritage" and conferring the symbolic capital that comes with it. But other events were sidelined. Books celebrating a local music shop—the Plug Inn—and a reunion of the bands from the scene of which it was a part in the 1970s were absent from the official narrative. Beyond this, the precinct that had been a training and socializing ground for those local musicians— derelict by 2010—was covered up to serve as a projection screen for the official performances of the People's Opening (Cohen 2013: 580).

Developments such as these are resonant of Europe-wide trends in using cultural history to drive urban and economic development. This is achieved by way of promoting cultural heritage and the cultural industries, as well as by developing international links (and tourism) through the fostering of cultural diversity (582–587). However, these strategies tend to privilege certain types of cultural activity: the commercially successful (the Beatles and Cream in Liverpool, rather than the unheralded musicians of the Plug Inn scene) and the "high cultural" (Mozart and waltz in Vienna, as opposed to Vienna's post-war popular culture). "Heritage," then, becomes refracted through commercial and civic considerations which inform particular kinds of cultural memory. The irony is that the broad sweep of cultural policy at the level of the city, in seeking to valorize diversity, integration and inclusion, can often marginalize the very groups that it aims to benefit: the economically deprived agents working outside the commercial mainstream.

From "Culture" to "Creative Industries"

Emphasizing the material benefits of cultural activity has underwritten another conceptual shift. The origins of city cultural policies and their provision of "cultural quarters" and "creative clusters" to drive growth (Cohen 2007: 191, Hesmondhalgh 2013: 170) were located in left-leaning local authorities. However, this was set against the broader retrenchment of the state and an emboldened private sector. Hesmondhalgh and Pratt (2005: 5) note the challenges to state involvement in media and communications in the 1980s, beginning in the United States and spreading internationally. Economic liberalization ran alongside the increasing marketization of the "cultural industries," increasing the globalization of intellectual property mechanisms and, from the 1990s, the rise of the web as a source of both disruption and the fuel-injected growth of transnational trade.[4]

While such developments have favored transnational business interests, a corollary has been their appeal to national governments seeking to portray themselves as inclusive while simultaneously favoring the free market over *dirigisme*. As Hesmondhalgh and Pratt put it:

> A great attraction of cultural industries policy . . . for many politicians and advisors, was that cultural policy, previously on the margins in many areas of government, could be seen to be economically relevant in an era when policy was judged primarily in terms of its fiscal rewards . . . Moreover, creative industries policy could be portrayed as democratising and anti-elitist, as opposed to the supposed elitism of arts policy aimed at subsidising cultural production that could not meet its costs through the market.
>
> (ibid.)

A tendency to focus on social and cultural concerns became, by the early twenty-first century, an emphasis on economic concerns. An emblematic change in the United Kingdom was the Labour government's replacement of the Department of National Heritage with the Department for Culture, Media and Sport. Besides the tonal shift away from high culture, this also served to bring cultural pursuits under the same policy roof as the burgeoning internet businesses. Conflating these categories broadened the scope of "creativity," aligning music, television, cinema and so on with software, blurring the boundaries between support for artists and business development.

This trend is not specific to the United Kingdom. The international harmonization of copyright regimes accompanies a general shift toward creative industries policies. Homan (2013: 389), for example, describes the echoes of this shift in Australia as, concomitantly, "the cultural [being] increasingly called upon to pull its weight as part of GDP considerations." Neither is it restricted to the global west. Hesmondhalgh (2013: 178–179) describes the role of creative industries in the emergence of China as a world power in the marketplace. Flew (2012: 42) in addition notes the "uptake of creative industries as a nodal policy concept in East Asia, notably the fast developing 'tiger' economies of Singapore, Hong Kong, Korea and Taiwan."

However, by folding together under the "creative" umbrella the work of the technical, financial and symbolic domains—such as the work of the software developer, record label boss, independent bass guitarist and institutionally employed opera singer—creative industries policy poses a raft of difficult questions for a wide range of practitioners. The creative industries' drift toward the center of economic policy is fraught with theoretical and practical complications over both what *counts* as culture—or creativity—and how such activity is *counted*.

Creativity and Cultural Value

The basis of much thinking on creativity and culture lies in a Romantic view of artistic endeavor (Bennett 2006) and Kantian aesthetics (O'Connor 2010: 15). However, the privileging of artistic autonomy (not least from the market) implied in this view sits uneasily with the drive toward marketization, even while this latter tendency retains—indeed deploys—the rhetorical tropes of cultural value.

This trend was evident in Scotland with the reconfiguration of its Arts Council (previously broadly aligned with Keynesian values) into "Creative Scotland," a more creative industries- (and therefore market-) oriented funding body. The creation of this agency caused an imbroglio, pitting a significant section of the artistic community against its own state support agency (Stevenson 2013). While this has brought popular culture—certainly popular music—more firmly into the realm of state funding, there remains a lack of clarity over the distinction between commercial activity (a matter for enterprise and industry boards) and creative work (a cultural matter). Additionally, the fact that a large proportion of "creative" workers are either self-employed or part of small to medium enterprises—and often support such activities with paid work in other sectors—makes their contribution difficult to measure. In any case, key issues such as copyright and the Standard Industrial Classification codes used to account for the contributions of different sectors reside in the purview of international bodies and treaties (Behr and Brennan 2014: 175–176).

However, the arguments over how to support creative work—and whose job it is in the first place—reveal a more fundamental tension in cultural policy. For throughout the turn toward "creative industries," the tension between instrumental and intrinsic cultural value remained improperly addressed by policymakers. The democratizing urge to include popular (and commercial) as well as high culture (and potentially elitist) work within cultural policy goes hand in hand with a move away from *ars gratia artis*: "art for art's sake."

Even when not predicated on specifically economic values, the discourse of support for the arts on social grounds collapses into what Belfiore (2012) calls a "defensive instrumentalism," whereby appeals to (ideally measurable) benefits—such as falling crime rates or mental health outcomes—cut the discussion adrift from fundamental questions of ideology. Or they at least render them overly mechanistic, reframing them as a battle between particular sorts of material benefit and abandoning a *positive* case for the arts to the winds of quantification. As Belfiore observes (2012: 107), "the exquisitely ideological question of making the (political) case for the arts has been translated in the rather more technical (and therefore apparently neutral) issue of arts impact assessment, with the focus firmly on the methodological problems of evaluation rather than on thorny questions of cultural value."

There is a pragmatic case to be made for this strategy. O'Brien (2010) argues that the distinction between "instrumental" and "intrinsic" values is unhelpful, and that the arts must speak a language that policymakers understand in order to secure funding. This need not entail an appeal to economics, but should recognize the real priorities of policymakers—the allocation of resources—and the cost–benefit analyses by which they assess them. (It will always be difficult to make a case for, say, funding opera in the face of calls for new schools and hospitals if it relies on the allure of intrinsic cultural value.)

Nevertheless, the overarching relationship between culture and policy connects to matters of power and society that frame and inform the structure within which pragmatic concerns such as O'Brien's operate. As Street (2013: 284) puts it, "The value of music (and culture more generally) needs to be debated in explicitly political terms . . . the question is how we understand and assess that value, which is what is entailed by the making of cultural policy."

Looking beyond either a purely intrinsic or instrumental notion of value reveals the common ground between market-driven and romantically infused experiences of the arts. As Stanbridge notes:

> the arts have always been a profoundly social activity, have always had instrumental benefits, have always been part of a mixed economy of subsidized and commercial activity that the outmoded discourse of "aesthetic experience" and "intrinsic benefits" only serves

to obscure . . . It is perhaps in this pragmatic blend of human experience that arts and cultural activities find their most convincing justifications for government support, succumbing neither to the blatant economism of "instrumental benefits," nor to the traditional aestheticism of "intrinsic benefits."

(2008: 6)

For Stanbridge, this blend includes the capacity of art forms that are marginal to the marketplace— contemporary jazz and improvised music are his examples—to nevertheless inform broader socio-cultural debates. And these debates speak to the conditions on the ground in which artistic, economic and social activity all takes place.

Citizens, Consumers, and Culture

Just as Cohen's example of Liverpool's celebration shows how particular types of cultural memory can be privileged in specific policy applications, the case of the merger between Live Nation and Ticketmaster illustrates how the prevailing policy climate feeds into regulatory and legal decisions. Concerns about the concentration of ownership and its possible effect on diversity and access to provision were overridden by competition authorities in the United States, the United Kingdom and Norway, all of whose primary criterion was the likely effect on the price of tickets in the market (Street 2012: 582). The regulators viewed the key rights associated with live music provision as "property rights," which trumped other considerations—plurality, access and expression. Music (culture) was afforded no dispensation beyond its status as a (financially) transactional good. The consequences of this are far-reaching. A political environment that places cultural transactions into the same category as financial ones suggests a notion of cultural stakeholders as consumers first, and active citizens (with rights beyond those that apply to property) second. Street puts it this way:

> The law is important to the form, content and quality of live music, but only within the confines of a political and legal order that sees live music as unrelated to the issues of plurality and freedom of expression that apply to other cultural forms or other jurisdictions . . . if we live a bad or inadequate cultural theory, we see the production and consumption of live music in the same terms that we see the production of insurance or banking services.
>
> (2012: 584)

This issue also bleeds into cultural policy research. A notable effect of both the disruptions caused by digital technology and the policy turn toward the creative industries is that industry bodies have become more active and effective in lobbying governments. Nation states in the west have, to follow Cloonan's formula, moved from a broadly "benign" strategy to one that is more "promotional." This leads to a closer involvement with industry. The call on evidence-based policy coincides with industry's need to protect its interests, a key means for this being the production of evidence for its contribution to the economy. The subsidized sector is represented in this equation too. If it is to apply O'Brien's strategy, it must also provide evidence to justify support. This provides both opportunities and challenges for academics. Theorizing and researching culture and cultural policy require sensitivity to a couple of key concerns.

First, this theorizing and research are taking place against a background of rapid technological development that has broadened the reach of capital. In a creative economy of digital products increasingly predicated on experience rather than physical commodities, consumers, as Thrift points out, "contribute their intellectual labor and all kinds of work to production in the cause of making better goods, in a kind of *generalized outsourcing*." In this way, "migrations regularly occur between production and consumption and vice versa" (Thrift 2006: 282; emphasis in original). The constant feedback between users of social media, games, apps and their parent brands is, effectively, a form of research and development (R&D). The situation is fluid. Research occurs in an environment which "is being constructed by business, and furthermore by a business that uses theory as an instrumental *method*, as a source of *expertise* and as an *affective register* to inform an everyday life that is increasingly built from that theory" (2006: 301; emphasis in original).

Second, empirical research involves negotiating between the diverse requirements of policymakers and industry with a view to whom, ultimately, is being served. The subsidized arts is not the only sector that needs to show "impact" to stake a claim to resources. The academic drive to make evidence relevant to policy makers means engaging with industry and cultural organizations, as well as their agendas. This can be a fraught process. Williamson, Cloonan and Frith (2011: 466–467) classify as "knowledge resistance" situations such as the Recording Industry Association of America's (RIAA) flat-out rejection of research claiming a minimal effect on sales from illegal downloading. Similar issues arose when their own mapping exercise of the music industry in Scotland ran into complaints from royalty collection societies about their sources of information and pressure from funding body Scottish Enterprise (which had commissioned the report) about the wording of the executive summary (463). Their prescription that academic work should ultimately benefit "citizens . . . who have no one else lobbying policymakers on their behalf" (462) aligns with Street's concern for an adequate cultural theory that serves the public interest rather than interested parties. Cultural policy research, in other words, needs to work with its subjects—policymakers and the creative industries—without lapsing into advocacy.

Conclusion

Cultural policy entails a balance between blunt expediency in a complex network of economic and social concerns and value systems that, as Churchill's apocryphal statement suggests, reach beyond them. An account of the "instrumental" value of the arts—particularly beyond their economic worth—and due consideration of appeals to their "intrinsic" value—which speak to a more sophisticated experience than raw numbers can capture—are both necessary for the formulation of a policy framework that does justice to the full spectrum of social rights, needs and agents. But neither is, in itself, sufficient. Attention to the "cultural industries" plays a valuable role in mitigating elitism and exclusivity in the symbolic domain although, if untempered, it risks tipping the balance toward a different type of exclusivity, one that puts the needs of capital—and transnational capital with scant concern for civic or social goods—above access to the potential benefits of those industries' cultural products.

If, as Stanbridge suggests, the rhetoric of "excellence" and the duty to foster democratic cultural experiences are compatible, then the question of subsidy versus the market becomes less about the private *versus* the public sector, and more about how to effectively—and fairly—manage their relationship. By the same token, while it must handle the competing demands of often self-interested industry and sometimes distracted policymakers, cultural policy research can open up a space for a discussion of how to negotiate the political discourses with which culture itself is imbricated— the politics of culture in tandem with the culture of politics. None of these are simple tasks but they need not be attempted in isolation. Neither should competing claims degenerate into a zero-sum game. Recognizing the political dimension of culture and the cultural seedbed of the creative industries is ultimately not just a theoretical exercise. Rather, it is a precondition to achieving the goal of a balanced cultural policy.

Notes

1   Cloonan (2007: 7–38) provides a more detailed history of British policy changes, while Loosely (2012) offers useful points of comparison with the experience of France.
2   "Neoliberalism" is a contested term. Proponents use the term to refer to a revival of the classical liberal economic belief in the benefits of the market. Critics, on the other hand, see radical economic reforms, the diminution of the state and of welfare spending, as well as the spread of capitalism more generally. Here, I take it to refer to "The view that human needs are best served by an unregulated 'free market'" (Hesmondhalgh 2013: 99) and the policies of deregulation and spending-cuts that are associated with it.
3   The competition was launched in 1985 as "City of Culture" and re-named "Capital of Culture" in 1999. Through this competition, the European Commission selects a city to host and run an annual cultural program from nominations made to the European Parliament (Cohen 2013: 577).
4   Notable developments include agreements on Trade-Related Aspects of Intellectual Property rights as part of the General Agreement on Trade and Tariffs in 1994, the Digital Millennium Copyright Act in the United States (1998) and the EU Copyright Directive (2001), all of which sought to protect corporate interests in the face of the internet's growth. See Hesmondhalgh (2013: 160–163) and Laing (2004: 80–84) for detailed accounts.

References

Behr, A. and M. Brennan. 2014. "The Place of Popular Music in Scotland's Cultural Policy." *Cultural Trends* 23(3): 169–177.

Behr, A., M. Brennan and M. Cloonan. 2014. *The Cultural Value of Live Music from the Pub to the Stadium: Getting Beyond the Numbers*. Research by the University of Edinburgh and the University of Glasgow: Part of the Arts and Humanities Research Council's Cultural Value Project. http://livemusicexchange.org/wp-content/uploads/The-Cultural-Value-of-Live-Music-Pub-to-Stadium-report.pdf.

Belfiore, E. 2012. "'Defensive Instrumentalism' and the Legacy of New Labour's Cultural Policies." *Cultural Trends* 21(2): 103–111.

Bennett, O. 2006. "Intellectuals, Romantics and Cultural Policy." *Cultural Trends* 12(2): 117–134.

Cloonan, M. 1999. "Pop and the Nation-State: Towards a Theorisation." *Popular Music* 18(2): 193–207.

_____. 2007. *Popular Music and the State in the UK: Culture, Trade or Industry?* Aldershot: Ashgate.

Cohen, S. 2007. *Decline, Renewal and the City in Popular Music Culture: Beyond the Beatles.* Aldershot: Ashgate

_____. 2013. "Musical Memory, Heritage and Local Identity: Remembering the Popular Music Past in a European Capital of Culture." *International Journal of Cultural Policy* 19(5): 576–594.

Flew, T. 2012. *Creative Industries: Culture and Policy.* London: Routledge.

Frith, S. 1993. "Popular Music and the Local State." In *Rock and Popular Music: Politics, Policies, Institutions*, eds. T. Bennett, S. Frith, L. Grossberg, J. Shepherd and G. Turner, 15–24. London: Routledge.

_____. 2013. "The Social Value of Music (in the Context of European Regeneration Policy)." Address to the European Music Council Annual Forum in Glasgow on 19 April 2013. http://livemusicexchange.org/blog/the-social-value-of-music-in-the-context-of-european-regeneration-policy-simon-frith.

Hesmondhalgh, D. 2013. *The Cultural Industries*, 3rd ed. London: Sage.

Hesmondhalgh, D. and A. Pratt. 2005. "Cultural Industries and Cultural Policy." *International Journal of Cultural Policy* 11(1): 1–13.

Homan, S. 2013. "From Coombs to Crean: Popular Music and Cultural Policy in Australia." *International Journal of Cultural Policy* 19(3): 382–398.

Laing, D. 2004. "Copyright, Politics and the International Music Industry." In *Music and Copyright*, eds. S. Frith and L. Marshall, 70–85. Edinburgh: Edinburgh University Press.

Loosely, D.L. 2012. "Democratising the Popular: the Case of Pop Music in France and Britain." *International Journal of Cultural Policy* 18(5): 579–592.

O'Brien, D. 2010. *Measuring the Value of Culture: a Report to the Department for Culture, Media and Sport.* London: Department for Culture, Media and Sport. https://www.gov.uk/government/uploads/system/uploads/attachment_data/file/77933/measuring-the-value-culture-report.pdf.

O'Connor, J. 2010. *The Cultural and Creative Industries: a Literature Review*, 2nd ed. Newcastle upon Tyne: Creativity, Culture and Education (CCE).

Scullion, A. and B. Garcia. 2005. "What is Cultural Policy Research?" *International Journal of Cultural Policy* 11(2): 113–115.

Stanbridge, A. 2008. "From the Margins to the Mainstream: Jazz, Social Relations, and Discourses of Value." *Critical Studies in Improvisation* 4(1): www.criticalimprov.com/article/view/361/959.

Stevenson, D. 2013. "What's the Problem Again? The Problematisation of Cultural Participation in Scottish Cultural Policy." *Cultural Trends* 22(2): 77–85.

Street, J. 2011. "The Popular, the Diverse and the Excellent: Political Values and UK Cultural Policy." *International Journal of Cultural Policy* 17(4): 380–393.

_____. 2012. "From Gigs to Giggs: Politics, Law and Live Music." *Social Semiotics* 22(5): 575–585.

_____. 2013. "Music, Markets and Manifestos." *International Journal of Cultural Policy* 19(3): 281–297.

Sutherland, R. 2013. "Why Get Involved? Finding Reasons for Municipal Interventions in the Canadian Music Industry." *International Journal of Cultural Policy* 19(3): 366–381.

Thrift, N. 2006. "Re-Inventing Invention: New Tendencies in Capitalist Commodification." *Economy and Society* 35(2): 279–306.

Williamson, J., M. Cloonan and S. Frith. 2011. "Having an Impact? Academics, the Music Industries and the Problem of Knowledge." *International Journal of Cultural Policy* 17(5): 459–474.

27

Copyright

LEE MARSHALL

Anyone who wants even a rudimentary understanding of how the music industry works needs to have some understanding of copyright. Whereas once such a statement may have been deemed an exaggeration, it is today more commonly accepted as the fortunes of the music industry since the digital turn have garnered almost as much media coverage as the music stars it supports. However, what is also true is that anyone who wants even a rudimentary understanding of copyright needs to have some understanding of the workings of the music industry (or a similar creative industry such as film or publishing) because copyright is not a fixed, abstract, legal principle but is, rather, an outcome of negotiations between interested parties and something re-negotiated in the daily practices of those in the creative industries. While the discourse surrounding copyright often concerns "creativity," copyright is much more to do with business and, as such, the nuances and inflections of copyright change with the circumstances of those involved in the copyright industries.

Writing an introduction to copyright is a hazardous business. For one thing, copyright can be ridiculously complicated, so full of jargon and acronyms that it might be suggested that current laws have been designed for the specific purpose of muddying the principles of copyright and keeping copyright lawyers in employment. There is also the problem that copyright, and the music industry more generally, are fairly fast-moving phenomena (at least compared to academic publishing). The danger here lies in providing details of specific copyright acts or piracy initiatives that may have been superseded well before this chapter is published, let alone in five or ten years' time. Finally, there is the complication that copyright is not really one thing. This is true in a very specific sense— legally, "copyright" is actually a series of different rights that offers the rights holder the exclusive right to do various things to the work in question (and not just the right to copy)—but it is true in a broader sense, too, because different countries have traditionally had their own copyright traditions (or, in many non-western countries, no tradition of copyright at all). Over time, through international agreements, copyright has become increasingly "harmonized" (a musical term that disguises a great deal of discord), a process that accelerated once intellectual property rights were brought under the remit of the World Trade Organization (WTO) through the Agreement on Trade-Related Aspects of Intellectual Property Rights (TRIPS) of 1994. Even so, there remains a great deal of international variation about how copyright is implemented and enforced, dependent upon different cultural traditions and industrial structures. Truly understanding copyright in the music industry, therefore, involves understanding how it works in Brazil, South Korea, Mexico, Poland, Ukraine and so on, not just how it affects the major US and western European music companies and their music consumers.[1]

To circumvent these hazards, this chapter, as much as possible, deals with the broad principles of copyright. In the next section I will outline and define some of the fundamental terms required to understand the basics. The section after explicitly considers some of the ways that copyright works in the music industry. Following this, I shall move on to some more theoretical discussions, considering the rationale and justifications for copyright before considering some criticisms of copyright and particular controversies within the music industry. Finally, there will be a brief discussion of piracy as well as some concluding comments about understanding copyright in the music industry sociologically.

Copyright Basics

This section is essentially broken down into three questions: what does copyright protect, what does it enable and how long does it last? To begin with the first question, copyright offers protection for cultural expressions that are original (generally referred to as "works").[2] The word original is extremely important and I will return to it later but, for the time being, I want to concentrate on another important word: "expression." Copyright protects expressions of ideas, not the ideas themselves. That someone had the idea to write a song about, say, surfing does not mean that someone else cannot write a song on the same topic; what it does mean is that they cannot use the same words, or the same chords or melody, to express that idea. In theories of copyright, this is known as the idea/expression dichotomy. The idea/expression dichotomy exists to ensure that the flow of ideas in society is not restricted by copyright (Vaidhyanathan 2003: 28–34).

Because copyright protects expressions, those expressions have to be "fixed," which means that they have to be recorded in some way so that they have a material reality. When the first copyright act was enacted (the Statute of Anne in the United Kingdom in 1709), the idea of something being fixed was unproblematic—it meant something had to be written down. The kind of culture being protected was also relatively uncontroversial too—it was basically assumed to protect writing (novels, treatises, poems, play scripts and so on). As technology has advanced, however, more and more forms of "fixation" have been brought under the protection of copyright, from plate engraving to photography, moving pictures, sound recording, video games and so on. Forms of culture other than literature also began to be protected, including music, which was protected from 1831 in the United States and from 1842 in the United Kingdom.

So, copyright protects original expressions. To whom is copyright granted and what rights does it grant? Copyright comes into being the moment a work is created (a common misconception, especially in the United States—because it was true here until 1976—is that one must register for copyright). It is initially vested in "the author" of a work. Again, in 1709, the idea of the author was relatively unproblematic; it meant the man (it was almost always a man) who wrote the words. As time has gone on, however, this has become more complicated: today companies can be considered as authors and many works are produced under the "work for hire" doctrine whereby companies are treated as the author of works created by their employees.[3]

Copyright is much more than just the right to copy; it grants the rights holder the exclusive right to perform (or to license another party to perform) certain actions in relation to the work. As well as the right to copy, the most significant rights enabled by copyright include the right to adapt the work, to make "derivative works" (such as making a television show based on a stage play), the right to issue copies of the work to the public, the right to broadcast the work, and the right to perform the work in public. Copyright is therefore sometimes said to consist of a "basket of rights."

Although copyright grants owners the exclusive right to reproduce the work, there are some limits placed on rights holders' powers. First, a number of countries have defined certain actions that the public can perform without infringing copyright. These are generally known as "fair use" or "fair dealing" provisions. Fair use provisions include the right to reproduce part of a work for criticism or review, for news reporting or for the purpose of parody. In some countries, consumers are entitled to make a backup copy of copyrighted works that they have purchased (Marshall 2004: 197–199). Second, there are a small number of "compulsory licenses," whereby states have determined that some acts do not have to be authorized by the rights holder so long as "equitable remuneration" is made (often at a rate determined by the government). The most significant compulsory licenses relate to broadcasting (broadcasters do not have to request permission to broadcast a song but, in most countries, are required to pay a "set rate" for any song they broadcast) and to the ability to record a song (as soon as a composition has been recorded once, anyone else can record that song without permission so long as they pay the copyright holder the mandatory rate).

A third, and very significant, limitation on copyright is that it lasts for a finite period. The rationale for a finite period emphasizes copyright's cultural rather than economic dimensions. It reflects the understanding that works subject to copyright are actually part of a shared cultural heritage that should be freely accessible to everyone and be available for contemporary creators to use when creating new works (a similar rationale as for the idea/expression dichotomy). Works that have fallen out of copyright (or where copyright was never enforced in the first place) are, therefore, said to be in the "public domain." However, the duration of copyright has continually expanded, stretching the definition of what might be considered "finite." This will be discussed further below.

Copyright initially vests in the author of a work. However, a vital element of copyright is that it is transferrable—it can be sold.[4] This is why copyright is so important to the business of culture. An aspiring novelist or songwriter may own the copyright to their new creation, but it is financially worthless if they do not have the financial capital to print and distribute the work. Intermediaries such as publishing companies thus offer to provide the necessary infrastructure to turn the novel or song into a bestseller but require the transferal of copyright in return (or, if the author has more bargaining power, perhaps just a proportion of the copyright income).[5] This exchange is why copyright can only be considered within the context of business; it does not really exist in the abstract as it only becomes valuable in a commercial context in which authors are expected to transfer their copyrights to publishers (this was the situation right from the beginning: when petitioning for protection in the 1700s, it is clear that the publishers saw the right as *de facto* belonging to them rather than the authors). For that reason, as Kretschmer and his colleagues (2010) argue, contract is more important than copyright for most creators.

This section has been written in as neutral and abstract a manner as possible, but what should be clear from the preceding paragraphs is that copyright is riven with controversy and disagreement. What should be protected by copyright, for how long they should be protected, what the scope of protection should be, what rights the public should have, what should be considered a "work for hire," whether moral rights should exist or not are all political decisions, with parties on both sides arguing vigorously for their vested interests. These interests come from existing business practices, with new technologies and new practices repeatedly resisted by those well served by existing laws.

Copyright in the Music Industry

With that in mind, let us now consider some of the key ways in which copyright operates in the music industry specifically. The aim here is to keep things as simple as possible (not easy, as shall be seen) so let's begin with an individual songwriter who has written a new song. As the author of the song, she is the first owner of the copyright (though both the lyrics and the music are protectable separately—someone else cannot simply put new lyrics to the same tune and call it a new song: it would be a derivative work). As copyright owner, the songwriter has the exclusive right to do all of the things mentioned in the previous section. In most cases, however, because they want their song to be heard by the public or because they want to make money from it, she will enlist the help of third parties to help "exploit" the rights. To do this, she can either "assign" (usually by selling outright) or license the rights to other parties. Things get complicated at this point because rights are limited by territory (although international treaties have harmonized many standards). Thus it is possible to license the right to publicize the work to one party in India and to another party in Canada, and for different periods of time. Because of these complications, the songwriter is likely to enlist the support of a music publisher. The publisher offers expertise and networks that the songwriter may lack (as well as actively promoting the songwriter's work) and will normally ask for a percentage of any income generated by the rights to that song (what the percentage is depends upon the relative power of the songwriter, whether they have had previous success and so on).

Financially, one of the most significant rights is the right to record the song. If a recording artist would like to record the song they must license the right from the copyright owner. Once a recording of the song is made, then a second copyright emerges—the right in the specific sound recording (in many countries, this right is known as a "neighboring right"). Recognizing that there are two distinct copyrights in music is extremely important. When music first became eligible for copyright protection, what was understood as "music" was straightforward—the written score. Economically, this made sense as "the music industry," at least until the 1920s, was dominated by the music publishing industry, with publishers selling sheet music to professional and amateur performers alike. During the course of the twentieth century, however, the record rather than the score became commonly understood as "the song," "the music industry" became dominated by the recording industry and copyright law adapted to reflect this by creating a new right in sound recordings.[6] Ownership gives rights holders (which are mainly record labels) the exclusive right to reproduce the recording, to cause the recording to be heard in public, to broadcast the recording, or to create new recordings that include the original recording, or any part of it.

There thus exist two copyrights in any popular record: one in the underlying composition and one in the specific recording. The initial owner of the copyright in the sound recording is the party responsible for making the recording (known in legal terms as the "producer"). This has conventionally been the record label, and the record labels' dominance of the music industry in the latter half of the twentieth century resulted from their ownership of most rights in sound recordings (Laing 2002: 185). The different beneficiaries (the songwriter and the recording company) lead to slightly different emphases: neighboring rights tend to last for less time than copyright (currently seventy years in the European Union and ninety-five years in the United States) but they also tend to be less flexible (meaning more strictly enforceable) than copyright in compositions and there are no statutory license restrictions.[7]

As might already be apparent, there are innumerable ways in which copyrights in music can be "exploited." Some of the most common are:

- Selling records: for example, when Apple sells an MP3 on iTunes, approximately 60 percent of the price will be returned to the owners of the copyright in the sound recording, with a further 10 percent or so being returned to the owners of the copyright in the underlying composition (the return to songwriters is often known as "mechanical royalties" because it is payment for the mechanical reproduction of the song).[8]
- Live performance: results in a payment to the owners of the composition copyright (at the end of a show, a performer is expected to submit a list of songs performed so that a royalty can be paid to the copyright owners).
- Broadcasting: in most countries, broadcasting songs on the radio, television or the internet results in a payment to the owners of both the songwriting and the recording copyright.[9]
- Licensing music for use in TV shows, movies, video games, advertisements and anything else that includes music: for example, if a TV producer wants to use a recording in a show, then they have to get the agreement of (and agree a fee with) the owners of both copyrights.

In some instances, because rights for sound recordings tend to be more expensive than rights for songs, TV producers will choose to re-record the song for use in their film or advertisement, using a "soundalike" band. They would thus only have to pay the owners of the songwriting copyright as the producers themselves would own the rights to the new sound recording!

- Ringtones: a polyphonic ringtone would be considered a derivative work and result in a payment to the owner of the copyright in the composition; a ringtone using the original recording would also result in a payment to the owner of the right in the sound recording.
- Licensing music for use in other recordings: particularly since the rise of hip hop, "sampling" records (repeatedly using small snatches of other records) has become a more common element of popular music. When an artist uses a sample in their song, they will often have to get agreement (known as "clearance") from both the rights holder in the sound recording and the composition (often for a fee).

When one considers all the different rights, the ways in which they can be exploited and the fact that the rights exist independently for different territories, then it becomes apparent that keeping track of the uses of one's music is beyond the scope of any individual musician, or even publisher or record label. Things are simplified (at least a little) by the use of compulsory licenses. However, most rights are handled collectively, with "collecting societies" handling the licensing of specific rights such as performance rights (the Performing Rights Society [PRS] in the United Kingdom, the American Society of Composers, Authors and Publishers [ASCAP] and Broadcast Music, Inc. [BMI] in the United States) and mechanical rights (the Mechanical-Copyright Protection Society [MCPS] in the United Kingdom). The collecting societies keep track of all uses of copyright music, collect the fees and distribute the income to rights holders (keeping 8–10 percent of the income for their efforts).[10]

Justifications for Copyright

When considering the justifications and rationales offered for copyright, the warning given at the start of this chapter—that copyright has to be understood in the context of business—becomes most important as it is at this point that arguments about copyright sometimes drift away from the business of culture. At its core, copyright exists to ease an economic obstacle to a public policy objective. It has long been accepted that the dissemination of knowledge is socially beneficial: scientific knowledge enhances humanity's practical abilities and, through public debate, generates further knowledge, while cultural knowledge enhances our collective and individual capacities for qualities such as reflexivity and compassion. However, knowledge (information) is different from most other kinds of goods because one person's use of the good does not diminish someone else's potential enjoyment of it (unlike, say, a hamburger). Indeed, the second person's enjoyment of, say, a book may actually be enhanced by the first person having "consumed" it, as it means that they can discuss it, share their views and so on. In economic terms, this quality is described as being "non-rivalrous," and it is a characteristic of what are known as "public goods" (Towse 2004: 58–59). Information is a public good, as are such things as fresh air and street lighting. A second characteristic of a public good is that it is "non-excludable." This means that it is impossible to prevent someone from enjoying the good even though they have not paid for it (so, for example, you cannot prevent a person from making use of street lighting even though they have not paid their taxes). This is where we get to the nub of the economic problem: if someone can benefit from a product without paying for it (and we therefore assume that they will not pay for it), the producer's potential reward for producing the good is undermined, reducing the likelihood that they will produce it (this is the circumstance in which the recording industry currently finds itself).

We are thus left with a dilemma: something exists that has been acknowledged to be socially beneficial, but conventional free-market economics does not adequately provide an incentive for its production. Copyright is the mechanism that attempts to resolve the dilemma. To achieve the socially desirable goal of making cultural work and other information available to the public, copyright gives the copyright owner a time-limited monopoly to make reproductions and distribute to the public, creating a situation whereby consumers cannot access the good for free and other producers cannot simply undercut the prices of the copyright holder.

Because copyright exists to provide an incentive for the publication of information, it originally focused on publishers. Over time, however, copyright has come to be justified in terms of *authorship* rather than publication which, many critics argue, has fundamentally changed the nature of copyright law (for example, Patterson and Lindberg 1991). The first way in which authors are used as a justification for copyright is a simple "just desserts" argument. It seems inherently fair that someone who writes a book or composes a song should receive some reward for their effort, and that the promise of reward should provide an incentive for them to create new works. However, while artists certainly need some form of income, it is not entirely clear that they are incentivized in the same manner as those seeking to make a profit from publishing. Neither is it clear that copyright is economically beneficial for the majority of creators, given that they exist in a context in which they have to trade away the majority of their rights. Furthermore, it can plausibly be argued that an individual writing a new song and then keeping it to themselves is not socially beneficial; it only becomes socially beneficial once the public get to hear the song. From this perspective, copyright should remain a reward for publication, not creation.

In response to such criticisms, those in favor of strengthening and extending copyright law use a stronger form of justification grounded in a specific understanding of authorship that developed during the nineteenth century (not coincidentally, alongside the development of copyright). This understanding, known as "romantic authorship," emphasizes an organic relationship between the author and the work, with the work interpreted as emerging wholly out of the author's imagination in much the same way as an infant emerges out of a mother's womb. Romantic authors thus become recognized as special individuals who create things out of nothing and their works become understood as being like their children, containing within them the seeds of the creator's genius. When understood this way, copyright can easily be interpreted as a monument to authors, offering some small recognition to these heroic figures and, from nineteenth century romantic poets to twenty-first-century session musicians, this trope of the deserving author has been a key element in copyright debates (Jaszi 1991, Boyle 1996, Toynbee 2001, Marshall 2005).

Criticisms and Controversies

The rhetorical shift from understanding copyright as an incentive for publication to understanding it as a reward for authorship has a number of significant implications. Many of them stem from the problematic concept of "originality." Actually, within copyright law, the threshold for originality is very low: it basically means "has not been copied." Ideologically, however, the idea is more significant: "originality" is one of the keystones of romantic authorship, emphasizing the author's ability to create things from nothing. Originality thus becomes a term signifying considerable aesthetic value (read a few album reviews and you can quite clearly see this within popular music discourse). Added to this are numerous other, complementary, notions relating to the work's "paternity": art as self-expression and so on.

The problem is that creativity rarely, if ever, occurs in the manner characterized in the ideal of romantic authorship. For one thing, new cultural works are never "purely" original: even the most radical and groundbreaking works make use of themes, motifs and concepts from already-existing works. No one writes a song without having heard other songs. This is a fact long-acknowledged by both authors[11] and critics[12] though, within the study of literature, criticisms of "author-centric" understandings of creativity only really accelerated as post-structuralism spread throughout the humanities and social sciences (for example, see Barthes 1977, Foucault 1984). A second weakness of the romantic model is that authors rarely work in isolation—writers talk to friends and colleagues, are given advice by editors and so on. As Toynbee (2001) argues, authorship is something inherently social, shaped by collective as much as individual forces.

If one considers the history of popular music, then it is quite easy to see how these "alternative" forms of creativity dominate. The daily practices by which new music is created are inherently collective, with input from band members and session musicians as well as producers, sound engineers and so on. At a broader cultural level, one can easily see how specific melodies and phrases were used interchangeably across hundreds of folk and blues songs, while particular styles and phrases become widely imitated in more commercial contexts. All in all, it is hard to justify an argument that a popular song is a purely individual creation. This would not be a problem (no one really believes that it could be) were it not for the fact that copyright is based upon a model of authorship that exaggerates individual creativity and thus, critics argue, awards too much power to copyright holders. This ultimately restricts creativity rather than rewarding it. "Sampling" is one area of popular music where this problem is brought into focus.

Sampling is the act of taking a portion of an already-existing recording, manipulating it (through repeating it, for example) and recontextualizing it in a new song. The practice of sampling first became popular among rap artists in the late 1970s and early 1980s, emerging from the practice of what is now called turntabling (DJs scratching and sliding records to create new grooves). It became more popular as digital recording devices became more readily available, enabling artists to reproduce, manipulate and repeat virtually any pre-existing recording. In the early days of hip hop, bands like Public Enemy and De La Soul liberally used samples throughout their songs, creating sonic encapsulations of the fragmented world around them in albums such as *It Takes a Nation of Millions to Hold Us Back* (1987) and *Three Feet High and Rising* (1989).

Sampling can be seen as a continuation of some of the forms of creative practice well-established in popular music, such as the jazz saxophonist repeating part of someone else's solo in their own or the blues singer incorporating lyrics from a song such as "John Henry" into their new song. What differs in sampling, however, is the use of recordings (rather than compositions): it is bits of recordings, not just songs, that are borrowed and reproduced within new contexts. Copyright tends to protect recordings more strictly than compositions (because a recording is very clearly an "expression" and therefore unequivocally protected, and because there is no compulsory license allowing for the reuse of recordings in order to create derivative works). Very soon, therefore, rights holders of the sound recordings were accusing sampling artists of infringing their rights. A landmark case occurred in 1991 when rapper Biz Markie (more specifically, Markie's label, Warner Bros. Records) was sued by 1970s British rock star Gilbert O'Sullivan, who alleged that Markie's sampling of the introduction to the O'Sullivan's song "Alone Again (Naturally)" in the introduction to Markie's song "Alone Again" was copyright infringement (O'Sullivan was in the relatively unusual position of being an artist who owned the rights to his own recordings).

This episode reflects a consistent pattern in the business of copyright. When sound recordings were given protection in the United States, it was on the basis that manufacturers of recordings needed protection against bootlegging and counterfeiting, not because of problems caused by sampling. However, once the right was granted, rights holders were able to find a new way to commercially exploit it. And, once a legal precedent had been set, the business of copyright swung into action, as new business practices emerged to structure the licensing of, and payment for, sampling. Without government-set standard rates for the cost of sampling (unlike in song publishing) and with rights holders having no requirement to permit the use of their records, the costs of sampling dramatically increased, as did the administrative burden of obtaining agreements. Entire divisions of record labels can be given over to the obtaining and granting of licenses to sample. The sum total of this is that sampling has become less widespread and, many would argue, less creative than it was in the past. This negative impact is sometimes referred to as a "chilling effect" whereby creators, either priced out of making use of previous cultural works in their projects or intimidated by the threat of expensive legal action, are unable to create new works. (For more on sampling and its relation with copyright, see Sherman and Bentley 1992, Vaidhyanathan 2003: 132–145, McLeod 2005, McLeod and DiCola 2011, Morey 2012).

A second criticism of copyright is that private interest has come to dominate copyright at the expense of the public interest. When copyright first emerged it was for a very limited period of time and covered a few restricted acts. The rationale for creating copyright was that cultural and intellectual works were socially valuable but that the market did not adequately provide an incentive for their production. The state thus allowed publishers a monopoly over the right to reproduce the cultural work for a limited time and, at the end of that time, the work became free for all to use, providing raw materials for future creativity. Over time, however, a number of different trends have occurred that threaten these public policy goals. The first is a transformation from copyright existing to ensure that owners *get paid* for usage to copyright existing so that rights holders can *control* usage. The sampling example above is one example of where rights holders now have the right to say "no, you can't use that record" and there are many other cases where copyright owners have attempted to use copyright in order to prevent usage, or for the purposes of censorship (Gordon 1990, Boyle 1996: 145–148). The second detrimental trend has been the continual expansion and extension of copyright. Copyright now "protects" against far more acts and different types of acts than it did in its early days. This is not merely because copyrighted works are now used in many more ways than before (though this is true). It also reflects the trend toward rights holders seeking to "extract value" from any and all actions that make use of cultural works, a problem exacerbated by how much copyright has been extended since its initial incarnation: from fourteen years to the life of the author plus seventy years. Furthermore, there is evidence that, whenever the rights to valuable properties are due to expire, major rights holders lobby for further extensions. Legislators seem easily persuaded by these large corporations. For example, The Copyright Term Extension Act (CTEA), which extended copyright in the United States for a period of a further twenty years, was enacted in 1998 following intensive lobbying from Disney (among others), probably connected to the fact that copyright in the earliest Mickey Mouse animations were shortly due to expire (Drahos and Braithwaite 2002: 177). More recently, with copyright in sound recordings from the early 1960s (including the Beatles' early albums) due to expire in the European Union (where the term of protection was "only" fifty years), the recording industry embarked upon an extensive lobbying campaign that, ultimately, got the term of protection extended to seventy years (Harkins 2012, Laing 2012). When the Beatles recorded their first albums, the term of protection was actually twenty-five years.

Because of issues such as those outlined here, there are many who are critical of copyright and, over the last two decades or so, there has been considerable opposition to the actions of copyright holders from academics, artists, pressure groups and, in various ways, the public. Alternative forms of licensing have arisen, such as Copyleft[13] and Creative Commons,[14] which maintain attribution of authorship but, to varying degrees, allow the creative and non-commercial reuse of cultural works. Such social criticism of copyright has accelerated since the widespread adoption (in the global North at least) of the internet which, it is argued, is an inherently open system, encouraging collaborative creativity and limiting the ability of rights holders to restrict copying (Lessig 2000, 2009). This development has led to much public discussion about increasing levels of "piracy," and it is to this issue that I now turn.

Piracy

It may seem odd to have got this far through a chapter on copyright without there being a discussion of piracy. This is partly because piracy is only one part of copyright, and the daily practices of those in the music industry are structured by more mundane copyright matters, the "legitimate" licensing of music for use between businesses. The issue of "illegitimate" music distribution is really its own topic, and there is no space in this chapter to discuss the intricacies of piracy, to consider the different types of piracy, whether it affects record sales or so on.[15] Instead, I shall limit myself to a few short comments intended to prompt some reflection on the idea of piracy in light of the content of this chapter.

Although its use has become much more pervasive within the structures and processes of the creative industries, copyright was actually invented to address specifically the issue of piracy: it was brought into being to alleviate the commercial problems faced by early-eighteenth century book publishers—third parties reproducing works issued by the publisher and selling them for a lower price than the publisher could afford. The invention of copyright provided publishers with a legal tool with which they could protect themselves against copycats. This reinforces an important point: that copyright was initially about publishing not authorship, prohibiting the commercial reproduction of published works rather than one author copying from another.[16] I bring it up here to reintroduce the key theme of this chapter: that copyright is about business more than culture. Copyright emerged as the legal regulation of commercial practices, as one set of entrepreneurs (the "pirate" publishers) started moving into areas where existing entrepreneurs were already practicing. This pattern has repeated throughout the last 300 years, with new commercial innovations (often, but not always, linked to new technological developments) being seen as a threat to existing commercial interests and being labeled by those with vested interests as "piracy." In his analysis of popular music piracy throughout the twentieth century, Kernfeld (2011) recounts this cyclical pattern but he makes a distinction between "equivalent" forms of piracy (in which the pirate merely replicates a function already fulfilled by the rights holder) and "transformative" forms of piracy (in which the pirate provides a new service to consumers, such as the "song sheets" which made lyrics of popular songs available to music fans in the 1920s). Each time an existing industry is threatened, Kernfeld (2011: 4–7) argues, copyright holders claim that the new act is equivalent piracy. However, consumers generally recognize genuinely transformational uses and, more often than not, the official industries are forced to incorporate the new uses into their own business practices.

Two implications are worth highlighting here. The first is that, for most of copyright's existence, debates about piracy have centered on competing businesses rather than about individual consumer behavior (although many of the "pirate" businesses were extremely small scale, often one-man operations). It was only with the invention of home recording equipment in the 1960s (becoming much more common in the early 1980s) that individual music consumers were themselves accused of piracy (most memorably with the infamous "home taping is killing music" campaign). The arguments made by record labels in the late 1970s and early 1980s was that individuals recording songs from the radio, or recording their friends' records, were responsible for the decline in record sales.[17]

The distinction between organized, commercial piracy and individual non-commercial piracy was fairly easy to maintain in the 1980s and 1990s. The internet made it more complicated, however, as the boundary between who is a producer and who is a consumer became increasingly blurred.

Using P2P technology, individual downloaders also became uploaders (publishers) and the dramatic increase in individual "piracy" made it harder to claim that "non-commercial" forms of copying have negligible economic impact on rights holders. In recent years, the recording industry has been more aggressive toward individual consumers, suing or threatening legal action against many thousands of individuals (Marshall 2012: 57–58). Yet, despite claims from rights holders that downloaders are the same class of criminal as car-thieves and shoplifters, it is clear that most of the population do not see it this way. In particular, the distinction between commercial and non-commercial forms of "piracy" remains ideologically significant.

This brings me to a final point: namely that the notion of piracy depends upon the existence of copyright. Prior to the Statute of Anne (and skipping over a number of metaphysical arguments) the "pirates" were doing nothing illegal. If piracy is understood as certain acts that infringe copyright, then it logically makes sense that no acts were piracy before there was a copyright law to infringe. Piracy is, in other words, ideological, with rights holders having to argue, persuade and continually reinforce the idea that certain acts infringe copyright. Radio broadcasting, for example, was initially presented by record labels as piracy (why would anyone buy records if they could just listen to them for free on the radio?). However, as Kernfeld highlights, many activities that are originally described as piracy are eventually incorporated into the business practices of the dominant industry. This can be seen in the contemporary situation: despite legal threats to individuals, publicity campaigns and digital rights management systems, P2P sharing has only begun to diminish once the recording industry developed alternative music delivery systems that match consumer behavior (though this story is far from finished). This is why it is important to understand copyright from a sociological perspective. While copyright does provide much of the structure for the industrial production of music, copyright itself is shaped by existing social and cultural practices at least as much as it shapes them. Copyright is, in other words, a social construction subject to continuous negotiation by all of those involved in the production and consumption of music.

Notes

1 For Ukraine, see Helbig (2012); for a study of piracy in a range of emerging economies, see Karaganis (2011).

2 Because copyright depends upon the existence of a work then, technically, it *subsists* rather than exists, as its coming into being depends upon the existence of the work.

3 For a sophisticated account of how work for hire principles exist in the US recording industry, see Stahl (2012), Chapter 5.

4 In most countries, particularly those from a civil law tradition such as France and Germany, copyright also includes something called "moral rights." These moral rights are connected to the personality of the author and the integrity of the work, such as the right to be acknowledged as the author of the work and the right to reject any adaptation of the work that the author deems to injure his or her reputation. These moral rights are not transferrable, but they are of negligible economic significance (Kretschmer 2000: 214).

5 I am here skipping over the argument that the internet allows creators the opportunity to sell their work without the need for publishers/record labels. In practice, there have not been many cases of creators selling a lot of their work without relying on traditional intermediaries.

6 This right actually occurred remarkably late in the United States—it was not until 1972 that sound recordings were protected nationally by US Copyright law (although some states offered their own protection). The right occurred after lengthy lobbying by record labels concerned about the new phenomenon of bootlegging. Sound recordings were generally granted protection much earlier in other countries (1911 in the United Kingdom).

7 There is a further right that should be mentioned: the performer's right (not to be confused with "performance rights"). The performer's right provides protection for the performer in their live performances, so that no one else can record and distribute the live performance without permission.

8 Streaming music follows the same model, although what income gets distributed is less straightforward.

9 Different standards and laws may regulate broadcasting on different platforms (radio, satellite, internet and so on). For example, at the time of writing, there is a controversy in the United States because satellite broadcaster

Pandora has to pay a higher statutory royalty rate than conventional radio broadcasters. There are very few countries where the broadcasting of records on the radio does not require a payment to the owners of the sound recording (known as a "public performance right"). By far the most significant of these is the United States.

10 For more on collecting societies, see Wallis (2004).

11 T.S. Eliot: "Immature poets borrow; mature poets steal."

12 Northrop Frye: "Poetry can only be made out of other poems; novels out of other novels."

13 www.gnu.org/copyleft/

14 http://creativecommons.org/

15 I discuss these elsewhere in Marshall (2004) and Marshall (2012).

16 This does not mean that there was no conception of plagiarism before this point—there definitely was—just that it was a matter separate from copyright.

17 The record labels' campaigns were not purely focused on individuals. They also targeted the industries making blank tapes and stereos with tape-to-tape recording facilities. In many countries, the recording industry was successful in getting a tax applied to the sale of blank tapes in order to compensate for "lost" sales. A similar strategy was attempted for hard drives in the early 2000s, but with less success.

References

Barthes, R. 1977. "The Death of the Author." In *Image, Music, Text*, 142–148. London: Fontana.

Boyle, J. 1996. *Shamans, Software, and Spleens: Law and the Construction of the Information Society*. London: Harvard University Press.

Drahos, P. and J. Braithwaite. 2002. *Information Feudalism: Who Owns the Knowledge Economy?* London: Routledge.

Foucault, M. 1984. "What Is An Author?" In *The Foucault Reader*, ed. P. Rabinow, 101–120. London: Penguin.

Gordon, W. 1990. "Toward a Jurisprudence of Benefits: The Norms of Copyright and the Problem of Private Censorship." *University of Chicago Law Review* 57(3): 1009–1049.

Harkins, P. 2012. "Extending the Term: The Gowers Review and the Campaign to Increase the Length of Copyright in Sound Recordings." *Popular Music and Society* 35(5): 629–649.

Helbig, A. 2012. "Ukraine." In *The International Recording Industries*, ed. L. Marshall, 193–206. London: Routledge.

Jaszi, P. 1991. "Toward a Theory of Copyright: The Metamorphoses of 'Authorship'." *Duke Law Journal* 40(2): 455–503.

Karaganis, J. 2011. *Media Piracy in Emerging Economies*. Social Science Research Council. www.ssrc.org/publications/view/C4A69B1C-8051-E011-9A1B-001CC477EC84.

Kernfeld, B. 2011. *Pop Song Piracy: Disobedient Music Distribution since 1929*. Chicago: University of Chicago Press.

Kretschmer, M. 2000. "Intellectual Property in Music: a Historical Analysis of Rhetoric and Institutional Practices." *Studies in Cultures, Organizations and Societies* 6(2): 197–223.

Kretschmer, M., E. Derclaye, M. Favale and R. Watt. 2010. *The Relationship between Copyright and Contract Law*. London: SABIP.

Laing, D. 2002. "Copyright as a Component of the Music Business." In *The Business of Music*, ed. M. Talbot, 171–194. Liverpool: Liverpool University Press.

_____. 2012. "Copyright in the Balance: Notes on Some 21st-Century Developments." *Popular Music and Society* 35(5): 617–627.

Lessig, L. 2000. *Code: And Other Laws of Cyberspace*. New York: Basic Books.

_____. 2009. *Remix: Making Art and Commerce Thrive in the Hybrid Economy*. Harmondsworth: Penguin Books.

McLeod, K. 2005. "Confessions of an Intellectual (Property): Danger Mouse, Mickey Mouse, Sonny Bono, and My Long and Winding Path as a Copyright Activist-Academic." *Popular Music and Society* 28(1): 79–93.

McLeod, K and P. DiCola. 2011. *Creative License: The Law and Culture of Digital Sampling*. Durham: Duke University Press.

Marshall, L. 2004. "Infringers." In *Music and Copyright*, 2nd ed., eds. S. Frith and L. Marshall, 189–208. Edinburgh: Edinburgh University Press.

_____. 2005. *Bootlegging: Romanticism and Copyright in the Music Industry*. London: Sage.

_____. 2012. "The Recording Industry in the Twenty-First Century." In *The International Recording Industries*, ed. L. Marshall, 53–74. London: Routledge.

Morey, J. 2012. "The Bridgeport Dimension: Copyright Enforcement and Its Implications for Sampling Practice." In *Music, Business and Law: Essays on Contemporary Trends in the Music Industry*, eds. A.-V. Kärjä, L. Marshall and J. Brusila, 21–45. Turku: IIPC Publications.

Patterson, L.R. and S. Lindberg. 1991. *The Nature of Copyright: A Law of Users' Rights*. Athens: University of Georgia Press.

Sherman, B. and L. Bently. 1992. "Cultures of Copying: Digital Sampling and Copyright Law." *Entertainment Law Review* 3(5):158–163.

Stahl, M. 2012. *Unfree Masters: Recording, Artists and the Politics of Work*. Durham: Duke University Press.

Towse, R. 2004. "Copyright and Economics." In *Music and Copyright*, 2nd ed., eds. S. Frith and L. Marshall, 54–69. Edinburgh: Edinburgh University Press.

Toynbee, J. 2001. *Creating Problems: Social Authorship, Copyright and the Production of Culture. Pavis Papers in Social and Cultural Research*. Milton Keynes: Open University.

Vaidhyanathan, S. 2003. *Copyrights and Copywrongs: The Rise of Intellectual Property and How It Threatens Creativity*. New York: New York University Press.

Wallis, R. 2004. "Copyright and the Composer." In *Music and Copyright*, 2nd ed., eds. S. Frith and L. Marshall, 103–122. Edinburgh: Edinburgh University Press.

V

TECHNOLOGY AND MEDIATION

The study of sound technology and mediation has in recent years become one of the most vital subfields in the sociology of music. In this section Pinch and Bijsterveld provide an overview of the key themes and insights of such scholarship, suggesting that the introduction of new technologies into musical culture can fundamentally unsettle notions of what counts as a musical instrument and about what constitutes musical talent, musical creativity—and even the very definition of music itself.

Such work builds on a generation of scholarship in the sociology of science and technology (SST). The development of actor-network-theory (ANT) is particularly important in this context, because it draws attention to the ways that human social arrangements are impossible to sustain without an abundance of non-human objects and technologies (see for example Latour 1992, Law 1992). In this way, humans and things are seen to exist in relations of mutual constitution, or co-construction, which resonates strongly with music sociology's interest in the co-construction of social action and aesthetic conventions (see also the general Introduction and Section VI).

Working implicitly within this paradigm, Baade provides a critical introduction to radio as a key form of musical mediation. She argues that radio as a technological system has evolved in tandem with shifts in music's audiences, in how wider institutional frameworks have afforded public availability for some musics and not others, as well as in the co-constitutive role between radio as a medium and the genre formations of music.

Similarly, Wright argues that the institutional demands and aesthetic conventions of Hollywood cinema together exert a powerful (but not deterministic) influence on the sonic signature of contemporary film practices. Wright's work is deeply informed by interactionism and executed with careful ethnographic precision, while also demonstrating a keen ear for the aesthetic nuances of the film soundtrack. In this way, he provides an exemplary study of how "the social and the aesthetic" (Born 2010) are inextricable. His chapter evokes some of the debates about musical aesthetics covered in the general Introduction and Section VI.[1]

Science and technology scholars also move away from reductionist notions of technological determinism and "progress," which suggest that technologies inevitably govern their own uses and outcomes, and march toward sophistication. The alternative critical SST perspective is evident in Théberge's chapter, where he rejects the simplistic narratives of "impact" and "revolution" that typically accompany discussions of music and digitalization. The digitalization of music, Théberge suggests, is better understood as a long, contingent and uneven process through which both musical and technical possibilities have reconfigured one another. While Théberge focuses primarily on the western world, digitalization is of course also a global phenomenon, with particular musical and cultural manifestations in different contexts. The sociology of music is only beginning to understand what musical digitalization means on a global scale, and this can be seen as a pressing task for future research (see for example the work of Born's Music and Digitization Research Group: musdig.music.ox.ac.uk).

Note

1   It is worth noting two additional ways in which Wright advances film-related sociological and musicological scholarship. First, he builds on an ethnographic tradition that stretches back to Faulkner's (1971) work on Hollywood studio musicians, while also drawing on the key insights of sound studies, which is to focus not only on music but the entire soundtrack, including sound effects (see also Théberge 2008). Second, Wright's empiricism decisively breaks with the speculative, psychoanalytic paradigm that has governed mainstream film studies since the 1970s.

References

Born, G. 2010. "The Social and the Aesthetic: For a Post-Bourdieuian Theory of Cultural Production." *Cultural Sociology* 4(2): 171–208.

Faulkner, R. 1971. *Hollywood Studio Musicians: Their Work and Careers in the Recording Industry*. Chicago: Aldine-Atherton.

Latour, B. 1992. "Where are the Missing Masses? The Sociology of a Few Mundane Artifacts." In *Shaping Technology /Building Society: Studies in Sociotechnical Change*, eds. W. Bijker and J. Law, 225–258. Cambridge: MIT Press.

Law, J. 1992. "Notes on the Theory of the Actor-Network: Ordering, Strategy and Heterogeneity." *Systems Practice* 5(4): 379–393.

Théberge, P. 2008. "Almost Silent: The Interplay of Sound and Silence in Contemporary Film and Television." In *Lowering the Boom: Critical Studies in Film Sound*, eds. J. Beck and T. Grajeda, 51–67. Champaign: University of Illinois Press.

28

Instruments and Innovation

TREVOR PINCH AND KARIN BIJSTERVELD

Technology plays an increasingly prominent role in music. Today most music is produced or consumed with the aid of technological devices. The recording industry is founded upon a series of technological innovations, ranging from the original Edison phonograph to the latest MP3 software compression algorithms (Chanan 1995, Day 2000, Morton 2000).[1] Even a live concert by a symphony orchestra is scarcely possible without microphones, mixing consoles, amplifiers, loudspeakers, and so forth. New electronic and computer technologies have left their mark, and have sparked the development of new sorts of instruments, such as the electric organ, the electric guitar, the synthesizer, and the digital sampler.

But the impact of technology upon music is not solely a twentieth-century phenomenon. Throughout history, new instruments and instrument components drawing upon the technological possibilities of the day have often incited debates as to their legitimacy and place within musical culture. The arrival of the pianoforte into a musical culture that revered the harpsichord was for some an unwarranted intrusion by a mechanical device (DeNora 1995a).

Scholars in the fields of musicology and the sociology of music are increasingly analyzing the role played by technology in music (Prieberg 1960, Jones 1992, Schafer 1994 [1977], Born 1995, Frith 1996, Théberge 1997, Waksman 1999, DeNora 2000, Taylor 2001). There is also growing interest within science and technology studies (including the history of technology) in sound, noise, and music (Hennion 1989; Ungeheuer 1991; Braun 1992, 1994, 2002 [2000]; Kraft 1994, 1996; Siefert 1995; Thompson 1995, 1997, 2002; Pinch and Trocco 1999, 2002; Bijsterveld 2000; Schmidt-Horning 2000; Pinch 2001). Arguably, music technologies are amenable to the same sorts of analytical insights as technologies in general. In particular, the influence of technology in music raises questions as to the boundary between "instruments" and "machines" and the place of the latter within musical culture.[2] New technologies sharpen the perennial issue of what makes for good music and "art." They also challenge our notion of what counts as live entertainment: should one applaud when the performer is a machine?

One way of thinking about the approach we adopt in this article is to see the introduction of new technologies into music as a set of "breaching experiments." Such experiments, first introduced into sociology by Harold Garfinkel, serve as probes into how everyday social order is maintained. Garfinkel (1967) got his students (the experimenters) to breach taken-for-granted interactional conventions, such as routine greetings, and observe what happened.[3] We want to treat the introduction of new machines as prima facie cases of breaches in musical culture. Such interjections provide an opportunity to rehearse arguments about what counts as part of music and art and, conversely, what is appropriately delegated to machines; breaches of convention reveal underlying norms and values.[4] Indeed, our argument about the breaches new musical instruments produce can be extended to technology in general. That is to say, reactions to new technologies could provide a fertile research site for investigating how technologies in general are embedded within conventional normative frameworks (see Marvin 1988).

[. . .]

Early Mechanical Instruments

We will start with a brief examination of a relatively unknown debate arising from a mechanical innovation in an existing instrument. In the mid-nineteenth century, linked-key mechanisms and valves, such as are found on today's woodwind instruments, replaced the traditional method of controlling pitch on the flute—that is, using one's fingers to stop holes bored in the instrument. The new keys were easy to operate and facilitated the production of much more uniform and cleaner tones for individual notes. But they met with opposition, because they ruled out the possibility of making a "vibrato by simply moving the fingers over the sound holes" and diminished the player's ability to "correct out of tune sounds" by means of slightly altering finger positions.[5] One commentator, Heinrich Grenser, declared that improving tone quality by the use of keys was "neither complex nor art" (Henkel 1994).[6] According to Grenser, "the real art" of flute construction was to build flutes that would enable flutists to play whatever they wanted without the use of keys (Henkel 1994: 86).

The kinds of boundaries drawn in this example between art and non-art, and between control and the loss of that control, are the ones we are interested in. The opposition of some musicians to keys and valves did not stop the technology from changing. In other cases, however, resistance to change and the accompanying debates over what counts as "real" music and art have been of enormous importance.

One well-known example of such resistance is the introduction of the player piano at the turn of the twentieth century.[7] Player pianos, such as the Pianola and the Welte-Mignon, produced their music mechanically through a set of instructions stored on a perforated music roll. Their commercial success depended upon not only the standardization of music rolls but also important changes in cultural values.

The earlier success of the pianoforte was intimately related to the Victorian ideal of the so-called piano girl—the notion that every young, middle-class woman should learn to play music, preferably on the piano. To play the piano "demanded toil, sacrifice, and perseverance;" which, like work, "built character, fortitude, self-control." The home, with the woman and her piano at its center, was considered a haven in the heartless world of industrial society (Roell 1989: 3). Moreover, women were thought to be especially suited to producing such caring and restorative music.[8]

At first the piano trade thought of the idea of "a 'machine' to produce piano playing" as "ridiculous" and "preposterous" (Roell 1989: 40). Musicians, music teachers, and composers opposed the new machine, contending that one could copy sound but not interpretation; that mechanical instruments reduced the expression of music to a mathematical system; that amateur players would disappear; and that mechanized music diminished the ideal of beauty by "producing the same after same, with no variation, no soul, no joy, no passion" (54). One commentator was afraid that members of the "lower level" of society would copy the "cultivated class" in order to advance themselves (57). Others feared that music would "lose its distinctiveness, its uniqueness as an experience" (58). After "several months of mechanical music," a critic said, a listener would miss the "hesitating sounds which once charmed him, that human touch which said something to him, although imperfectly" (ibid.).

[. . .]

In mounting their opposition to mechanical instruments, critics made explicit their own views concerning real art and interesting music and music making. Their arguments centered on the need for mastery of technique and control over interpretation, for romantic passion, expression, variation, and uniqueness, and on the appearance of a frightening democratization. Performers and music teachers probably also feared for their jobs.[9]

Some European composers and musicians, however, welcomed the new mechanical instruments. The composer and well-known music critic H.H. Stuckenschmidt (1924, 1926a, 1926b, 1926c, 1926d, 1927) wrote that such instruments could replace expensive musicians, were superior as performers of increasingly complex music, and expressed the spirit of the age more fully. Others similarly stressed the need for clear and unsentimental music or saw particular potential in mechanical music composed for radio and gramophone—technologies that demanded rigorous, linear, and rhythmic music (e.g. Toch 1926, Schünemann 1931). Support also came from American music educators, piano manufacturers, and music publishers, who thought that the player piano would lead to "an almost universal music education" and would therefore democratize music (Roell 1989: 39).

[. . .]

These debates over the introduction of new technologies into music, like breaching experiments, make visible norms and values concerning the art of music and music making that are often taken for granted. We have seen the importance placed on control and personal achievement, the links drawn between irregularity, unpredictability, and creativity, and the part played by the new value perceived in democratized leisure (a point raised by both critics and proponents of mechanical instruments). These values and norms were strategically adapted by the promoters of the new musical instruments.[10] The blending of personal achievement (the loss of which had been feared by opponents of mechanical instruments) with democratized leisure (which had been seen as an advantage by proponents of mechanical instruments) in effect helped create a market for the player piano.

Electric and Electronic Instruments

In the twentieth century, electricity and electronics offered new opportunities for innovation. The telharmonium, the theremin, the Ondes Martenot, and the Trautonium were welcomed by composers for the variations in sound and tone color they created.[11] But most of these early instruments failed to gain widespread acceptance. . . .

[. . .]

The Synthesizer

The most successful electronic instrument of the twentieth century is the synthesizer.[12] It offers a far greater range of sounds and more ways of controlling sound than instruments like the theremin, Trautonium, and Ondes Martenot. Since its development in the early 1960s it has been widely used in many musical genres and become part of the leisure and entertainment industries broadly conceived. We will briefly describe the early development of the synthesizer before turning to examine a debate among synthesists as to what synthesizers can and cannot do.[13]

[. . .]

The Moog and Buchla synthesizers consisted of sound generators (oscillators that produced different wave forms and white noise) and processors (filters and envelope generators) connected by patch wires in endless combinations.[14] Analog voltage control technology enabled the pitch of an oscillator to be varied according to its input voltage. The output from one oscillator could also control the frequency of a second oscillator, providing a form of vibrato. Feeding back voltages produced a great variety of sounds that moved dynamically in pitch and/or amplitude. Moog offered a monophonic keyboard and a ribbon controller (a continuous-resistance strip played by sliding the finger along it) as further variable sources of control voltages. In appearance the early synthesizers resembled analog telephone exchanges . . .

Buchla rejected the use of standard keyboards . . . Not wanting to be limited by the conventional twelve-tone scale, he favored an array of touch-sensitive plates to control various parameters and devices. In his view, the new source of sound—electronics—should not be controlled by an old technology that stemmed from hammers and strings. Buchla, himself an avant-garde artist, was interested in aleatoric composition. He incorporated a source of random control voltages into his design, and his instruments allowed the user to set off complex chains of events that could feed back on each other.[15] He mainly sold his synthesizers to like-minded experimental composers; Vladimir Ussachevsky, for example, bought three, one for each of his identically equipped Columbia-Princeton studios.

[. . .]

Jon Weiss, a Moog studio musician who played both instruments, perceptively captures the difference between Moog and Buchla: "[Buchla] didn't want his machine to be a glorified electric organ . . . His designs were wild and wonderful. Moog's were conservative, rigorous and well-controlled . . . Everything under exact control of one-volt-per-octave, and everything will change exactly the same, and laying everything out in octaves, dividing twelve discrete steps, all that he carried through in the whole design of the machine."[16] Buchla saw himself as making instruments rather than machines: "I'm an instrument builder . . . I don't build machines, I never have built a machine, I build only things that you play."[17] For Buchla, who refused to mass produce his synthesizers, each individual had its own characteristics, idiosyncrasies, and ways of responding to human senses and touch.[18] By asserting the distinction between machines and instruments, Buchla was drawing attention to what he considered the underlying values of genuine musical endeavors. The debate as to whether the synthesizer is a machine or a musical instrument is encapsulated in the differences between Moog and Buchla. Buchla is at the instrument end of the spectrum, stressing uncertainty, idiosyncrasy, the "wild and wonderful"; Moog is at the machine end, stressing control, reliability, and repeatability. This tension between "machine" and "instrument," and between the values and norms reflected in these different conceptions, resurfaces throughout the history of the synthesizer.

[. . .]

By the mid-1970s, as the synthesizer became more like an electronic organ with a polyphonic keyboard and preset sounds, the era of exploring new sounds was coming to an end. By the time the first commercially successful digital instrument, the Yamaha DX7 (lifetime sales of two hundred thousand), appeared in 1983 with an astonishing range of presets (including most acoustic instrument sounds), synthesizers were too complicated for most users to program themselves, and a separate cottage industry of "plug in" sound cards developed. The adoption of the MIDI (Musical Instrument Digital Interface) standard in 1982, enabling synthesizers from different manufacturers to be connected together and/or connected to personal computers, and the subsequent waves of digital synthesizers marked a geographical shift in the industry, with Japanese companies like Yamaha, Roland, and Korg becoming the dominant players in this new global industry. In the 1990s the Japanese company Casio sold millions of its keyboards for home entertainment. The dissemination of the synthesizer during the 1980s and 1990s reflected the same norms of democratized leisure apparent in the success of the player piano.

[. . .]

There is no doubt that the synthesizer is a unique musical instrument because of its capacity to reproduce the sound of other instruments. But interestingly enough, many synthesists themselves reject the idea that it can actually replace musicians. In the late 1970s and early 1980s; with the growing power of synthesizers to emulate acoustic instruments threatening musicians' livelihoods, synthesists started to debate what the synthesizer could and could not do. Perhaps surprisingly, skeptics appealed again to the same norms concerning the nature of art that critics of earlier technological innovations had cited. As Michael Boddicker commented: "They [the union] think I can replace a trumpet player . . . who's been playing for twenty or thirty years on just that instrument. They know all the styles indigenous to that instrument. . . . I would have to live as a trumpet player for twenty years like those cats to have that much knowledge" (Darter and Armbruster 1984: 246). This remark draws a boundary in terms of musicianship; what counts is not being able to make the sound of a trumpet but being able to play all the different trumpet styles. Such an argument against the encroachment of machines relies on irredeemable human features of musicianship that cannot be captured by machines. It is similar in form to the arguments made by critics of artificial intelligence (Dreyfus 1972, Collins 1990).[19]

It is in the area of performance that the synthesizer is often seen as lacking the qualities necessary to produce proper musical art. John Chowning, a percussionist and engineer (and the inventor of the digital algorithms used in the Yamaha DX7) makes the point this way: "There's a special relationship between performance and the literature and the players and their instruments that is not going to be violated, no matter what kind of a futurist view one might hear . . . The commercial view of the effect of synthesis [in replacing conventional instruments] I just think is absolutely beyond belief. It's bullshit" (Darter and Armbruster 1984: 109). Human control over performance and interpretation sets the boundary between what synthesizers can and cannot do. Similarly, Klaus Schulze of Tangerine Dream remarks, in a comment reminiscent of the earlier criticisms of the player piano: "Computers will never replace the human touch in music. . . . Even if you could program a computer to add that human variable element, it wouldn't be the same. Otherwise, you could just program a symphony and it would always sound the same" (Darter and Armbruster 1984: 185).

Of course, listening culture is not itself static. As Emily Thompson (2002) has shown, at the start of the twentieth century audiences had to learn to listen to the music they experienced in the new concert halls in new ways. Similarly, with listeners constantly exposed to synthesized sounds, as they are in movies and with techno music, their expectations for what counts as credible sound, and hence what counts as musicianship, will also change. Indeed, as virtuoso DJs take center stage in techno and dance music, we are reminded that what counts as a "musician" also can change.

Stability and Change

One aspect of this story that deserves attention is the presence of stability in the midst of change. Indeed, it would appear that elements of musical culture are remarkably persistent. Part of the explanation for this may lie in the musical institutions that dominate western societies—schools, conservatories, concert halls, critics, and so on—and reproduce these values. It is also clear that within musical culture the relationship between producers and users of new, machine-like instruments has been extremely close. Instrument makers often were (amateur) musicians, composers, or artists themselves, whether or not they also worked with engineers.[20] Because of this, values central to musical culture have helped inform the production, acceptance, and transformation of new technologies. Within the context of musical culture, especially the world of composing and live, onstage performance, personal achievement has been of enduring importance: machines or machine-like instruments have been incorporated in ways that permit personal achievement to remain visible and audible.

At the same time, again because of the importance of personal achievement, the control over sound and interpretation that machines have enabled has also been embraced. Moreover, machines have been incorporated in the contexts of musical performances and compositions by blending old values with new, as in "recreation for all plus personal achievement" or "uncertainty re-controlled." This has paradoxically served to sometimes strengthen the norm of personal achievement.

There is little question that the synthesizer has changed the face of much popular music, or that it has put some musicians, particularly session musicians in New York and Los Angeles, out of work. Indeed, the role of the profit motive is notably understated in this article because of our focus on art versus machine. Work displacement and the synthesizer is a topic that merits its own study. But, as always, the story of technical change and work is a complicated one, with new opportunities opening up as well. The mass-production of affordable versions of these instruments and the consequent democratization of musical opportunity, so to speak, has been an important development, too. Musicians have, however, been able to keep some areas of musicianship from the encroaching machines by defining machine-instruments in such a manner that the artistic dimension of their practice can be kept alive.

Within the world of composing and onstage performance, the value ascribed to skill has restricted the role of the machine. Even where the threat of the machine seems greatest, in digital sampling, the aesthetic system founded on control and personal achievement has not vanished but rather been reworked.[21] Techno bands, too, have found that in the domain of live performance, audiences expect some displays of virtuosity. New instruments are important because they allow people to do new things in new ways. But acceptance seems to depend on an alignment between old values and new practices. Old norms and values, it seems, die hard.

Notes

1 MP3 refers to MPEG Layer 3, an audio compression standard for encoding music; MPEG stands for Moving Picture Experts Group, which operates under the auspices of the International Organization for Standardization to develop standards for digital video and digital audio compression.

2 For work on boundaries in science and technology, and between science and technology and society, see Gieryn (1995), and Star and Griesemer (1989).

3 A useful discussion of Garfinkel's work can be found in Heritage (1984).

4 We are not interested here in the foundational issue of what the proper role of machines in music is but rather in what the introduction of machines tells us about what different groups of historical actors have taken to be essential features of musical creation, production, and dissemination.

5 For discussion of this case, see Ahrens (1996).

6 All quotations from German and Dutch sources have been translated by the authors.

7 The player piano was far from being the first "automated" musical instrument. According to Helmut Kowar's recent bibliography on mechanical music, which encompasses 1,819 references, mechanical instruments date back as far as antiquity; see Kowar (1996).

8 That is, as long as the music was performed at home. Tia DeNora (1995b) claims that in public performances in Vienna between 1780 and 1810 the female pianist became less and less common. This may have been due to the style of piano playing inspired by Beethoven; in contrast to older playing technique, which favored physical reserve, the new style created a virtuoso-culture that prized an aggressive, dramatic, manly, and physically emphatic manner of playing.

9 As Howard Becker (1982: 306) notes in *Art Worlds*, innovations in art often threaten art world participants who have acquired their conventions and mastered their skills through time-consuming learning processes.

10 Our view of norms here is not static and deterministic. Norms can both constrain and enable.

11 For overviews of these instruments, see Bode (1984), Chadabe (1997), Roads (1996), Simms (1986), Braun (2000/2002: introduction), and Davies (2000). For a detailed account of the history of the telharmonium, see Weidenaar (1995); for the theremin, see Glinsky (2000). See also Rebling (1939); Weiskopf (1926); and van Dantzig (1937).

12 One should note here also two other very successful electric instruments, the Hammond organ (which, like the telharmonium, uses an electromechanical source of sound, the spinning tone wheel) and the electric guitar. The Hammond organ was very popular in churches in the 1950s and then later as a pop instrument: see Théberge (1997). On the development of the electric guitar, see Waksman (1999) and McSwain (2000).

13 Our research on the synthesizer focuses primarily on the period 1963–75 and has involved archival research and interviews with pioneering engineers and early users. See Pinch and Trocco (1999, 2002). For the attitudes of musicians concerning what synthesizers can't do, we rely upon interviews with well-known 1970s synthesists conducted for *Keyboard* magazine and collected in Darter and Armbruster, eds. (1984).

14 Moog and Buchla synthesizers used "subtractive synthesis," which made it easier to produce complex sounds by taking a waveform already rich in overtones and filtering out some overtones. These synthesizers, unlike the RCA Mark II, also worked in real time. Moog and Buchla initially rejected the word "synthesizer"; but in 1967 Moog's catalog featured for the first time his 900-series "Synthesizer"; see Pinch and Trocco (2002).

15 The best example of this effect is Morton Subotnick, *Silver Apples of the Moon* (Nonesuch, 1967).

16 Jon Weiss, interview by Trevor Pinch and Frank Trocco, Interlaken, New York, 8 May 1996.

17 Don Buchla, interview by Trevor Pinch, 4 April 1997.

18 Buchla did, however, license his designs to CBS for a short time around 1968–69.

19 Interestingly, in the case of artificial intelligence the arguments are made by outsiders—philosophers and sociologists inspired by phenomenology.

20 Moog and Buchla were both amateur musicians and worked closely with other musicians. See Pinch and Trocco (2002).

21 On sampling, see Goodwin (1988).

References

Ahrens, C. 1996. "Technological Innovations in Nineteenth-Century Instrument Making and Their Consequences." *Musical Quarterly* 80(2): 332–340.

Becker, H.S. 1982. *Art Worlds*. Berkeley: University of California Press.

Bode, H. 1984. "History of Electronic Sound Modification." *Journal of the Audio Engineering Society* 32(10): 730–739.

Born, G. 1995. *Rationalizing Culture: IRCAM, Boulez, and the Institutionalization of the Musical Avant-Garde*. Berkeley: University of California Press.

Braun, H.-J. 1992. "Technik im Spiegel der Musik des Frühen 20. Jahrhunderts." *Technikgeschichte* 59(2): 109–131.

_____. 1994. "'I Sing the Body Electric': Der Einfluss von Elekroakustik und Elektronik auf das Musikschaffen im 20. Jahrhundert." *Technikgeschichte* 61(4): 353–373.

_____., ed. 2002. *Music and Technology in the 20th Century*. Baltimore: Johns Hopkins University Press. Originally published as *"I Sing the Body Electric": Music and Technology in the 20th Century* (2000, Holheim: Wolke Verlag).

Bijsterveld, K. 2000. "'A Servile Imitation': Disputes about Machines in Music, 1910–1930. "In *"I Sing the Body Electric": Music and Technology in the 20th Century*, ed. H.-J. Braun, 121–147.

Chadabe, J. 1997. *Electric Sound: The Past and Promise of Electronic Music*. Saddle River: Prentice Hall.

Chanan, M. 1995. *Repeated Takes: A Short History of Recording and Its Effects on Music*. London: Verso.

Collins, H.M. 1990. *Artificial Experts: Social Knowledge and Intelligent Machines*. Cambridge: Harvard University Press.

Darter, T., and G. Armbruster, eds. 1984. *The Art of Electronic Music*. New York: W. Morrow.

Davies, H. 2000. "Electronic Instruments: Classifications and Mechanisms." In *"I Sing the Body Electric": Music and Technology in the 20th Century*, ed. H.-J. Braun, 43–58. Holheim: Wolke Verlag).

Day, T. 2000. *A Century of Recorded Music: Listening to Musical History*. New Haven: Yale University Press.

DeNora, T. 1995a. *Beethoven and the Construction of Genius: Musical Politics in Vienna, 1792–1803*. Berkeley: University of California Press.

_____. 1995b. "Gendering the Piano: Repertory, Technology and Bodily Discipline in Beethoven's Vienna." Paper presented to Center for Research into Innovation, Culture and Technology Workshop. Brunel University, London.

_____. 2000. *Music in Everyday Life*. Cambridge: Cambridge University Press.

Dreyfus, H.L. 1972. *What Computers Can't Do: A Critique of Artificial Reason*. New York: Harper and Row.

Frith, S. 1996. *Performing Rites: On the Value of Popular Music*. Cambridge: Harvard University Press.

Garfinkel, H. 1967. *Studies in Ethnomethodology*. Englewood Cliffs: Prentice Hall.

Gieryn, T.F. 1995. "Boundaries of Science." In *Handbook of Science and Technology Studies*, eds. S. Jasanoff, G.E. Markle, J.C. Petersen and T. Pinch, 393–443, Thousand Oaks: Sage.

Glinsky, A. 2000. *Theremin: Ether Music and Espionage*. Champaign: University of Illinois Press.

Goodwin, A. 1988. "Sample and Hold: Pop Music in the Digital Age of Reproduction." *Critical Quarterly* 30(3): 34–49.

Henkel, H. 1994. "Die Technik der Musikinstrumentenherstellung am Beispiel des klassischen Instrumentariums." In *Technik und Kunst*, ed. D. Guderian, 67–91. Düsseldorf: Springer.

Hennion, A.1989. "An Intermediary Between Production and Consumption: The Producer of Popular Music." *Science, Technology and Human Values* 14(4): 400–424.

Heritage, J. 1984. *Garfinkel and Ethnomethodology*. Cambridge: Polity Press.

Jones, S. 1992. *Rock Formation: Music, Technology, and Mass Communication*. London: Sage.

Kowar, H. 1996. *Mechanische Musik: Eine Bibliographie*. Vienna: Vom Pasqualatihaus.

Kraft, J.P. 1994. "Musicians in Hollywood: Work and Technological Change in Entertainment Industries, 1926–1940." *Technology and Culture* 35(2): 289–314.

_____. 1996. *Stage to Studio: Musicians and the Sound Revolution, 1890–1950*. Baltimore: Johns Hopkins University Press.

Marvin, C. 1988. *When Old Technologies Were New: Thinking about Electric Communication in the Late Nineteenth Century*. New York: Oxford University Press.

McSwain, R. 2000. "The Social Reconstruction of a Reverse Salient in Electric Guitar Technology: Noise, the Solid Body and Jimi Hendrix." In *"I Sing the Body Electric": Music and Technology in the 20th Century*, ed. H.-J. Braun, 198–211. Holheim: Wolke Verlag.

Morton, D. 2000. *Off the Record: The Technology and Culture of Sound Recording in America*. New Brunswick: Rutgers University Press.

Pinch, T. 2001. "Why You Go to a Piano Store to Buy a Synthesizer: Path Dependence and the Social Construction of Technology." In *Path Dependence and Creation*, eds. R. Garud and P. Karnøe, 381–401. Hillsdale: Lawrence Earlbaum Associates.

Pinch, T. and F. Trocco. 1999. "The Social Construction of the Electronic Music Synthesizer." *ICON: Journal of the International Committee for the History of Technology* 4: 9–31.

_____. 2002. *Analog Days: The Invention and Impact of the Moog Synthesizer*. Cambridge: Harvard University Press.

Prieberg, F.K. 1960. *Musica ex Machina: Über das Verhältnis von Musik und Technik*. Berlin: Ullstein.

Rebling, E. 1939. "Electrische Muziekinstrumenten." *Maandblad voor Hedendaagsche Muziek* 8: 335–340.

Roads, C. 1996. "Early Electronic Music Instruments: Time Line 1899–1950." *Computer Music Journal* 20(3): 20–23.

Roell, C.H. 1989. *The Piano in America 1890–1940*. Chapel Hill: University of North Carolina Press.

Schafer, R.M. 1994. *The Soundscape: Our Sonic Environment and the Tuning of the World*. Rochester, VT: Destiny Books. Originally published as *The Tuning of the World* (1977, New York: Knopf).

Schmidt-Horning, S. 2000. "Chasing Sound: The Culture and Technology of Recording Studios in Postwar America," *ICON: Journal of the International Committee for the History of Technology* 6: 100–118.

Schünemann, G. 1931. "Muziek en Techniek." *Maandblad voor Hedendaagsche Muziek* 1: 4–6.

Siefert, M. 1995. "Aesthetics, Technology, and the Capitalization of Culture: How the Talking Machine Became a Musical Instrument." *Science in Context* 8(2): 417–449.

Simms, B.R. 1986. "Electronic Music." In *Music of the Twentieth Century*. New York: Schirmer Books.

Star, S.L. and J.R. Griesemer. 1989. "Institutional Ecology, 'Translations' and Boundary Objects: Amateurs and Professionals in Berkeley's Museum of Vertebrate Zoology, 1907–39." *Social Studies of Science* 19(3): 387–420.

Stuckenschmidt, H.H. 1924. "Die Mechanisierung der Musik." *Pult und Takstock* 2: 1–8.

_____. 1926a. "'Aeroplansonate' (George Antheil)." *Der Auftakt* 6: 178–181.

_____. 1926b. "Mechanical Music." *Der Kreis* 3: 506–508.

_____. 1926c. "Mechanische Musik." *Der Auftakt* 6: 170–173.

_____. 1926d. "Mechanisierung." *Anbruch* 8: 345–346.

_____. 1927. "Machines—A Vision on the Future." *Modern Music* 4: 8–14.

Taylor, T.D. 2001. *Strange Sounds: Music, Technology, and Culture*. New York: Routledge.

Théberge, P. 1997. *Any Sound You Can Imagine: Making Music / Consuming Technology*. Hanover: Wesleyan University Press.

Thompson, E. 1995. "Machines, Music, and the Quest for Fidelity: Marketing the Edison Phonograph in America, 1877–1925." *Musical Quarterly* 79(1): 131–171.

_____. 1997. "Dead Rooms and Live Wires: Harvard, Hollywood, and the Deconstruction of Architectural Acoustics, 1900–1930." *Isis* 88(4): 597–626.

_____. 2002. *The Soundscape of Modernity: Architectural Acoustics and the Culture of Listening in America, 1900–1933*. Cambridge: MIT Press.

Toch, E. 1926. "Musik für Mechanische Instrumente." *Anbruch* 8: 346–349.

Ungeheuer, E. 1991. "Ingenieure der Neuen Musik—Zwischen Technik und Ästhetik: Zur Geschichte der elektronischen Klangerzeugung." *Kultur und Technik* 15: 34–41.

van Dantzig, J.F. 1937. "Electrische Muziek." *Maandblad voor Hedendaagsche Muziek* 6: 157–160.

Waksman, S. 1999. *Instruments of Desire: The Electric Guitar and the Shaping of Musical Experience*. Cambridge: Harvard University Press.

Weidenaar, R. 1995. *Magic Music from the Telharmonium*. Metuchen: The Scarecrow Press.

Weiskopf, H. 1926. "Sphaerophon, das Instrument der Zukunft." *Der Auftakt* 6:177–178.

29

Radio

CHRISTINA BAADE

Since Lee de Forest's first experimental music and voice broadcasts in 1914 (Douglas 1999: 51), music on the radio has meant many things: a Beethoven concert in a rural family's parlor, Chuck Berry on a teenager's transistor radio, Dionne Warwick underscoring a dentist visit, and Last.fm's "Lorde and Similar" playing on computer speakers. Such scenarios embody an array of new social possibilities, as well as the ways that radio has profoundly reshaped music's cultural role. In attempting to understand these changes, as well as the complex structural forces that shape radio programming, scholars have initiated numerous lines of inquiry. Cutting across a range of historical and cultural contexts, their questions cluster around four key concerns:

1. Audience: What individuals and groups constitute radio's listeners? How are their identities understood in terms of gender, age, race/ethnicity, nationality, class and taste? What agency do they have in interpreting—and influencing—music that is broadcast? Should they be conceptualized as consumers of a product, a market for advertisers, citizens participating in the public life of a democracy, a community or a brainwashed mass?
2. Production of Culture: How have structural factors—"technology, law and regulation, industry structure, organizational structure, occupational career, and market" (Peterson and Anand 2004: 313)—influenced what music is broadcast and the meanings that it takes on? What are the differences between public service and commercial radio? Between local stations and national networks?
3. Musical Genre: What role does musical genre play in shaping radio organizations and audiences? What roles do radio organizations and audiences play in constituting musical genres?
4. Listening Practices: How does music heard on the radio affect the everyday lives of listeners? How do listeners—and broadcasters—negotiate different modes of listening, ranging from attentive to distracted? How does radio listening affect music's cultural roles and meanings?

As might be expected for a medium that has been used around the world for the broadcasting of popular, classical and traditional musics, the answers to these questions vary significantly. A consideration of this variety yields a conceptual map of the significant changes that have occurred in radio, music and society over the past century, as well as of the different national, regional and local contexts in which radio developed and continues to be used. This changeable object of study is not only produced by different historical and cultural contexts. It is also produced by what are arguably the central challenges of radio studies: the ephemerality of radio sound, the dispersed nature of radio listening, and the incompleteness and inaccessibility that characterizes the archives of many broadcasting entities. The tasks of finding useful source materials and of developing methodological and theoretical frameworks for analysis are thus critical for researchers working on music and radio.

The literature on music and radio is characterized by a diversity of approaches, reflecting the disciplinary backgrounds, intellectual traditions and even political and industrial commitments that have informed researchers working in the field since the 1930s. Whereas commercial radio has long been dominated by quantitative audience research, academic researchers have utilized a range of critical, ethnographic, archival and quantitative methodologies. Since the early 2000s, research on music and radio has burgeoned, particularly with interdisciplinary dialogue between cultural studies and the sociology of culture, between media studies and music studies, and in the emergence of the vibrant interdisciplines of radio studies and sound studies.

This chapter offers an overview of sociologically informed research into music and radio, organized by the historical developments in music broadcasting upon which scholarship has focused: the 1930s, when radio broadcasting and listener research coalesced around the British public service model and the United States commercial model; the 1950s, when, with the rise of television, radio was reinvented as a secondary medium devoted primarily to recorded music; the 1970s, when commercial formats, defined by narrow demographics and specific musical genres, became dominant; and the 2000s, when terrestrial (as opposed to satellite and/or internet) radio was joined by what Hilmes (2013: 43–44) calls "soundwork": "the entire complex of sound-based digital media." The focus, it should be acknowledged, is largely upon radio in the United Kingdom and the United States, the nations that have produced the most globally influential broadcasting models and around which a preponderance of the (English-language) literature has clustered.

The 1930s: Defining the Audience

Radio transformed in the 1920s from the experimental domain of hobbyists into a modern mass medium, heard by a wide audience via an increasingly affordable domestic appliance. By the 1930s, its powerful influence on the public was recognized; indeed, with its "theoretically universal address," radio shaped new and contradictory conceptions of the public, as both citizens and consumers (Loviglio 2005: xxi). Social scientists and advertisers responded by developing new techniques for studying audiences. Their efforts intersected with several key dichotomies in radio discourse and policy: public service versus commercial radio; active versus passive listening; and local versus national broadcasting. Classical music became a touchstone for these discussions, because it emblemized radio's potential as a tool of cultural uplift, even as popular music embodied radio's links to commerce. This section will explore the implications of these dichotomies for music programming and research, focusing upon the British Broadcasting Corporation's (BBC's) Listener Research in the United Kingdom and the Princeton Radio Project in the United States.

As Hilmes (2012) has shown, the public service versus commercial dichotomy took shape by the end of the 1920s along national lines: in the United Kingdom, the publicly funded BBC played the role of mass educator and national unifier, whereas, in the United States, commercial networks competed for audiences and advertisers. The two systems defined themselves against each other, even as they influenced other nations: many Scandinavian, African and Antipodean nations followed the BBC's model whereas the US commercial models dominated in Central and South America (Hilmes 2012: 6, 19). Other nations, including Australia, Brazil, France and Canada, borrowed from both models to develop "mixed" systems (Goodman 2011: 15). The dualistic framing of public service versus commercial broadcasting obscured similarities between the systems. For example, although classical music was key to its educational mission, the BBC also aired, and thus promoted, dance bands, theater organs and crooners (Scannell and Cardiff 1991, Baade 2012). Meanwhile, US commercial networks embraced symphonic broadcasting, both for prestige and to satisfy public interest regulations (Goodman 2011).

Throughout the interwar period, listener letters represented a key source of information about audience tastes, and both commercial and public service broadcasters encouraged listeners to write in with feedback about what they heard. Although sometimes regarded as a crude system for tracking audience opinion before the advent of scientific measurement, listener correspondence provided rich qualitative data while also helping to constitute the role of radio in public life, with actively engaged audiences (Doctor 1999, Goodman 2011, Razlagova 2011). Nonetheless, there were also calls for more systematic research. During the 1930s, three US firms—Crossley, Hooper and Nielsen—pioneered independent audience measurement, using telephone surveys and other sampling techniques (Cox 2008: 43–49). Their ratings figures helped advertisers determine the reach of programs they sponsored, but they also revealed that educational and cultural programming attracted fewer listeners than popular music and entertainment.

At the BBC, with its mission of cultural uplift, concerns about ratings-driven programming fueled resistance to audience research, which was seen as a commercialized, US development. Nonetheless, several BBC staff appealed for more information about listener habits and the effectiveness of different modes of presentation. Meanwhile, the BBC's lack of systematic audience research gave critics ammunition to argue that it was unresponsive to the public and should lose its monopoly. The solution was to institute a Listener Research Department. Headed from 1936 by Robert Silvey, BBC Listener Research quickly became an innovative force. Silvey pioneered "random sampling techniques," but he also utilized "local correspondents" and panels to provide qualitative information on attitudes and listening practices, an approach aligned with the "quasi-anthropological" methods of the influential Mass-Observation social research organization, founded in the same year (Nicholas 2006). Listener Research soon produced a picture of the BBC's audience, finding that younger and working-class listeners (the majority) preferred variety and lighter music to classical music. A key condition for the Listener Research Department, however, was that it not be involved in "applying" its research. Thus, the classically oriented Music Department was able to ignore its findings, although the Variety Department worked closely with Listener Research to refine popular music presentation (Scannell and Cardiff 1991: 375–379, Nicholas 2006: 5–6). In essence, the BBC adopted audience research without becoming beholden to ratings.

Academic radio research in the United States took a very different shape, not only because of US radio's commercial orientation, but also because academic sociology was growing as a "scientific" discipline. One of the most notable of the period's many "large-scale, substantially financed research projects" was the Princeton Radio Research Project, which was started in 1937 (Calhoun 2007: 34). The project's director, Paul Lazarsfeld, aimed to develop industry-friendly approaches to measuring audience opinion, signaling a shift in US audience research from an engagement with open-ended listener feedback to a focus on easily quantified "knee-jerk preferences" (Razlagova 2011: 101–104). Despite his "administrative" orientation, Lazarsfeld hired Theodor Adorno, his fellow *émigré*, to explore theoretical approaches to radio's effect on audiences. He assigned Adorno and his section the topic of music because it was "the mildest and least explosive area of broadcasting" (Goodman 2011: 164–165). Adorno (1941) responded by asserting that radio contributed to "retrogressive" (passive) listening, challenging the assumption that broadcasting classical music was automatically a social good—and that measuring audience opinion could improve it. Ultimately, Adorno's dissonant perspectives led to his 1940 departure from the project.

During the 1930s and into the 1940s, both public service and commercial broadcasters embraced classical music as a vehicle for cultural uplift, even as they sought to better understand the audience they were hoping to educate. Despite their efforts, classical music remained a minority taste. Because of its public service mandate, the BBC continued to air classical music during the period following the Second World War, whereas US commercial radio largely left classical programming to university stations and the specialized realm of FM broadcasting. To frame the 1930s solely through the encounters between classical music, audience research and national radio systems would be a mistake, however, as the case of regional broadcasting in the United States demonstrates. First, its local orientation and pre-recorded content became the model for post-war commercial broadcasting (Russo 2010). Second, it played a key role in the development of the country music genre and (rural, white) audience (Peterson 1997). The recognition that radio—and the musical genres that it broadcast—reached a segmented, rather than mass, audience had a powerful impact on post-war broadcasting.

The 1950s: Localism, Top 40, and Rock 'n' Roll

In the United States after the Second World War, commercial radio assumed the characteristics that would come to define it globally: it featured recorded music, with disc jockeys (DJs) providing a live presence, it addressed a local and increasingly specific audience, and it developed close ties with the recording industry. These developments, coupled with the coalescence of teenagers as a distinct popular music audience, the emergence of rock 'n' roll as a distinct genre and the development of the Top 40 radio format, made US commercial radio in the 1950s a touchstone in histories of radio and popular music. Although relatively little sociologically informed research focuses exclusively on the topic, it is foundational to understanding the rise of music formats on commercial radio in the 1970s (Peterson and Davis 1974). This section will sketch key developments in radio and music during this period, focusing upon the often-mythologized dichotomy of the autonomous DJ and the standardized Top 40 format.

In the post-war era, the rise of television was the catalyst for transforming radio into a "secondary" medium. While television became a national medium that addressed a fully attentive audience, radio became a localized accompaniment to listeners' everyday activities. During the late 1940s, the number of independent local stations expanded five-fold, encouraged by US Federal Communication Commission efforts to limit monopolies and diversify ownership. Cost-conscious local stations turned to recorded music to fill airtime while, to compete for advertisers, they increasingly aimed for high ratings with distinct audience segments (Peterson and Davis 1974: 301). Throughout the 1950s and 1960s, radio advertising revenues and radio sales rose. Meanwhile, many local commercial stations served audiences that had been ignored by the networks, most notably African Americans, served by "black appeal" stations, and teenagers, especially as portable transistor radios became more affordable in the late 1950s (Barlow 1999, Douglas 1999: 223–226).

Both radio and the recording industry also embraced a distinct teenage market, particularly through the new genre of rock 'n' roll, which was linked to the crossover of African-American rhythm and blues to a white teenage audience. Modeling themselves after African-American DJs, Alan Freed and other white DJs became iconic figures in popularizing black music with white audiences (Keightley 2001). If classical music represented radio's "civic ambition" in the 1930s, rock 'n' roll embodied the democratic, anti-segregationist hopes of the civil rights era (Goodman 2011). Rock criticism of the 1960s further cast rock 'n' roll in masculinist terms as oppositional and serious, in contrast to vapid mainstream pop (Coates 2003). This dichotomy mapped onto the perceived opposition in 1950s radio between musically adventurous DJs and standardized, commercialized Top 40 music, contributing to the romanticization of DJs and the dismissal of pop music audiences as feminized teenyboppers.

As Killmeier (2001) argues, DJs balanced their roles as taste-making "surrogate consumers" with democratic claims that they were responsive to listeners' tastes, communicated through informal polls and community outreach. DJs in the 1950s enjoyed a relatively high level of control over their programming, but they were not fully autonomous. Through the payola system, record companies offered DJs a variety of inducements to play their discs—a practice that helped small labels gain access to the airwaves but also diverted income from musicians. Like the older practice of song plugging, payola underscored the importance of radio in marketing popular songs—not least because airplay offered a seemingly impartial confirmation of a song's popularity (Rossman 2012: 23). In 1960, the US Congress initiated a series of hearings on payola. Fueled by a moral panic about rock 'n' roll, race and the corruption of youth by unscrupulous DJs, the hearings led to the outlawing of payola and new limits on DJ autonomy (Douglas 1999: 250–251).

Beyond celebrity DJs, radio stations in the 1950s pursued ratings through more systematic means, most famously, the Top 40 format. Its invention is usually credited to Todd Storz, who, observing teenagers playing the same jukebox discs repeatedly, recognized the importance of familiarity and repetition in attracting—and keeping—listeners. Although early iterations featured a wide spectrum of pop, the Top 40 format was associated with rock 'n' roll and teenage listeners by the late 1950s. The format's key elements were a high-energy presentation style and hit songs played in "high rotation" (Eberly 1982: 200–206). Although it was criticized for being formulaic and commercialized, especially with the rise of independent freeform FM radio in the late 1960s, which valorized rock authenticity and DJ autonomy, the Top 40 format, with its increasingly tight playlists and intense "quality control," strongly influenced commercial radio from the 1970s onward.

1970s: Formats and the Public Interest

Terrestrial commercial radio assumed its modern form during the 1970s, as music formats proliferated on an expanded FM spectrum, which offered higher fidelity sound than the AM spectrum. A format defines a station's distinctive "sound": its playlist, musical genre(s), DJ patter and advertising—all of which are calculated to generate high ratings with a specific demographic, which are then used to market airtime to advertisers. Within the industry, formats are arguably defined as much by demographics as by musical genre, as is the case with Adult Contemporary, a format that targets women aged 24 to 54 with a blend of light rock and melodic pop. Format radio makes three key assumptions about audiences: they want to hear familiar music, they tend to listen distractedly and they can be understood through "typifications" (for example, young male rock fans do not want to hear women artists). Several scholars have offered useful accounts of the development and classifications of formats, along with their complicated interactions with musical genre, listener identities and practices, and the music industry (Barnes 1988, Berland 1994, Rothenbuhler 1996, Wollman 1998, Simpson 2011, Weisbard 2014).

A key concern in the literature is how music formats can serve the public interest, particularly with the concentration of station ownership following deregulation in the 1980s and 1990s (Berland 1994, Lee 2004). Determining what constitutes the public interest is, of course, a significant challenge. Is it *laissez faire* competition? Responsiveness to a local community? Representation of a nation's musicians? For many scholars, diversity—of formats, record labels or songs—is a key indicator that the public interest is being served, not only in terms of listener tastes but also, given radio's promotional importance, in ensuring that a wide range of musicians and labels have access to the airwaves. Such questions continue earlier debates about whether the audience is a public or a market, about who controls music programming and about music's status as commodity or form of cultural expression. To address these questions, many scholars have used communication theory and engaged a production-of-culture perspective, with methods ranging from interviews and ethnographies of radio personnel to analyses of playlist, station and market data.

The question of whether commercial radio programming is more responsive to local needs or national industries has been central to scholarship on format radio since the 1980s. In his ethnography of an Album Oriented Rock (AOR) station, Rothenbuhler (1985) found that programming decisions were primarily based upon airplay data published in national trade sheets, recommendations by record company promoters and artists' reputations; listeners and DJs had little input. Berland's influential essay on Canadian format radio argued that syndicated corporate radio, by centralizing production, had divorced programming decisions from local contexts. Both scholars asserted that the corporate drive for profits limited the diversity of what was aired and, ultimately, the community building potential of radio (Berland 1994, Rothenbuhler 1996).

Several scholars have examined the effect of corporate consolidation on musical diversity after the 1996 US Telecommunications Act, which allowed unlimited national ownership of radio stations and significant increases in local ownership. Lee (2004) found that, under consolidated ownership, programming was increasingly done at the regional level, which decreased song diversity in all major formats throughout the 1990s. On the other hand, consolidation contributed to greater format diversity in large markets, as owners of multiple stations bundled several formats to pursue as many "commercially valuable demographic segments" as possible (Lee 2004: 333). Rossman's diffusion analysis demonstrated that corporate routines and strategies, not deliberate top-down decision making, were driving the "sameness" of commercial radio—specifically, the genre parameters of formats and "record label promotions," including payola, which has remained a significant force in the industry, despite periodic scandals and regulatory crackdowns. Like Lee, Rossman (2012: 72, 100) identified a trend toward more formats with less song diversity, with the most successful songs cutting across formats and the least successful falling outside narrow generic conventions.

The US model has influenced commercial radio internationally (Ahlkvist 2001), as have multinational music corporations. Responding to concerns about Americanization, governments like Canada and France have instituted quotas for broadcasters, whereas others have adopted softer "promotional state" incentives (Cloonan 2007). Several studies have examined how policy affects national music industries, genres and identities. For example, Henderson (2008) argues that Canadian content quotas, in place since 1971, have not only supported the nation's music industry but also helped support vibrant independent music scenes. In contrast, New Zealand opted for a voluntary quota system, with the agency New Zealand on Air promoting local music, a strategy deemed most effective for mainstream, "radio-friendly" songs (Scott 2008).

In some nations, public service broadcasters remain influential, serving as "gatekeepers" between cultural producers and the public. In the United Kingdom, for example, BBC Radio 1 has been a dominant force in the nation's popular music industry since 1967 (Percival 2011). Under a "ratings by day, reputation by night" approach, it adopted a "Top 50" playlist for daytime programming in the early 1970s while its night-time DJs enjoyed a high degree of autonomy, programming progressive rock and other adventurous repertory. Barring offshore competitors, such as the legendary pirate stations of the 1960s, the BBC did not face competition from independent commercial radio until the 1970s, and such stations were slow to adopt US-style formats until deregulation in the 1980s (Barnard 1989: 50–62). During the 1990s, Radio 1 reframed its public service mandate to feature "new music first." Not only did this differentiate it from format-driven commercial stations but, Hendy (2000) argued, its new focus contributed to the global successes of Britpop in the late 1990s.

In Israel, a nation on the periphery of the multinational music industry, the situation was more complex. Kaplan (2012) describes how Galgalatz, the military's publicly funded second station, adopted an adult contemporary format in 1996 in order to compete with commercial stations. Offering a blend of English-language and Israeli soft rock, it soon became the nation's leading station, and its format came to be seen as an Israeli invention, not a globalized import. Meanwhile, it was commercial stations that diversified Israeli popular music by including Arab-influenced genres in their playlists (Kaplan 2012: 225–226).

The literature is generally pessimistic about the ability of commercial format radio to be musically diverse, respond to local communities and avoid blandness. Rationalized programming, cost cutting, payola and the prioritization of profit are all blamed for turning music radio into something to be overheard rather than listened to. Indeed, radio listenership has declined since the 1990s, although cheaper talk formats have expanded, even in US public radio, which historically aired less marketable genres, like classical, jazz and folk (Lee 2004, NEA 2006). Nonetheless, the music industry still treats terrestrial music radio as an important promotional outlet (Rossman 2012).

Many scholars, in fact, have argued for the continued relevance of terrestrial and/or commercial radio, particularly those investigating sites where music programming is not fully rationalized. This may be found at niche stations in North America (Ahlkvist 2001) and in nations like Peru, where commercial radio and DJs remain dominant forces in the industry, promoting a wide range of local, as well as cosmopolitan, popular genres (Tucker 2010). Finally, non-commercial, community radio stations are distinguished by their responsiveness to local communities, offering models for democratic musical engagement (Fairchild 2012). Clearly, focusing exclusively upon terrestrial format radio in the developed world obscures a wide range of exciting music radio.

The 2000s: Music Radio Online

As Loviglio and Hilmes (2013) note, radio has undergone a renaissance since the early 2000s. An upsurge of radio scholarship has examined terrestrial radio in the developing world, community radio, satellite radio, web radio and podcasting, and a range of digital music streaming services. Radio has even found its way onto screens through smartphone apps and station websites offering a range of content and discussion forums (Hilmes 2013). Many observers have celebrated the resurgence of radio documentary and the global reach of online radio. The investigation of music radio, however, remains a challenge, not least because the music industry itself is in an intense period of reinvention in response to digital media. This section will consider research on new forms of "music radio," focusing upon online music services and the ongoing tensions of rationalized programming versus DJ autonomy, playlist personalization and the constitution of the public interest in online environments.

In an extension of format radio's narrowcast address, online music services offer subscribers an extensive, "hyperfragmented" selection of formats. Algorithm-based music services like Last.fm further allow users to personalize playlists to their tastes (Lacey 2013: 15). Popular discourse often contrasts such "robot" services unfavorably with the curated experience provided by freeform DJs. Razlagova (2013: 63) argues, however, that the more important divide is "between open-access culture and corporate uses of intellectual property," citing industry-backed services, like Spotify, which pay musicians negligible royalties and serve only a few nations because of licensing restrictions. In contrast, independent web radio provides a wide range of open-access music to audiences around the globe, subverting the agendas, genres and formats of the music and radio industries.

The debate about open access versus corporate ownership on the internet recalls older questions concerning broadcasting and the public interest. Unlike the broadcast spectrum, which is regulated as a public resource, much of the internet's infrastructure is privately owned, rendering considerations of public interest and even of "the public" problematic (Wall, forthcoming). Online music services often "bypass the politics and regulation related to nation-building discourses" (Homan 2012: 1047). Many public service broadcasters have responded by developing significant online presences. For example, the Canadian Broadcasting Corporation's CBC Music, an online service and app, offers a wide spectrum of formats and other content with an emphasis on Canadian artists.

As Lacey (2013) argues, the notion of a public is a construction fostered through modern communications media. Online environments promote a dichotomous image of participation (for example, comments pages) and of personalized, privatized listening. Indeed, online radio and music services represent hyperfragmentation in formats and more intense narrowcasting—even as they make available a staggering diversity of genres, artists, periods and songs, necessitating in turn a new set of gatekeepers, whether they be recommendation algorithms or taste-making DJs. The question of how the public for these services is constituted—and its relation to the local, the national and the online community—remains open.

Conclusion

Sociologically informed scholarship on radio and music has focused largely upon production-of-culture concerns, ranging from regulations and industry organizations to studies of DJs and radio programmers. Researchers have also attended to audiences, considering how they are constituted and how they interact with musical sound. Finally, musical genre has also been key, often functioning as an organizing concept in investigations of listening habits, demographics and industry structures.

Relatively little of this literature attends closely to musical sound or the specific performances of musicians. There are several reasons for this: the disciplinary backgrounds of scholars in the field, the challenge of untangling the complex political economies of radio, and the quantitative nature of most readily available data. In many ways, the radio industry's tendency to treat music like a commodity has made it difficult for scholars interested in music as more than a commodity to find a foothold for their analyses. These challenges are amplified by the sheer quantity and ubiquity of music on radio, both on air and online—and its diversity throughout history and across cultures.

Thanks to music scholars' engagement with media, media scholars' engagement with sound, and the new fields of radio and sound studies, the literature investigating music on radio has grown significantly. This work offers not only a better understanding of music's role in society, but also an opportunity to understand how music on radio may (or may not) contribute to a more democratic public sphere.

References

Adorno, T.W. 1941. "The Radio Symphony." In *Radio Research 1941*, eds. P.F. Lazarsfeld and F.N. Stanton, 110–139. New York: Duell, Sloan and Pearce.

Ahlkvist, J.A. 2001. "Programming Philosophies and the Rationalization of Music Radio." *Media, Culture & Society* 23(3): 339–358.

Baade, C. 2012. *Victory through Harmony: The BBC and Popular Music in World War II*. New York: Oxford University Press.

Barlow, W. 1999. *Voice Over: The Making of Black Radio*. Philadelphia: Temple University Press.

Barnard, S. 1989. *On the Radio: Music Radio in Britain*. Milton Keynes: Open University Press.

Barnes, K. 1988. "Top 40 Radio: A Fragment of the Imagination." In *Facing the Music*, ed. S. Frith, 8–50. New York: Pantheon.

Berland, J. 1994. "Radio Space and Industrial Time: The Case of Music Formats." In *Canadian Music: Issues of Hegemony and Identity*, eds. B. Diamond and R. Witmer, 173–187. Toronto: Canadian Scholars' Press.

Calhoun, C. 2007. "Sociology in America: An Introduction." In *Sociology in America: A History*, ed. C. Calhoun, 1–38. Chicago: University of Chicago Press.

Cloonan, M. 2007. *Popular Music and the State in the UK*. Aldershot: Ashgate.

Coates, N. 2003. "Teenyboppers, Groupies, and Other Grotesques: Girls and Women and Rock Culture in the 1960s and early 1970s." *Journal of Popular Music Studies* 15(1): 65–94.

Cox, J. 2008. *Sold on Radio: Advertisers in the Golden Age of Broadcasting*. Jefferson: McFarland and Co.

Doctor, J. 1999. *The BBC and Ultra-Modern Music, 1922–1936: Shaping a Nation's Tastes*. Cambridge: Cambridge University Press.

Douglas, S.J. 1999. *Listening In: Radio and the American Imagination, from Amos 'n' Andy and Edward R. Murrow to Wolfman Jack and Howard Stern*. New York: Random House.

Eberly, P.K. 1982. *Music in the Air: America's Changing Tastes in Popular Music*. New York: Hastings House.

Fairchild, C. 2012. *Music, Radio and the Public Sphere: The Aesthetics of Democracy.* New York: Palgrave Macmillan.

Goodman, A. 2011. *Radio's Civic Ambition: American Broadcasting and Democracy in the 1930s.* New York: Oxford University Press.

Henderson, S. 2008. "Canadian Content Regulations and the Formation of a National Scene." *Popular Music* 27(2): 307–315.

Hendy, D. 2000. "Pop Music Radio in the Public Service: BBC Radio 1 and New Music in the 1990s." *Media, Culture and Society* 22(6): 743–761.

Hilmes, M. 2012. *Network Nations: A Transnational History of British and American Broadcasting.* New York: Routledge.

_____. 2013. "The New Materiality of Radio: Sound on Screens." In *Radio's New Wave: Global Sound in the Digital Era*, eds. J. Loviglio and M. Hilmes, 43–61. New York: Routledge.

Homan, S. 2012. "Local Priorities, Industry Realities: The Music Quota as Cultural Exceptionalism." *Media, Culture and Society* 34(8): 1040–1051.

Kaplan, D. 2012. "Institutionalized Erasures: How Global Structures Acquire National Meanings in Israeli Popular Music." *Poetics* 40(3): 217–236.

Keightley, K. 2001. "Reconsidering Rock." In *The Cambridge Companion to Pop and Rock*, eds. S. Frith, W. Straw, and J. Street, 109–142. Cambridge: Cambridge University Press.

Killmeier, M.A. 2001. "Voices between the Tracks: Disk Jockeys, Radio, and Popular Music, 1955–1960." *Journal of Communication Inquiry* 25(4): 353–374.

Lacey, K. 2013. "Listening in the Digital Age." In *Radio's New Wave: Global Sound in the Digital Era*, eds. J. Loviglio and M. Hilmes, 9–23. New York: Routledge.

Lee, S.S. 2004. "Predicting Cultural Output Diversity in the Radio Industry, 1989–2002." *Poetics* 32(3/4): 325–342.

Loviglio, J. 2005. *Radio's Intimate Public: Network Broadcasting and Mass-Mediated Democracy.* Minneapolis: University of Minnesota Press.

Loviglio, J. and M. Hilmes. 2013. "Introduction: Making Radio Strange." In *Radio's New Wave: Global Sound in the Digital Era*, eds. J. Loviglio and M. Hilmes, 1–6. New York: Routledge.

National Endowment for the Arts (NEA). 2006. *Airing Questions of Access: Classical Music Radio Programming and Listening Trends.* Washington, DC.

Nicholas, S. 2006. "Introduction." *BBC Audience Research Reports.* Part 1: *BBC Listener Research Department*, 1937–c. 1950. 1–14. Wakefield: Microform Academic Publishers.

Percival, J.M. 2011. "Music Radio and the Record Industry: Songs, Sounds, and Power." *Popular Music and Society* 34(4): 455–473.

Peterson, R.A. 1997. *Creating Country Music: Fabricating Authenticity.* Chicago: University of Chicago Press.

Peterson, R.A. and N. Anand. 2004. "The Production of Culture Perspective." *Annual Review of Sociology* 30: 311–334.

Peterson, R.A. and R.B. Davis, Jr. 1974. "The Contemporary American Radio Audience." *Popular Music and Society* 3(4): 299–313.

Razlagova, E. 2011. *The Listener's Voice: Early Radio and the American Public.* Philadelphia: University of Pennsylvania Press.

_____. 2013. "The Past and Future of Music Listening: Between Freeform DJs and Recommendation Algorithms." In *Radio's New Wave: Global Sound in the Digital Era*, eds. J. Loviglio and M. Hilmes, 62–76. New York: Routledge.

Rossman, G. 2012. *Climbing the Charts: What Radio Airplay Tells Us About the Diffusion of Innovation.* Princeton: Princeton University Press.

Rothenbuhler, E.W. 1985. "Programming Decision Making in Popular Music Radio." *Communication Research* 12(2): 209–232.

_____. 1996. "Commercial Radio as Communication." *Journal of Communication* 46(1): 125–143.

Russo, A. 2010. *Points on the Dial: Golden Age Radio beyond the Networks.* Durham: Duke University Press.

Scannell, P. and D. Cardiff. 1991. *A Social History of British Broadcasting*, Vol. 1: *Serving the Nation.* Oxford: Basil Blackwell.

Scott, M. 2008. "The Networked State: New Zealand on Air and New Zealand's Pop Renaissance." *Popular Music* 27(2): 299–305.

Simpson, K. 2011. *Early '70s Radio: The American Format Revolution.* New York: Continuum.

Tucker, J. 2010. "Music Radio and Global Mediation: Producing Social Distinction in the Andean Public Sphere." *Cultural Studies* 24(4): 553–579.

Wall, T. Forthcoming. "Music Radio Goes Online." In *Music and the Broadcast Experience: Performance, Production, and Audiences*, eds. C. Baade and J. Deaville. New York: Oxford University Press.

Weisbard, E. 2014. Top 40 Democracy: *The Rival Mainstreams of American Music.* Chicago: University of Chicago Press.

Wollman, E.L. 1998. "Men Music & Marketing at Q104.3 (WAXQ-FM New York)." *Popular Music and Society* 22(4): 1–23.

30

Music and the Moving Image
A Case Study of Hans Zimmer

BENJAMIN WRIGHT

All the naysayers for a while were going, "Oh, all you guys did was build a factory. It's just a factory." And at first I was really offended by that, but then I realized that, yes, that's exactly what we did. We built a factory where there's an infrastructure in place, there's technology, there's a constant support system that lets the artists be creative and do crazy things while having a sort of comfort level and support network.

Hans Zimmer (quoted in Rule and Gallagher 1999: 31)

In this 1997 interview with *Keyboard* magazine, film composer Hans Zimmer describes the critical reaction to Remote Control Productions, the music production facility he formed in 1989 with his producing partner Jay Rifkin. At the time, the company's Santa Monica, California facility boasted a 40,000 square-foot studio campus that functioned as a cooperative "think tank" for dozens of feature film, television, gaming and commercial composers to hone their craft and build careers in the entertainment industry. With its shared network of digital music samples and cutting-edge equipment, not to mention its communal sense of creative workflow, Zimmer suggests in the same interview, "There's a difference in the way scores sound that come out of here. Not so much a sound quality issue, but more because there's an infrastructure in place" (Rule and Gallagher 1999: 31). The aesthetic dimensions of this particular "sound" are shaped, in part, by a reliance on classical Hollywood scoring practices, and a synergy between electronic and orchestral musical structures. In large measure, the institutional organization of Zimmer's studio and the technological infrastructure that supports it has helped to create a distinct house style that has been instrumental in reorganizing the form and function of contemporary film music practices.

Of particular interest in this chapter is how the Remote Control "sound" developed out of a shared set of institutional demands and aesthetic structures specific to contemporary film and television music production and the stylistic imprimatur of Zimmer. To this end, I argue that this "group style" functions within a set of interrelated formal conventions and centralized labor structures modeled after scoring principles developed in the Hollywood studio era. More than this, however, the occupational identities of Remote Control musicians and composers are tied to not just the social and technical infrastructure of Zimmer's "factory" but also to Zimmer's aesthetic approach to film scoring. Ultimately, this infrastructure can tell us something about contemporary Hollywood music production and its relationship to narrative, digital technology and the business of modern filmmaking.

Industrial accounts of composers in Hollywood have emphasized the inherent conflict between corporate and creative demands of this commercial art. Film music historians Karlin and Wright argue that, in addition to the creative work of writing music for motion pictures, the work of a composer invariably involves the negotiation of a complex assortment of factors including narrative, directorial, visual and business demands (Karlin and Wright 2004: 21). According to Faulkner (1978: 100), film composing is "client dominant" where interference from producers, directors and studio executives pose distinct challenges to the creative autonomy of a composer and the creation of a unique artwork (the film score): "What a worker does about the problems of inappropriate demands and different definitions of the situation depends upon a number of factors, including the alternatives at his or her disposal, his or her power to define and control the actions of clients, and his or her power to select a clientele to work with." Underscoring this relationship is the extent to which a composer has leverage—or institutional power—to affect the creative direction of their work. At the same time, as Dowd (2004: 239) has noted, composers must also negotiate career opportunities in a field where very few individuals enjoy stable and consistent careers.

By the early 1960s, most major Hollywood studios had divested themselves of on-the-lot production and postproduction services, and began contracting out sound, music and picture editorial work to freelance practitioners. The Paramount decision of 1948, which effectively severed the studios' distribution and exhibition holdings from their production networks, led to widespread layoffs and reorganizations of studio personnel. Film studios, including Metro-Goldwyn-Mayer, Twentieth Century Fox, Warner Bros. and Paramount, announced they could no longer afford to staff large numbers of craft workers, including composers and music personnel, under multi-year contracts (Anon. 1970). In its place, studios began contracting on a per-picture basis. In economic terms, the short-term partnerships that developed between craft professionals and studio management constituted a form of industrial organization called "flexible specialization." According to Christopherson and Storper (1989: 55), flexibly specialized workers in the contemporary film industry provide sub-contracted, specialized services to producers and directors but remain open to changes in workflow, professional relationships and technical skills. For composers, who as a group continue to remain unaffiliated with a Hollywood guild or labor union, freelance work means occupational uncertainty and instability. In making the transition from full-time studio staff to freelance laborers over the last few decades, composers—in addition to most other postproduction personnel—negotiated their professional status within the industry by developing and nurturing relationships with producer and director clients that could potentially lead to recurring work and the prospect of a stable career. However, as Faulkner has shown, one of the symptoms of the unstable freelance system is that even though composers continue to develop and nurture relationships with filmmakers, and may even relinquish artistic control over their work when disagreements arise, the likelihood of their efforts positively affecting their career is never guaranteed.

In some sense, then, Remote Control Productions, which originally began as Media Ventures and underwent a name change in 2003, represents a social and creative anomaly within contemporary film music production, resembling the serial mode of production common to studio-era music practices. During their heyday of the 1930s and 1940s, major studios housed music departments with staff composers, arrangers, orchestrators, copyists, music editors, librarians and a musical director who oversaw daily operations and functioned as an intermediary between producers and composers (Prendergast 1992: 37). The production of studio-era film music, as Cooke (2008: 72) notes, was largely a collaborative affair involving multiple composers, arrangers and orchestrators where scores were routinely considered "team efforts" and those responsible were not given proper screen credit. Decades later, the Remote Control motto—"to nurture musically talented individuals into successful composers and recording artists"—suggests a training ground that is not otherwise available to composers within the current Los Angeles-based music production community.

The composition of the Remote Control facility reflects a decentralized mode of production with a small staff of salaried composers, sound designers, orchestrators, technicians and a growing collective of composers who lease studio space in the facility, including Steve Jablonsky (*Transformers*, 2007), Henry Jackman (*X-Men: First Class*, 2011), Ramin Djawadi (*Game of Thrones*, 2011), Rupert Gregson-Williams (*Winter's Tale*, 2014), Heitor Pereira (*Despicable Me 2*, 2013), Geoff Zanelli (*Disturbia*, 2007), Atli Orvarsson (*Season of the Witch*, 2011), Lorne Balfe (*Megamind*, 2010) and Junkie XL (*300: Rise of an Empire*, 2014). In a 2014 *Variety* profile, film music historian Jon Burlingame (2014) refers to Remote Control as a "loanout company" with an eighty-five-member team of independent freelancers who secure their own film projects and utilize the facility's four control rooms and numerous mixing suites to perform, record and mix their music. Former Remote Control composer Jeff Beal expresses the campus camaraderie in the following way: "This really is a collective of different people, each doing his own thing, and occasionally coming in to help and inspire one another when necessary and possible" (quoted in Rule and Gallagher 1999: 31). In addition to the facility's congenial atmosphere and open door policy, Remote Control composers benefit from two strongly centralized components, one based on studio technology and the other on the transactional nature of composer collaboration within the facility.

The company's infrastructure is anchored by its extensive digital sample library that houses thousands of sounds—from *taiko* hits to cello sustains to horn bursts to environmental ambiences—culled from recording sessions with world musicians, performers, sound artists and the London Symphony Orchestra. Among the sounds stored in the studio archive are raw selections created for dozens of Zimmer's own scores, including *Rain Man* (1988), *Black Rain* (1989), *The Lion King* (1994), *Crimson Tide* (1995), *Gladiator* (2000), the *Pirates of the Caribbean* series (2003–2011) and *The Dark Knight* trilogy (2005–2012). Linked by a central server, these recordings are available to every composer in the facility to use in the creation of temporary mock-ups or in a final score. Indeed, passages from Zimmer's scores to *The Peacemaker* (1997) and *The Thin Red Line* (1998) contain elements from the sample library that are interwoven with original orchestral and choral performances. Typically during the scoring process, a composer will audition a selection of musical sketches for a visiting director using the sample library in place of a more expensive orchestra. Once an approach is settled upon, the composer replaces the demo material with a live orchestra. In other cases, a director may become attached to the temporary track (known as "temp love") and request its use in the final track (Sadoff 2006: 166). What these samples provide, then, is a wellspring of proprietary sound material that is unavailable to musicians outside of Remote Control Productions. But, at the same time, the library network also fosters a dynamic workflow between Zimmer and other composers that strongly resembles the team-based method of studio-era music departments.

It is not uncommon for Zimmer to call on additional composers to "flesh out" his ideas after he has composed the principal motifs and themes for a particular cue, especially on large film projects with tight schedules. According to composer Henry Jackman, "Hans gives you a road map of the cue. He's written a 2:30 piano piece, with loads of key changes, the mood of the movement. So you've pretty much got all the ammunition, emotionally" (quoted in Hurwitz 2007: 49). Working from Zimmer's detailed sketches, Jackman performs the tasks of orchestrator, music editor and composer as he orchestrates the cue and times it to specific scenes. Jackman has received an additional composer credit on several Zimmer projects, including *The Holiday* (2006) and *The Simpsons Movie* (2007). What Burlingame's analysis does not account for is the way in which less experienced composers develop their craft by programming synthesized material, orchestrating cues and writing original music for Zimmer's projects before securing solo assignments with filmmakers and studios who have worked with Remote Control in the past.

In many ways, this technological and communal infrastructure is governed by the shared conventions and patterns of activity of contemporary film music practices. As Becker (1976) and Rosenblum (1978) have shown, aesthetic norms of artistic practice can tell us something about the social organization of such "art worlds." Here, aesthetic style consists of predictable combinations of materials that remain flexible to an artwork's organization of production. As Rosenblum (1978: 422) argues, these predictable features and conventional textures can tell us something about the structural characteristics, social milieu and creative constraints associated with the production of artworks. As artistic labor within a commercial industry, Hollywood composers work within a bounded set of options most often determined by four choices: replication, revision, synthesis and rejection. Film scholar David Bordwell (1997: 154) has shown that these options allow us to consider the ebb and flow of stability and change across the history of film style. While most creative decisions will consist of replicating traditional methods, composers can solve problems using innovative strategies that reject conventional wisdom. Style in this sense bears upon the composer to solve creative problems by repeating, revising, combining or rejecting aesthetic strategies that have been tried in the past. Musicologist Leonard Meyer (1987: 21) further posits that artistic style is based on a system of constraints—or rules—that are "learned and adopted as part of the historical-cultural circumstances of individuals or groups." One way to account for the social organization of Remote Control Productions and its distinctive "sound" is to consider the aesthetic functions and conventional norms of film music practices.

The bounded options Bordwell describes in his analysis of classical Hollywood cinema can be tied to Gorbman's foundational reading of studio-era film music practices. She outlines seven principles of scoring, sound editing and mixing that shaped the production of classical Hollywood sound tracks, described as: (1) invisibility; (2) inaudibility; (3) signifier of emotion; (4) narrative cueing; (5) continuity; (6) unity and (7) escape clause. The first two principles dovetail with the broader goals of classical continuity editing where the work of filmmaking does not call attention to its conditions of production. Likewise, classical film music functions as something that should not disrupt the illusion of seamless continuity. To accomplish this, music often serves to smooth over and unify the disruptive qualities of editing, which explains principles five and six. The third and fourth principles refer specifically to the ways music can convey narrative details and strengthen emotional connections to characters through themes, instrumentation and placement. The final rule—"escape clause"—is perhaps the most abstract one as it informs how composers implement the other six principles. In effect, it addresses the bounded but flexible system of continuity filmmaking where composers may choose to ignore any principle at the service of the other principles (Gorbman 1987: 73). The durability of this system and its enduring set of creative constraints and possibilities suggest a collection of shared conventions and coordinated activities that continue to find favor among contemporary composers and filmmakers primarily because they offer shared agreements, tacit knowledge and a common aesthetic language to a large community of freelance artists.

The stylistic characteristics central to the Remote Control aesthetic can be found in the replicated features, habits and scoring approach of Hans Zimmer. What Zimmer accomplishes is not so much a reinvention of film music conventions as a magnification of classical techniques and practices. Specifically, Zimmer composes material that often works to spotlight narrative details—what Gorbman (1987: 73) calls "narrative cueing"—and to create audiovisual continuity by unifying disparate shots and scenes with long cues that tie together notions of space, place and character. When asked to describe the stylistic aspects of his film music, Zimmer remarked, "I would have been just as happy being a recording engineer as a composer. Sometimes it's very difficult to stop me from mangling sounds, engineering, and doing any of those things, and actually getting me to sit down and write the notes" (Spitfire Audio 2013). For Zimmer, writing melodies and designing sounds using synthesizers are not mutually exclusive tasks. Having spent the early part of his career as a synthesizer programmer and keyboardist for new wave bands such as the Buggles and Ultravox, then as a *protégé* of English film composer Stanley Myers, Zimmer has cultivated a hybrid electronic-orchestral style that incorporates a range of analog and digital oscillators, filters and amplifiers alongside the ubiquitous sound of the symphony orchestra. His early Hollywood successes, *Driving Miss Daisy* (1989), *Black Rain* and *Days of Thunder* (1990), combined pop themes and electronic passages with propulsive rhythms and driving ostinatos, where musical performance and the texture of individual instruments cue narrative details through an emphasis on musical color.

Zimmer's writing process begins with a search for a film's musical identity, what he calls its "sonic landscape." To accomplish this, he often invites world musicians to Remote Control for impromptu jam sessions to find and hone the musical syntax of a particular project. Afterwards, he returns to his studio and layers the raw samples over orchestral performances, choral parts and electronic passages. In most cases, the partnerships between Zimmer and his performers have provided the equivalent of a pop hook to much of his output: Jeff Beck's Stratocaster riffs in *Days of Thunder*, Lebo M's opening vocal in *The Lion King*, Johnny Marr's reverb-heavy guitar licks in *Inception* (2010) and Lisa Gerrard's wordless vocals in *Gladiator* and *Black Hawk Down* (both 2001). The melodic hooks are simple but infectious—even Zimmer admits he writes "stupidly simple" melodies that can often be played with just one finger on the piano (Zimmer quoted in Greiving 2013). But what matters most are the musical colors that frame those simple melodies and the performances that imbue them with identifying marks that, in Zimmer's view, "seep into the pores of all the buildings, not just the characters" of a film's visual environment (Zimmer quoted in Greiving 2013).

Writing in 1946, musicologist Robert U. Nelson described the prevalence of musical color in Hollywood film scoring practices, especially in its ability to conjure associations to specific geographic locales, character types and dramatic situations. Color, in Nelson's (1946: 57) words, "may be taken to represent the sensuous or exotic side of music, in distinction to musical structure and line, which may be looked upon as representing the intellectual side." It is in this sense that musical color may offer the composer greater flexibility: "color is immediate in its effect, unlike thematic development, which makes definite time demands; infinitely flexible, color can be turned on and off as easily as water from a tap" (ibid.). Zimmer's expressive treatment of musical color through improvisation and collaborative recording sessions further characterizes his hybrid status as a composer and engineer, where film music meets the mixing studio. Music scholar Paul Théberge (1989) has noted that the recording engineer's interest in an aesthetic of recorded musical "sound" led to an increased demand for control over the recording process, especially in the early days of multitrack rock recording where overdubbing created a separate, hierarchical space for solo instruments. Likewise for Zimmer, it is not just about capturing individual sounds from an orchestra but also layering them into a synthesized product. Zimmer is also interested in experimenting with acoustic performances, pushing musicians to play their instruments in unconventional ways or playing his notes "the wrong way," as he instructed cellists and string players to do for the Joker's theme in *The Dark Knight*, which features an ascending pair of notes played slowly and roughly to produce a ragged, razor-like sound (Gotham Uncovered 2008).

The significance of the cooperative aspects of these musical performances and their treatment as colors to be modulated, tweaked and polished rests on a paradoxical treatment of sound. While he often finds his sound world among the wrong notes, mistakes and impromptu performances of world musicians, Zimmer is also often criticized for removing traces of an original performance by obscuring it with synthetic drones and distortion (Clemmensen 2008). In some cases, like in *The Peacemaker* (1997), the fusion of synth samples and symphony orchestra results in a mushy, canned sound; but in other cases, the trace of a solo performance serves the same function as a melodic *leitmotif*. Rejecting the ubiquitous need for musical line and complex melodic writing, Zimmer insists,

"A single note can be a performance" (Spitfire Audio 2013). Compare, for instance, the opening title music for two different Batman films. Danny Elfman's opening title music for Tim Burton's *Batman* (1989) introduces a suite of densely orchestrated, Wagnerian themes, while Zimmer's main title for Christopher Nolan's *The Dark Knight* opts for a micro sound world featuring the Joker's cello sustain. In Zimmer's case, it is the timbre of the cello, not its melody, which carries its identifying features. Not surprisingly, when describing the sound world of *The Dark Knight*, Zimmer claims that the music should immediately conjure an audiovisual image of a particular film: "I think if you put on *Dark Knight* you know this is Gotham City. And, from the first note to the last note, that holds true. I think that's partly why I sometimes use unconventional instruments, because it stops it from just being a generalization. It becomes very specific to those movies and to that world" (Zimmer quoted in Greiving 2013).

Similarly, the sound world for *Man of Steel* (2013), Zack Snyder's Superman remake, had Zimmer thinking about telephone wires stretching across the plains of Clark Kent's boyhood home in Smallville, Kansas. Zimmer asked himself, "That wind making those telephone wires buzz—how could I write a piece of music out of that?" (Zimmer quoted in Greiving 2013). He found a solution in the sliding scales of a pedal steel guitar, those twangy lap instruments of country music (Greiving 2013). In recording sessions, Zimmer instructed a group of pedal steel players to experiment with sustains and reverb that, when mixed into the final sound track, accompanies Superman leaping over tall buildings at a single bound.

The thread running through these statements about color is an attention to music as a stabilizing system that supports the dramatic development of the narrative. This occurs in much the same way as the classical scoring methods borrowed from the Wagnerian principle of unity between music and dramatic text. Indeed, as Flinn (1992: 34) has argued, Hollywood's investment in the synthesis of image and sound, where music works toward the goals of the narrative, is indebted to Richard Wagner's notion of *Gesamtkunstwerk*, or "total work of art," which required music to serve the text in such a way that it would remain subservient to the dramatic goals of the production. The legacy of music that underscores visual drama, especially in film, is one that treats its subordination to narrative as something that should not be consciously heard but *felt* as an effect of the entire audiovisual drama. Inasmuch as musical color remains an immediately identifiable feature of the sound track, Zimmer's hybrid electronic-orchestral sound worlds also underscore and cohere narrative development with a technique that expands upon the classical Hollywood practice of unifying visual action by incorporating repetitive electronic drones and slowly changing tonal harmonies.

In *The Thin Red Line* (1998), Terrence Malick's poetic Second World War drama, Zimmer's original score works, on the one hand, to unify aspects of the elliptical narrative with lengthy cues, and supply the film with an identifiable sound world on the other. According to Zimmer, he wrote most of the score before the film was edited, leaving Malick and his editorial staff with suites of music that could be tracked into the film. In this way, Zimmer could compose long passages that were not timed to particular scenes. One of the score's standout cues—known as "Journey to the Line" on the soundtrack album—features wooden percussion, *taiko* drums and a mournful harmonic texture comprised of three descending tones first carried by low strings and then by brass and electronic pulses. The E-flat minor figure intensifies throughout its nine-minute duration and reaches its crescendo with a bold statement from the brass, *taikos* and synthetic drones. What is most interesting about this cue—aside from its simplicity—is the way it works within the film, untethered from the visual action but still able to unify an intentionally disorienting sequence. When US soldiers storm a Japanese bivouac, they are immediately confronted by a chaotic scene: Japanese soldiers returning fire, a makeshift infirmary with wounded men writhing in pain, a soldier standing in the middle of the war zone with hands covering his ears and screaming. The handheld camera moves through the carnage, capturing a series of dramatic vignettes without a unified point of view. Zimmer's music synthesizes these vignettes into a cohesive rise-and-fall structure that ends with a plaintive voiceover asking, "Who's doin' this? Who's killin' us?"

What differentiates the cue from other examples of Hollywood action music is its focus on mood instead of tightly timed bursts of line and melody that serve to explain through music the generic sound of Hollywood wartime combat: snares, trumpets and military hymns. In contradistinction to this trend, Zimmer fashioned a solution by composing against the action, not for it, creating what he calls "minimalist music taken to a romantic level" (Zimmer quoted in Goldwasser 2006). This self-described *romantic minimalism* neatly collapses the two dominant functions of his film music into one stylistic device. Building on Wagnerian codes of dramaturgic unity and classical Hollywood continuity, as well as sampled colors that clarify narrative details, Zimmer's scoring habits derive, in some respects, from a popular definition of minimalism offered by Demers (2010: 69) in her study of experimental electronic music: "minimalist music has become synonymous with predominantly American music featuring rhythmic and melodic repetition, tonal harmonies, and textural transformations that unfold slowly through a process of accretion." In the context of musical technique, romantic minimalism is illustrative of a larger trend in contemporary scoring practices, especially among Remote Control composers, that replicates the stretched out tonal harmonies, sampled percussion and unifying logic of the "Journey to the Line" cue.

In subsequent scoring assignments, Zimmer returned to this particular aesthetic on *The Da Vinci Code* (2006), *The Dark Knight, Inception* and *Rush* (2013), where the final moments of each film feature similar rise-and-fall tonal harmonies, slowly evolving *ostinatos* and rich orchestral-electronic colors. In particular, the finale of *The Da Vinci Code* was originally written not with any scene in mind, but as a suite of musical ideas that was tracked into the last few minutes of the film. Recalls Zimmer:

> One day I could see that [director Ron Howard] was really worried, so I said, "Okay, I'll tell you what. I've written something, so let's put it up against the picture, just slap it up and start the CD and the picture at the same time." And it hit every cut, and it did everything, and that was the piece and we never adjusted it—and he never adjusted a frame of picture, it just happened to work.
>
> (Quoted in Goldwasser 2006)

In bridging the final scenes of the film, the music not only imbues the visual action with movement and rhythm, but also appears perfectly synchronized to it, reflecting what sound theorist Michel Chion (1994: 62) calls *synchresis*: "the mental fusion between a sound and a visual when these occur at exactly the same time."

On an industrial level, however, Zimmer's romantic minimalism proved popular with filmmakers and major studios throughout the 2000s as specific cues and textural colors from *The Thin Red Line* and *Inception* were appropriated for use in numerous movie trailers (Jagernauth 2013, Davis 2013) and other film scores. In many cases, the films that borrowed this aesthetic were scored by composers under the Remote Control banner, further highlighting the factory analogy embraced by Zimmer, and the aesthetic imprimatur of the company's group style. Consider, for instance, the final battle sequence in *X-Men: First Class*, which shares the same three-chord harmonic structure and rise-and-fall development with Zimmer's "Journey to the Line" cue; or the climax of *Ender's Game* (2013) by Steve Jablonsky, which features a percussive *ostinato* and brass blasts not unlike the same cyclical figures in Zimmer's *Inception*; or the training sequences in *Pacific Rim* (2013), where Ramin Djawadi underscores the film's action with stretched out, cyclical string figures that share the same textural colors with some of Zimmer's *Dark Knight* material, especially the propulsive rhythms of its action scenes. The aesthetic has become so ubiquitous in action spectacles that filmmakers Trey Parker and Matt Stone hired Remote Control composer Harry Gregson-Williams to compose a score for their action film parody *Team America: World Police* (2004) that spoofed the company's signature sound.

One way to account for the pervasiveness of romantic minimalism in Remote Control music is the industry's long-standing practice of creating "temp tracks" using pre-existing music for the purpose of screening presentations of films-in-progress, and providing composers with a blueprint for their eventual score. As Sadoff (2006: 166) has shown, temp tracks often rehearse a "ghostly version" of the score that "survives only in its role for audience previews—discarded immediately following the preview phase." However, "temp love" can often hinder a composer's ability to stretch out aesthetically when he or she is requested to emulate the temporary track. And it is not surprising that the commercial success of Zimmer's films—at least in the eyes of financially minded studio executives—has led to the industry's tendency to replicate what has worked in the past. To put it another way, a casual glance at domestic box office grosses for 2014 reveals that four of the year's top-ten grossing films feature scores from current and former Remote Control composers (Box Office Mojo 2014).

On the other hand, the same tendency to imitate these structural and textural elements can be located in the occupational infrastructure of Remote Control, where aesthetic style is intrinsically linked to the collaborative workflow embedded in its technical and communal organization. In effect, romantic minimalism and the aesthetic treatment of musical sound are both the cause and effect of its relationship to musical form and function in Hollywood cinema. As client dominant work, composing for film may be negotiated artistic labor but it is also dependent on the legacy of music conventions within the film industry. What this says about the house Zimmer built is that the enduring legacy of studio-era conventions, especially the signifying aspects of musical color and the relationship between music and narrative development, continues to influence the ways in which composers reject, revise, synthesize and innovate elements of musical expression. By creating an infrastructure that offers centralized access to digital samples, library tracks and the collaborative workflow between Zimmer and his associates, Remote Control has also reorganized the way a group of freelance composers negotiate their occupational identities within the film industry. The studio is a platform for composers to establish relationships with filmmakers, secure solo assignments and most importantly refine their craft by assisting Zimmer on major film projects. Despite its flexibly specialized network of freelancers, Remote Control is organized around a centralized group style so identifiable and ubiquitous within the industry that its electronic-orchestral tonal harmonies, foregrounded percussion, cyclical string figures and experiments with musical color are part of a shared lexicon of conventions that define a particular group style and, perhaps more importantly, the current sound of popular cinema.

References

Anon. 1970. "The Day the Dream Factory Woke Up." *Life* 68(7): 38–46.

Becker, H.S. 1976. "Art Worlds and Social Types." *American Behavioral Scientist* 19(6): 703–718.

Bordwell, D. 1997. *On the History of Film Style*. Cambridge: Harvard University Press.

Box Office Mojo. 2014. "2014 Domestic Grosses." www.boxofficemojo.com/yearly/chart/?yr=2014&p=.htm.

Burlingame, J. 2014. "Remote Control Prods.: Hans Zimmer's Music Factory as a Breeding Ground." *Variety* (07 May): http://variety.com/2014/music/news/remote-control-prods-music-factory-as-breeding-ground-1201173763.

Chion, M. 1994. *Audio-Vision: Sound on Screen*. New York: Columbia University Press.

Christopherson, S. and M. Storper. 1989. "The Effects of Flexible Specialization on Industrial Politics and the Labor Market: The Motion Picture Industry." *Industrial and Labor Relations Review* 42(3): 331–348.

Clemmensen, C. 2008. "'The Peacemaker' Soundtrack Review." *Filmtracks.com*: www.filmtracks.com/titles/peacemaker.html.

Cooke, M. 2008. *A History of Film Music*. Cambridge: Cambridge University Press.

Davis, E. 2013. "BRAAM! 10 Trailers That Use and Abuse the 'Inception' BRAAAM!" *The Playlist: IndieWire* (12 April): http://blogs.indiewire.com/theplaylist/braaam-10-trailers-that-use-abuse-the-inception-braaam-20130412.

Demers, J. 2010. *Listening Through Noise: the Aesthetics of Experimental Electronic Music*. Oxford: Oxford University Press.

Dowd, T.J. 2004. "Production Perspectives in the Sociology of Music." *Poetics* 32 (3/4): 235–246.

Faulkner, R.R. 1978. "Swimming With Sharks: Occupational Mandate and the Film Composer in Hollywood." *Qualitative Sociology* 1(2): 99–129.

Flinn, C. 1992. *Strains of Utopia: Gender, Nostalgia, and Hollywood Film Music*. Princeton: Princeton University Press.

Goldwasser, D. 2006. "Hans Zimmer: Interview." *Soundtrack.net*: www.soundtrack.net/content/article/?id=206.

Gorbman, C. 1987. *Unheard Melodies: Narrative Film Music*. Bloomington: Indiana University Press.

Gotham Uncovered. 2008. *The Dark Knight*. DVD Featurette. Warner Bros.

Greiving, T. 2013. "Hans Zimmer: Steel Reinventing." *Projector and Orchestra* (24 June): http://projectorandorchestra.com/hans-zimmer-steel-reinventing.

Hurwitz, M. 2007. "Hans Zimmer's Scoring Collective." *Mix* 31(9): 49.

Jagernauth, K. 2013. "Hans Zimmer Feels 'Horrible' When His 'Inception' BRAMMS Are Used in Movie Trailers." *The Playlist: IndieWire* (06 November): http://blogs.indiewire.com/theplaylist/hans-zimmer-feels-horrible-when-his-inception-bramms-are-used-in-movie-trailers-20131106.

Karlin, F. and R. Wright. 2004. *On the Track: A Guide to Contemporary Film Scoring*, 2nd ed. New York: Routledge.

Meyer, L.B. 1987. "Toward a Theory of Style." In *The Concept of Style*, ed. B. Lang, 21–71. Ithaca: Cornell University Press.

Nelson, R.U. 1946. "Film Music: Color or Line?" *Hollywood Quarterly* 2(1): 57–65.

Prendergast, R. 1992. *Film Music: A Neglected Art*, 2nd ed. New York: W.W. Norton and Co.

Rosenblum, B. 1978. "Style as Social Process." *American Sociological Review* 43(3): 422–438.

Rule, G. and M. Gallagher. 1999. "Movie Music: Inside Media Ventures with Hans Zimmer." *Keyboard* 25(4): 30–40.

Sadoff, R.H. 2006. "The Role of the Music Editor and the 'Temp Track' as Blueprint for the Score, Source Music, and Source Music of Films." *Popular Music* 25(2): 165–183.

Spitfire Audio. 2013. "Spitfire Presents . . . In Conversation with Hans Zimmer." www.youtube.com/watch?v=me_8pWY2HpQ.

Théberge, P. 1989. "The 'Sound' of Music: Technological Rationalization and the Production of Popular Music." *New Formations* 8: 99–111.

31

Digitalization

Paul Théberge

The digitalization of music is not a "revolution." Contrary to the inflated rhetoric that has accompanied the rise of the information technology sector in the early years of the twenty-first century, digitalization has been, in fact, a relatively long, transformative process of economic, technological, social and cultural change that has taken place over a half-century or more. In this sense, the digitalization of music should be regarded not as the result of a singular technological innovation (the development of MP3 file compression or the internet) nor the apparent rise of new forms of consumer power (file-sharing) but, rather, as a series of more or less distinct transformations that have occurred at different times and across a number of different areas of musical practice, including the composition, performance, recording, distribution and reception of music. Furthermore, while it could be argued that virtually every form of music making has been affected in some way by the processes of digitalization, these transformations have taken place unevenly across different genres of music, and across different social groups and industrial sectors. Taken as a whole, however, the digitalization of music has deep implications not only for how we make and experience music, but also for how we conceive of it as a form of cultural activity and as an object of study. This chapter will provide an understanding of processes of digitalization from the perspective of musicians as social actors engaged in the production of music through technological means, the recording and representation of digital audio, the institutional and economic organization of music as a commodity form, and the activities of audiences as they experience music and negotiate their relationships as fans.

Making Music Digitally

Technology is deeply embedded within the practice of music making: from the most rudimentary musical instruments, to notation, to the most sophisticated recording devices, musicians engage with technology as an essential part of their music making activities. For Weber (1958), musical instruments and notation were as important to the development of western music as were the fundamental building blocks of melody, rhythm and harmony. Furthermore, Weber understood that the development of musical instruments, as a form of methodic experimentation, provided a key link between music and science as otherwise distinct types of rational human behavior.

Not surprisingly, the earliest experiments in the digitalization of music involved the combined efforts of musicians and scientists: for example, in the early days of mainframe computing (the late 1950s and early 1960s), experimentation with sound and music at Bell Labs benefitted from the collaboration of musicians and composers (such as James Tenny, Jean-Claude Risset, Laurie Spiegel and others) and engineers such as Max Mathews. Along with his various collaborators, Max

Mathews' ongoing efforts to develop digital music and sound synthesis tools resulted in a series of important early software programs: the MUSIC-n series of programs began with MUSIC I in 1957 and culminated in MUSIC IV and V a decade later (Howe 1975). The programs were widely influential and formed the basis for further developments in music software by other researchers working at a variety of institutions. While the MUSIC-n series of programs was based on a fairly conventional conception of musical sound and structure (the program separated the calculation of "instruments" and "score" as compositional elements), subsequent developments in computer music during the 1970s placed computation and statistical methods at the heart of compositional practice. Based on an aesthetic whose origins lay in Xanakis's early experiments with mathematical models and probability in his musical compositions, so-called "granular synthesis" techniques, for example, brought mathematical operations to the micro-construction of tones as well as large-scale compositional structures (Roads 2001). In these ways, the digitalization of avant-garde music represented a significant departure from conventional materials and methods of composition.

From a sociological point of view, the process of re-conceptualizing music from an art of instrumental sound, performance and compositional technique to one of mathematics, digital technologies and algorithmic operations also had the effect of redefining the role of the musician from that of a composer or performer to something more closely aligned with that of the computer scientist—in short, redefining the "artist" as a "researcher." These new roles were further reinforced by periodicals such as the *Computer Music Journal*. Published continuously since 1977 by MIT Press, the journal has been dedicated to promoting rigorous research in acoustics, computer science, music composition and technology. Through the journal and its spin-offs (see for example Roads and Strawn 1985, Roads 1989) MIT Press has helped to define the history of computer music as both science and art, and its practice as a form of serious research.

This early research into the digitalization of music required sophisticated computing equipment and could only be supported through the auspices of large, privately or publicly funded institutions such as Bell Labs in the United States, dedicated state-funded research facilities such as the Institut de Recherche et Coordination Acoustique/Musique (IRCAM) in Paris, or major post-secondary educational institutions such as MIT and Stanford University. In her ethnography of IRCAM, Born (1995) studied the effects of this institutionalization of the musical avant-garde and found ideological contradictions between the roles of art and science as well as the formation of hierarchies of knowledge, expertise and technology that often separated composers and technical staff.

While these institutional contexts allowed, at least initially, the digitalization of music and sound to take place outside the immediate pressures of industry and commerce, over time many turned to limited forms of commercial production to justify the high costs of operation. In the case of IRCAM, government pressure has led to the development of products for a wide range of applications: from music to automobile sound systems to cinema. At Stanford, John Chowning's early work in creating the algorithms for digital FM synthesis became the basis for an exclusive licensing deal with Yamaha and led, after much further research and development, to the release of their popular DX-7 line of FM keyboard synthesizers during the early 1980s. This netted the university royalties amounting to over $20 million over the life of the patent (Stanford News Service 1994). In these ways, while the aesthetics and social and institutional formation of avant-garde computer music separate it from popular music and culture, economic and industrial pressures have, to some extent, brought these two art worlds together at the level of technological development.

The commercial release of the DX7 synthesizer in 1983 and the simultaneous introduction of the Musical Instrument Digital Interface (MIDI) mark a watershed in the digitalization of music. MIDI, the result of an unprecedented collaboration between commercial synthesizer manufacturers, facilitated the interconnection of digital musical instruments (synthesizers, drum machines, sequencers and samplers) and personal computers. This created the basis for affordable, integrated digital production environments for popular music (see Théberge 1997). Whereas avant-garde computer music had been located within elite institutional environments and based on hierarchies of scientific knowledge and technical expertise, MIDI technologies allowed for the spread of digitalization throughout the popular music industry (not to mention other educational institutions) and at every level, from professional to amateur. "Democratization" came to be equated with the availability of consumer technologies and prefabricated musical resources (ibid.). The conflation of democracy, consumption and ease of use is, of course, a hallmark of contemporary capitalism. This ideology continues to dominate the promotional discourses of digital culture (musical and otherwise) in the early twenty-first century.

As with the avant-garde, the digitalization of popular music making also had an impact on the roles of various players in the production of popular music. The proliferation of drum machines and other MIDI devices opened up the question of the relevance of traditional performance skills and the need for new definitions of musicianship. Many of the initial concerns voiced by critics of the technology—for example, that drum machines would replace live drummers—were largely exaggerated. Countering such critiques, recent scholars have examined more closely the mutual influences between live drumming and digital programming (Zagorski-Thomas 2010) together with the ways in which sampling and programming shape overall musical structure (as in Butler's 2006 analysis of "multimeasure patterning" in electronic dance music). At the same time, Warner (2003) has argued that the adoption of the MIDI technologies—especially digital sampling and sequencing—in conjunction with multitrack recording placed increased importance on the role of the producer as a creative force in the recording studio. Warner regards the work of pop producer Trevor Horn (with the Buggles, Malcolm McLaren, Yes, the Art of Noise, Grace Jones and others) as emblematic of the role of the producer during this period. In addition, digital production during the 1980s and 1990s brought to the fore early controversies (and legal battles) over copyright. While copyright is dealt with elsewhere in this volume, it is important in this context to recognize that digital sampling (a technique where brief sound elements from existing recordings are digitally reproduced within the context of a new musical composition) was one of the first areas of cultural production in which a sustained and highly publicized argument for the creative reuse of copyright material was articulated, along with a questioning of the role of the "artist" and notions of "originality." While industry interests may have prevailed in many of the cases brought before the courts, Beadle (1993) has argued that sampling practice was nevertheless reflective of larger currents in popular production and consumption and must be regarded as a key expression of popular sensibility during the late twentieth century.

Digital Recording, Visualization, and Digital Humanities

In tandem with the digitalization of musical composition and instrument technologies, digital audio recording developed slowly over the period of about two-and-a-half decades. Digital mastering had already been introduced into the world of sound recording by the late 1970s, as was the use of computer controlled mixing consoles. However, the demands of multitrack recording required much more sophisticated and powerful digital technologies and only the largest studio complexes were able to invest in the specialized hardware and software—the so-called "Digital Audio Workstations" (DAWs)—that began to appear during the 1980s. By the mid-1990s and early 2000s, however, general-purpose computers had become powerful enough to not only record multiple tracks of digital audio but to also offer digital signal processing capabilities and the possibility of full integration with software-based MIDI sequencing and synthesis. The development of these technologies contributed to the emergence of small-scale "project" studios that could rival the capabilities of the larger complexes, creating increased competition within the studio marketplace and thus transforming the character of independent record production (Théberge 2012). Contemporary DAW software can now be housed within a laptop computer and it is not uncommon to find musicians using sophisticated software packages in live performance contexts.

In many ways, the basic practices used in DAW recording are similar to those associated with multitrack tape recording, overdubbing and mixing. In this sense, DAW software is a classic example of what Bolter and Grusin (2000) have referred to as "remediation"—the refashioning and extension of earlier analog media and techniques in the digital realm. While DAW software has certainly offered greater levels of precision in audio editing and processing and new, non-linear ways of assembling and rearranging recorded material (bringing the flexibility of MIDI sequencing to the audio realm), these capabilities were, at least initially, perhaps less significant than the level of continuity offered to musicians and engineers in terms of their previously acquired sensibilities and skills. Even the look of DAW software is designed to resemble the hardware devices and controls familiar to multitrack recording: consoles and racks of processing devices, faders and knobs.

But perhaps one of the most significant and overlooked aspects of DAW software is the many ways in which audio, MIDI and multitrack data are represented in visual form on the computer display. In addition to the familiar depictions of analog hardware, audio is represented in waveform displays, spectral analyses, graphic displays of frequency and dynamic processing and so on. MIDI and track data are represented in a variety of drum machine formats, piano-roll scrolls, conventional notation and graphic layouts derived from earlier MIDI sequencer software. In essence, DAW software provides popular musicians and engineers a new kind of musical and sonic notation—a notation that describes actual sonic events (as opposed to instructions for performance) and allows for the detailed manipulation and control of both the micro and macro levels of a musical recording (Théberge 2013). Indeed, Kvifte (2010: 214–15) has argued that DAW software offers a much richer environment for the manipulation of music and sound than conventional notation and has analyzed the multiple, hierarchical levels of representation available in DAW displays as well as the various degrees of precision and detail offered at each level. Books devoted to the techniques of digital audio recording rely heavily on these visual displays for pedagogical purposes and place a great deal of emphasis on the waveform display itself as the central means by which the engineer engages with audio. Furthermore, the visual display of processes as familiar as equalization (EQ) allows engineers to visually analyze these processes in ways that are impossible by ear alone (Savage 2011). The sheer quantity and complexity of the visual data presented to the engineer has led some to argue for the need to understand and intelligently "manage" the multiple windows of information contained in the computer display (Savage 2011: 130–131).

The ability to analyze music and sound in new ways through visual representations has had implications for music, science and scholarship beyond the confines of the recording studio. Even before DAW software was taken up in popular music production, composers at institutions such as IRCAM used spectrum analysis (originally developed by scientists interested in sound and acoustics) as part of their compositional strategies as early as the 1970s. So-called "spectral music" used visual representations and mathematical analysis to identify key aspects of sound spectra that could then be used to manipulate and transform sounds over time. More significantly, the ability to visualize and analyze music with a high degree of precision has been taken up by a wide range of scientists and musicologists interested not so much in the production of electronic music but in coming to a new understanding of the subtleties of musical performance. For example, MIDI can be used to program musical sequences or to capture performances. In the case of the latter, MIDI (and digital recording more generally) renders the performances with a degree of precision that allows for a deeper understanding of the dynamics and rhythmic placement of both individual events and musical phrases as performed by musicians in real time. In her work on rhythm, Danielsen (2010: 4–7) argues that the use of digital technology challenges our understanding of musical performance and allows us to re-think the relationships between music as performed and felt (the "groove") and music as structure (the implied, and more abstract relationships between measures, beats, subdivisions and syncopations).

In a manner similar to that of Danielsen's work, but focusing less on contemporary dance music than on jazz, rock and other genres, Iyer (2002) has examined the effect of the "microtiming" of beats, accents and phrasing as an aspect of "embodied" musical performance. For Iyer, playing "in the groove" means playing simultaneously in and out of time. He argues that this ability is an essential feature of many African-American musical styles and, furthermore, that this mode of performance is not confined to drummers alone but is also common among jazz pianists and other instrumentalists. Iyer's work is part of an area of interdisciplinary study that combines music research and methodologies derived from cognitive science and psychoacoustics. What is significant about this work within the current context, however, is its dependence on digital tools of recording and analysis: indeed, as Geoffrey and James Collier (2002: 281) have argued, our present understanding of the temporal inflections and subtle discrepancies present in live performance has been aided by our very ability to digitally record and measure these phenomena at the level of the microsecond.

The work by Danielsen, Iyer and others can perhaps be considered part of a growing body of research questions and methodologies that have emerged in recent years under the general rubric of "digital humanities" (see Schreibman, Siemens and Unsworth 2004). While the term "digital humanities" has often been narrowly applied to recent research and to the networks of individuals working in the field since the advent of the internet, digital tools and methodologies have in fact been explored in various fields within the humanities since the earliest attempts to establish large-scale indexes, databases and concordances for written texts during the 1950s (ibid.). In music, digital scholarship includes work that has used optical recognition to create computer-readable versions of music notation and the use of databases for the analysis of both scores and written texts. These and other techniques have extended and enhanced the work of many traditional musicologists. Going beyond the notated score, more recent work at the Centre for Digital Music at Queen Mary College (University of London) has led to the development of the "Sonic Visualizer," a set of free software tools for the analysis of the pitch, timing and timbrel characteristics of recorded music (www.sonicvisualizer.org). Again, what is interesting for the arguments presented here is that the digitalization of music and sound has resulted in the use of a common set of digital visualization tools—albeit, customized, fine-tuned and used differently and for different purposes—by a range of social groups, from scientists interested in the physics of sound, to musicians, producers and engineers engaged in the production of recordings, to researchers interested in the study and analysis of music and performance.

Digital Distribution and Commodity Form

The most common usage of the term "digitalization" in music has come about since the advent of technical means for the distribution of digital audio through telecommunications networks. Indeed, for many, digitalization is virtually synonymous with the development of MP3 files and their proliferation through the internet. This conflation of digitalization and the internet has not been limited to music, but is also generally prevalent in discussions of new media and the cultural industries (see for example Hesmondhalgh 2013: 310–363). In addition to the various ways in which digitalization can be understood in relation to music (as discussed above), it can be argued that the introduction of MP3 files and the internet should not be thought of as the beginning of digitalization in music, or even digital distribution, but rather as a significant shift in the *meaning* of digitalization.

In understanding this shift in meaning, it is important to recognize that the digital distribution of music actually begins in the early 1980s with the introduction of the compact disc. The CD was a technological format designed to carry digital audio, something that neither LPs nor audio cassettes—the two major vehicles for music distribution at the time—could do. The CD (and digital audio more generally) was marketed as a major advancement in audio fidelity: uniform frequency response, the elimination of background and surface noise through the use of high technology (lasers), more than double the playing time on a single side and the ability to make multiple copies without apparent signal loss all made the CD the logical successor to the LP (even over the protests of audiophiles who argued that the sound quality of early CD recordings was inferior to analog). The MP3 compression format, on the other hand, was designed for compactness, not audio fidelity and, in this sense, marks one of several breaks that have occurred in the discourses of fidelity and progress that have largely dominated histories of sound reproduction (see Sterne 2003: 215–286). The principles behind audio compression were based, in part, on decades-old research in psychoacoustics (some of which had been conducted at Bell Labs) that shifted the question of audio quality away from notions of fidelity and external, objective measurement, to the listening subject, the peculiarities of human hearing and the problem of intelligibility. As Sterne (2012) has argued, in this regard the MP3 file owes more to the history of telephony than it does to the sound recording industry. In bracketing the idea of fidelity, the MP3 file format presented consumers with a different definition of digitalization, one based on the values of speed of access, minimized storage requirements and convenience—values that were more compatible with the limitations both of personal computers and the internet during the mid-1990s.

The limitations of early internet access were an important factor in the adoption of MP3 files: data compression was necessary if the promises of the World Wide Web were to be achieved. Indeed, the digital transmission of high-quality audio and video had already been realized through the use of Integrated Services Digital Network (ISDN). Faster, secure, private and more reliable than most internet connections, ISDN was and continues to be used in broadcasting and other industries. However, ISDN was expensive and access to it limited. While the speed of ISDN would eventually be exceeded by broadband internet connections, domestic access to the internet, even during the heyday of Napster (1999–2001), was limited by the speed of analog modems.

Equally important, CDs, like many commodity forms (digital or otherwise), were based on a system of artificial scarcity—a system in which record companies could exert a significant level of control over the availability of recorded music. MP3s, on the other hand, were defined within an emergent virtual economy characterized by abundance. Initially, MP3 files traded by music enthusiasts often contained independent music, old records, bootleg concert recordings and other types of music that circulated outside the mainstream record industry. Later, with the commercialization of the internet, music sites promoted their services based on their ability to provide access to databases containing millions of songs. The ideal of immediate and unlimited access to recorded music of the present and past is one of the key ways in which the idea of "digitalization" was redefined in the age of the internet.

With the introduction of MP3 files, the status of recorded music as a commodity form appeared to be at risk, but perhaps not entirely in the ways in which the debate about it was constructed at the time. While the terms of the debate centered on copyright infringement, piracy and file-sharing, none of these things were entirely new, nor unique to MP3s and the internet. Unauthorized LP and cassette duplication was common in the 1970s, as was the availability of pirated CDs in the 1990s, and the industry had only limited success in halting any of these illegal activities. Similarly, music copying and sharing had been a significant part of the popular culture surrounding audio cassettes since the 1970s. Unable to control such practices or to "educate" consumers about the values of copyright, the industry lobbied governments for compensation through levies on blank tape, thus exacting payment *before* any alleged "crime" had been committed.

The sheer scale of MP3 file-sharing was, however, something quite extraordinary. The fact that it proliferated within the record industry's most profitable markets was cause for concern. However, the industry strategy of pursuing litigation against the purveyors of MP3 files—websites such as Napster and MP3.com—was only partially intended to stem the flow of digital music files; it was also intended as a message to the web's financial backers. The role of venture capital in the early days of Napster and other file-sharing sites is not widely acknowledged but, as Hesmondhalgh (2009: 60) has argued, "It is sometimes forgotten, in a rush to portray these companies as radical challenges to corporate power, that these networks were commercial enterprises, supported by advertising, and usually backed by venture capital." In the case of Napster, the company would never have survived as long as it did nor reached as many users had it not received millions of dollars from venture capitalists such as Hummer Winblad. As a condition of their investment, a member of the firm was installed as CEO of Napster, further cementing their relationship with the company (Alderman 2001: 124). The battle over file-sharing was thus not simply between the music industry, fans and a few "renegade" web portals but, to a large extent, a conflict between two industrial sectors and the financial interests that supported them.

The record industry was portrayed throughout this period as a villain (the choice of litigating against individual file-sharers was especially damaging to its image) and the representative of a dying corporate structure; ironically, it has survived. While the industry has suffered greatly from the loss of CD sales, its profitability has never been entirely dependent on the sale of commodities but has always had a more or less significant secondary stream of income from the sale of copyrights and licensing (Hesmondhalgh 2013: 345). In recent years, the industry has shifted its attention to the large, dominant players on the internet, negotiating rights with Apple, YouTube and music streaming services. In some cases, it may have profited more from these deals than the internet companies themselves: for example, the digital music streaming service, Spotify, despite its own difficulties in generating adequate subscription and advertising revenues, is reported to have paid royalties amounting to over $500 million to recording artists in 2013 alone (Luckerson 2013). Of course, royalties seldom go directly to artists and, in the face of a destabilized industry, record companies have moved to increase their share of artist revenues through so-called "360 deals," contracts that ensure them access to income derived from every aspect of an artists' work (Stahl 2010). In these ways, while the advent of MP3 files and competition from the highly capitalized players on the internet have greatly challenged the record industry, it has nevertheless managed to negotiate its way through and profit from these challenges.

Reception—the Digitalization of Fandom

Consumers have also greatly benefitted from the digitalization of music. They have access to a vast archive of recorded music, greater than at any time in history. Much of it is available to them for free (even legally so) or at low cost through the internet on their computers, portable music players and cell phones. Beyond simple consumption, music fans have found new ways to engage with music, artists and other fans through new technologies, websites, blogs and social networking. At the same time, however, their activities have come under increasing scrutiny and exploitation by website developers and advertisers. Taken together, it can be suggested that these various possibilities for new levels of access, interaction and invasive marketing might be characterized as "the digitalization of fandom."

Much of the academic discourse surrounding new media has been influenced by cultural theorists such as Henry Jenkins (1992), who has argued that the possibilities for appropriation and transformation of digital commodities work against simple ideas of consumption and lead to more "participatory" forms of cultural practice. In some of his work, Jenkins described television fans who used video editing as a means of appropriating television texts and giving them new meanings. However, his ideas are equally applicable to music on the internet. For example, when DJ Danger Mouse released his mashup of music by the Beatles and rapper Jay-Z in 2004 (his so-called *Grey Album*), he was immediately faced with an injunction from the record industry and forced to remove the album from the internet. Before this could be accomplished, however, fans held an international day of protest, making the album available for download on a great number of sites and, in some cases, offering software that enabled enthusiasts to make their own mashups. The latter gesture suggested that digital sampling and mashup techniques were no longer the sole preserve of DJs and music producers; they belonged to consumers as well.

As noted by Hesmondhalgh (2013: 313–320), however, the "digital optimism" of theorists such as Jenkins and others needs to be tempered by a degree of realism regarding the possibilities offered by new technology, consumer habits and the internet as a medium. (After all, one might ask, how many fans in 2004 had an interest in heeding the call of Danger Mouse's supporters and actually learned how to use mashup software?) Even with respect to sites such as YouTube, which is known for its encouragement of user-generated content, Hesmondhalgh (2013: 351–352) cites studies that suggest that the most-watched videos are often produced not by users but by the entertainment industries themselves. In this regard, for the record industry, YouTube is the new MTV: a convenient and effective vehicle for promoting its products (even if artists receive little direct revenue in the process).

The internet has also become an important vehicle for fans who wish to follow artists and to interact with them and with other fans. Indeed, fan websites have largely replaced the activities of conventional fan clubs (themselves a kind of "social network") that have been in operation for decades producing newsletters and fan-centered events (Théberge 2005: 492). What is especially interesting in these fan-sites is not simply the character of the online exchanges that they facilitate, but also their interaction with live touring and other offline activities. The daily character of social interaction on the internet helps to generate sustained interest in live concerts, tours and releases—events that are, by their very nature, ephemeral. In this way, fan-sites can have a significant impact on fans and their affective engagement with artists and the fan community by anticipating, intensifying and prolonging their relationship with these events (494–496). For their part, artists and their management have often used fan-sites as secondary sources of profit by promoting artists' work and selling merchandise.

The potential for ongoing, even daily interactions between artists and fans through fan-sites and blogs is in many ways unprecedented in the history of popular culture, and constitutes a new forum for the exercise and exchange of social power between these groups. Of course, artists and fans have always had an ambivalent relationship: their devotion and need for one another can be both a source of empowerment and vulnerability. And, at the very least, the ways in which power circulates within fan-sites is more or less direct and transparent. The same cannot be said for more recent developments on the internet in which special-interest portals, such as fan-sites and music-oriented social networks such as MySpace, have given way to general-purpose social networks such as Facebook and Twitter.

The sheer magnitude of the user base—numbering in the hundreds of millions—for networks sponsored by large-corporations such as Google and Facebook has given them a special appeal to advertisers across virtually all industry sectors, including the music industry. But beyond advertising, the information routinely gathered by the owners of these networks has come to be seen as a potentially rich source of marketing information for their advertising clients. Most of this data about consumers, their habits, interests and interactions with others is obtained without their knowledge and has been critiqued as an invasion of personal privacy. However, internet providers have not been deterred by these critiques and they continue to look for new ways to use and profit from the information they gather. "Big data" has become a common term for the gathering of such data and the development of algorithmic techniques for extracting useful (that is to say, profitable) information from it.

It is not always obvious how this profit is to be realized, however, especially within sectors such as the music industry where the prediction of new tastes and trends is notoriously difficult. In early 2014, it was announced that Twitter would enter into an exclusive relationship with "300," a venture company founded by former music promoter and label executive Lyor Cohen in an attempt to find ways to exploit its vast databanks of user messages for the purpose of determining new trends in music (Sisario 2014). In true internet fashion, the relationship was characterized as challenging the traditional ways in which the record industry has done business. But as a music industry insider, Cohen's partnership with Twitter perhaps marks a new level of cooperation between these industry sectors, one based on a mutual interest in the digitalization of fandom.

Conclusion

The term "digitalization" has been applied not only to music in recent years but also to a range of cultural practices, media and artistic institutions. Given the centrality of the internet and mobile communications in contemporary economic and social life, it is not surprising that many of the applications of the term "digitalization" have often been limited to the discussion and analysis of trends emerging since the late 1990s and early 2000s. As I have argued, however, the digitalization of music is a phenomenon that can be understood as numerous, intersecting histories that cut across a range of social, cultural, institutional and industrial practices. Digitalization has been a means through which musicians have rethought the role of sound in music, a means for creating new kinds of musical instruments and for recording sounds, and a way of understanding older performance practices. Digitalization has also become a means of musical distribution and exchange, providing an environment in which we organize our musical experiences and our relations with one another. In this sense, digitalization should be thought of not simply as digital audio files, circulated through the networks of cyberculture and accumulated on hard drives and mobile devices, but as a phenomenon that permeates virtually every aspect of how we think about, make and experience music in contemporary culture.

References

Alderman, J. 2001. *Sonic Boom: Napster, MP3 and the New Pioneers of Music*. New York: Basic Books.
Beadle, J.J. 1993. *Will Pop Eat Itself?* London: Faber and Faber.
Bolter, J.D. and R. Grusin. 2000. *Remediation: Understanding New Media*. Cambridge: MIT Press.
Born, G. 1995. *Rationalizing Culture: IRCAM, Boulez, and the Institutionalization of the Musical Avant-Garde*. Berkeley: University of California Press.
Butler, M. 2006. *Unlocking the Groove: Rhythm, Meter, and Musical Design in Electronic Dance Music*. Bloomington: Indiana University Press.
Collier, G.L. and J.L. Collier. 2002. "Introduction." *Music Perception: An Interdisciplinary Journal* 19(3): 279–284.
Danielsen, A., ed. 2010. *Musical Rhythm in the Age of Digital Reproduction*. Farnham: Ashgate.
Hesmondhalgh, D. 2009. "The Digitalisation of Music." In *Creativity, Innovation and the Cultural Economy*, eds. A.C. Pratt and P. Jeffcutt, 57–73. London: Routledge.
_____. 2013. *The Cultural Industries*, 3rd ed. Los Angeles: Sage.
Howe Jr., H.S. 1975. *Electronic Music Synthesis: Concepts, Facilities, Techniques*. New York: W.W. Norton and Company.
Iyer, V. 2002. "Embodied Mind, Situated Cognition, and Expressive Microtiming in African-American Music." *Music Perception: An Interdisciplinary Journal* 19(3): 387–414.

Jenkins, H. 1992. *Textual Poachers: Television Fans and Participatory Culture.* New York: Routledge.

Kvifte, T. 2010. "Composing a Performance: The Analogue Experience in the Age of Digital (Re)Production." In *Musical Rhythm in the Age of Digital Reproduction*, ed. A. Danielsen, 213–230. Farnham: Ashgate.

Luckerson, V. 2013. "Here's How Much Money Top Musicians are Making on Spotify." *Time* (03 December): http://business.time.com/2013/12/03/heres-how-much-money-top-musicians-are-making-on-spotify.

Roads, C., ed. 1989. *The Music Machine: Selected Readings from Computer Music Journal.* Cambridge: MIT Press.

_____. 2001. *Microsound.* Cambridge: MIT Press.

Roads, C. and J. Strawn, eds. 1985. *The Foundations of Computer Music.* Cambridge: MIT Press.

Savage, S. 2011. *The Art of Digital Audio Recording: A Practical Guide for Home and Studio.* Oxford: Oxford University Press.

Schreibman, S., R. Siemens and J. Unsworth, eds. 2004. *A Companion to Digital Humanities.* Oxford: Blackwell.

Sisario, B. 2014. "Venture Will Mine Twitter for Music's Next Big Thing." *New York Times* (02 February): Available online: www.nytimes.com/2014/02/03/business/media/twitter-and-300-team-up-to-find-musical-talent.html?_r=0>

Stahl, M. 2010. "Primitive Accumulation, the Social Common, and the Contractual Lockdown of Recording Artists at the Threshold of Digitalization." *Ephemera: Theory and Politics in Organization* 10(3/4): 337–355.

Stanford News Service. 1994. "Music Synthesis Approaches Sound Quality of Real Instruments." News Release (07 June): http://news.stanford.edu/pr/94/940607Arc4222.html.

Sterne, J. 2003. *The Audible Past: Cultural Origins of Sound Reproduction.* Durham: Duke University Press.

_____. 2012. *MP3: The Meaning of a Format.* Durham: Duke University Press.

Théberge, P. 1997. *Any Sound You Can Imagine: Making Music/Consuming Technology.* Hanover: Wesleyan University Press.

_____. 2005. "Everyday Fandom: Fan Clubs, Blogging, and the Quotidian Rhythms of the Internet." *Canadian Journal of Communication* 30(4): 1–18.

_____. 2012. "The End of the World as We Know It: The Changing Role of the Studio in the Age of the Internet." In *The Art of Record Production: An Introductory Reader for a New Academic Field*, eds. S. Frith and S. Zagorski-Thomas, 77–90. Farnham: Ashgate.

_____. 2013. "Visualizing Music and Sound in the Digital Domain." Presented at "Music, Digitisation, Mediation: Towards Interdisciplinary Music Studies." University of Oxford: 11–13 July.

Warner, T. 2003. *Pop Music—Technology and Creativity: Trevor Horn and the Digital Revolution.* Aldershot: Ashgate.

Weber, M. 1958. *The Rational and Social Foundations of Music.* Translated and edited by D. Martindale, J. Riedel and G. Neuwirth. Carbondale: Southern Illinois University Press.

Zagorski-Thomas, S. 2010. "Real and Unreal Performances: The Interaction of Recording Technology and Rock Drum Kit Performance." In *Musical Rhythm in the Age of Digital Reproduction*, ed. A. Danielsen, 195–212. Farnham: Ashgate.

VI

NEW DIRECTIONS

These chapters represent some of the most significant conceptual interventions in music sociology at the outset of the twenty-first century. One of the main themes across the chapters is how to navigate a path between what Born (2010) elsewhere calls "the social and the aesthetic." The authors in this section are thus searching for *social* approaches to music that are also social approaches to *music*— that is, resolutely non-reductive accounts of the realities of social processes and the specifics of musical sound. This problematic relationship between the social and the aesthetic has been an enormously productive tension in music sociology since its earliest days. DeNora and Prior navigate this tension by reviewing and expanding the contributions of two key figures in music sociology: Adorno and Bourdieu, respectively. Both DeNora and Prior present strong arguments about the limitations of Adorno and Bourdieu, focusing especially on their misconceptions and lack of attention to the question of how the social gets into the musical. Yet in advocating for new approaches to such an issue, neither DeNora nor Prior wishes to throw out the baby with the bathwater: Adorno and Bourdieu remain, for them, valuable keystones in music sociology. Born, meanwhile, departs more strongly from earlier work and forges her own conception of musical mediation. Drawing on a rich range of concepts and writers, Born's goal is to theorize, in terms of four intermediating levels of sociality, "the generative nature of the imbrication of musical formations and social formations." Gilbert addresses most thoroughly a question that also forms part of the three preceding chapters: affect, or musical feeling and embodiment. He argues that interpreting music in terms of linguistic discourse is to subscribe to a limited view of how music works in culture: "Music has *physical effects* which can be identified, described and discussed but which are not the same thing as it having *meanings*" (emphases in original; see also Shepherd and Wicke 1997). Each chapter thus works to expand the conceptual and empirical horizons of music sociology. What is more, new work is emerging all the time that refines and extends previous insights into this relationship between music as a sonic form and a social activity. One especially promising direction is represented by critically-oriented deployments of actor-network-theory (see Piekut 2011, 2014).

Of course, there are many other emerging paradigms in music sociology—ones that stretch well beyond theoretical and empirical statements on the social and the aesthetic. As outlined in the Introduction and elsewhere in this volume, such directions relate to: the rise of "big data," the digital humanities and the attendant proliferation of new methodological possibilities; shifting forms of capitalism and new questions in policy, arts funding and the uncertainty or precariousness of cultural and creative work; issues of popular music heritage, cultural memory and urban space; the role of music in ageing, health, wellbeing and death; the materiality and political ecology of musical manufacturing and waste; as well as posthumanist erosions of the boundaries between people and animals, represented in the emerging field of "zoomusicology" (see for example Martinelli 2009). In the early years of the twenty-first century, the musical–sociological imagination thus seems not only highly energetic but also increasingly diffuse and interdisciplinary. Even if, as we suggested at the outset, this might raise questions about the phrase "sociology of music" as a distinct academic discipline, we are confident that it also increases the richness of music sociology as an intellectual endeavor.

References

Born, G. 2010. "The Social and the Aesthetic: For a Post-Bourdieuian Theory of Cultural Production." *Cultural Sociology* 4(2): 171–208.

Martinelli, D. 2009. *Of Birds, Whales and Other Musicians: An Introduction to Zoomusicology*. Scranton: University of Scranton Press.

Piekut, B. 2011. *Experimentalism Otherwise: The New York Avant-Garde and Its Limits*. Berkeley: University of California Press.

———. 2014. "Actor-Networks in Music History: Clarifications and Critiques." *Twentieth-Century Music* 11(2): 191–215.

Shepherd, J. and P. Wicke. 1997. *Music and Cultural Theory*. Cambridge: Polity.

32

After Adorno

TIA DeNora

Music Sociology, the "New" Musicology, and Adorno

While Adorno has been all but forgotten by music sociologists (though not by social and cultural theorists), his work is alive and well in musicology. Indeed, the vicissitudes of Adorno's reputation within music scholarship highlight just how dramatically that field has changed since the 1970s, when Rose Rosengard Subotnik's (1976) uncanny sensitivity to his thought was virtually the only torch to be carried for Adorno there. Subotnik's work has since been vindicated and interest in Adorno's work burgeons. This interest can, I suggest, be read as part of a wider paradigm shift within musicology.

Today—or so it seems looking in from the outside—most musicologists would probably agree with Donald Randel's (1992) observation that musicology's more traditional "toolbox" had been designed for the work of constructing and maintaining a canon of acceptable topics—works, great works, great composers. In roughly the past fifteen years, and in response to developments in other disciplines such as literary theory, philosophy, history, anthropology, and, to a much smaller extent, sociology, the field of musicology has been thoroughly revised. Today the "new" musicologists (a term dating to at least to the middle 1980s) have called into question the separation of historical issues (biography and the social contexts of music-making) and musical form. They have focused instead on music's role as a social medium. This move, once controversial, has now, it seems fair to say, been institutionalised within the discipline. It is now "normal," or at least acceptable, to pursue questions about the interrelation between musical works on the one hand, and categories and hierarchies of social structure—identity, power, and the practices of ruling—on the other. One could argue that the "new" musicology is now, for all practical purposes, "musicology" writ large, or, if not, then part of what is officially recognised as part of musicology's forefront. From a sociological perspective this development is welcome. But there is still more work to be done before musicology and sociology can operate in tandem. This work involves rethinking both music sociology and musicology so as to highlight what, within each discipline, has been ignored.

What is missing, then, from music sociology? . . . [W]ork on music by sociologists can be characterised almost entirely as a sociology *of* music, that is, a sociology about how musical activity (composition, performance, distribution, reception) is socially shaped. This work has not correspondingly dealt with the problem of how music "gets into" social reality; how music is a dynamic medium of social life. In this respect its empirically grounded focus is directed away from Adorno's key concerns. Most sociologists do not bother with the question of music's specifically *musical* properties and how these properties may "act" upon those who encounter them. Indeed, sociologists tend to infuriate musicologists when they suggest that musical meaning—music's perceived associations, connotations, and values—derive *exclusively* from the ways in which music is framed and appropriated, from what is "said" about it. Musicologists often assume (and in some cases correctly) that this notion overrides any concept of music's own properties (conventions, physical properties of sound) as active in the process of perceived meanings.

The problem with the new musicology viewed from the perspective of music sociology is that it has been too tightly committed to the interpretation and criticism of musical texts. This commitment in turn has constrained musicology's conception and interrogation of the social. This focus is perhaps hardly surprising, given the traditional concerns of musicology as a discipline. It also helps to explain why Adorno's work is more highly valued by music scholars than by music sociologists. Richard Leppert's and Susan McClary's influential edited collection, *Music and Society: The Politics of Composition, Performance and Reception* (1987), a paradigmatic work in the field of new musicology, helps to clarify these points.

Musicology's Society Paradigm

As the editors put it in their Introduction, the volume was oriented to "presenting alternative models to the reading of music history and music criticism—models that strive to permit social context and musical discourse to inform one another" (1987: xiii–xiv). Analytically, this aim was addressed in ways that resonated with two aspects of Adorno's methodology.

The first of these resonances was described by Rose Subotnik, whose essay ("On Grounding Chopin") outlined the techniques to be employed for illuminating music's "mediating role." "The problem of trying to relate music to society *is*," Subotnik wrote, "fundamentally, a problem of criticism, requiring very much the same sorts of means that one would take to the interpretation of a literary text" (1987: 107). The second resonance involved the technique . . . of juxtaposing "microscopies of musical detail" (as Merquior put it, quoted in Martin 1995: 115) with broad-brush depictions of the social whole. This strategy was the primary strategy within musicology at the time for illuminating music's ideological role. Its usefulness was linked to its ability to point to structural *patterns* between musical and social forms—to make suggestions about how music—in and through its compositional practices—might be related to ideas or social arrangements.

For example, in "On Talking Politics during Bach Year," Susan McClary wrote, "[t]he values it [functional tonality] articulates are those held most dear by the middle class: beliefs in progress, in expansion, in the ability to attain ultimate goals through rational striving, in the ingenuity of the individual strategist operating both within and in defiance of the norm" (1987: 22). Similarly, John Shepherd's discourse (in "Music and Male Hegemony") also alluded, in a general way, to music's ability to afford social action. He described what he regarded as rare forms of music that manage, "to subvert, if only partially, the bureaucratised norms of 'classical' music. *The structure of many Afro-American and Afro-American influenced 'popular' musics reflects the situation of proletarianized peoples* contained by social institutions that they cannot influence or affect in any consequential fashion" (1987: 162, emphasis added).

As a strategy, the juxtaposition of micro-musical and macro-social analysis helped reorient scholars to music's social dimension—and it required a good deal of professional courage at the time. But this strategy also constrained the possibilities for theorising society (and with it, available modes of, and rationale for, empirical socio-musical investigation). This constraint can be seen as linked to the tactic of positing social structure as a backdrop or foil for detailed musical analysis— a resource for musical analysis but not a topic of socio-musical analysis. By this I mean that the social was not theorised in a manner that could highlight the mechanisms of its making and remaking. As such, music comes to be seen as reflecting society, a conception that, at least implicitly, forfeits a theory of dynamism between music and society (and within which links between the two can only be stated hypothetically). In short, we never see music *in the act of* articulating social structure or as it is mobilised for this articulation. Instead, through reference to "middle-class beliefs" or "proletarianised peoples" social structure is (at least implicitly) posited as extant (objectified).

Society in a Pumpkin Shell?

In his seminars at the University of California, the sociologist Bruno Latour used to describe how the macro-oriented sociologists critical of his work (theorists of global systems, the various quantitative analysts and statistical modellers) would often ask him where, within his focus on the networks, strategies, and campaigns through which scientific "facts" were established, was the "big picture"? Where, for example, were the "systems"—legal, political, economic? Where were the historical "eras," "epochs," and "regimes"? Sociology, they would argue, had to consider "the big picture." When they uttered these words ("the big picture"), Latour recounted, their voices would (reverentially) drop an octave and their arms would sweep upwards to describe a circle. At this point Latour would say (and I paraphrase), "you see? They make reference to 'the big picture' but that picture turns out to be no bigger than a pumpkin [i.e., the size of the arm span used in the gesture]." By this Latour meant that the "wider society" to which these scholars alluded (democracy, revolution, norms, criminality, the family, indeed society itself) was an extrapolation of the known, an attribution, in part, of imagination and faith. The "bigger picture" was, in short, a literary production, one that came to be performed (indexed) through statements "about" it.

While one might counter this position by pointing to the ways in which these "fictions" nevertheless manage to produce highly tangible signs of their presence (state-sponsored violence and war; apartheid; purdah; the caste system; systematic forms of discrimination), Latour's point remains, on *methodological* grounds, unchallenged. There, lessons to be drawn from Latour are straightforward: it will not do to "sociologise" social structure. Instead, all claims about "structures," social forces, and the like need to be examined in terms of mechanisms of operation, in terms of the agents or (to use the terminology employed by this perspective) "actor networks" within which social patterns and institutions are performed and, for varying lengths of time, consolidated. These mechanisms include people's day-to-day activities, their meaningful orientation to the things that they understand as "society," "law," "government," the "economy," "family life," and many others.

Such questions imply a grounded focus on the connections between culture (including ideas of structure) and agency (activity). Doing science, or music (which includes consuming these things) is simultaneously doing social life, and it was precisely this point that Latour sought to make in *The Pasteurization of France* (1989). It should be clear by now that this paradigm is concerned with how, *at the level of situated* activities, science and society do not "reflect" each other (as if they are distinct) but are rather "co-produced." The term, "co-production" highlights how it is possible to, as it were, *do things with science* (one could substitute here, music), that is, how the form that scientific knowledge takes has *consequences* for, is part of the ecosystem of, the various worlds within which it is formulated, received, and used. This idea, while linked to a methodological programme fundamentally different from Adorno's, nonetheless resonates with his concern with cultural products as active ingredients in relation to consciousness and to ruling.

In sum, Latour's notion of co-production offers lessons for both the new musicology and for music sociology. For the former, the lesson is that, on its own, the analysis of the discursive properties of texts is not enough. It leaves in shadow the actual workings of "society," that is, the question of how music and non-musical features of social life can be seen to interact. It also sidesteps issues concerning the construction of musical meaning in actual contexts of reception and thus the issue of *contested* meanings (including resistance to particular musicological interpretations—for example, disputes within and between "expert" and "lay" respondents to music). Music's mechanisms of operation within this model are unspecifiable—that is, there is no methodology for describing music as it "acts" within actual social settings, eras and spaces, and in real time.

For music sociology, the lesson is that the new musicology's concern with music as a dynamic medium within social life cannot be ignored. Music is not simply "shaped" by "social forces"—such a view is not only sociologistic, it also misses music's active properties and thus diminishes the potential of music sociology by ignoring the question of music's discursive and material powers.

In what follows, I attempt to build upon these lessons to develop a programme for socio-musical research that draws together the concerns of musicology and sociology and sets them on an empirical plane. This programme takes to heart Howard Becker's disarmingly clear observation that society (or music) is, "what a lot of people have done jointly" (1989: 282). Its focus is on music as (and in relation to) social *process*, on how musical materials (and the interpretations and evaluations of these materials) are created, revised, and undercut with reference to the social relations and social contexts of this activity. It also is concerned with how music provides constraining and enabling resources for social agents—for the people who perform, listen, compose, or otherwise engage with musical materials.

This focus attends to the question of *how* links between music and agency, music and forms of community, music and ideas, come to be forged. It takes as its first commandment Antoine Hennion's stricture that "it must be strictly forbidden to create links when this is not done by an identifiable intermediary" (1995: 248). By this, Hennion means that while music may be, or may seem to be, interlinked to "social" matters—patterns of cognition, styles of action, ideologies, institutional arrangements—these links should not be presumed. Rather, they need to be specified (observed and described) at their levels of operation (e.g., in terms of how they are established and come to act). We need, in short, to follow actors in and across situations as they draw music into (and draw on music as) social practice. And *this* is where empirical methods come into their own within the sociology of music. It should be obvious at this point that I am seeking to move the argument on to a level where social life can be portrayed in less general, more socially located, terms. I suggest that this is a theoretical advance for music sociology, a move towards greater nuance in keeping with Adorno's own critique of reason—it is a move towards specificity.

Grand Theory and Everyday Experience

In her novel *The Good Apprentice*, Iris Murdoch (1985: 150) has a character exclaim "the modern world is full of theories which are proliferating at a wrong level of generality, we're so *good* at theorising, and one theory spawns another, there's a whole industry of abstract activity which people mistake for thinking." The argument developed so far has led to this point: too much of socio-musical studies (and too much of sociology as well) has been conducted on this "wrong level." By the term "wrong level," I mean a level of theorising that does not address or attempt to document the *actual* mechanisms through which music plays a mediating role in social life. In this suggestion, I am by no means original.

Olle Edström clarifies this point. Describing how his musicology study group at Gothenburg became frustrated after many months of Adorno Study-Group, Edström (1997: 19) says, "... we gradually gained a deeper insight into the pointlessness of instituting theoretical discourses on music without a solid ethnomusicological knowledge of the everyday usage, function and meaning of music."

The focus on "use" described by Edström entails certain shifts. First, as described already, it involves a shift away from a sole preoccupation with "works" and towards, instead, the ways that works are incorporated into practice. There is most assuredly a place for "readings" here, but they are used either as heuristic aids or as topics in their own right, as I describe below. Second it involves a shift from "what" to "how" questions—that is a shift from a concern with "what" musical works might "tell" us to a concern with "how," as they are incorporated into practice (whether through the ways they are consumed or performed or through the ways that they may provide resources for the composition and/or interpretation of new or other works) they may come to have "causal" or structuring powers, effects. In short, to understand music as a constitutive ingredient of social ordering (and this is ultimately Adorno's concern), it is necessary to gain distance from the prevailing models of music's relation to "society," common within musicology, cultural studies, and socio-cultural theory. By contrast, what is required is a focus on actual musical *practice*, on how specific agents use and interact with music. Such an approach makes no assumptions about "what" music can do but examines music's social "content" as it is constituted through musical practices in real time and in particular social and material spaces. Only through observation of these practices is it possible to document music's mechanisms of operation, to follow agents as they *do things with music*. It is only through this empirical work that theories can be extended beyond the "wrong level" of generality. . . .

Music does function discursively—the new musicologists are right. Music's recipients may, in other words, identify with particular aspects of music or see themselves in particular features of compositions. When they do this, music can be said to "do" things, in this case, to "get into" (inform, lend form to, structure) subjectivity. Musicological readings of works may thus help us to see how musical structures give rise to subjective orientations (subject positions) and their relations; may help us to see how cultural artefacts may serve as object lessons in social relations and may be associated with particular patterns of reception. . . .

But [such issues also need to be explored] in grounded, methodologically rigorous ways. The question arises, then, how should this be done? Is it sufficient, for example, to use the traditional methods of reception study, simply to ask people to "talk about" what this music means? I have been suggesting that these traditional methods are insufficient to the task, that we need to explore music as it functions *in situ*, not as it is "interpreted" but rather as it is *used*. Such a focus, I argue in what follows, helps to situate socio-musical study at the "right" level of generality—it preserves a concern with the fine-grained texture of, on the one hand, social practices of musical appropriation and, on the other, music's musical features as they are relevant to this process.

What Can Music Afford?

Reception and media studies have been useful. They have taught us how the meanings of cultural media (including their perceived "value")—come to be articulated through the ways people (media consumers) interact with media products (for sociological discussions of this point see, for example, Van Rees 1987, Moores 1990, Tota 2001). Among these "consumers" are music scholars, analysts, and critics who are just one sub-set (albeit perhaps a prominent and often influential sub-set) of music consumers and music users. This *emergent* aspect of cultural-textual meaning includes both the meanings found "in" texts by amateur or lay consumers, and the meanings divined by "expert" analysts and readers.

At the same time, as the new musicologists have sought to demonstrate, it is wrong to suggest that texts make no contribution to the ways they are received. Musical texts, or, more broadly, musical materials, are by no means neutral. They are created and distributed in ways that employ and reinforce meanings. There are many aspects of music that can serve as examples here: music's physical features, such as volume and pace; the physical requirements of performance (e.g., solo violin or massed strings); conventions such as genres, styles, melodic devices, or topoi; and, in the case of repeated hearings, accumulated connotations, institutionalised interpretations. While no musical unit, passage, or work may guarantee its reception under all circumstances (even the most conventional of materials can still be, in Eco's term (1992), "over-interpreted"), musical materials are nonetheless part of, and contribute to, their circumstances of hearing (see DeNora 2000: 21–45 for a more detailed discussion of these points). To take a very basic example, it is unlikely that any listener will hear a march tune as "dreamy" or Debussy's *Prélude à l'après-midi d'un faune* as suitable music for marching.

Particular musical materials may thus be perceived, often with regularity, as commensurate with a variety of "other things." These "things" may be other works (how we come to recognise the "style" of an era, composer, region, for example) but, more interesting for socio-musical analysis, they may be some extra-musical phenomenon, such as values, ideas, images, social relations, or styles of activity. The *sociological* significance of this last point is intensified when music's social "content" is not merely hailed (as a representation of a reality or imagined reality) but is rather acted upon, when music comes to serve in some way as an organising material for action, motivation, thought, imagination, and so forth. It is here that we can begin to speak of music as it "gets into" action. And it is here that socio-musical study can be extended beyond notions (derived from textual analysis) of music's symbolic character, its interpretations and perceived *meaning(s)*.

There are precedents here in the work of scholars—prominent in the American context here is Robert Wuthnow—who have been concerned with the *interrelationships between* (rather than *meanings of)* cultural elements, an emphasis that seeks to retain the sociological impetus within cultural studies by redirecting our focus on culture's organising properties and away from the individualistic focus on meaning and its reception. As Wuthnow (1987) has observed, meanings emerge from cultural systems and fields that provide "categories in which formal thinking about ourselves" may be conducted. This is, again, a focus on how meanings and forms "get into" action— how they provide, in the words of other theorists, *repertoires* for action . . . The focus on meaning systems leads, at least implicitly, to a focus upon actors as they engage with and mobilise cultural materials, as they move through particular cultural fields and so configure themselves as conscious agents. Such a perspective is in line, I believe, with the focus, within organisational studies, on structuration and agency—work such as DiMaggio's (1982) that has consisted of an abiding focus on agents as they mobilise cultural structures to produce and reproduce organisations. Here, then, music can be understood as a resource for getting things done and, in this sense, the sociology of music can not only learn from existing theoretical and empirical work on institutions, it can also advance that work through its potential to reveal the aesthetic and non-cognitive dimensions of social agency.

In short, the "right level" of generality in socio-musical studies consists of a focus on music-as-practice, and music as providing a basis for practice. It deals with music as a formative medium in relation to consciousness and action, as a resource for—rather than medium about—world-building. Within this dynamic conception of music's social character, focus shifts from *what* music depicts, or what it can be "read" as saying "about" society, to what it *makes possible*. And to speak of "what music makes possible" is to speak of what music "affords."

Adapted from social psychology, the concept of "affordance" captures music's role as, to use Antoine Hennion's (2001) term, a "mediator" of the social. And, depending upon how it is conceptualised, the concept of "affordance" highlights music's potential as an organising medium, as something that helps to structure such things as styles of consciousness, ideas, or modes of embodiment. To speak of music as affording things is to suggest that it is a material against which things are shaped up, elaborated through practical and sometimes non-conscious, action. . . .

[M]usic "causes" nothing; it "makes nothing happen," as Auden said of poetry, and certainly it does not "give rise," in and of itself, to either marching or ideas about social organisation. That is, to speak of music as an affordance structure is by no means the same as to speak of music as "cause" or "stimulus" of action, thought, or emotional response. It also does not imply that there is some "set" of things that a particular music may afford, since what comes to count as the musical "object" emerges in relation to how that object is handled by its recipients.

By contrast, the concept of affordance extends developments within reception theory, emphasising music's effects as dependent upon the ways that those who hear it respond to it; how they incorporate it into their action; and how they may adapt their action (not necessarily or in most cases consciously) to its parameters and qualities. It posits music as something acted with and acted upon. It is only through this appropriation that music comes to "afford" things, which is to say that music's affordances, while they might be anticipated, cannot be pre-determined but rather depend upon how music's "users" connect music to other things; how they interact with and in turn act upon music as they have activated it. It is here, then, that we can sustain socio-music analysis at a "right" level of generality. . . .

Music as a Resource for Agency

The notion of musical affordance that I have sought to develop in this chapter is dynamic; it points to a conception of music as resource for doing, thinking, and feeling "other things." Contra Adorno, however, music's affordances cannot be regarded as residing "in" musical texts, and it is for this reason that socio-musical analysis cannot proceed on a general level. Rather, what music "does" is dependent upon the ways in which music is heard and perceived; how its meanings are, to use Lucy Green's (1997) phrase, delineated. It is the job of the socio-musical analyst, therefore, to examine this process of delineation, to follow the terms of musical engagement. Music comes to afford things when it is perceived as incorporating into itself and/or its performance some property of the extra-musical, so as to be perceived as "doing" the thing to which it points. Music is active, in other words, as and when its perception is acted upon, and this circularity is precisely the topic for socio-musical research into music's power. Thus, music is much more than a structural "reflection" of the social. Music is constitutive of the social in so far as it may be seen to enter action and/or conception when "things" take shape in relation to music; when actors move in ways that are oriented to music's rhythms (e.g., making the body move "like" marching rhythm); or when actors employ musical structures as models or analogies for elaborating conceptual awareness. And, by contrast, action may be said to "get into" music when music takes shape in relation to things outside itself, as when music incorporates aspects of the physical, conceptual, or imaginative world. It is here that socio-musical analysis can develop Adornoian questions. How, for example, does music enter into fantasy life, as in the case of Adorno's essay on the conductor and the orchestra? How does music facilitate cognition, as in the case of Adorno's analysis of Schoenberg? How does other music come to pacify its listeners, to inculcate modes of consciousness that are amenable to particular regimes—political or social—as in the case, according to Adorno, of popular music?

The answers to these questions need to be framed in specific terms. If they are, it is possible to see acts of musical engagement simultaneously constituting both music's power and extra-musical modes of sociality. And it is here that *both* earlier music sociology and the new musicology erred. The one focused on how society shaped music; the other on how musical discourse could shape or reflect society. By contrast, I suggest that we consider both questions at once, melding them together as a theory of musical affordance and a practice of ethnographic investigation, historically informed, devoted to the study of how music's affordances are accessed and deployed. If, on the other hand, we are willing to observe actors as they engage in the acts of drawing music into extra-musical realms and vice versa (and not always with deliberation), as music is employed for world-building, and as aspects of non-musical realms and materials are employed for building and responding to music, we arrive at a "right" level of generality. This level calls for new methodologies, particularly qualitative techniques that focus on music production and consumption in specific spaces and over time. And this in turn suggests case studies.

Case studies are useful, I suggest, not simply because they are empirically rich and as such make for good history (their usual rationale) but also because close attention to the details of musical practice makes good theory, that is, provides a means for describing the mechanisms of culture (music) in-action, for specifying *how* music works. This focus on practice leads us further away from a concern with musical textual objects and towards the materiality of music as event, its relations, circumstances and technologies of production/reception, its uses. From here it is possible to consider how music "performs" social life, in the sense that its performance and appropriation provide resources for the production of social life, that it affords modes of thinking and feeling . . .

References

Adorno, T. 1976. *Introduction to the Sociology of Music*. Translated by E.B. Ashton. New York: Continuum.

Becker, H.S. 1989. "Ethnomusicology and Sociology: A Letter to Charles Seeger." *Ethnomusicology* 33(2), 275–285.

DeNora, T. 2000. *Music in Everyday Life*. Cambridge: Cambridge University Press.

DiMaggio, P. 1982. "Cultural Entrepreneurship in Nineteenth-Century Boston." *Media, Culture and Society* 4 (1/4): 35–50 and 303–322.

Eco, U. with R. Rorty, J. Culler and C. Brooke-Rose. 1992. *Interpretation and Overinterpretation*. Cambridge: Cambridge University Press.

Edström, O. 1997. "Fr-a-g-me-n-ts: A Discussion on the Position of Critical Ethnomusicology in Contemporary Musicology." *Svensk Tidskrift for Musikforskning (Swedish Journal of Musicology)* 79(1): 9–68.

Green, L. 1997. *Music, Gender and Education*. Cambridge: Cambridge University Press.

Hennion, A. 1995. "The History of Art—Lessons in Mediation." *Réseaux: The French Journal of Communication* 3(2): 233–262.

_____. 2001. "Music Lovers: Taste as Performance." *Theory, Culture and Society* 18(5): 1–22.

Latour, B. 1989. *The Pasteurization of France*. Cambridge: Harvard University Press.

Leppert, R. and S. McClary, eds. 1987. *Music and Society*. Cambridge: Cambridge University Press.

Martin, P. 1995. *Sounds and Society: Themes in the Sociology of Music*. Manchester: Manchester University Press.

McClary, S. 1987. "On Talking Politics During the Bach Year." In *Music and Society*, eds. R. Leppert and S. McClary, 13–62. Cambridge: Cambridge University Press.

Moores, S. 1990. *Interpreting Audiences*. London: Sage.

Murdoch, I. 1985. *The Good Apprentice*. London: Chatto and Windus.

Randel, D. 1992. "The Canon in the Musicological Toolbox." In *Disciplining Music: Musicology and its Canons*, eds. K. Bergeron and P. Bohlman, 10–23. Chicago: University of Chicago Press.

Shepherd, J. 1987. "Music and Male Hegemony." In *Music and Society*, eds. R. Leppert and S. McClary, 151–172. Cambridge: Cambridge University Press.

Subotnik, R.R. 1976. "Adorno's Diagnosis of Beethoven's Late Style." *Journal of the American Musicological Society* 29 (2): 242–275.

_____. 1987. "On Grounding Chopin." In *Music and Society: The Politics of Composition, Performance and Reception*, eds. R. Leppert and S. McClary, 105–131. Cambridge: Cambridge University Press.

Tota, A.L. 2001. "When Orff Meets Guinness: Music in Advertising as a Form of Cultural Hybrid." *Poetics* 29(2): 109–124.

Van Rees, C.J. 1987. "How Reviewers Reach Consensus on the Value of Literary Works." *Poetics* 16(3/4), 275–294.

Wuthnow, R. 1987. *Meaning and Moral Order*. Berkeley: University of California Press.

33

Bourdieu and Beyond

Nick Prior

Recent developments in the sociology of music have presaged a significant shift in approaches to the relationship between music and society. Alongside an emerging focus on intellectual copyright, technological change and a globalized media system, scholars have begun the task of questioning the grounds on which an orthodox sociology of music is built (Born 2005). Once a central strut in strong constructivist approaches to culture, where genre, taste and practice were shown to be profoundly social accomplishments, current trends have thrown into doubt sociological analyses of music that do not sufficiently engage with the specificities of musical objects and which fail to take the cognitive affordances of music seriously (DeNora 2003). Instead, an emerging strand of new music sociology has attached to the complex ways the social and the aesthetic are embedded in and activate one another, implying a more open relationship to the material and sensuous properties of the work and a scepticism towards accounts that gloss these properties (Gomart and Hennion 1999).

Precisely because he is a lynchpin in the field of cultural sociology, the figure of Pierre Bourdieu looms large in this movement. In many ways, Bourdieu has set the agenda for post-Marxist investigations of socio-musical practices as they play out relationally. His concepts of cultural capital, field and *habitus* in particular, have been central to the formation of a critical paradigm in music sociology that demonstrates how the social penetrates, produces or contextualizes music. Bourdieu-inspired studies of both popular and classical music now occupy a good chunk of the field of music sociology. His most canonical text, *Distinction* (1984), has provided an empirical benchmark for explorations of the nature and formation of musical taste in places like France, America and the UK. And even in the less hallowed realms of music journalism, Bourdieu's terms are finding currency, with influential critics like Simon Reynolds deploying Bourdieusian categories to examine logics of populism and elitism in contemporary pop (Reynolds 2009).

This paper reviews the status, position and legacy of Bourdieu in the sociology of music, the waxing and waning of his influence, and the recent move away from Bourdieu towards something like a post-critical engagement with musical forms and practices. The idea is to show the reaction to and treatment of Bourdieu's ideas as a gauge of where we are in the sociology of culture. Certainly, along with Howard Becker (1982), Bourdieu has been representative of a devoutly sociological approach to cultural production that has placed the aesthetic object in a network of social forces and determinants. This puts him in the line of fire as far as non-reductive accounts of culture are concerned. How, then, should we assess the impact of Bourdieu's ideas on the sub-fields of art and music sociology? What various strands of influence emanate from his work? And what is at stake in this "post-Bourdieu" moment when a position once considered progressive and critical now acts as the foil against which new work is being conducted?

... [T]he article will discuss the impact of Bourdieu's work on music sociology in the UK and beyond. It will then move towards a discussion of newer approaches to music after Bourdieu ... and point to the significant ways these contributions move debates on musico-social relations into territories more sensitive to the complex mediating qualities of music. While varying in tone and tenor, the paper will show how such work combines at a critical juncture in the development of a sociology of culture that does not reduce its object to a simple determination or resource for domination. Such work is better placed, therefore, to represent music as an animating force in everyday life, including its specific mediating qualities "in action." At the same time, however, the construction of a new sociology of music is not without its perils, particularly when one considers issues of analytical coverage and conceptual adequacy. The article will conclude with some potential problems with these approaches, and will take stock of what might be lost as well as gained by adherence to them.

[. . .]

Bourdieu and the Sociology of Music

... Music sociology ... constitutes one of the biggest growth areas in cultural sociology, and one where Bourdieu's presence has been crucial. What specific challenges, then, are thrown up by an engagement with musical forms, attachments and processes? And to what extent can recent developments in the sociology of music be said to constitute a drift away from Bourdieu? Before I attempt to answer these questions, let me first briefly take stock of Bourdieu's influence on the corpus of music sociology in order to examine what it is the "new" sociology of music is responding to.

Bourdieu rarely engaged with music directly or in any detail. In contrast to an almost obsessive preoccupation with modern literature and the visual arts—in particular, the "heroic modernism" of Flaubert, Manet and Baudelaire—Bourdieu is relatively quiet on musical forms, practices and practitioners. This is somewhat surprising given the bold statement in *Distinction* that "nothing more clearly affirms one's 'class,' nothing more infallibly classifies, than tastes in music" (Bourdieu 1984: 18).[1] Sure enough, Bourdieu does show music to be a relational set of objects bound to logics of social differentiation. On the basis of interview and questionnaire data, he plots class-based preferences for a selection of more or less well-disseminated musical works including Strauss' "Blue Danube" (popular and therefore favoured by manual workers) and Bach's "Well-Tempered Clavier" (less popular and therefore preferred by those with higher levels of cultural capital).[2] Elsewhere, he makes scattered references to composers like Debussy and Berlioz in order to locate them in the late 19th-century field of cultural production and notes the "hagiographic exaltation" of Beethoven as the archetypal "pure" artist (Bourdieu 1996: 149).

Apart from these sporadic engagements, however, Bourdieu largely avoids music's social life and location. Certainly as far as popular music is concerned, Bourdieu pays no attention to the emergence of a developed commercial system, jazz is given short shrift and music-based youth formations are glossed. Of course, much of this neglect has to do with the local context that was France in the 1950s and 1960s, with its specific cultural reference points and field dynamics. Rock 'n' roll was a distinctly Anglo-American configuration, after all, and one that was only beginning to make waves outside of that axis. But the neglect also has to do with Bourdieu's emphasis on legitimate culture as the basis for distinction and his relative ignorance of the complexity of popular art and culture, as some notable commentators have argued (Fowler 1997, Shusterman 1992). A culture that Bourdieu dismisses as high art's poor monolithic cousin was certainly, by the 1950s and 1960s, a more fissured, idiosyncratic and developed set of forms than Bourdieu allows. And he is hardly symmetrical when it comes to understanding how "high" and "low" cultures function. On the other hand, even on "classical" or "art" music, where one might expect some engagement with the avant-garde position-takings of composers like Boulez, Bourdieu is coy.

In any case, it's been largely left to sympathetic scholars to fill the gap left by this neglect and develop a sociology of music broadly influenced by Bourdieu's work. That they have done so expansively and with such enthusiasm speaks not only of the fertility of Bourdieu's concepts across a range of cultural forms, but also what Heinich calls the "Bourdieu effect," the almost mythical status accorded to an increasingly dominant player in European scholarship (Danko 2008). From the late 1970s onwards, a kind of Bourdieu paradigm of critical music sociology has materialized, based on a love of certain key texts, a following for a figure of intellectual authority and a fascination for concepts deemed suitable for application in empirical settings. From quantitative examinations of musical taste to political economies of the music industry, and from Quebecois *chansonniers* to Japanese *nihon ongaku*, a Bourdieusian terminology has lubricated the circuits of music scholarship (De Ferranti 2002, Ollivier 2006). It is nowadays rare to find a study of musical taste that does not start with or evoke Bourdieu's ideas, while key works such as *Distinction* and *The Field of Cultural Production* have become touchstones for studies that examine music and social structure. Meanwhile, a substantial Bourdieu culture industry has developed via the scholarly accoutrements of translation, application and interpretation. This is evident in recent texts like *Opera and Society in Italy and France from Monteverdi to Bourdieu* (Johnson et al. 2007), where Bourdieu plays the role of both theoretical interlocutor and guide to new understandings of the operatic form.

Not that this presence has been internationally uniform. As Santoro (2009) notes, there has been a curious neglect of Bourdieu in Italian sociology, where conditions in the academic field have typically resisted the incursions of foreign authors whose works are considered a threat to existing positions. It's also the case that different national fields have appropriated Bourdieu's work in subtly different ways. In North America, Bourdieu has been used most keenly for quantitative studies of consumption and taste, although he has also been an emergent reference point for studies of Indian American dance music, studio technologies and the history of sound reproduction (Maira 2002, Sterne 2003, Théberge 1997). The influential journal *Poetics*, while heavily inflected by the production-of-culture approach, has also set the agenda for Bourdieu-influenced sociologies of music with an empirical focus (Dowd 2007). Most recently, the journal has published articles on hip-hop (Cheyne and Binder 2010), "heritage rock" (Bennett 2009) and jazz (Pinheiro and Dowd 2009), each making some reference to Bourdieu's work. Meanwhile, older American studies of cultural production and organization remain classic reference points for an examination of the dynamics of musical content in complex social systems (DiMaggio 1977, Peterson and Berger 1975).

In Israel and South America, it is Bourdieu's later work on the field concept that has been most consistently applied to glocalized styles of pop and rock music. In Regev's (2007) comparative study of "pop-rock" fields in Israel and Argentina, for instance, the author describes the historical legitimacy of an amplified electronic aesthetic among critics and other field agents. Regev claims that a cosmopolitan "pop-rock *habitus*" among these agents disposes them to straddle both global and ethno-national fields in the construction of innovative strategies of production. Other studies in this vein are also worth noting. Frota's (2006) analysis of canon formation in the case of *Música Popular Brasileira* shows how the constitution of the popular musical field in Brazil is linked to the advent of commercial radio stations and record companies, as well as the position- takings of musicians from the 1960s. Lopes's (2000) study of the genealogy of the modern jazz para-digm in America, on the other hand, demonstrates the fecundity of the field concept as a tool to show how new aesthetic practices among jazz musicians were legitimated in the first half of the 20th century.

What unites many of these studies is the strategic deployment of Bourdieu's theories as a necessary first move away from orthodox histories of music in particular (national) cases. Bourdieu's work is recognized as providing critical leverage in re-writing eulogizing narratives of music that fail to incorporate questions of power, struggle and exclusion. His function, in this sense, has been to help modernize studies of music by providing ammunition against internalist histories. But Bourdieu-inspired studies have had deeper and wider coverage. In some cases, scholars have examined the acquisition of specific musical practices such as vocal styles and melodic-rhythmic techniques using Bourdieu's categories (De Ferranti 2002). In other cases, such categories are employed to map relations between broad economic contexts and cultural hierarchies in the formation of genres of popular music, including identifying the crucial role played by what Bourdieu called "cultural intermediaries" in the symbolic production of musical goods and services (Negus 1999).

Of course, it would be wrong to suggest that Bourdieu is always used in such extensive ways in the sociology of music or that he is used uncritically. Indeed, a related axis of differentiation is the extent to which various studies deploy Bourdieu's ideas in relation to others in the sociology of music. As a crude indicator here we can draw on a distinction made by Goldthorpe (2007) between "wild" and "domesticated" uses of Bourdieu. Goldthorpe argues, in the context of discussions of educational achievement, that the concept of cultural capital has been used in two ways. First, in domesticated form, subject to qualifications and triangulated with a number of other positions. Second, in wild form, as part of a grand paradigmatic statement that explains relations between cultural capital and large-scale social reproduction in modern societies. Goldthorpe's argument is that the wild version of Bourdieu is more faithful to the spirit of Bourdieu's own explanatory system, but that this system itself is flawed.

Putting aside Goldthrope's critique of Bourdieu, we can nevertheless recognize a distinction between relative weights of analysis—Bourdieu-lite and Bourdieu-heavy—in the field of music sociology. On the one hand, making reference to Bourdieu's concepts is part of the currency of ideas in music scholarship. Concepts like *habitus* are regularly cited in order to give academic gloss to arguments about musical practice, even if the study does not pivot on this concept. Equally, music sociologists will cast Bourdieu as one of several influential authors (including Weber, Adorno, Benjamin, Peterson and Becker) whose ideas need to be parsed in order to pay due attention to the tradition of cultural sociology itself. On the other hand, music sociologists have utilized Bourdieusian concepts more extensively to construct overarching frameworks for how the whole music/society jigsaw fits together. As Goldthorpe (2007) recognizes, Bourdieu had grand theoretical ambition in suggesting a meta-sociological narrative to explain the nature of modern social configurations. It is unsurprising, therefore, that the spirit of these grand ambitions is also present in Bourdieu-inspired examinations of music which aim to trace the social determinations of musical practices within a system of overlapping social, economic and political fields.

[. . .]

The Post-Bourdieu Moment

In the domain of music sociology, the call for a more sophisticated engagement with musical objects has become increasingly insistent. Here, sociologists from France and the UK, in particular, have begun the task of building something like a post-critical approach to music that aims to give due credence to the rich complexities of aesthetic expression, materiality and attachment. While varying in voice, tenor and trajectory, such contributions share a determination to move the intellectual agenda on music into territories unencumbered by over-simplified accounts of cultural production and consumption. In many respects, therefore, they constitute something like a new wave of theoretically informed positions set against previous orthodoxies in the sociology of culture, in which an interest in the specific properties of music has inflected the outcome in important ways.

In a recent paper outlining a "post-Bourdieuian theory of cultural production," Georgina Born (2010: 7) writes: "if we look to Bourdieu to fill out a sociological aesthetics and to address the specificity of the art object, we look in vain." Bourdieu's impoverished analysis of popular aesthetics is compounded, for Born, by an inability to address important questions around creative agency and artistic purpose. This is because Bourdieu's theorization of aesthetic qualities is a negatively sceptical one, even in books like *The Rules of* Art which claim to show the historical autonomization of aesthetic positions. Here, questions of form are collapsed, for Born, into an account of conflict between positions hierarchically arranged in a way that refuses to admit either the mediating effects of art or the creative decisions of the producer. This translates into a denial of artistic value beyond the *social* value of art in cementing certain taste clusters or positions.

The requirement to move beyond Bourdieu is therefore announced as an explicit principle for broadening the grounds on which a complete theory of the social and the aesthetic can be based. Born (2010: 16) gravitates to anthropologists of culture such as Alfred Gell, Christopher Pinney and Steven Feld as supports for an analysis of the "distinctive ontologies that inform expressive practices." Such practices are intimately bound, for these authors, to both the authorial subjectivities of creators and to the material properties of works themselves. It is to this less socialized version of the interplay between objects and agency that Born is attracted. Hence, as far as music is concerned, it is the concept of "mediation" that serves Born best in getting at how objects afford a continual relay of translation of distinct processes and effects. Mediation hints at how music's properties are in a constant state of assemblage and production, "continually, immanently open to re-creation" as she puts it in an earlier paper (Born 2005: 26). Indeed, while music is said to be a medium that disrupts dualisms around the separation of subject and object, present and past, production and reception, musical works also possess "careers" in that they condense creative labour just as they are subject to temporal change. Born's (2005: 7) argument, then, hinges on the promotion of a complex, multiform analysis that takes its cue from music as a "paradigmatic multiply-mediated, immaterial and material, fluid quasi-object, in which subjects and objects collide and intermingle." At an advanced theoretical level, she makes a case for replacing the rusty frameworks of *habitus*, field and capital with a more eclectic space of theorizing the work and the subject across time and space.

The theme of musical mediations is also apparent in Antoine Hennion's neo-phenomenological analysis of cultural encounters. Here, Hennion attempts to show what musical works do and what they make us do in their affordances, occurrences and effects. Hennion argues that if we start from the assumption that taste is an activity rather than a socially determined stock of capital, then we can begin to demonstrate how direct contact with objects (wine, art works, pieces of music) necessitates a shift from self to object. In other words, such objects are involved in an intensified contact that implies that they interrupt us and offer themselves up to us—for instance, they are able to surprise us and announce their presence to us. In short, taste is a practice of attachment in which we exchange properties with the object and in which what counts is what happens in the encounter, rather than what is determined by external social forces. This returns Hennion (1999: 1) to the importance of describing specific engagements among real-world audiences actively involved in practices of playing and listening, "with its moments, its tools, its arrangements and emotional effects." The figure of the musical amateur is interjected by Hennion because it is in the passionate techniques of attachment between amateurs and their objects of desire (records, instruments, scores, playback devices) that one can recognize both the material sensations sparked by objects and the modalities of passion characteristic of the pull of music itself (Gomart and Hennion 1999). Such a shift from determinism to action forces us to attend to the significant adjustments and gestures that mark themselves in the inner details of consumption and to deliver to the sociology of music taste a chance to properly register its object rather than to reduce it to an effect of the social.

This emphasis on the affective and sensual qualities of musical encounters is fully developed in Tia DeNora's *Music and Everyday Life* (2000). Here, DeNora illustrates how music is a technology of self-regulation bound up with the modification and management of emotional states. Based on ground level data on the uses of music in local settings (from commuting to aerobics classes), DeNora shows how a focus on the creative contours of agency gives us a richer understanding of how music possesses ordering properties vis-à-vis the activities and scenes that compose everyday life (see also Bull 2007). The fact that actors actively deploy music to craft their ongoing emotional and biographical selves shows how music "gets into action," for DeNora, shaping the "inner sonorous life" of individual subjectivities. Or as she puts it, "respondents make . . . articulations between musical works, styles and materials on the one hand and modes of agency on the other" (2000: 53).

Here, DeNora's theoretical debt is to Adorno, particularly the latter's emphasis on music as a potentially transformative (and manipulative) force of consciousness and cognitive praxis. Identifying music's formal properties is crucial, to this extent, because the immanent qualities of music (tone, structure, timbre and so on) are distinct to how they act upon those who come into contact with them. All of which implies that we need to move away from a sociology *of* music—"a sociology about how musical activity (composition, performance, distribution, reception) is socially shaped" (DeNora 2003: 36)—towards a sociology *with* music—one that does not ignore music's 'discursive and material powers' (DeNora 2003: 39). Like Hennion, then, DeNora argues for a shift from an analysis of "what" music does to "how" it matters in particular social settings. This, DeNora argues, would constitute a desired theoretical advancement towards a more nuanced music sociology fit for its objects of analysis.

The Challenges of Critique and Renewal

This triumvirate of figures offers a compelling and innovative attempt to push the edifice of cultural sociology—a field that has made little headway in tackling the thorny issue of the social and the aesthetic over the last 20 years—into relatively unchartered territories. In tailoring their conceptual schemes to tackle new ontologies of musical processes, such authors demonstrate what was missing in strong constructivist approaches to culture. Returning to Bourdieu after reading Hennion, one is struck by how flat Bourdieu's analysis of the work of art is, how synoptic, inert and mechanical the cultural encounter can seem. Equally, Born and DeNora's accounts lend themselves to thoughtful strategies of engagement with aesthetic processes and objects by treating these engagements and objects seriously rather than dismissing them as weapons of bourgeois power or manifestations of deep social forces. But, of course, with innovation comes danger and, at the very least, these new approaches have to be both wary of the potential pitfalls of their endeavours and reflexive about their own auspices—what drives the analysis, but also what new problems may arise in this moment of critique and renewal. Three issues are worth highlighting in particular.

First, there is the problem of finding the precise terminology and language in the absence of an established sub-discipline of sociological aesthetics. What was notable about the critical paradigm in arts sociology was the way it replaced a vocabulary of "creativity," "artist" and "expression" with that of "cultural production," "cultural producer" and "cultural work." This was, as Wolff (1981: 138) notes, "a way of ensuring that the way in which we talk about art and culture does not allow or encourage us to entertain mystical, idealised and totally unrealistic notions about the nature of this sphere." The question is, which terms, metaphors and tropes best fit the new aesthetic agenda in sociology and how adequate are they in relaying both the subtleties and sociologies of these objects?

A key dilemma is that in forging new ground one inevitably falls onto terms that are already inscribed with meanings sedimented by pre-existing traditions and disciplines. How possible, after all, is it to evoke ideas of "creativity," "expression," "creative agency" and "form" without ghosting into 19th-century ideologies of Romanticism? How does one separate the "thing itself" from discourses of the thing? The content of these terms is, in other words, already heavily loaded with sets of assumptions about the world. As Frith has recently noted, for instance, the term "creativity" can only be understood as a discursive effect of particular social institutions that equate the term with ideas of unique selfhood, originality and innovation (Frith, unpublished). As a result, creativity is both an explanation and justification for the authority of certain musicians (such as composers) over others (such as session musicians). One way around this terminological tethering is, of course, to bring in a *new* set of terms, such as "mediation," "assemblage," "contingency" and "attachment." This allows authors to construct new tools without being too weighed down with historical inter-pretation. But at times, it is clear that these authors still rely on concepts and terms redolent of less sophisticated approaches, inevitably evoking outmoded terms and traditions.

A related danger is that in giving at least some ground to art history, musicology or aesthetics, a concession unwittingly becomes a sliding into very traditional, unreconstituted and reactionary analyses that resurrect universalist ideas of creativity, judgment and independent aesthetic value (Zangwill 2002). Indeed, the call for a rapprochement between humanities and sociology alluded to by Born, Wolff and others, while laudable on paper, can create cumbersome combinations rather than productive dialogues. There's the danger, here, of creating a false harmony for the sake of a very muddy inter-disciplinarity that dilutes the projects of all concerned: a little musicology for formal analysis of the work, a little Husserl for temporality, a little Merleau-Ponty to bring in the body, a touch of Foucault for subjectivity, a whiff of Deleuze for some difference, some cultural anthropology and Actor Network Theory for the object. All of which can end up in a mish-mash theoretical pragmatism that wants the best of all worlds. While theoretical eclecticism can be a useful corrective to siding with a single theorist, it can also end up as a marriage of inconsistent premises.

Second, in staking out a position in part in opposition to a conventional critical account of music, there is a danger of moving too far in the opposite direction purely in order to make the point. In other words, in eschewing approaches couched in traditional ideas of ideology, power or distinction, there could be a tendency to over-cook the alternative and ignore what might have been salvageable in previous positions. Should we never, as many Bourdieusians do, use statistics? Is it never the case that taste is a social weapon? There is an appealing element in traditions like phenomenology and disciplines like anthropology and aesthetics because they appear to offer a way out of determinism. The question is, how much do they replace orthodox sociology with a kind of micro-aestheticism? And how much do they assert the primacy of agency by collapsing social context into a series of inter-subjectively negotiated interpretations of the aesthetic object? After all, it is one thing to say what is currently "good" as a critique of Bourdieu, it is another to dismiss everything he says as outside the limits of what can possibly be known from a critical sociological standpoint. If all that happens is "in the encounter," as Hennion argues, then is this not another (albeit rather scintillating) form of aesthetic individualism? To flip the question around, if it is the case that there is more to art and culture than crude social class determinisms, then does that mean we are merely left to describe singular aesthetic moments of attachment?

Finally, in seeking alternatives to Bourdieu, it could be argued that the post-critical analysis replaces one form of theoretical imperialism with another, in the name of a post-imperialist reconstruction that makes an exception of itself. What I mean by this is that Bourdieu, as already noted, is held as a figure who wields sociology as a weapon to deconstruct all domains of knowledge and practice—a sociological imperialist who seems immune from his own critique of knowledge as interested and inseparable from power (Inglis 2005). But those who make this charge are often just as wont to construct theoretical edifices that, while post-Bourdieusian in some senses, are still making truth claims that end up offering a similarly substantialist attempt to explain the world. Indeed, while the new sociology of culture might claim to be less imperialist than its predecessor, one could argue that it is precisely in its attempt to capture the domain of the aesthetic that it continues this imperialism. For if one casts the aesthetic as the sociology of culture's erstwhile "other" then would it be too much of a stretch to suggest that this might just be the latest move in a (post-colonial) logic of tolerance and assimilation?

This might be an unfair analogy. After all, there is no sense that the new sociologists of music are setting out to conquer other disciplinary territories in the name of a post-positivist superpower. What it does do, however, is raise the important question of how intellectual strategizing is inseparable from the business of professionalized cultural production in academic settings.

Conclusion

In attempting to engage with what was, up to recently, thought of as a discredited domain of the aesthetic, sociologists have made great strides in moving debates around art, music and society forward. Not only have they conceptualized cultural production in ways that are more faithful to the precise contours of cultural works, attachments and practices, but they have revealed deep lacunae in previous accounts that secreted their objects before properly engaging with them. But in the brave new world of the sociology of aesthetics, there are costs and benefits. The drift away from Bourdieu involves elements of both. For while Bourdieu's programme for a sociology of art leaves important questions unanswered, particularly regarding questions of form, style and content, it nevertheless remains one of the most comprehensive and generative frameworks of sociological analysis. Ignoring the continuing applicability and relevance of Bourdieu's ideas to art and culture can therefore leave a hole where a treatment of power-mediated artistic relations might be found. This is particularly the case when the disciplinary limits driving the odd and often incommensurable relationship between humanities and social sciences point up instances of failed integration.

All of which suggests a call, before ditching him completely (or forgetting him), of entertaining the agonistic element in Bourdieu, of twisting and skewing him, of deploying him strategically in battle to overly internalist readings of culture as well as cultural sociologies that give culture too much autonomy (Mouffe 1993). In short, of making him part of the ammunition in an open dialogue between sociologists, art historians and musicologists. If this dialogical battle is missing, conflict can too easily be replaced by a weak, murky and anodyne middle ground, the analytical equivalent to liberal individualism or the politics of a "third way" that assumes that there is nothing left to fight for but details. There is clearly much to be gained by a critical engagement with aesthetics, but also much to lose if sociology attempts to leapfrog its own grounds in an attempt to move beyond itself. Bourdieu's is not the only game in town when it comes to the analysis of art and culture, but it is clearly the most developed, sophisticated and, most importantly, sociological. And that's something still worth holding on to.

Notes

1   For Bourdieu, this is less to do with the nature of musical works themselves than the fact that the means of acquiring musical capital (in the form of playing "noble" instruments, for instance) is more invisible than, say, visiting an art museum and displaying one's knowledge of painting. It is the most "spiritual" of the arts precisely because listening is considered an "inner" quality of deep, and spiritual engagement. Hence, as he puts it: "Music is the 'pure' art par excellence. It says nothing and has *nothing to say* . . . Music represents the most radical and most absolute form of the negation of the world, and especially the social world, which the bourgeois ethos tends to demand of all forms of art" (Bourdieu 1984: 19).

2   A taste for the French singer Jacques Brel is placed somewhere in between. Lower social groups are also identified as less able to name the 16 composers of classical works read out to them in interview, while higher groups struggle to dignify "songs" (Bourdieu's shorthand for popular music) as legitimate, so they end up preferring the most consecrated, but essentially middle-brow, works of Edith Piaf and Charles Trénet.

References

Becker, H. 1982. *Art Worlds*. Berkeley: University of California Press.

Bennett, A. 2009. "'Heritage Rock': Rock Music, Representation and Heritage Discourse." *Poetics* 37(5/6): 474–489.

Born, G. 2005. "On Musical Mediation: Ontology, Technology and Creativity." *Twentieth-Century Music* 2(1): 7–36.

_____. 2010. "The Social and the Aesthetic: For a Post-Bourdieuian Theory of Cultural Production." *Cultural Sociology* 4(2): 1–38.

Bourdieu, P. 1984. *Distinction: A Social Critique of the Judgement of Taste*. London: Routledge and Kegan Paul.

_____. 1996. *The Rules of Art*. Cambridge: Polity.

Bull, M. 2007. *Sound Moves: iPod Culture and Urban Experience*. London: Routledge.

Cheyne, A. and A. Binder. 2010. "Cosmopolitan Preferences: The Constitutive Role of Place in American Elite Taste for Hip-Hop Music, 1991–2005." *Poetics* 30(3): 336–364.

Danko, D. 2008. "Natalie Heinich's Sociology of Art—and Sociology from Art." *Cultural Sociology* 2(2): 242–256.

De Ferranti, H. 2002. "'Japanese Music' Can Be Popular." *Popular Music* 21(2): 195–208.

DeNora, T. 2000. *Music and Everyday Life*. Cambridge: Cambridge University Press.

_____. 2003. *After Adorno: Rethinking Music Sociology*. Cambridge: Cambridge University Press.

DiMaggio, P. 1977. "Market Structure, the Creative Process and Popular Culture: Toward an Organizational Reinterpretation of Mass Culture Theory." *Journal of Popular Culture* 11(2): 436–452.

Dowd, T. 2007. "Innovation and Diversity in Cultural Sociology." *Sociologica* 1.

Fowler, B. 1997. *Pierre Bourdieu and Cultural Theory: Critical Investigations*. London: Sage.

Frith, S. Unpublished Paper. "Creativity as a Social Fact."

Frota, W. 2006. "The Enactment of the Field of Cultural and Artistic Production of Popular Music in Brazil: A Case Study of the 'Noel Rosa Generation' in the 1930s." *Popular Music* 25(1): 117–125.

Goldthorpe, J. 2007. "Cultural Capital: Some Critical Observations." *Sociologica* 2.

Gomart, É. and A. Hennion. 1999. "A Sociology of Attachment: Music Amateurs, Drug Users." In *Actor Network Theory and After*, eds. J. Law and J. Hassard, 220–247. Oxford: Blackwell.

Hennion, A. 1999. "Music Industry and Music Lovers, Beyond Benjamin." *Soundscapes* 2. Available at: www.icce.rug.nl/~soundscapes/DATAB SES/MIE/Part2_chapter06.shtml.

Inglis, D. 2005. "The Sociology of Art: Between Cynicism and Reflexivity." In *The Sociology of Art: Ways of Seeing*, eds. D. Inglis and J. Hughson, 98–112. Basingstoke: Palgrave Macmillan.

Johnson, V., J. Fulcher and T. Ertman. 2007. *Opera and Society in Italy and France from Monteverdi to Bourdieu*. Cambridge: Cambridge University Press.

Lopes, P. 2000. "Pierre Bourdieu's Fields of Cultural Production: A Case Study of Modern Jazz." In *Pierre Bourdieu: Fieldwork in Culture*, eds. N. Brown and I. Szeman, 165–185. Oxford: Roman and Littlefield.

Maira, S. 2002. *Desi in the House: Indian American Youth Culture in New York City*. Philadelphia: Temple University Press.

Mouffe, C. 1993. *The Return of the Political*. London: Verso.

Negus, K. 1999. *Music Genres and Corporate Cultures*. London: Routledge.

Ollivier, M. 2006. "Snobs and Quétaines: Prestige and Boundaries in Popular Music in Quebec." *Popular Music* 25(1): 97–116.

Peterson, R.A. and D.G. Berger. 1975. "Cycles in Symbol Production: The Case of Popular Music." *American Sociological Review* 40(2): 158–173.

Pinheiro, D.L. and T.J. Dowd. 2009. "All That Jazz: The Success of Jazz Musicians in Three Metropolitan Areas." *Poetics* 37(5/6): 490–506.

Regev, M. 2007. "Ethno-National Pop-Rock Music: Aesthetic Cosmopolitanism Made From Within." *Cultural Sociology* 1(3): 317–341.

Reynolds, S. 2009. "Stuck in the Middle with You: Between Pop and Pretension." *The Guardian* (6 February).

Santoro, M. 2009. "How 'Not' to Become a Dominant French Sociologist: Bourdieu in Italy, 1996–2009." *Sociologica* 2–3.

Shusterman, R. 1992. *Pragmatist Aesthetics*. Oxford: Blackwell.

Sterne, J. 2003. "Bourdieu, Technique and Technology." *Cultural Studies* 17(3–4): 367–389.

Théberge, P. 1997. *Any Sound You Can Imagine: Making Music / Consuming Technology*. London: Wesleyan University Press.

Wolff, J. 1981. *The Social Production of Art*. London: Macmillan.

Zangwill, N. 2002. "Against the Sociology of the Aesthetic." *Cultural Value* 6(4): 443–452.

34

Mediation Theory

GEORGINA BORN

In this primarily conceptual article I offer some answers to the question: how does music materialize identities? I will argue that music is instructive in relation to conceptualizing the materialization of identity because it opens up new perspectives with regard to theories both of materiality and of affect; and moreover, that these perspectives are intimately related to the copious socialities of music, which themselves necessitate a novel social analytics—one that responds to current interests in re-theorizing the social. I will suggest that together these developments offer a framework for understanding the generative nature of the imbrication of musical formations and social formations.[1]

I open with four observations that situate music as a distinctive medium in relation to common thematics in the anthropology of material culture and art. First, beyond the visual and artefact-centrism that characterizes theories of art and material culture, music indicates that there need not be a physical artefact or a visual object or symbol at the centre of the analysis of materiality, mediation and semiosis. Indeed, music has its own particular material and semiotic properties. Musical sound is non-representational, non-artefactual and alogogenic. In most human cultures, in the absence of a denotative or literal level of meaning, musical sound engenders a profusion of extra-musical connotations of various kinds—visual, sensual, emotional and intellectual. These connotations are naturalized and projected into the musical sound object, yet they tend to be experienced as deriving from it. Ethnomusicologists, in the face of such a profusion of significa-tion, have analyzed the universal existence of linguistic metaphors for music (Feld 1984, Feld and Fox 1994). In my own ethnographies I have extended this approach through a focus on how metaphors for music combine and cohere into wider discursive formations, raising questions of power—the differential power to define, circulate and institutionalize the meanings attributed to music (Born 1995).

A second observation is that if the linguistic mediation of music is pervasive, it cannot be reduced simply to language. Music has no material essence but a plural and distributed materiality. Its multiple simultaneous forms of existence—as sonic trace, discursive exegesis, notated score, technological prosthesis, social and embodied performance—indicate the necessity of conceiving of the musical object as a constellation of mediations. Music requires and stimulates associations between a diverse range of subjects and objects—between musician and instrument, composer and score, listener and sound system, music programmer and digital code. Compared with the visual and literary arts, which we associate with a specific object, text or representation, music may therefore appear to be an extraordinarily diffuse kind of cultural object: an aggregation of sonic, social, corporeal, discursive, visual, technological and temporal mediations—a musical assemblage, where this is understood as a characteristic constellation of such heterogeneous mediations. In Deleuzian thought an assemblage is defined as a multiplicity made up of heterogeneous components, each having a certain auton-omy, a multiplicity "which establishes liaisons [or] relations between them ... The assemblage's only unity is that of a co-functioning" (Deleuze and Parnet 1987: 69), while the interactions between components are non-linear and mutually catalysing, "only contingently obligatory" (DeLanda 2006: 12; Deleuze 1988).

A third point, following on, is that a number of writers—from Adorno onwards—have pointed to music's mediation of subject–object relations. Such an approach is central to the recent sociology of music. Antoine Hennion (2003: 90) stresses the intimate mediation between music lover and musical sound in the co-production of taste, where taste is grasped as a mutually transformative relation cultivated through a range of practices and techniques. As he proposes, "bodies, spaces, durations, gestures, regular practice, technical devices"—all point to taste as an accomplishment. Music therefore "transforms those who take possession of it," resulting in "the co-formation of a music and of those who make it and listen to it." Tia DeNora (2000: 40) takes a similar stance, arguing that "music is active within social life: just as music's meanings may be constructed in relation to things outside it, so, too, things outside music may be constructed in relation to music." Such analyses make palpable the bidirectional nature both of music's mediation and of human and non-human agency: music generating and conditioning human subjectivities and socialities, while music is constituted in discourse and practice, as well as through its manifold socialities and socio-technical arrangements.

My fourth opening observation, however, is that the kind of microsociology favoured by DeNora and Hennion, which finds its anthropological equivalent in Alfred Gell's (1998) adoption of a biographical "depth of focus" in his analysis of art's social mediation in *Art and Agency*, is insufficient when accounting for music's complex social mediation. Indeed, music necessitates an expansion of the conceptual framework of social mediation. In this sense it compounds the challenge to reconceptualize the social issued by Marilyn Strathern when she called for a concern with the "constant movement ... from one type of sociality to another," socialities constituted either by processes of "de-pluralization" (Strathern 1988: 14, 13) or by the elaboration of heterogeneity, as well as by Bruno Latour (2005: 34) in his manifesto for a "sociology of associations" that traces the "many ... contradictory cartographies of the social." For if music generates myriad social forms, it requires a social analytics that encompasses four planes of social mediation. In the first plane, music produces its own diverse social relations—in the intimate socialities of musical performance and practice, in musical ensembles, and in the musical division of labour. In the second, music conjures up and animates imagined communities, aggregating its listeners into virtual collectivities and publics based on musical and other identifications. In the third plane, music is traversed by wider social identity formations, from the most concrete and intimate to the most abstract of collectivities—music's refraction of the hierarchical and stratified relations of class and age, race and ethnicity, gender and sexuality. In the fourth, music is bound up in the social and institutional forms that provide the grounds for its production, reproduction and transformation, whether elite or religious patronage, market or non-market exchange, the arena of public and subsidized cultural institutions, or late capitalism's cultural economy. All four planes of social mediation enter into the musical assemblage. All four are irreducible to one another, while being articulated in contingent and non-linear ways through relations of synergy, affordance, conditioning or causality. The first two planes amount to socialities engendered by musical practice and experience; whereas the last two amount to social and institutional conditions that themselves afford certain kinds of musical practice—although they enter into the nature of musical experience, permeating music's intimate socialities and imagined communities. By adopting the topological metaphor of the plane to stand for distinctive forms of sociality mediated by music, I intend to highlight both their autonomy and their mutual interference or interrelations, while combating any reading of them merely in terms of scale or level.[2] The metaphor, of course, has limitations: it fails to register their fleshy, demotic nature as well as their dynamic and temporal qualities—issues that develop later in the article.

[. . .]

[I]n the remainder of the article I develop three additional arguments concerning music's capacities to mediate and mobilize identity formations. To do this I draw on theories both of genre and of affect, which further illuminate the mutual entanglement of musical and social formations—in particular through music's powers to create aggregations of the affected.

My first argument concerns the benefits of analysing cross-scalar relations between the first and third planes: how the socialities engendered by musical performance are traversed by broader social relations. Salient here are studies that demonstrate the mutual modulation between performance socialities and formations of race and class, such as Charles Keil's *Urban Blues* (1970), Ingrid Monson's *Saying Something* (1996) and Louise Meintjes's *Sound of Africa!* (2003). Keil's account of the socialities manifest in the interactions between the Chicago blues singer Bobby Bland, his band and their club audiences in the 1960s shows how social solidarities and collective catharsis were generated in performance through the use of voice, gesture, humour and ambiguous sexual and spiritual innuendo, all of them enlivened by the "stylistic common denominators" (Keil 1970: 143) that crossed between blues performance and preaching in the lives of black Chicagoans. Other studies show how musical performance is not only entangled in wider social identity formations, but has the capacity to reconfigure or catalyze those formations. In her research on live soca performance in Trinidad, Jocelyne Guilbault stresses its transformative capacities as it produces "public intimacies." With this term she refers to the socialities and spatial proximities of performance as they unfold between musicians on stage, between musicians and audience, and between audience members. Guilbault (2010: 17) argues that these embodied and performative social interactions "reiterate identities," while also enabling "new points of connection [to be] developed (for example among artists and audience members of different ethnicities, nationalities and generations, and across musical genres)." The socialities created between artists and crowd at a soca gig range from the affirmation of a common sense of national belonging to the establishment of "'affective alliances' through the sharing of feelings—exuberance, joy, and exhaustion" (21). If soca artists on stage "enjoy crossing entrenched divides of ethnicity, race, and nation" (27), they also reinforce "heteronormative relations" and exclude homosexual expression (19). Performance socialities, she contends, can therefore work either to reinforce or to reconfigure social norms and social antagonisms.

An expansion of this perspective comes from research pointing to cross-scalar relations between the four planes of sociality as formative of the political in music. Louise Meintjes (2003), in her study of recording in apartheid and post-apartheid South Africa, shows how the recording studio amounts to a microcosm that incubates its own social relations, while it also refracts wider social relations. The politics of recording occur on two intersecting planes: first, in the socialities of the studio—manifest in who is able to exercise power and control, whose musical imagination determines how things will sound; and second, in how these socialities are crossed by broader formations of race and class, given that black musicians work in a "white-controlled industry" personified in white sound engineers who are largely ignorant of black musical styles. Meintjes shows the struggles manifest in aesthetic judgements in the mediation by white engineers of Zulu styles for world music markets. Minute shifts in intonation or timbre determine whether a track is deemed to merit international distribution; moreover, aesthetic imperatives issued by producers serving international markets can tempt black musicians to proffer Zulu stereotypes, pandering to essentialist and primitivist imaginaries. The racialized dynamics of the studio thus mediate the very sounds that circulate globally as "authentic" Zulu music. Recording practices are therefore the site of struggles over musical inflections and sound qualities, struggles in which black musicians engage covertly in attempts to wrest back musical control.

[. . .]

In sum, evidence from both historical and anthropological research suggests that it is the autonomy of the socialities of musical performance and practice that renders them potential vehicles for social experimentation or for the exercise of a musico-political imagination, in the sense that they may enact alternatives to or inversions of, and can be in contradiction with, wider forms of hierarchical and stratified social relations. These are performed contradictions that can contribute powerfully to the nature of socio-musical experience by offering a compensatory or utopian social space—one that fashions experience differently, even as it may fail to overturn or counter broader social hierarchies and inequalities (although such an outcome is not foreclosed). Not only these cases but many forms of the political in music require a social analytics that addresses music's multiple socialities and their complex and contingent interrelations.

My next observation concerns the second plane of music's social mediation: music's capacity to animate imagined communities, aggregating its adherents into virtual collectivities and publics based on musical and other identifications. These are musically imagined communities that, as I have shown elsewhere, may reproduce or memorialize extant identity formations, generate purely fantasized identifications, or prefigure emergent identity formations by forging novel social alliances (Born 2000). Here, in turn, I offer two comments. First, music seems to be ever more significant in its powers to generate imagined or virtual communities. Whether manifest in music's central contributions in internet-based social networks to the personalization of online identity constructions, or in peer-to-peer file sharing and ramifying music-exchange networks, music has become a medium both of identity formation and of social aggregation (Baym 2007, Baym and Ledbetter 2009), aggregations that may be irreducible to other dimensions of socio-cultural identity. This property of music was first theorized by Will Straw (1991) in his concept of musical "scene." Straw develops the concept through the comparative analysis of two genres–alternative rock and electronic dance musics—insisting that the social universes produced by them cannot be reduced to any pre-given social ontology. Instead, he argues, scene points to music's capacity to construct "affective alliances" (374), propagating musically imagined communities that are irreducible to prior categories of social identity. Scene points to the significance and the autonomy of the first two planes: the socialities of musical performance, which Straw portrays through the engrossing corporeality of the dance floor, and the imagined communities summoned into being by musical tastes and experiences, which he addresses through the "coalitions" of dance music audiences created in the late 1980s between "black teenagers, young girls listening to Top 40 radio, and urban club-goers" (384–385). But the idea of scene recognizes also their mutual mediation: how the socialities of performance catalyze music's imagined communities, just as those imagined communities imbue the socialities of performance with collective emotion. Straw connects these two planes in turn to the social relations of class, race and gender, proposing that the politics of popular music stem from music's capacity to create affective coalitions that reconfigure the boundaries between pervasive social categories. He then introduces a further plane of social mediation: the institutions—such as radio, dance clubs and record stores—which provide "the conditions of possibility of [those affective] alliances" (384). Straw's concept of scene thus invokes all four planes of sociality, as well as pointing to the contingency of their interrelations. The notion of scene is important as an attempt to move beyond the idea that music (and culture) articulate only pre-existing identity formations. Rather, it is clear that music can become a primary vehicle of collective identification—even if this is traversed by other vectors of identity (race, class, ethnicity, gender, sexuality). This remains an invaluable insight and bears out a co-constitutive theory of social mediation: music both producing its own affective and aggregative identity effects, its own modes of "imitation" or contagion (Tarde 1969, 2001 [1890]), while also responding to and transforming pre-existing social formations.

A second comment on musically imagined community concerns the now dominant way of conceiving of the public-making qualities of culture and music. This is in the terms of Michael Warner's (2005: 67) Althusserian formulation of the public interpellated through practices of cultural production—a public that, as he puts it, "exists by virtue of being addressed." In Warner's approach the public aggregated by cultural production is equated with virtual or stranger publics *tout court*; the very fact of the production and circulation of textuality is taken to conjure up and attach a community of interest. But the assumption here of a sturdily *achieved* public is surely questionable. My research on widely varying spheres of cultural production suggests both that they have quite different projections of audience-hood, which influence the kinds of audience that can result, and that in practice these expectations are often frustrated, indicating a split between anticipated and achieved public.[3] Similar arguments are made for anthropology by Karin Barber (2007), and for cultural history by Roger Chartier (1995); they are also made by Jacques Rancière (2010: 151) when, questioning any a priori assumption about the political efficacy of critical art practices, he notes that "they cannot avoid the aesthetic cut that separates consequences from intentions." Genre theory, to which I come shortly, offers a better way of conceiving of the mutual articulation of cultural production and publics. But we can also augment Warner by recognizing another type of publicness animated by cultural production, one that is illuminated by music's privileged relation with performance. This entails holding the textual-interpellation model up against an alternative conception of the co-present public that is potentialized by performance events. Such a co-present public cannot be guaranteed; it *may* be constituted by the socialities of musical performance—socialities that should not be idealized,[4] just as their public-making qualities cannot be adjudged in advance (cf. Born and Barry, 2010: 112–116).[5]

My final argument turns on another relation between distinctive planes of musical socialities, the one most commonly drawn in existing literatures. It is the interaction between the third and second planes: between wider social relations and systems of musical genre, where genre is taken to be the primary mechanism for the mutual articulation of musically imagined communities and social identities—communities that are often taken to derive from those social identities. Already obvious here is how genre theory luxuriates in teleology—a tendency apparent in the temptation to elide mimetic and mediation accounts of music's articulation of social identities. In Eric Drott's (2011: 7) succinct take, extracted from a rich discussion of genre and mediation, "genres . . . both constitute social groups and are constituted by them"—an expansion of the mutual mediation of musical object and subject on to the plane of the historical co-production of musical genres and social formations. . . .

Here David Brackett's (2005: 82) stress, in his research on black American popular musics, on the "paradoxes (and tautologies) of genre" is salutary. Brackett brings out both the processual instability and the generativity of genre. In his words, "the notion of genre speaks to transitory divisions in the musical field that correspond in discontinuous and complex ways to a temporally defined social space" (75). Moreover, he contends, "a linkage between social identity and a practice of music making (as in "black music") need not depend on the reproduction of a negative stereotype but may function as a positive marker, a chiastic turn" (87). Brackett shows how historically labile have been the apparently established links between black musical genres and African American social formations; yet he cautions against over-arbitrary accounts of genre categories as mere "social constructions" (75). He demonstrates how this perspective requires a dual focus on both the temporalities and the *real attempted teleologies* of genre. That is to say: genre works by projecting temporally, into the unruly, ongoing cauldron of alternative socio-cultural formations, potential moves and reconfigurations of those formations coded materially as aesthetic moves and transformations that are proffered as analogous to the social. When the teleology works, then music may effect a redirection or a new affective coalition of the identity formations that it set itself to mediate. For Brackett, Bakhtin's (1986: 95) concept of addressivity illuminates how, through aesthetic gestures in any genre, musicians attempt to attract and attach an envisaged audience to the musical object; his example is Isaac Hayes's 1969 cross-over soul version of Jimmy Webb's 1967 middle-of-the-road ballad, "By the time I get to Phoenix." Given the instabilities and contingencies of genre, Hayes's aesthetic gestures reveal "how intersubjective awareness of the audience—addressivity—is in play on both musical and verbal levels" (86).

In sum, my discussion of genre as an assumed point of convergence or translation between aesthetic figure, musically imagined community and wider identity formation is intended to destabilize what is too often taken as smoothly conjoined. Rather than any assured linkage between music and wider social formations, it is by analysing genre as entailing a mutual mediation between two self-organizing historical entities—musical formations (on the one hand) and social identity formations (on the other)—that we can grasp the way that wider social identity formations are refracted in music, and that musical genres entangle themselves in evolving social formations. In this analysis, both musical and social identity formations are conceived as being in process of becoming; both are reliant on the collective production of memory as well as the anticipation of futures. In other words, genre is understood as a radically contingent and material process—one that is, however, oriented to the production of teleology and thus the erasure of its own contingency.

In theorizing, with reference to notions of affective alliances, the uncertain imbrication in genre of the dynamics of both musical and social identification, it may be that Gabriel Tarde's relational sociology is apposite, with its vision of the contagion of affect as constitutive of the social. Recently rediscovered in anthropological and social theory (Barry and Thrift 2007, Candea 2010), Tarde's (2001[1890]: 203) dictum that "invention and imitation are the elementary social acts" (my translation) is predicated on a rejection of the foundational dualism of individual and social, and of the separation of psychology from sociology. Instead, Tarde advocates an "inter-psychology" attentive to the way "that subjects [are] open to affecting and being affected" (Blackman 2007: 576), positing imitation and suggestion as twin motors of the diffusion of affect, desire and habit through a population. It is perhaps no surprise, then, that music—given its hyper-connotative, hyper-affective propensities—promotes the formation of social bonds in the guise of what I have called aggregations of the affected. Moreover rhythm, dance, bodily proximity and corporeal experience—all components of both music and performance—are considered by writers in this area to promote the intensification of affect and the creation of affective associations (Brennan 2004, Thrift 2008: ch. 6). More acutely, it is striking that the notion of entrainment appears to provide a conceptual bridge between music and affect. It is central to Teresa Brennan's (2004: ch. 3) attempts to extend the ideas of crowd theorists and group psychoanalysts to the transmission of affect. Brennan aims to overcome another foundational dualism—that of the social and the biological—by hypothesizing the existence of physiological mechanisms that underlie affective contagion, which she locates in transmissible hormonal changes triggered by particular "atmospheres" and social environments. In Brennan's persuasive anti-neo-Darwinian account, "certain biological and physical phenomena themselves require a social explanation. While its wellsprings are social, the transmission of affect is deeply physical in its effects" (23). But entrainment is also invoked in present ethnomusicological attempts to link physiological and social processes in the analysis of musical performance (Clayton et al., 2004).[6] Once again rhythm, movement and embodied experience, along with synchronicity, are given privileged place in this discussion; questions raised include:

> Since certain degrees of entrainment between individuals seem to be associated with positive affect, is it the case that particular patterns, periodicities, hierarchies or intensities of

entrainment afford particular affects? Could positive affect be associated with a greater degree of self-synchrony as well as closer synchrony with a social group?

(Clayton et al. 2004: 21[7])

Bringing together the consideration of theories of genre and of affect, what we have is a potent conceptual cluster: genre as a point of contingent convergence between musical formations and social formations; entrainment, in turn, as a putative link between affect, music, the biological and social. Yet against the backdrop of the arc of arguments in this article, the perspectives provided by Tarde, Brennan and others—while they add insight into how affective dimensions of musical experience may fuel social aggregation—provide only part of the answer to theorizing music's mediation of social identities. For when detached from the analysis of larger social formations and enduring musical, cultural and historical processes, they are reductive in the literal sense of the evasion of ineluctable complexity. We might ask: can we account for the social—in the guise, for example, of the enduring but evolving armatures of class relations in Britain today as they continue to mediate and be mediated by music (Bennett et al. 2009: ch. 5)—solely through the transmission of affect (with Brennan) or a sociology of associations (with Latour and the neo-Tardeians)? These perspectives may contribute to an analysis of the mutual mediation of musical and social identity formations, but they are not sufficient. For they fail to bring into the calculus an awareness of the several distinctive planes of sociality mobilized and mediated by musical assemblages. It is the novel analytics of the mutual modulation of four planes of social mediation proposed in this article, working resiliently against the reification of both musical and social formations, and attuned to the significance of the autonomy and the contingent interrelations between the four planes for analysing socio-musical complexity, that enables us to understand how music materializes identities.

Notes

1 I use the term "musical formations" to indicate the specificity of long-term musical systems which exhibit both a certain unity and continuity and an evolving heterogeneity. This is the approach advocated by David Brackett, a leading theorist of genre and scholar of 20th-century black American popular musics, when he writes of "black popular music as part of a long-range historical discourse and as part of an ever-changing genre system" (2005: 80).

2 The Deleuzian concept of assemblage is again apposite, now encompassing music's social mediation, evoking as it does a heterogeneous unity composed of elements that have a certain autonomy while being brought into relation and fuelling emergence; in this sense the assemblage is a "whole [that] may be both analysable into separate parts and at the same time have irreducible properties, properties that emerge from the interactions between parts" (DeLanda 2006: 10). Despite DeLanda's cogent exposition of assemblage theory, his application of it to social analysis is unconvincing, centred as it is on linear and nested social forms of increasing scale: persons and networks, organizations and governments, cities and nations.

3 My research on cultural production has encompassed ethnographies of computer music and of the musical avant-garde (Born 1995), of the production of popular television and radio at the BBC (Born 2005), and of the experimental field of art-science (Born and Barry 2010) and other interdisciplinary knowledge practices (Barry et al. 2008).

4 For influential and idealizing accounts of the socialities of musical performance, see Schutz (1971) and Small (1998).

5 Elsewhere (Born 2013) I develop the idea of the co-present public afforded by musical performance with reference to Dana Villa's (1996) interpretation of Hannah Arendt's thought. Villa pursues the implications of Arendt's adoption of the performing arts as her preferred idiom for the renewal of the public realm. By using a performance model for the analysis of political action and its constitution of the public realm, Arendt understood such action as autonomous and artificial, non-teleological and non-instrumental. Its essence was nothing less than continuous, direct participation, while such participation was always embedded in the "already existing web of human relationships" (Arendt 1989 [1958]: 184; cited in Villa 1996: 84). Dueck (2013) illustrates the fertility of this approach to musical publics in his ethnography of Aboriginal communities in Manitoba, exploring the potent interrelations between the intimate publics of performance and the virtual public afforded by Aboriginal music radio.

6   The ethnomusicological discourse on entrainment sees itself as building on earlier models of the connection between rhythm, movement and musical socialities in the work of John Blacking, Alan Lomax, Charles Keil and Steven Feld (Clayton et al. 2004: 19–20).

7   The concern in this discussion with the interplay between musical aesthetics and affect in mobilizing social identity formations echoes the current interest in the same dynamic as it animates nationhood; see Mookherjee and Pinney (2011).

References

Arendt, H. 1989 [1958]. *The Human Condition*. Chicago: University of Chicago Press.

Bakhtin, M. 1986. *Speech Genres and Other Late Essays*, eds. C. Emerson and M. Holquist. Austin: University of Texas Press.

Barber, K. 2007. *The Anthropology of Texts, Persons and Publics: Oral and Written Culture in Africa and Beyond*. Cambridge: Cambridge University Press.

Barry, A. and N. Thrift. 2007. "Gabriel Tarde: Imitation, Invention and Economy." *Economy and Society* 36(4): 509–525.

Barry, A., G. Born, and G. Weszkalnys. 2008. "Logics of Interdisciplinarity." *Economy and Society* 37(1): 20–49.

Baym, N.K. 2007. "The New Shape of Online Community: The Example of Swedish Independent Music Fandom. *First Monday* 12(8). Available at: http://firstmonday.org/htbin/cgiwrap/bin/ojs/index.php/fm/article/view/1978/1853.

Baym, N.K. and A. Ledbetter. 2009. "Tunes that Bind? Predicting Friendship Strength in a Music-Based Social Network." *Information, Communication & Society* 12(3): 408–427.

Bennett, T., M. Savage, E. Silva, A. Warde, M. Gayo-Cal, and D. Wright. 2009. *Culture, Class, Distinction*. London: Routledge.

Blackman, L. 2007. "Reinventing Psychological Matters: The Importance of the Suggestive Realm of Tarde's Ontology." *Economy and Society* 36(4): 574–596.

Born, G. 1995. *Rationalizing Culture: IRCAM, Boulez, and the Institutionalization of the Musical Avant-Garde*. Berkeley: University of California Press.

_____. 2000. "Music and the Representation/Articulation of Sociocultural Identities." In *Western Music and Its Others: Difference, Representation, and Appropriation in Music*, eds. G Born and D. Hesmondhalgh, 31–37. Berkeley: University of California Press.

_____. 2005. *Uncertain Vision: Birt, Dyke and the Reinvention of the BBC*. London: Vintage.

_____. 2013. "Introduction: Music, Sound, and the Transformation of Public and Private Space." In *Music, Sound, and the Transformation of Public and Private Space*, 1–70. Cambridge: Cambridge University Press.

Born, G. and A. Barry. 2010. "Art-Science: From Public Understanding to Public Experiment." *Journal of Cultural Economy* 3(1): 103–119.

Brackett, D. 2005. "Questions of Genre in Black Popular Music." *Black Music Research Journal* 25(1/2): 73–92.

Brennan, T. 2004. *The Transmission of Affect*. Ithaca: Cornell University Press.

Candea, M. 2010. *The Social after Gabriel Tarde*. London: Routledge.

Chartier, R. 1995. *Forms and Meanings: Texts, Performances, and Audiences from Codex to Computer*. Philadelphia: University of Pennsylvania Press.

Clayton, M., R. Sager, and U. Will. 2004. "In Time with the Music: The Concept of Entrainment and its Significance for Ethnomusicology." Paper read at European Meetings in Ethnomusicology 11/ ESEM Counterpoint.

DeLanda, M. 2006. *A New Philosophy of Society: Assemblage Theory and Social Complexity*. London: Continuum.

Deleuze, G. 1988. *Foucault*. London: Athlone.

Deleuze, G. and C. Parnet. 1987. *Dialogues*. London: Athlone.

DeNora, T. 2000. *Music in Everyday Life*. Cambridge: Cambridge University Press.

Drott, E. 2011. *Music and the Elusive Revolution: Cultural Politics and Political Culture in France, 1968–1981*. Austin: University of Texas Press.

Dueck, B. 2013. "Civil Twilight: Country Music, Alcohol, and the Spaces of Manitoban Aboriginal Sociability. In *Music, Sound, and the Transformation of Public and Private Space*, ed. G. Born, 239–256. Cambridge: Cambridge University Press.

Feld, S. 1984. "Communication, Music, and Speech about Music." *Yearbook for Traditional Music* 16: 1–18.

Feld, S. and A.A. Fox. 1994. "Music and Language." *Annual Review of Anthropology* 23(1): 25–53.

Gell, A. 1998. *Art and Agency: An Anthropological Theory*. Oxford: Clarendon Press.

Guilbault, J. 2010. "Music, Politics, and Pleasure: Live Soca in Trinidad." *Small Axe* 14(1): 16–29.

Hennion, A. 2003. "Music and Mediation: Toward a New Sociology of Music." In *The Cultural Study of Music*, eds. M. Clayton, T. Herbert and R. Middleton, 80–91.London: Routledge.

Keil, C. 1970. *Urban Blues*. Chicago: University of Chicago Press.

Latour, B. 2005. *Reassembling the Social: An Introduction to Actor-Network-Theory*. Oxford: Oxford University Press.

Meintjes, L. 2003. *Sound of Africa! Making Music Zulu in a South African Studio*. Durham: Duke University Press.

Monson, I.T. 1996. *Saying Something: Jazz Improvisation and Interaction*. Chicago: University of Chicago Press.

Mookherjee, N. and C. Pinney. 2011. *The Aesthetics of Nations: Anthropological and Historical Approaches*. London: Royal Anthropological Institute.

Rancière, J. 2010. *Dissensus: On Politics and Aesthetics*. London: Continuum.

Schutz, A. 1971. "Making Music Together." In *Collected Papers II: Studies in Social Theory*. 159–178. The Hague: Nijhoff.

Small, C. 1998. *Musicking: The Meanings of Performing and Listening*. Middletown: Wesleyan University Press.

Strathern, M. 1988. *The Gender of the Gift: Problems with Women and Problems with Society in Melanesia*. Berkeley: University of California Press.

Straw, W. 1991. "Systems of Articulation, Logics of Change: Communities and Scenes in Popular Music." *Cultural Studies* 5(3): 368–388.

Tarde, G. 1969. *On Communication and Social Influence*, ed. T.N. Clark. Chicago: University of Chicago Press.

_____. 2001 [1890]. *Les Lois de l'Imitation*. Paris: Les Empecheurs de Penser en Rond/Editions du Seuil.

Thrift, N.J. 2008. *Non-Representational Theory: Space, Politics, Affect*. London: Routledge.

Villa, D. 1996. *Arendt and Heidegger: The Fate of the Political*. Princeton: Princeton University Press.

Warner, M. 2005. *Publics and Counterpublics*. New York: Zone.

35

From Signification to Affect

JEREMY GILBERT

Two words are so indispensable to the vocabulary of the contemporary humanities that they barely seem to warrant discussion: "culture" and "discourse." The one has been argued over endlessly in the past, and while it continues to form the subject of studies both learned and polemical by leading scholars (Mulhern 1999, Eagleton 2000), few if any of them ever actually challenge the received usage of the term. The other has become at least as ubiquitous but more, it seems, by default than by design. Having slipped out of a corner of Foucault's work that he never expected anyone to see (he remarked more than once that he never expected *The Archaeology of Knowledge* to be widely read), and having long-ago escaped the rigorous limitations of socio-linguistics (e.g. the work of Norman Fairclough), "discourse" is a term which is now everywhere used and nowhere adequately defined. My contention in this paper will be that the vectors which these two terms—"culture" and "discourse"—have travelled on converge in a conceptual space that is still difficult to delineate using the vocabularies of mainstream cultural theory, but which is crucial to any effective understanding of the dynamics of culture in the twenty-first century (or, for that matter, any other century), and which is exactly that being opened up by the search for a cultural theory which can properly address the experiential dimension of "affect."

Firstly, "culture." In an interview published in *Radical Philosophy* at the end of 1997, Stuart Hall is asked if there is any new notion of culture regulating the field of cultural studies in a manner similar to the way in which he identified the culturalist and semiotic paradigms regulating it before and after the structuralist break of the 1970s. He replies as follows:

> I am not sure that there is, or ever was, one regulative notion of culture, although the shift you are talking about was a very substantial one. The Williams appropriation "a whole way of life" as opposed to "the best that has been thought and said" and high ideas, raised questions from the very beginning. He'd hardly written the sentence before a critique of the organicist character of that definition emerged. It was an important move, the sociological, anthropological move, but it was cast in terms of a humanist notion of social and symbolic practices. The really big shift was the coming of semiotics and structuralism: not because the definition of culture stopped there, but that remains the defining paradigm shift, nonetheless; signifying practices, rather than a whole way of life.
>
> There had to be some relative autonomy introduced into the study of signifying practices. If you want to study their relation to a whole way of life, that must be thought of as an *articulation*, rather than the position Williams had which is that "everything is expressive of everything else": the practices and the signification, they're all one; the family and ideas about the family are all the same thing. For Williams, everything is dissolved into practice.

Of course, the new model was very linguistic, very Saussurean, but nevertheless, that was the definitive break. Everything after that goes back to that moment. Post-structuralism goes back to the structuralist break. Psychoanalytic models are very influenced by the Lévi-Straussian moment, or the Althusserian moment. If I were writing for students, those are still the two definitions I'd pick out, and I wouldn't say there is a third one. I suppose you might say that there is a postmodern one. A Deleuzian one, which says that signification is not meaning, it's all a question of affect, but I don't see a break in the regulative idea of culture as fundamental as the earlier one.

(Hall 1997)

If Hall is thinking of anyone in gesturing towards this possible third, postmodern, Deleuzian paradigm, then it is probably his former student and long-term colleague, Lawrence Grossberg. It's Grossberg (1992, 1997a, 1997b) who has tried in recent years to develop such a "postmodern" practice. What I want to present here is a set of theoretical reflections, complementary to rather than critical of Grossberg's, on both the logical grounds and the necessary consequences of making such a move; and to suggest that on some level it does indeed necessitate the modification of existing regulative notions of "culture."

In doing this, I'm not proposing here to posit such a third, postmodern, Deleuzian paradigm as offering a wholly new regulative idea of culture. Indeed, I'm not proposing to posit such a third paradigm as constituting any radical break with the past at all, although a break with the history of breaks, with the insistence on always seeking out paradigm shifts where more subtle processes of change and continuity may in fact be effective, might be on the agenda. What I am going to try to do is map out some of the issues raised by the possibility of this third paradigm and the question of its relationships with those models Hall identifies as preceding it. One observation I would like to make here is that while there is an obvious danger implicit in Hall's criticism of Williams' attempt to dissolve everything into practice—a danger of drawing too rigid a distinction between practice and other dimensions of experience—I don't think that this is a danger of which Hall and his colleagues have ever been ignorant. Ernesto Laclau—the key theorist of "discourse" on whose work Hall and others have drawn—recently remarked that he saw no fundamental difference between the statements "everything is discourse" and "everything is practice" (both of which he agrees with), other than the fact that nobody can be found to dispute the latter statement.[1]

Thought in these terms, Hall is clearly right to say that one of the necessary effects of the structuralist break in cultural studies was to make possible a differentiation between the different practices, signifying and otherwise, which constitute cultural life. It may be, as he himself suggests, that this resulted in an excessive emphasis on linguistic models of cultural experience, and it may be that a new emphasis on the affective, non-linguistic dimension of cultural experience is required by a new approach. However, what is really at stake in the possibility of a paradigm which focuses not just on meaning but on affect, I will suggest, is the question of how to move this process of conceptual differentiation on (rather than any idea of reversing it), by addressing the issue of the precise nature and rigidity of those differentiations between different types of practice and the different elements making up a whole way of life. A third paradigm, informed by such concerns, rather than moving even further from the work of Raymond Williams might want rather to recapture something of the spirit of Williams' refusal to draw firm distinctions between practice and meaning, but it should also avoid abandoning the gains made by the structuralist moment, and indeed seek to build on them while subjecting them to their own problematising logic.

To get a better sense of the issues at stake here, we need to address this term "affect." It is one sign, literally, of its increasing significance that the meanings attached to this term seem to proliferate and slip around. Frederic Jameson (1991) famously characterised postmodern culture in terms of the "waning of affect," the apparent decline in passionate engagement between subjects and texts. In recent work influenced by English psychoanalysis, such as that of Wendy Wheeler (1999: 71, 117), the term is used more or less synonymously with "emotion." On the other hand, a more precise but rather more difficult definition is offered by Deleuze and Guattari's appropriation of the work of Spinoza (via Nietzsche and Bergson). Probably the most influential figure in transmitting these ideas to an Anglophone audience has been Deleuze and Guattari's translator Brian Massumi, whose essay "The Autonomy of Affect," remains a key starting point for any consideration of the implications of the concept. Massumi's own explanation of the term, from his translator's preface to Deleuze and Guattari's *A Thousand Plateaus*, is as follows:

> Affect/Affection. Neither word denotes a personal feeling . . . *Affect* (Spinoza's *affectus*) is an ability to affect and be affected. It is a prepersonal intensity corresponding to the passage from one experiential state of the body to another and implying an augmentation or diminution of that body's capacity to act.
>
> (Deleuze and Guattari 1988: xvi)

Elsewhere, Massumi (1996: 237) writes that "affect is indeed unformed and unstructured but that it is nevertheless highly organised and effectively analysable (it is not entirely containable in knowledge, but is analysable in effect, as effect)." So "affect" is a term which denotes a more or less organised experience, an experience probably with empowering or disempowering consequences, registered at the level of the physical body, and not necessarily to be understood in linguistic terms. So why might we be interested in this term and its possible usages today?

The Sound of Music: "Discourse" and the Limits of Signification

It's no accident that it should be Lawrence Grossberg who has looked for this other paradigm. For perhaps more than any other senior figure in the Birmingham-derived mainstream of Anglophone cultural studies, it is Grossberg who has attempted to get to grips with music as a cultural form: not as an adjunct to studies of the visual iconography of youth culture, but as a medium in its own right, with its own tendencies and its own potentialities. Here is a problem familiar to anyone who has tried to do the same. It was until recently a commonplace that cultural studies has had relatively little to say about music as such. Plenty had been written about the spectacular world of youth subcultures and their relationships with the media, but on the subject of music itself, sonic experience, cultural studies had been relatively silent (Gilbert and Pearson 1999: 38–53). It isn't hard to see why this should be the case. Music is not amenable to analysis using methodologies that prioritise language as the model form of communication. The godfather of structuralism himself, Claude Lévi-Strauss (1994), was one of many commentators to remark that music's specificity lies in the fact that it is registered not just cognitively but at the level of the physical body, in ways in which visual and linguistic media are not. Sound vibrations are registered by parts of the body which do not register changes in vibrations of light. Music has *physical effects* which can be identified, described and discussed but which are not the same thing as it having *meanings*, and any attempt to understand how music works in culture must, as many commentators over the years have acknowledged, be able to say something about those effects without trying to collapse them into meanings. . . .

[T]he fact that sound is difficult to talk about in linguistic terms does not make it desirable, as has been thought by earlier thinkers, simply to consign music to a realm of sublime mystery, impossible to even discuss in any terms, having no purpose beyond its own pristine existence, expressing nothing but its own logic. The problem we have is that music is by definition an *organised* form of experience, one whose effectivity is strictly delimited by sedimented cultural practices, but it is one whose structured effects cannot be fully understood in terms of meanings; precisely, they cannot be understood according to the structural logic of language. It is to this point that I think this set of reflections leads us—to the observation that, at least as far as music is concerned, a notion of "culture" which sees in it only "signifying practices" is quite simply not up to the job. Music is obviously cultural, but its "culturality" is not limited to its capacity to signify. Music's sonic-corporeal effectivity is not universal and transhistorical, a fact registered by the simple observation that what is musical for some cultural groups is merely "noise" for others. Of course, music's capacity to cross cultural barriers which signifying media cannot is famous, and is clearly one of the reasons why music is so central to post-national cultural formations (Gilroy 1993, Gilbert 2001). In this sense, music clearly exhibits a great deal of what might be called, following Derrida, "iterative force" (Derrida 1988; cf. Gilbert 1999)—that is, the capacity to escape its originary context and become operable in another—and its capacity to exhibit such force is obviously connected to its non-significatory affective power. Nonetheless, any detailed attention to the history of such trans-cultural crossings would demonstrate that there are always cultural and historical limits to what can be heard as music, and how it can be experienced. So music is clearly an element of cultural experience, an experience which is subject to relatively high levels of organisation, but which does not necessarily signify as such. We are left with a problem for the idea of culture as made up of signifying practices.

What we are left with, rather, is a notion of culture not merely as the site of "symbolic activity" or "signifying practice," but as the site at which human experience achieves a certain level of organisation, however minimal. Such organisation of experience is, to be sure, the very form and substance of power relationships, and is always irreducibly social in character. Moving far from any notion of culture as somehow "expressing" social relations from which it derives but which it does not constitute, such a model would, as Grossberg has suggested, see power relations as utterly immanent to culture, and vice-versa. Grossberg draws on the Deleuzian vocabulary of affect in his study of American rock culture for just the purpose of delineating such a notion of culture as affectively organised and organising, using "affect" as a term which denotes a more or less organised experience, an experience probably with empowering or disempowering consequences, registered at the level of the physical body, and not necessarily to be understood in linguistic terms.[2]

The place where such vocabularies have proved most indispensable, however, is in recent writing on dance music culture. The emergence into mainstream popularity (or, more accurately, popularity with those young, white, middle-class men whom the music press, "serious" broadcasters and broadsheet newspapers have traditionally regarded as the core audience for "music") of styles of music which did not have lyrics or which used lyrics obviously as purely musical elements, like bass and rhythm tracks, played by anonymous DJs and listened to in darkened rooms, posed obvious problems in the 1990s for any model which tried to understand music's significance in terms of the clearly coded meanings which it could communicate (Redhead 1993, Gilbert and Pearson 1999). In fact, this was an issue that had been taken up long before. Richard Dyer's (1979) seminal 1979 essay "In Defence of Disco," written at the moment when punk rock and semiotics were each at the high point of their prestige among scholars affiliated to cultural studies, takes an approach to understanding disco music which focuses on its sonic qualities in so far as they enable certain physical effects. Dyer's praise for the "all-body eroticism" which the lush polyrhythms of disco makes possible, contrasted with the thrusting phallocentrism of rock, can easily be read as a Spinozan account of gay, even straight-male-feminist bodies empowered by sound (try *David Mancuso Presents The Loft*, Nuphonic 1999, or *Classic Salsoul Mastercuts Volume Two*, Mastercuts, 1999, for evidence). Indeed, the very existence of musics which exist primarily to be danced to suggests that any attempt to talk about music-in-culture must have recourse to an understanding of music as effective at the corporeal level, and not merely as an exercise in signification. Indeed, even the most cerebral music of the concert tradition must be understood as working affectively, at least in part:

unless music is merely read as an unheard [melody], the strings which vibrate the air which vibrates our skin, membranes and bones communicate a force which is not the same as the cognisable message encoded in the pitch intervals and rhythm (McClary 1994: 32–33).

Perhaps a historical example will bring the point home. It has long perplexed commentators inside and outside hip-hop culture that militant black nationalists Public Enemy acquired a huge following among white youth in North America in the 1980s. This most unexpected and unlikely example of black–white "crossover" was notable for the complete indifference white audiences demonstrated towards the explicit political content of Public Enemy's lyrics, appearance, record sleeve designs, public pronouncements and so forth. Semiotics simply has no answer to this riddle. Everything about the music and the self-presentation of Public Enemy was explicit in its advocacy of revolutionary politics—so explicit as to leave no discernible room for creative "decoding" on the part of consumers. And yet their following during their commercial peak in the late 1980s was largely made up of politically conservative suburban white males. What was going on here? From the point of view of an affective analysis, the answer is quite simple. The affective qualities of Public Enemy's music were never that different from those of the heavy rock which was the most popular form with this audience: loud, fast, aggressive, offering the male participant an experience of exciting empowerment and battle-ready determination, at the level of affect this simply *was* rock music. Although the popularity of Public Enemy, like that of black male artists before and since their heyday, was no doubt also subtended by traditional fantasies about the erotic power and autonomous aggression of black men, it's clearly missing the point to see that as the main issue. It was the speed and power—the affective specificity—of the music that was the support for such fantasies, at least as much as they have offered access to it. This is another example of a complex political situation that cannot be properly understood by reference to music as merely meaningful.

Of course, to argue that music's effects cannot be reduced to meanings is not to say that the issue of meaning is irrelevant to an understanding of those effects. Effects have meanings, even if the two things are not identical. For example, the potentially empowering/subversive affective qualities of disco and its musical descendants or the supposedly phallomorphic "mattering maps" of the "Rock Formation" (Grossberg 1992) can be at least partially reconfigured by specific discursive practices. For the Riot Grrrls (bands like Hole, Bikini Kill, Babes in Toyland), a masculine rock sound with screaming aggressive vocals and guitars was a means by which to occupy the corporeal-affective space of masculinity, and so challenge the gendered distribution of power in 1990s America (Reynolds and Press 1995). Disco's sensuality is easily contained by an exclusionary apparatus (dress codes, guest-lists, expensive drugs) which turns it into an indulgence for the wealthy rather than an enacted riposte to all normativity, and this particular mode of territorialisation has been imposed and resisted repeatedly since the 1970s (Lawrence 2003). The political struggles at stake in the formation and dissolution of such assemblages can only be understood by reference *both* to the affective specificities of the musics in question, *and* to the semiotic contexts in which they are fought over. To try to read disco in terms of its "significations" (its banal lyrics, its often simplistic and standardised structures) would tell us nothing about why it was important for gay men like Dyer in the 1970s, or how its wordless descendants—house and techno—came to transform the musical milieu of the 1990s. To talk about what Riot Grrrl *meant* without explaining what it *felt like* would be to rob it of all specificity, hearing it as identical either to every other feminist musical project (Tori Amos? Patti Smith? Aretha Franklin? Carla Bley?) or to the masculinist strands of hardcore punk and heavy rock whose forms it appropriated.

The question, therefore, is how to talk about music in a way which takes account of the elaborated physicality of its material effects while acknowledging that such effects will always be mediated by the cultural—and indeed narrowly discursive—conditions in which they occur. An influential solution to this problem is proposed by Robert Walser in his book on heavy metal. Walser, like anyone taking a Spinozan approach, sees music as having corporeal effects that are experienced by musicians and listeners as experiences of empowerment (or, presumably, disempowerment). However, Walser clearly wishes to avoid any naive idea that these physical effects can be understood as wholly "raw," as somehow acultural, and he does not refer at all to the Spinoza-Nietzsche-Deleuze tradition (just to be clear: this is not a criticism of Walser). Instead, locating his work in the mainstream of Anglophone cultural theory, he mobilises a Foucauldian vocabulary of discourse. For Walser, "Music Discourse" includes both the actual concrete sounds of music—the notes, the rhythms, the textures—and the linguistic and visual codes which lend those sounds particular meanings in particular contexts:

> The analytical notion of discourse enables us to pursue an integrated investigation of musical and social aspects of popular music. By approaching musical genres as discourses, it is possible to specify certain formal characteristics of genres but also a range of understandings shared by musicians and fans concerning the interpretation of these characteristics. The concept of discourse enables us to theorise beyond the artificial division between "material reality" and consciousness.
>
> (1993: 45)

Walser here neatly brings us to our second keyword, because he uses the term "discourse" in a way that has become commonplace, explicitly taking the term to imply that there is no ultimate distinction to be made between the material and the ideal, the physical and the mental, between practice and meaning. It is important to be aware of just where this usage of the word does and does not come from. It is not, actually, how Foucault—normally credited with popularising the term—uses the word "discourse." Both he and Derrida refer in their work to the existence of "discursive" and "non-discursive" forces, and it is quite clear from a careful reading of those parts of Foucault's work where he is actually interested in the term "discourse" (which are not that many, it has to be said), that he has no interest in defending the assertion that there is no distinction to be made between the discursive and the non-discursive. The people who *do* actually make this claim explicitly are Ernesto Laclau and Chantal Mouffe, the leading exponents of that methodology which is referred to within political studies as "discourse analysis," but which is rather different from the "discourse analysis" of socio-linguists such as Norman Fairclough and actually no different at all from dominant paradigms of post-structuralist cultural studies (Laclau and Mouffe 1985, Torfing 1999). Under the influence of deconstruction, it is Laclau and Mouffe who make the explicit claim that there is no such distinction to be made, that in effect "everything is discourse" (a statement which, as already mentioned, Laclau has asserted to be no different in its implications from "everything is practice"). Laclau and Mouffe write:

> The main consequence of a break with the discursive/extra-discursive dichotomy is the abandonment of the thought/reality opposition, and hence a major enlargement of the field of those categories which can account for social relations. Synonym, metonymy, metaphor are not forms of thought that add a second sense to a primary, constitutive literality of social relations; instead, they are part of the primary terrain itself in which the social is constituted. Rejection of the thought/reality dichotomy must go together with a rethinking and interpretation of the categories which have until now been considered exclusive of one or the other.
>
> (Laclau and Mouffe 1985: 110)

The issue which this influential claim raises, but which is rarely if ever addressed, is this: if the term "discourse" no longer refers exclusively to the linguistic-cognitive dimension of social experience then it must refer to something much broader. If, in fact, everything is discourse, then the term "discourse," if it is to have any meaning at all, can only be understood, like a post-logocentric notion of "culture," as designating some basic organisational level of all human experience. "Discourse," in this sense, is any form of experience—linguistic or otherwise—which is even minimally organised. However, even where "discourse analysis" is informed by this explicit claim, it continues to prioritise linguistic constructions as its analytical object and a linguistic vocabulary as its primary theoretical resource, if only by continuing to use the word "discourse" in this way, with its clear etymological allusion to speech, in preference to any other term. The logical implication of this practice, even if it is never made explicit, is a claim that verbal language is the most adequate systemic metaphor by which to understand the organisational level of all social experience. . . .

Force and Signification: Affect on the Experiential Continuum

But . . . is there any reason *why* we would want to provoke such a change in cultural studies' sense of identity? Is there any reason why we should want to displace the centrality of meaning to culture's sense of itself? Well, for some of us, as I hope will be apparent by now, there is. Music is that cultural form which most obviously has its specific qualities erased by any attempt to understand it as a language, and whether or not they have actually used the term, almost all theoretical work which has tried to engage with this fact has had to use or develop a model of music as a generator of affects. Just to be clear: this is not a question of disputing the fact that music is also always meaningful. Rather it is to emphasise the extent to which the music cannot be thought without an appreciation of its affective dimension, and to emphasise the extent to which, in the tradition of Spinoza and Nietzsche (1968: 354, 427–429), this dimension must be understood as bound up with the corporeal nature of musical experience. In this sense, the affective dimension of musical experience is no doubt bound up with what Barthes (1977) calls "the grain" of music: those tangible qualities of timbre and tone which are derived from music's irreducible materiality (Gilbert and Pearson 1999). . . .

Notes

1 This remark was made at an event celebrating the 15th anniversary of the publication of Laclau and Mouffe's *Hegemony and Socialist Strategy* (1985) at the Tate Modern gallery, London.
2 Elsewhere I have taken a slightly different route, drawing on Luce Irigaray, Judith Butler and feminist and queer musicology in an attempt to develop models with which to describe and discuss music and its organised effects, but the issues at stake are precisely the same (Gilbert and Pearson 1999).

References

Barthes, R. 1977. "The Grain of the Voice." *Image Music Text.* Translated by S. Heath. London: Fontana.
Deleuze, G. and F. Guattari. 1988. *A Thousand Plateaus.* Translated by B. Massumi. London: Athlone.
Derrida, J. 1988. *Limited Inc.* Evanston: Northwestern University Press.
Dyer, R.1979. "In Defence of Disco." In *On Record: Rock, Pop, and the Written Word*, eds. S. Frith and A. Goodwin, 351–358. London: Routledge.
Eagleton, T. 2000. *The Idea of Culture.* Oxford: Blackwell.
Gilbert, J. 1999. "White Light/White Heat: Jouissance Beyond Gender in the Velvet Underground." In *Living Through Pop*, ed. A. Blake, 31–48. London: Routledge.
_____. 2001. "Against the Empire: Thinking the Social and (Dis)locating Agency Before, Across and Beyond any National Determination." *Parallax* 7(3): 96–113.
Gilbert, J. and E. Pearson. 1999. *Discographies: Dance Music, Culture and the Politics of Sound.* London: Routledge.
Gilroy, P. 1993. *The Black Atlantic.* London: Verso.
Grossberg, L. 1992. *We Gotta Get Out of this Place: Popular Conservatism and Popular Culture.* New York: Routledge.
_____. 1997a. *Bringing it All Back Home: Essays on Cultural Studies.* Durham: Duke University Press.

_____. 1997b. *Dancing in Spite of Myself: Essays on Popular Culture*. Durham: Duke University Press.

Hall, S. 1997. "Culture and Power." *Radical Philosophy* 86 (November/December): 24–41.

Jameson F. 1991. *Postmodernism or the Cultural Logic of Late Capital*. London: Verso.

Laclau, E. and C. Mouffe. 1985. *Hegemony and Socialist Strategy: Towards a Radical Democratic Politics*. London: Verso.

Lawrence, T. 2003. *Love Saves the Day: A History of American Dance Music Culture 1970–1979*. Durham: Duke University Press.

Lévi-Strauss, C. 1994. *The Raw and the Cooked*. London: Pimlico.

Massumi, B. 1996. "The Autonomy of Affect." In *Deleuze: A Critical Reader*, ed. P. Patton, 217–239. Oxford: Blackwell.

McClary, S. 1994. "Same as it Ever Was." In *Microphone Fiends: Youth Music and Youth Culture*, eds. A. Ross and T. Rose, 29–40. New York: Routledge.

Mulhern, F. 1999. *Culture/Metaculture*. London: Routledge.

Nietzsche, F. 1968. *The Will to Power*. Translated by W. Kaufman. New York: Vintage.

Redhead, S., ed. 1993. *Rave Off: Politics and Deviance in Contemporary Youth Culture*. Aldershot: Avebury.

Reynolds, S. and J. Press. 1995. *The Sex Revolts: Gender, Rebellion and Rock 'n' Roll*. London: Serpents Tail.

Torfing, J. 1999. *New Theories of Discourse*. Oxford: Blackwell.

Walser, R. 1993. *Running with the Devil: Power, Gender and Madness in Heavy Metal Music*. Hanover: Wesleyan University Press.

Wheeler, W. 1999. *A New Modernity?* London: Lawrence and Wishart.

Williams, R. 1977. *Marxism and Literature*. Oxford: Oxford University Press.

Contributors

Christina Baade is Associate Professor of Communication Studies and Music at McMaster University in Hamilton.

Adam Behr is a Research Associate at the University of Edinburgh and a Senior Research Associate on the CREATe project at the University of East Anglia.

Andy Bennett is Professor of Cultural Sociology and Director of the Griffith Centre for Cultural Research at Griffith University in Queensland, Australia.

Karin Bijsterveld is Professor of Science, Technology and Modern Culture at Maastricht University, the Netherlands.

Georgina Born is Professor of Music and Anthropology at the University of Oxford and a Professorial Fellow of Mansfield College.

Sara Cohen is Professor in the School of Music at the University of Liverpool, where she is also Director of Research and Director of the Institute of Popular Music.

Tia DeNora is Professor of Sociology of Music and Director of Research (Sociology/Philosophy) at Exeter University.

Kyle Devine is Lecturer in Music at City University London, and a research associate with the Music and Digitization Research Group at the University of Oxford.

Eric Drott is Associate Professor of Music Theory and the Head of the Division of Theory/ Composition at the University of Texas at Austin.

Mary Fogarty is Assistant Professor in the Department of Dance at York University in Toronto and an invited Visiting Scholar at New York University's Hip Hop Education Centre.

Simon Frith is Tovey Professor of Music at the University of Edinburgh.

Jeremy Gilbert is Professor of Cultural and Political Theory at the University of East London and is Editor of the journal New Formations.

David Grazian is Associate Professor of Sociology at the University of Pennsylvania.

Anthony Kwame Harrison is Associate Professor and Gloria D. Smith Professor of Africana Studies in the Department of Sociology at Virginia Polytechnic Institute.

Antoine Hennion is Research Director at the Center for the Sociology of Innovation at Mines ParisTech.

Dave Laing is Honorary Research Fellow at the Institute of Popular Music, University of Liverpool and Executive Editor of *Popular Music History*.

Marion Leonard is Senior Lecturer in the School of Music, a member of the Institute of Popular Music and Director of the MA Popular Music Studies program at the University of Liverpool.

Peter Martin is formerly Professor of Sociology at the University of Manchester.

Lee Marshall is Reader in Sociology at the University of Bristol.

Susan McClary is Professor in the Department of Music at Case Western Reserve University.

Lisa McCormick is Assistant Professor of Sociology at Haverford College.

Morten Michelsen is Associate Professor of Musicology in the Department of Arts and Cultural Studies at the University of Copenhagen.

Trevor Pinch is Goldwin Smith Professor of Science and Technology Studies at Cornell University.

Nick Prior is Senior Lecturer in Sociology and Head of Department at the University of Edinburgh.

Motti Regev is Professor of Sociology at the Open University of Israel, where he currently heads the MA program in Cultural Studies and the Department of Literature, Language and the Arts.

Marco Santoro is Associate Professor of Sociology at the University of Bologna.

John Shepherd is Vice-Provost and Associate Vice-President (Academic) at Carleton University in Ottawa, where he is also Chancellor's Professor of Music and Sociology.

Paul Théberge is Professor in the Institute for Comparative Studies in Literature, Art and Culture, as well as the School for Studies in Art and Culture, at Carleton University in Ottawa.

William Weber is Emeritus Professor of History at California State University, Long Beach.

Benjamin Wright is Lecturer in Cinema Studies at the University of Toronto.

Index

CPSIA information can be obtained
at www.ICGtesting.com
Printed in the USA
BVHW081314090120
569008BV00006B/17/P

9 781138 856363